MARKET ABUSE REGULATION

Commentary and Annotated Guide

MARKET ABUSE REGULATION

Commentary and Annotated Guide

Edited by

Marco Ventoruzzo
Sebastian Mock

OXFORD
UNIVERSITY PRESS

OXFORD
UNIVERSITY PRESS

Great Clarendon Street, Oxford, OX2 6DP,
United Kingdom

Oxford University Press is a department of the University of Oxford.
It furthers the University's objective of excellence in research, scholarship,
and education by publishing worldwide. Oxford is a registered trade mark of
Oxford University Press in the UK and in certain other countries

First Edition published in 2017
Impression: 2

Published in the United States of America by Oxford University Press
198 Madison Avenue, New York, NY 10016, United States of America

British Library Cataloguing in Publication Data
Data available

Library of Congress Control Number: 2017943889

ISBN 978–0–19–881175–6

Printed and bound by
CPI Group (UK) Ltd, Croydon, CR0 4YY

Alla piccola Giulia, con amore—M.V.
Für Friedrich—S.M.

PREFACE

The Market Abuse Regulation (MAR) is one of the centrepieces of the new Capital Market Union (CMU) of the European Union. In terms of legislative technique, the choice of a direct-ly applicable regulation to replace the old Market Abuse Directive (MAD), which had to be implemented by the single Member States with ad hoc statutes, is itself a major step towards a more uniform legal framework. The impacts on law practice and research are far-reaching. From now on, the focus of the interpreters, no matter in what jurisdiction they operate, will be on a single text, with very limited, if at all, local variations. This will inevitably foster a more international legal debate and contribute to lower the barriers that still now might separate jurists from different countries within the European Union. Of course, path dependence and inertia will still determine differences among Member States in the way the Directive is read and interpreted, but it is now fair to say that continental Europe now speaks a common legal language in the area of market abuse and that the cross-border dialogue will contribute to make these differences fade away.

We decided to contribute to this pan-European dialogue with an approach that aspires to bring together different legal genera used in different legal traditions. The book you are holding has in fact a 'mixed format': part essays on specific concepts, and part analytical commentary, provision by provision, of the MAR, an approach that is not equally common in all jurisdictions. Our goal is to combine a thorough technical analysis of the provisions of the MAR, which hopefully will be helpful for practitioners, academics, and law students; with a general part on selected topics that cuts across more specific details, offering a broader systematic view.

The book is inherently international also because we were fortunate enough to obtain contributions from leading authors in the field from several European jurisdictions. We believe that the diverse perspectives and voices of the different authors has enriched the polyphony of the analysis, and we owe them special gratitude for the passion with which they have engaged in our shared effort.

Marco Ventoruzzo/Sebastian Mock

Milan/Hamburg

TABLE OF CONTENTS

TABLE OF CASES

UNITED KINGDOM

COURT OF JUSTICE OF THE EUROPEAN UNION

INTERNATIONAL TRIBUNALS

European Court of Human Rights

NATIONAL JURISDICTIONS

France

Germany

Netherlands

Switzerland

United States

TABLE OF LEGISLATION

EUROPEAN UNION

European Regulations

Treaties

LIST OF ABBREVIATIONS AND LEGISLATION

AFM	Netherlands Authority for the Financial Market
BaFin	German Federal Financial Supervisory Authority
Brussels I bis Regulation (2012/1215/EU)	Regulation (EU) No 1215/2012 of the European Parliament and of the Council of 12 December 2012 on jurisdiction and the recognition and enforcement of judgments in civil and commercial matters (OJ L 351 (20 December 2012) 1)
Buy-back Programmes and Stabilisation Regulation (2273/2003/EC)	Commission Regulation (EC) No 2273/2003 of 22 December 2003 implementing Directive 2003/6/EC of the European Parliament and of the Council as regards exemptions for buy-back programmes and stabilisation of financial instruments (OJ L 336 (23 December 2003) 33)
Capital Maintenance Directive (2012/36/EU)	Directive 2012/30/EU of the European Parliament and of the Council of 25 October 2012 on coordination of safeguards which, for the protection of the interests of members and others, are required by Member States of companies within the meaning of the second paragraph of Article 54 of the Treaty on the Functioning of the European Union, in respect of the formation of public limited liability companies and the maintenance and alteration of their capital, with a view to making such safeguards equivalent (OJ L 315 (14 November 2012) 74)
Capital Requirements Directive (CRD IV) (2013/36/EU)	Directive 2013/36/EU of the European Parliament and of the Council of 26 June 2013 on access to the activity of credit institutions and the prudential supervision of credit institutions and investment firms, amending Directive 2002/87/EC and repealing Directives 2006/48/EC and 2006/49/EC (OJ L 176 (27 June 2013) 338)
Capital Requirements Regulation (CRD IV) (2013/575/EU)	Regulation (EU) No 575/2013 of the European Parliament and of the Council of 26 June 2013 on prudential requirements for credit institutions and investment firms and amending Regulation (EU) No 648/2012 (OJ L 321 (30 November 2013) 6)
CFR	Charter of Fundamental Rights of the European Union

CRIM MAD	See Market Abuse Directive on Criminal Sanctions (2014/57/EU)
Data Protection Directive (95/46/EC)	Directive 95/46/EC of the European Parliament and of the Council of 24 October 1995 on the protection of individuals with regard to the processing of personal data and on the free movement of such data (OJ L 281 (23 November 1995) 31)
EBLR	European Business Law Review
EBOR	European Business Organization Law Review
ECFR	European Company and Financial Law Review
ESMA	European Securities and Markets Authority
ESMA Regulation (1095/2010/EU)	Regulation (EU) No 1095/2010 of the European Parliament and of the Council of 24 November 2010 establishing a European Supervisory Authority (European Securities and Markets Authority), amending Decision No 716/2009/EC and repealing Commission Decision 2009/77/EC (OJ L 331 (15 December 2010) 84)
FCA	Financial Conduct Authority—United Kingdom
FSA	Financial Services Authority—United Kingdom
Greenhouse Gas Emission Allowances Directive (2003/87/EC)	Directive 2003/87/EC of the European Parliament and of the Council of 13 October 2003 establishing a scheme for greenhouse gas emission allowance trading within the Community and amending Council Directive 96/61/EC (OJ L 275 (25 October 2003) 32)
Greenhouse Gas Emission Allowances Regulation (1031/2010/EU)	Commission Regulation (EU) No 1031/2010 of 12 November 2010 on the timing, administration and other aspects of auctioning of greenhouse gas emission allowances pursuant to Directive 2003/87/EC of the European Parliament and of the Council establishing a scheme for greenhouse gas emission allowances trading within the Community (OJ L 302 (18 November 2010) 1)
Insider Dealing Directive Proposal	Commission, Proposal for a council directive coordinating regulations on insider trading, COM(87) 111 final
Insider Dealing Directive (1989/592/EEC)	Council Directive 89/592/EEC of 13 November 1989 coordinating regulations on insider dealing (OJ L 334 (18 November 1989) 30)

Investment Recommendations Directive (2003/125/EC)	Commission Directive 2003/125/EC of 22 December 2003 implementing Directive 2003/6/EC of the European Parliament and of the Council as regards the fair presentation of investment recommendations and the disclosure of conflicts of interest (OJ L 339 (24 December 2003) 73)
IOSCO	International Organization of Securities Commissions
(former) Market Abuse Directive (2003/6/EC)	Directive 2003/6/EC of the European Parliament and of the Council of 28 January 2003 on insider dealing and market manipulation (market abuse) (OJ L 96 (12 April 2003) 16)
Market Abuse Implementation Directive (2003/124/EC)	Commission Directive 2003/124/EC of 22 December 2003 implementing Directive 2003/6/EC of the European Parliament and of the Council as regards the definition and public disclosure of inside information and the definition of market manipulation (OJ L 339 (24 December 2003) 70)
Market Abuse Directive on Criminal Sanctions (2014/57/EU)	Directive 2014/57/EU of the European Parliament and of the Council of 16 April 2014 on criminal sanctions for market abuse (market abuse directive) (OJ L 173 (12 June 2014) 179)
Market Abuse Regulation (2014/596/EU)	Regulation (EU) No 596/2014 of the European Parliament and of the Council of 16 April 2014 on market abuse (market abuse regulation) and repealing Directive 2003/6/EC of the European Parliament and of the Council and Commission Directives 2003/124/EC, 2003/125/EC and 2004/72/EC (OJ L 173 (12 June 2014) 1)
Market Abuse Regulation Proposal	Commission, Proposal for a Regulation of the European Parliament and of the Council on insider dealing and market manipulation (market abuse), COM(2011) 651 final
Markets in Financial Instruments Directive I (2004/39/EC)	Directive 2004/39/EC of the European Parliament and of the Council of 21 April 2004 on markets in financial instruments amending Council Directives 85/611/EEC and 93/6/EEC and Directive 2000/12/EC of the European Parliament and of the Council and repealing Council Directive 93/22/EEC (OJ L 145 (30 April 2004) 1)
Markets in Financial Instruments Directive II (2014/65/EU)	Directive 2014/65/EU of the European Parliament and of the Council of 15 May 2014 on markets in financial instruments and amending Directive 2002/92/EC and Directive 2011/61/EU (OJ L 173 (12 June 2014) 349)

Markets in Financial Instruments Implementation Regulation (1287/2006/EC)	Commission Regulation (EC) No 1287/2006 of 10 August 2006 implementing Directive 2004/39/EC of the European Parliament and of the Council as regards record-keeping obligations for investment firms, transaction reporting, market transparency, admission of financial instruments to trading, and defined terms for the purposes of that Directive (OJ L 231 (2 September 2006) 241)
Markets in Financial Instruments Regulation (2014/600/EU)	Regulation (EU) No 600/2014 of the European Parliament and of the Council of 15 May 2014 on markets in financial instruments and amending Regulation (EU) No 648/2012 (OJ L 173 (12 June 2014) 84)
MTFs	multilateral trading facilities
Omnibus I Directive (2010/78/EU)	Directive 2010/78/EU amending Directives 98/26/EC, 2002/87/EC, 2003/6/EC, 2003/41/EC, 2003/71/EC, 2004/39/EC, 2004/109/EC, 2005/60/EC, 2006/48/EC, 2006/49/EC and 2009/65/EC in respect of the powers of the European Supervisory Authority (European Banking Authority), the European Supervisory Authority (European Insurance and Occupational Pensions Authority) and the European Supervisory Authority (European Securities and Markets Authority) (OJ L 331 (15 December 2010) 120)
OTF	organized trading facility
PRIIPs Regulation (2014/1286/EU)	Regulation (EU) No 1286/2014 of the European Parliament and of the Council of 26 November 2014 on key information documents for packaged retail and insurance-based investment products (PRIIPs)
Prospectus Directive (2003/71/EC)	Directive 2003/71/EC of the European Parliament and of the Council of 4 November 2003 on the prospectus to be published when securities are offered to the public or admitted to trading and amending Directive 2001/34/EC (OJ L 345 (31 December 2003) 64)
Prospectus Regulation (2017/1129/EU)	Regulation on the prospectus to be published when securities are offered to the public or admitted to trading (hereafter Prospectus Regulation), as approved by the European Parliament in first reading on 5 April 5 2017
Rome II Regulation (864/2007/EC)	Regulation (EC) No 864/2007 of the European Parliament and of the Council of 11 July 2007 on the law applicable to non-contractual obligations (Rome II) (OJ L 199 (31 July 2007) 40)

Short Selling Regulation (236/2012/EU)	Regulation (EU) No 236/2012 of the European Parliament and of the Council of 14 March 2012 on short selling and certain aspects of credit default swaps (OJ L 86 (24 March 2012) 3)
SME	small and medium-sized enterprises
SSM Regulation (1024/2013/EU)	Regulation 1024/2013 conferring specific tasks on the European Central Bank concerning policies relating to the prudential supervision of credit institutions (OJ L 287 (29 October 2013) 63)
Stock Exchange Listing Directive I (1979/279/EEC)	Council Directive 79/279/EEC of 5 March 1979 coordinating the conditions for the admission of securities to official stock exchange listing (OJ L 66 (16 March 1979) 21)
Stock Exchange Listing Directive II (2001/34/EC)	Directive 2001/34/EC of the European Parliament and of the Council of 28 May 2001 on the admission of securities to official stock exchange listing and on information to be published on those securities (OJ L 184 (6 July 2001) 1)
STORs	Suspicious Transaction and Order Reports
STRs	Suspicious Transaction Reports
Takeover Directive (2004/25/EC)	Directive 2004/25/EC of the European Parliament and of the Council of 21 April 2004 on takeover bids (OJ L 142 (30 April 2004) 12)
(former) Transparency Directive (2004/109/EC)	Directive 2004/109/EC of the European Parliament and of the Council of 15 December 2004 on the harmonisation of transparency requirements in relation to information about issuers whose securities are admitted to trading on a regulated market and amending Directive 2001/34/EC (OJ L 390 (31 December 2004) 48)
Transparency Directive (2013/50/EU)	Directive 2013/50/EU of the European Parliament and of the Council of 22 October 2013 amending Directive 2004/109/EC of the European Parliament and of the Council on the harmonisation of transparency requirements in relation to information about issuers whose securities are admitted to trading on a regulated market, Directive 2003/71/EC of the European Parliament and of the Council on the prospectus to be published when securities are offered to the public or admitted to trading and Commission Directive 2007/14/EC laying down detailed rules for the implementation of certain provisions of Directive 2004/109/EC (OJ L 294 (6 November 2013) 13)

UCITS V (2014/91/EU)	Directive 2014/91/EU of the European Parliament and of the Council of 23 July 2014 amending Directive 2009/65/EC on the coordination of laws, regulations and administrative provisions relating to undertakings for collective investment in transferable securities (UCITS) as regards depositary functions, remuneration policies and sanctions (OJ L 257 (28 August 2014) 186)
Wholesale Energy Market Integrity and Transparency Regulation (2011/1227/EU)	Regulation (EU) No 1227/2011 of the European Parliament and of the Council of 25 October 2011 on wholesale energy market integrity and transparency (OJ L 326 (8 December 2011) 93)

LIST OF CONTRIBUTORS

Editors

Marco Ventoruzzo is professor of law at Bocconi University in Milan, Italy, where he also directs the Department of Legal Studies, and professor of law at the Pennsylvania State University Law School, State College, USA. He is a scientific member of the Max Planck Institute in Luxembourg. His academic interests, research, and teaching include corporate governance, corporate finance, financial markets regulation, takeovers, and banking law. He serves on the boards of several peer-reviewed academic journals in his field, and has taught and lectured in several different countries. He regularly consults private and public entities on corporate law and securities regulation issues.

Sebastian Mock is an associate professor of law at the University of Hamburg in Germany (since 2013). He teaches corporate law, securities regulation, and commercial and bankruptcy law. After studying at the Universities of Jena and Hamburg (both in Germany), Montpellier (France), and the New York University School of Law, Sebastian obtained a PhD in Law from the University of Hamburg in 2007 and finished his Habilitation in 2012. In addition to teaching in Germany, Sebastian has also taught corporate and bankruptcy law in China, Russia, and Italy. His books and articles have been published in the United States and Europe.

Contributors

Danny Busch is professor of financial law and director of the Institute for Financial Law (IFL), University of Nijmegen, the Netherlands, visiting professor at the Università Cattolica del Sacro Cuore di Milano, visiting professor at the Università degli Studi di Genova, and member of the Dutch Banking Disciplinary Committee (Tuchtcommissie Banken). From 2002 until 2010 he was an attorney-at-law (advocaat) with the leading Dutch international law firm De Brauw Blackstone Westbroek in Amsterdam, where he practised banking and securities law (both the private law and regulatory aspects). In 2002 he defended his PhD in Utrecht. In 1998 he was awarded the degree of Magister Juris in European and Comparative Law by the University of Oxford (St John's College).

Sofie Cools is a senior research fellow at the Max Planck Institute for Comparative and International Private Law in Hamburg, and an affiliated senior researcher at the University of Leuven. She holds law degrees from the University of Leuven and Harvard. Her academic work focuses on company law and financial regulation, and the comparative and economic analysis thereof, and was awarded several prizes, including the Irving Oberman Memorial Award at Harvard Law School and the Fernand Collin Prize of the Belgian University Foundation. She has been an attorney at Cleary Gottlieb Steen & Hamilton Brussels, a teaching fellow at the University of Leuven, and a visiting lecturer at the Torcuato Di Tella University in Buenos Aires.

Marco Dell'Erba is a post-doctoral fellow at the Groningen Center for financial services (University of Groningen), research associate at LabEx ReFi-Financial Regulation Laboratory of Excellence (University of Paris I Panthéon-Sorbonne, ENA, ESCP, CNAM) (Paris), and LLM candidate (2017–2018) at the New York University (Hauser Global Scholar). He holds a PhD in private law (financial law) from the University of Paris I Sorbonne Panthéon and a PhD in commercial law from the University of Rome. He practised law in the departments of Banking and Finance and Litigation and Dispute Resolution at Clifford Chance LLP (Rome office) and as an independent consultant (Paris). He previously held research positions at the LabEx ReFi, National University of Singapore (Singapore) and as a research assistant in the department of law of the London School of Economics (London). He graduated from the University of Rome La Sapienza and is a fellow of the Lamaro Pozzani University College of Excellence (Rome). His main interests lie in the field of financial and banking regulation, corporate law, and securities law (ie hedge funds, derivatives, clearing houses, and blockchain).

Jesper Lau Hansen, dr juris & LLM (Cantab), is a professor of company law and financial regulation at the University of Copenhagen. His main areas of research in recent years have been Nordic corporate governance, takeovers, and the regulation of market abuse. He has served on national committees on subjects including the Danish 2009 Companies Act, insider dealing and SIFI regulation. He was a member of the Commission's Reflection Group on the future of EU company law and is presently a member of the successor group ICLEG. He served the first two terms of the Stakeholder Group connected to ESMA after its establishment in 2011, the last term as its chair.

Chiara Mosca is assistant professor at Bocconi University in Milan where she teaches company law and securities regulation. She holds a PhD from the Università Cattolica del Sacro Cuore in Milan and a Master of Science in Law and Accounting from the London School of Economics. Her main areas of research are takeover regulation in Italy and, in Europe, market abuse regulation and corporate governance, investment services, and investor protection.

Chiara Picciau is a post-doctoral research fellow in company law at Bocconi University in Milan. She holds a law degree from Bocconi University and a PhD in commercial law from the University of Milan. She has written contributions in the field of corporate and financial markets law. Her current research focuses on market abuse regulation, corporate governance, and securities regulation.

Alain Pietrancosta is professor of law at the Sorbonne Law School (University of Paris). He earned his PhD from the University of Paris 1 Panthéon-Sorbonne and passed the *Concours d'agrégation* in private law in 2001. He is the founder and director of the Masters in Financial Law programme at the Sorbonne Law School. Among other activities, he is a member of: the Legal High Advisory Committee for Financial Markets of Paris; the Legal High Advisory Committee for Corporate law; the Issuers Committee of the French Financial Market Authority (AMF); the Labex (Excellence Research Center) Financial Regulation; the Paris Europlace legal committee; and the European Company Law Experts Group (ECLE).

Arad Reisberg joined Brunel University London in May 2016 as the head of the Brunel Law School and professor of corporate law and finance. Previously, he was a reader in corporate and financial law at UCL Faculty of Laws (2009–2016), and a lecturer in law (2006–2009) acting as Director, UCL Centre for Commercial Law (2009–2016) and UCL Laws Vice Dean (Research) (2009–2012). He held visiting appointments at a number of institutions including Oxford University (2005), Brooklyn Law School (2012), and the National University of Singapore (NUS) (2013 and 2014). Arad is the recipient of numerous academic scholarships and awards and has written widely on shareholder remedies and directors' duties. He is the author of *Derivative Actions and Corporate Governance* (Oxford University Press 2007) and currently the Consultant Editor, *Halsbury's Laws of England* (Companies Title). Since July 2016 he has been a Member of the Financial Markets Law Committee (FMLC) Advisory Group at the Bank of England convened to consider and address the legal uncertainties which may ultimately result from the UK's vote to leave the European Union. He sits on the editorial Boards of the Journal International Corporate Rescue and the Journal of Corporate Ownership and Control.

Johannes Zollner has been professor for Austrian and international corporate and commercial law at the University of Graz since April 2013. Between 2011 and 2013 he was professor for private law at the University of Klagenfurt. His research activities have concentrated on corporate law, capital markets law, and foundation law.

Part A

ANNOTATED GUIDE

1

HISTORY, APPLICATION, INTERPRETATION, AND LEGAL SOURCES OF THE MARKET ABUSE REGULATION

I. The Market Abuse Regulation as a European Regulation

The Market Abuse Regulation is a European Community legal instrument under the EC Treaty. As a Community regulation, it has general application, and is binding in its entirety and directly applicable in all Member States (Article 288 TFEU). *General application* means that the Market Abuse Regulation applies to objectively determined situations and produces legal effects on categories of persons envisaged in the abstract.[1] *Binding in their entirety* means that all **A.1.01**

[1] Case 244/88 *Usines Coopératives de Déshydratation du Vexin v EC Commission* [1989] ECR I-3811 and Case 299/88 *Cargill v EC Commission* [1990] ECR I-1303.

provisions of the Market Abuse Regulation apply in identical terms throughout the Community. Finally, *directly applicable* means that the Market Abuse Regulation has direct effect in all Member States and does not have to be transposed into national law. However, clearly the accompanying directives must be transposed into national law.

A.1.02 The Market Abuse Regulation is based on the competence of the Union in Article 114 of the Treaty on the Functioning of the European Union (TFEU). The choice for a regulation instead of a directive is based on the idea that a regulation is the most appropriate legal instrument to define the market abuse network in the Union.[2] This assessment of the Commission is based mainly on the experiences with the (former) Market Abuse Directive (2003/6/EC), which failed to create a truly level playing field with regard to market abuse.[3] The Market Abuse Regulation also meets the requirements set out under the principle of subsidiarity and of proportionality (Article 5(3) TEU). In particular, the previous experiences in connection with the harmonization of national capital markets law created by the (former) Market Abuse Directive (2003/6/EC) made it obvious that the practice of regulatory arbitrage still remained in the Common Market.

II. Historical Development

A.1.03 The regulation of market abuse has a long history in the Union, dating back to the 1960s.[4]

The Segré Report of 1966

A.1.04 The initial ideas for regulating the European capital markets were proposed in the Segré Report of 1966,[5] which was in fact merely an analysis of the situation in the European capital markets at that time. In this regard, the Segré Report pointed out a number of weaknesses in the securities markets in Europe and made several political recommendations. However, the regulation of market abuse and its underlying principles were not addressed in the report.

---

[2] Commission, Proposal for a Regulation of the European Parliament and of the Council on insider dealing and market manipulation (market abuse), COM(2011) 651 final 5.

[3] See Part B—art 8 n 33 ff.

[4] For an historical overview see Niamh Moloney, *EU Securities and Financial Markets Regulation* (3rd edn, OUP 2014) 706 ff.

[5] European Commission, 'The Development of a European Capital Market—Report of a Group of Experts Appointed by the EEC Commission' (1966).

The (original) Stock Exchange Listing Directive (1979/279/EEC)

The first regulation of market abuse in the European Union was the (original) Stock Exchange Listing Directive (79/279/EEC), which introduced in Article 17 the obligation to disclose important single events, which were defined in Schedules C and D of that directive. Although this obligation might be considered as a forerunner of the obligation to disclose inside information as set out in Article 17 of the Market Abuse Regulation, this obligation was extremely limited and did not cover all aspects of (inside) information. **A.1.05**

The Insider Dealing Directive (1989/592/EEC)

The next major step was the Insider Dealing Directive (1989/592/EEC) of 1989.[6] However, in contrast to the Market Abuse Regulation the Insider Dealing Directive (1989/592/EEC) focused only on the definition and prohibition of insider dealing. This limitation to the prohibition of insider dealing alone therefore failed to seize the opportunity of creating a strict liability obligation to disclose inside information and to prohibit market manipulation. This was as a result of the fact that, in the 1960s, there was no regulation of insider trading at all in the capital markets laws of most of the Member States. Therefore, the limited approach of the Insider Dealing Directive (1989/592/EEC) was clearly nothing more than the most basic form of legislation concerning European capital markets law. However, it should be pointed out that the structure and some of the basic concepts included in the Market Abuse Regulation were in fact addressed by the Insider Dealing Directive (1989/592/EEC), particularly with regard to the definition of inside information (Article 1),[7] the transactions and the behaviour covered by the prohibition (Article 2),[8] and the exemptions regarding monetary and public debt management activities (Article 4).[9] **A.1.06**

The (new) Stock Exchange Listing Directive II (2001/34/EC)

A brief episode in the regulation of market abuse was the (subsequent) Stock Exchange Listing Directive II (2001/34/EC) of 2001, whereby listed companies issuing new shares and undertakings issuing debt securities were obliged to inform the public with immediate effect of any major new developments in their business activities or changes regarding their share capital that were not information that was within the public domain and which might, by virtue of their **A.1.07**

---

[6] See eg Paul L Davies, 'The European Community's Directive on Insider Dealing: From Company Law to Securities Markets Regulation?' (1991) 11 Oxford Journal of Legal Studies 92, 101 ff; Klaus J Hopt, 'The European Insider Dealing Directive' (1990) 27 Common Market Law Review 51; see Moloney (n 4) 707 ff.

[7] See Part B—art 7 n 25 ff.

[8] See Part B—art 8 n 33 ff.

[9] See Part B—art 6 n 3 ff.

effect on the assets and liabilities or financial position or in the general course of business, lead to substantial movements in the market prices of their shares (Articles 68(1) and 81(1) of the (new) Stock Exchange Listing Directive II (2001/34/EC)). This obligation was supported by a number of additional disclosure requirements. However, the prohibition of insider dealing and market manipulation was entirely unaffected by the (new) Stock Exchange Listing Directive II (2001/34/EC).

The (former) Market Abuse Directive (2003/6/EC)

A.1.08 The first major piece of legislation addressing not only insider dealing but also certain other aspects of market abuse was the (former) Market Abuse Directive (2003/6/EC), which addressed the same aspects as the Market Abuse Regulation.[10] Although recital (12) of the (former) Market Abuse Directive (2003/6/EC) defined market abuse only as insider dealing and market manipulation, the (former) Market Abuse Directive (2003/6/EC) not only covered these two forms of market abuse in its Articles 2 and 5 but also required the issuers of financial instruments to inform the public as soon as possible of inside information that directly concerned the issuer (Article 6 (former) Market Abuse Directive (2003/6/EC)). In comparison with earlier directives, the (former) Market Abuse Directive (2003/6/EC) provided a very comprehensive framework for the regulation of market abuse. However, since the (former) Market Abuse Directive (2003/6/EC) had to be transposed into national law by each of the Member States, huge differences regarding the application of the law on market abuse was thereby created in the Member States and which remained in place. These differences had a correspondingly large negative impact in terms of market integrity and investor protection and led to anything but a level playing field.[11] Despite this, at the time the (former) Market Abuse Directive (2003/6/EC) was considered as a general success, owing to the fact that it introduced a comprehensive market abuse regime in all Member States and, particularly, in those Member States which had until then pursued a more reluctant approach.

[10] See eg E Avgouleas, 'The Mechanics and Regulation of Market Abuse' (OUP 2005); Helena Bolina, 'Market Manipulation and Insider Dealing in the New Market Abuse Directive (2003/6/EC)' (2001–2002) 4 Revue Européenne de Droit Bancaire et Financier 555; Guido A Ferrarini, 'The European Market Abuse Directive' (2004) 41 Common Market Law Review 711; Jesper Lau Hansen, 'MAD in a Hurry: The Swift and Promising Adoption of the EU Market Abuse Directive' (2004) 15 European Business Law Review 183; Niamh Moloney, 'New Frontiers in EC Capital Market Law: From Market Construction to Market Regulation' (2003) 40 Common Market Law Review 809.

[11] See Commission, Proposal for a Regulation of the European Parliament and of the Council on insider dealing and market manipulation (market abuse) (n 2) 2 ff; see also Moloney (n 4) 709 ff.

The Market Abuse Regulation as part of the capital markets union

These factors, namely the lack of uniformity, several new developments regarding insider trading and market manipulation, the limited scope of application and the financial crises of 2007/2008 led, in the later 2000s, to a discussion regarding the reform of the (former) Market Abuse Directive (2003/6/EC). This led, in turn, to the enactment of the Market Abuse Regulation.[12] The deployment of a regulation rather than a directive was one of the major features of this reform, because harmonization under the (former) Market Abuse Directive (2003/6/EC) could not provide the legal framework necessary to create the Capital Markets Union. However, it is questionable whether the mere transformation of the (former) Market Abuse Directive (2003/6/EC) into the Market Abuse Regulation can truly provide such a framework. This is the case because the application of the Market Abuse Regulation is basically in the domain of the competent national authorities and the European Securities Market Authority (ESMA), neither of which has the power directly to refer cases to the Court of Justice of the European Union (CJEU) for a preliminary ruling. Only the national courts of the Member States have that right under Article 267 of the TFEU. Since market participants are often extremely reluctant to challenge actions taken by the competent national authorities, such preliminary rulings dealing with the Market Abuse Regulation will probably be as rare as they were under the (former) Market Abuse Directive (2003/6/EC). Consequently, the application of the Market Abuse Regulation will principally be influenced by the administrative practices of the competent national authorities and the ESMA and will not be subject to the control of the CJEU. **A.1.09**

III. Interpretation of the Market Abuse Regulation

As a European regulation, the Market Abuse Regulation must be directly applicable, and subject to the interpretation by the CJEU in the last instance. In this regard, autonomous interpretation is the core principle for the interpretation of the Market Abuse Regulation.[13] However, the interpretation of the Market Abuse Regulation, as is true of all EU legislation, faces the problem of so-called *divided interpretation*.[14] **A.1.10**

---

[12] See Commission, Proposal for a Regulation of the European Parliament and of the Council on insider dealing and market manipulation (market abuse) (n 2) 3; see also the so-called de Larosière Group Report of the High-level Group on Financial Supervision in the EU www.ec.europa.eu/internal_market/finances/docs/de_larosiere_report_en.pdf.

[13] See n 11.

[14] See n 12.

Autonomous interpretation as the core principle for the interpretation of the Market Abuse Regulation

A.1.11 The interpretation of the Market Abuse Regulation is first of all driven by the fact that the European legislator wanted to increase market integrity and investor protection, whilst simultaneously ensuring a single rule book and a level playing field, thereby increasing the attractiveness of securities markets for raising capital.[15] This underlines the general principle of an autonomous interpretation of European law, which means in the context of the Market Abuse Regulation that all of its provisions must be interpreted autonomously and without reference to national capital markets or corporate law. In addition, the former practices of the competent national authorities in the application of national law implementing the (former) Market Abuse Directive (2003/6/EC) are no longer relevant or applicable, unless they can be seen to comply with (autonomous) interpretation of the Market Abuse Regulation. However, the case law of the CJEU regarding the (former) Market Abuse Directive (2003/6/EC) remains relevant for the interpretation of the Market Abuse Regulation, owing to the fact that it is partially based on this case law, especially regarding the requirement for the disclosure of inside information, as set out in Article 7.[16] Another unresolved question regarding the interpretation of the Market Abuse Regulation is its application in the context of civil matters, largely because it does not address civil law issues at all.[17]

The problem of 'divided' interpretation

A.1.12 The Market Abuse Regulation establishes a common regulatory framework on market abuse. As is the case for any form of regulation in capital markets law, it touches not only aspects of administrative (capital markets) law dealing with the competences of a supervisory authority but also aspects of criminal law and—even though not explicitly dealt with[18]—of civil law and especially of civil liability for violations of the prohibitions it sets out. This broad approach of the Market Abuse Regulation, however, has led to the problem that standards for the interpretation of the Market Abuse Regulation are different for each area of law. This is especially the case for criminal law, where a rather strict interpretation of the law must usually be applied. Additionally, in the administrative law of (some) Member States a different but also strict interpretation must be applied to meet constitutional or other restrictions for administrative authorities. Finally, in civil law in the context of capital markets law very often specific standards of proof are applied to protect investors who have suffered losses, which also has an indirect

[15] See Commission, 'Proposal for a Regulation of the European Parliament and of the Council on insider dealing and market manipulation (market abuse)' (n 2) 3.
[16] See Part B—art 7 n 16 ff.
[17] See Part A—Private Enforcement of the Market Abuse Regulation in European Law.
[18] ibid.

influence on the interpretation of the Market Abuse Regulation as the underlying regulation.[19] The consequences of these three different standards for the interpretation of the Market Abuse Regulation (so-called *divided interpretation*) remain an unresolved problem.

IV. Legal Sources of the (New) Market Abuse Regime

Level 1—Legislation

Market Abuse Regulation

The first and most important piece of legislation of the (new) market abuse regime is the Market Abuse Regulation itself, which entered into force on 2 July 2014 (Article 39(1) Market Abuse Regulation). However, large parts of the Market Abuse Regulation only came into effect on 3 July 2016 (Article 39(2) Market Abuse Regulation). The Market Abuse Regulation replaces the (former) Market Abuse Directive (2003/6/EC).[20] **A.1.13**

Market Abuse Directive on Criminal Sanctions (2014/57/EU)

Although the European legislator enacted the market abuse regime as a regulation rather than as a directive, several aspects of this new regime are not covered by the regulation but are instead governed by the Market Abuse Directive on Criminal Sanctions (2014/57/EU). It should be borne in mind that the European legislator avoided including certain aspects in the Market Abuse Regulation and decided to implement them in a directive on criminal sanctions, although this approach has often been considered to be insufficient for the (general aspects of the) market abuse regime. This somewhat reluctant and negative approach is attributable to the fact that the European legislator has only a very limited ability to adopt rules on criminal law. Pursuant to Article 83(2) of the TFEU, the European legislator can only adopt minimum rules in criminal matters, and only when such rules are essential to ensure the effective implementation of EU policy. **A.1.14**

The Market Abuse Directive on Criminal Sanctions (2014/57/EU) sets out the general framework for criminal sanctions for violations of the prohibitions of the Market Abuse Regulation.[21] In this regard, the Market Abuse Directive on Criminal Sanctions (2014/57/EU) requires Member States to ensure that insider dealing, recommending or inducing another person to engage in insider dealing, the unlawful disclosure of inside information, and market manipulation **A.1.15**

---

[19] For the influence of the Market Abuse Regulation on the civil liability for the violation of the prohibitions set out by it see Part A—Private Enforcement of the Market Abuse Regulation in European Law.

[20] See n 8.

[21] For an overview see eg Moloney (n 4) 766 ff.

constitute criminal offences in all cases when committed intentionally (Articles 3, 4, and 5 of the Market Abuse Directive on Criminal Sanctions (2014/57/EU)). Moreover, inciting, aiding, and abetting of these offences is punishable as a criminal offence (Article 6 Market Abuse Directive on Criminal Sanctions (2014/57/EU)). In addition to these definitions for criminal offences, the Market Abuse Directive on Criminal Sanctions (2014/57/EU) also sets out a general framework for the respective penalties (Article 7) and establishes liability for legal persons (Articles 8 and 9). Finally, Article 10 sets out the jurisdictions for these offences since they affect the capital markets of several Member States.

Level 2—Rules adopted by the Commission

A.1.16 Furthermore, in Article 35 of the Market Abuse Regulation the power to adopt delegated acts is granted to the Commission. These so-called Level 2 Legislative Acts usually deal with specific technical aspects. To date, the Commission has adopted nine delegated acts and one implementing act.[22]

Level 3—Guidelines and recommendations

A.1.17 Finally, the European Securities Market Authority (ESMA) can issue so-called Level 3 guidelines and recommendations. These guidelines and recommendations are intended to support the competent national authorities and market participants in the application of the Market Abuse Directive. Although these guidelines and recommendations are non-binding, Article 16(3) of the ESMA Regulation (1095/2010/EU) states that the competent national authorities and market participants must use their best endeavours to comply with them.[23]

V. Additional Regulation of Market Abuse by the Member States

A.1.18 A complex problem of the Market Abuse Regulation is whether it governs market abuse in the Member States exclusively. Under the (former) Market Abuse Directive (2003/6/EC), most Member States did not consider the directive as a maximum harmonization measure, and one therefore giving them the opportunity to expand its scope of application or to create additional rules for market abuse outside its scope. Although it is a directly applicable European regulation, this problem also occurs in the context of the Market Abuse Regulation. This is

[22] See art 35.

[23] Marloes van Rijsbergen, 'On the Enforceability of EU Agencies' Soft Law at the National Level: The Case of the European Securities and Markets Authority' (2014) 10 Utrecht Law Review 116; Edoardo Chiti, 'European Agencies' Rulemaking: Powers, Procedures and Assessment' (2013) 19 European Law Journal 93.

especially relevant regarding the detailed scope of application set out by Article 2 of the Market Abuse Regulation, owing to the fact that some Member States would prefer that the regulation were to have a broader scope of application and rules prohibiting market abuse than it actually does. As for the (former) Market Abuse Directive, under the new market abuse regime contained in the Market Abuse Regulation, it is necessary to distinguish in this context those aspects covered by the scope of application of Article 2 of the Market Abuse Regulation and those outside its scope. The rules set out by the Market Abuse Regulation within its scope of application (Article 2 of the Market Abuse Regulation) must be considered as exclusive. Therefore, Member States have no competence to create additional rules on market abuse regarding financial instruments already traded on markets covered by Article 2 of the Market Abuse Regulation. This is because Article 1 of the Market Abuse Regulation explicitly states that the Market Abuse Regulation establishes a common regulatory framework on market abuse. The ability of the Member States to create additional rules within the scope of application of the Market Abuse Regulation would undermine in particular the confidence of investors in those markets, since they would be faced with competing rules. Moreover, it should be borne in mind that the lack of uniformity in the market abuse regime under the (former) Market Abuse Directive (2003/6/EC) was the major reason for the European legislator to replace the directive with the Market Abuse Regulation. However, Member States are not limited in their ability to expand the scope of application of the Market Abuse Regulation to financial instruments or markets currently outside the scope of application covered by Article 2 of the Market Abuse Regulation. In this regard, Member States can choose between referring simply to the Market Abuse Regulation in national law or to create their own national laws for market abuse. If a Member State makes a reference to the Market Abuse Regulation that is outside its scope of application, the interpretation of these rules—including those referred to in the Market Abuse Regulation—is a matter of national law alone. Consequently, national courts of Member States cannot directly refer a case involving the interpretation of such a provision to the CJEU for a preliminary ruling under Article 267 of the TFEU.

2

THE CONCEPT OF INSIDER DEALING

I. Introduction

In a nutshell, and possibly oversimplifying, the rules governing insider dealing prohibit, and punish with administrative and criminal sanctions, trading in certain securities and financial assets while in possession of non-public information that is considered price sensitive, meaning that the information, if known by other investors, would affect the market price of the securities. This essential definition is sufficient to introduce the issue, but it requires several qualifications. **A.2.01**

The first qualification is that, notwithstanding the theoretically very clear goals of insider dealing regulation, the scope of the prohibition varies significantly depending on the jurisdiction and the legal tradition. Consider, for example, the two major models of insider trading regulation: The 'parity of information' approach adopted in the European legislation and in most European countries; and the US 'fiduciary-duty-based' theory of insider trading. The former has a potentially much broader reach. In fact, under the 'parity of information' approach, virtually everyone in possession of privileged information and aware of its character cannot trade, including for instance a bystander who by chance overheard a conversation between the executives of a listed corporation. Under the American approach, on the other hand, the prohibition operates only if additional requirements are met, such as the existence of a fiduciary relationship with the source of the information, or a misappropriation of the information. In addition to these macroscopic differences, jurisdictions of course present many other distinctions in how they define, interpret, and especially enforce insider dealing. **A.2.02**

A.2.03 A second qualification of the general definition offered above is that the basic prohibition is at the centre of a system, a web of rules whose complexity and extension has grown significantly over the last few decades. Depending again on the jurisdiction, trading while in possession of inside information is only one among many prohibited conducts, ranging from tipping inside information to conducting market soundings without proper protections of confidentiality. What is noticeable, however, is the additional number of compliance obligations, aimed at preventing unlawful behaviours, that the legislative evolution has imposed on issuers, investors, intermediaries, and executives, for example with respect to the creation of an appropriate 'insiders' list'.

A.2.04 The connection between the prohibition of insider trading and the duty to disclose price-sensitive information augments the complexity of the field. A common expression used in this context used to be 'disclose or abstain', meaning that—in the absence of confidentiality obligations—the insider can either disclose the information, therefore eliminating its inside nature, and be free to trade; or keep it confidential, but in this case she is not allowed to trade. The evolution and intertwine of statutory rules and case law has, however, profoundly altered the principle succinctly expressed by the formula 'disclose or abstain'. Several legal systems, including that of the European Union, have in fact generalized and anticipated the 'duty to disclose' to the very emergence of price-sensitive information. For example, under the EU Market Abuse Regulation, inside, price-sensitive information must be made public 'as soon as possible', unless there is a legitimate reason to delay the disclosure, and only under specific conditions aimed at protecting investors. The consequence of the different regulatory approach is that, today, in several jurisdictions, a more accurate expression to describe the essence of insider dealing rules might be 'abstain *and* disclose'.[1] The interrelation between the basic prohibition of insider trading and an extensive set of provisions

---

[1] More precisely, of course, you must abstain from trading until disclosure occurs. At this point, the information loses its confidential nature, the market can discount it, and everybody can trade. The moment at which disclosure takes place relates to the notion of inside information. Within the European Union, the anticipation of the duty to disclose has been achieved by adopting a single notion of inside information, which is applicable to both the insider dealing prohibition and the issuer's disclosure obligation. On the approach chosen by Regulation (EU) No 596/2014 see Jesper Lau Hansen, 'Say When: When Must an Issuer Disclose Inside Information?' Nordic & European Company Law Working Paper No 16-03 (19 September 2016) 19–27 https://papers.ssrn.com/sol3/papers.cfm?abstract_id=2795993 (last accessed 28 January 2017); Niamh Moloney, *EU Securities and Financial Markets Regulation* (3rd edn, OUP 2014) 730–3; Christian Kersting, 'Insider Dealing and Ad Hoc Disclosure Requirements in the New EU Market Abuse Regulation' (2014) 33 Banking & Financial Services Policy Report 15, 17. More generally for an overview of the disclosure regime under the first Market Abuse Directive see Carmine Di Noia and Matteo Gargantini, 'Issuers at Midstream: Disclosure of Multistage Events in the Current and in the Proposed EU Market Abuse Regime' (2012) 4 European Company and Financial Law Review 484, 507–15, who provide a comparative overview of some of the national rules adopted under the Directive of 2003; Mathias M Siems and Matthijs Nelemans, 'The Reform of the EU Market Abuse Law: Revolution or Evolution?' (2012) 19 Maastricht Journal of European and Comparative Law 195, 201; Jesper Lau Hansen and David Moalem, 'The MAD Disclosure

concerning the treatment of financial information is now essential to understand fully the legal framework we are considering.

Insider dealing is a controversial issue. On the one hand, it attracts extensive media attention, and is one of few securities regulation issues providing good material for movies and fiction. Insiders, together with Ponzi-schemers, are the archetypal financial villains, but the economic and ethical bases of the prohibition are or have been debated and raise complex legal, but also economic and philosophical questions, as demonstrated by the opposition to the prohibition of insider trading voiced by prominent scholars.[2] The following pages offer a general background for the analytical discussion of the single provisions of the Market Abuse Regulation contained in the second part of the book. The goal here is to take a broad view of the evolution of the phenomenon and the legal discourse surrounding it, rather than dwelling in the technicalities. This requires adopting an historical perspective and comparing and contrasting different regulatory approaches (in the interest of brevity, the focus is on the US and Europe, which offer a good proxy for most existing regulatory models). The economic and ethical basis invoked to support—or criticize—the prohibition will then be briefly discussed. **A.2.05**

Finally, this introduction will mention a few open questions or regulatory challenges that might be relevant in the next few years. **A.2.06**

II. An Historical and Comparative Perspective

Taking a sufficiently ample historical perspective, the repression of insider dealing is a relatively recent phenomenon. This is true not only with respect to the law in the books, but also, and especially, in terms of enforcement. According to a 2002 study, until the 1990s prosecution of insider trading was sporadic at best. Before 1990, only thirty-four countries had insider trading laws and enforcement. In terms of actual prosecution, this had occurred in only nine of them. **A.2.07**

Regime and the Twofold Notion of Inside Information: The Available Solution' (2009) 4 Capital Markets Law Journal 323, 328–9.

[2] Some of the most famous arguments against the introduction of insider dealing prohibitions have been put forward by Henry G Manne, 'In Defense of Insider Trading' (1966) 44 Harvard Business Review 113; Henry G Manne, *Insider Trading and the Stock Market* (The Free Press 1966). In this regard see also Dennis W Carlton and Daniel R Fischel, 'The Regulation of Insider Trading' (1983) 35 Stanford Law Review 857. See more recently Robert W McGee and Walter Block, 'An Ethical Look at Insider Dealing' (2014) https://papers.ssrn.com/sol3/papers.cfm?abstract_id=2419738 (last accessed 28 January 2017). Cf also Jonathan R Macey, 'The Genius of the Personal Benefit Test' (2016) 69 Stanford Law Review 64; Jonathan R Macey, 'Beyond the Personal Benefit Test: The Economics of Tipping by Insiders' (2016) https://papers.ssrn.com/sol3/papers.cfm?abstract_id=2870738 (last accessed 28 January 2017), who argued that certain trading conducts on the basis of inside information should be permitted to the extent that they reveal fraud or make markets more efficient.

In 1998, among the one hundred and three countries with (very diverse) stock markets, these numbers rose to eighty-seven and thirty-eight respectively.[3]

A.2.08 Of course, using confidential information for personal gain has always raised ethical issues, but it is only in the last thirty years that prosecuting the phenomenon has become a tenet of financial regulation. In the writings of Cicero, the great Roman politician, advocate and thinker, we find a brief discussion of the issue, although not surprisingly referring to commodities markets. Cicero considers the case of a grain merchant who arrives at a Greek port during a terrible famine, after having seen, on his voyage there, a large fleet bound for the same port and carrying grain. Should he disclose this piece of information, and be content with a lower price for his commodities? The author suggests that this would be the moral thing to do, but he seems to indicate the ethically desirable course of action, rather than to invoke the rigours of the law.[4]

A.2.09 With a leap of almost eighteen centuries, the US Supreme Court confirmed the legitimacy of insider trading in an 1817 decision, *Laidlaw v Organ*.[5] During the war between Britain and the US of 1812, the British blockade of the American ports—and in particular of New Orleans—had depressed the price of tobacco. A Mr Organ learned before others of the end of the hostilities, and purchased tobacco at a low price without disclosing the confidential information. While the analogies between this behaviour and the conduct currently prohibited under the laws governing insider trading are of course limited, if nothing else because Mr Organ dealt in commodities, it is interesting to note that Chief Justice Marshall concluded that the contract was perfectly valid and enforceable. Almost in the same years, an apocryphal story spread the legend that Nathan Rothschild, the founder of the fortunes of the famous family of bankers, speculated on British treasury bonds thanks to inside information on the defeat of Napoleon at Waterloo.[6] The source of this account was in fact a French anti-Semitic pamphlet aimed at tarnishing the reputation of the Rothschilds, but the very fact that the anecdote was fabricated indicates the social stigma against the exploitation of non-public information.

A.2.10 Until a few decades ago, however, not only in most countries was insider trading legally permissible, but many argued that using price-sensitive information was almost a normal and necessary component of the 'remuneration package' of corporate executives and directors.[7]

---

[3] Utpal Bhattacharya and Hazem Daouk, 'The World Price of Insider Trading' (2002) The Journal of Finance 75.

[4] Marcus Tullius Cicero, *De Officiis* Liber III, XII, 50.

[5] 15 US 178 (1817).

[6] Frederic Morton, *The Rothschilds: A Family Portrait* (1962) as cited in Marco Ventoruzzo and others, *Comparative Corporate Law* (West Academic 2015) 581–2.

[7] Among those who considered as 'compensation' for managers the profits obtained through dealing in financial instruments on the basis of inside information see Carlton and Fischel, 'The Regulation of Insider Trading' (n 2) 870, who, for instance, also argued that: '[t]he unique

The United States might be considered the first country to enact rules designed to curb the phenomenon with the New Deal legislation. The only provision explicitly regulating the matter, however, is not the most-commonly invoked Section 10(b) of the 1934 Securities and Exchange Act—which, in fact, does not include one single word clearly prohibiting insider trading—but Section 16(b), the so-called prohibition of short-swing profits.[8] This crude provision simply imposes the disgorgement to the issuer of profits obtained by buying and selling, or selling and buying securities in a period of six months when obtained by a narrowly defined group of primary insiders (directors, officers, and principal shareholders).[9] Section 10(b) and Rule 10b-5 thereunder, the broad 'anti-fraud' provisions that today constitute the basis of insider trading enforcement in the US, on the other hand, were also introduced in 1934, but for several decades were irrelevant for the repression of insider trading. **A.2.11**

It is only in the 1960s that the SEC, and federal courts, started interpreting these rules as including a prohibition of insider trading, even if enforcement remained quite exceptional at least through the 1980s. In Europe, until the 1980s and 1990s few countries regulated the phenomenon, and several Member States did so only due to EU obligations. In the UK, the first comprehensive regulation came in 1980; in Italy in 1991. In Japan, insider trading was criminalized at the end of the 1980s, and in China only in 1993. Several other countries still do not have insider-trading laws or, if they have them, enforcement is extremely rare. **A.2.12**

The United States, as the 'first-mover' on the issue, however, soon took a very peculiar path, leading to a convoluted approach that differs significantly from the one currently adopted by the Market Abuse Regulation. A detailed discussion of **A.2.13**

advantage of insider trading is that it allows a manager to alter his compensation package in light of new knowledge, thereby avoiding continual renegotiation'; Manne, *Insider Trading* (n 2) 138–41; Manne, 'In Defense' (n 2) 118–19; Henry G Manne, 'Insider Trading and Property Rights in New Information' (1985) 4 Cato Journal 933, 935–7; Kenneth E Scott, 'Insider Trading: Rule 10b-5, Disclosure and Corporate Privacy' (1980) 9 Journal of Legal Studies 801, 808. On the contrary see eg Stephen M Bainbridge, 'The Insider Trading Prohibition: A Legal and Economic Enigma' (1986) 38 University of Florida Law Review 35, 47–8.

[8] On the limited reach of Section 16(b) see Manne, 'In Defense' (n 2) 120. For further discussion on Section 16(b), Hsiu-Kwang Wu, 'An Economist Look at Section 16 of the Securities Exchange Act of 1934' (1968) 68 Columbia Law Review 260; Ellen Taylor, 'Teaching an Old Law New Tricks: Rethinking Section 16' (1997) 39 Arizona Law Review 1315; Marc I Steinberg and Daryl L Landsdale Jr, 'The Judicial and Regulatory Constriction of Section 16(b) of the Securities Exchange Act of 1934' (1999) 68 Notre Dame Law Review 33; Michael J Kaufman and John M Wunderlich, 'Section 16(b) and Its Limitations Period: The Case for Equitable Tolling' (2011) 39 Securities Regulation Law Journal 169, 169–72.

[9] It is interesting to note that the peculiar formula used to calculate the 'virtual profits' is not based on the actual difference in price of the securities sold, but rather applies a mechanism that might determine a 'gain' even when the insider actually had a loss or, at least, a lower gain. This element underlines the 'punitive' nature of this type of 'confiscation', which goes to the issuer rather than to the state or federal government (it is, in fact, generally enforced through derivative actions), something in line with the American idea of the 'Private Attorney General'. See Stephen M Bainbridge, *Insider Trading. Law and Policy* (Foundation Press 2014) 227.

these differences would require more space than the one available here, but a few insights should be sufficient to illustrate the general issue. In short, the very first applications of Section 10(b) of the 1934 Securities and Exchange Act and SEC Rule 10b-5 adopted the so-called 'parity of information' theory, meaning that no one in possession of privileged, price-sensitive information, could trade in securities.[10] In the seminal case of *Chiarella v United States*, however, the Supreme Court—one might argue, concerned with the policy implications of such a broad prohibition—concocted, without any real textual basis in the law, the so-called 'fiduciary duty' theory of insider trading.[11] Under this approach, in order to commit insider trading a fiduciary relationship between the insider and the source of the information was necessary. The problem, of course, is that the existence of a fiduciary relationship can be difficult to define, and the precise boundaries of the illicit conduct have since been, to use an expression of Judge Cardozo in a famous case, enveloped in the mist of the common law.[12]

A.2.14 From this moment on, the legal history of insider trading in the US is a long and complex tug-of-war among the legislature, the SEC, prosecutors, defendants, and judges, in which several new rules have been introduced, and doctrines developed, or bent, in the effort of creating a more rational system and closing the several loopholes created by the fiduciary-duties theory, or attempting to escape liability. Probably the most important development of this often-confusing evolution is the 'misappropriation theory' introduced with the 1997 Supreme Court decision of *United States v O'Hagan*.[13] As opposed to the 'classic theory' of insider dealing, the misappropriation theory extends the prohibition to whoever 'misappropriates' information belonging, for example, to his or her principal. In the specific case decided, O'Hagan was a lawyer who came to know of an acquisition on which another partner of the firm was working and traded based on this information. Once again, however, what precisely constitutes misappropriation was not rigorously defined: what about, for example, information obtained hacking into a computer? Courts have concluded that it might fit the definition, but not without some acrobatic hermeneutics.[14]

A.2.15 Uncertainty has also surrounded the relevance of tipping, in particular because of precedents indicating that the tipper had to obtain some 'personal benefit' from tipping, also an ambiguous notion. In 1983, the Supreme Court (*Dirks v SEC*[15]) took the position that a tippee assumes a fiduciary obligation not to trade only

---

[10] *In re Cady, Roberts and Co* 40 SEC 907 (1961); *SEC v Texas Gulf Sulphur Co* 401 F 2d 833 (2d Cir, 1968).

[11] 445 US 222 (1980).

[12] *Meinhard v Salmon* 249 NY 458 (1928).

[13] 521 US 642 (1997).

[14] The issue was expressly addressed, for instance, in *SEC v Dorozhko*, 574 F 3d 42 (2d Cir, 2009).

[15] 463 US 646 (1983).

when the insider tipping the information has breached her fiduciary duties, and the tippee knows or should have known this. In addition, pursuant to the same decision, the tippee is liable only if the insider receives a direct or indirect 'personal benefit' from the disclosure. The question of what kind of 'personal benefit' is relevant has been debated for almost three decades now but, in December of 2016, the Supreme Court stepped in to resolve, or at least limit a split among circuit courts. The Court of Appeals for the Second Circuit (*US v Newman*, 2014[16]) had in fact adopted a rather narrow interpretation, according to which the personal benefit of the tipper required at least a potential gain of a pecuniary or similarly valuable nature. The judges of the Ninth Circuit (*US v Salman*, 2015[17]), on the other hand, took a broader approach, holding that the 'intent to benefit a trading relative or friend' is sufficient for the tippee's liability. The Supreme Court shared the latter interpretation, but limited the relevant benefit of the insider to a gift to a trading 'relative or friend' (another slippery expression), stopping short of the more expansive view that a gift of inside information to anyone might be a ground for liability.[18] The stricter position of the government, closer to the European-style parity of information approach, was not embraced by this decision.

The two examples of the boundaries of the misappropriation theory and the ambiguities surrounding the definition of tipping demonstrate the complex and problematic nature of the US approach to insider dealing. This is hardly surprising. In the US insider dealing is based on very general 1930s statutory provisions, ground-breaking at the time of their enactment, but probably in need of updating. In addition, not-always-settled and often-convoluted judicial doctrines, SEC regulatory provisions enacted to fix enforcement problems or legislative *lacunae*, and creative interpretations of defendants and their brilliant attorneys have further complicated the body of applicable rules. **A.2.16**

The difficulties briefly evoked did not and do not prevent the SEC and the Department of Justice from aggressively prosecuting insider trading in the US, also thanks to the significant resources dedicated to this activity. The 'morass' of insider trading, to borrow the title of a *New York Times* article criticizing the American approach,[19] is also, at least in part, the inevitable consequence of the role played by case law in the US, but undoubtedly this lack of clarity, especially when criminal sanctions are involved, deserves to be stigmatized. In this perspective, the parity-of-information theory followed in Europe (and in many other parts of the world) might be too broad, but has the undeniable advantage of a **A.2.17**

[16] 773 F 3d 438 (2d Cir, 2014), *cert denied*, 136 S Ct 242 (2015).
[17] 792 F 3d 1087 (9th Cir, 2015), *cert granted*, 136 S Ct 899 (2016).
[18] *Salman v United States*, 137 S Ct 420 (2016).
[19] James B Stewart, 'Delving into Morass of Insider Trading' *New York Times* (19 December 2014).

comparatively clearer and more rigorous framework. As we will see throughout this book, while interpretative problems and uncertainties abound also in EU law, many of the complex problems raised in the US by concepts such as fiduciary duties, misappropriation of information, and tippee's benefit, do not exist on this side of the Atlantic. The paradox is that parity of information was, in fact, the first approach followed also in the United States, but eventually abandoned in its home country.

A.2.18 Many European countries, in fact, adopted insider trading rules only after the European Community (now Union) imposed them with the Insider Dealing Directive (1989/592/EEC). Germany with its WpHG, enacted in 1994, is a case in point; but the same is true for Italy, whose first comprehensive regulation of the phenomenon was introduced in 1991.[20]

III. The Rationale of the Prohibition: Economic and Ethical Perspectives

A.2.19 If the history of the rules governing insider trading teaches us something, it is that the rationale for the criminalization of the conduct is at the same time intuitive and problematic: intuitive because the predatory behaviour of a person taking advantage of an information asymmetry immediately raises ethical concerns and evokes fairness considerations; but also problematic because the desirability and scope of the prohibition have been and are questioned. Several authoritative scholars, in fact, have argued that allowing insiders to trade is in fact beneficial in terms of market efficiency and favours the price-discovery mechanism.[21] One question among the others that might be raised is why trading in securities on generally liquid markets should be treated differently from other transactions. For example, and depending on the legal system, only in limited circumstances does the buyer or seller of real estate have a statutory and mandatory duty to disclose information not available to her counterparty, and of course nothing similar to the 'disclose or abstain' rule applies to most transactions involving different assets.

A.2.20 Of course, the explanation has to do with the extreme difficulty of correctly pricing securities and evaluating the businesses and assets represented by shares, bonds, and other financial instruments. A good starting point to put things

[20] See Bhattacharya and Daouk, 'The World Price' (n 3) 75, who also observe that until 1967, when France introduced rules on insider trading, the United States was the only country that had already established them (at 88). For further discussion on the rules enacted in Europe at the national level before the Insider Dealing Directive (1989/592/EEC) see Emmanuel Gaillard (ed), *Insider Trading: The Laws of Europe, the United States and Japan* (Kluwer Law and Taxation Publishers 1992).

[21] See the authors cited in n 2.

into perspective is the famous definition of information efficiency formulated by Eugene Fama.[22] In short, Fama distinguished between weak, semi-strong, and strong efficiency, depending on the fact that market prices were able to reflect promptly all past information, all publicly available information, or also inside information. A different way to express the same concept is that, in a weakly efficient market, traders would be able to obtain extra profits simply by observing and interpreting past asset prices. In a semi-strong market, extra profits would be possible by factoring public information into investment decisions. Finally, a strong market is so 'efficient', so rapid, and effective in adjusting prices, that not even insiders would be able to speculate based on their information advantage, because market forces would promptly adjust prices. Empirical evidence suggests that most modern stock exchanges and financial markets have weak efficiency, while—not surprisingly—results are more ambiguous with respect to semi-strong efficiency. What seems undisputed, however, is that no market is efficient in the strong sense: in other words, insiders can generally always gain an extra profit when trading on the basis of non-public information.[23]

Nevertheless, occasionally markets have appeared effective in promptly— **A.2.21**
sometimes even within minutes—identifying and pricing new information. An interesting anecdote on the mechanisms of market efficiency concerns, for instance, the market reaction to the explosion of the space shuttle *Challenger* in 1986. The crash of the *Challenger* caught many by surprise and it took several months to investigate its causes. A commission of technical experts finally identified a faulty seal in the shuttle's rocket boosters supplied by a listed corporation named Morton Thiokol. Market reactions, however, did not wait until the end of the investigations. On the very day of the crash, the price of Morton Thiokol's stock experienced a sharp decrease, while the same did not happen, at least with that magnitude, to the stock of other NASA contractors involved in the building of the shuttle. Arguably, the market behaved efficiently in correctly allocating responsibility more quickly than the public authorities, but the question remains

[22] Eugene F Fama, 'Efficient Capital Markets: A Review of Theory and Empirical Work' (1970) 25 Journal of Finance 383; Eugene F Fama, 'Efficient Capital Markets: II' (1991) 46 Journal of Finance 1575.

[23] The idea that markets are efficient is also relevant for the so-called 'Fraud-on-the-Market' Theory, which is essential to facilitate private enforcement of liability for false or misleading financial information. The theory, as adopted in the leading case of *Basic v Levinson*, 485 US 224, 238 (1988), recently confirmed in *Halliburton Co v Erica P John Fund, Inc*, 134 S Ct 2398 (2014), holds that market prices of shares, in well-developed markets, reflect all publicly available information. The consequence is that investors trade relying on the integrity of prices, and this might allow a presumption of reliance, which lowers the burden of the proof of investors in securities litigation. In reality, the theory presents profound problems. First, relying on the fact that market prices reflect all publicly available information does not, in any way, imply relying on the completeness or truthfulness of that information: there is plenty of false public information, and even the dumbest of investors knows this. Secondly, and possibly even more importantly, investors trade *exactly* because they believe that market prices are not correct and that they have a better interpretation of the available information, because other investors are wrong in selling etc.

on how particularly informed trades have induced these price adjustment mechanisms. The line between strong-form market efficiency and insider trading can be, as in this case, extremely blurred.[24]

A.2.22 If we take the view that markets are not and cannot be efficient in a strong sense, the prohibition of insider dealing, and its corollaries, is a way to level the playing field by eliminating the very possibility of exploiting the absence of strong information efficiency on the market.

A.2.23 This explanation, however, does not really clarify why insider dealing should be prohibited, and in fact raises a second (provocative) question. Assuming that it is possible to obtain extra profits analysing public information (eg financial statements of listed corporations, macroeconomic variables etc), why should a sophisticated investor with significant resources devoted to market analysis be able to exploit his position, and someone possessing privileged information be required to abstain from trading? The intuitive answer is that, in the first case, the extra profits are the result of an investment that deserves to be protected and incentivized, with the side benefit of promoting analysis of information with (indirect) positive consequences for market transparency. Insiders, on the other hand, passively take advantage of other positions of trusts: they are the unproductive rentiers of market information.

A.2.24 This is, however, only a partial and not entirely satisfactory rationale. After all, as some criminal law experts say, insider trading could be deemed to be a 'victimless crime'. The hypothetical seller, unaware of the inside information, in fact wants to sell at that price, and he or she simply does not obtain the additional gain that might be obtained by insiders. The prohibition of insider trading, in fact, affects wealth distribution. An example might clarify. Let us assume that Bob has inside information indicating that tomorrow the price of X Inc shares will be €10, against a current price of €8. If he buys today shares from Linda, who wants to sell, at €8, keeps them for 24 hours, and then sells for €10 to Mike, Bob has made a profit of €2. By preventing Bob's trade, it is possible that Linda will enjoy the price increase selling to Mike when prices have risen, but it is also possible that Linda will still sell for €8 before the price increase and someone else—let us say a lucky non-insider—will pocket the €2 profit. Linda, in other words, is not necessarily negatively affected by the activity of the insider Bob and, to the extent she is, the consequence is only loss of profit, not actual monetary damages.

---

24 On the crash of the space shuttle *Challenger* in 1986 and on its implications in terms of market efficiency see Michael T Maloney and J Harold Mulherin, 'The Complexity of Price Discovery in an Efficient Market: the Stock Market Reaction to the *Challenger* Crash' (2003) 9 Journal of Corporate Finance 453.

It can be argued, therefore, that the primary, or at least an important goal of insider trading is distributive justice. There is possible merit to the argument that, at least under certain conditions, allowing insiders to trade might facilitate or speed up price discovery; that it might, in other words, render markets more efficient. The point, however, is that the advantage of the insider would undermine confidence in the fairness of the game, and potentially alienate non-insiders from the market, with negative consequences on liquidity. The real public good protected by insider regulation is trust in financial markets. The counterparties of an insider might not be victims of a crime in a traditional sense, but this does not mean that internal dealing is a victimless crime: the victim, simply, is the belief or feeling that the market is a levelled playing field. **A.2.25**

Seeing insider regulation as a way to foster fairness—actual or perceived— underlines the importance of distributive justice as a fundamental value ingrained in human beings and essential for social cohesion. Behavioural studies on dogs and monkeys confirm the value that social animals attribute to equality. In a series of clever experiments, for example, two dogs sitting next to each other were required to perform a simple task, such as giving the paw, but rewarded very differently for the same activity (for example, one was given more treats and cuddles than the other). They showed that they were sensitive to fairness, and the animal unjustly rewarded in a less generous way became uninterested in performing.[25] This is quite extraordinary, especially when both subjects were rewarded, although differently. In economic terms, we might say that cooperating with the experimenter (exchanging the paw for the treat) was Pareto efficient: both dogs obtained something and the total wealth, or utility, of the miniature pack of dogs. However, dogs, like investors, tend to disengage if they feel that they are treated unfairly, and that other participants in the game receive an unjust advantage. Whether this is rational or not depends on how crude and simplistic our notion of rationality is. The logic of insider trading prohibitions relies on a similar mechanism: the disincentives for dogs giving the paw, and for investors participating in the market, are not so different after all. **A.2.26**

The unfairness of insider trading has however also a price in terms of efficiency. Empirical evidence seems to suggest, for example, that vigorous enforcement of the prohibition of insider trading reduces the cost of equity by as much as 5 per cent.[26] **A.2.27**

---

[25] See eg in this line of research Friederike Range and others, 'The Absence of Reward Induces Inequity Aversion in Dogs' (2009) 106 Proceedings of the National Academy of Sciences of the United States of America 340 http://www.pnas.org/content/106/1/340.full.pdf (last accessed 28 January 2017).

[26] See Bhattacharya and Daouk, 'The World Price' (n 3).

IV. Insider Trading in the Market Abuse Regulation

A.2.28 As mentioned above, the first European regulation of insider trading dates back to 1989, and set in motion the widespread adoption of insider trading laws in Member States, which at the time existed only in three countries.[27] This first directive was followed by the (former) Market Abuse Directive (2003/6/EC), which profoundly changed the regulatory landscape in the area, essentially because it shifted the regulatory perspective from prohibiting a single unlawful conduct to fostering market transparency through a series of coordinated instruments, which included an entirely new market manipulation regime and a general disclosure obligation upon issuers regarding inside information. Notably, the (former) Market Abuse Directive (2003/6/EC) was a central component of the Financial Services Action Plan of 1999, which, as a whole, aimed to provide a more comprehensive legislative framework to the financial sector.

A.2.29 In July 2016, however, the new Market Abuse Regulation and Market Abuse Directive on Criminal Sanctions (2014/57/EU) came into effect, almost thirty years after the first harmonized regulatory framework.

A.2.30 The first thing to notice, of course, is the circumstance that two sources, a regulation and a directive, now govern the issue. As provided by its Article 1, the regulation, which is the subject of this book, establishes 'a common regulatory framework on insider dealing, the unlawful disclosure of inside information and market manipulation (market abuse) as well as measures to prevent market abuse to ensure the integrity of financial markets in the Union and to enhance investor protection and confidence in those markets'. It contains all the fundamental definitions and sets forth the prohibitions. The directive, on the other hand, complements the regulation by establishing minimum rules concerning criminal sanctions for insider dealing, unlawful disclosure of inside information, and market manipulation, referring to the definitions and provisions of the regulation.

A.2.31 The adoption of a regulation, instead of a directive, clearly serves the purpose of an effective and rapid maximum harmonization. With respect to criminal sanctions, on the other hand, a minimum harmonization approach was followed using the tool of a directive. The Market Abuse Directive on Criminal Sanctions (2014/57/EU) is, in fact, the first case of EU legislation on criminal matters based on new Article 83(2) TFEU as amended by the Lisbon Treaty, which allows the enactment of EU-wide minimum rules on criminal offences and sanctions if

27 Before the enactment of the Insider Dealing Directive (1989/592/EEC) only France, the United Kingdom, and Denmark had adopted specific rules on the subject: see Raffaello Fornasier, 'The Directive on Insider Dealing' (1989) 13 Fordham International Law Journal 149, 165.

these are essential to ensure that an EU policy is effectively implemented in the same way across the EU.

When compared to the (former) Market Abuse Directive (2003/6/EC), the Market Abuse Regulation has introduced important substantive innovations, for example significantly expanding its scope of application beyond financial instruments traded on EU regulated markets, and now including, for example, also instruments traded in multilateral trading facilities (MTF) or over the counter (OTC) and commodities markets and derivatives on commodities. The broader scope of application imposes costs and risks on a number of transactions previously exempted from complying with insider trading rules, and might in fact create disincentives, for example, to list securities on MTFs, especially for smaller issuers. It is unclear if, and in fact doubtful at all, that the European legislator fully considered the costs and benefits of such an ample application of the Market Abuse Regulation and the (former) Market Abuse Directive (2003/6/EC). **A.2.32**

With specific respect to the definition of insider dealing (and market manipulation), however, the new rules have not introduced profound changes, even if the Market Abuse Regulation now directly defines concepts such as 'information of a precise nature', 'significant effect on price', or 'reasonable investor test' previously left to delegated legislation. Some of the most innovative elements of the new framework can be found not so much in the definition of insider dealing, but rather in the set of rules surrounding the core definition and aimed at limiting the risk of violations, facilitating enforcement, or, more generally, governing confidential, price-sensitive information, such as rules on insider lists or market sounding. **A.2.33**

V. Open Questions and New Challenges

Going back to broader issues, insider dealing, as a still recent set of rules and theories, presents several open questions and challenges for scholars, regulators, enforcement authorities, judges, practitioners, and business people. Let us consider some of the most interesting ones. **A.2.34**

One important and delicate issue is that of double jeopardy or, to use an expression more common in continental Europe, *ne bis in idem*. The problem has been addressed by some very important decisions of the highest judicial bodies in both Europe and the United States, and it is quite simple to describe in general terms. Most modern legal systems include, in some cases at the constitutional level, a prohibition against substantive double jeopardy: none can be punished twice for the same facts. The protection often extends to procedural protections, prescribing also that none can be tried or be subject to investigation or adjudication twice for the same facts. This principle has profound and complex historical roots, and has been extensively studied by academics and judges. For our purposes, however, this simple definition might suffice. **A.2.35**

A.2.36 In virtually all jurisdictions, enforcement of insider trading relies on a combination of administrative (or 'civil') sanctions—usually monetary fines and possibly prohibitions or limitations to exercising certain professions—and criminal sanctions—which might also include prison time. Market authorities, such as the SEC in the United States, ESMA in the European Union, or one of the existing national agencies of the Member States generally administer and impose administrative sanctions. Prosecutors are, on the other hand, responsible for criminal sanctions, which can be imposed only after an adjudication procedure in front of a state or federal court, with the full protections of due process. This double track is considered by most commentators essential for effective enforcement, especially because the technical complexities of insider trading investigations require market authorities to play a role in the prosecution of the illicit conduct.

A.2.37 A first problem is that several systems distinguish between an administrative and a criminal sanction based on rather formal criteria represented by the 'name', the 'label' that the legislature has attributed to the sanction. Substantively, however, administrative and criminal sanctions for insiders in the form of pecuniary fines are quite similar. Administrative sanctions can easily amount to millions of euros, and the very measure of them is often the same as the one of criminal sanctions. In this perspective, some courts have concluded that the formal distinction between the two types of sanctions was a 'labelling fraud', and that in reality sanctions defined as 'administrative' in nature also had a punishing effect indistinguishable from that of a 'criminal' sanction. If this is true, people accused of insider trading and prosecuted by both regulatory agencies and public prosecutors might be subject to double jeopardy.

A.2.38 This reasoning—applicable not only to insider trading, but also to other issues such as violations of tax laws—can hardly be criticized. It raises, however, very practical problems both because if brought to its inevitable consequences it makes repression of insider trading very difficult, and because distinguishing substantively between sanctions that can be combined determines uncertainties and confusion. Both the United States Supreme Court and the European Court of Human Rights (ECtHR), have in fact tackled the issue with contradictory results. The US Supreme Court, in the 1980s, adopted a broad notion double jeopardy by recognizing that the labels 'criminal' or 'civil' attached by the law to a specific sanction 'are not of paramount importance', if both penalties have, in fact, a punitive intent.[28] This decision was, however, overruled in the 1990s in the case of *Hudson v United States*, where the US Supreme Court adopted a more formalistic approach.[29] The ECtHR, on the other hand, in *Grande Stevens*

[28] *United States v Halper*, 490 US 435 (1985).
[29] 522 US 93 (1997).

and Others v Italy, took a substantive stance, according to which 'administrative' sanctions may be considered of criminal nature independently from their 'label', in light of their severity, whenever they pursue a comparable punitive and deterrence function.[30] Also, the case law of the ECtHR has, however, followed an unsteady course. Recently, the Strasbourg Court came back to the issue in a tax law case, in which two Norwegian taxpayers claimed that they were prosecuted and punished twice for the same offence. Significantly, the ECtHR concluded that dual criminal and administrative proceedings are admissible as long as they are 'combined in an integrated manner so as to form a coherent whole'.[31] Clearly, however, this provides a much less defined standard, which for sure will bring uncertainty to the table, if not actually overrule *Grande Stevens*.

In addition, procedural double jeopardy, ie the right not to be subject twice to adjudication for the same facts, raises delicate problems, also in terms of coordination between enforcement actions. An even subtler problem concerns due process in administrative enforcement actions. Should the same protections of a criminal investigation and trial be also granted to a person facing the risk of an administrative sanction for insider trading? The answer is negative only if we exclude the criminal nature of sanctions formally labelled as administrative: certain protections are granted, but not the full panoply of extensive due process rights that characterize criminal enforcement. **A.2.39**

Even if we conclude that administrative sanctions are not criminal, and do not require the full due process protections of a criminal sanction, we are still left with a very concrete conundrum. The problem is that, as a practical matter, very often the results of the 'administrative' investigation conducted by supervision authorities—without the full protection of due process—are at least partially shared with prosecutors, and end up playing a (persuasive) role in the possible subsequent criminal investigation and trial. This might undermine the position of the accused in criminal litigation following administrative action for insider trading. One of the challenges faced by policy-makers, therefore, is to find the right balance between protecting the accused and ensuring an effective and economically sustainable enforcement apparatus, which requires the coexistence of prosecutors and administrative enforcement agencies. An apparently easy way to resolve this conflict might be to prohibit prosecutors from using, or even accessing, the information collected by supervisory authorities, but a similar solution would be highly inefficient and impracticable. **A.2.40**

A different type of challenge for insider trading regulation and enforcement, related to technological developments, comes from algorithmic and high-frequency **A.2.41**

[30] *Grande Stevens et autres c Italie* (Application nos 18640/10, 18647/10, 18663/10, 18668/10) (2014) ECtHR (4 March 2014).

[31] *A et B c Norvège* (Application nos 24130/11, 29758/11) (2016) ECtHR (15 November 2016).

trading. The expression refers to the use of supercomputers and extremely fast connections to execute, through specifically engineered software and hardware, thousands of transactions in order to exploit very small price changes; or to elaborate at high-speed available information, eg on price differences among different trading venues, and engage in arbitrage. This development, which nowadays constitutes a very significant percentage of all trades, has raised numerous issues. In brief, concerns have been expressed on its effect on volatility and transparency, and equal access to the market. Empirical studies have indicated mixed results, but it is fair to say that high-frequency trading does not seem to deserve outright prohibition.[32]

A.2.42 From the point of view of insider trading (and, from a different perspective, market manipulation), high-frequency trading in itself does not change the regulatory paradigm. If considered as simply a technology that allows operating at a speed unthinkable even a few years ago, and obviously impossible to reach for human traders, it is not radically different from the introduction of telegraph, fax machines, computers, or mobile phones. In other words, as long as the algorithms employed only use publicly available information, they should not raise a problem in terms of insider trading, at least not theoretically. From a more practical standpoint, however, they do raise a significant problem in terms of enforcement. When a computer is able to use even publicly disclosed information close to the speed of light, for example to factor in an announcement of the Federal Reserve to sell, less than a second later, securities, at a minimum regulators need to be able to track orders and activities of market participants at intervals of milliseconds. A difference of a fraction of a second might in fact separate an illegal trade from a legitimate one. Coherently with these technological breakthroughs, regulators have recently required stock exchanges and trading venues to use atomic clocks to time market activities and orders precisely.[33]

A.2.43 This problem is interesting but it is largely a factual issue, a question of effective enforcement. An additional and somehow more philosophical question, however, is whether the new technology, which creates profound differences among market participants in terms of their ability to take advantage of (public) information,

---

[32] Consob, 'Il trading ad alta frequenza. Caratteristiche, effetti, questioni di policy' (December 2012) *Quaderno No 5*; Charles R Korsmo, 'High-Frequency Trading. A Regulatory Strategy' (2014) 48 University of Richmond Law Review 523; Matt Prewitt, 'High-Frequency Trading: Should Regulators Do More?' (2012) 19 Michigan Telecommunications and Technology Law Review 131; Peter Gomber and others, 'High-Frequency Trading' (2011) https://papers.ssrn.com/sol3/papers.cfm?abstract_id=1858626 (last accessed 19 November 2016).

[33] For instance, within the European Union, in compliance with art 50 of the Markets in Financial Instruments Directive II (2014/65/EU), ESMA has developed draft regulatory technical standards to specify the level of accuracy to which clocks are to be synchronized, taking into account the relevant international standards: ESMA, 'Final Report: Draft Regulatory and Implementing Technical Standards MiFID II/MiFIR' ESMA/2015/1464 (28 September 2015), especially para 7.4. See also ESMA, 'Guidelines on Transaction Reporting, Order Record Keeping and Clock Synchronisation under MiFID II' ESMA/2016/1452 (10 October 2016).

raises concerns similar to the ones of insider trading in terms of perceived fairness and levelled playing field. The answer seems negative for at least a couple of reasons. First, it is desirable not to discourage investments in technology and information analysis, which might contribute to information efficiency. We do not want to limit the ability of investors to hire an extensive team of qualified analysts to understand better the financial positions of listed corporations. Similarly, we do not want to create obstacles to technological investment, and the possible advantages of high-frequency traders can be considered the reward for their investments. In addition, and somehow simplifying, the gains of these types of market participants are so miniscule on the individual transaction (although significant in the aggregate), that it can hardly be argued that they speculate on transactions in which, on the other side, there is an individual trader who suffers a disadvantage. The price adjustments determined by high frequency trading accelerate price discovery, but through tiny price movements that are almost unnoticeable for counterparties not using these technologies.

Accordingly, it is doubtful that distinctions should be made in the enforcement **A.2.44**
of the insider trading ban depending on the technology available to traders. In this regard, one could also wonder whether the fact that the Market Abuse Regulation has extended the scope of the insider dealing prohibition to the cancellation of orders might constitute a problem for high-frequency traders. Recent studies, however, suggest that the cancellation of orders might not be that much more frequent for high-frequency traders than for other market operators.[34] As a consequence, there is yet no clear evidence that the revised insider dealing prohibition will target high-frequency traders with greater severity now that its scope has been broadened.

One final issue worth mentioning, addressed by scholars and courts, but in our **A.2.45**
opinion not settled yet, concerns the possibility of insider trading based on highly personal and confidential information affecting the insider as an individual that can, however, have an impact on the market. Sometimes referred to, with a misnomer, as 'self-insider', the situation can be exemplified with the case of the charismatic CEO of an important public corporation who discovers she is seriously ill. Would she be responsible for insider trading if she sells shares before the disclosure of this clearly non-public and potentially price-sensitive information? Unless we conclude that this information does not relate, either directly or indirectly, to an issuer or to financial instruments (to use the wording of the Market Abuse Regulation), the response might be affirmative. However, the case raises very delicate privacy and individual freedom concerns. It is hard to pinpoint the rationality of the position, but there is something inherently problematic in

---

[34] Avanidhar Subrahmanyam and Hui Zheng, 'Limit Order Placement by High-frequency Traders' (2016) https://papers.ssrn.com/sol3/papers.cfm?abstract_id=2688418&download=yes (last accessed 31 January 2017).

prohibiting someone from trading in light of information concerning his or her own personal health or status. It might become difficult to draw precisely a line between personal choices and opinions that do not limit trading activities in any way, and information subject to insider prohibitions. In the previous hypothetical, for example, the CEO might argue that she decided to sell some of her assets foreseeing a disengagement with her professional activities, and possible medical expenses. Several legal systems, in fact, set forth exemptions that might be applicable to these situations, especially if the person can prove that the reason for selling securities at a certain time was the need of liquidity.

A.2.46 Notwithstanding this somehow instinctual reaction, we must conclude also that 'personal' information that has all the features of inside information can be relevant for insider purposes. If information, including on the health of executives, concerns directly or indirectly the issuer or the securities, is not public, and might have an impact on market prices, it is included in the scope of the prohibition, and cannot be treated differently on the basis of vague and uncertain criteria.

VI. Conclusions

A.2.47 Whether and when trading in securities based on privileged or price-sensitive information should be banned has long constituted the subject of vivid discussions. Even nowadays, with most legal systems prohibiting insider dealing, its rationale and scope are debated. Some scholars still argue that allowing insiders to trade might be beneficial for price discovery. Nevertheless, there are also solid arguments to support the idea that insider regulation fosters the creation of a level playing field for investors, with positive effects on market efficiency and the cost of capital. The risk, in fact, is that the edge enjoyed by insiders would undermine public confidence in the integrity of the markets.

A.2.48 Accordingly, while there is a broad consensus on the need to regulate insider dealing, different legal systems have regulated the issue in different ways. In the US, the 'parity of information' approach was soon abandoned in favour of the 'fiduciary-duty-based' theory of insider trading, according to which insider trading requires (the breach of) a fiduciary relationship between the insider and the source of the information. From this moment on, a complex web of rules and doctrines has developed, rendering insider trading one of the most arcane, and sometimes irrational, fields of securities and corporate law practice.

A.2.49 In Europe, the opposite approach has prevailed. From the introduction of EU-wide insider trading prohibitions with the Insider Dealing Directive (1989/592/EEC), 'parity of information' has been the hallmark of European law in this area. The (former) Market Abuse Directive (2003/6/EC) clearly adopted the 'parity of information' approach by requiring virtually everyone in possession of privileged information and aware of its character to abstain from trading. This position has been strengthened by the Market Abuse Regulation of 2014, which significantly anticipated the general 'duty to disclose' to the very emergence of price-sensitive information and extended the scope of application of the whole market abuse regime previously limited to financial instruments traded on EU regulated markets.

As a consequence, certain types of conduct that, under the European rules, would certainly fall under the insider dealing ban, could be permitted in the US as long as they do not constitute a violation of fiduciary duties or a misappropriation by the agent of information belonging to the principal. **A.2.50**

The problems that both systems face are, however, comparable, and the responses have sometimes been incredibly similar. For instance, on the issue of double jeopardy, both the US and the EU jurisprudence moved from a substantive approach, in which also sanctions defined as 'administrative' could be considered de facto 'criminal' and be subject to double jeopardy limitations, towards a more nuanced position that allows, within certain limits, dual criminal and administrative proceedings. **A.2.51**

Technological developments and, in particular, the widespread use of algorithmic trading and high-frequency trading might raise, however, new problems, if not in terms of substantive rules, at least in the hard-fought arena of enforcement actions. Consequently, with the Market Abuse Regulation the European regulator has also tried to adjust its market abuse regime to these sophisticated trading strategies, but the impact and the effectiveness of the new rules is still to be seen, at least with respect to the insider dealing prohibition. **A.2.52**

3

THE CONCEPT OF MARKET MANIPULATION

I. Historical Development of the Prohibition of Market Manipulation

Market manipulation is the oldest form of market abuse. Insider trading and the unlawful disclosure of inside information are a rather new phenomenon, having only been developed in the twentieth century.[1] In contrast, market manipulation can and did indeed occur on every market where the market prices are determined by supply and demand.[2] From almost from every epoch of human history, market manipulations are reported as being mainly based on the publishing of false or misleading statements.[3] While the problem of market manipulation was initially **A.3.01**

[1] See Part A—The Concept of Insider Dealing n 6 ff.

[2] For the general phenomenon of market manipulation see Franklin Allen and Douglas Gale, 'Stock Price Manipulation' (1992) 5 Review of Financial Studies 503; Daniel R Fischel and David J Ross, 'Should the Law Prohibit "Manipulation" in Financial Markets?' (1991–1992) 105 Harvard Law Review 503; Emilios Avgouleas, 'The Mechanism and Regulation of Market Abuse' (OUP 2005).

[3] See Jerry W Markham, *Law Enforcement and the History of Market Manipulation* (Sharpe 2014) giving an overview of market manipulations from ancient history to the present day.

considered as a problem of contract law—especially in the context of an obligation of the contractual parties to share certain information—it only later became a general concern of the regulation of markets. The first regulation and, in particular, prohibition of market manipulation dates back to the late nineteenth century, when this phenomenon became a general problem. Since at this time market manipulation was considered as a type of *fraud*, many jurisdictions simply expanded the application of this criminal offence to stock markets, which still leads today to the question of whether market manipulation can (also) constitute criminal fraud.[4]

II. Prohibition of Market Manipulation in European Capital Markets Law

A.3.02 In European law, the prohibition of market manipulation is a relatively new phenomenon. The Insider Trading Directive (1989/592/EEC) did not include this prohibition but focused instead only on insider trading.[5] The first European piece of legislation regarding market manipulation was drafted by the Forum of European Securities Commission (FESCO) in 1999, which developed a first standard with a definition of market abuse.[6] Also in 1999, the Commission published its action plan on 'Implementing the Framework for Financial Markets',[7] discussing the enactment of a directive including—among other things—a prohibition of market manipulation. Moreover, the 'Final Report of the Committee of Wise Men on the Regulation of European Securities Markets' (the so-called Lamfalussy Report) of 2001[8] pointed out that the common market needed a clear and concise definition of market manipulation, especially since the prohibition of market manipulation was completely unknown to the national law of some Member States.

(Former) Market Abuse Directive

A.3.03 Based on these reports, the Commission published its first draft for a Market Abuse Directive in May 2001,[9] which was later adopted as the (former) Market

[4] Case C-445/09 *IMC Securities BV gegen Stichting Autoriteit Financiële Markten* [2011] ECR I-5917, stating that the (former) Market Abuse Directive (2003/6/EC) did not state a duration requirement and that even a single abusive transaction is captured.

[5] Klaus J Hopt, 'The European Insider Dealing Directive' (1990) 27 Common Market Law Review 51, 80 ff.

[6] FESCO, 'Market Abuse'—FESCO's response to the call for views from the Securities Regulators under the EU's Action Plan for Financial Services.

[7] Commission, 'Implementing the Framework for Financial Markets: Actions Plan' COM(1999) 232 final. For further details see Jesper Lau Hansen, 'MAD in a Hurry: The Swift and Promising Adoption of the EU Market Abuse Directive' (2004) 15 European Business Law Review 183; Niamh Moloney, 'New Frontiers in EC Capital Market Law: From Market Construction to Market Regulation' (2003) 40 Common Market Law Review 809, 813 ff.

[8] See http://ec.europa.eu/internal_market/securities/docs/lamfalussy/wisemen/final-report-wise-men_en.pdf.

[9] 'Proposal for a Directive of the European Parliament and of the Council on insider dealing and market manipulation (market abuse)' COM(2001) 281 final.

Abuse Directive (2003/6/EC).[10] Pursuant to Article 5, Member States were obliged to prohibit any person from engaging in market manipulation. Article 1(2) of the (former) Market Abuse Directive (2003/6/EC) provided a general definition of market manipulation, following the general distinction between *transaction-based market manipulation*[11] and *information-based market manipulation*.[12,13] Although it included a detailed definition of market manipulation,

[10] Helena Bolina, 'Market Manipulation and Insider Dealing in the New Market Abuse Directive (2003/6/EC)' (2001–2002) 4 Revue Européenne de Droit Bancaire et Financier 555 ff; Guido A Ferrarini, 'The European Market Abuse Directive' (2004) 41 Common Market Law Review 711 ff.

[11] Article 1(2) of the (former) Market Abuse Directive (2003/6/EC) stated:

'Market manipulation' shall mean:

(a) transactions or orders to trade:

- which give, or are likely to give, false or misleading signals as to the supply of, demand for or price of financial instruments, or
- *which secure, by a person, or persons acting in collaboration, the price of one or several financial instruments at an abnormal or artificial level, unless the person who entered into the transactions or issued the orders to trade establishes that his reasons for so doing are legitimate and that these transactions or orders to trade conform to accepted market practices on the regulated market concerned;*

(b) transactions or orders to trade which employ fictitious devices or any other form of deception or contrivance;

...

[12] Article 1(2) of the (former) Market Abuse Directive (2003/6/EC) stated:

'Market manipulation' shall mean:

...

(c) dissemination of information through the media, including the Internet, or by any other means, which gives, or is likely to give, false or misleading signals as to financial instruments, including the dissemination of rumours and false or misleading news, where the person who made the dissemination knew, or ought to have known, that the information was false or misleading. In respect of journalists when they act in their professional capacity such dissemination of information is to be assessed, without prejudice to Article 11, taking into account the rules governing their profession, unless those persons derive, directly or indirectly, an advantage or profits from the dissemination of the information in question.

In particular, the following instances are derived from the core definition given in points (a), (b) and (c) above:

- conduct by a person, or persons acting in collaboration, to secure a dominant position over the supply of or demand for a financial instrument which has the effect of fixing, directly or indirectly, purchase or sale prices or creating other unfair trading conditions,
- *the buying or selling of financial instruments at the close of the market with the effect of misleading investors acting on the basis of closing prices,*
- *taking advantage of occasional or regular access to the traditional or electronic media by voicing an opinion about a financial instrument (or indirectly about its issuer) while having previously taken positions on that financial instrument and profiting subsequently from the impact of the opinions voiced on the price of that instrument, without having simultaneously disclosed that conflict of interest to the public in a proper and effective way.*

[13] For this general distinction see n 6 ff.

taking into account all kinds of behaviour relating to market manipulation, the practical impact of the (former) Market Abuse Directive (2003/6/EC) was—in this regard—somewhat limited. However, particularly during the financial crises and owing to certain scandalous events that occurred in the capital markets of some Member States, it turned out that a number of behavioural and trading techniques were not covered by the definition. This applied principally to short selling[14] and the manipulation of the rate in the so-called LIBOR scandal, where major European banks engaged in manipulation of the London Interbank Offered Rate (LIBOR), the interest rate that banks pay on money they borrow from one another, in order to increase the interest rate charges for borrowers.

Market Abuse Regulation and accompanying directions and regulations

A.3.04 Owing to problems with the implementation and application of the (former) Market Abuse Directive (2003/6/EC), in October 2011 the Commission published its first draft for a Market Abuse Regulation to replace the (former) Market Abuse Directive (2003/6/EC).[15] This new draft Market Abuse Regulation also followed the general distinction between transaction-based market manipulation (Article 12(1)(a) and (b))[16] and information-based market manipulation (Article 12(1)(c) and (d)).[17]

Specific (other) regulations of market manipulation

A.3.05 Market manipulation is not only a phenomenon of capital: it is also prohibited by regulations governing other markets. This is especially the case for the energy market, in respect of which there is a special prohibition of market manipulation (Article 5 Wholesale Energy Market Integrity and Transparency Regulation (1227/2011/EU)). Like Article 12 of the Market Abuse Regulation, the Wholesale Energy Market Integrity and Transparency Regulation (1227/2011/EU) also provides in its Article 2(2) a detailed definition of market manipulation.[18]

III. Forms of Market Manipulation

A.3.06 In contrast to the prohibition of insider dealing, market manipulation is not a single act or a set of different behaviours but is more of a multi-layer phenomenon

---

[14] See n 9.

[15] For further details see Part A—History, Application, Interpretation, and Legal Sources of the Market Abuse Regulation n 8.

[16] See art 12 n 3 ff.

[17] ibid.

[18] See also art 1 n 12 for a further discussion of the relation of the prohibition of market manipulation in art 5 Wholesale Energy Market Integrity and Transparency Regulation (1227/2011/EU) to the Market Abuse Regulation in general.

covering all kinds of behaviour generally not accepted in a market. In capital markets law, four different forms of market manipulation have developed, which can also be found in the Market Abuse Regulation (and other European legislation). These are information-based manipulation (see A.3.07), transaction-based manipulation (see A.3.08), short selling (see A.3.09), and other forms of manipulation (see A.3.10). However, the Market Abuse Regulation does not refer expressly to each of these forms of market manipulations but defines market manipulation in its Article 12 in general.

Information-based manipulation

The first form of market manipulation is the so-called information-based manipulation, where the person acting usually publishes false or misleading signals regarding financial instruments, knowing that the information being published is false or misleading. The motivation for information-based manipulation is to influence the market price of a financial instrument to place an order in advance or afterwards gaining some profit from this manipulation, owing to the creation of an artificial price level. Thus, the financial professional tries to persuade other participants in the market that the price or volume of a security or financial product is not at the actual or current value. Whether such an artificial price level exists or not can be very difficult to determine, since this requires a determination of the right market price for the financial instruments. However, in the case of information-based manipulation, this determination is usually less problematic, because only an abnormal increase or decrease in the market price of the financial instrument has to be deemed to be closely connected with the publication of the false or misleading signals or rumours. Since the publishing of false or misleading statements does not require large resources and is relatively simple, information-based manipulation is the most common form of market manipulation. Moreover, the numerous publication requirements (eg financial statements, disclosure of inside information, and transparency regarding major shareholdings and financial instruments pursuant to the Transparency Directive [(2013/50/EU)]) can easily lead to an unintended information-based manipulation by the issuer.[19] Because it is based on the publication of false or misleading signals, information-based manipulation can constitute not only market manipulation but also insider dealing, raising the difficult question of whether the prohibition of these two forms of market conduct are related to each other.[20] Typical forms of information-based manipulation are so-called *painting the tape*[21] or *scalping*.[22] **A.3.07**

[19] For the intent requirement for committing market manipulation see n 12 ff.

[20] See n 11 for further details.

[21] *Painting the tape* usually means presenting non-existent orders on the price tape to feign (non-existent) strong demand (see eg Lars Teigelack, 'Market Manipulation' in Rüdiger Veil (ed), *European Capital Markets Law* (1st edn, Hart Publishing 2012) para 14 n 16).

[22] See n 11.

In the Market Abuse Regulation, information-based manipulation is considered as market manipulation pursuant to Article 12(1)(c) and (d) and Article 12(2)(d).

Transaction-based manipulation

A.3.08 Another form of market manipulation is the so-called transaction-based manipulation, where somebody enters in a transaction, placing an order to trade to influence the market price of a financial instrument. Here, the manipulator tries to create an—even if very short-lived[23]—artificial price level for the financial instruments. However, in contrast to the information-based manipulation,[24] the determination of the *right* price level compared to the artificial price level can be extremely difficult and sometimes even impossible to establish. Nevertheless, it should be borne in mind that the determination of the *right* price level in contrast to the artificial price level is not usually necessary. Particularly with regard to administrative sanctions[25] and criminal sanctions,[26] it is sufficient that the manipulator committed a market manipulation in general. Only in the context of the civil liability of the manipulator[27] will such a determination be mandatory, usually putting a severe burden of proof on the claimant. In contrast to the information-based manipulation,[28] transaction-based manipulation usually concerns huge investments, since only large transactions have the potential to influence the market price of a financial instrument. Therefore, transaction-based manipulation can often be found in small markets regarding financial instruments with small daily trading volumes. Prominent examples of transaction-based manipulation are *wash sales*,[29] *marking the close*,[30] *spoofing*,[31] or *improper match orders*.[32]

[23] Case C-445/09 *IMC Securities BV gegen Stichting Autoriteit Financiële Markten* [2011] ECR I-5917, stating that the (former) Market Abuse Directive (2003/6/EC) did not state a duration requirement and that even a single abusive transaction is captured.

[24] See n 7.

[25] See Part A—Public Enforcement of the Market Abuse Regulation.

[26] See art 15 n 8 ff.

[27] See Part A—Private Enforcement of Market Abuse Regulation in European Law.

[28] See n 7.

[29] In a *wash sale*, the seller and the buyer of financial instruments are—from an economic point of view—the same person. In this case, the buyer or seller is usually a company wholly owned by the seller or buyer.

[30] *Marking the close* focuses on the close of trading in a market by influencing the closing price by executing purchase or sales orders immediately prior to the market closing, since orders are often executed at the closing price. See also art 12(2)(b) Market Abuse Regulation.

[31] *Spoofing* describes a technique where a manipulator who is holding a long position submits several orders, signalling to the market that there is an increase in demand. As soon as the market price for the financial instruments increases, the orders are cancelled prior to execution. The concept of this manipulation technique is that other market participants also submit orders for these financial instruments owing to the increasing demand and market price. See also art 12(2)(c)(iii) Market Abuse Regulation.

[32] By using *improper matched orders* several persons place a huge amount of orders at identical conditions. This usually gives a signal to the market that there is a higher demand, although the trades actually executed are not based on market conditions but on agreements between these

A very common form of market manipulation involves stabilization measures undertaken during an initial or secondary offering of securities, since the issuer usually agrees with one or several financial institutions or investment firms to undertake the necessary volume of transactions to keep the price of the financial instruments for a fixed period up to a certain level, which is usually above the initial offer price. However, since these transactions are widely accepted in all modern capital markets, Article 5 of the Market Abuse Regulation provides a *safe harbour* exempting them from the prohibitions of Articles 14 and 15 of the Market Abuse Regulation.[33] Even though the safe harbour provision of Article 5 of the Market Abuse Regulation also applies to buy-back-programmes for shares, this kind of transaction does not necessarily constitute a market manipulation, even though it creates an artificial price level for shares.[34]

The transaction-based market manipulations are covered by the Market Abuse Regulation in its Article 12(1)(a) and Article 12(2)(a) to (c) and (e). The definitions set out in Article 12(1)(a) of the Market Abuse Regulation are completed by a list of indicators in Annex I of the Market Abuse Regulation.

Short selling

A specific form of market manipulation is short selling. While this trading technique was not addressed in the (former) Market Abuse Directive (2003/6/EC), especially during the financial crises of 2007/2008 an intense discussion started in Europe whether short selling should be considered as market manipulation or completely banned.[35] This discussion came to an end when the Short Selling Regulation (236/2012/EU) was enacted in 2012, establishing reporting requirements for short positions and restrictions especially for uncovered short sales. Although having created a specific regulation for short selling, the European legislator failed to address the relation of these requirements and restrictions to the (former) Market Abuse Directive (2003/6/EC). Consequently, the relation of the Market Abuse Regulation—and especially its prohibition of market manipulation (Articles 12, 15)—to the Short Selling Regulation (236/2012/EU) remains unclear. However, according to the general principle of *lex specialis derogat legi generali*, an application of the Market Abuse Regulation is excluded when a transaction or a behaviour falls within the application of the Short Selling Regulation (236/2012/EU). Nevertheless, the extent of that principle remains untested in the current practice and is still open to debate. **A.3.09**

---

persons. Also in this case, the manipulators hope that other market participants also place buy orders, resulting in an increase of the market price of the financial instruments involved.

[33] See art 5 n 3.

[34] See art 5 n 5.

[35] See Jennifer Payne, 'The Regulation of Short Selling and Its Reform in Europe' (2012) 13 European Business Organization Law Review 413, 421 ff.

Other forms of manipulation

A.3.10 Since market manipulation can already occur in many different forms, often being constantly improved and replaced by new forms, the (former) Market Abuse Directive (2003/6/EC) included a catch-all provision in its Article 5(2)(b) that transactions or orders to trade employing fictitious devices or any other form of deception or contrivance constitutes market manipulation. The Market Abuse Regulation follows that approach by stating the same principle in its Article 12(2)(b). The definition set out in Article 12(1)(b) of the Market Abuse Regulation is completed by a list of indicators in Annex I of the Market Abuse Regulation.

IV. Market Manipulation and Insider Trading

A.3.11 Although the Market Abuse Regulation distinguishes explicitly between market manipulation and insider trading, these two forms of market abuse can overlap. This is especially the case for so-called *scalping*, where typically a person known to the public for a certain expertise in capital markets and investments publicly recommends the acquisition or the disposal of a certain financial instrument which he or she had previously acquired. After the public recommendation—typically based on incorrect information—this person realizes the profit based on the changed price of the financial instrument. The term *scalping* is based on the idea that this person *scalps* other market participants. Such behaviour combines elements of insider trading and market manipulation, since the person so acting gives a false statement to the public (information-based market manipulation) without disclosing that he or she owns a position of that financial instrument he or she wants to dispose of afterwards (insider trading). In some jurisdictions (eg Germany[36]), such behaviour is considered to amount to information-based market manipulation and not as insider trading because the information (acquiring financial instruments knowing that a personal recommendation will be published later) used to acquire the relevant financial instruments is only information about the person acting himself and not about the issuer or the financial instruments. Although this interpretation is generally doubted, to be considered as insider dealing, it is usually necessary to ascertain an obligation for the person acting to disclose his or her conflict of interest. This problem of an overlap between insider trading and market manipulation regarding scalping is also pointed out in the development of the Market Abuse Regulation itself. While the proposal for the Market Abuse Regulation considered scalping as insider trading (Article 8(3)(d) Market Abuse Regulation Proposal), pursuant to Article 12(2)(d) scalping is now

[36] See German Federal Court of Justice of 6 November 2003, 1 StR 24/03 (*Sascha Opel*), BGHSt 48, 373 = NJW 2004, 202; affirmed by German Federal Court of Justice of 4 December 2013, 1 StR 106/13, BGHSt 59, 105 = NJW 2014, 1896.

considered as market manipulation. Although this problem is settled for scalping in Article 12(2)(d) of the Market Abuse Regulation, the general problem of distinguishing market manipulation and insider trading still remains under the new regime. However, it should be noted that such a clear and precise differentiation between these two forms of market abuse is relevant *only* for the criminal sanctions, since in criminal law the conviction must be based on a clearly defined criminal offence.

V. The 'Missing' Intent Requirement for Market Manipulation

One remaining puzzle of the new market abuse regime of the Market Abuse Regulation is the requirement for intention to commit market manipulation. Neither the (former) Market Abuse Directive (2003/6/EC)[37] nor the Market Abuse Regulation clearly states whether an act, trade, or behaviour must be committed intentionally to constitute a market manipulation as defined in Article 12 of the Market Abuse Regulation. Apart from the fact that the definition of intent in the (criminal and civil) law of the Member States is far from homogenous and is also not harmonized in other areas of the Capital Market Union (CMU), the question of whether intention to commit market manipulation is necessary or not becomes even more puzzling when considering the requirements set out in the Market Abuse Directive on Criminal Sanctions (2014/57/EU). Pursuant to Article 5(1) of the Market Abuse Directive on Criminal Sanctions (2014/57/EU), Member States are only obliged to ensure that market manipulation is treated as a criminal offence only for serious cases *and* when they are committed *intentionally*. Although it could be argued with an *argumentum e contrario* that the intention to commit a crime is not required for committing market manipulation under Article 5(1) of the Market Abuse Directive on Criminal Sanctions (2014/57/EU), where intention is expressly required for criminal offences, it must be doubted that—outside the scope of criminal sanctions—intention is generally not necessary. This is the case since, in the end, every act, trade, or behaviour requires at least some kind of intent. **A.3.12**

The problem of the intent requirement for market manipulation must be solved within the context of the respective sanction. For administrative sanctions,[38] the Market Abuse Regulation does not require intent, instead leaving this question to be resolved by the national administrative laws of the Member States. The same **A.3.13**

[37] Article 1(1)(1)(2)(c) of the (former) Market Abuse Directive (2003/6/EC) stated that for an information-based manipulation the manipulator who made the dissemination knew, or ought to have known, that the information was false or misleading. Therefore, intent at least was required for this form of market manipulation.

[38] See Part A—Public Enforcement of the Market Abuse Regulation.

applies for civil liability for committing market manipulation,[39] since usually the national tort laws of the Member States provide that not only must the tort itself be committed intentionally but that the person committing the market manipulation had some form of intent regarding the damage caused by his or her act. For criminal sanctions, this problem is addressed in Article 5(1) of the Market Abuse Directive on Criminal Sanctions (2014/57/EU), leaving the regulation of the intent requirement itself for criminal sanctions to the Member States.[40]

VI. Enforcement of the Prohibition of Market Manipulation

A.3.14 In its current state, the Market Abuse Regulation and the accompanying directives focus on criminal sanctions (see A.3.15) and administrative sanctions (see A.3.20). In contrast, civil liability for the violation of the prohibition of market manipulation is completely omitted from the Market Abuse Regulation (see A.3.21).

Criminal sanction

A.3.15 The regime of the Market Abuse Regulation is mainly based on criminal sanctions for the violation of the prohibition of market manipulation. However, criminal sanctions are not directly set out by the Market Abuse Regulation itself but by the Market Abuse Directive on Criminal Sanctions (2014/57/EU). By choosing a directive instead of a regulation in this context, the European legislator deviated from the general idea of the new market abuse regime as part of the Capital Market Union (CMU) to govern it directly by regulations. However, the detailed characteristics of market manipulation set out in the Market Abuse Directive on Criminal Sanctions (2014/57/EU) state that market manipulation is a criminal offence, providing general principles for the penalties for committing market manipulation and dealing with the jurisdiction over these offences. Hence, the Market Abuse Directive on Criminal Sanctions (2014/57/EU) sets out solid and common ground regarding criminal sanctions under the European market abuse regime. In this regard, the new market abuse regime takes a giant step further than the (former) Market Abuse Directive (2003/6/EC), since the latter directive did not impose any obligation for the Member States to impose criminal sanctions.

A.3.16 The basic characteristics are that the Member States must ensure that a serious case of market manipulation committed intentionally constitutes a criminal offence (Article 5 Market Abuse Directive on Criminal Sanctions (2014/57/EU)). It is worth noting that the Market Abuse Directive on Criminal Sanctions (2014/

[39] See Part A—Private Enforcement of Market Abuse Regulation in European Law.

[40] See art 15 n 8 ff.

57/EU) provides a specific definition for market manipulation, and does not refer to Article 12 of the Market Abuse Regulation. Moreover, inciting, aiding, and abetting engagement in market manipulation and attempting to commit market manipulation must be punishable as a criminal offence under national law (Article 6 Market Abuse Directive on Criminal Sanctions (2014/57/EU)).

In addition to the requirement to establish market manipulation as a criminal offence, the Market Abuse Directive on Criminal Sanctions (2014/57/EU) also determines the general framework for the penalties for committing the offence of market manipulation, which must be effective, proportionate, and dissuasive (Article 7(1) Market Abuse Directive on Criminal Sanctions (2014/57/EU)). This means that the criminal offence of committing market manipulation must be punishable by a maximum term of imprisonment of at least four years (Article 7(1) Market Abuse Directive on Criminal Sanctions (2014/57/EU)). **A.3.17**

In addition, Member States must also take the measures necessary to ensure that both legal natural persons can be held liable for offences committed for their benefit by any person, acting either individually or as part of an organ of the legal person (Article 8(1) Market Abuse Directive on Criminal Sanctions (2014/57/EU)). In this regard, the Market Abuse Directive on Criminal Sanctions (2014/57/EU) not only addresses natural but also legal persons. Pursuant to Article 8(1) of the Market Abuse Directive on Criminal Sanctions (2014/57/EU), legal persons can be held liable for offences committed for their benefit by any person, acting either individually or as part of an organ of the legal person. **A.3.18**

Finally, Article 10 of the Market Abuse Directive on Criminal Sanctions (2014/57/EU) states that the Member State shall have jurisdiction over an offence when this offence has been committed in whole or in part within that Member State's territory or by one of its nationals, at least in cases where the act is an offence where it was committed. **A.3.19**

Administrative sanctions

Like the (former) Market Abuse Directive (2003/6/EC), the Market Abuse Regulation also addresses administrative sanctions. However, in this regard the administrative sanctions governed by Article 30 onwards of the Market Abuse Regulation are more far-reaching than those of the (former) Market Abuse Directive (2003/6/EC). The Member States must ensure that the competent authority shall: order the person responsible for the infringement to cease the conduct and to desist from any repetition of that conduct; ensure that the person responsible for the infringement reimburses any illegal profits or losses avoided owing to the infringement; warn the public by identifying the person responsible for the infringement and the nature of the infringement; withdraw or suspend the authorization of an investment firm; discharge a person from managerial responsibilities within an investment firm; and order administrative pecuniary **A.3.20** sanctions of at least three times the amount of the profits gained or losses avoided because of the infringement (Article 30(2) Market Abuse Regulation).[41] Also, the European legislator introduced a naming-and-shaming-mechanism under which the identity of the person subject to the decision of the competent authority is published, together with the decision imposing the administrative sanction (Article 34 Market Abuse Regulation).[42] See also in general Part A—Chapter 6 for further details on the public enforcement of the Market Abuse Regulation.

Civil liability

A.3.21 In contrast to criminal and administrative sanctions, the new market abuse regime does not deal at all with the problem of civil liability for committing market manipulation. Therefore, in this regard the national laws of the Member States apply, which are mostly based on tort law or some tort law-related principles especially developed for capital markets law. However, it should be noted that the international jurisdiction for these claims being based on market manipulation is governed neither by the Market Abuse Regulation nor by the national laws of the Member States but by the Brussels I bis Regulation (2012/1215/EU). Although, the Brussels I bis Regulation does provide a specific regulation for the determination of the international jurisdictions for these claims, its general rule for tort law in Article 7(2) of the Brussels I bis Regulation (2012/1215/EU) applies in this context. Therefore, the national courts of the Member States have jurisdiction where market manipulation has occurred. However, it is still not settled whether this is the place where the market manipulation is committed or where the loss of the affected market participants originates.

A.3.22 The lack of regulation of civil liability for market manipulation in the Market Abuse Regulation constitutes one of its major weak spots. This is especially the case since, in the last decade or so, market manipulation has occurred in a number of Member States,[43] thus raising the question of whether the investors being harmed by such market manipulation can claim damages from the person or persons committing market manipulation. Since these developments are not based on European capital markets law and usually deviate from Member State to Member State, a competition for the most investor (=claimant)-friendly capital markets tort law could develop, thereby questioning the general purpose of the Market Abuse Regulation to establish a common regulatory framework on market manipulation (Article 1 Market Abuse Regulation).

[41] For further details see art 30 Market Abuse Regulation n 10 ff.

[42] For further details see art 34 Market Abuse Regulation n 7 ff.

[43] See eg the *Porsche-Volkswagen-Takeover* involving the failed takeover of Volkswagen by Porsche, causing huge losses for investors with short positions (for further details see eg Teigelack, 'Market Manipulation' (n 21) n 17).

VII. Market Manipulation and General Criminal Law

Market manipulation can also be relevant in the context of general criminal law, especially regarding the criminal offence of fraud. In the criminal law of some Member States, market abuse—especially insider trading and market manipulation—does not constitute a criminal fraud, since the monetary benefit of the person committing the market abuse does not necessarily equate to the damage that the other market participants suffer. However, it is worth noting that, in some legal systems, market manipulation is nevertheless considered as fraud,[44] which has a tremendous influence on the problem of civil liability, since most legal systems provide civil claims for the victim of a fraud. Also, the intention necessary to commit a fraud could be problematic since, in the case of insider trading and market manipulation, the perpetrator does not necessarily intend to defraud a certain person suffering from the market abuse but only the market itself and therefore all (other) market participants in general. Since this problem is neither covered by the Market Abuse Regulation nor by the Market Abuse Directive on Criminal Sanctions (2014/57/EU), the Member States are not limited by European law to sanction market manipulation with the criminal offence of fraud. **A.3.23**

[44] See eg the old case law of the Swiss Federal Court of Justice of 27 September 1996, BGE 122 II, 422 later abandoned by Swiss Federal Court of Justice of 18 January 2010, BGE 134 IV, 210 requiring that the benefit equals the damage (so-called *Stoffgleichheit*).

4

PUBLIC DISCLOSURE OF INSIDE INFORMATION AND MARKET ABUSE

I. Overview

Articles 17 to 21 of the Market Abuse Regulation, and their predecessor—Article 6 of the (former) Market Abuse Directive (2003/6/EC)—have in common that they mandate positive behaviours, contrasting with the abstention requirements laid down in Articles 14 and 15 on insider dealing, unlawful disclosure of inside information and market manipulation. **A.4.01**

In this sense, Articles 17 to 21 appear to complement the main market abuse prohibitions, serving the ancillary purpose of reducing the potential occurrences of insider dealing or market manipulation, through special, prompt, or objective disclosure requirements weighing on persons categorized according to the sensitivity of their professional positions.[1] **A.4.02**

Articles 17 to 19 mainly concern issuers and their managers: they require the former to inform the public as soon as possible of inside information which **A.4.03**

[1] To be contrasted with preventative measures resulting in reporting requirements to the competent authorities: see Article 16.

directly concerns them (Article 17) and, on a continuous basis, to draw up lists of their insiders (Article 18); they mandate the latter to notify the significant transactions they enter into relating to the instruments of their companies (Article 19).

A.4.04 Articles 20 and 21 impose objectivity and transparency requirements on persons producing or disseminating investment recommendations and on public institutions disseminating statistics or forecasts.

II. Impact of the Market Abuse Regulation

A.4.05 Considering the overwhelming evidence of a high level of market abuse activity, even in countries where the prohibitions are the toughest,[2] one may claim that the preventative measures represent in fact the market abuse regulation's main contribution.

A.4.06 Undoubtedly, the general evolution of EU market abuse law directly and specifically impacts the disclosure requirements laid down in Chapter 3 of the Market Abuse Regulation. As indicated, this evolution does not so much relate to the general philosophy of the market abuse offences and of their preventative measures, which remains based on macro-financial imperatives, especially investors' confidence in the fairness and efficiency of the price-formation process, secured through the imposition of a minimal level of market egalitarianism regarding access to and use of information.[3] This evolution mostly concerns the legal status, the scope, the volume, and the technicalities of the different prohibitions and disclosure requirements arising from EU market abuse law, which represent important practical issues for listed companies, their managers, and, beyond, for everyone possessing inside information. The assessment process of the (former) Market Abuse Directive (2003/6/EC) review identified a number of problems—eg negative impacts in terms of market integrity and investor protection; uneven

---

[2] See eg See A Bris, 'Do Insider Trading Laws Work?' Yale School of Management, European Corporate Governance Institute, European Financial Management (2005) Vol 11, No 3 267–312; J Cox, 'Illegal Insider Trading: How Widespread Is the Problem and Is There Adequate Criminal Enforcement?' Hearing before the Committee on the Judiciary US Senate, One Hundred Ninth Congress, Second Session (26 September 2006); FSA Occasional papers series no 25, Updated Measuring Market Cleanliness (March 2007) http://www.fsa.gov.uk/pubs/occpapers/op25.pdf; Capital Markets CRC Limited, 'Enumerating the Cost of Insider Trading' (unpublished 2010); P Augustin, 'Detecting Illegal Insider Trading' HLS Forum on Corporate Governance and Financial Regulation (27 November 2016).

[3] For a comparison see A Pietrancosta and C A Umhoefer, 'Le délit d'initié: Insider Trading Law in France' (1992) 30 Columbia Journal of Transnational Law 89; S M Bainbridge, 'An Overview of US Insider Trading Law: Lessons for the EU?' UCLA School of Law, Law-Econ Research Paper No 05-5, 2005; M Ventoruzzo, 'Comparing Insider Trading in the United States and in the European Union: History and Recent Developments' ECGI, Law Working Paper No 257/2014 (May 2014); Niamh Moloney, *EU Securities and Financial Markets Regulation* (3rd edn, OUP 2014) 700 (Moloney, *EU Securities and Financial Markets Regulation*); J Armour and others, *Principles of Financial Regulation* (OUP 2016) 160 ff. (Armour and others, *Principles*).

playing field; compliance costs and disincentives for mid-sized issuers to raise capital—that needed to be dealt with.[4]

Increase of uniformity

First, the replacement of the (former) Market Abuse Directive (2003/6/EC) by a Market Abuse Regulation certainly helps addressing the insufficient cohesion of the previous regulatory framework resulting from the options and discretions offered to Member States and the numerous differences in the interpretation and implementation at national level of the 2003 market abuse minimum harmonization directive.[5] However, this effort towards uniformity faces limitations: intrinsically, it does not eliminate the risk of divergence in national interpretations of the new European provisions, whose key concepts remain open and abstractly defined; more directly, the Market Abuse Regulation grants discretion either to the Member States or their competent authorities to decide on important practical matters, especially the explanations that issuers delaying public disclosure of inside information have to provide *ex post* to the NCAs, the threshold for notification of managers' transactions or the author of the publication of managers' transactions. **A.4.07**

Secondly, as the desire to create a level playing field among trading venues has led to a significant extension of scope of the disclosure requirements, the will to clarify certain key issues, and provide a more comprehensive, precise, and detailed regime in order to offer greater legal certainty for investors operating on a pan-European basis, has resulted in a remarkable amplification and refinement of the disclosure requirements' specifications. At level 1, such requirements, which were enshrined in the single, one-page long Article 6 of the (former) Market Abuse Directive (2003/6/EC), are now detailed in the eight-page long Articles 17 to 21. Such detail facilitates the comprehension of the new regime and allows for a better distinction among the different categories of persons subject to the requirements, although the prescriptions remain substantially the same. Despite the fact that the increase in the level 1 provisions is partly due to the absorption of much of the content of the previous level 2 provisions, the amplification is also palpable at level 2, where the three implementing directives of the (former) Market Abuse Directive (2003/6/EC), all entirely or partially devoted to its Article 6,[6] **A.4.08**

---

4 See EU Commission, 'Staff Working Paper: Impact Assessment', SEC(2011) 1217 final.

5 See ESME, 'Report EC Call for Evidence: Review of the MAD' (2007) 3 ff www.ec.europa.eu (ESME Report); C di Noia and M Gargantini, 'The Market Abuse Directive Disclosure Regime in Practice' (2009) Rivista delle Società 24; CESR, 'Review Panel Report Options and Discretions 2009 (CESR/09-1120) (29 March 2010) www.cesr.org.

6 Commission Directive 2003/124/EC of 22 December 2003 implementing Directive 2003/6/EC as regards the definition and public disclosure of inside information and the definition of market manipulation, OJEU, L 339/70 (24 December 2003); Commission Directive 2003/125/EC of 22 December 2003 implementing Directive 2003/6/EC as regards the fair presentation of investment recommendations and the disclosure of conflicts of interest, OJEU, L 339/73 (24 December 2003); Commission Directive 2004/72/EC of 29 April 2004 implementing Directive

are repealed and replaced by two delegated regulations and three implementing regulations,[7] adopted by the Commission either by way of ordinary delegation or through implementing technical standards or regulatory technical standards submitted by ESMA.

Increase in scope and in weight of the disclosure requirements

A.4.09 The increase in scope and in weight of the disclosure requirements raises a number of concerns. One relates to the application in time of the new legal regime, since the severity of the new provisions may play a determinative role in this regard. Indeed, even though the relevant provisions fall out of the 2014 (former) Market Abuse Directive (2003/6/EC) remit, their criminal nature, as autonomously characterized by the European Court of Human Rights and the European Court of Justice, triggers for the accused the special protection regime expressed through the double principle of the non-retrospective application of criminal law *in pejus* and of the retroactive application of criminal law *in mitius*.[8]

Rigidification of the new disclosure requirements

A.4.10 Another concern lies in the rigidification of the new disclosure requirements, the burdens and costs entailed by their increased level of detail or their over-inclusiveness that can no longer be eased nationally. The benefits of this evolution are not self-evident in terms of efficiency and not even in terms of legal certainty. Paradoxically, the replacement of a directive with a regulation may in some instances end up creating more uncertainty where detailed implementing prescriptions bringing some relief to actors subject to disclosure requirements have disappeared in the process of their transfer to the level 1 regulation, or where general national legislators as well as national competent authorities (NCAs) had provided for particular relief or safe harbours that they were or felt obliged to repeal in achieving the 'negative transposition' required by the Market Abuse Regulation. In addition, more rigid rules governing issuers' disclosure requirements may play a significant role when assessing the burden of the new Market Abuse Regulation requirements and may push issuers to consider listing alternatives: for example, issuers may evaluate delisting from their EU multilateral trading facility or selecting a listing or trading venue on a non-EU market for

---

2003/6/EC as regards accepted market practices, the definition of inside information in relation to derivatives on commodities, the drawing up of lists of insiders, the notification of managers' transactions and the notification of suspicious transactions, OJEU, L 162/70 (30 April 2004).

[7] See Article 35.

[8] See Article 49 European Union's Charter of Fundamental rights; Article 7 European Convention on Human rights, as extended by recent case law (Grand Chamber, *Scoppola v Italy* (No 2)) (Application no 10249/03) judgment Strasbourg (17 September 2009); *Del Rio Prada v Espagne* (no 42750/09) paras 77–80, CEDH 2013; *Rohlena v Czech Republic* (no 59552/08) para 50 (27 January 2015); Fourth section, *Contrada v Italy* (No 3) (no 66655/13) (14 April 2015).

future transactions, with a consequent negative impact in terms of overall competitiveness of the European financial markets.[9]

Special provisions for small and medium-sized enterprises

The only counter-reaction to the expansion in the scope and depth of the issuers' disclosure requirements lies in the introduction of special provisions designed for small and medium-sized enterprises (SMEs) in order to adapt legislation to their particular needs, alleviate their administrative burdens and facilitate their access to financing.[10] However, the ambit of the simplified regime aimed at issuers whose financial instruments are admitted on SME growth markets may disappoint their beneficiaries, as it is limited to only two technical provisions, relating to the website where inside information should be posted and the obligation to draw up insider lists. Finding the right balance here is not an easy task since markets for SMEs' financial instruments are less liquid and transparent and therefore present a higher level of risk for investors. **A.4.11**

This general evolution only accentuates the problems associated with fundamental choices made in the past decade when reshaping some particular market abuse preventative measures. This is especially the case for the main prophylactic tool used in this chapter, ie the requirement imposed on listed issuers to disclose publicly and as soon as possible of all inside information which directly concerns them. The alleged assignment of such a broad public disclosure requirement to the mere function of market abuse prevention is indeed problematic and creates an ambiguity which has important repercussions on its legal regime. **A.4.12**

III. Ad Hoc Disclosure (Article 17)

Rather than a mere ancillary provision, Article 17, successor to Article 6 of the (former) Market Abuse Directive (2003/6/EC), in spelling out the so-called 'ad hoc', 'continuous', or 'ongoing' public disclosure of inside information requirement, appears as one of the cornerstone provisions of EU securities regulation. Its reach goes far beyond the mere preventative function of insider dealing induced by its inclusion in the Market Abuse Regulation[11] as it forms the European legal general basis for ad hoc disclosure, one of the three pillars of listed issuers' **A.4.13**

---

9 See Shearman & Sterling, 'EU Market Abuse Regulation—Implications for Non-EU Issuers with Securities Traded on an EU Market' (23 June 2016) www.shearman.com.

10 According to the Commission, a number of provisions contained in the (former) Market Abuse Directive (2003/6/EC) 'impose administrative burdens on issuers, notably those whose financial instruments are admitted to trading on SME growth markets, that should be reduced', Proposal for a regulation on insider dealing and market manipulation, 2011/0295 (20 October 2011) recital (6).

11 See recital (49).

transparency, beside periodic and occasional disclosure. By construction, this continuous transparency requirement is of the utmost practical importance for the day-to-day life of issuers, investors, regulators, and financial markets in general, which tends to follow an endlessly accelerating pace.

A.4.14 The legislative history of the issuer ad hoc disclosure regime is here to underline the absence of entire subjection of the ad hoc disclosure requirement to market abuse prevention. This transparency requirement is indeed as old as the EU securities regulation itself and its consecration occurred a decade before the adoption of a European prohibition of insider dealing. It is only with the (former) Market Abuse Directive (2003/6/EC) that, departing from the path initiated and followed from the outset, it was decided to transfer the issuer ad hoc disclosure regime into the new market abuse directive.[12]

A.4.15 Unquestionably, the issuer ad hoc disclosure legal duty serves a greater purpose than the mere prevention of market abuses. The fact that this requirement has been enshrined since 2003 in a market abuse directive and is now part of a market abuse regulation may distort the perception and comprehension of its various functions. Indeed, from this angle, such a requirement appears essentially as a mere complement to the main market abuse prohibitions, serving the ancillary purpose of reducing the potential occurrences of insider dealing or market manipulation. As underlined by recital (49) of the Market Abuse Regulation, '[t]he public disclosure of inside information by an issuer is essential to avoid insider dealing and ensure that investors are not misled'. The reasoning is implicitly based on the realistic assumption that the market abuse prohibitions and their direct preventative measures, such as the duty of confidentiality weighing on insiders or the reporting requirements of their suspicious transactions, are only relatively effective and should be supported by an overarching plain disclosure requirement aimed at reducing the amount of available inside information and consequentially its use and abuse.

A.4.16 If the prophylactic function is undisputable, as is the indirect contribution to the fairness of the market, the ad hoc disclosure requirement can hardly be reduced to this single goal. Along with all the other disclosure requirements imposed on listed issuers, it serves the greater purpose of enhancing the transparency and, therefore, efficiency of capital markets. As elegantly put by the 1966 Segré Report, ongoing disclosure specifically ensures 'a steady flow of intelligence to shareholders and the public … indispensable if investors and their advisers are to be enabled to take fully informed investment decisions'.[13] History and geography amply show that, although they may be aligned to a certain extent, these two functions should

[12] See art 20 of the (former) Market Abuse Directive (2003/6/EC), repealing arts 68(1) and 81(1) of Directive 2001/34.

[13] European Commission, 'The Development of a European Capital Market: Report of a Group of Experts Appointed by the EEC Commission' (1966) 228.

not be confused.[14] As indicated, the European compulsory publication of inside information has existed long before the introduction of an insider dealing prohibition and for broader purposes; in the United States, these two functions are dealt with through separate sets of requirements. To be sure, even if no insider dealing could be perpetrated due to strong direct preventative measures or deterrence, there would still exist a case for the imposition of a positive duty of on-going transparency in order to increase the efficiency of capital markets through the improvement of the price-formation process and the reduction of the negative effects of the asymmetrical distribution of information between issuers and investors on the functioning of the markets. Reverting the perspective, some may view the market abuse prohibitions as complementary safeguards for capital market full transparency,[15] in the sense that transparency reduces the possibilities for insiders willing to trade on inside information to postpone unduly its disclosure, or to disclose information prematurely in order to cash in on their inside trading or to disclose false information and abuse the market.

The complexity of the ad hoc disclosure requirement's functions shed a broader light and helps to understand the legal regime. This combination of functions explains why the persons subject to this positive obligation are not necessarily the same as the ones subject to the market abuse prohibitions; why this disclosure obligation only weighs on issuers and not on any type of insiders; how European law departs from a 'duty to disclose *or* abstain' logic, as non-issuers are in general simply under a duty to abstain, whereas issuers find themselves in a position to abstain *and* disclose or sometimes even in a position to abstain *without* disclosing where they can show a legitimate interest to delay publication. **A.4.17**

The incorporation of the ad hoc disclosure requirement in the (former) Market Abuse Directive (2003/6/EC) also led to the use of a unified event, namely 'inside information', for triggering both the duty to abstain and the duty to disclose. The (former) Market Abuse Directive (2003/6/EC) put an end to the previous 'two-step model', characterized by the existence of a distinct definition of private information that has to be publicly disclosed by issuers and private information that may not be unduly used or circulated by insiders. Departing from the path initiated and followed from the outset, and finally dismissing the idea to align the definition of price-sensitive information to be published on an ad hoc basis with the definition of material information to be included in the listing particulars or prospectuses, the (former) Market Abuse Directive (2003/6/EC) endorsed a 'one-step model', erecting the notion of inside information as a common constituent element from which derive all the duties set out in the Directive ie the prohibition **A.4.18**

[14] See Philipp Koch, 'Disclosure of Inside Information' in Rüdiger Veil (ed), *European Capital Markets Law* (1st edn, Hart Publishing 2012) para 19 note 3 ff; Armour and others, *Principles* (n 3) 161 ff.

[15] See recital (15) (former) Market Abuse Directive (2003/6/EC).

to enter into transactions, the confidentiality duty and the disclosure duty placed upon the issuers.

A.4.19 This reorientation has generated wide criticism, owing to the costly risk of confusion between these duties' partly distinct functions that this single-step model can engender. In its evaluation of the (former) Market Abuse Directive (2003/6/EC) and its implementation by Member States, published in 2007, the European Securities Markets Expert Group (ESME) characterized the application of a common definition of inside information to both the prohibition of insider dealing and duty of publication by the issuer as 'a fundamental flaw of the directive'.[16] The report stated that this flaw had led to national resistance, becoming a significant source of national inconsistencies in the interpretation, implementation, and enforcement of the (former) Market Abuse Directive (2003/6/EC) across Europe. Indeed, whereas a one-step model prevailed in Germany and France, other Member States including the UK, Italy, and the Nordic countries leaned towards a two-step model that either restricted the definition of inside information adopted for disclosure purposes to actual decisions and events that have already occurred (Nordic countries and Italy) or extended the definition of inside information for insider dealing purposes (UK).[17] Curiously, after the Commission recalled, in its 2009 solicitation for evidence, the 'important advantages' of a disclosure requirement based on a somewhat broad definition of inside information, as an 'incentive for improving public availability of information regarding the issuers and their financial instruments', investors' confidence, liquidity, and efficiency of financial markets, and 'as an effective means to reduce the possibilities of insider dealing',[18] the Commission's 2011 draft Market Abuse Regulation

---

[16] ESME Report (n 5) 5; P Staikouras, 'The Conundrum of the Market Abuse Directive Preventative Measures for EU Financial Services' Integration' in 'Search of Equilibrium between Market Integrity Enhancement and Undue Regulatory Encumbrance' (2008) 35 Legal Issues of Economic Integration 351, 356; C di Noia, M Milič, and P Spatola, 'Issuer Obligations under the New Market Abuse Regulation and the Proposed ESMA Guideline Regime: A Brief Overview' *ZBB* (2014) 96, mentioning 'a fatal flaw'; R Veil and P Koch, 'Towards a Uniform European Capital Markets Law: Proposals of the Commission to Reform Market Abuse' Bucerius Law School, Working Paper Series 1/2012; Koch, 'Disclosure of Inside Information' (n 14) para 19; Moloney, *EU Securities and Financial Markets Regulation* (n 3) 73.

[17] See di Noia and Gargantini, 'The Market Abuse Directive Disclosure Regime in Practice' (n 5); J L Hansen and D Moalem, 'The MAD Disclosure Regime and the Two-Fold Notion of Inside Information: The Available Solution' (2009) 4 Capital Markets Law Journal 323; Jelena Lepetic, 'Public Disclosure of Inside Information' (2012) 3 Belgrade Law Review 188; Hartmut Krause and Michael Brellochs, 'Insider Trading and the Disclosure of Inside Information after Geltl v Daimler' (2013) Capital Markets Law Journal 283; Koch, 'Disclosure of Inside Information' (n 14) para 19; L Hellstén, *Disclosure and Delayed Disclosure of Inside Information in the Light of the EU Market Abuse Regulation* (University of Helsinki Faculty of Law, Master's thesis, February 2015); Jesper Lau Hansen, 'Say When: When Must an Issuer Disclose Inside Information?' Nordic & European Company Law Working Paper No 16–03 (19 September 2016), 5 https://papers.ssrn.com/sol3/papers.cfm?abstract_ id=2795993 (last accessed 12 November 2016).

[18] EU Commission, 'Call for Evidence: Review of Directive 2003/6/EC on Insider Dealing and Market Manipulation' (April 2009) 9 www.ec.europa.eu; CESR, 'CESR's Response to the European Commission's Call for Evidence' (2009) 4 www.cesr.org.

proposed a move towards a UK-style two-step model, through an expansion of the definition of 'inside information' exclusively applicable in the field of insider dealing.[19] Such a change would have directly contradicted the ESME's conclusion that the definition of 'inside information' worked well as an element of the insider dealing prohibition but gave rise to problems when determining when an issuer had a duty to make information public, underlining the risk of insider dealing and market manipulation caused by the disclosure of premature information.[20] The Commission proposal did not survive the opposition of one-step-model countries, in particular Germany,[21] to the creation of a 'light' notion of inside information for insider dealing purposes. Compared to the proposed dualist model, the one-step model could claim to be a lesser burden for its users. As a result, the choice for a common definition of inside information as a triggering event of the insider dealing prohibition and of the issuer disclosure requirement, ie the rejection of a distinction between information whose vocation is to remain private but that may not be unlawfully used by insiders and information whose vocation is to be made public and contribute in the price-formation process, was clearly reaffirmed.

The one-step model certainly comes out stronger from the Market Abuse **A.4.20**
Regulation. The replacement of the (former) Market Abuse Directive (2003/6/EC) by a European regulation will leave less room for manoeuvre in two-step-model countries. Moreover, with regard to events that have not yet occurred, the repealing of the safe harbour provision allowing issuers to postpone disclosure until the triggering event comes into existence, following what has been called a 'principle of reality',[22] will weaken national resistance in favour of a two-step model.

Coupled with the extension of the notion of inside information, the strength- **A.4.21**
ening of the one-step model will certainly make its drawbacks more acute and therefore intensify criticism. The risk of confusion between the distinct functions of the ad hoc disclosure requirement and the market abuse prohibitions has already materialized. The Court of Justice of the European Union (CJEU) in *Markus Geltl v Daimler AG*[23] showed how the interpretation of the notion of inside information in a disclosure case can be contaminated by considerations related to insider dealing. Undoubtedly, the extension of the notion, which is understandable in the context of the insider dealing prohibition, gives rise to problems when determining when an issuer had a duty to make information

[19] See Moloney, *EU Securities and Financial Markets Regulation* (n 3) 733; C Kersting, 'Insider Dealing and Ad Hoc Disclosure Requirements in the New EU Market Abuse Regulation' (2014) 33 Banking and Financial Services Policy Reports 15.

[20] See ESME Report (n 5); di Noia, Milič, and Spatola, 'Issuer Obligations' (n 16).

[21] See K Langenbucher, 'Insider Trading: An Exercise in (Economic and Legal) Transplants' (2013/2014) Remediation Technologies Development Forum 35.

[22] See Hellstén, *Disclosure and Delayed Disclosure of Inside Information in the Light of the EU Market Abuse Regulation* (n 17).

[23] Case C-19/11 *Markus Geltl gegen Daimler AG* [2012] ECR I-0000, ECLI:EU:C:2012:397.

public, underlining the risk of insider trading and market manipulation caused by the disclosure of premature information.[24] The issuer's requirement to disclose intermediate steps in protracted processes may even disrupt the overall balance of the issuer disclosure regime, in the sense that it reduces the use of occasional insiders' lists and increases the pressure on the supposedly limited possibilities for an issuer to delay the publication of insufficiently mature information.

A.4.22 The principle-based characteristic of the European ad hoc disclosure duty will make the problem more acute. Suffice it to say that Article 17, as its predecessor in the (former) Market Abuse Directive (2003/6/EC), imposes on issuers listed on EU financial markets a transparency requirement that is far more demanding than the corresponding obligations in the United States, disclosure regulation's homeland.

A.4.23 The European general obligation to disclose publicly as soon as possible all inside information which concerns directly the issuer contrasts negatively, from a legal certainty viewpoint, with the event-specific approach favoured in the US, where there exists a closed list of particular events that issuers should report under the 1934 Securities and Exchange Act, through a Form 8-K.[25] Even if the number of the reportable events increased significantly in 2004,[26] after the passing of the Sarbanes-Oxley Act, somewhat reducing the gap between the two systems, these events remain specifically defined. Not only is there a limited number of disclosable events but the SEC has detailed at length, specifying the triggering events for disclosure, the content of disclosure, the timing of disclosure, which should happen within four business days after the occurrence of the event, and provide for a safe harbour to protect issuers against potential civil liability. Under the famous Rule 10b-5, prohibiting any act or omission resulting in fraud or deceit in connection with the purchase or sale of securities, and incidentally the primary instrument for regulating insider trading, the US Supreme Court decided in 2011 that companies are not subject to 'an affirmative duty to disclose any and all material information', disclosure being only required 'when necessary to make … statements made, in the light of the circumstances under which they were made, not misleading'.[27] The reluctance to create such a general duty lies precisely in the uncertainty as to when information becomes material and must

---

[24] ESME Report (n 5); di Noia, Milič, and Spatola, 'Issuer Obligations' (n 16).

[25] See T L Hazen, *The Law of Securities Regulation* (7th edn, West Academic Publishing 2017) 330 ff.

[26] See SEC, 'Additional Form 8-K Disclosure Requirements and Acceleration of Filing Date' (25 March 2004) www.sec.gov.

[27] *Matrixx Initiatives, Inc v Siracusano* 131 S Ct 1309 (2011). See ESMA, reminding 'that when there is a change in a published inside information, and the change itself constitutes a new inside information, this new information is covered by the inside information's provisions within the Market Abuse Regulation, and the full process of public disclosure would have to take place (again)'. ESMA, 'Draft Technical Standards on the Market Abuse Regulation (ESMA/2015/1455)' (28 September 2015) www.esma.org.

be disclosed, and the risks of judicial second-guessing and of excessive liability imposed on listed companies owing to an effective private litigation system.[28] A cynical mind would wonder whether the comparatively strong stance taken by the European Union on disclosure requirements only has a chance to emerge and survive in a low enforcement environment.

The enlargement and intensification of the ad hoc disclosure requirement directly lead to a stronger emphasis on the issuer's right to delay disclosure. Having abolished the informal deferred mechanism in case of events not yet occurred,[29] the Market Abuse Regulation imposes as the only recourse the ordinary delay in disclosure, which is subject to a series of strict substantial, organizational, and procedural conditions. **A.4.24**

There is no question that the existence of such a possibility is an absolute necessity for issuers submitted to an ad hoc disclosure requirement. Given its particular nature, ad hoc disclosure of inside information increases significantly the overall amount of available information related to listed securities, which can only add to the economic benefits ordinarily attached to transparency in terms of market efficiency, market liquidity, cost of capital, agency relationship, corporate fraud, and, of course, market abuse. However, as much as its continuous characteristic makes it highly valuable compared to other types of information, it is also the source of inherent boundaries. Real-time information can indeed be destructive for an issuer: it may harm its property rights, compromise ongoing deals, weaken its competitive positions, destabilize its internal organizational structure, accelerate its financial difficulties, add unduly to market volatility, fuel perverse strategic behaviours,[30] create false expectations for its investors and/or mislead the market. A proper balance of interests is therefore to be set in order to accommodate the necessary dose of privacy inherent to business life without compromising the general requirement of listed issuers' transparency. If this compromise appears to mark a relative victory of the issuers' micro-interest against the capital markets' macro-interest, this opposition should not be overstated since it is likely that no issuer would ever accept the listing of its securities on a market under the drastic condition that it has to remain under the public eye continuously, without any hiatus, and live in a modern-type financial Panopticon, even as concerns inside information. Nonetheless, the ways in which this necessary compromise **A.4.25**

---

[28] E Greene and O Schmid, 'Duty-Free Insider Trading?' (2013) Columbia Business Law Review 369.

[29] See para A.4.20.

[30] See eg W Schön, 'Corporate Disclosure in a Competitive Environment: the ECJ's Axel Springer Case and the Quest for a European Framework for Mandatory Disclosure, Max Planck Institute for Intellectual Property, Competition and Tax Law, Law Working Paper No 55/2006' (February 2006); A Shleifer, *Inefficient Markets: An Introduction to Behavioral Finance* (OUP 2000) 112–52.

materializes show that the cursor is everywhere depending on the state and influence of the opposing forces.

A.4.26 From the outset, before insider dealing law even emerged, the European compromise took the form of the possibility for issuers to delay public disclosure where such disclosure would jeopardize their legitimate interests, under the supervision of their NCAs. Only the definition of such legitimate interests and the role devoted to NCAs changed over time.

A.4.27 Article 17 Market Abuse Regulation largely maintains the previous legislative framework, only changing the distribution of competences between level 2 and level 3 authorities, explicitly underlining its exceptionality,[31] setting forth a rule on rumours as well as on protracted processes, mandating the *ex post* information of NCAs and introducing a specific case of delay based on financially systemic reasons. Besides these direct modifications, the legislative tipping point is altered, at least as importantly, by the aforementioned extension of disclosable inside information and reinforcement of the one-step model. This evolution, coupled with the strengthening of the delaying regime, creates a scissors effect that puts issuers under an increasing pressure. A more frequent use of delaying, even more crucial in a one-step model that ignores the simple deferred disclosure mechanism,[32] will in turn add to the stress on this ultimate safety valve for issuers and on NCAs called on to draw clear and reliable boundaries between disclosure and legitimate temporary privacy.

A.4.28 The Market Abuse Regulation only introduces an additional possibility to withhold inside information when it comes to preserving financial stability, an imperative that the last financial crisis has placed at the centre of all attention. Responding to the difficulties experienced by systemic financial firms during the crisis and dictated by the public interest, this special delaying mechanism, reserved to credit or financial institutions, differs from the 'ordinary delay', both substantially and procedurally. It is a regime in its own right, whose use requires the *ex ante* approval of the national competent authority.

A.4.29 From a regulatory viewpoint, the ad hoc transparency requirement is the product of major policy options taken at EU level reflecting a certain faith in an ever-increasing mandatory public disclosure[33] destined to increase capital markets' efficiency and mitigate the problem of information asymmetries on those markets and within listed issuers. Like any other legal choice between colliding values, transforming proprietary information into a public good is not cost-free.

[31] See recital (49) referring to 'special circumstances'.

[32] See art 17 n 11.

[33] See eg Koch, 'Disclosure of Inside Information' (n 14) para 19; L Enriques and S Gilotta, 'Disclosure and Financial Market Regulation' ECGI Working Paper Series in Law, Working Paper No 252/2014 (April 2014); A Sotiropoulou, *Les obligations d'information des sociétés cotées* (Larcier 2012).

It entails major consequences borne by listed issuers in terms of internal organization or external competition,[34] which can only fuel criticism. In the attempt to set an optimal balance between insiders and outsiders' interests, the ultimate criterion lies in the measure of the aforementioned drawbacks against the contribution of the prompt disclosure of inside information to the attractiveness of capital markets. One may be therefore sceptical as to the ability to set an optimal and fine-tuned enough balance between issuers and investors' expectations only through limited alleviations designed for listed SMEs or though national interpretation/enforcement accommodations of Article 17, where this European provision intrinsically carries a one-size-fits-all approach as it is directly applicable to all issuers listed on all EU capital markets despite the major differences existing in the structure of their corporate ownership.

IV. Additional Legislative Measures to Prevent Market Abuse

The strengthening of the legal framework is also evident when considering the subsequent Articles 18 to 21. The Market Abuse Regulation has significantly increased the level of details for insider lists (Article 18), the disclosure of managers' and closely associated persons' transactions (Article 19), investment recommendations and statistics (Article 20), as well as the disclosure or dissemination of information in the media (Article 21). **A.4.30**

Insider lists (Article 18)

Although their effectiveness is debated,[35] insider lists, introduced with the (former) Market Abuse Directive (2003/6/EC), have been confirmed as a major prophylactic measure against insider dealing.[36] In this respect, European authorities reaffirmed that insider lists are beneficial both for competent authorities, to effectively investigate potential market abuses in the view of protecting the market integrity, and for issuers, 'to control the flow of inside information and thereby help manage their confidentiality duties'. Consequently, Article 18 requires issuers as well as any person acting on their behalf to draw up and update insider lists, in compliance with specific requirements (including a format and a template), pursuing a model of full harmonization at the European level. Article 18(6) sets out a lighter regime only for issuers whose financial instruments are admitted to trading on SME growth markets, which are exempted from drawing up insider lists under certain conditions. **A.4.31**

---

34 See eg Schön, 'Corporate Disclosure' (n 30).

35 ESME Report (n 5).

36 Jesper Lau Hansen, 'MAD in a Hurry: The Swift and Promising Adoption of the EU Market Abuse Directive' (2004) 15 European Business Law Review 183.

Disclosure of managers' and closely associated persons' transactions (Article 19)

A.4.32 In order to increase the transparency of financial markets and prevent insider dealing, Article 19 mandates public disclosure of certain transactions entered into by persons discharging managerial responsibilities (PDMRs) within an issuer. PDMRs have a duty to notify the issuer and the national competent authority of every transaction conducted on their own account relating to the shares or debt instruments of that issuer. In addition, the issuer itself is responsible for ensuring that the information is made public, unless national law provides that the NCA makes the information public. The public disclosure of such transactions contributes to the information available to investors and to the effectiveness of the competent authorities' supervision. As has been correctly noted, 'corporate managers generally do not act in isolation of social context. Therefore, inside managers typically have a sphere of both natural and legal outside persons, which can be more or less under the managers' influence, and with whom managers' personal economic interests may be significantly aligned'.[37] For this reason, the Market Abuse Regulation extends the disclosure regime on managers' transactions to closely associated persons (CAPs), in order to 'curb the possible circumvention by the prime target of the disclosure regime, ie, the inside manager'.[38]

Investment recommendations and statistics (Article 20)

A.4.33 Article 20 Market Abuse Regulation applies to persons who produce or disseminate investment recommendations or other information recommending or suggesting an investment strategy. It contains specific requirements connected to the concerned information and deals with potential conflicts of interests. The Market Abuse Regulation now comprises the relevant definitions that formerly were included in the Investment Recommendations Directive (2003/125/EC). The 2016 level 2 Commission Implementing Regulation provides for a first layer of general obligations applicable to all persons who produce recommendations and for a second layer applicable to qualified persons. With regard to key issues, including inter alia general standard of objective representation, non-written recommendations and the identity of the producers of recommendations, the level 2 Commission Implementing Regulation has maintained the same approach adopted under the (former) Market Abuse Directive (2003/6/EC).

A.4.34 Journalists do not fall within the scope of the technical arrangements laid down in the regulatory technical standards if they are subject to appropriate equivalent regulation in a Member State. Article 20 includes appropriate self-regulation in

[37] M Knuts, 'The Optimal Scope of Disclosure by Association Regime under MAR' (2016) European Company and Financial Law Review 495.

[38] ibid.

the notion of appropriate equivalent regulation, under the condition that such regulation achieves similar effects as those technical arrangements.

Disclosure or dissemination of information in the media (Article 21)

Article 21 focuses on disclosure or dissemination of information and recommendations produced or disseminated for the purpose of journalism or any other form of expression in the media, and the application of the rules governing the freedom of the press and freedom of expression in other media as well as the rules or codes governing journalists' profession. Under the (former) Market Abuse Directive (2003/6/EC), the content of the current Article 21 was included in the definition of 'market manipulation', laid down in Article 1(2)(c). The Market Abuse Regulation emphasizes the difficulties of identifying a fair balance between freedom of press (safeguarded by professional rules, including those of a self-regulatory nature) and market disclosure requirements.[39] **A.4.35**

[39] See Guido A Ferrarini, 'The European Market Abuse Directive' (2004) 41 Common Market Law Review 711 ff.

5

PUBLIC ENFORCEMENT OF THE MARKET ABUSE REGULATION

I. Introduction

Public enforcement has long been a relatively neglected part of EU securities legislation. Typically, relevant legislative instruments would confine themselves to allocating some supervisory powers to national authorities, providing for basic cooperation mechanisms, and requiring in general wordings that effective administrative sanctions be available.[1] The financial crisis of 2007–2008 has been a watershed, painfully demonstrating the inadequacy of nationally shaped supervision and enforcement. The proposal for a Market Abuse Regulation was the first post-crisis EU legislative initiative with an encompassing approach to enforcement. Two features stand out in this regard. First, the Market Abuse Regulation grants national competent authorities additional powers with regard to supervision, investigation, and—especially—sanctioning. Minimum standards are to ensure that enforcement practices no longer diverge excessively between Member States. Secondly, competent authorities are embedded in a network of **A.5.01**

[1] Niamh Moloney, 'EU Financial Market Regulation after the Global Financial Crisis: "More Europe" or More Risks?' (2010) 47 Common Market Law Review 1364.

cooperation, with market actors, trading platforms, authorities of other Member States and third countries, and the European Securities and Markets Authority (ESMA).

A.5.02 This chapter is organized as follows. Section II describes the historical evolution of public enforcement of market abuse and securities regulation more generally. This is followed by a sketch of the innovations of the Market Abuse Regulation relating to public enforcement, with Sections III to V consecutively dealing with the enhanced powers of the competent authorities, the closer involvement of market actors, and the improved cooperation between authorities. Section VI rounds off with an economic assessment of the effectiveness of the new enforcement regime and its impact at the micro and macro level. Criminal sanctions do not fall within the ambit of this chapter.

II. History

Enforcement of the (former) Market Abuse Directive (2003/6/EC)

A.5.03 Traditionally, insider trading regulations and other securities laws have been more assiduously enforced in the United States than in Europe. Several studies have found noticeable differences both in terms of actual public enforcement actions brought and sanctions imposed (output)[2] and in terms of enforcement budget and staff size of competent authorities (input).[3] Nevertheless, one must be careful in interpreting these data (and they may need qualification),[4] as international comparisons of the intensity of enforcement are fraught with difficulties due to differences with regard to the scope of competence of regulatory agencies, regulatory priorities, levels of compliance with the law, geographical scale, sophistication of the financial industry etc.[5] Also, low levels of enforcement actions and sanctions could be interpreted both as indicating effective deterrence and as reflecting poor enforcement.[6]

A.5.04 In addition to formal enforcement, financial authorities may also revert to informal enforcement methods. This brings us to a related point of difference between Europe (or at least the UK) and the United States. While the American SEC is

[2] John C Coffee Jr, 'Law and the Market: The Impact of Enforcement' (2007) 156 University of Pennsylvania Law Review 268–74; Howell E Jackson, 'Variation in the Intensity of Financial Regulation: Preliminary Evidence and Potential Implications' (2007) 24 Yale Journal on Regulation 278.

[3] See paras A.5.36–A.5.37.

[4] Marco Ventoruzzo, 'Comparing Insider Trading in the United States and in the European Union: History and Recent Developments' (2014) European Company and Financial Law Review 591.

[5] See Coffee, 'Law and the Market' (n 2) 263–4; Jackson, 'Variation in the Intensity of Financial Regulation' (n 2) 263–5.

[6] John Armour et al., *Principles of Financial Regulation* (Oxford University Press 2016) 594.

clearly an enforcement-led agency, the same could not be said of the Financial Services Authority (FSA, predecessor of the current Financial Conduct Authority (FCA)) in the UK prior to the financial crisis. When possible, the FSA followed a 'light touch' approach, with a clear preference for supervision and informally negotiated compliance over formal sanctions.[7] The FSA, as well as the German Federal Financial Supervisory Authority (BaFin), also spent less of their budgets on formal enforcement than the SEC.[8] An influential theory that helped justify this approach was Ayres and Braithwaite's theory of responsive regulation.[9] According to this theory, regulators must adapt their regulatory style to firms' behaviour and choose their sanctions accordingly from a 'regulatory pyramid'. The assumption is that most firms genuinely want to comply with the law. When they do not, it suffices for regulators to impose a cooperative measure from the bottom of the pyramid, such as persuasion or, in a next step, a warning. Only in exceptional cases should a regulator, under the theory of responsive regulation, resort to severe enforcement measures, such as suspending or even revoking licences.[10]

Before the financial crisis, the legal framework itself was not conducive to strong public enforcement in Europe either, as enforcement was not a main concern in European capital markets regulation at that time.[11] Traditionally, the EU harmonized only substantive law, largely leaving enforcement matters to the Member States.[12] Comparatively speaking, the (former) Market Abuse Directive (2003/6/EC) devoted much attention to supervision, enforcement, and cooperation, and noticeably enhanced it.[13] While a step forward, important deficiencies remained in all three areas. **A.5.05**

Compared to other areas of securities regulation, the (former) Market Abuse Directive (2003/6/EC) had effectuated a relatively high degree of supervisory **A.5.06**

[7] John Tiner, 'Keynote Address—Enforcement Law Conference' (16 June 2006) http://www.fsa.gov.uk/library/communication/speeches/2006/0616_jt.shtml; Margaret Cole, 'Enforcing Financial Services Regulation: The UK FSA Perspective' European Policy Forum (4 April 2008) http://www.fsa.gov.uk/pages/Library/Communication/Speeches/2008/0404_mc.shtml. See John Armour, 'Enforcement Strategies in UK Corporate Governance: A Roadmap and Empirical Assessment' in Alessio M Pacces (ed), *The Law and Economics of Corporate Governance* (Edward Elgar Publishing 2010) 231–2 and 248; Iain MacNeil, 'Enforcement and Sanctioning' in Niamh Moloney, Eilís Ferran, and Jennifer Payne (eds), *The Oxford Handbook of Financial Regulation* (Oxford University Press 2015) 281, 284, and 290.

[8] See Coffee, 'Law and the Market' (n 2) 277–81.

[9] See MacNeil, 'Enforcement and Sanctioning' (n 7) 286.

[10] Ian Ayres and John Braithwaite, *Responsive Regulation: Transcending the Deregulation Debate* (Oxford University Press 1992).

[11] Niamh Moloney, *EU Securities and Financial Markets Regulation* (3rd edn, Oxford University Press 2014) 762.

[12] Miroslava Scholten, 'Mind the Trend! The Enforcement of EU Law is Moving to "Brussels"' International Conference on Public Policy (ICPP) (2 July 2015) 1–2.

[13] Niamh Moloney, *EC Securities Regulation* (2nd edn, Oxford University Press 2008) 993 and 994.

convergence.[14] The (former) Market Abuse Directive (2003/6/EC) listed a good number of minimal powers for the competent authorities.[15] However, it did not include a few crucial powers, such as the power to enter private premises or to require data traffic records from telecommunications operators.[16]

A.5.07 With regard to sanctioning powers, the (former) Market Abuse Directive (2003/6/EC) confined itself to requiring Member States to ensure that effective, proportionate, and dissuasive administrative sanctions and measures could be taken.[17] It did not specify which sanctions should be available, for which infringements they should be possible, or how the severity of the sanction should be determined, thus leaving a vast amount of discretion to the Member States. In addition, in the absence of European competence in the field of criminal law at that time,[18] the (former) Market Abuse Directive (2003/6/EC) merely allowed the imposition of criminal sanctions.[19] As a consequence, in a 2007 report, the Committee of European Securities Regulators (CESR) found significant disparities between Member States with regard to the range of sanctions available, the size of pecuniary sanctions, the infringements to which they were applied, and the criteria for determining the sanctions.[20] The (former) Market Abuse Directive (2003/6/EC) also merely allowed, but did not mandate the publication of sanctions.[21] The fact that not all national authorities made use of this possibility,[22] contributed to the perception that market abuse was not effectively enforced, thus possibly also affecting compliance rates.[23]

A.5.08 With regard to international cooperation, the (former) Market Abuse Directive (2003/6/EC) had brought improvement by requiring competent authorities to cooperate whenever necessary to carry out their duties, particularly with regard to the exchange of information and requests to carry out investigations.[24] CESR

---

[14] Moloney, *EU Securities and Financial Markets Regulation* (n 11) 756 and 758.

[15] Article 12 (former) Market Abuse Directive (2003/6/EC).

[16] See Commission, 'Staff Working Paper: Impact Assessment' SEC(2011) 1217 final, 24–5.

[17] Article 14(1) (former) Market Abuse Directive (2003/6/EC).

[18] See Michael G Faure and Claire Leger, 'The Directive on Criminal Sanctions for Market Abuse: A Move Towards Harmonizing Insider Trading Criminal Law at the EU Level?' (2014–2015) 9 Brooklyn Journal of Corporate, Financial, and Commercial Law 389.

[19] Article 14(1) (former) Market Abuse Directive (2003/6/EC).

[20] CESR, 'An evaluation of equivalence of supervisory powers in the EU under the Market Abuse Directive and the Prospectus Directive' (June 2007) 07-334, 3–4. See also ESME, 'Market abuse EU legal framework and its implementation by Member States: a first evaluation' (6 July 2007) 19 http://ec.europa.eu/internal_market/securities/docs/esme/mad_070706_en.pdf; CESR, 'Report on administrative measures and sanctions as well as criminal sanctions available in Member States under the Market Abuse Directive' (17 October 2007) (CESR/07-693) http://www.esma.europa.eu/sites/default/files/library/2015/11/07_693_u_2_.pdf.

[21] Article 14(4) (former) Market Abuse Directive (2003/6/EC).

[22] See commentary to art 34 at B.34.05.

[23] ESME, 'Market abuse EU legal framework and its implementation by Member States: a first evaluation' (n 20).

[24] Article 16 (former) Market Abuse Directive (2003/6/EC). See also CESR, 'An evaluation of equivalence of supervisory powers in the EU under the Market Abuse Directive and the Prospectus Directive' (n 20) 4.

also played an important role in enhancing cooperation and coordination in market abuse enforcement efforts.[25] In 2006, CESR established a new operational structure for CESR-Pol 'to promote closer cooperation and to ensure the consistent and effective application of EU key directives, particularly the (former) Market Abuse Directive (2003/6/EC)'.[26] Coordination between competent authorities from different Member States functioned relatively well with regard to supervision, but failed with regard to the imposition of sanctions, due to considerable differences in the sanctioning practices of the Member States and in the absence of any specific obligation to coordinate in this regard.[27] Another predicament of international cooperation stemmed from the fact that, in some Member States, investigatory and sanctioning powers in relation to market abuse are exercised by criminal authorities, while the (former) Market Abuse Directive (2003/6/EC) only required administrative authorities to cooperate.[28] As a consequence, judicial and administrative authorities could only cooperate indirectly, through the administrative authorities, but they were not explicitly required to do so.[29]

Responses to the financial crisis

The financial crisis of 2007–2008, and in particular the lack of enforcement in its early years, brought the importance of effective supervision and enforcement as well as the weakness of the existing system into the limelight.[30] Worldwide, securities regulators were found to lack sufficient sanctioning powers and credible enforcement programmes, and to fail to cooperate effectively with their foreign counterparts.[31] This triggered an international shift in regulatory emphasis from the law on the books to achieving actual compliance with the law by means of enhanced enforcement and harsher sanctions.[32] As a G20 working group put **A.5.09**

[25] See Moloney, *EU Securities and Financial Markets Regulation* (n 11) 954.

[26] CESR, 'CESR changes its profile and starts operational tasks to deliver effective supervisory convergence in the EU' Press Release (2 August 2006) http://www.esma.europa.eu/sites/default/files/library/2015/11/06_303.pdf.

[27] European Securities Committee, Minutes (26 June 2005) 3 http://ec.europa.eu/finance/securities/docs/esc/meetings/2006-06-26-report_en.pdf.

[28] Article 16 (former) Market Abuse Directive (2003/6/EC).

[29] The latter could then pass on information in accordance with art 16(2), fifth subparagraph (former) Market Abuse Directive (2003/6/EC) (see M J J P Luchtman, 'Europese handhavingssamenwerking bij de bestrijding van marktmisbruik' [2006] SEW 264–5).

[30] Commission Communication, 'Reinforcing sanctioning regimes in the financial services sector' (8 December 2010) COM(2010) 716 final, 2; MacNeil, 'Enforcement and Sanctioning' (n 7) 281; see Moloney, *EU Securities and Financial Markets Regulation* (n 11) 944.

[31] See the IOSCO assessments, described in Ana Carvajal and Jennifer Elliott, 'The Challenge of Enforcement in Securities Markets: Mission Impossible' (2009) IMF Working Paper 09/168, 20–4.

[32] Commission Communication, 'Reinforcing sanctioning regimes in the financial services sector' (n 30) 3; Moloney, *EU Securities and Financial Markets Regulation* (n 11) 944–5. See also Christopher P Montagano, 'The Global Crackdown on Insider Trading: A Silver Lining to the "Great Recession"' (2012) 19 Indiana Journal of Global Legal Studies 577, 577–81 and 591–5.

it: 'No matter how sound the rules are for regulating the conduct of market participants, if the system of enforcement is ineffective—or is perceived to be ineffective—the ability of the system to achieve the desired outcome is undermined'.[33] In 2008, the G20 leaders set out an action plan which included putting appropriate sanctioning regimes in place to combat financial misconduct.[34] In the US, enforcement was an important component of the 2010 Dodd Frank reform of the financial system.[35] In Europe, the change in the regulatory climate was spearheaded by the FSA in the UK.[36] In 2008–2009, it abandoned its former light touch approach for a strategy of credible deterrence and made more frequent use of formal enforcement actions.[37]

A.5.10 Supervision and enforcement have become an important part of the EU post-crisis reform agenda as well.[38] As part of a general effort to further develop an area of freedom, security, and justice through its 'Stockholm programme', the European Council urged the Member States and the European Commission to improve the early detection of fraudulent market abuse and to consider approximating national criminal laws.[39] In the context of financial supervision, the High-level Group chaired by Jacques de Larosière made the case for strong supervisory and sanctioning regimes in 2009. In particular, the Group recommended, with specific reference to insider trading, that supervisory authorities be equipped with sufficient powers to act and that sanctions regimes against financial crimes should be strengthened, harmonized, and enforced effectively.[40] In the ensuing establishment of a new European System of Financial

---

[33] G-20 Working Group 1, 'Enhancing Sound Regulation and Strengthening Transparency' Final Report (25 March 2009) 44 http://www.iasplus.com/en/binary/resource/0903g20.pdf.

[34] G20, 'Declaration Summit on Financial Markets and the World Economy' (15 November 2008) 4 http://www.g20.org/English/Documents/PastPresidency/201512/P020151225609230748803.pdf. See also G-20 Working Group 1, 'Enhancing Sound Regulation and Strengthening Transparency' (n 33) 44, http://www.iasplus.com/en/binary/resource/0903g20.pdf (recommending that the effective enforcement of regulation be a priority of all financial regulators).

[35] Dodd-Frank Wall Street Reform and Consumer Protection Act of 2010, Pub L 111-203.

[36] Pierre-Henri Conac, 'Is Europe Finally Converging with the US on Sanctions for Insider Trading and Other Market Abuses?' *CLS Blue Sky Blog* (2 April 2013).

[37] Margaret Cole, 'Delivering Credible Deterrence' FSA Annual Financial Crime Conference speech (27 April 2009) http://www.fsa.gov.uk/library/communication/speeches/2009/0427_mc.shtml. See MacNeil, 'Enforcement and Sanctioning' (n 7) 284 and 286; Christine Astaniou, Shoshana Wainer, and Nikunj Kiri, 'UK Market Abuse Update: FSA Continues to Demonstrate Resolve to Tackle Market Abuse' (2010) 4(6) Law and Financial Markets Review 582.

[38] Niamh Moloney, 'Supervision in the Wake of the Financial Crisis: Achieving Effective "Law in Action"—A Challenge for the EU' in Eddy Wymeersch, Klaus Hopt, and Guido Ferrarini (eds), *Financial Regulation And Supervision: A Post-crisis Analysis* (Oxford University Press 2012) 77–9.

[39] Council of the European Union, 'The Stockholm programme. An open and secure Europe serving and protecting the citizen' (2 December 2009) 48 resp 28–9 http://register.consilium.europa.eu/pdf/en/09/st17/st17024.en09.pdf.

[40] High-level Group on Financial Supervision in the EU, Report (25 February 2009) 23 and 50–1 http://ec.europa.eu/internal_market/finances/docs/de_larosiere_report_en.pdf (De Larosière Report).

Supervision in January 2011, CESR was replaced with ESMA. ESMA was granted the authority to carry out peer reviews of national authorities (including sanctioning powers),[41] to fulfil a coordination role between national authorities,[42] to promote a common supervisory culture,[43] and to propose technical standards to the European Commission in order to develop a single rulebook applicable to all financial market participants in the internal market.[44] At the same time, national competent authorities were required to cooperate with ESMA and to provide it with information regarding the sanctions and measures they imposed.[45]

In its Communication on 'Driving European recovery', the European Commission announced an ambitious reform programme with more effective sanctions against market wrongdoing as one of its five key objectives (including a review of the (former) Market Abuse Directive (2003/6/EC)).[46] In 2010, the Commission outlined its new approach in its communication on 'Reinforcing sanctioning regimes in the financial services sector' based on CESR's findings referred to above (para A.5.07) and with reference to the de Larosière report.[47] It stated that: '[e]fficient and sufficiently convergent sanctioning regimes are the necessary corollary to the new supervisory system'.[48] For that reason, the Commission considered a legislative initiative prescribing a core set of administrative sanctions and possibly some criminal sanctions, a sufficiently high level of administrative fines, the possibility of imposing sanctions on both individuals and financial institutions, criteria to be taken into account when applying sanctions, publication of imposed sanctions, and mechanisms supporting the effective application of sanctions, such as whistle-blowing.[49] In parallel with the Commission Communication, ESMA has been mapping the actual use of sanctioning powers under the (former) Market Abuse Directive (2003/6/EC) in the period 2008–2010. The main takeaway message was that strong divergences had persisted with regard to, among others, investigatory powers of competent authorities, the imposition of non-pecuniary administrative sanctions, and the levels of pecuniary sanctions. Nevertheless, there has also been some improvement. Since the CESR mapping of 2007, for **A.5.11**

[41] Article 30 ESMA Regulation (1095/2010/EU).

[42] ibid art 31.

[43] ibid art 29.

[44] ibid art 15 and recital (22).

[45] Article 3 Omnibus I Directive (2010/78/EU).

[46] Commission Communication, 'Driving European recovery' (4 March 2009) COM(2009) 114 final, vol 1, 7–8.

[47] Commission Communication, Reinforcing sanctioning regimes in the financial services sector (n 30).

[48] ibid 2. See also ibid 15 ('In order to ensure an effective, proportionate and dissuasive sanctioning regime, it is essential that the sanctions provided for by the law are effectively applied, that violations are detected, that investigations and sanctioning procedures are carried out expediently and that appropriate sanctions are imposed where this is warranted').

[49] ibid 11–15.

instance, eight Member States have increased the maximum amounts for pecuniary sanctions for market abuse.[50]

A.5.12 The topic of enforcement played an important role in the Market Abuse Regulation.[51] The European Commission had already identified strengthening enforcement and international cooperation as some of its key objectives in its public consultation for a revision of the (former) Market Abuse Directive (2003/6/EC) in 2010.[52] The Commission opined that a new instrument on market abuse should include stronger investigation powers for competent authorities, including the power to obtain telephone and data traffic records and to enter private premises; effective and deterrent sanctions, including injunctions to put an end to an infringement, temporary prohibition of an activity, and fines of at least twice the gain or the avoided loss; and cooperation between competent authorities and with third countries, with the assistance of ESMA.[53] The European Commission's Market Abuse Regulation proposal in 2011 elaborated on these elements in more detail, and included additional features, such as protection for whistle-blowers. It was the first post-crisis reform that drastically revised the pre-crisis sanctioning regime and opted for a tougher and more prescriptive approach (after earlier post-crisis reforms, such as AIFMD, EMIR, and the Short Selling Regulation (236/2012/EU), had been limited to relatively mild reforms in this regard).[54] Not surprisingly, for that reason, several aspects, in particular the level of pecuniary sanctions, the publication of sanctions, and the treatment of whistle-blowers, were heavily debated during the Parliament and Council negotiations (with many proposed amendments aiming at even more severe sanctions).[55] Since the Market Abuse Regulation proposal, however, similar provisions on the specific breaches for which administrative sanctions can be imposed, the range of sanctions, the criteria for determining sanctions, mandatory naming and shaming, publication of sanctions and reporting thereof to ESMA, and/or whistle-blower protection, have been included in the Transparency Directive (2013/50/EU),[56] the Capital Requirements Directive (CRD IV) (2013/36/EU),[57] the

[50] ESMA, 'Report: Actual use of sanctioning powers under MAD' (26 April 2012), ESMA/2012/270, esp 11 and 46–7.

[51] See recital (70) Market Abuse Regulation.

[52] Commission, 'Public consultation on a revision of the Market Abuse Directive (MAD)' (25 June 2010) 2–3 http://ec.europa.eu/finance/consultations/2010/mad/docs/consultation_paper_en.pdf. See also Commission, 'Impact Assessment' (n 16) 63.

[53] Commission, 'Public consultation on a revision of the Market Abuse Directive (MAD)' (n 52) 8–12. See also Commission, 'Impact Assessment' (n 16) 23–7.

[54] Moloney, *EU Securities and Financial Markets Regulation* (n 11) 764 and 967.

[55] Draft report, 'Amendments 332–401' (11 May 2012) 2011/0295 (COD); Presidency Compromise (22 May 2012) 2011/0295 (COD) no 10198/12; 'Presidency Progress Report on the Market Abuse Regulation' 2011/0295 (COD) (21 June 2012) 4.

[56] Articles 28–29 Transparency Directive (2013/50/EU).

[57] Articles 66 and 68–71 Capital Requirement Regulation (CRD IV) (2013/575/EU).

PRIIPs Regulation (2014/1286/EU),[58] UCITS V (2014/91/EU),[59] the Markets in Financial Instruments Directive II (2014/65/EU),[60] the Securities Financing Transaction Regulation (2015/2365/EU),[61] the Insurance Distribution Directive (2016/97/EU),[62] and the Prospectus Regulation (2017/1129/EU).[63] The Market Abuse Regulation proposal thus marked the beginning of a new European approach to sanctioning in securities and markets regulation, which—following the FSA's policy reversal in the UK (see para A.5.09)—is now based on credible deterrence.[64]

III. Enhanced Powers of Competent Authorities

Supervision and investigation

The effective enforcement powers of competent authorities heavily depend on their capacity to detect and investigate infringements. Under the (former) Market Abuse Directive (2003/6/EC), competent authorities generally had to have the necessary supervisory and investigatory powers, and in particular the power to access documents, to interview any person, to inspect non-private premises, to require existing telephone and existing data traffic records, to require the cessation of an infringement, to suspend trading of financial instruments, to request the freezing and/or sequestration of assets, and to request temporary prohibition of professional activity (see para A.5.06). In almost all Member States, competent authorities possessed these powers.[65] **A.5.13**

The Market Abuse Regulation provided some much-needed additional powers. First, competent authorities must have the power to enter the premises of natural and legal persons in order to seize documents and data in any form.[66] Such power is indispensable when someone fails or may be expected to fail to comply with a demand for information or may tamper with or remove pieces **A.5.14**

58 Articles 24–29 PRIIPs Regulation (2014/1286/EU).

59 Article 1(16)–(17) UCITS V (2014/91/EU).

60 Articles 70–73 Markets in Financial Instruments Directive II (2014/65/EU).

61 Articles 22–27 Securities Financing Transaction Regulation (2015/2365/EU).

62 Articles 31–36 Insurance Distribution Directive (2016/97/EU).

63 Articles 38–43 Prospectus Regulation (2017/1129/EU).

64 Moloney, *EU Securities and Financial Markets Regulation* (n 11) 967–8; Sarah Wilson, 'The New Market Abuse Regulation and Directive on Criminal Sanctions for Market Abuse: European Capital Markets Law and New Global Trends in Financial Crime Enforcement' (2015) 16 ERA Forum 446.

65 CESR, 'An evaluation of equivalence of supervisory powers in the EU under the Market Abuse Directive and the Prospectus Directive' (n 20) 2–3. See also ESMA, 'Supervisory Practices under MAD' (1 July 2013) ESMA/2013/805; ESMA, 'Peer Review on Supervisory Practices against Market Abuse' (22 December 2015) ESMA/2015/1905.

66 Article 23(2)(e) Market Abuse Regulation.

of information.[67] This is a far-reaching measure—bearing close resemblance to the dawn raids carried out in competition law cases—that may interfere with the fundamental rights to privacy and family life.[68] For that reason, a competent authority may only exercise this power where a reasonable suspicion exists that documents related to the subject-matter of the inspection may be relevant to proving a case of insider dealing or market manipulation and, if required under national law, after having obtained prior judicial authorization.[69] Secondly, where there is a reasonable suspicion of an infringement and where such records may be relevant to the investigation of insider dealing or market manipulation, competent authorities should be able to require existing data traffic records from a telecommunications operator.[70] Such records are often the only way to establish who has disseminated false or misleading information or whether an insider has transferred inside information to someone who subsequently made a suspicious trade.[71] The power to require these records must be exercised in accordance with national law, which may thus require prior judicial authorization. Furthermore, in the absence of transparency rules or reporting obligations for spot commodity markets, competent authorities must be able to request information from market participants on commodity derivatives related spot markets, obtain reports on transactions, and have direct access to traders' systems.[72] They must also be able to refer matters for criminal investigation;[73] and to take all necessary measures to ensure that the public is correctly informed, for instance by correcting false or misleading disclosed information.[74] The language of the relevant provisions in the Market Abuse Regulation is directive-like, in order to respect different legal traditions in Member States and to prevent the provisions being interpreted as limiting the powers of competent authorities.[75] Finally, the Markets in Financial Instruments Regulation (2014/600/EU) contributed to the detection of market abuse by extending the MiFID transaction reporting regime, which requires investment firms and, to some extent, trading venues to record

[67] Proposal for a Regulation on insider dealing and market manipulation (market abuse) 2011/0295 (COD) 11.

[68] Article 7 CFR. See Opinion of the European Data Protection Supervisor on the Commission proposals for a Regulation of the European Parliament and of the Council on insider dealing and market manipulation, and for a Directive of the European Parliament and of the Council on criminal sanctions for insider dealing and market manipulation [2012] OJ C177/2, 4.

[69] Article 23(2)(e) and (2) second subparagraph Market Abuse Regulation.

[70] ibid art 23(2)(h).

[71] Commission Proposal (n 67) 11–12.

[72] Article 23(2)(c) Market Abuse Regulation.

[73] ibid art 23(2)(f).

[74] ibid art 23(2)(m).

[75] Presidency Progress Report on the Market Abuse Regulation, 2011/0295 (COD) (21 June 2012) 3–4.

transactions in financial instruments and provide detailed reports to the competent authority.[76]

Sanctioning

The Market Abuse Regulation replaced the general requirement for effective, proportionate, and dissuasive administrative sanctions in the (former) Market Abuse Directive (2003/6/EC) (see para A.5.07) with clear minimum standards regarding the breaches for which sanctions must be imposed, the types of sanctions and measures that must at least be available, their maximum levels, and the criteria to be taken into account when determining the type and level of administrative sanctions.[77] The possible measures and sanctions must include a cease and desist order; disgorgement of the profits gained or losses avoided; a public warning; withdrawal or suspension of the authorization of an investment firm; a temporary or permanent ban from exercising management functions in investment firms; and a temporary ban from dealing on own account.[78] The most radical change compared to current practices, however, follows from the new maximum amounts for administrative pecuniary sanctions. These must now be at least three times the amount of the profits gained or losses avoided as a result of the infringement, or up to €15 million or 15 per cent of the annual (consolidated group) turnover for legal persons and up to €5 million for natural persons.[79] This is another (see para A.5.14)) drastic change in the market abuse regime that bears some resemblance to competition law enforcement. When selecting the sanction and its level, competent authorities must consider the gravity and duration of the infringement, the degree of responsibility of the offender, the offender's financial capacity, size of the profits gained or losses avoided, recidivism, and the level of cooperation with the competent authorities.[80] **A.5.15**

Member States that, on 3 July 2016, already had criminal sanctions in place for infringements requiring administrative sanctions under the Market Abuse Regulation (eg Denmark) were allowed—but not required—to decide against adding administrative sanctions.[81] In any case, the Market Abuse Directive on Criminal Sanctions (2014/57/EU) requires that serious cases of market abuse that have been committed intentionally must be punished by certain minimal criminal penalties. A consequence of these rules is that the same behaviour may be punished with both administrative and criminal sanctions.[82] Member States **A.5.16**

[76] Articles 25–26 Markets in Financial Instruments Regulation (2014/600/EU).
[77] Articles 30–31 Market Abuse Regulation.
[78] ibid art 30(2)(a)–(g).
[79] ibid art 30(2)(h)–(j) and (2) second subparagraph.
[80] ibid art 31(1).
[81] ibid art 30(1), second subparagraph.
[82] See, under the MAD: ESMA, 'Report: Actual use of sanctioning powers under MAD' (n 50) 10 (between 2008 and 2010, in nine Member States criminal and administrative fines could be imposed cumulatively for the same facts).

will therefore need to carefully assess how to respect the *non bis in idem* principle contained in the Charter of Fundamental Rights of the European Union (CFR).[83]

A.5.17 Although it was not primarily meant as a sanction, the harshest punishment—in terms of reputational damage—may well follow from the obligation for competent authorities to immediately publish decisions imposing administrative sanctions or measures,[84] a practice frequently referred to as 'naming and shaming'.[85] The primary rationale behind this provision is to inform market participants of what behaviour is permitted and of the fact that other behaviour is effectively punished.[86] Nevertheless, when publication would be disproportionate or would jeopardize an ongoing investigation or the stability of the financial markets, the competent authority may defer, anonymize, or forgo publication.[87]

Cross-market competence

A.5.18 An important expansion of the powers of the competent authorities ensues from the general widening of the scope of application of the market abuse regime. While the (former) Market Abuse Directive (2003/6/EC) only applied to trading on regulated markets, the Market Abuse Regulation—in response to the increasing fragmentation of trading across multiple venues—also covers trading on multilateral trading facilities (MTF) and organized trading facilities (OTF).[88] At the same time, the Market Abuse Regulation sticks to the rule of one single administrative competent authority per Member State, that is competent for all covered financial products and markets.[89] Cross-market surveillance is indispensable for effective enforcement of market abuse regulations. With the proliferation of trading venues and of financial products that allow trading of the same underlying economic interest, it has become easier for offenders to disguise market abuse by splitting their trades strategically.[90] A centralized system of enforcement is also efficient with regard to sanctioning, since it increases predictability.[91]

---

[83] See commentary to art 30 at paras B.30.22–B.30.23.

[84] Article 34 Market Abuse Regulation. Under the Market Abuse Directive, this was merely optional (art 14(4) Market Abuse Directive).

[85] See commentary to art 34 (n 22).

[86] See recital (73) Market Abuse Regulation.

[87] ibid art 34(1), third subparagraph.

[88] ibid art 2.

[89] ibid art 22. This rule was introduced by art 11 Market Abuse Directive.

[90] Janet Austin, 'Protecting Market Integrity in an Era of Fragmentation and Cross-Border Trading' (2014–2015) 46 Ottawa Law Review 38–9 and 41.

[91] See Chase Foster, 'Governing Financial Markets after the Crisis: European and American Approaches to Securities Enforcement' Working Paper (September 2016) 18 (arguing that the divided regulatory powers in the US render pecuniary sanctions more unpredictable). In the US, not only the SEC, but also the CFTC can enforce insider trading rules within its sphere of competence.

IV. Closer Involvement of Market Actors

Because market abuse does not visibly harm its victims and abusive orders or trades are hard to differentiate from legitimate ones, it is very difficult for public authorities to detect errant behaviour. This was already the case on the traditional stock exchanges, but the problem has been aggravated by the advent of multilateral trading facilities and firms that operate as systematic internalizers and manage so-called 'dark pools'[92] (and the increased possibility of splitting trades over different brokers, venues, and instruments[93]), direct access trading without the need for a broker who can act as a gatekeeper, and high-frequency traders who can manipulate markets by placing and withdrawing orders in fractions of a second.[94] Cooperation of competent authorities with market operators and market participants is therefore an important part of effective enforcement programmes. While this was already recognized in the (former) Market Abuse Directive (2003/6/EC), the Market Abuse Regulation places responsibility on market undertakings even more squarely and all economic actors to contribute to market integrity.[95] It strengthens existing obligations and introduces whistle-blowing mechanisms as efficient and low-cost additional sources of information for regulators about possible cases of market abuse,[96] thus tending towards an almost hybrid system of enforcement, whereby private individuals cooperate with public authorities. Engaging private market actors in public enforcement has become a more general trend in financial regulation. In some ways, this represents a return to the pre-crisis cooperative model of enforcement.[97] However, there is an important distinction in that private monitoring is now intended as a mere complement to public oversight, thus avoiding the pre-crisis mistake of overreliance on self-regulation.[98] **A.5.19**

Without any doubt, the main innovation in the Market Abuse Regulation with regard to the involvement of private actors in public enforcement is the mandatory introduction of whistle-blower programmes.[99] Competent authorities, as well as employers who carry out activities regulated by financial services regulation, must have programmes in place to enable whistle-blowing. Where a person is not under an obligation to report, Member States may even provide financial **A.5.20**

[92] Kern Alexander, 'Market Structures and Market Abuse' in Gerard Caprio (ed), *Handbook of Safeguarding Global Financial Stability* (Elsevier 2013) 380.
[93] See para A.5.18 above.
[94] See Austin, 'Protecting Market Integrity in an Era of Fragmentation and Cross-border Trading' (n 90) 38.
[95] See recital (63) Market Abuse Regulation.
[96] Commission, 'Impact Assessment' (n 16) 50.
[97] See para A.5.04 above.
[98] See Moloney, 'Supervision in the Wake of the Financial Crisis' (n 38) 90–4.
[99] Article 32 Market Abuse Regulation.

rewards for new and relevant information that results in the imposition of a sanction or administrative measure for market abuse, a move clearly inspired by the American SEC's whistle-blower bounty programme. The inclusion of private actors in public enforcement by means of whistle-blower programmes will probably at the same time require and contribute to a shift in the public opinion about 'denouncing' fellow citizens.[100] That this form of cooperation with the government has a longer history of acceptance in the US, should not come as a surprise in light of the higher prominence of private enforcement there.[101]

A.5.21 The Market Abuse Regulation also strengthened existing obligations for private actors to support competent authorities' investigation efforts. The first of these are the obligations under the (former) Market Abuse Directive (2003/6/EC) for market operators to adopt structures aimed at preventing and detecting market manipulation[102] and for brokers to notify the competent authority of reasonable suspicions that a transaction might constitute insider dealing or market manipulation.[103] Under the Market Abuse Regulation, the first obligation also applies to investment firms that operate a trading venue, and the reporting obligation has been extended to cover unexecuted orders and attempts at insider dealing or market manipulation.[104] Brokers must also have systems in place to detect and report suspicious orders and transactions, while their reporting obligation has been expanded to unexecuted orders and attempts, and OTC trading.[105] Moreover, the scope of reporting obligations has widened along with the general application of the market abuse regime (including MTFs and OTFs).[106]

A.5.22 Secondly, under the (former) Market Abuse Directive (2003/6/EC), issuers (or persons acting on their behalf or for their account) had to compile and regularly update a list of persons with access to inside information.[107] These insider lists have been a very useful tool for competent authorities to identify insiders who might have committed market abuse and for raising awareness about market abuse risks in the issuer's organization and environment.[108] Under the Market Abuse Regulation, more extensive data must be included in the list and the

---

[100] See commentary to art 32 at para B.32.04.

[101] See MacNeil, 'Enforcement and Sanctioning' (n 7) 287–8.

[102] Article 6(6) (former) Market Abuse Directive (2003/6/EC) and art 43(2) MiFID I.

[103] Article 6(9) (former) Market Abuse Directive (2003/6/EC) and arts 7–11 Directive 2004/72/EC.

[104] Article 16(1) Market Abuse Regulation.

[105] Partially reflecting these changes, the reports are no longer referred to as Suspicious Transaction Reports (STRs) but as Suspicious Transaction and Order Reports (STORs).

[106] Article 16 Market Abuse Regulation.

[107] Article 6(3) (former) Market Abuse Directive (2003/6/EC); art 5 implementing Directive 2004/72/EC.

[108] Commission, 'Call for evidence: Review of Directive 2003/6/EC on insider dealing and market manipulation' (Market Abuse Directive) 12 http://ec.europa.eu/internal_market/consultations/docs/2009/market_abuse/call_for_evidence.pdf.

acknowledgement by persons included on the insider list of the concomitant legal and regulatory duties must henceforth be made in writing.[109]

Thirdly, the scope of the regime for notification of transactions by persons discharging managerial responsibilities and closely associated persons has changed in both directions. At first glance, the Market Abuse Regulation appears to have reined in the notification requirements. Because of the administrative burden associated with this measure under the (former) Market Abuse Directive (2003/6/EC),[110] the Market Abuse Regulation only requires notification once the total amount of transactions has reached €5,000 per calendar year (or a higher threshold up to €20,000 to be determined by the competent authorities).[111] By the same token, however, the notification obligation now also applies to managers of companies that only issued debt instruments, managers of issuers of financial instruments traded on an MTF or OTF, and managers of emission allowance market participants.[112] **A.5.23**

Although possibly unintended,[113] the punishment ensuing from the publication of sanctions also in practice depends on 'cooperation' from private market actors. Only through their refusal to do business with (or invest in) the offender does 'naming and shaming' actually cause reputational damage. **A.5.24**

V. Improved Cooperation between Authorities

Cooperation between competent authorities

A national competent authority is to ensure compliance with the Market Abuse Regulation 'regarding all actions carried out on its territory, and actions carried out abroad relating to instruments admitted to trading on a regulated market, for which a request for admission to trading on such market has been made, auctioned on an auction platform or which are traded on an MTF or an OTF or for which a request for admission to trading has been made on an MTF operating within its territory'.[114] The competent authorities' territorial scope of competence reflects the fact that market abuse can easily be orchestrated from abroad.[115] Splitting transactions over various markets and several jurisdictions can also be **A.5.25**

---

109 Article 18 Market Abuse Regulation.

110 Commission, 'Call for evidence: Review of Directive 2003/6/EC on insider dealing and market manipulation' (Market Abuse Directive) http://ec.europa.eu/internal_market/consultations/docs/2009/market_abuse/call_for_evidence.pdf 13. See art 6(4) (former) Market Abuse Directive (2003/6/EC) and art 6 implementing Directive 2004/72/EC.

111 Article 19 Market Abuse Regulation.

112 ibid arts 2(1) and 19.

113 See para A.5.17.

114 Article 22 Market Abuse Regulation.

115 See ibid recital (67).

used as a conscious strategy to disguise market abuse.[116] International cooperation therefore constitutes an indispensable part of an effective enforcement strategy.

A.5.26 In light of these considerations, the Market Abuse Regulation strengthens the cooperation obligations contained in the (former) Market Abuse Directive (2003/6/EC). As before, competent authorities must generally cooperate with each other and ESMA where necessary for the purpose of the Market Abuse Regulation, and can refuse cooperation only in limited circumstances (relating to national security, or impact on or existence of that authority's own investigation or enforcement activities).[117] They must also render assistance to each other and, without undue delay, exchange information and cooperate in investigation activities, and now also in supervision and enforcement activities.[118] The Market Abuse Regulation addresses the hurdles to international cooperation between administrative and judicial authorities that existed under the (former) Market Abuse Directive (2003/6/EC) (para A.5.08)) by requiring Member States who apply criminal sanctions to provide their competent authorities with all necessary powers to liaise with the relevant judicial authorities in order to receive specific information related to criminal investigations and proceedings on market abuse and to provide this information to other competent authorities.[119] Competent authorities may also require the assistance from competent authorities of other Member States regarding onsite inspections or investigations and can request ESMA to coordinate the investigation or inspection.[120] If a request for information or assistance is rejected or not complied with in a reasonable timeframe, ESMA can intervene with more conciliation and enforcement powers (including binding decisions) than its predecessor CESR.[121] Competent authorities must now not only inform and consult with each other, but also coordinate their enforcement actions, when they are convinced that infringements are being, or have been, carried out on the territory or with regard to financial instruments traded on trading venue of another Member State.[122] Reflecting the Market Abuse Regulation's cross-market approach, competent authorities must also cooperate with relevant authorities in relation to spot markets and emission allowances.[123]

A.5.27 The stronger cooperation obligations under the Market Abuse Regulation, while being a step forward, do not accomplish an integration of enforcement structures

[116] See Austin, 'Protecting Market Integrity in an Era of Fragmentation and Cross-border Trading' (n 90) 41. See para A.5.18.
[117] Article 25(2) Market Abuse Regulation.
[118] ibid art 25(1). See also ibid art 31(2).
[119] ibid art 25(1), fourth subparagraph.
[120] ibid art 25(6).
[121] ibid art 25(7).
[122] ibid art 25(5).
[123] ibid art 25(8).

on par with the integration seen in today's financial markets. The Market Abuse Regulation does not prescribe a priority rule with regard to which jurisdiction can take the lead in enforcement of market abuse. This could result in incomplete enforcement, whereby the enforcement authority that strikes first, bars further proceedings due to the rule of *non bis in idem*.[124] In the best case scenario, the harmonization of sanctions can be expected to mitigate the importance of which jurisdiction sanctions first.

Cooperation with third countries

With intensifying cooperation between Member State authorities, the risk **A.5.28** arises that market abuse will increasingly be carried out from non-EU Member States (while still falling under the—extraterritorial—reach of the Market Abuse Regulation). The Market Abuse Regulation therefore contains new provisions with regard to cooperation with third countries. Competent authorities of Member States shall, where necessary, conclude cooperation arrangements with supervisory authorities of third countries concerning information exchange and enforcement of the Market Abuse Regulation. Where possible, ESMA must also facilitate and coordinate the development of cooperation arrangements and the exchange of information between Member State authorities and third country authorities.[125] The Market Abuse Regulation also requires compliance with professional secrecy and data protection rules where information is exchanged with third countries.[126]

The European Union is, of course, not alone in its concern about international **A.5.29** cooperation. The International Organization of Securities Commissions (IOSCO) has traditionally fostered such cooperation by means of its general benchmark document 'Objectives and Principles', as well as specific resolutions and by encouraging its members to sign bilateral Memoranda of Understanding. In 2002, the IOSCO adopted a Multilateral Memorandum of Understanding (MMoU) relating to information exchange and assistance, among others in the field of insider dealing and market manipulation, which has been signed by most of its eligible members.[127]

---

[124] Michiel Luchtman and John Vervaele, 'Enforcing the Market Abuse Regime: Towards an Integrated Model of Criminal and Administrative Law Enforcement in the European Union?' (2014) 5 New Journal of European Criminal Law 192, 201.

[125] Article 26(1) and (2) Market Abuse Regulation. See also art 25(8) first and last subparagraph Market Abuse Regulation with regard to spot markets.

[126] Article 26(3) and 29 Market Abuse Regulation.

[127] See Antoine Van Cauwenberge, 'Developments Regarding Global Cooperation in Supervision of Financial Markets' in Eddy Wymeersch, Klaus J Hopt, and Guido Ferrarini (eds), *Financial Regulation and Supervision: A Post-Crisis Analysis* (Oxford University Press 2012) 401–2. See also the IOSCO website http://www.iosco.org/about/?subsection=mmou.

Extended role of ESMA

A.5.30 ESMA's role in international cooperation began to take shape under the (former) Market Abuse Directive (2003/6/EC), as amended by the Omnibus I Directive (2010/78/EU) upon the establishment of the new European System of Financial Supervision (para A.5.10). The Omnibus I Directive (2010/78/EU) and the Market Abuse Regulation have significantly increased ESMA's powers with regard to cooperation between national authorities, compared to the limited powers of CESR in this regard.[128] Since the Omnibus I Directive (2010/78/EU), competent authorities have been required to cooperate with ESMA in the field of market abuse and provide ESMA with all information necessary for carrying out its duties.[129] The Market Abuse Regulation added that ESMA will draft implementing technical standards for the exchange of information,[130] that the obligations described above[131] for cooperation and assistance between competent authorities also must be observed by competent authorities in their relationship with ESMA,[132] and that competent authorities must also notify ESMA of possible infringements[133] in other Member States.[134] Since the Omnibus I Directive (2010/78/EU), ESMA can also intervene when a request for information or assistance from one competent authority to another one is not complied with.[135] The Market Abuse Regulation also assigned ESMA the role of facilitator and coordinator for the development of cooperation arrangements and the exchange of information between Member State authorities and third country authorities.[136] ESMA was also to draft a template cooperation arrangement, but at the time of writing it has not done so or started consultations. ESMA must still be kept informed by competent authorities about investigations they have undertaken, as well as any sanctions and administrative measures they have imposed, so that ESMA can publish these data in its annual report.[137] ESMA's central role, when used proactively, may provide an important counterbalance to the absence of fully integrated enforcement structures (para A.5.27).

A.5.31 The ESMA Regulation (1095/2010/EU) also authorized ESMA to conduct peer reviews of competent authorities to assess the adequacy of the resources and the

---

128 CESR's role was limited to discussing conflicts between competent authorities with regard to the exchange of information and cooperation with an investigation (art 16(2), fourth subparagraph and 16(4), fifth subparagraph (original) Market Abuse Directive).

129 Article 15a Consolidated Market Abuse Directive; art 24 Market Abuse Regulation.

130 Article 24(3) Market Abuse Regulation.

131 See para A.5.26.

132 Article 25(1) Market Abuse Regulation.

133 See para A.5.26.

134 Article 25(5) Market Abuse Regulation.

135 Article 16(2), fifth subparagraph Consolidated Market Abuse Directive; art 25(7) Market Abuse Regulation.

136 Article 26(1) and (2) Market Abuse Regulation. See also art 25(8) first and last subparagraph Market Abuse Regulation with regard to spot markets.

137 Article 14(5) Consolidated Market Abuse Directive; art 33 Market Abuse Regulation.

governance arrangements of competent authorities, the degree of convergence, the competent authorities' best practices, as well as the effectiveness of, and the degree of convergence with regard to, enforcement.[138] While ESMA has spent its first years focusing on developing a single rulebook, it is now increasingly busy with promoting supervisory convergence.[139] One of the first examples of this strategic shift has been its peer review on supervisory practices in the field of market abuse.[140]

VI. Efficiency and Importance

Factors determining effectiveness

The Market Abuse Regulation addresses almost all of the seven factors underpinning credible deterrence identified by IOSCO in a recent report.[141] First, it aims to enhance the quality of legal and regulatory frameworks to provide legal certainty. Secondly, as described in Section III, it strengthens competent authorities' ability to detect misconduct and increase offenders' expectation that they will get caught. Thirdly, by improving cooperation between competent authorities of different Member States among themselves and with third countries' authorities (Section V), the Market Abuse Regulation renders it more difficult for offenders to hide behind borders. The effectiveness of the Market Abuse Regulation's new tools for international cooperation will of course depend on competent authorities' willingness to use them,[142] but it appears that such willingness is strong.[143] Fourthly, the Market Abuse Regulation widens the array of sanctions and measures available to competent authorities, thus adding further to effective deterrence. Fifthly, through publication of sanctions and related reports and peer reviews, the Market Abuse Regulation regime aims to promote public understanding and transparency about enforcement practices. Sixthly, the Market Abuse Regulation provides for a review of its appropriateness by the European Commission and a mapping exercise on the effective application of sanctions by ESMA.[144] A regular evaluation and adaptation of enforcement governance, strategy, priorities, and tools makes regulators more responsive to new types of risks. **A.5.32**

[138] Article 30 ESMA Regulation (1095/2010/EU).

[139] ESMA, Annual Report 2015, 3.

[140] ESMA, Supervisory Practices under MAD (1 July 2013) ESMA/2013/805; ESMA, Peer Review on Supervisory Practices Against Market Abuse (22 December 2015) ESMA/2015/1905.

[141] IOSCO, 'Credible Deterrence in the Enforcement of Securities Regulation' (June 2015).

[142] See André Dao, Andrew Godwin, and Ian Ramsay, 'From Enforcement to Prevention: International Cooperation and Financial Benchmark Reform' (2016) 10 Law and Financial Markets Review 95.

[143] Moloney, *EU Securities and Financial Markets Regulation* (n 11) 759.

[144] Article 38 Market Abuse Regulation.

A.5.33 The one remaining factor underpinning credible deterrence in IOSCO's list is the rigorous and swift investigation and prosecution of misconduct, which should include the possibility for competent authorities to enter into settlements. While the latter possibility is not mandated in the Market Abuse Regulation, its Preamble does refer to settlements.[145] Neither does the Market Abuse Regulation require an increased emphasis on formal enforcement or an aggressive pursuit of their new investigation and sanctioning powers. We have seen (in paras A.5.04 and A.5.09) that, for instance, the FSA has in the past been reluctant to use its authority and that a conscious shift to more credible deterrence has had at least as much impact as statutory changes could have. Whether such a development will spread over Europe will depend on competent authorities' choices regarding their regulatory style. The enactment of tougher rules in the Market Abuse Regulation has sent a political message that may influence these choices.[146] ESMA has an important role to play in this regard. Through its peer reviews, mapping exercises, and publication of sanctions and measures in its annual report, it has some important means to fulfil its task of promoting a common supervisory culture.[147]

A.5.34 An important condition for enforcement to be effective, even if all of the above factors are fulfilled, is that competent authorities dispose of sufficient budget, skilled staff, and specialized equipment. Traditionally, common law countries (including the UK) have expended vastly greater resources on enforcement of securities regulation than civil law countries.[148] Under the regime of the (former) Market Abuse Directive (2003/6/EC), Member State practices differed widely in this regard.[149] The de Larosière report had already generally recommended deploying more resources and more sophisticated detection processes where needed.[150] The expansion of competent authorities' power to new markets provided by the Market Abuse Regulation will also necessitate additional financial resources.[151] In its 2010 Communication on sanctioning in the financial services sector, however, the European Commission considered that resource allocation could better be addressed at national level.[152] Although in the wake of the crisis, several

---

[145] See recital (71) Market Abuse Regulation.

[146] See Conac, 'Is Europe Finally Converging with the US on Sanctions for Insider Trading and Other Market Abuses?' (n 36).

[147] See para A.5.10.

[148] See Coffee, 'Law and the Market' (n 2) 264–6; Jackson, 'Variation in the Intensity of Financial Regulation' (n 2) 272–3.

[149] CESR, 'An evaluation of equivalence of supervisory powers in the EU under the Market Abuse Directive and the Prospectus Directive' (n 20) 6–7 (with regard to special supervisory IT tools); ESMA, 'Report: Actual use of sanctioning powers under MAD' (n 50) 8 and 21–3 (with regard to the number of staff).

[150] De Larosière Report (n 40) 23.

[151] Mathias Siems and Matthijs Nelemans, 'The Reform of the EU Market Abuse Law: Revolution or Evolution?' (2012) 19 Maastricht Journal of European, and Comparative Law 205.

[152] Commission Communication, 'Reinforcing sanctioning regimes in the financial services sector' (n 30) 15.

competent authorities have recruited more staff,[153] it remains to be seen whether resource constraints will hinder supervisory convergence and effectiveness.

Impact of strong enforcement

At the level of individual market actors and competent authorities, the effects of strong enforcement are generally straightforward, but difficult to measure empirically, due to the same difficulties as those faced by supervisors seeking to verify actual compliance by individual market actors.[154,155] Several studies have circumvented this problem by looking at abnormal returns in the period preceding the announcement of a transaction or, better, the existence of rumours about a possible transaction, but these studies relate to time periods before entry into effect of the Market Abuse Regulation.[156] However, there is anecdotal evidence that the increased sanctions in the Market Abuse Regulation have had an immediate effect in encouraging listed firms and financial sector firms to take compliance more seriously. Theoretically, strong enforcement also buttresses competent authorities' credibility in the exercise of their supervisory tasks and when making compliance demands.[157] Enforcement thus not only depends on supervision (see para A.5.13 above), but it also strengthens supervision. **A.5.35**

The impact of increased enforcement at a macro-economic level, such as financial market development, has been debated more intensely. La Porta, Lopez-de-Silanes, and Shleifer famously found that their measurements of public enforcement did not correlate well with financial development and concluded that public enforcement does not play an important role in the development of securities markets. In contrast, private enforcement did and was also better developed in common law jurisdictions. Through this avenue, the authors argued, legal origin influences the development of financial markets.[158] However, the authors looked exclusively at formal attributes of competent authorities, such as their independence and powers.[159] Although these do play a role in the effectiveness of public enforcement,[160] **A.5.36**

[153] See Moloney, 'Supervision in the Wake of the Financial Crisis' (n 38) 86–7.

[154] See para A.5.19 above.

[155] MacNeil, 'Enforcement and Sanctioning' (n 7) 291.

[156] See eg Ben Dubow and Nuno Monteiro, 'Measuring Market Cleanliness' FSA Occasional Paper Series No 23 (March 2006); Tyas Prevoo and Bas Ter Weel, 'The Effects of a Change in Market Abuse Regulation on Abnormal Returns and Volumes: Evidence From the Amsterdam Stock Market' (2010) 158 De Economist 237; Brendan John Lambe, 'The Efficacy of Market Abuse Regulation in the UK' (2016) 24 Journal of Financial Regulation and Compliance 248.

[157] See Carvajal and Elliott, 'The Challenge of Enforcement in Securities Markets' (n 31) 5, fn 2.

[158] Rafael La Porta, Florencio Lopez-de-Silanes, and Andrei Shleifer, 'What Works in Securities Laws' (2006) 61 Journal of Finance 20. See also Simeon Djankov, Rafael La Porta, Florencio Lopez-de-Silanes, and Andrei Schleifer, 'The Law and Economics of Self-Dealing' (2008) 88 Journal of Financial Economics 430 (finding no relationship between public enforcement and stock market development).

[159] See La Porta, Lopez-de-Silanes, and Shleifer, 'What Works in Securities Laws' (n 158) 11.

[160] See Carvajal and Elliott, 'The Challenge of Enforcement in Securities Markets' (n 31) 11 and 25.

they do not reflect actual enforcement efforts and are probably not a reliable proxy for enforcement intensity.[161]

A.5.37 Later studies mostly found the other opposite, namely that the public enforcement of market abuse and other securities laws is related to financial market development. Jackson and Roe measured the intensity of public enforcement of securities laws by looking at regulatory budgets and staffing levels and showed a significant correlation with financial depth (with causation probably being bi-directional). They also found that, controlling for enforcement intensity, legal origins were not significantly related to stock market capitalization. Public enforcement of securities laws overall was a better explanation for financial market outcomes around the world than private enforcement. This may be explained by the fact that centralized oversight of trading markets, the development and enforcement of disclosure requirements and consistent accounting rules, and the imposition of a wide array of sanctions are all impossible for private market actors.[162] Other studies have found evidence that enforcement intensity can better explain national differences in the cost of capital (as evidenced by valuation premiums in case of cross-listing) than legal origins,[163] that in developed markets, the enforcement of insider trading laws enhances price informativeness,[164] and that jurisdictions with more prohibitive insider trading laws (including stronger public enforcement powers) have more diffuse equity ownership, more accurate stock prices, and more liquid stock markets.[165] In the EU, Member States with stricter implementation and enforcement experienced significantly larger capital market effects of the introduction of the (former) Market Abuse Directive (2003/6/EC).[166] In fact, enforcement of the law may be more important than the substantive law itself. Merely legislating against insider trading has been shown not to reduce the cost of equity, while proactive enforcement of insider trading laws did.[167] Enacting but not enforcing insider trading laws might even increase the cost of capital, due to varying levels of compliance by economic actors, whereby those who do not comply will cause those who do comply more harm than they would incur if there were no law at all.[168]

---

[161] See Coffee, 'Law and the Market' (n 2) 250; Howell E Jackson and Mark J Roe, 'Public and Private Enforcement of Securities Laws: Resource-based Evidence' (2009) 93 Journal of Finance and Economics 207.

[162] See Jackson and Roe, 'Public and Private Enforcement of Securities Laws' (n 161) 207.

[163] See Coffee, 'Law and the Market' (n 2) 231.

[164] Nuno Fernandes and Miguel A Ferreira, 'Insider Trading Laws and Stock Price Information' (2009) 22 Review of Financial Studies 1845.

[165] Laura N Beny, 'Do Insider Trading Laws Matter? Some Preliminary Comparative Evidence' (2005) 7 American Law and Economics Review 144.

[166] Hans B Christensen, Luzi Hail, and Christian Leuz, 'Capital-market Effects of Securities Regulation: Prior Conditions, Implementation and Enforcement' (2016) 20 Review of Financial Studies 2885.

[167] Utpal Bhattacharya and Hazem Daouk, 'The World Price of Insider Trading' (2002) 57 Journal of Finance 75.

[168] Utpal Bhattacharya and Hazem Daouk, 'When No Law is Better than a Good Law' (2009) 13 Review of Finance 577.

6

PRIVATE ENFORCEMENT OF THE MARKET ABUSE REGULATION IN EUROPEAN LAW

I. Introduction

The Market Abuse Regulation has been applicable in the EU/EEA since 3 July 2016. As regulatory provisions of this nature are classified as public law, any failure to comply with provisions of the Market Abuse Regulation will primarily affect the infringer's relationship with the competent financial supervisor. In other words, the relevant financial supervisor can enforce these provisions under administrative law in the event of an infringement, for example by imposing an administrative fine. This is essentially no different from the situation under the **A.6.01**

Market Abuse Regulation's predecessor— Market Abuse Directive (2003/6/EC), as implemented in the various national legal systems.

A.6.02 However, an infringement of the key provisions of the Market Abuse Regulation in any event also has an important effect on the private law relations between the infringer and the investing public. By 'key provisions' I mean (i) the prohibition of insider dealing (Article 14(a) in conjunction with Article 8(1) of the Market Abuse Regulation); (ii) the prohibition of unlawful recommendation and disclosure (Article 14(b) in conjunction with Article 8(2) of the Market Abuse Regulation and Article 14(c) in conjunction with Article 10(1) and (2) of the Market Abuse Regulation, respectively); (iii) the prohibition of market manipulation (Article 15 in conjunction with Article 12 of the Market Abuse Regulation); and (iv) the requirement of prompt public disclosure of inside information (Article 17 Market Abuse Regulation).[1]

A.6.03 In Dutch case law and literature, it is now commonly accepted that an infringement of the key provisions of the (former) Market Abuse Directive (2003/6/EC), as implemented in the Dutch Financial Supervision Act (Wet op het financieel toezicht) until 3 July 2016, constitutes a tort (unlawful act) on account of contravention of a statutory duty (Article 6:162(2) Burgerlijk Wetboek or Dutch Civil Code (DCC)[2]). Above all, a breach of the requirement of prompt public disclosure of inside information has proved to be a popular ground in Dutch legal practice for bringing liability proceedings not only against the issuer itself but also against its directors.[3] All of this will remain essentially unchanged in the Netherlands under the Market Abuse Regulation, although it should be noted that it will now be much easier for aggrieved investors to prove a breach of the

[1] It should be noted, however, that the European legislator in fact regards the public disclosure obligation not as a key provision but mainly as an ancillary (or 'flanking') measure. This is evident, for example, from the fact that the Community obligation to introduce criminal sanctions is limited to the prohibition of insider dealing, the prohibition of unlawful recommendation and disclosure and the prohibition of market manipulation. The Dutch government clearly sees this differently. It regards the obligation to provide public disclosure of inside information as a key provision which is of the same level of importance as the three prohibitions just mentioned. See D R Doorenbos, 'Openbaarmaking van voorwetenschap onder de Verordening Marktmisbruik' *Ondernemingsrecht* 2016/83 para 5 (with further references).

[2] Article 6:162(2) DCC reads as follows: 'As a tortious act is regarded a violation of someone else's right (entitlement) and *an act or omission in violation of a duty imposed by law* [italics added by the author] or of what according to unwritten law has to be regarded as proper social conduct, always as far as there was no justification for this behaviour'. Translation taken from http://www.dutchcivillaw.com/civilcodebook066.htm.

[3] See recently Amsterdam Court of Appeal (11 November 2014) *JOR* 2015/71, with note by Hoff (*VEB v Super de Boer*); Amsterdam Court of Appeal (29 July 2014) *JOR* 2014/300, with note by Doorenbos (*VEB v Fortis*); Midden-Nederland Court (27 July 2016) ECLI:NL:RBMNE:2016:4094 (*VEB v Ziggo*). With regard to the liability of directors for failure to provide prompt public disclosure of inside information see Utrecht District Court (15 February 2012) ECLI:NL:RBUTR:2012:BV3753, *JOR* 2012/243, with note by Willems; *Ondernemingsrecht* 2012/51, with note by De Jong; *AA* 2012/744, with note by Raaijmakers; *NTBR* 2012/37, with note by Arons (*X v Votron and Others*) paras 4.40, 4.51.

obligation to provide public disclosure of inside information. However, in some other jurisdictions within the EU/EEA, the knock-on effect of the European market abuse rules in civil liability law is taken much less for granted.[4] To this extent, the Netherlands would appear to be leading the way within Europe in recognising the direct effect of EU market abuse rules in civil liability law. Frequent references will therefore be made to Dutch law below. Dutch case law on the collapse of Fortis, the Belgian–Dutch banking and insurance group, will play a central role in this connection.

II. Questions under Consideration

This chapter examines the extent to which the civil courts are bound under EU law by the key provisions of the Market Abuse Regulation. The following questions are considered in this context: (1) May civil courts apply standards that are less strict than the key provisions of the Market Abuse Regulation? (2) May civil courts apply standards that are stricter than the key provisions of the Market Abuse Regulation? (3) What effect do the key provisions of the Market Abuse Regulation have on the requirement of proximity or relativity in the Member States where this is a requirement for liability in tort? (4) What effect do the key provisions of the Market Abuse Regulation have on the proof of causal link? (5) Should civil courts apply the key provisions of the Market Abuse Regulation of their own motion? Afterwards, I consider how the Market Abuse Regulation makes it easier to establish proof in civil proceedings of a breach of the requirement of public disclosure of inside information. In the final section I draw some conclusions. **A.6.04**

III. May Civil Courts Be Less Strict than the Market Abuse Regulation?

General

May civil courts apply standards that are less strict than the key provisions of the Market Abuse Regulation? Let me concentrate on four categories of case: **A.6.05**

(1) The civil courts refuse a claim for damages brought for a breach of a key provision of the Market Abuse Regulation because under private law they apply a principle that is less strict and has not been infringed (category 1).

[4] See eg for Germany: A Hellgardt, 'Europarechtliche Vorgaben für die Kapitalmarkt informationshaftung—de lege lata und nach Inkrafttreten der Marktmissbrauchverordnung' *Aktiengesellschaft* 5/2012, 154–68; D Poelzig, 'Private enforcement im deutschen und europäischen Kapitalmarktrecht' *ZGR* 2015, 801–48. See eg for the UK: P L Davies, S Worthington, and E Micheler, *Gower's Principles of Modern Company Law* (10th edn, Sweet & Maxwell 2016) paras 26.24, 16.29, 30.7–30.10, 30.53, 30.55.

(2) The civil courts refuse a claim for damages brought for a breach of a key provision of the Market Abuse Regulation, but not because in private law they apply a principle that is less strict and has not been infringed. In this case, they recognise the European rule. Breach of a key provision of the Market Abuse Regulation constitutes a tort as it is a contravention of a statutory duty.[5] Nonetheless, the civil courts refuse the claim for damages in the specific case because there is a ground of justification for the breach.[6] This means that the infringement is not unlawful (category 2).

(3) An issuer breaches the requirement that inside information must be disclosed as soon as possible (Article 17 Market Abuse Regulation[7]). This requirement is binding only on the issuer and—unlike, say, the prohibition of market manipulation (Article 15 in conjunction with Article 12 of the Market Abuse Regulation[8])—not on anyone else. The director who is in actual control of the issuer when it commits this breach therefore acts, by definition, in his capacity of director of the issuer. In keeping with the prevailing doctrine in the Netherlands, the increased liability threshold for serious personal culpability then applies in full under Dutch law (category 3).[9]

(4) A person who commits market manipulation (Article 15 in conjunction with Article 12 of the Market Abuse Regulation[10]) is a person who makes

---

[5] See under Dutch law art 6:162(2) DCC: 'As a tortious act is regarded a violation of someone else's right (entitlement) and *an act or omission in violation of a duty imposed by law* [italics added by the author] or of what according to unwritten law has to be regarded as proper social conduct, always as far as there was no justification for this behaviour.' Translation taken from http://www.dutchcivillaw.com/civilcodebook066.htm.

[6] As referred to in art 6:162(2) (last words) DCC: 'As a tortious act is regarded a violation of someone else's right (entitlement) and an act or omission in violation of a duty imposed by law or of what according to unwritten law has to be regarded as proper social conduct, *always as far as there was no justification for this behaviour* [italics added by the author]'. Translation taken from http://www.dutchcivillaw.com/civilcodebook066.htm.

[7] The corresponding provision of the (former) Market Abuse Directive (2003/6/EC) was implemented in Dutch law in s 5:25i of the Dutch Financial Supervision Act until 3 July 2016 and prior to this in s 5:59 of the Dutch Financial Supervision Act. When the Transparency Directive was transposed on 1 January 2009 into ch 5.1A of the Dutch Financial Supervision Act (rules for the provision of information by issuers), the public disclosure obligation was moved from s 5:59 to s 5:25i of the Dutch Financial Supervision Act. With regard to the private law consequences of a breach of the public disclosure obligation under Dutch liability law see G T J Hoff, 'Aansprakelijkheid bij niet-naleving van de openbaarmakingsplicht van koersgevoelige informatie' in D Busch, C J M Klaassen, and T M C Arons (eds), *Aansprakelijkheid in de financiële sector* (Serie Onderneming en Recht vol 78, Kluwer 2013) 711–72.

[8] Until 3 July 2016, the corresponding provision of the (former) Market Abuse Directive (2003/6/EC) was implemented in the Netherlands in s 5:58 of the Dutch Financial Supervision Act.

[9] See also T M C Arons and D Busch, 'Bestuurdersaansprakelijkheid bij schending van financieelrechtelijke toezichtregels' (2016) *WPNR* 7125 893–906 at 902 (no 44); Utrecht District Court (15 February 2012) ECLI:NL:RBUTR:2012:BV3753, *JOR* 2012/243, with notes by J H M Willems; *Ondernemingsrecht* 2012/51 B J de Jong; AA20120744 M J G C Raaijmakers; *NTBR* 2012/37 T.M.C. Arons (*X v Votron and Others*) paras 4.40 and 4.51.

[10] Incorporated in Dutch legislation until 3 July 2016 in s 5:58 of the Dutch Financial Supervision Act, by way of implementation of the equivalent provision of the (former) Market Abuse Directive (2003/6/EC).

misleading statements in his capacity of director of an issuer. In keeping with the prevailing doctrine in the Netherlands, the increased liability threshold for serious personal culpability then applies in full under Dutch law (category 4).[11]

Category 1

The judgment of the Dutch Supreme Court (Hoge Raad der Nederlanden or HR) in the case of *FortisEffect and Others v Netherlands* is of particular interest in illustrating category 1.[12] For an international readership, it is important first of all to pause and consider the background to the *Fortis* case. **A.6.06**

In October 2007 a greatly weakened ABN AMRO had fallen prey to an international banking consortium consisting of the Belgian–Dutch banking and insurance group Fortis, the Royal Bank of Scotland, and the Spanish company Banco Santander. Against the background of the global financial crisis and the bankruptcy of Lehman Brothers on 15 September 2008, the planned takeover soon proved to be a crippling financial burden on Fortis. On 3 October 2008, the Fortis Group had to be broken up along national lines and parts were nationalized. In this way, ABN AMRO came into the hands of the Dutch state. What followed was an avalanche of legal proceedings in Belgium and the Netherlands.[13] **A.6.07**

One of the legal actions brought in the Netherlands was instituted by *Stichting FortisEffect and Others*. They applied to the Utrecht District Court for a declaratory judgment that Fortis and the State of the Netherlands had acted unlawfully by furnishing incorrect and misleading information. They also requested the court to order Fortis and the Netherlands to pay compensation for the resulting loss and damage and to direct that this should be quantified. The court rejected the applications. On appeal, the Court of Appeal upheld the judgment of the lower court in relation to the claim against the Netherlands. However, in relation to Fortis the Court of Appeal quashed the judgment and gave—inter alia—a declaratory ruling that Fortis had acted unlawfully in the period from 29 September 2008 to 1 October 2008, in breach of sections 5:58 (prohibition **A.6.08**

[11] See Arons and Busch, 'Bestuurdersaansprakelijkheid bij schending van financieelrechtelijke toezichtregels' (n 9) 900 (no 32); L Timmerman, 'Beginselen van bestuurdersaansprakelijkheid' (2016) *WPNR* 7105 no 23. But see also Utrecht District Court (15 February 2012) ECLI:NL:RBUTR:2012:BV3753, *JOR* 2012/243, with note by Willems; *Ondernemingsrecht* 2012/51, with note by de Jong; *AA*20120744, with note by Raaijmakers; *NTBR* 2012/37, with note by Arons (*Kortekaas and Others v Votron and Others*) paras 4.7 and 4.49.

[12] Dutch Supreme Court (30 September 2016) ECLI:NL:HR:2016:2213.

[13] With regard to the collapse of ABN AMRO see J Smit, *De Prooi. Blinde trots breekt ABN AMRO* (Prometheus 2008). See also the stage play and three-part TV series (both dramatized) based on this book. With regard to the fall of Fortis see P Depuydt, *De kloof. Hoe de breuk tussen Belgen en Nederlanders Fortis fataal werd* (Prometheus 2010). For a list of law suits in the Netherlands and Belgium see *Annual Report Ageas 2015*, 209–13 https://www.ageas.com/en/text/annual-report-2015. Fortis was later renamed Ageas.

of market manipulation) and 5:59 (old) (requirement to provide prompt public disclosure of inside information) of the Dutch Financial Supervision Act.[14]

A.6.09 The only part of the Dutch Supreme Court's judgment relevant to the present discussion is the dismissal of the claim against the Netherlands. Initially, an appeal in cassation had also been lodged against the Court of Appeal's decision to allow the claim against Fortis, but this matter was settled out of court before the Dutch Supreme Court could give judgment.[15] The legal battle on which the spotlight is now focused is therefore not the proceedings against Fortis but those against the State of the Netherlands.

A.6.10 On Thursday 2 October 2008, the Minister of Finance made statements in the House of Representatives of the Dutch parliament (Tweede Kamer) about the first rescue operation for Fortis. According to *FortisEffect and Others*, these statements were incorrect and/or misleading within the meaning of what was then section 5:58 of the Dutch Financial Supervision Act (now Article 15 in conjunction with Article 12 of the Market Abuse Regulation). It was argued that during the Thursday debate the minister had failed to divulge that the transaction on the preceding Sunday evening had not had the desired effect and that more far-reaching measures were necessary and the negotiations to achieve this were already at an advanced stage. The Court of Appeal held as follows on this point:

> 4.2.16. As noted above, the State was aware on Thursday 2 October 2008 that the transaction concluded on Sunday 28 September 2008 had not had the desired effect. Nonetheless, this does not alter the fact that it was appropriate for the State to inform the House of Representatives about the background to the transaction in the manner in which it did. In the Court of Appeal's view, it was reasonable for the State—given the great importance to the financial system—to decide at that time that information about the more far-reaching measures it was planning did not yet need to be disclosed as this—in its reasonable estimation—would have immediately led to a further undermining of confidence in Fortis, possibly triggering events beyond the control of Fortis and the banking system. The statements made during the debate in the House of Representatives were not of such a nature that the average informed, prudent and observant investor—bearing in mind, among other things, the falling price of Fortis shares—could have concluded that the problems with Fortis had been resolved and that the rescue operation had been a success.

---

[14] Section 5:59 (old) Dutch Financial Supervision Act is addressed to the issuer, in this case Fortis. The provision does not therefore play a role in the proceedings against the State of the Netherlands. Following the transposition of the Transparency Directive into ch 5.1A of the Dutch Financial Supervision Act (rules for the provision of information by issuers) on 1 January 2009, the duty of public disclosure was transferred from s 5:59 Dutch Financial Supervision Act to s 5:25i Dutch Financial Supervision Act. Since 3 July 2016 this duty has been contained in art 17 Market Abuse Regulation.

[15] See Ageas's press release of 14 March 2016 https://www.ageas.com/en/press-release/ageas-deminor-stichting-fortiseffect-sicaf-and-veb-reach-agreement-aiming-settling-all.

> 4.2.17. It follows that the State did not breach section 5:58 of the Dutch Financial Supervision Act or otherwise act unlawfully by making the statements discussed above.[16]

FortisEffect and others are appealing in cassation against the judgment of the Court of Appeal and have submitted, among other things, that the finding expressed above is insufficiently (clearly) reasoned (ground of cassation 9.3). In his Opinion in this case, Advocate General Timmerman wonders how paragraph 4.2.16 of the Court of Appeal's judgment as set out above should now be interpreted.[17] According to him, the Court of Appeal's finding is essentially that, leaving aside the question of whether or not the investor was misled by the failure to disclose the relevant information, the actions of the Netherlands were *justifiable* (or, in any event, *not culpable*) because it was faced with events beyond its control (*force majeure*). The Advocate General points out that this interpretation of paragraph 4.2.16 is in keeping with what is said in paragraph 4.3.5, at (a): **A.6.11**

> The question of the extent to which the State (wrongly) disseminated incorrect, incomplete or misleading information about Fortis (and its rescue) has already been considered in relation to the submission by FortisEffect and Others that the State contravened the Dutch Financial Supervision Act. The conclusion was that *no blame could be attached* to the State in that respect [italics added by the Advocate General].

Advocate General Timmerman notes in his Opinion that there is no scope for an *argument based on grounds of justification* in the context of an assessment of compliance with section 5:58 of the Dutch Financial Supervision Act. A statement does not become less incorrect or misleading because the party that made it was faced with events beyond its control. Moreover, a precise interpretation of the rule contained in section 5:58 of the Dutch Financial Supervision Act is all the more important because the Netherlands Authority for the Financial Markets (AFM)[18] and the administrative courts are also called upon to interpret and apply this provision in the context of their supervision under public law.[19] **A.6.12**

Advocate General Timmerman notes in passing that, although the Court of Appeal held that in the circumstances the actions of the Netherlands could be justified (or were not culpable), this does not mean, in his view, that the Court of Appeal intended to treat this as a *ground of justification within the meaning of Article 6:162(2) of the Dutch Civil Code.*[20] The finding in question in paragraph **A.6.13**

---

[16] Amsterdam Court of Appeal (29 July 2014) ECLI:NL:GHAMS:2014:3005, *JOR* 2014/300, with note by Doorenbos, paras 4.2.16–4.2.17.

[17] Opinion of Advocate General Timmerman (25 March 2016) ECLI:NL:PHR:2016:163 no 3.112.

[18] The AFM is the Dutch business conduct regulator for the financial services industry.

[19] Opinion of Advocate General Timmerman (25 March 2016) ECLI:NL:PHR:2016:163 no 3.112.

[20] Article 6:162(2) DCC reads as follows: 'As a tortious act is regarded a violation of someone else's right (entitlement) and an act or omission in violation of a duty imposed by law or of what according to unwritten law has to be regarded as proper social conduct, *always as far as there was*

4.2.16 has been placed in the context of assessing whether there were misleading statements within the meaning of section 5:58 Dutch Financial Supervision Act, and the term 'ground of justification' was not used by the Court of Appeal. He also refers to paragraph 4.7.3, in which the Court of Appeal held that since, in its view, the State had not acted unlawfully, 'any application of the ground of justification (is) no longer relevant'.[21]

A.6.14 All things considered, Advocate General Timmerman concludes as follows:

> In view of the above, I believe that the submission put forward in part 9.3 ... of the appeal in cassation succeeds. In the light of arguments put forward by FortisEffect and Others, I consider that the reasons given by the Court of Appeal for finding that section 5:58 of the Dutch Financial Supervision Act was not contravened during the Thursday debate are not sufficiently clear. Although the statements that *were* made by the Minister were not—according to the Court of Appeal—misleading, the Court of Appeal did not recognise—or did not sufficiently recognise—that the average investor may also have been misled (within the meaning of section 5:58 of the Dutch Financial Supervision Act) since essential information was omitted when providing the information. There can be no doubt, in my view, that the information to which FortisEffect and Others refer (including the fact that it was already clear on the Thursday that the first rescue operation had not had the desired effect and would no longer be implemented and that negotiations were under way about much more far-reaching measures) constituted essential information of this kind. It also follows from the above that a finding that the actions of the State were *justified* cannot also support a finding that there was no contravention of section 5:58 of the Dutch Financial Supervision Act.[22]

A.6.15 According to Advocate General Timmerman, what the Court of Appeal did was, in short, to read an additional requirement into section 5:58 of the Dutch Financial Supervision Act which cannot be found either in that provision or in the (former) Market Abuse Directive (2003/6/EC) on which it was based, and then to conclude that there had been no contravention of the rule. It is clear from this that the Court of Appeal in fact applied a standard which was less strict than the provision actually contained at that time in section 5:58 of the Dutch Financial Supervision Act implementing the (former) Market Abuse Directive (2003/6/EC) and which now follows directly from Article 15 in conjunction with Article 12 of the Market Abuse Regulation. The Court of Appeal's reasoning can be seen as a 'veiled' example of a category 1 case.

A.6.16 However this may be, category 1 cases are at odds with the European principle of effectiveness, as formulated, inter alia, by the Court of Justice of the European

no justification for this behaviour [italics added by the author].' Translation taken from http://www.dutchcivillaw.com/civilcodebook066.htm.

[21] Opinion of Advocate General Timmerman (25 March 2016) ECLI:NL:PHR:2016:163 no 3.113.

[22] Opinion of Advocate General Timmerman (25 March 2016) ECLI:NL:PHR:2016:163 no 3.114.

Union (CJEU) in its *Immofinanz* judgment.[23] That case concerned the private law consequences of rules from the Prospectus Directive (2003/71/EC), the Transparency Directive (2013/50/EU), and the (former) Market Abuse Directive (2003/6/EC). In paragraph 40 of the judgment the CJEU held as follows:

> While it is true that, unlike Article 25(1) of the Prospectus Directive, Article 28(1) of the Transparency Directive and Article 14(1) of the Market Abuse Directive do not expressly refer to the civil liability regimes in the Member States, the fact remains that the Court has previously ruled that, in respect of the award of damages and the possibility of an award of punitive damages, in the absence of European Union rules governing the matter, it is for the domestic legal system of each Member State to set the criteria for determining the extent of the damages, *provided that the principles of equivalence and effectiveness are observed* [italics added by the author] (see, by analogy, Joined Cases C-295/04 to C-298/04 *Manfredi and Others* [2006] ECR I-6619, paragraph 92, and the judgment of 6 June 2013 in Case C-536/11 *Donau Chemie and Others* [2013] ECR, paragraphs 25 to 27).

The CJEU had previously taken a similar line in relation to the Markets in Financial Instruments Directive I (2004/39/EC) in the *Genil* case.[24] In this judgment the CJEU had held that in the absence of EU legislation it is for the Member States themselves to determine the contractual consequences of non-compliance with the know-your-customer (KYC) rules under MiFID I, but that the principles of equivalence and effectiveness must be observed (paragraph 57).[25] The Court of Justice referred in this connection to paragraph 27 of a judgment of 19 July 2012 concerning a tax matter (*Littlewoods Retail and Others*, Case C-591/10) and the case law cited there. This paragraph reads as follows: **A.6.17**

> In the absence of EU legislation, it is for the internal legal order of each Member State to lay down the conditions in which such interest must be paid, particularly the rate of that interest and its method of calculation (simple or compound interest). Those conditions must comply with the principles of equivalence and effectiveness; that is to say that they must not be less favourable than those concerning similar claims based on provisions of national law *or arranged in such a way as to make the exercise of rights conferred by the EU legal order practically impossible* [italics added by the author] (see, to that effect, previously cited cases *San Giorgio*, paragraph 12; *Weber's Wine World*, paragraph 103; and Case C-291/03 *MyTravel* [2005] ECR I-8477, paragraph 17).[26]

[23] CJEU (19 December 2013) no C-174/12, *NJ* 2014/184, with note by Mok; *Ondernemingsrecht* 2014/71, with note by Arons; *V&O* 2014 no 7/8, pp. 109–14, with note by Beckers (*Alfred Hirmann v Immofinanz AG*).

[24] CJEU (30 May 2013) no C-604/11, *AA* (2013) 663, with note by Busch; *JOR* 2013/274, with note by Busch (*Genil 48 SL and Others v Bankinter SA and Others*).

[25] CJEU (30 May 2013) no C-604/11, *AA* (2013) 663, with note by Busch; *JOR* 2013/274, with note by Busch (*Genil 48 SL and Others v Bankinter SA and Others*).

[26] See now also the explicit provision in art 69(2), last paragraph Markets in Financial Instruments Directive II (2014/65/EU): 'Member States shall ensure that mechanisms are in place to ensure that compensation may be paid or other remedial action be taken in accordance with national law for any financial loss or damage suffered as a result of an infringement of this Directive or [Markets in Financial Instruments Regulation (2014/600/EU)].' The rules implementing MiFID II will come into force on 3 January 2018. For the effect of Markets in Financial

A.6.18 The principle of effectiveness therefore means that the conditions which an investor must fulfil in order to bring a civil liability action may not be such that success is practically impossible or even extremely difficult. The judgment appears to mean, in so far as relevant here, that civil courts may not be *less strict* than is possible under the EU market abuse rules. Where, according to the EU rules, there is market manipulation in a specific case and the aggrieved investors bring a civil action for damages, the civil courts may not dismiss this claim by holding that in the particular circumstances the rule applied in private law is less strict. As the market abuse rules are intended to achieve maximum harmonization, this would, after all, clash with the principle of effectiveness.

A.6.19 If this were not the case, the principles of legal certainty and the European level playing field would be put under great strain, particularly since the EU market abuse rules themselves provide for a detailed list of situations in which the prohibition of market manipulation does not apply, such as stabilization of market prices.[27] All of this applies to an even greater extent under the Market Abuse Regulation. The instrument of a regulation was expressly chosen since the requirements would then be directly applicable, which would thus 'provide more legal certainty' and 'ensure uniform conditions by preventing diverging national requirements as a result of the transposition of a directive'. The Market Abuse Regulation 'will require that all persons follow the same rules in all the Union'.[28] This approach can be extended to claims for damages for non-compliance with the prohibition of insider dealing, the prohibition of unlawful recommendation and disclosure, and the requirement of public disclosure of inside information.

Category 2

A.6.20 This brings me to category 2 cases. Here the basis for rejection by the civil courts of a claim for damages is not (as in category 1 cases) that a less strict rule is applicable and has not been infringed. The civil courts recognise the EU criterion. Infringement of the market abuse rules constitutes a tort for contravention of a statutory duty. Nonetheless, the civil courts reject the claim for damages because the existence of a ground of justification exists as referred to in Article 6:162(2) (last words), DCC means that the infringement is not unlawful.[29]

Instruments Directive II (2014/65/EU) in private law see D Busch, Chapter 20: 'The Private Law Effect of MiFID: Genil and Beyond' in D Busch and G Ferrarini (eds), *Regulation of the EU Financial Markets: MiFID II and MiFIR* (OUP 2017).

[27] See now arts 5, 6, and 13 Market Abuse Regulation.

[28] Recitals (4) and (5) Market Abuse Regulation.

[29] Article 6:162(2) DCC reads as follows: 'As a tortious act is regarded a violation of someone else's right (entitlement) and an act or omission in violation of a duty imposed by law or of what according to unwritten law has to be regarded as proper social conduct, *always as far as there was no justification for this behaviour* [italics added by the author].' Translation taken from http://www.dutchcivillaw.com/civilcodebook066.htm.

Although the Amsterdam Court of Appeal did not, according to Advocate General Timmerman, view the case of *FortisEffect and Others v Netherlands* as a category 2 case, the issue of whether or not this category was consistent with the European principle of effectiveness was nonetheless sufficiently intriguing for the Advocate General to devote a passage in his Opinion to it. According to the Advocate General, category 2 cases are not inconsistent with the European principle of effectiveness: **A.6.21**

> In my view, the principle of effectiveness does not warrant the general conclusion that the ground of justification rule should not be applied in the case of a claim for damages for breach of section 5:58 of the Dutch Financial Supervision Act. The legitimacy of this rule of general Dutch tort law, under which in (very) special circumstances a tortious act need not necessarily result in liability, does not mean that Dutch law does not provide for adequate legal redress in the event of an infringement of section 5:58 of the Dutch Financial Supervision Act.[30]

I do not share the Advocate General's conviction that category 2 cases are not inconsistent with the European principle of effectiveness. The possibility of invoking a ground of justification within the meaning of Article 6:162(2) (last words) DCC enables Dutch civil courts to introduce exceptions to the European market abuse rules which do not have a statutory basis in EU law. I am all the more hesitant because the European market abuse rules themselves contain a detailed list of exceptions to which the prohibition of market manipulation is not applicable.[31] As the aim of the European market abuse rules is to achieve maximum harmonization, civil courts should, in my view, be very cautious about introducing national exceptions, for example by assuming a ground of justification within the meaning of Article 6:162(2) (last words) DCC. As noted previously, this applies even more following the introduction of the Market Abuse Regulation, since the decision to have a regulation was made precisely in order to ensure legal certainty and a level playing field ('uniform conditions'). Whether the reasoning used by the civil courts must be regarded as a category 1 or category 2 case is immaterial. In both cases, the court concerned would be making a substantive exception to the European market abuse rules which is not covered by one or more of the exceptions provided for in these rules themselves. **A.6.22**

Intermezzo

Naturally, however, it would be unsatisfactory if the State of the Netherlands were to be liable to aggrieved investors for damage suffered by them because the Minister of Finance had been guilty of market manipulation in the House of Representatives. When the Minister was called to the House of Representatives to **A.6.23**

---

[30] Opinion of Advocate General Timmerman (25 March 2016) ECLI:NL:PHR:2016:163 no 3.30.

[31] See note 29.

report on the first rescue operation of Fortis, he decided not to disclose information about the plans for more far-reaching measures. I agree with the Amsterdam Court of Appeal that it was entirely understandable and indeed sensible not to disclose the information at that stage. After all, it was reasonable to suppose that any such disclosure would have immediately undermined confidence in Fortis still further, possibly triggering events that would be beyond the control of Fortis and the banking system.

A.6.24 The Dutch Supreme Court has extricated itself from this problem in a way that avoids getting caught up in complicated discussion about the European principle of effectiveness. It does so by interpreting the judgment of the Court of Appeal as follows:

> 3.9.4. [t]he view of the Court of Appeal . . . is essentially that although the Minister did not always disseminate full information, this did not give—nor was it likely to give—a misleading signal to investors since they were aware of the context in which the rescue operations and the disclosure of information were taking place, and the Minister's decision not to provide full information was also justified by the importance of maintaining the stability of the financial system, especially in the second period.
>
> . . .
>
> 3.11. It is implicit in the judgment of the Court of Appeal that the investors should have realised that the Minister was reporting on the transaction of Sunday 28 September 2008 and not on the current state of the rescue operation. In this light, and taking into account the wording chosen by the Minister . . ., it was not unreasonable for the Court of Appeal to hold that what was said by the Minister during the parliamentary debate did not create the impression that the problems with Fortis had been resolved and that the rescue operation was a success.[32]

A.6.25 In short, in view of the context of the financial crisis and the wording chosen by the Minister of Finance in the debate in the House of Representatives on 2 October 2008, the information he provided could not be said to have been misleading within the meaning of what was then section 5:58 of the Dutch Financial Supervision Act and is now Article 15 in conjunction with Article 12 of the Market Abuse Regulation. The Dutch Supreme Court does not in fact answer the question of whether the minister's actions were justified (ie whether this was a category 1 or category 2 case). In this way, it circumvents the pitfalls of EU law which it would otherwise have to negotiate if it were accepted that the minister misled the House of Representatives and hence the public too within the meaning of section 5:58 of the Dutch Financial Supervision Act, which is now Article 15 in conjunction with Article 12 of the Market Abuse Regulation.

A.6.26 The conclusion that the State of the Netherlands is not liable to aggrieved investors for market manipulation is to be welcomed in a social sense. But in a legal

32 Dutch Supreme Court (30 September 2016) ECLI:NL:HR:2016:2213.

sense it is hard to accept. Can it really be argued that the minister was not guilty of market manipulation on 2 October 2008? For the sake of the future, it would in any event be preferable for the Netherlands to push for an amendment to the Market Abuse Regulation to enable an exception to be made to the prohibition of market manipulation in the interests of protecting the stability of the financial system. Nor is this idea so far-fetched when one thinks that an issuer which is a bank or other financial institution may delay public disclosure of inside information if this is necessary to maintain the stability of the financial system.[33] As matters stand, it is therefore permissible to stay silent in the interests of the stability of the financial system, but not to tell half-truths. Where staying silent is not an option (ie because the Minister is bound to report to the House of Representatives), telling half-truths too should be permissible in the interests of the stability of the financial system.

Categories 3 and 4

Let us now move on to category 3 cases. An issuer breaches the requirement of prompt public disclosure of inside information. This is a provision that is binding exclusively on the issuer and not—as, say, in the case of the prohibition of market manipulation—on everyone. The director who is in actual control of the issuer at the time of this conduct therefore acts, by definition, in his capacity of director of the issuer. In keeping with the prevailing doctrine in the Netherlands, the increased liability threshold for serious personal culpability then applies in full under Dutch law (category 3 case).[34] **A.6.27**

Finally, we come to category 4 cases. A person who commits market manipulation is a person who makes misleading statements in his capacity of director of an issuer. In keeping with the prevailing doctrine in the Netherlands, the increased liability threshold for serious personal culpability then applies in full under Dutch law (category 4 case).[35] **A.6.28**

---

[33] See art 17(5) Market Abuse Regulation: 'In order to preserve the stability of the financial system, an issuer that is a credit institution or a financial institution, may, on its own responsibility, delay the public disclosure of inside information, including information which is related to a temporary liquidity problem and, in particular, the need to receive temporary liquidity assistance from a central bank or lender of last resort, provided that all of the following conditions are met: (a) the disclosure of the inside information entails a risk of undermining the financial stability of the issuer and of the financial system; (b) it is in the public interest to delay the disclosure; (c) the confidentiality of that information can be ensured; and (d) the competent authority specified under para 3 has consented to the delay on the basis that the conditions in points (a), (b) and (c) are met.'

[34] For more information see Arons and Busch, 'Bestuurdersaansprakelijkheid bij schending van financieelrechtelijke toezichtregels' (n 9) 902 (no 44); Utrecht District Court (15 February 2012) ECLI:NL:RBUTR:2012:BV3753, *JOR* 2012/243, with note by Willems; *Ondernemingsrecht* 2012/51, with note by de Jong; AA20120744, with note by Raaijmakers; *NTBR* 2012/37, with note by Arons (*X v Votron and Others*) paras 4.40 and 4.51.

[35] See Arons and Busch, 'Bestuurdersaansprakelijkheid bij schending van financieelrechtelijke toezichtregels' (n 9) 900 (no 32); L Timmerman, 'Beginselen van bestuurdersaansprakelijkheid'

A.6.29 Cases in categories 3 and 4 do not involve the application by the civil courts of criteria that are less strict than the European market abuse rules, although this may perhaps not be apparent at first sight.

A.6.30 Where the requirement of prompt public disclosure of insider information is infringed, in a legal sense, the infringer in category 3 cases is not the director in his capacity of a natural person but the legal person at whom the provision is exclusively targeted. The requirement of serious culpability is not imposed in respect of that legal person, nor is there a higher liability threshold than that prescribed by the European prohibition of market manipulation.

A.6.31 Where market manipulation is committed in a legal sense, the infringer in category 4 cases is not the director in his capacity of natural person but the legal person to whom the unlawful act must be imputed. The requirement of serious culpability is not imposed in respect of that legal person, and the liability threshold is not higher than that prescribed by the European prohibition of market manipulation. Nor, in my view, would the position be any different if, in the meantime, the legal person has become bankrupt and no longer provides any opportunity for recovery.

IV. May Civil Courts Be Stricter than the Market Abuse Regulation?

General

A.6.32 Another question of both theoretical and practical importance is whether the rules that civil courts apply may be stricter than the key provisions of the Market Abuse Regulation and the (former) Market Abuse Directive (2003/6/EC). In practice, this question could become topical in civil liability proceedings or in an investigation procedure (*enquêteprocedure*) before the Enterprise Court (*Ondernemingskamer* or OK) at the Amsterdam Court of Appeal. An example would be where an issuer delays disclosure of inside information in accordance with the requirements imposed by the European market abuse rules. Under EU law, would it nonetheless be permissible for a civil court to hold that as a result of the delay a rule of private law has been breached or for the Enterprise Court to hold that the delay constitutes mismanagement?

A.6.33 An example of an investigation procedure before the Enterprise Court in which this issue arose was the *Fortis* case. Here this very question was expressly raised

2016 *WPNR* 7105 no 23. But see also Utrecht District Court (15 February 2012) ECLI:NL:RBUTR:2012:BV3753, *JOR* 2012/243, with note by Willems; *Ondernemingsrecht* 2012/51, with note by de Jong; *AA*20120744, with note by Raaijmakers; *NTBR* 2012/37, with note by Arons (*Kortekaas and Others v Votron and Others*) paras 4.7 and 4.49.

by Fortis's lawyers in one of the grounds of cassation set out in their appeal against the decision of the Enterprise Court.[36] The company investigation procedure before the Enterprise Court will be dealt with in more detail later on in this chapter. For now it is sufficient to note that the aim of the procedure is to allow a company's affairs to be investigated with a view to possibly reorganising the company, restoring sound relations within it, allowing proper disclosure and, where applicable, allocating responsibility for any mismanagement.[37] In its final ruling on Fortis, the Enterprise Court formulated this as follows:

> The Enterprise Court should assess whether the report of the investigation shows that the acts or omissions of Fortis, its organs or their members, as alleged by the Association of Stockholders (VEB) and others, constitute mismanagement. This will be the case if Fortis's acts or omissions have been so negligent or reprehensible that they must be held to have breached fundamental principles of sound business practice.[38]

I would point out that it is not yet entirely clear whether the Enterprise Court actually held in the *Fortis* case that certain acts constitute mismanagement, given that the acts in question are covered by and permissible under the (former) Market Abuse Directive (2003/6/EC) and the rules of the Dutch Financial Supervision Act based on it. From the cautious wording of the relevant ground of appeal in cassation ('if and in so far as'[39]) it might even be inferred that Fortis was of the same opinion. In any event, the Dutch Supreme Court has not explicitly answered the question raised in the cassation appeal against the decision of the Enterprise Court, even by way of obiter dictum. The Dutch Supreme Court simply dismisses the ground of appeal concerned without expressly answering the question raised in it. **A.6.34**

In dismissing the ground for appeal in cassation, the Dutch Supreme Court merely held in a general sense that whether or not certain acts by Fortis were permissible under the (former) Market Abuse Directive (2003/6/EC) and the rules of the Dutch Financial Supervision Act based on it was not decisive in determining whether there had been mismanagement.[40] Naturally, this finding is, broadly speaking, unobjectionable. The mere fact that the European market **A.6.35**

[36] Dutch Supreme Court (6 December 2013) ECLI:NL:HR:2013:1586, with note by Busch *FR* 2014/1, 30–35 (*Ageas NV (previously Fortis NV) v VEB NCVB and Others*) para 4.3.1.

[37] Dutch Supreme Court (10 January 1990) *NJ* 1990, 466 (*Ogem*); Asser-Maeijer/Van Solinge/Nieuwe Weme 2-II* (2009) no 728.

[38] Enterprise Court (5 April 2012) *JOR* 2013/41, with note by Bulten; *AA* (2012) 744, with note by Raaijmakers; *Ondernemingsrecht* (2012) 71, with note by Bartman, para 4.2; cf Dutch Supreme Court (10 January 1990) *NJ* 1990, 466 (*Ogem*); Asser-Maeijer/Van Solinge/Nieuwe Weme 2-II* (2009) no 790.

[39] Dutch Supreme Court (6 December 2013) ECLI:NL:HR:2013:1586, *FR* 2014/1, 30–35, with note by Busch (*Ageas NV (previously Fortis NV) v VEB NCVB and Others*) para 4.3.1.

[40] Dutch Supreme Court (6 December 2013) ECLI:NL:HR:2013:1586, *FR* 2014/1, 30–35, with note by Busch (*Ageas NV (previously Fortis NV) v VEB NCVB and Others*) para 4.3.3.

abuse rules are infringed by the company or by its senior management does not itself warrant the conclusion of mismanagement. Naturally, it would be different if the acts in question were to involve serious and/or systematic breaches of supervisory legislation. Neither the Enterprise Court nor the Dutch Supreme Court explicitly makes this distinction, but the wording of their judgments does leave scope for such a conclusion. And it should also be noted, of course, that even where European market abuse rules are not infringed mismanagement may still exist for other reasons.

A.6.36 However, this means that the Dutch Supreme Court has not yet resolved the specific issue raised in the ground of appeal in cassation in the *Fortis* case as outlined above, namely where a given act is covered by and permissible under the European market abuse legislation but the Enterprise Court holds that the act in question constitutes mismanagement.[41] This brings us back to the question I raised at the end of paragraph A.6.32, namely whether a civil court (including the Enterprise Court) may apply stricter standards than those prescribed by the European market abuse rules.

Immofinanz and *Genil*

A.6.37 The judgments in the *Immofinanz* and *Genil* cases do not in any event seem to provide a definitive answer to the question of whether civil courts may apply *stricter* standards than the European market abuse rules.[42] If, for example, a civil court holds that although an issuer is admittedly entitled to delay public disclosure of inside information under the European market abuse rules this is not possible in private law, this does not deprive an aggrieved investor of a claim for breach of the European market abuse rules. Where a civil court applies stricter standards than the European market abuse rules this does not appear to be at odds with the principle of effectiveness as formulated by the Court of Justice in the *Immofinanz* and *Genil* judgments. It should be noted, however, that the question whether civil courts may apply stricter standards than the European market abuse rules was not at issue in the *Immofinanz* and *Genil* cases, and was therefore not answered explicitly. The *Immofinanz* judgment was solely about the private law consequences of a breach of, among other things, the market abuse rules, and the *Genil* case was solely about the private law consequences of non-compliance with the MiFID I KYC rules. However, none of this precludes the possibility that

[41] On this point see my previous notes on Dutch Supreme Court (6 December 2013) ECLI:NL:HR:2013:1586, *FR* 2014/1, 35 nos 22 t/m 24 (*Ageas NV (previously Fortis NV) v VEB NCVB and Others*).

[42] CJEU (19 December 2013) no C-174/12, *NJ* 2014/184, with note by Mok; *Ondernemingsrecht* 2014/71, with note by Arons; *V&O* 2014 no 7/8, pp. 109–14, with note by Beckers (*Alfred Hirmann v Immofinanz AG*); CJEU (30 May 2013) no C-604/11, *AA* (2013) 663, with note by Busch; *JOR* 2013/274, with note by Busch (*Genil 48 SL and Others v Bankinter SA and Others*).

it could be argued on the basis of other principles of EU law that civil courts may not apply stricter standards than the European market abuse rules. Some pointers can be found in the CJEU's judgment in the case of *Nationale-Nederlanden v Van Leeuwen* concerning exorbitant management costs charged in connection with life insurance policies.[43]

Nationale-Nederlanden v Van Leeuwen

The *Nationale-Nederlanden* judgment appears to show that European law is blind to the distinction between public and private law in relation to European legal standards.[44] In *Nationale-Nederlanden* the CJEU did not, after all, have any difficulty in accepting that Annex II to the Third Life Assurance Directive[45] was implemented in the Netherlands in Article 2 of the Regulation regarding the provision of information to policyholders 1998 (*Regeling informatieverstrekking aan verzekeringsnemers 1998/RIAV 1998*) (public law), whereas the option for Member States in Article 31(3) of the Third Life Assurance Directive to require assurance undertakings to furnish additional information could be implemented through the requirements of reasonableness and fairness (*redelijkheid en billijkheid*) of Article 6:2 DCC (private law). **A.6.38**

If it is correct that European law is blind to the distinction between public and private law, this also has an important impact on whether civil courts, including the Enterprise Court, may apply stricter standards than those of the European market abuse rules. The European market abuse rules provide for maximum harmonization. If European law is truly blind to the distinction between public and private law in relation to European legal standards, the principle of maximum harmonization must also apply to civil courts, including the Enterprise Court. This would mean that they cannot impose stricter duties under private law than the criteria resulting from the market abuse rules, regardless of whether they are included in a directive or a regulation. In the *Immofinanz* and *Genil* judgments, the Court of Justice admittedly held that in the absence of EU legislation it is for the Member States themselves to determine what effect non-compliance with European directives has under private law (provided that it is not practically impossible to recover compensation for the loss or damage suffered), but this refers to the sanction and not to the legal rule itself. **A.6.39**

[43] CJEU (29 April 2015) C-51/13, *AA* (2015) 696, with note by Busch and Arons (*Nationale Nederlanden v Van Leeuwen*).

[44] CJEU (29 April 2015) C-51/13, *AA* (2015) 696, with note by Busch and Arons (*Nationale Nederlanden v Van Leeuwen*) para 28.

[45] Directive 92/96/EEC, OJ EU L 360 (9 December 1992) 1–27. This has since been repealed and replaced by more recent versions; see CJEU (29 April 2015) C-51/13, *AA* (2015) 696, with note by Busch and Arons (*Nationale Nederlanden v Van Leeuwen*) para 3.

V. Influence of the Market Abuse Regulation on the Requirement of Relativity

A.6.40 In some European jurisdictions a tort claim based on breach of statutory duty cannot succeed in the absence of 'proximity' or 'relativity'.[46] This means that the relevant duty must not only serve the general interest, but also the claimant's proprietary interests. In the jurisdictions imposing a relativity requirement the question therefore arises whether this requirement is met where there is a breach of a key provision of the Market Abuse Regulation.

A.6.41 In the Netherlands the requirement of relativity must have been met if there is to be liability in tort (Article 6:163 DCC). In so far as relevant here, this means that one of the aims of the key provision of the European market abuse rules that has been infringed must be to offer protection for the loss or damage suffered by the investor. Although the *Immofinanz* and *Genil* judgments admittedly show that in the absence of EU legislation it is for the Member States themselves to determine the private law consequences of non-compliance with, among other things, the market abuse rules, various requirements including the principle of effectiveness must always be fulfilled. In this context, the principle of effectiveness means that the conditions on which an investor may sue an infringer of a key provision of European market abuse rules may not be such as to make it impossible or extremely difficult to mount a successful action in practice.

A.6.42 It is submitted that the European principle of effectiveness means that a claim for damages for infringement of the key provisions of the European market abuse rules may not fail by virtue of the requirement of relativity. After all, these rules are intended to promote not only market integrity but also, very emphatically, investor protection.[47] This interpretation is also in keeping with what is said on this subject in the Explanatory Memorandum to the Dutch Financial Supervision Act, namely that all provisions of the Dutch Financial Supervision Act are intended to protect the proprietary interests of clients. The same applies to other company stakeholders under private law, for example shareholders and bond holders.[48] Although the European market abuse rules have been removed

---

[46] For example, the requirement of relativity in the Netherlands (*relativiteitsvereiste*) and the *Schutznorm* requirement in Germany (art 6:163 DCC and para 823 *Bürgerliches Gezetsbuch*, respectively).

[47] See eg para 3 (market integrity) and para 8 (investor protection) Market Abuse Regulation. See also *Dutch Parliamentary Papers II*, 2015/16, 34 455 no 3 (Explanatory Memorandum) 1–2.

[48] See *Dutch Parliamentary Papers II*, 2005/2006, 29 708 no 19, 393, where it is noted in a general sense that '[w]here consumers suffer damage as a consequence of a breach of a provision of this bill ..., the requirement of relativity of art 6:163 DCC will also be deemed to have been complied with. One of the aims of this bill is to protect consumers from misconduct by financial undertakings'. For this purpose, the term consumer must be broadly interpreted. Basically, it means anyone who obtains financial services, ie anyone who is a 'client', whether in a private or non-private capacity. This interpretation is confirmed, for example, by the paragraph in the

from the Dutch Financial Supervision Act since 3 July 2016 and now appear in a regulation that has direct effect in the Netherlands, the scope of the protection afforded by the rules has remained unchanged.

VI. Influence of the Market Abuse Regulation on Proof of Causal Link

Another interesting question concerns the impact of a breach of the European market abuse rules on the proof of causal link, a universal requirement for liability in all EU Member States and far beyond.[49] **A.6.43**

Let us first consider a judgment of the Dutch Supreme Court concerning the internet company *World Online*.[50] That case concerned loss allegedly suffered by investors in World Online as a consequence, among other things, of a misleading prospectus published on the occasion of the company's flotation. In brief, the **A.6.44**

legislative history of the Dutch Financial Supervision Act prior to the passage just quoted above, where reference is made to 'consumers or other contacts of financial undertakings under private law'. Whatever the case, it is apparent from the Dutch legislative history that whether the rule that has been infringed is a rule of prudential supervision or a rule of market conduct supervision is immaterial to the application of the requirement of relativity. All provisions of or under the Dutch Financial Supervision Act are intended to protect the proprietary rights of clients and other contacts of financial undertakings under private law. This interpretation is in keeping with other passages from the legislative history of the Dutch Financial Supervision Act, where it is noted that the prudential supervision by the Dutch central bank (DNB) is performed not only in the public interest but also in order 'to protect those obtaining services offered or provided by the financial undertakings concerned'. Similarly, the market conduct supervision by the AFM is performed not only in the public interest but also to protect the proprietary rights of 'clients'. With regard to prudential supervision see *Dutch Parliamentary Papers II* 2003–2004, 29 708 no 3 (Explanatory Memorandum), pp. 28–29. The fact that prudential supervision is intended to protect the proprietary rights of policy holders (a *species* of the *genus* client) is also apparent from Dutch Supreme Court judgment HR (13 October 2006) *NJ* 2008/529, with note by Van Dam; *JOR* 2006/295, with note by Busch; *JA* 2007/2, with note by Van Boom (*DNB v Stichting Vie d'Or*) para 4.2.2. With regard to market conduct supervision see *Dutch Parliamentary Papers II* 2003/04, 29 708 no 3 (Explanatory Memorandum) 29. With regard to the relativity requirement in relation to infringements of market abuse rules see also Utrecht District Court (15 February 2012) *JOR* 2012/243, with note by Willems; *Ondernemingsrecht* 2012/267, with note by De Jong; *NTBR* 2012/262, with note by Arons. Finally, the principle described above can be extended to cover investors who are solely contractual counterparties (and hence not clients) of a financial undertaking. If supervision rules are infringed in this situation, the relativity requirement is also automatically fulfilled. For a detailed consideration of how this relates to infringement of the requirement of prompt public disclosure of inside information see Hoff, 'Aansprakelijkheid bij niet-naleving van de openbaarmakingsplicht van koersgevoelige informatie' (n 7) 756–9.

[49] See first and foremost the all-time classic of H L A Hart and Tony Honoré, *Causation in the Law* (2nd edn, Oxford University Press 1985). See, more recently, Michael S Moore, *Causation and Responsibility: An Essay in Law, Morals, and Metaphysics* (Oxford University Press 2009).

[50] Dutch Supreme Court (27 November 2009) *NJ* 2014/201, with note by Du Perron; *AA* (2010) 336, with note by Raaijmakers; *JOR* 2010/43, with note by Frielink (*Vereniging van Effectenbezitters and Others v World Online International NV*).

Dutch Supreme Court held as follows. As it is often hard to prove a *condicio sine qua non* link (the 'but for' test) in relation to liability for a prospectus, the investor protection which the Prospectus Directive (2003/71/EC) is intended to provide may prove illusory in practice. Although this Directive admittedly contains detailed provisions about what information must be included in the prospectus, it does not regulate civil liability if the prospectus is misleading because it is incomplete or incorrect. It does, however, require the Member States to ensure that their laws, regulations, and administrative provisions on civil liability apply to those persons responsible for the information given in a prospectus (Article 6(2), first paragraph). According to the Dutch Supreme Court, this means that effective legal protection must be provided in accordance with the rules of national law.[51] The Dutch Supreme Court also held as follows:

> With a view to that effective legal protection and having regard to the protection which the prospectus rules are intended to provide for investors and potential investors against misleading information in the prospectus, the basic principle should be that a *condicio sine qua non* link ('but for' link) must exist between the misleading information and the decision to invest. This means that it must be assumed, in principle, that if there had been no misleading information the investor would not have proceeded with the purchase of the securities or, in the event of purchase on the secondary market, would not have done so on the same conditions. However, the court may conclude—from the submissions of the parties (either party being free to prove the correctness of the alleged facts) and any further information available—that the basic principle referred to above does not apply in the specific circumstances. This will be the case, for example, if it is shown that the investment decision was made before disclosure of the misleading information. It should be noted by the way that as professional investors have knowledge and experience of the relevant market and of analysing the available information, there will generally be more reason than in the case of retail investors to conclude that, despite the

[51] See Dutch Supreme Court (27 November 2009) *NJ* 2014/201, with note by Du Perron; *AA* (2010) 336, with note by Raaijmakers; *JOR* 2010/43, with note by Frielink (*Vereniging van Effectenbezitters and Others v World Online International NV*) para 4.11.1. For the record, it should be noted that the Prospectus Directive has subsequently been amended as a consequence of Directive 2010/73/EU. The changes had to be transposed into national law by 1 July 2012 at the latest (art 3, Directive 2010/73/EU). This was achieved in the Netherlands. For a detailed discussion of the obligation to publish a prospectus see K A Kralj, *De prospectusplicht* (FR 10 Kluwer 2012). Directive 2010/73/EU does not make any changes to art 6(2), first paragraph, of the Prospectus Directive. However, the text of art 6(2), second paragraph, has been supplemented. The text in italics below is the addition made by Directive 2010/73/EU: 'However, Member States shall ensure that no civil liability shall attach to any person solely on the basis of the summary, including any translation thereof, unless it is misleading, inaccurate or inconsistent, when read together with the other parts of the prospectus, *or it does not provide, when read together with the other parts of the prospectus, key information in order to aid investors when considering whether to invest in such securities. The summary shall contain a clear warning to that effect* [italics added by the author].' From 21 July 2019 onwards the bulk of the new Prospectus Regulation will directly apply in the Member States, at which point national implementation of the current Prospectus Directive can cease. See art 49(2) of Regulation (EU) 2017/1129, OJ L 168, 30 June 2017, pp. 12–82 (Prospectus Regulation). The text of art 6 Prospectus Directive can be found in art 11 of the Prospectus Regulation.

misleading information in the prospectus, they were not actually influenced by it in making their investment decision.[52]

In short, the Dutch Supreme Court proceeds on the assumption that the *condicio sine qua non* link between the misleading information and the decision to invest is present. In the case of professional investors, their knowledge and experience may warrant the conclusion that they were not actually influenced by the misleading information. In such cases, the court may apply the basic rule that the investor has the burden of proving the *condicio sine qua non* link. **A.6.45**

A question of particular relevance in assessing the influence of the European market abuse rules on proof of causal link is whether the Dutch Supreme Court's reasoning in the *World Online* case as described above can also be applied where investors suffer damage as a consequence of infringement of one or more of the key provisions of the market abuse rules. I believe that a good case could certainly be made for this, especially in relation to the prohibition of market manipulation and the requirement of public disclosure of inside information. One of the main aims of the European market abuse rules is investor protection.[53] Although the European market abuse rules do not contain a provision comparable to Article 6(2) Prospectus Directive (2003/71/EC), we may assume that the European legislator intended the Member States to offer effective legal protection in relation to the market abuse rules as well. The principle of effectiveness is, after all, a fundamental principle of EU law.[54] The *Immofinanz* judgment provides support for this idea. It is apparent from the judgment that although in the absence of EU legislation it is admittedly left to the Member States to determine the private law consequences of non-compliance with market abuse obligations they must still ensure observance of (inter alia) the principle of effectiveness. In this connection, this principle means that the conditions an investor must fulfil in order to bring a civil action against a firm that infringes a key provision of the European market abuse rules may not be such that in practice success is impossible or extremely difficult. **A.6.46**

---

[52] See Dutch Supreme Court (27 November 2009) *NJ* 2014/201, with note by Du Perron; *AA* (2010) 336, with note by Raaijmakers; *JOR* 2010/43, with note by Frielink (*Vereniging van Effectenbezitters and Others v World Online International NV*) para 4.11.2. With regard to this aspect of the judgment see A C W Pijls and W H van Boom, 'Handhaving prospectusaansprakelijkheid niet illusoir: vermoeden van causaal verband bij prospectusaansprakelijkheid' (2010) *WPNR* 6834, 194–200, 196–7; B J de Jong, 'Liability for Misrepresentation: European Lessons on Causation from the Netherlands' (2011) European Company and Financial Law Review 352, 364–6.

[53] See recitals (3) (market integrity) and (8) (investor protection) Market Abuse Regulation. See also *Dutch Parliamentary Papers II*, 2015/16, 34 455 no 3 (Explanatory Memorandum) 1–2.

[54] Regarding the question of how the principle of effectiveness affects the impact of EU law on private law in a general sense see for example: A S Hartkamp, *European Law and National Private Law. Effect of EU Law and European Human Rights Law on Legal Relationships between Individuals* (2nd edn, Intersentia 2016) 98–116; T Tridimas, *The General Principles of EU Law* (Oxford University Press 2006) 418–76; W van Gerven, 'Of Rights, Remedies and Procedures' (2000) Common Market Law Review 501.

A.6.47 If effective legal protection (to use the terminology of the *World Online* judgment) is to be provided, a good case can be made, particularly in relation to infringements of the prohibition of market manipulation and the requirement of public disclosure of inside information, for taking the causal link between the infringement of the rule and the loss or damage as the starting point, since the investor protection which the market abuse rules are intended to provide may otherwise prove illusory in practice.[55] At present, however, it is unclear whether the Dutch Supreme Court or other civil courts would adopt this approach. Naturally, other approaches that help the client in proving a causal link may also be in keeping with the principle of effectiveness.[56]

VII. Are the Courts Obliged to Apply the Market Abuse Regulation of their Own Motion?

A.6.48 This brings me, finally, to what I regard as an intriguing question that has a bearing on the intensity with which the European market abuse rules impact private law. Are the civil courts obliged to determine of their own motion whether the European market abuse rules have been infringed? I would certainly not wish to exclude this possibility in advance.

A.6.49 It is apparent from the settled case law of the CJEU that the national courts must determine of their own motion whether, on the basis of the European principle of effectiveness, unreasonably onerous clauses in contracts between businesses and consumers are 'unfair' within the meaning of Directive 93/13/EEC. The Court of Justice may also direct the civil courts to determine of their own motion whether the legislation is applicable.[57]

A.6.50 Indeed, it would seem to be extending the protection to the entire field of consumer protection directives. Recently, the Court of Justice gave such a direction in the case of the consumer purchases directive.[58] In any event, the key provisions

[55] See also B J de Jong, *Schade door misleiding op de effectenmarkt* (dissertation Radboud University, VHI series vol 103 Kluwer 2010) 271–2; Hoff, 'Aansprakelijkheid bij niet-naleving van de openbaarmakingsplicht van koersgevoelige informatie' (n 7) 760–70, both of which refer to the Transparency Directive and the obligation of prompt public disclosure of inside information under the (former) Market Abuse Directive (2003/6/EC).

[56] With regard to the last point see C J M Klaassen, 'Bewijs van causaal verband tussen beweerdelijk gelden beleggingsschade en schending van een informatie- of waarschuwingsplicht' in D Busch, C J M Klaassen, and T M C Arons (eds), *Aansprakelijkheid in de financiële sector* (Serie Onderneming en Recht, vol 78 Kluwer 2013) 127–74, 151.

[57] See CJEU (26 October 2006) no case 168/05, *NJ* 2007/201, with note by Mok (*Mostaza Claro*); CJEU (4 June 2009) no case 243/08, *NJ* 2009/395, with note by Mok (*Pannon*); CJEU (6 October 2009) no case 40/08, *NJ* 2010/11 (*Asturcom*); CJEU (30 May 2013) *NJ* 2013/487, with note by Mok (*Asbeek Brusse and De Man Garabito*); CJEU (28 July 2016) no case 168/15, *AA* 2016/658, with note by Hartkamp (*Milena Tomášová* v *Ministerstvo spravodlivosti SR ea*).

[58] See CJEU (3 October 2013) no case 32/12, *AA* 2015/222, with note by Hartkamp (*Soledad Duarte Hueros v Autociba*); CJEU (4 June 2014) no case 497/13, *Ars Aequi* 2015/816, with note

of the European market abuse rules can, in my view, be treated as consumer protection provisions in so far as they must be observed in relation to private investors.[59] National civil courts should in that case determine of their own motion whether there has been an infringement of the key provisions of the market abuse rules in disputes between infringers and private investors.

VIII. Proof of Failure by Civil Parties to Provide Prompt Public Disclosure of Inside Information

General

As already noted in the introduction, in the Netherlands, a failure to provide prompt public disclosure of inside information often serves as a basis for liability claims against issuers and even their directors.[60] This path does not appear to be very popular in the other Member States of the EU, at least for the time being. In Dutch legal practice, when bringing a claim for damages against an issuer, investors often support their case by citing the fact that the AFM has imposed an administrative fine on the issuer for breach of the disclosure obligation. They may also invoke (i) the investigation report produced for the Enterprise Court in the context of an investigation procedure, or (ii) the final decision of the Enterprise Court in which it provides a description of and/or makes a declaratory ruling on the issuer's communication policy, for example that it amounts to mismanagement.[61] **A.6.51**

by Hartkamp (*Froukje Faber v Autobedrijf Hazet Ochten BV*). See also A Ancery and B Krans, 'Ambsthalve toepassing van consumentenrecht: grensbepaling en praktische kwesties' (2016) *Ars Aequi* 825.

[59] One of the main aims of the European market abuse rules is investor protection. See recital (8) Market Abuse Regulation. See also *Dutch Parliamentary Papers II*, 2015/16, 34 455 no 3 (Explanatory Memorandum) 1–2.

[60] See recently Amsterdam Court of Appeal (11 November 2014) *JOR* 2015/71, with note by Hoff (*VEB v Super de Boer*); Amsterdam Court of Appeal (29 July 2014) *JOR* 2014/300, with note by Doorenbos (*VEB/Fortis*); Midden-Nederland Court (27 July 2016) (ECLI:NL:RBMNE:2016:4094) (*VEB v Ziggo*). With regard to the liability of directors for failure to provide prompt public disclosure of inside information see Utrecht District Court (15 February 2012) ECLI:NL:RBUTR:2012:BV3753, *JOR* 2012/243, with note by Willems; *Ondernemingsrecht* 2012/51, with note by De Jong; *AA* 2012/744, with note by Raaijmakers; *NTBR* 2012/37, with note by Arons (*X v Votron and Others*) paras 4.40, 4.51. As public disclosure is an obligation that is binding only on the issuer (unlike, for example, the prohibition of market manipulation which applies to everyone), the director who is in actual control of this conduct acts by definition in his capacity of director of the issuer. According to the prevailing doctrine, the requirement of serious personal culpability of the director applies in full under Dutch law. For more detail see Arons and Busch, 'Bestuurdersaansprakelijkheid bij schending van financieelrechtelijke toezichtregels' (n 9) 902 (no 44).

[61] Cf Hoff, 'Aansprakelijkheid bij niet-naleving van de openbaarmakingsplicht van koersgevoelige informatie' (n 7) 743.

Imposition of fine by the AFM

A.6.52 A decision by the AFM to impose a fine will generally be a fairly major element of proof in civil proceedings. After all, a decision of this kind may be imposed only if the AFM has found that the obligation of prompt public disclosure of inside information has been infringed. To be able to determine whether such an infringement has taken place, the AFM has extensive investigative powers which a civil party does not possess.[62] Investors may request the AFM to take enforcement action and thus 'elicit' the imposition of a fine. In principle, the AFM must make any such decision public, including the reasons for the decision (section 1:97 et seq. Dutch Financial Supervision Act). In the *Fortis* case, the AFM imposed fines on Fortis for infringing the prohibition of market manipulation and failing to make prompt public disclosure of inside information. This decision was contested by Fortis all the way up to the highest Dutch administrative court (the Trade and Industry Appeals Tribunal/CBB), albeit in vain.[63]

A.6.53 Strictly speaking, however, the civil courts are not bound by a decision of the AFM or by the ruling of an administrative court to which the AFM's decision has been referred for judicial review. In civil proceedings the AFM's decision or a ruling on it by an administrative court has whatever evidentiary value the court gives it. Nonetheless, a decision of the AFM or a ruling on it by an administrative court will, in practice, have persuasive authority.[64]

The Dutch company investigation procedure

General

A.6.54 For an international readership the Dutch company investigation procedure needs some explanation. To provide this, I will discuss the investigation procedure in the *Fortis* case. For the general background to the *Fortis* case, see paragraphs A.6.07 ff above.[65]

A.6.55 The aim of the procedure is allow a company's affairs to be investigated with a view to a possible reorganization, restoration of sound intra-company relations, proper disclosure and, where applicable, allocation of responsibility for any mismanagement. The possibility of instituting an investigation also has

[62] Examples are the power of the AFM to obtain information (s 1:74 Dutch Financial Supervision Act) and the supervisory powers of the AFM's staff, such as the power to demand information (s 5:16 General Administrative Law Act), the power to inspect business data and papers (s 5:17 General Administrative Law Act), and the duty of the issuer to cooperate (s 5:20 General Administrative Law Act).

[63] CBB (4 March 2014) ECLI:NL:CBB:2014:67, *JOR* 2014/133, with note by Stevens (*Ageas v AFM*).

[64] See also Hoff, 'Aansprakelijkheid bij niet-naleving van de openbaarmakingsplicht van koersgevoelige informatie' (n 7) 747–8.

[65] See para III.3.2.

preventive effect.[66] Where a procedure is requested solely to resolve a pecuniary dispute (for example, whether the company and its directors are liable for loss or damage suffered), the application is not admissible; and where a procedure is requested to resolve a pecuniary dispute as well as one or more of the other matters referred to above but the reasoning is not plausible, the application is admissible but should be refused.[67] In practice, these limitations are scarcely an impediment to the successful institution of an investigation procedure.[68] Indeed, the investigation procedure regularly serves as a prelude to liability proceedings.[69]

The following are competent to apply for an investigation into the affairs of a private or public company: (i) shareholders (provided that they fulfil, individually or together, strict absolute or relative capital requirements); (ii) the company itself (represented by the managing board, supervisory board or non-executive directors) and, in the event of the company's bankruptcy, its liquidator; (iii) an employees' association, provided that certain requirements are met; (iv) persons granted this power in the articles of association or in an agreement with the company; (v) the Advocate General at Amsterdam Appeal Court Public Prosecution Office in cases where an investigation would be in the public interest.[70] **A.6.56**

[66] Dutch Supreme Court (10 January 1990) *NJ* 1990, 466 (*Ogem*); Asser-Maeijer/Van Solinge/Nieuwe Weme 2-II* (2009) no 728.

[67] Dutch Supreme Court (18 November 2005) *NJ* 2006, 173; *JOR* 2005/295 (*Unilever*); Asser-Maeijer/Van Solinge/Nieuwe Weme 2-II* (2009) no 728.

[68] Cf B Winters and P N Ploeger, 'Kroniek Enquêterecht' in M Holtzer, A F J A Leijten, and D J Oranje (eds), *Geschriften vanwege de Vereniging Corporate Litigation 2006-2007* (Serie vanwege het Van der Heijden Instituut, vol 93 Kluwer 2007) 11–47, 18–21; Asser-Maeijer/Van Solinge/Nieuwe Weme 2-II* (2009) no 728.

[69] Asser-Maeijer/Van Solinge/Nieuwe Weme 2-II* (2009) no 442; for example see also Willems in his note no 1 to the judgment of Utrecht District Court (15 February 2012) *JOR* 2012/243 (*Kortekaas and Others v Lippens and Others*).

[70] See arts 2:345–347 DCC, as these provisions have read since 1 January 2013 as a consequence of the Investigation Right (Amendment) Act (*Bulletin of Acts and Decrees* 2012, 274). This amending legislation has introduced stricter requirements to be fulfilled by providers of capital to large companies and listed companies in order to be able to apply for an investigation (art 2:346(1)(c) DCC). As a result, activist shareholders will find it harder to request an investigation into large companies and listed companies. It should be noted that the access threshold can be set lower in the articles of association. At the time when the Fortis investigation was requested, the statutory requirements were less strict. The right of the company itself and, in the event of its bankruptcy, its liquidator to apply for an investigation (arts 2:346(1)(d) and 2:346(3) DCC respectively) was introduced on 1 January 2013 when the Investigation Right (Amendment) Act referred to above came into force. These possibilities did not therefore yet exist at the time of the application for the *Fortis* investigation. With regard to the amendments see eg P van Schilfgaarde, J Winter, and J B Wezeman, *Van de BV en de NV* (16th edn, Kluwer 2013) no 117. For a more detailed account of the amending legislation in its draft form see A F J A Leijten and M P Nieuwe Weme, 'Het wetsvoorstel aanpassing enquêterecht' in M Holtzer, A F J A Leijten, and DJ Oranje (eds), *Geschriften vanwege de Vereniging Corporate Litigation 2011-2012* (Serie vanwege het Van der Heijden Instituut, vol 112 Kluwer 2012) 123–73.

A.6.57 As the shareholders participated in the two top holding companies Fortis and Fortis SA/NV through a so-called twinned share arrangement,[71] they remained shareholders despite the nationalization (which took place at a lower level) and were therefore fully able in that capacity to apply for an investigation into Fortis pursuant to Article 2:346, opening words and (b), DCC.[72] Represented in part by the Association of Stockholders (VEB), this is what they did.[73]

The investigation phase

A.6.58 The investigation procedure consists of two separate phases. In the first phase the Enterprise Court decides whether there should be an investigation into the policy and affairs of a legal person (Article 2:345(1) DCC). It grants the application only if there are good reasons for doubting the correctness of the policy (or affairs) of the company (Article 2:350(1) DCC).[74] In the case of Fortis, this criterion was met.[75] The Enterprise Court then appoints one or more external, independent investigators who have practical experience and whose task is to establish the facts concerning the company's policy and affairs (Article 2:345(1) DCC).[76] For this purpose they have far-reaching investigative powers. They are entitled, for example, to inspect the accounts and records of the company, and the directors, supervisory and non-executive directors, and other officers of the company have a duty to furnish them with information (Article 2:351(1) DCC).

A.6.59 The first phase of the investigation concludes when the investigation report is deposited at the registry of Amsterdam Court of Appeal (Article 2:353(1) DCC).

---

[71] Shareholdership in the Fortis Group took the form of a 'twinned share'. Under the articles of association of both Fortis SA/NV and Fortis, a share in either of these companies could be issued, subscribed for, cancelled, and encumbered only together with a share in the other company, this being in the form of a unit. A unit consisted of an ordinary share in Fortis SA/NV and an ordinary share in Fortis. The Fortis share compiled in this way was listed on the stock exchange of Euronext Amsterdam NV. See, for example, Enterprise Court (24 November 2008) *JOR* 2009/9, with note by Josephus Jitta, para 2.2.

[72] As this provision read prior to 1 January 2013, ie prior to the date on which the Investigation Right (Amendment) Act (*Bulletin of Acts and Decrees* 2012, 274) came into force. Now they would have to make an application under art 2:346(1), opening words and (c), DCC. Please note that in the meantime the Dutch Supreme Court has ruled that even shareholders who lost ownership of their shares owing to a nationalization of the relevant company may have capacity to apply for an investigation. See Dutch Supreme Court (4 November 2016) ECLI:NL:HR:2016:2456 (*Netherlands and Others v Association of Stockholders (VEB) and Others*) para 3.

[73] The VEB does not have an independent power to apply for an investigation. Although, during the recent revision of the law on company investigations, proposals were made for lobbying organizations within the meaning of art 3:305a DCC—and hence the VEB too—to be given this power, the proposal was not adopted. See *Dutch Parliamentary Papers II* 2010/11, 32 887 no 3 (Explanatory Memorandum) 17.

[74] The words 'or correct state of affairs' were added to art 2:350(1) DCC with effect from 1 January 2013 as a consequence of the entry into force of the Investigation Right (Amendment) Act (*Bulletin of Acts and Decrees* 2012, 274). These words did not therefore appear in the provision as it read at the time of the application for the Fortis investigation.

[75] See Enterprise Court (24 November 2008) *JOR* 2009/9, with note by Josephus Jitta.

[76] Three investigators were appointed in the Fortis case.

It is by no means uncommon for these investigation reports to be very lengthy. The report of the Fortis investigation had no less than 582 pages, excluding the appendices. In the case of Fortis, the Enterprise Court decided that the report and three appendices should be open to public inspection. The remaining appendices could be inspected only by interested parties.[77]

In view of the above, an investigation report prepared by investigators for the Enterprise Court as part of an investigation procedure is clearly eminently suitable for use as evidence in substantiating an allegation that an issuer has failed to provide prompt public disclosure of inside information.[78] However this may be, in the case of Fortis a group of investors did not await publication of the investigation report and instead brought liability proceedings against Fortis and its directors and policy-makers before Utrecht District Court, with partial success.[79] When framing its judgment, Utrecht District Court already had the investigation report in its possession, but did not consider it necessary to await the final decision of the Enterprise Court, which was published less than two months after **A.6.60**

[77] See Enterprise Court (16 June 2010) ECLI:NL:GHAMS:2010:BM8183 (depositing of Fortis investigation report) para 3. The appendices form an integral part of the investigation report. In any event the Advocate General at Amsterdam Court of Appeal, the legal person itself, and the applicants and their lawyers receive a copy of the report (art 2:353(2) DCC). If the legal person, as in this case, is subject to the supervision of the Dutch central bank (DNB), the bank too receives a copy (art 2:353(2) in conjunction with art 2:348 DCC). Since 1 January 2013 (following the entry into force of the Investigation Right (Amendment) Act referred to above), the AFM has also been entitled to receive a copy if the legal person is subject (or partially subject) to its supervision (art 2:353(2) in conjunction with art 2:348 DCC). The major banks in the Eurozone have come under the direct supervision of the European Central Bank (ECB) in November 2014. It would therefore be logical to add the ECB in art 2:353 (2) and 2:348 DCC. The Enterprise Court *may* also determine that all or part of the report will be available for inspection by other persons designated by it or by everyone (art 2:353(2) DCC). As most of the appendices, as noted in the main body of the text, are available for inspection only by interested parties, the VEB requested the Enterprise Court to authorize it pursuant to art 2:353(3) DCC to divulge information to third parties from these appendices to which access is restricted. The VEB needed this authorization in order to be able to use these appendices in a law suit which at the time was pending before the Amsterdam District Court. In these proceedings, Fortis, a number of former directors of Fortis, and banks involved in the issue of shares announced on 21 September 2007 had been sued by Fortis which, in its capacity of representative of the interests of other persons within the meaning of art 3:305a DCC, had requested the Court to give a declaratory ruling that the defendants acted unlawfully in a number of respects and that they are liable for the loss and damage suffered as a result by everyone who acquired shares in Fortis in the relevant period. The Enterprise Court granted this authorization; see Enterprise Court (6 November 2013) ECLI:NL:GHAMS:2013:4745. As regards the first phase of the investigation procedure see Asser-Maeijer/Van Solinge/Nieuwe Weme 2-II* (2009) nos 730, 774–789.

[78] Cf Hoff, 'Aansprakelijkheid bij niet-naleving van de openbaarmakingsplicht van koersgevoelige informatie' (n 7) 747–8.

[79] Utrecht District Court (15 February 2012) *JOR* 2012/243, with note by Willems; *Ondernemingsrecht* (2012) 51, with note by De Jong; *NTBR* (2012) 37, with note by Arons (*Kortekaas and Others v Lippens and Others*). See also Amsterdam Court of Appeal (29 July 2014) ECLI:NL:GHAMS:2014:3005, *JOR* 2014/300, with note by Doorenbos (*Stichting Fortis Effect and Others v State of the Netherlands and Ageas (previously Fortis)*).

the court's judgment. In establishing the facts of the case, Utrecht District Court did, however, base its reasoning on the public part of the investigation report.[80]

Determination of mismanagement

A.6.61 The second phase (referred to in Article 2:355 DCC) starts once the investigation report is deposited at the court registry. In the second phase the initiative lies with the Enterprise Court itself, which is required to assess—assuming that a request to this effect has been made—on the basis of the investigation report whether there has been mismanagement. In its final decision on *Fortis*, the Enterprise Court described its task as follows (as noted previously):

> The Enterprise Court should assess whether the investigation report shows that the acts or omissions of Fortis, its constituent organs or those who staffed them constituted mismanagement as alleged by the VEB and others. This will be the case if the acts or omissions of Fortis were negligent or so serious as to be contrary to fundamental principles of responsible business practice.[81]

A.6.62 The Enterprise Court came to the conclusion that the report prepared by the investigators appointed by it showed evidence of mismanagement by the Dutch company Fortis NV in the period from September 2007 to September 2008 in respect of (i) the implementation of its solvency planning in 2008, (ii) the disclosure of information about its subprime portfolio in the issue prospectus published on 24 and 25 September 2007 and the trading update, and (iii) its communication policy in the same period.[82]

A.6.63 After finding that mismanagement occurred, the Enterprise Court *may*—but is not bound to—take measures based on the investigation report.[83] In the case of Fortis the Enterprise Court not only held that the report showed evidence of mismanagement but also acted to quash the resolution passed by the general meeting of shareholders in which the directors were discharged from liability for the policy they had pursued in 2007, in so far as the discharge related to the provision of information about Fortis's subprime portfolio (and the risks it entailed)

---

[80] On this point see also Willems in his note no 3 to the judgment of Utrecht District Court (15 February 2012) *JOR* 2012/243 (*Kortekaas and Others v Lippens and Others*).

[81] Enterprise Court (5 April 2012) *JOR* 2013/41, with note by Bulten; *AA* (2012) 744, with note by Raaijmakers; *Ondernemingsrecht* (2012) 71, with note by Bartman, para 4.2; cf Dutch Supreme Court (10 January 1990) *NJ* 1990, 466 (*Ogem*); Asser-Maeijer/Van Solinge/Nieuwe Weme 2-II* (2009) no 790.

[82] Enterprise Court (5 April 2012) *JOR* 2013/41, with note by Bulten; *AA* (2012) 744, with note by Raaijmakers; *Ondernemingsrecht* (2012) 71, with note by Bartman, para 7.

[83] See Dutch Supreme Court (27 September 2000) *NJ* 2000, 653; *JOR* 2000/217 (*Gucci*); Asser-Maeijer/Van Solinge/Nieuwe Weme 2-II* (2009) no 730. The judgment in Dutch Supreme Court (18 April 2003) *JOR* 2003/110, with note by Blanco Fernandez, para 3.3, shows, incidentally, that in finding that there has been mismanagement the Enterprise Court need not rely solely on the investigation report, but can base its findings in part on what has been submitted or found in the proceedings themselves. Cf Bulten in her note 5 to Enterprise Court (5 April 2012) *JOR* 2013/41.

in the issue prospectus published on 24 and 25 September 2007 and the trading update.[84]

The Enterprise Court's assessment that an issuer has been guilty of mismanagement is probably of less value in civil liability proceedings.[85] As is apparent from the above, the concept of 'mismanagement' as referred to in Article 2:355(1) DCC has its own very specific meaning. Mismanagement does not in itself imply liability. In liability proceedings the facts established by the Enterprise Court are not assumed proven in advance, not even subject to proof to the contrary. However, a finding by the Enterprise Court that there has been mismanagement may be accorded some evidential value in the proceedings. The court hearing the liability proceedings can hold that it has been proven in advance that the person concerned failed to properly perform his duties to the legal person, taking into account the investigation report and the debate conducted about this in the second phase of the investigation.[86] **A.6.64**

Proving claims for damages under the Market Abuse Regulation

Whatever the case may be, proving claims for damages for a failure to provide prompt public disclosure of inside information will be a good deal easier under the Market Abuse Regulation. This will work as follows in practice in the Netherlands. **A.6.65**

Under the Market Abuse Regulation an issuer is obliged (i) to keep a careful record of internal decisions on inside procedures, and (ii) to draw up and, on request, produce an explanation of any decision it takes to delay disclosure, with explicit mention of the persons responsible for the decision.[87] **A.6.66**

An investor who feels prejudiced by the lack of disclosure may try to obtain the information by requesting the AFM to enforce the provisions. He may do so by lodging an objection to a refusal by the AFM and then, in the context of the administrative law procedure, request leave to inspect the documents in the action, including the explanatory notes.[88] However, the investor must then be **A.6.67**

---

[84] Enterprise Court (5 April 2012) *JOR* 2013/41, with note by Bulten; *AA* (2012) 744 with note by Raaijmakers; *Ondernemingsrecht* (2012) 71, with note by Bartman, para 7.

[85] See also Hoff, 'Aansprakelijkheid bij niet-naleving van de openbaarmakingsplicht van koersgevoelige informatie' (n 7) 748.

[86] Dutch Supreme Court (8 April 2005) *NJ* 2006/443, with note by Van Solinge; *JOR* 2005/119, with note by Brink (*Laurus*) paras 3.8 and 3.9; Asser-Maeijer/Van Solinge/Nieuwe Weme 2-II* (2009) nos 442–444, 799.

[87] Article 17(4) Market Abuse Regulation in conjunction with arts 4 and 5 Commission Implementing Regulation (EU) 2016/1055 of 29 June 2016 laying down implementing technical standards with regard to the technical means for appropriate public disclosure of inside information and for delaying the public disclosure of inside information in accordance with Regulation (EU) No 596/2014 of the European Parliament and of the Council, OJ EU 2016, L 173/47.

[88] Cf ss 7:4 and 8:42 General Administrative Law Act (Awb).

designated as an interested party (*belanghebbende*) under Dutch administrative law, but that would seem to be reasonable.[89]

A.6.68 Quite apart from this, every investor who claims to have been prejudiced may also try to obtain access to the records by bringing a claim under Article 843a of the Dutch Code of Civil Procedure (obligation to produce exhibits) in order to strengthen his case. The existence of this evidence may be assumed, given the fact that the obligation to keep records is defined so explicitly in the EU legislation. The investor is therefore able to state with sufficient certainty what data he wishes to inspect.[90]

IX. Conclusion

A.6.69 The last word has not been spoken about the effect of the Market Abuse Regulation on private law. The Market Abuse Regulation—like the (former) Market Abuse Directive (2003/6/EC)—says nothing about this. Although the judgments in the *Immofinanz*, *Genil*, and *Nationale-Nederlanden* cases make the contours rather clearer, a number of important questions have not yet been explicitly answered by the CJEU. Further decisions of the CJEU must be awaited for more definite answers. Despite these uncertainties, the number of civil actions for breach of market abuse provisions, particularly for failure to provide prompt public disclosure of inside information, is not expected to diminish, at any rate in the Netherlands. The Market Abuse Regulation is of great assistance to aggrieved investors in obtaining evidence to support their case.

[89] Cf CBB (7 June 2012) ECLI:NL:CBB:2012:BW7748, *JOR* 2012/254, with note by Affourtit and Van den Broek (*AFM and Others v Trafalgar Asset Managers and Others*) para 5.

[90] Cf in this connection Dutch Supreme Court (26 October 2012) *JOR* 2013/30, with note by Jansen. For further references on this subject see D R Doorenbos, 'Openbaarmaking van voorwetenschap onder de Verordening Marktmisbruik' *Ondernemingsrecht* 2016/83 para 5 in conjunction with para 4.7.

Part B

COMMENTARY

1

GENERAL PROVISIONS

Article 1: Subject matter

This Regulation establishes a common regulatory framework on insider dealing, the unlawful disclosure of inside information, and market manipulation (market abuse), as well as measures to prevent market abuse to ensure the integrity of financial markets in the Union and to enhance investor protection and confidence in those markets.

I. General Remarks

Overview

Article 1 defines the subject matter of the Market Abuse Regulation and distinguishes in this regard between the establishment of a common regulatory framework on insider dealing, the unlawful disclosure of inside information and market manipulation, and measures to prevent market abuse to ensure the integrity of financial markets in the Union and to enhance investor protection and confidence in those markets. **B.1.01**

Historical development

B.1.02 The explicit definition of the subject matter of the Market Abuse Regulation in its Article 1 had no equivalent in the (former) Market Abuse Directive (2003/6/EC). However, the (former) Market Abuse Directive (2003/6/EC) referred to the subject matter now explicitly governed by Article 1 in its recitals.[1]

II. Subject Matter of the Market Abuse Regulation

B.1.03 The subject matter of the Market Abuse Regulation is, pursuant to Article 1, the establishment of a common regulatory framework on market abuse,[2] the establishment of measures to prevent market abuse to ensure the integrity of financial markets in the Union,[3] and the enhancement of investor protection and confidence in those markets.[4] Although defined as the subject matter of the Market Abuse Regulation, these objectives are mainly of political significance and have barely any relevance for the interpretation of the Market Abuse Regulation. This is especially the case since the scope of the Market Abuse Regulation is—in contrast to many other European Regulations—separately governed by its Article 2.

Establishment of a common regulatory framework

B.1.04 The major purpose of the Market Abuse Regulation is the establishment of a common regulatory framework for market abuse. Because the (former) Market Abuse Directive (2003/6/EC) already established such a common regulatory framework,[5] the major precise purpose of the Market Abuse Regulation is the enhancement or improvement of the common regulatory framework by replacing the previously existing regulatory framework in the Member States by a directly applicable regulation (Article 288(2) TFEU).[6]

B.1.05 Article 1 contains the general definition of market abuse, which consists of insider dealing, the unlawful disclosure of inside information, and market manipulation. The actual meaning of this definition is somewhat limited, since the term market manipulation as defined by Article 12 covers almost all kinds of transactions with influence on the price of financial instruments on financial markets. However, a specific definition of market abuse for the purposes of the Market

[1] See especially recital (1) (former) Market Abuse Directive (2003/6/EC).
[2] See n 2 ff.
[3] See n 5.
[4] See n 6.
[5] See Part A—History, Application, Interpretation, and Legal Sources of the Market Abuse Regulation n 8.
[6] For the consequences of this change from a directive to a regulation see Part A—History, Application, Interpretation, and Legal Sources of the Market Abuse Regulation n 10 ff.

Abuse Regulation is necessary, since market abuse also exists in other areas of law such as competition law.[7]

The single elements of market abuse are defined throughout the Market Abuse Regulation. Insider dealing is defined by Article 8, unlawful disclosure of inside information by Article 10, and market manipulation by Article 12. However, these general definitions are encompassed by further regulation limiting or broadening the scope of these definitions. **B.1.06**

Establishment of measures to prevent market abuse to ensure the integrity of financial markets in the Union

Furthermore, the Market Abuse Regulation establishes measures to prevent market abuse and to ensure the integrity of financial markets. This additional subject matter of the Market Abuse Regulation must be understood as a general authorization of the ESMA and the single administrative competent authorities of the Member States (Article 3(12)[8]). Since the powers of ESMA and these competent authorities are defined in Article 23, the actual meaning of this additional subject matter is somewhat limited. **B.1.07**

Enhancement of investor protection and confidence

Finally, Article 1 states that the subject matter of the Market Abuse Regulation is also the enhancement of investor protection and confidence in the financial markets in the Union. Like the subject matter discussed in note 5, this subject is also of rather limited importance and has more of a political meaning. **B.1.08**

III. Related Subjects Outside the Subject Matter of the Market Abuse Regulation

Takeover law

Market abuse is particularly relevant in takeover situations. The Market Abuse Regulation also addresses takeover law and refers to the Takeover Directive (2004/25/EC). Pursuant to recital (27), the Market Abuse Regulation should be interpreted in a manner consistent with the laws, regulations, and administrative provisions adopted in relation to takeover bids, merger transactions, and other transactions affecting ownership or control of companies regulated by the supervisory authorities appointed by Member States pursuant to Article 4 of the Takeover Directive (2004/25/EC). Also, Article 9(4) and recital (30) state that the **B.1.09**

[7] See n 8.
[8] See art 3 n 16.

use of inside information in the context of a public takeover bid for the purpose of gaining control should not be deemed to constitute insider dealing.[9] Finally, the disclosure of inside information by a person intending to make a takeover bid for the securities of a company or a merger with a company to parties entitled to the securities can constitute a market sounding and therefore be exempt from the prohibition of insider trading.[10]

Competition law

B.1.10 Pursuant to recital (80), the Market Abuse Regulation is without prejudice to the application of Union rules on competition. Therefore, a trade, act, or behaviour constituting a market abuse as set out in the Market Abuse Regulation can also violate the rules on competition in Articles 101 ff of the Treaty on the Functioning of the European Union (TFEU). The relevance of recital (80) remains unclear, however, since the Market Abuse Regulation—as a piece of secondary European legislation—cannot override the application of Articles 101 ff TFEU. However, since there are also other (secondary) sources of European competition law, the significance of recital (80) seems to be not to exclude their application. The relation of market abuse and competition law has become especially relevant in several Member States, where the civil liability for a violation of competition law is expressly stated in (general) civil law but not for committing market abuse.

Law of unfair business practices

B.1.11 Also, the relation of the Market Abuse Regulation to the national law of unfair business practices remains unclear. This is especially the case for the prohibition of market manipulation as set out in Articles 12 and 15, since certain transactions or behaviours regarding financial instruments within the scope of the Market Abuse Regulation[11] can also constitute a violation of the national law on unfair business practices. The practical relevance of that problem is the absence of a detailed regulation of civil liability in the context of market abuse, since such a regulation usually exists or is generally recognized in the national law on unfair business practices.

Accounting law and law of financial reporting

B.1.12 The Market Abuse Regulation and especially the disclosure requirements pursuant to Articles 17 ff do not affect the disclosure requirements set out by accounting law and the law of financial reporting. Therefore, both requirements must be fulfilled independently by the persons responsible. Moreover, pursuant to

---

9 See art 9 n 61 ff.
10 See art 11 n 6 ff.
11 See art 2 n 3 ff.

Article 19(11), a person discharging managerial responsibilities within an issuer shall not conduct any transactions relating to financial instruments of the issuer during a closed period of thirty calendar days before the announcement of an interim financial report or a year-end report, which the issuer is obliged to make.[12]

Another issue of the relation of accounting law and law of financial reporting to the Market Abuse Regulation is whether certain accounting techniques can constitute a market manipulation as defined in Article 12. This is especially the case for so-called *window dressing*, where transactions are delayed or pushed through so that they can be included in a financial statement for a certain accounting period. Although this behaviour affects the price of the financial statement of the issuer publishing these financial statements only indirectly, it is still far from clear whether such transactions can constitute a market manipulation. In this context, the problem of aiding and abetting a market manipulation can also become relevant, since usually these transactions involve a third party.[13] **B.1.13**

Specific (other) regulations on market abuse

Market abuse is also addressed by other European regulations. Pursuant to Article 5 of the Wholesale Energy Market Integrity and Transparency Regulation (1227/2011/EU), any engagement in, or attempt to engage in, market manipulation on wholesale energy markets is prohibited. Also, Article 3 of the Wholesale Energy Market Integrity and Transparency Regulation (1227/2011/EU) prohibits insider trading and its Article 4 states an obligation to publish inside information. Although provided as a separate set of rules on market abuse without referring to the Market Abuse Regulation, the interpretation of Articles 3 to 5 of the Wholesale Energy Market Integrity and Transparency Regulation (1227/2011/EU) is influenced by the Market Abuse Regulation. This is especially the case since the Wholesale Energy Market Integrity and Transparency Regulation (1227/2011/EU) was adopted before the Market Abuse Regulation and is therefore mainly based on the (former) Market Abuse Directive (2003/6/EC). Moreover, the Market Abuse Regulation applies to financial instruments only related to wholesale energy products and therefore being outside the scope of Articles 3 to 5 of the Wholesale Energy Market Integrity and Transparency Regulation (1227/2011/EU).[14] **B.1.14**

---

[12] See art 19 n 42 ff for further details.

[13] See Mark C Hilgard and Sebastian Mock, 'Stoneridge and Its Impact on European Capital Markets Law' (2008) European Company and Financial Law Review 453 ff for the situation under the (former) Market Abuse Directive (2003/6/EC). See also art 15 n 5 for further details.

[14] See recitals (20) and (44).

Article 2: Scope

1. This Regulation applies to the following:
   (a) financial instruments admitted to trading on a regulated market or for which a request for admission to trading on a regulated market has been made;
   (b) financial instruments traded on an MTF, admitted to trading on an MTF or for which a request for admission to trading on an MTF has been made;
   (c) financial instruments traded on an OTF;
   (d) financial instruments not covered by point (a), (b) or (c), the price or value of which depends on or has an effect on the price or value of a financial instrument referred to in those points, including, but not limited to, credit default swaps and contracts for difference.

This Regulation also applies to behaviour or transactions, including bids, relating to the auctioning on an auction platform authorized as a regulated market of emission allowances or other auctioned products based thereon, including when auctioned products are not financial instruments, pursuant to Regulation (EU) No 1031/2010. Without prejudice to any specific provisions referring to bids submitted in the context of an auction, any requirements and prohibitions in this Regulation referring to orders to trade shall apply to such bids.

2. Articles 12 and 15 also apply to:
   (a) spot commodity contracts, which are not wholesale energy products, where the transaction, order or behaviour has or is likely or intended to have an effect on the price or value of a financial instrument referred to in paragraph 1;
   (b) types of financial instruments, including derivative contracts or derivative instruments for the transfer of credit risk, where the transaction, order, bid or behaviour has or is likely to have an effect on the price or value of a spot commodity contract where the price or value depends on the price or value of those financial instruments; and
   (c) behaviour in relation to benchmarks.
3. This Regulation applies to any transaction, order or behaviour concerning any financial instrument as referred to in paragraphs 1 and 2, irrespective of whether or not such transaction, order or behaviour takes place on a trading venue.
4. The prohibitions and requirements in this Regulation shall apply to acts and omissions, in the Union and in a third country, concerning the instruments referred to in paragraphs 1 and 2.

I. General Remarks

Overview

Article 2 defines the scope of the Market Abuse Regulation. In this regard, Article 2 distinguishes between the primary scope of application governed by Article 2(1)[1] and the extended scope of application solely for the prohibition of market abuse governed by Article 2(2).[2] However, Article 2(3) sets almost no limitation for the scope of application for certain transactions, orders, or behaviour on trading venues.[3] Finally, Article 2(4) defines the territorial scope of application.[4] **B.2.01**

Historical development

The scope of application of the (former) Market Abuse Directive (2003/6/EC) was less extensive. Pursuant to its Article 9, the directive applied only to financial instruments admitted to trading on a regulated market in at least one Member State. Therefore, the (former) Market Abuse Directive (2003/6/EC) was not applicable to financial instruments traded on a multilateral trading facility (MTF) or an organized trading facility (OTF). Also, credit default swaps, contracts for difference, and markets of emission allowances or other auctioned products were not covered by it. Finally, the territorial scope of application was **B.2.02**

[1] See n 3 ff.
[2] See n 9 ff.
[3] See n 13.
[4] See n 14 ff.

not explicitly set out in the (former) Market Abuse Directive (2003/6/EC), since its Article 9(1) stated only that it applied to financial instruments, irrespective of whether or not the transaction itself actually took place on that market.

II. Primary Scope of Application (Article 2(1))

B.2.03 For its primary scope of application, Article 2(1) distinguishes between financial instruments admitted to trading on a regulation market,[5] on a MTF,[6] on an OTF,[7] and other financial instruments.[8] Financial instruments are defined in Article 3(1)(1) by referring to the Markets in Financial Instruments Directive II (2014/65/EU).[9]

Financial instruments admitted to trading on a regulated market (Article 2(1)(a))

B.2.04 The Market Abuse Regulation applies to all financial instruments admitted to trading on a regulated market. The term regulated market is defined in Article 3(1)(6) and refers to the Markets in Financial Instruments Directive II (2014/65/EU).[10] However, the Market Abuse Regulation also applies if the financial instruments are not admitted to trading on a regulated market but when a request for admission to trading has been made. This extension of the scope of application is necessary, because insider trading and market manipulation can occur when a request for admission has been made beforehand. In this context, it is required that all necessary steps for an application were made and that the application was successfully filed. Furthermore, the Market Abuse Regulation remains applicable even if the application is later withdrawn.

Financial instruments traded on a multilateral trading facility (MTF) (Article 2(1)(b)

B.2.05 Furthermore, the Market Abuse Regulation applies to financial instruments traded on a MTF (Article 3(1)(7)[11]). As in Article 2(1)(a), the request for admission is also already sufficient.[12]

---

[5] See n 4.
[6] See n 5.
[7] See n 6.
[8] See n 7.
[9] See art 3 n 4 ff.
[10] See art 3 n 10.
[11] See art 3 n 11.
[12] See n 4 for further details.

Financial instruments traded on an organized trading facility (OTF) (Article 2(1)(c))

The Market Abuse Regulation applies to financial instruments traded on an OTF (Article 3(1)(8)[13]). As in Article 2(1)(a), the request for admission is also already sufficient.[14] **B.2.06**

Other financial instruments (Article 2(1)(d))

The Market Abuse Regulation also applies to all financial instruments not covered by Article 2(1)(a), (b), or (c), the price or value of which depends on or has an effect on the price or value of a financial instrument referred to in those points. As examples, Article 2(1)(d) states that these include credit default swaps and contracts for difference, without limiting the scope of application to these financial instruments. This extension of the scope of application of the Market Abuse Regulation is necessary, owing to the fact that many financial instruments refer to the value or price of other financial instruments traded on regulated markets, MTFs, or OTFs. Since the use of insider information, their unlawful disclosure or the manipulation of these financial instruments not traded on a market covered by the Market Abuse Regulation would not constitute a market abuse in regulated markets, MTFs, or OTFs and such behaviour would not be punishable or forbidden by the Market Abuse Regulation. To protect the integrity of the markets where these financial instruments are traded, Article 2(1)(d) also extends the scope of application to these financial instruments. **B.2.07**

Extension to regulated markets of emission allowances (Article 2(1) subs. 2)

Finally, the Market Abuse Regulation applies also to regulated markets of emission allowances or other auctioned products, even when the auctioned products are not financial instruments. In particular, but not exclusively, greenhouse gas emission allowances under the Greenhouse Gas Emission Allowances Regulation (1031/2010/EU) are covered. In contrast to the regulation on the scope of application for financial instruments, Article 2(1), the regulation in Article 2(2) does not merely extend the scope of application of the Market Abuse Regulation to emissions allowances but only specifies that it should apply to behaviours or transactions relating to emissions allowances. However, particularly since the general behaviour is mentioned in Article 2(1) subs. 2, all forms of market abuse are covered. This is especially the case for orders or trades, since Article 2(1) subs. 2 sent. 2 explicitly states that the requirements and prohibitions of the Market Abuse Regulation should apply in this context. **B.2.08**

---

[13] See art 3 n 12.
[14] See n 4 for further details.

III. Extended Scope of Application for the Prohibition of Market Manipulation (Article 2(2))

B.2.09 In Article 2(2), the scope of application of the Market Abuse Regulation is extended for (and solely for) the prohibition of market manipulation of Articles 12 and 15. This limited extension of the scope of application is based on the problem that the manipulation of the prices of a financial instrument takes place not only in a regulated market or other market covered by Article 2(1), but also outside the market in relation to products or benchmarks that have a direct effect on financial instruments in a regulated market or other market covered by Article 2(1). Although these indirect manipulations could theoretically be covered by the prohibition of market manipulation itself, this explicit extension of the scope of application is necessary to impose criminal sanctions for these violations to meet the requirements of the legal principle of *nulla poena sine lege certa*.

Application to spot commodity contracts (Article 2(2)(a))

B.2.10 The prohibition of market manipulation (Articles 12 and 15) applies also to spot commodity contracts, which are defined in Article 3(1)(15).[15] However, the only transactions that are covered are ones that have or are likely or intended to have an effect on the price or value of the financial instruments referred to in Article 2(1).[16] Wholesale energy products are explicitly excluded from the extended scope of application in Article 2(2)(a), since such manipulative transactions are already forbidden by Article 5 of the Wholesale Energy Market Integrity and Transparency Regulation (1227/2011/EU).

Financial instruments for the transfer of credit risk (Article 2(2)(b))

B.2.11 Moreover, the prohibition of market manipulation (Articles 12 and 15) applies also to financial instruments not traded on a regulated market[17] or other market covered by Article 2(1)(b) or (c)[18] when the transaction, order, bid, or behaviour has or is likely or intended to have an effect on the price or value of spot commodity contracts,[19] where the price or value depends on the price or value of those financial instruments referred to in Article 2(2)(a).[20] Therefore, Article 2(2)(b) extends the scope of application of Article 2(2)(a) and not of Article 2(1).

[15] See art 3 n 19.
[16] See n 4.
[17] See n 4.
[18] See nn 5 and 6.
[19] See n 10.
[20] ibid.

If a transaction, order, bid, or behaviour has or is likely or intended to have an effect on the price or value of financial instruments traded on a regulated market[21] or other market covered by Article 2(1)(b) or (c)[22] to which already Article 2(1)(d) applies, then Articles 12 and 15 shall also apply.[23]

Behaviour in relation to benchmarks (Article 2(2)(c))

Finally, the prohibition of market manipulation (Articles 12 and 15) applies also to behaviour in relation to benchmarks. This extension of the scope of application was introduced owing to the so-called LIBOR scandal, where major European banks engaged in a manipulation of the London Interbank Offered Rate (LIBOR), the interest rate that banks pay on money they borrow from one another, in order to increase the interest rate charges for borrowers. Although Article 2(2)(c) only requires behaviour in relation to benchmarks, it is also necessary that these benchmarks have an impact on financial instruments traded in a regulated market[24] or other market covered by Article 2(1)(b) or (c).[25] This is indeed the case, since Article 1 clearly states that the Market Abuse Regulation ensures the integrity of financial markets in the Union.[26] **B.2.12**

IV. No Limitation to Transactions, Orders, or Behaviour on Trading Venues (Article 2(3))

Although being a market regulation the Market Abuse Regulation does not simply apply to market-related behaviour only, but to all transactions, orders, or behaviour that have an impact on the price or value of financial instruments. This principle is explicitly set out in Article 2(3). Therefore, the Market Abuse Regulation is not limited to transactions, orders, or behaviour taking place at trading venues. In fact, the place where or the way in which a violation of the Market Abuse Regulation is committed does not matter and does not limit the scope of its application. If a transaction, order, or behaviour has an impact on the price or value of financial instruments covered by Article 2(1)[27] or Article 2(2),[28] the Market Abuse Regulation applies. **B.2.13**

21 See n 4.
22 See nn 5 and 6.
23 See n 7.
24 See n 4.
25 See nn 5 and 6.
26 See art 1 n 5.
27 See n 3 ff.
28 See n 9 ff.

V. Territorial Scope of Application (Article 2(4))

B.2.14 Finally, Article 2(4) sets the territorial scope of application for the Market Abuse Regulation. In this regard, Article 2(4) distinguishes between acts and omissions in the Union and in third countries. When it comes to acts and omissions in the Union, the Market Abuse Regulation applies without any reservations.

B.2.15 However, acts and omissions in third countries (ie, those not being Member States of the Union) are not completely within the scope of application of the Market Abuse Regulation. Although Article 2(4) does not explicitly set any further requirements for the application of the Market Abuse Regulation in these cases, it is necessary that the acts and omissions in a third country have an impact on the price or value of financial instruments traded in a regulated market[29] or other market covered by Article 2(1)(b) or (c).[30] This limitation of the scope of application of the Market Abuse Regulation derives from general international law, since the European legislator cannot govern acts or omissions that take place outside the European Union without any direct relation to it (the requirement of the so-called *genuine link*). Therefore, the impact of acts or omissions on the price or value of financial instruments traded in a regulated market[31] or other market covered by Article 2(1)(b) or (c)[32] is the necessary link of these acts or omissions to the Union. If such an impact is missing, the Market Abuse Regulation does not apply and such behaviour is not punishable under the European market abuse regime. However, Member States can extend the application of their national market abuse regime to these cases, since they are not covered by European law. If such an extension constitutes a violation of international law or constitutional law of the respective Member State, this constitutes a problem of this respective Member State only and does not involve European law.

B.2.16 The territorial scope of application for the Market Abuse Regulation set out in Article 2(4) has no influence on the determination of the applicable civil law governing damages or other aspects related to market abuse. In this regard, the applicable civil law (on non-contractual obligations) must usually be determined in accordance with the Rome II Regulation (864/2007/EC). The same applies to the determination of the international jurisdiction for civil claims, which is determined by the Brussels I bis Regulation (2012/1215/EU).

[29] See n 4.
[30] See nn 5 and 6.
[31] See n 4.
[32] See nn 5 and 6.

Article 3: Definitions

1. **For the purposes of this Regulation, the following definitions apply:**
   - **(1) 'financial instrument' means a financial instrument as defined in point (15) of Article 4(1) of Directive 2014/65/EU;**
   - **(2) 'investment firm' means an investment firm as defined in point (1) of Article 4(1) of Directive 2014/65/EU;**
   - **(3) 'credit institution' means a credit institution as defined in point (1) of Article 4(1) of Regulation (EU) No 575/2013 of the European Parliament and of the Council;**(1)
   - **(4) 'financial institution' means a financial institution as defined in point (26) of Article 4(1) of Regulation (EU) No 575/2013;**
   - **(5) 'market operator' means a market operator as defined in point (18) of Article 4(1) of Directive 2014/65/EU;**
   - **(6) 'regulated market' means a regulated market as defined in point (21) of Article 4(1) of Directive 2014/65/EU;**
   - **(7) 'multilateral trading facility' or 'MTF' means a multilateral system as defined in point (22) of Article 4(1) of Directive 2014/65/EU;**
   - **(8) 'organised trading facility' or 'OTF' means a system or facility in the Union as defined in point (23) of Article 4(1) of Directive 2014/65/EU;**
   - **(9) 'accepted market practice' means a specific market practice that is accepted by a competent authority in accordance with Article 13;**
   - **(10) 'trading venue' means a trading venue as defined in point (24) of Article 4(1) of Directive 2014/65/EU;**
   - **(11) 'SME growth market' means SME growth market as defined in point (12) of Article 4(1) of Directive 2014/65/EU;**
   - **(12) 'competent authority' means an authority designated in accordance with Article 22, unless otherwise specified in this Regulation;**
   - **(13) 'person' means a natural or legal person;**
   - **(14) 'commodity' means a commodity as defined in point (1) of Article 2 of Commission Regulation (EC) No 1287/2006;**(2)
   - **(15) 'spot commodity contract' means a contract for the supply of a commodity traded on a spot market which is promptly delivered when the**

[1] Regulation (EU) No 575/2013 of the European Parliament and of the Council of 26 June 2013 on prudential requirements for credit institutions and investment firms and amending Regulation (EU) No 648/2012 (OJ L 176 (27 June 2013) 1).

[2] Commission Regulation (EC) No 1287/2006 of 10 August 2006 implementing Directive 2004/39/EC of the European Parliament and of the Council as regards record-keeping obligations for investment firms, transaction reporting, market transparency, admission of financial instruments to trading, and defined terms for the purposes of that Directive (OJ L 241 (2 September 2006) 1).

transaction is settled, and a contract for the supply of a commodity that is not a financial instrument, including a physically settled forward contract;

(16) 'spot market' means a commodity market in which commodities are sold for cash and promptly delivered when the transaction is settled, and other non-financial markets, such as forward markets for commodities;

(17) 'buy-back programme' means trading in own shares in accordance with Articles 21 to 27 of Directive 2012/30/EU of the European Parliament and of the Council;([3])

(18) 'algorithmic trading' means algorithmic trading as defined in point (39) of Article 4(1) of Directive 2014/65/EU;

(19) 'emission allowance' means emission allowance as described in point (11) of Section C of Annex I to Directive 2014/65/EU;

(20) 'emission allowance market participant' means any person who enters into transactions, including the placing of orders to trade, in emission allowances, auctioned products based thereon, or derivatives thereof and who does not benefit from an exemption pursuant to the second subparagraph of Article 17(2);

(21) 'issuer' means a legal entity governed by private or public law, which issues or proposes to issue financial instruments, the issuer being, in case of depository receipts representing financial instruments, the issuer of the financial instrument represented;

(22) 'wholesale energy product' means wholesale energy product as defined in point (4) of Article 2 of Regulation (EU) No 1227/2011;

(23) 'national regulatory authority' means national regulatory authority as defined in point (10) of Article 2 of Regulation (EU) No 1227/2011;

(24) 'commodity derivatives' means commodity derivatives as defined in point (30) of Article 2(1) of Regulation (EU) No 600/2014 of the European Parliament and of the Council;([4])

(25) 'person discharging managerial responsibilities' means a person within an issuer, an emission allowance market participant or another entity referred to in Article 19(10), who is:

[3] Directive 2012/30/EU of the European Parliament and of the Council of 25 October 2012 on coordination of safeguards which, for the protection of the interests of members and others, are required by Member States of companies within the meaning of the second paragraph of art 54 of the Treaty on the Functioning of the European Union, in respect of the formation of public limited liability companies and the maintenance and alteration of their capital, with a view to making such safeguards equivalent (OJ L 315 (14 November 2012) 74).

[4] Regulation (EU) No 600/2014 of the European Parliament and of the Council of 15 May 2014 on markets in financial instruments and amending Regulation (EU) No 648/2012 (see page 84 of this Official Journal).

(a) a member of the administrative, management or supervisory body of that entity; or

(b) a senior executive who is not a member of the bodies referred to in point (a), who has regular access to inside information relating directly or indirectly to that entity and power to take managerial decisions affecting the future developments and business prospects of that entity;

(26) 'person closely associated' means:

(a) a spouse, or a partner considered to be equivalent to a spouse in accordance with national law;

(b) a dependent child, in accordance with national law;

(c) a relative who has shared the same household for at least one year on the date of the transaction concerned; or

(d) a legal person, trust or partnership, the managerial responsibilities of which are discharged by a person discharging managerial responsibilities or by a person referred to in point (a), (b) or (c), or which is directly or indirectly controlled by such a person, or which is set up for the benefit of such a person, or the economic interests of which are substantially equivalent to those of such a person;

(27) 'data traffic records' means records of traffic data as defined in point (b) of the second paragraph of Article 2 of Directive 2002/58/EC of the European Parliament and the Council;([5])

(28) 'person professionally arranging or executing transactions' means a person professionally engaged in the reception and transmission of orders for, or in the execution of transactions in, financial instruments;

(29) 'benchmark' means any rate, index or figure, made available to the public or published that is periodically or regularly determined by the application of a formula to, or on the basis of the value of one or more underlying assets or prices, including estimated prices, actual or estimated interest rates or other values, or surveys, and by reference to which the amount payable under a financial instrument or the value of a financial instrument is determined;

(30) 'market maker' means a market maker as defined in point (7) of Article 4(1) of Directive 2014/65/EU;

(31) 'stake-building' means an acquisition of securities in a company which does not trigger a legal or regulatory obligation to make an announcement of a takeover bid in relation to that company;

---

[5] Directive 2002/58/EC of the European Parliament and of the Council of 12 July 2002 concerning the processing of personal data and the protection of privacy in the electronic communications sector (Directive on privacy and electronic communications) (OJ L 201 (31 July 2002) 37).

(32) 'disclosing market participant' means a person who falls into any of the categories set out in points (a) to (d) of Article 11(1) or of Article 11(2), and discloses information in the course of a market sounding;

(33) 'high-frequency trading' means high-frequency algorithmic trading technique as defined in point (40) of Article 4(1) of Directive 2014/65/EU;

(34) 'information recommending or suggesting an investment strategy' means information:

(i) produced by an independent analyst, an investment firm, a credit institution, any other person whose main business is to produce investment recommendations or a natural person working for them under a contract of employment or otherwise, which, directly or indirectly, expresses a particular investment proposal in respect of a financial instrument or an issuer; or

(ii) produced by persons other than those referred to in point (i), which directly proposes a particular investment decision in respect of a financial instrument;

(35) 'investment recommendations' means information recommending or suggesting an investment strategy, explicitly or implicitly, concerning one or several financial instruments or the issuers, including any opinion as to the present or future value or price of such instruments, intended for distribution channels or for the public.

2. For the purposes of Article 5, the following definitions apply:

(a) 'securities' means:

(i) shares and other securities equivalent to shares;

(ii) bonds and other forms of securitised debt; or

(iii) securitised debt convertible or exchangeable into shares or into other securities equivalent to shares.

(b) 'associated instruments' means the following financial instruments, including those which are not admitted to trading or traded on a trading venue, or for which a request for admission to trading on a trading venue has not been made:

(i) contracts or rights to subscribe for, acquire or dispose of securities;

(ii) financial derivatives of securities;

(iii) where the securities are convertible or exchangeable debt instruments, the securities into which such convertible or exchangeable debt instruments may be converted or exchanged;

(iv) instruments which are issued or guaranteed by the issuer or guarantor of the securities and whose market price is likely to materially influence the price of the securities, or vice versa;

(v) where the securities are securities equivalent to shares, the shares represented by those securities and any other securities equivalent to those shares;

(c) **'significant distribution' means an initial or secondary offer of securities that is distinct from ordinary trading both in terms of the amount in value of the securities to be offered and the selling method to be employed;**

(d) **'stabilisation' means a purchase or offer to purchase securities, or a transaction in associated instruments equivalent thereto, which is undertaken by a credit institution or an investment firm in the context of a significant distribution of such securities exclusively for supporting the market price of those securities for a predetermined period of time, due to a selling pressure in such securities.**

I. General Remarks

Overview

B.3.01 Article 3 sets out the definitions which are the basis for the interpretation and application of the Market Abuse Regulation. The definitions in Article 3 are binding for the application of the Market Abuse Regulation. Furthermore, the references in Article 3 to other regulations and directives of the Union are *frozen*, meaning that any change in these regulations or directives does not affect the application or interpretation of the definitions in Article 3 or the meaning within the interpretation and application of the Market Abuse Regulation, unless stated otherwise in the respective directive or regulation.

Historical development

B.3.02 Several definitions set out in Article 3 were already part of the Market Abuse Directive (2003/6/EC). This is especially the case for the definitions of financial instruments (Article 3(1)),[6] regulated markets (Article 3(6)),[7] accepted market practices (Article 3(9)),[8] competent authorities (Article 3(12)),[9] and trading venues (Article 3(13)).[10]

II. General Definitions (Article 3(1))

B.3.03 Article 3(1) contains general definitions that are relevant for all of the provisions of the Market Abuse Regulation.

Financial instrument (Article 3(1)(1))

B.3.04 For the definition of a *financial instrument*, Article 3(1)(1) refers to the definition of Article 4(1)(15) of the Markets in Financial Instruments Directive II (2014/65/EU), which refers to those instruments specified in Annex I, Section C of the Markets in Financial Instruments Directive II (2014/65/EU). Therefore, financial instruments are transferable securities, money-market instruments, units in collective investment undertakings, certain options, futures, swaps, forward rate agreements and any other derivative contracts, derivative instruments for the transfer of credit risk, financial contracts for differences, and emission allowances. Since the list in Annex I, Section C of the Markets in Financial Instruments Directive II (2014/65/EU) is exclusive, the Market Abuse Regulation does not apply

6 See n 3 ff.
7 See n 10.
8 See n 13.
9 See n 16.
10 See n 17.

to other financial instruments. The definition of financial instruments is of general importance for the application of the Market Abuse Regulation since almost all of its provisions refer to it. All financial instruments are registered with ESMA, owing to the notification requirement for market operators and investment firms (Article 4 (1)).[11] This register is available at https://registers.esma.europa.eu.

However, Member States are free to permit the application of the Market Abuse Regulation to financial instruments not covered by Article 3(1)(1). See Part A—History, Application, Interpretation, and Legal Sources of the Market Abuse Regulation note 18. **B.3.05**

Investment firm (Article 3(1)(2))

Article 3(1)(2) refers to the definition of *investment firm* in the general definition of that term in the Markets in Financial Instruments Directive II (2014/65/EU). Therefore, an investment firm is any legal person whose regular occupation or business is the provision of one or more investment services to third parties and/or the performance of one or more investment activities on a professional basis (Article 4(1)(1) Markets in Financial Instruments Directive II (2014/65/EU)). The definition of investment firm is relevant for Article 4(1),[12] Article 16(1),[13] Article 17(6)(a),[14] Article 23(2)(g),[15] Article 30(2)(d) to (g),[16] and Article 33(4). A register of all investment firms is available at https://registers.esma.europa.eu. **B.3.06**

Credit institution (Article 3(1)(3))

For the definition of *credit institution*, Article 3(1)(3) refers to the definition of that term given in the Capital Requirements Regulation (CRD IV) (575/2013/EU). Pursuant to Article 4(1)(1) of the Capital Requirements Regulation (CRD IV) (575/2013/EU), a credit institution is an entity undertaking the business of taking deposits or other repayable funds from the public and granting credits for its own account. The definition of credit institutions is relevant for Article 17(5) and (6)(a)[17] and Article 23(2)(g).[18] **B.3.07**

Financial institution (Article 3(1)(4))

Also, for the definition of *financial institutions*, Article 3(1)(4) refers to the definition of that term given in the Capital Requirements Regulation (CRD IV) (575/ **B.3.08**

[11] See art 4 n 3 ff.
[12] See art 4 n 3 f.
[13] See art 16 n 3.
[14] See art 17 n 101.
[15] See art 23 n 18.
[16] See art 30 n 14.
[17] See art 17 n 96.
[18] See art 23 n 16 ff.

2013/EU), according to which a financial institution is an undertaking other than an institution, the principal activity of which is to acquire holdings or to pursue one or more of the activities listed in Annex I points 2 to 12 and point 15 of Directive 2013/36/EU. This definition also includes financial holding companies, mixed financial holding companies, payment institutions (within the meaning of Directive 2007/64/EC), and any asset management company, but not insurance holding companies and mixed-activity insurance holding companies as defined in Article 212(1)(g) of Directive 2009/138/EC. The definition of financial institution is relevant for Article 6(2)(g),[19] Article 17(5),[20] and Article 23(2)(g).[21]

Market operator (Article 3(1)(5))

B.3.09 The term *market operator* is defined in Article 3(1)(5) pursuant to Article 4(1)(18) of the Markets in Financial Instruments Directive II (2014/65/EU) as a person or persons who manages and/or operates the business of a regulated market and maybe the regulated market itself. The definition of market operator is only relevant for the regulation on the notification and list of financial instruments in Article 4(1)[22] and Article 16(1).[23]

Regulated market (Article 3(1)(6))

B.3.10 *Regulated market* is defined by reference in Article 3(1)(6) to Article 4(1)(21) of the Markets in Financial Instruments Directive II (2014/65/EU) as a multilateral system operated and/or managed by a market operator, which brings together or facilitates the bringing together of multiple third-party buying and selling interests in financial instruments—in the system and in accordance with its non-discretionary rules—in a way that results in a contract, in respect of the financial instruments admitted to trading under its rules and/or systems, and which is authorized and functions regularly and in accordance with Articles 44 ff of the Markets in Financial Instruments Directive II (2014/65/EU). The definition of regulated market is relevant for Article 2(1),[24] Article 4(1) and (3)(a),[25] Article 17(1) and (4),[26] Article 18(7), Article 19(4)(a),[27] and for Article 22.[28] A register of all regulated markets is available at https://registers.esma.europa.eu.

---

[19] See art 6 n 4.
[20] See art 17 n 94 ff.
[21] See art 23 n 16 ff.
[22] See art 4 n 3 ff.
[23] See art 16 n 3.
[24] See art 2 n 3 ff.
[25] See art 4 n 3 ff.
[26] See art 17 n 28 ff.
[27] See art 19 n 10.
[28] See art 22 n 13.

Multilateral trading facility (Article 3(1)(7))

For the definition of *multilateral trading facility* (MTF), Article 3(1)(7) refers to Article 4(1)(22) of the Markets in Financial Instruments Directive II (2014/65/EU), which defines it as a multilateral system, operated by an investment firm or a market operator, which brings together multiple third-party buying and selling interests in financial instruments—in the system and in accordance with non-discretionary rules—in a way that results in a contract in accordance with Articles 5 ff of the Markets in Financial Instruments Directive II (2014/65/EU). This definition is relevant for Article 4(3)(a),[29] Article 17(1),[30] Article 18(7), Article 19(4)(b),[31] and for Article 22.[32] A register of all MTFs is available at https://registers.esma.europa.eu. **B.3.11**

Organized trading facility (Article 3(1)(8))

An *organized trading facility* (OTF) is—pursuant to Article 3(1)(8) and Article 4(1)(23) of the Markets in Financial Instruments Directive II (2014/65/EU)—a multilateral system that is not a regulated market or a MTF and in which multiple third-party buying and selling interests in bonds, structured finance products, emission allowances, or derivatives are able to interact in the system in a way that results in a contract in accordance with Articles 5 ff of the Markets in Financial Instruments Directive II (2014/65/EU). This definition is relevant for Article 4(1) and (3)(a),[33] Article 17(1),[34] Article 18(7), Article 19(4)(b),[35] Article 22,[36] and for Article 39. A register of all OTFs is available at https://registers.esma.europa.eu. **B.3.12**

Accepted market practice (Article 3(1)(9))

An *accepted market practice* is a unique feature of the Market Abuse Regulation and is defined as a specific market practice that is accepted by a competent authority in accordance with Article 13. Since the requirements for official recognition of an accepted market practice are defined in Article 13,[37] the definition in Article 3(1)(9) has no significant meaning. **B.3.13**

[29] See art 4 n 7.
[30] See art 17 n 28 ff.
[31] See art 19 n 10.
[32] See art 22 n 13.
[33] See art 4 n 7.
[34] See art 17 n 28 ff.
[35] See art 19 n 10.
[36] See art 22 n 13.
[37] See art 13 n 2 ff.

Trading venue (Article 3(1)(10))

B.3.14 A *trading venue* is—pursuant to Article 3(1)(10) and Article 4(1)(24) of the Markets in Financial Instruments Directive II (2014/65/EU)—a regulated market, a MTF, or an OTF.[38] The definition of trading venue is of general importance for the application of the Market Abuse Regulation since almost all of its provisions refer to it.

SME growth market (Article 3(1)(11))

B.3.15 *SME growth markets* are defined by reference in Article 3(1)(11) to Article 4(1)(12) Markets in Financial Instruments Directive II (2014/65/EU) as MTFs that are registered as an SME growth market in accordance with Article 33 of the Markets in Financial Instruments Directive II (2014/65/EU). This definition is relevant for Article 17(8), Article 18(6),[39] and for Article 39.

Competent authority (Article 3(1)(12))

B.3.16 A *competent authority* is an authority designated in accordance with Article 22 (Article 3(1)(12)). The definition of competent authority is of general importance for the application of the Market Abuse Regulation since almost all its provisions refer to it.

Person (Article 3(1)(13))

B.3.17 Pursuant to Article 3(1)(13), a *person* means a natural or legal person. Since this is the basic understanding in all Member States of the Union this definition is of almost no importance.

Commodity (Article 3(1)(14))

B.3.18 A *commodity* is—pursuant to Article 3(1)(14) and Article 2(1) of the Markets in Financial Instruments Implementation Regulation (2006/1287/EC)—defined as any good of a fungible nature that is capable of being delivered, including metals and their ores and alloys, agricultural products, and energy such as electricity. This definition is relevant for Article 2(2)(b),[40] Article 7,[41] Article 12,[42] and Article 23(2)(c).[43]

---

[38] See nn 10, 11, and 12 for further details.
[39] See art 18 n 6.
[40] See art 2 n 11.
[41] See art 7 n 5 ff.
[42] See art 12 n 6.
[43] See art 23 n 18.

Spot commodity contract (Article 3(1)(15))

The term *spot commodity contract* is defined in Article 3(1)(15) as a contract for the supply of a commodity traded on a spot market, which is promptly delivered when the transaction is settled, and a contract for the supply of a commodity that is not a financial instrument, including a physically settled forward contract. This definition is relevant for Article 2(2)(b),[44] Article 7,[45] Article 12,[46] and Article 23(2)(c).[47] See Article 3(1)(14) (note 18) for the definition of commodity. **B.3.19**

Spot market (Article 3(1)(16))

A *spot market* is commodity market in which commodities are sold for cash and promptly delivered when the transaction is settled, and other non-financial markets, such as forward markets for commodities. This definition is relevant for Article 2(2)(b),[48] Article 7(5),[49] Article 23(9)(c),[50] and Article 25(8).[51] See Article 3(1)(14) (note 18) for the definition of commodity. **B.3.20**

Buy-back programme (Article 3(1)(17))

A *buy-back programme* is trading in own shares in accordance with Articles 21 to 27 of the Capital Maintenance Directive (2012/30/EU). Although trading in own derivatives, bonds, and all kinds of options is highly relevant for issuers, buy-back programmes for these kinds of instruments are not covered by this definition. By referring to the requirements of the Capital Maintenance Directive, trading in own shares can only constitute a buy-back programme within the meaning of the Market Abuse Regulation when all of the requirements of Articles 21 to 27 of the Capital Maintenance Directive are met. See Article 5 for further details. See also the definitions in Article 3(2).[52] **B.3.21**

Algorithmic trading (Article 3(1)(18))

Algorithmic trading is—pursuant to Article 3(1)(18) and Article 4(1)(39) of the Markets in Financial Instruments Directive II (2014/65/EU)—defined as trading in financial instruments where a computer algorithm automatically determines individual parameters of orders such as whether to initiate the order, the timing, price, or quantity of the order or how to manage the order after its submission, **B.3.22**

---

44 See art 2 n 11.
45 See art 7 n 5 ff.
46 See art 12 n 6.
47 See art 23 n 18.
48 See art 2 n 11.
49 See art 7 n 20.
50 See art 23 n 18.
51 See art 25 n 39.
52 See n 48 ff.

with limited or no human intervention, and does not include any system that is only used for the purpose of routing orders to one or more trading venues or for the processing of orders involving no determination of any trading parameters or for the confirmation of orders or the post-trade processing of executed transactions.[53] This definition is only relevant for the definition of high-frequency trading in Article 3(1)(33).[54]

Emission allowance (Article 3(1)(19))

B.3.23 An *emission allowance* is—pursuant to Article 3(1)(19) and Annex I, Section C(11) of the Markets in Financial Instruments Directive II (2014/65/EU)—a unit recognized for compliance with the requirements of the Emissions Trading Scheme Directive (2003/87/EC). The definition of emission allowance is of general importance for the application of the Market Abuse Regulation since almost all of its provisions refer to it. See also Article 3(1)(20) for the definition of an allowance market participant.[55]

Emission allowance market participant (Article 3(1)(20))

B.3.24 An *emission allowance market participant* is defined in Article 3(1)(20) as a person who enters into transactions, including the placing of orders to trade in emission allowances, auctioned products based thereon, or derivatives thereof and who does not benefit from an exemption pursuant to Article 17(2)(2).[56] The definition of an emission allowance market participant is of general importance for the application of the Market Abuse Regulation since almost all of its provisions refer to it. For the definition of emission allowances, see also Article 3(1)(19).[57]

Issuer (Article 3(1)(21))

B.3.25 Pursuant to Article 3(1)(21), *issuer* means a legal entity governed by private or public law, which issues or proposes to issue financial instruments, the issuer being, in case of depository receipts representing financial instruments, the issuer of the financial instrument represented. The definition of issuer is of general importance for the application of the Market Abuse Regulation since almost all of its provisions refer to it.

[53] See Pierre-Henri Conac, 'Algorithmic Trading and High Frequency Trading' in Danny Busch and Guido Ferrarini (eds), *Regulation of the EU Financial Markets: MiFID II and MiFIR* (OUP 2017) ch 17.

[54] See n 44.

[55] See n 24.

[56] See art 17 n 64 ff.

[57] See n 23.

Wholesale energy product (Article 3(1)(22))

Wholesale energy products are—pursuant to Article 3(1)(22) and Article 2(4) of the Wholesale Energy Market Integrity and Transparency Regulation (2011/1227/EU)—contracts for the supply of electricity or natural gas where delivery is within the Union, derivatives relating to electricity or natural gas produced, traded, or delivered in the Union, contracts relating to the transportation of electricity or natural gas in the Union, and derivatives relating to the transportation of electricity or natural gas in the Union. However, contracts for the supply and distribution of electricity or natural gas for the use of final customers are generally not wholesale energy products. This definition is relevant for Article 2(2)(a),[58] Article 7(5), and Article 25(3) and (5).[59] **B.3.26**

National regulatory authority (Article 3(1)(23))

National regulatory authorities—pursuant to Article 3(1)(23) and Article 2(10) of the Wholesale Energy Market Integrity and Transparency Regulation (2011/1227/EU)—are regulatory authorities designated in accordance with Article 35(1) of Directive 2009/72/EC or Article 39(1) of Directive 2009/73/EC. This definition is only relevant for Article 25(3).[60] **B.3.27**

Commodity derivatives (Article 3(1)(24))

Pursuant to Article 3(1)(24), *commodity derivatives* means commodity derivatives as defined in Article 2(1)(30) of the Regulation on markets in financial instruments (2014/600/EU), which is based on the definition of derivatives in Article 4(1)(44(c) of the Markets in Financial Instruments Directive II (2014/65/EU), according to which all securities giving the right to buy or sell any such transferable securities or giving rise to a cash settlement determined by reference to transferable securities, currencies, interest rates, or yields, commodities, or other indices or measures are covered.[61] However, additionally these derivatives must relate to a commodity or an underlying good as defined in Annex I, Section C(10) of the Markets in Financial Instruments Directive II (2014/65/EU) or as defined in Annex I, Section C(5) to (7) of the Markets in Financial Instruments Directive II (2014/65/EU). This definition is relevant for Article 7(1)(b) and (5),[62] and for Article 23(2)(c).[63] **B.3.28**

---

[58] See art 2 n 10.

[59] See art 25 n 10 ff.

[60] See art 25 n 10 ff.

[61] See Antonella Sciarrone Alibrandi and Edoardo Grossule, 'Commodity Derivatives' in Danny Busch and Guido Ferrarini (eds), *Regulation of the EU Financial Markets: MiFID II and MiFIR* (OUP 2017) ch 16.

[62] See art 7 n 5 ff.

[63] See art 23 n 18.

Person discharging managerial responsibilities (Article 3(1)(25))

B.3.29 A *person discharging managerial responsibilities* is, pursuant to Article 3(1)(25), a member of the administrative, management, or supervisory body of that entity (note 30 ff) or senior executive (note 32). This definition is especially relevant for managers' transactions governed by Article 19[64] but also for Article 30(2)(e) to (g).[65]

Member of the administrative, management, or supervisory body of that entity (Article 3(1)(25)(a))

B.3.30 Persons discharging managerial responsibilities are first—pursuant to Article 3(1)(25)(a)—*members of the administrative, management, or supervisory body* of an entity. Since this definition serves as a basis for the regulation of managers' transactions in Article 19, a broad interpretation is necessary to establish effective measures to prevent market abuse (Article 1) and especially insider dealing.[66] Therefore, it does not make a difference whether the supervisory board of the entity is mandatory or not, as in both cases there is a high risk of insider dealing. However, the definition only covers acting and not former members of these bodies since former members usually do not have access to insider information. Whether a person belongs to the bodies mentioned in Article 3(1)(25)(a) or not has to be determined by the applicable corporate law and not by the Market Abuse Regulation. If a person has a strong influence on these bodies but is not a member, Article 3(1)(25)(a) does not apply. However, this person could qualify as a senior executive pursuant to Article 3(1)(25)(b).

B.3.31 Shareholders are not covered by Article 3(1)(25)(a), regardless of whether they are majority shareholders or not. Article 3(1)(25)(a) clearly refers only to members of an administrative, management, or supervisory body of the entity. If a (majority) shareholder is not a member of these bodies but uses his power to influence the decisions being made by these bodies, Article 3(1)(25)(a) does not apply. Since Article 3(1)(25) serves only as a basis for the regulation of managers' transactions in Article 19, an application of Article 3(1)(25) to (majority) shareholders is not necessary to establish effective measures to prevent market abuse (Article 1), since in these cases the general prohibition of insider dealing (Article 14) applies.

Senior executive (Article 3(1)(25)(b))

B.3.32 Furthermore, pursuant to Article 3(1)(25)(b), *senior executives* are persons discharging managerial responsibilities and who can undertake managers' transactions. However, a senior executive within the meaning of the Market Abuse

[64] See art 19 n 18 ff.
[65] See art 30 n 14 ff.
[66] See recital (58).

Regulation is only a person who is not a member of the bodies referred to in Article 3(1)(25)(a), who has regular access to inside information relating directly or indirectly to that entity and who has the power to take managerial decisions affecting the future developments and business prospects of that entity. Since the definition in Article 3(1)(25)(b) requires in particular access to insider information, the concrete form of employment and the applicable labour law is of no relevance in this context. It is also of no importance whether the person is supposed to have access to inside information relating directly or indirectly to that entity, as long as he or she actually has some access and takes managerial decisions affecting the future development and business prospects of that entity.

Person closely associated (Article 3(1)(26))

Persons closely associated are—pursuant to Article 3(1)(26)—spouse or partner (note 34), a dependent child (note 35), other relatives (note 36), and legal persons, trusts, or partnerships (note 37). This definition is especially relevant for managers' transactions governed by Article 19.[67] **B.3.33**

Spouse or partner (Article 3(1)(26)(a))

A person closely associated is, pursuant to Article 3(1)(26)(a), a *spouse*. Also, a partner must be considered as a person closely associated if he or she is equivalent to a spouse in accordance with national law. Although Article 3(1)(26)(a) does not clearly state which national law applies, Article 3(1)(26)(a) refers to the national family law of the member of the administrative, management, or supervisory body (Article 3(1)(25)(a)), or senior executive (Article 3(1)(25)(b)), since the definition of a person closely associated is only relevant for managers' transactions governed by Article 19.[68] This is also the case since Article 3(1)(26)(d) explicitly refers to the members of the administrative, management, or supervisory body (Article 3(1)(25)(a)), and senior executives (Article 3(1)(25)(b)). **B.3.34**

Dependent child (Article 3(1)(26)(b))

Furthermore, a *dependent child*, in accordance with national law, must be considered as a person closely associated. Also—as in Article 3(1)(26)(a)—the reference to national law means the national family law of the member of the administrative, management, or supervisory body (Article 3(1)(25)(a)), or senior executive (Article 3(1)(25)(b)).[69] **B.3.35**

67 See art 19 n 18 ff.
68 ibid.
69 See n 32.

Other relatives (Article 3(1)(26)(c))

B.3.36 Also, *other relatives* who have shared the same household for at least one year on the date of the transaction concerned are persons closely associated (Article 3(1)(26)(c)).

Legal persons, trusts, or partnerships (Article 3(1)(26)(d))

B.3.37 Finally, a person closely associated is also a *legal person, trust, or partnership*, the managerial responsibilities of which are discharged by a person discharging managerial responsibilities or by a person referred to in Article 3(1)(26)(a) to (c), which is directly or indirectly controlled by such a person, which is set up for the benefit of such a person, or the economic interests of which are substantially equivalent to those of such a person. Whether these conditions are met must be determined by the national law applicable to this legal person, trust, or partnership. The applicable law for managers' transactions is of no relevance in this regard.

Data traffic records (Article 3(1)(27))

B.3.38 *Data traffic records* are—pursuant to Article 3(1)(27) and Article 2(2)(b) of the Data Protection Directive (2002/58/EC)—any data processed for the purpose of the conveyance of a communication on an electronic communications network or for the billing thereof. This definition is only relevant for Article 23(2)(g)–(h).[70]

Person professionally arranging or executing transactions (Article 3(1)(28))

B.3.39 A *person professionally arranging or executing transactions* is, pursuant to Article 3(1)(28), a person professionally engaged in the reception and transmission of orders for, or in the execution of transactions in, financial instruments. Since Article 3(1)(28) does not refer to the definitions in the Markets in Financial Instruments Directive II (2014/65/EU) or to its scope, this definition is not limited to firms or entities providing investment services under the Markets in Financial Instruments Directive II (2014/65/EU).[71] Therefore, investment management firms (AIFs and UCITS managers) and firms professionally engaged in trading for their own account (proprietary traders) are also covered by the definition.[72] This definition is only relevant for the regulation of the prevention and detection of market abuse under Article 16(2).[73]

---

[70] See art 23 n 18.

[71] ESMA, 'Questions and Answers on the Market Abuse Regulation' 6 www.esma.org.

[72] ibid.

[73] See art 16 n 4.

Benchmark (Article 3(1)(29))

A *benchmark* is defined in Article 3(1)(29) as any rate, index, or figure made available to the public or published that is periodically or regularly determined by the application of a formula to, or on the basis of, the value of one or more underlying assets or prices, including estimated prices, actual or estimated interest rates or other values, or surveys, and by reference to which the amount payable under a financial instrument or the value of a financial instrument is determined. This definition is relevant for the regulation of the scope of application of the Market Abuse Regulation in Article 2(2)(c),[74] the definition of market manipulation in Article 12(1)(d), and Article 38. **B.3.40**

Market maker (Article 3(1)(30))

A *market maker* is—pursuant to Article 3(1)(30) and Article 4(1)(7) of the Markets in Financial Instruments Directive II (2014/65/EU)—a person who holds himself out on the financial markets on a continuous basis as being willing to deal on his own account by buying and selling financial instruments against that person's proprietary capital at prices defined by that person. This definition is only relevant for the regulation of legitimate behaviour in Article 9(2)(a).[75] **B.3.41**

Stake-building (Article 3(1)(31))

Stake-building is defined in Article 3(1)(31) as an acquisition of securities in a company which does not trigger a legal or regulatory obligation to make an announcement of a takeover bid in relation to that company. This definition is only relevant for the regulation of legitimate behaviour in Article 9(4)(2).[76] **B.3.42**

Disclosing market participant (Article 3(1)(32))

A *disclosing market participant* means, pursuant to Article 3(1)(32), a person who falls into any of the categories set out in Article 11(1)(a) to (d)[77] or in Article 11(2),[78] and who discloses information in the course of a market sounding. This definition is only relevant for the regulation of market soundings in Article 11.[79] **B.3.43**

High-frequency trading (Article 3(1)(33))

High-frequency trading is—pursuant to Article 3(1)(33) and Article 4(1)(40) of the Markets in Financial Instruments Directive II (2014/65/EU)—an algorithmic **B.3.44**

74 See art 2 n 12.
75 See art 9 n 32 ff.
76 See art 9 n 61 ff.
77 See art 11 n 12.
78 See art 11 n 13.
79 See art 11 n 12 ff.

trading technique characterized by an infrastructure intended to minimize network and other types of latencies, including at least one of the following facilities for algorithmic order entry: co-location, proximity hosting, or high-speed direct electronic access; a system-determination of order initiation, generation, routing, or execution without human intervention for individual trades or orders; and high-message intraday rates, which constitute orders, quotes, or cancellations.[80] This definition is only relevant for the definition of market manipulation in Article 12(2)(c).[81]

Information recommending or suggesting an investment strategy (Article 3(1)(34))

B.3.45 *Information recommending or suggesting an investment strategy* is defined in Article 3(1)(34)(i) as information produced by an independent analyst, an investment firm, a credit institution, any other person whose main business is to produce investment recommendations, or a natural person working for them under a contract of employment or otherwise, which, directly or indirectly, expresses a particular investment proposal in respect of a financial instrument or an issuer. In this context, it is of no relevance whether the production of the investment recommendation is the main business of the investment firm, since this criteria is only relevant for the *other person* mentioned in Article 3(1)(34)(i).[82]

B.3.46 Also, information produced by persons other than those referred to in Article 3(1)(34)(i), which directly proposes a particular investment decision in respect of a financial instrument, is information recommending or suggesting an investment strategy (Article 3(1)(34)(ii)). This definition is only relevant for the regulation of investment recommendations and statistics in Article 20.[83] See also Commission Delegated Regulation (EU) 2016/958.[84]

Investment recommendations (Article 3(1)(35))

B.3.47 *Investment recommendations* is defined in Article 3(1)(35) as information recommending or suggesting an investment strategy, explicitly or implicitly, concerning one or several financial instruments or the issuers, including any opinion as to the present or future value or price of such instruments, intended for distribution

[80] See Conac, 'Algorithmic Trading' (n 53) ch 17.

[81] See art 12 n 10 f.

[82] ESMA, 'Questions and Answers on the Market Abuse Regulation' 13 ff www.esma.org.

[83] See art 20 n 12 ff.

[84] Commission Delegated Regulation (EU) 2016/958 of 9 March 2016 supplementing Regulation (EU) No 596/2014 of the European Parliament and of the Council with regard to regulatory technical standards for the technical arrangements for objective presentation of investment recommendations or other information recommending or suggesting an investment strategy and for disclosure of particular interests or indications of conflicts of interest (OJ L 160 (17 June 2016) 15).

channels or for the public. In this context, it is of no relevance whether the recommendation was made orally or by electronic means such as telephone calls or face-to-face conversations. Also, so-called morning notes and sales notes can be considered as an investment recommendation if the criteria mentioned in Article 3(1)(35) are met.[85] If a communication does not refer to one or several financial instruments it is not an investment recommendation within the meaning of Article 3(1)(35). However, if a communication allows a reasonable investor to deduce that it is implicitly recommending specific financial instruments, it constitutes an investment recommendation.[86] This definition is only relevant for the regulation of investment recommendations and statistics in Article 20.[87]

Exemptions for buy-back programmes and stabilization (Article 3(2))

Article 3(2) sets out special definitions that are only relevant for the exemption for buy-back programmes and stabilization measures in Article 5. **B.3.48**

Securities (Article 3(2)(a))

Article 3(2)(a) defines *securities* as shares and other securities equivalent to shares (Article 3(2)(a)(i)), bonds and other forms of securitized debt (Article 3(2)(a)(ii)), and securitized debt convertible or exchangeable into shares or into other securities equivalent to shares (Article 3(2)(a)(iii)). This definition is more narrow than the one for financial instruments in Article 3(1)(1)[88] because the conditions set out in Article 5 can only be met by transactions in securities and not generally by transactions in financial instruments. The definition of securities in Article 3(2)(a) seems to conflict with the definition of buy-back-programmes in Article 3(1)(17),[89] since Article 3(1)(17) covers only trading in own shares and not in the other securities mentioned in Article 3(2)(a)(ii) to (iii). However, since the definition of securities in Article 3(2)(a) is only relevant for stabilization (Article 5(3)),[90] this definition has no influence on buy-back-programmes. **B.3.49**

Associated instruments (Article 3(2)(b))

Associated instruments are defined pursuant to Article 3(2)(b) as financial instruments (Article 3(1)(1))[91] that are limited to: (i) contracts or rights to subscribe for, acquire, or dispose of securities; (ii) financial derivatives of securities; (iii) where the securities are convertible or exchangeable debt instruments, the securities into which such convertible or exchangeable debt instruments may be converted or **B.3.50**

[85] ESMA, 'Questions and Answers on the Market Abuse Regulation' 11.
[86] ibid 12.
[87] See art 20 n 12 ff.
[88] See n 4 f.
[89] See n 21.
[90] See art 5 n 26.
[91] See n 4 f.

exchanged. Moreover also (iv) instruments which are issued or guaranteed by the issuer or guarantor of the securities and whose market price is likely to influence materially the price of the securities, or vice versa; and (v) where the securities are securities equivalent to shares, the shares represented by those securities, and any other securities equivalent to those shares are covered. For the definition of associated instruments, it is of no relevance whether they are admitted to trading or traded on a trading venue or not. Also, a request for admission to trading on a trading venue is not necessary. This definition is only relevant for the regulation of stabilization in Article 5(4).[92]

Significant distribution (Article 3(2)(c))

B.3.51 Pursuant to Article 3(2)(c), *significant distribution* means an initial or secondary offer of securities that is distinct from ordinary trading both in terms of the amount in value of the securities to be offered and the selling method to be employed. This definition is only relevant for the definition of stabilization in Article 3(2)(d).[93]

Stabilization (Article 3(2)(d))

B.3.52 *Stabilization* is—pursuant to Article 3(2)(d)—a purchase or offer to purchase securities, or a transaction in associated instruments equivalent thereto, which is undertaken by a credit institution or an investment firm in the context of a significant distribution of such securities exclusively for supporting the market price of those securities for a predetermined period of time, owing to selling pressure in such securities. This definition is of utmost importance for the regulation of stabilization in Article 5(4).[94]

B.3.53 The scope of the definition in Article 3(2)(d) is rather limited and covers only the overallotment in combination with a *Greenshoe option* as one common form of stabilization measure.[95] However, since the acquisition of the financial instruments by the issuer himself has the same effect on the prices of financial instruments, the safe harbour for buy-back programmes[96] must also be considered as a stabilization measure. Other forms of stabilization measures, such as *lock-up agreements* or agreements between the shareholders—not to increase the capital of the issuer or not to issue new shares—can also have the same effect on the prices of financial instruments not covered by the definition and which are therefore not exempted by the prohibitions of Articles 14 and 15.

[92] See art 5 n 35 ff.
[93] See n 52.
[94] See art 5 n 35 ff.
[95] See art 5 n 33.
[96] See n 21.

Article 4: Notifications and list of financial instruments

1. Market operators of regulated markets and investment firms and market operators operating an MTF or an OTF shall, without delay, notify the competent authority of the trading venue of any financial instrument for which a request for admission to trading on their trading venue is made, which is admitted to trading, or which is traded for the first time.

They shall also notify the competent authority of the trading venue when a financial instrument ceases to be traded or to be admitted to trading, unless the date on which the financial instrument ceases to be traded or to be admitted to trading is known and was referred to in the notification made in accordance with the first subparagraph.

Notifications referred to in this paragraph shall include, as appropriate, the names and identifiers of the financial instruments concerned, and the date and time of the request for admission to trading, admission to trading, and the date and time of the first trade.

Market operators and investment firms shall also transmit to the competent authority of the trading venue the information set out in the third subparagraph with regard to financial instruments that were the subject of a request for admission to trading or that were admitted to trading before 2 July 2014, and that are still admitted to trading or traded on that date.

2. Competent authorities of the trading venue shall transmit notifications that they receive pursuant to paragraph 1 to ESMA without delay. ESMA shall publish those notifications on its website in the form of a list immediately on receipt. ESMA shall update that list immediately on receipt of a notification by a competent authority of the trading venue. The list shall not limit the scope of this Regulation.
3. The list shall contain the following information:
   (a) the names and identifiers of financial instruments which are the subject of a request for admission to trading, admitted to trading or traded for the first time, on regulated markets, MTFs and OTFs;
   (b) the dates and times of the requests for admission to trading, of the admissions to trading, or of the first trades;
   (c) details of the trading venues on which the financial instruments are the subject of a request for admission to trading, admitted to trading or traded for the first time; and
   (d) the date and time at which the financial instruments cease to be traded or to be admitted to trading.

4. In order to ensure consistent harmonisation of this Article, ESMA shall develop draft regulatory technical standards to lay down:
(a) the content of the notifications referred to in paragraph 1; and
(b) the manner and conditions of the compilation, publication and maintenance of the list referred to in paragraph 3.

ESMA shall submit those draft regulatory technical standards to the Commission by 3 July 2015.

Power is delegated to the Commission to adopt the regulatory technical standards referred to in the first subparagraph in accordance with Articles 10 to 14 of Regulation (EU) No 1095/2010 of the European Parliament and of the Council ([1]).

Relevant Technical Standards:
Commission Delegated Regulation (EU) 2016/909 of 1 March 2016 supplementing Regulation (EU) No 596/2014 of the European Parliament and of the Council with regard to regulatory technical standards for the content of notifications to be submitted to competent authorities and the compilation, publication and maintenance of the list of notifications (OJ L 153 (10 June 2016) 13);
Commission Implementing Regulation (EU) 2016/378 of 11 March 2016 laying down implementing technical standards with regard to the timing, format and template of the submission of notifications to competent authorities according to Regulation (EU) No 596/2014 of the European Parliament and of the Council (OJ L 72 (17 March 2016) 1).

I. General Remarks

Overview

B.4.01 Although the Market Abuse Regulation is directly applicable in all Member States and ESMA is the central administrative agency for its enforcement, the

[1] Regulation (EU) No 1095/2010 of the European Parliament and of the Council of 24 November 2010 establishing a European Supervisory Authority (European Securities and Markets Authority), amending Decision No 716/2009/EC and repealing Commission Decision 2009/77/EC (OJ L 331 (15 December 2010) 84).

national (competent) authorities[2] play a key role in its application. In addition, the Market Abuse Regulation assigns a number of tasks to market operators.[3] To ensure a sufficient exchange of information between market operators, the competent authorities, and ESMA, Article 4 sets out numerous notification requirements establishing a system for the centralization of all necessary information at ESMA.

Historical development

The notification requirements in Article 4 were not part of the (former) Market Abuse Directive (2003/6/EC), since the Market Abuse Directive required Member States only to give the competent authorities all supervisory and investigatory powers that were necessary for the exercise of their functions. Therefore, it was at the discretion of Member States to introduce the reporting obligations necessary to comply with these requirements. **B.4.02**

II. Notification (Article 4(1))

Article 4(1) establishes the general notification requirement for all market operators of regulated markets, investment firms, and market operators of an MTF or an OTF. These market operators (Article 3(1)(5)[4]) or investment firms (Article 3(1)(2)[5]) must notify the competent authorities (Article 3(1)(12)[6]) of any financial instrument for which a request for admission to trading on their trading venue is made, which is admitted to trading, or which is traded for the first time. With this notification requirement, the Market Abuse Regulation ensures the establishment of measures to prevent market abuse, thereby ensuring the integrity of financial markets in the Union (Article 1). The market operators and investment firms trading on this market must fulfil this notification requirement without delay. **B.4.03**

The notification requirement also applies when the financial instrument in question ceases to be traded or is no longer admitted to trading (Article 4(1)(2)). However, if the date on which the financial instrument ceases to be traded or to be admitted to trading is already known to the competent authority and was referred to in the notification made in accordance with Article 4(1)(1), no additional notification is necessary. This additional notification requirement is **B.4.04**

[2] For a definition see art 3(12)—see art 3 n 16.
[3] For a definition see art 3(5)—see art 3 n 9.
[4] See art 3 n 9.
[5] See art 3 n 6.
[6] See art 3 n 16.

necessary because ceasing to trade in a financial instrument increases the likelihood of insider trading, especially if the trade cease is only temporary.

B.4.05 For the notification, market operators must disclose the names and identifiers of the financial instruments to the competent authority. In addition, they must submit the date and time of the request for admission to trading or the date and time of the admission to trading and the date and time of the first trade (Article 4(1)(3)). However, this notification requirement does not apply when the request for admission to trading was made before 2 July 2014 (Article 4(1)(4)). The same applies when the financial instruments were admitted to trading before 2 July 2014 and are still admitted or traded (Article 4(1)(4)).

III. Transfer to ESMA (Article 4(2))

B.4.06 The competent authorities must transmit the notifications by the market operators and the investment firms under Article 4(1) to ESMA without delay (Article 4(2)). ESMA publishes these notifications immediately on its website (Article 4(2)(2)) and updates that list immediately on receipt of a notification by a competent authority of the trading venue (Article 4(2)(3)). The fact that financial instruments are not on that list does not limit the scope of application of the Market Abuse Regulation (Article 4(2)(4)).

IV. Content of the Transferred List (Article 4(3))

B.4.07 The list being published by ESMA[7] must contain:

a. the names and identifiers of financial instruments which are the subject of a request for admission to trading, admitted to trading, or traded for the first time, on regulated markets, MTFs, and OTFs
b. the dates and times of the requests for admission to trading, of the admissions to trading, or of the first trades
c. details of the trading venues on which the financial instruments are the subject of a request for admission to trading, admitted to trading, or traded for the first time, and
d. the date and time at which the financial instruments cease to be traded or to be admitted to trading.

[7] See n 6.

V. Competence to Develop Regulatory Technical Standards (Article 4(4))

ESMA has, pursuant to Article 4(4), the competence to develop regulatory technical standards on the content of the notifications referred to in Article 4(1) and the manner and conditions of the compilation, publication, and maintenance of the list referred to in Article 4(3). The power to adopt the regulatory technical standard is delegated to the Commission (Article 4(4)(3)). This technical standard (Commission Delegated Regulation (EU) 2016/909) was adopted by the Commission on 1 March 2016. **B.4.08**

VI. Adoption of the Technical Standards (Article 4(5))

Finally, ESMA has the competence to develop regulatory technical standards on the timing, format, and template of the submission of notifications under Article 4(1) and (2). The power to adopt the regulatory technical standard is delegated to the Commission (Article 4(5)(3)). This technical standard (Commission Implementing Regulation 2016/378/EU) was adopted by the Commission on 11 March 2016. **B.4.09**

Article 5: Exemption for buy-back programmes and stabilisation

1. The prohibitions in Articles 14 and 15 of this Regulation do not apply to trading in own shares in buy-back programmes where:
   (a) the full details of the programme are disclosed prior to the start of trading;
   (b) trades are reported as being part of the buy-back programme to the competent authority of the trading venue in accordance with paragraph 3 and subsequently disclosed to the public;
   (c) adequate limits with regard to price and volume are complied with; and
   (d) it is carried out in accordance with the objectives referred to in paragraph 2 and the conditions set out in this Article and in the regulatory technical standards referred to in paragraph 6.
2. In order to benefit from the exemption provided for in paragraph 1, a buy-back programme shall have as its sole purpose:
   (a) to reduce the capital of an issuer;
   (b) to meet obligations arising from debt financial instruments that are exchangeable into equity instruments; or
   (c) to meet obligations arising from share option programmes, or other allocations of shares, to employees or to members of the administrative, management or supervisory bodies of the issuer or of an associate company.
3. In order to benefit from the exemption provided for in paragraph 1, the issuer shall report to the competent authority of the trading venue on which the shares have been admitted to trading or are traded each transaction relating to the buy-back programme, including the information specified in Article 25(1) and (2) and Article 26(1), (2) and (3) of Regulation (EU) No 600/2014.
4. The prohibitions in Articles 14 and 15 of this Regulation do not apply to trading in securities or associated instruments for the stabilisation of securities where:
   (a) stabilisation is carried out for a limited period;
   (b) relevant information about the stabilisation is disclosed and notified to the competent authority of the trading venue in accordance with paragraph 5;
   (c) adequate limits with regard to price are complied with; and
   (d) such trading complies with the conditions for stabilisation laid down in the regulatory technical standards referred to in paragraph 6.

5. **Without prejudice to Article 23(1), the details of all stabilisation transactions shall be notified by issuers, offerors, or entities undertaking the stabilisation, whether or not they act on behalf of such persons, to the competent authority of the trading venue no later than the end of the seventh daily market session following the date of execution of such transactions.**
6. **In order to ensure consistent harmonisation of this Article, ESMA shall develop draft regulatory technical standards to specify the conditions that buy-back programmes and stabilisation measures referred to in paragraphs 1 and 4 must meet, including conditions for trading, restrictions regarding time and volume, disclosure and reporting obligations, and price conditions.**

ESMA shall submit those draft regulatory technical standards to the Commission by 3 July 2015.

Power is delegated to the Commission to adopt the regulatory technical standards referred to in the first subparagraph in accordance with Articles 10 to 14 of Regulation (EU) No 1095/2010.

Relevant Technical Standards:
Commission Delegated Regulation (EU) No 2016/1052 of 8 March 2016 supplementing Regulation (EU) No 596/2014 of the European Parliament and of the Council with regard to regulatory technical standards for the conditions applicable to buy-back programmes and stabilisation measures (OJ L 173 (30 June 2016) 34).

I. General Remarks

Overview

B.5.01 Although constituting a market manipulation, buy-back programmes and stabilization measures are widely accepted in most jurisdictions because they can be justified and be carried out for legitimate reasons. Therefore, Article 5 states that the prohibition of insider dealing and market manipulation as set out in Articles 14 and 15 does not apply to these kinds of transactions and establishes a safe harbour.[1] To limit the effect of these transactions on the market price of the relevant financial instruments, Article 5 sets out several conditions for buy-back programmes[2] and stabilization measures.[3]

Historical development

B.5.02 The (former) Market Abuse Directive (2003/6/EC) had already recognized the need for a safe harbour rule for buy-back programmes and stabilization measures by generally exempting the prohibition in its Article 8. In addition, the Commission adopted specific implementation measures by enacting the Buy-back Programmes and Stabilisation Regulation (2273/2003/EC). This regulation was repealed by Article 37, with effect from 3 July 2016. However, Article 5 is based on this regulation to a large extent and hardly deviates from it.

Article 5 as limited *safe harbour*

B.5.03 The exemption established by Article 5 constitutes a so-called *safe harbour*, since the prohibitions in Articles 14 and 15 do not apply if the requirements of Article 5 are met. Therefore, the competent authorities cannot sanction any trades, actions, or behaviour in accordance with the requirements of Article 5. However, if these requirements are not met, such trades, actions, or behaviour do not automatically violate the prohibitions in Articles 14 and 15. Although Article 5(1) and (4) refer to the prohibitions in Articles 14 and 15 without any reservations, not all transactions, actions, or behaviour are generally exempted. This is especially the case for the prohibition of insider trading (Article 14(a) and (b)[4]), since the execution of a buy-back programme and stabilization measures can constitute insider information if the requirements of Article 7 are met. Since buy-back programmes and stabilization measures typically have a significant effect on the price of financial instruments, this is usually the case. If a person other than the issuer himself uses this information to acquire or dispose of financial instruments (Article 8(1)[5]) or

---

[1] See n 3:
[2] See n 10 ff.
[3] See n 33 ff.
[4] See art 14 n 4 ff.
[5] See art 8 n 33 ff.

recommends this to another person (Article 8(2)[6]), the safe harbour of Article 5 does not apply. See also note 30 for the relation of Article 5 to the public disclosure of inside information pursuant to Article 17. See also notes 27 and 28 for the (limited) influence of the safe harbour of Article 5 on other capital market regulations.

Economic background and limits

Buy-back programmes and the stabilization of financial instruments are common instruments of capital markets and, as such, are widely accepted. The Market Abuse Directive and the accompanying Buy-back Programmes and Stabilisation Regulation had already established a similar safe harbour which was, however, generally broader in its application. **B.5.04**

Buy-back programme

Buy-back programmes are necessary for issuers to fulfil contractual obligations to deliver their own shares.[7] Such obligations can result especially from the issuance of stock options. Moreover, the issuer can use his own shares for the acquisition of other corporations. Also, buy-back programmes can be used as a signal from the issuer to the capital markets that—pursuant to his own assessment—the shares are undervalued. Furthermore, buy-back programmes are a substitute for distributions to shareholders since they have the same effect. Although all of these purposes for buy-back programmes are common and widely accepted on international capital markets, only some of them are recognized by Article 5(2).[8] **B.5.05**

However, the execution of buy-back programmes can have a negative effect on capital markets. This is the case since their execution has a direct influence on the price of financial instruments because it reduces the number of shares being traded in the market. In addition, the influence of the other shareholders also increases, since the shares of the issuer owned by him do not usually—pursuant to corporate law—grant him any additional rights. Finally, the execution of buy-back programmes is necessarily based on an informational advantage of the issuer since he has unlimited access to all the information related to him. Consequently, buy-back programmes must be transparent to inform the other market participants about the irregular demand created by the issuer. By establishing broad and **B.5.06**

[6] See art 8 n 106 ff.

[7] See Jesper Lau Hansen, 'MAD in a Hurry: The Swift and Promising Adoption of the EU Market Abuse Directive' (2004) 15 European Business Law Review 183, 212 for the motives of an issuer for a buy-back programme. See also Niamh Moloney, *EU Securities and Financial Markets Regulation* (3rd edn, OUP 2014) 752 ff; Mathias Siems and Amadeo de Cesari, 'The Law and Finance of Share Repurchases in Europe' (2012) 12 Journal of Corporate Law Studies 33; Lars Teigelack, 'Market Manipulation' in Rüdiger Veil (ed), *European Capital Markets Law* (1st edn, Hart Publishing 2012) para 14 n 52 ff.

[8] See n 25.

wide transparency of the buy-back programme, Article 5(1) to (3)[9] constitutes a compromise between the interests of the issuer and the interests of other market participants.

Stabilization measures

B.5.07 Stabilization measures are a common feature of initial or secondary offers of securities. The basic idea of stabilization measures is to prevent excessive fluctuation of the price of financial instruments in the initial period of their listing. In an initial or secondary offer of securities, usually a so-called oversubscription takes place, because the number of shares offered for subscription exceeds the number of shares available.[10] Since this frequently leads to a massive increase in the price of the financial instrument in question in the first few days or weeks of its listing, many investors sell their shares to realize this profit. Consequently, the increase in the price of the financial instruments is often followed by a sudden decrease in the price (so-called *flipping*). To prevent such fluctuations, the issuer usually undertakes stabilization measures.

B.5.08 The most common form of stabilization is the so-called overallotment, combined with a Greenshoe option. In the event of an overallotment, the issuer agrees with an investment firm or credit institution that they accept subscriptions from investors for more financial instruments of the issuer than are offered in the initial or secondary offering. If the price of the financial instrument drops within the first weeks of the initial or secondary offering to less than a certain threshold, the investment firm or credit institution acquires the financial instruments in the market since they need the financial instruments to fulfil their obligations from the overallotment to the investors. This acquisition usually leads to an increase in the price of the financial instruments and therefore to its stabilization. However, if the market price of the financial instruments in question exceeds the offer price, the investment firm or credit institution can exercise the so-called *Greenshoe* option,[11] which allows them to subscribe for a certain number of the financial instrument in question from the issuer at the offer price. Therefore, the

---

[9] See n 10 ff.

[10] See Reena Aggarwal, 'Stabilization Activities by Underwriters after Initial Public Offerings' (2000) 55 Journal of Finance 1075–103; Rajesh K Aggarwal, Laurie Krigman, and Kent L Womack, 'Strategic IPO Underpricing, Information Momentum, and Lockup Expiration Selling' (2002) 66 Journal of Financial Economics 105–37; Stefano Lombardo, 'The Stabilisation of the Share Price of IPOs in the United States and the European Union' (2007) 8 European Business Organization Law Review 521 See also Moloney, *EU Securities and Financial Markets Regulation* (n 7) 752 ff; Teigelack, 'Market Manipulation' (n 7) n 63 ff.

[11] A *Greenshoe option* is defined in art 1(g) of the Commission Delegated Regulation for Buy-back-Programmes and Stabilisation Measures (Regulation 2016/1052/EU) and refers to the American corporation Green Shoe Manufacturing Company, where such an option was used for the first time in 1924. In the context of an initial public offering (IPO), a greenshoe option is a provision contained in an underwriting agreement that gives the underwriter the right to sell investors more shares than originally planned by the issuer if the demand for a particular security issue proves higher than expected.

Greenshoe option is a safeguard for the investment firm or credit institution that their obligation from the overallotment cannot be covered with financial instruments acquired in the market.

Although stabilization measures are generally accepted, they constitute a market manipulation. Their exemption from the prohibitions in Articles 14 and 15 is justified because otherwise initial or secondary offerings of securities would face a serious risk of failing, which would lead to an increase in the costs of initial or secondary offerings, especially since investment firms and credit institutions in particular would bear the risk. Since stabilization measures create an artificial price for the financial instruments, they are limited to a certain period of time and must be disclosed to all market participants before the initial or secondary offering starts[12] and after the respective transactions have taken place.[13] **B.5.09**

II. Buy-back Programmes (Article 5(1) to (3))

Definition

Buy-back programmes are defined in Article 3(1)(17)[14] as 'trading in own shares' in accordance with Articles 21 to 27 of the Capital Maintenance Directive (2012/30/EU). Therefore, the exemption in Article 5 is based on European corporate law, which especially limits its scope of application.[15] In contrast to the Market Abuse Directive, the Market Abuse Regulation does not distinguish between (regular) buy-back programmes and time-scheduled buy-back programmes, as defined in former Article 2(4) of the Buy-back Programmes and Stabilisation Regulation (Regulation 2273/2003/EC). **B.5.10**

Scope of application

In contrast to the general scope of application of the Market Abuse Regulation, Article 5 does not apply to all financial instruments as defined in Article 3(1)(1)[16] but sets its own scope of application. Pursuant to Article 5(1), the safe harbour for buy-back programmes applies only to shares. **B.5.11**

Therefore, the safe harbour does not apply to the acquisition of other financial instruments of the issuer. This is especially the case for bonds and options. This limitation of the safe harbour is debatable, since the issuer can also have an interest in acquiring these kinds of financial instruments. Without the application of **B.5.12**

[12] See n 34.
[13] See n 34.
[14] See art 3 n 21.
[15] See n 11 ff.
[16] See art 3 n 4 ff.

the safe harbour, the issuer risks a violation of the prohibition of Article 14 and Article 15 by executing a buy-back programme for these financial instruments. Because the European legislator expressly limited the scope of application of the safe harbour to shares, it is doubtful that the safe harbour can be applied in the same way as it can to other financial instruments. This is especially the case where the problem of the narrow scope of application already existed under the old regime of the (former) Market Abuse Directive (2003/6/EC).

B.5.13 The applicability (or not) of Article 5(1) to (3) to buy-back programmes of credit institutions remains unclear. This is because Article 77 of the Capital Requirements Regulation (Regulation 575/2013/EU) states that a credit institution shall require the prior permission of the competent authority to repurchase Common Equity Tier 1 instruments permitted under applicable national law. In this regard, the Capital Requirements Regulation does not relate or refer to the Market Abuse Regulation. However, since Article 77 of the Capital Requirements Regulation expressly governs the repurchase of shares of credit institutions, a repurchase in accordance with the requirements set out by Article 77 of the Capital Requirements Regulation cannot violate the prohibition in Articles 14 and 15 (*lex specialis derogat legi generali*).

B.5.14 Finally, the safe harbour for buy-back programmes of Article 5(1) to (3) is exclusive. Since the Market Abuse Regulation (and therefore the prohibitions in Articles 14 and 15) have priority over national law, any additional requirements or exemptions established by national law are irrelevant.

Exemption for buy-back programmes (Article 5(1))

B.5.15 Article 5(1) sets out the general requirements necessary for a buy-back programme not to violate the prohibitions in Articles 14 and 15. The general characteristics of these requirements are to establish broad and complete transparency of the buy-back programme to the market[17] and generally to limit the buy-back programme.[18] Also, the buy-back programme must have a certain purpose, as set out in Article 5(2).[19] These conditions are very similar to those of the (former) Buy-back Programmes and Stabilisation Regulation (Regulation 2273/2003/EC).

Disclosure of the full details of the programme (Article 5(1)(a))

B.5.16 The buy-back programme must be fully disclosed to the market. Pursuant to Article 5(1)(a), all details of the programme must be disclosed prior to the start of trading. With this requirement, market participants are informed and can anticipate that a certain amount of the trading volume in the market is attributable to

[17] See n 16 ff.
[18] See n 21 ff.
[19] See n 25.

the buy-back programme and not to an increasing demand from other market participants.[20] Therefore, Article 5(1)(a) requires that the full details of the buy-back programme must be disclosed prior to the start of trading and before the market opens. If the issuer commences the buy-back programme before this disclosure, the safe harbour does not apply. However, this does not necessarily constitute an actual violation per se of the prohibitions in Articles 14 and 15.

The details for the disclosure are set out in Article 2(1) of the Commission Delegated Regulation for Buy-back Programmes and Stabilisation Measures (Regulation 2016/1052/EU). Pursuant to this regulation, the issuer must disclose the purpose of the programme,[21] the maximum pecuniary amount allocated to the programme, the maximum number of shares to be acquired, and the period for which authorization for the programme has been granted. **B.5.17**

Reporting of the trades (Article 5(1)(b))

In addition to the disclosure of the full details of the buy-back programme, the issuer must report all trades of the buy-back programme to the competent authority, in accordance with the Article 5(3).[22] Afterwards, all trades must be reported to the public. This requires specific disclosure on the website of the issuer, where the information must be available to the public for at least a five-year period from the date of adequate disclosure having been given (Article 2(3)(2) Commission Delegated Regulation for Buy-back Programmes and Stabilisation Measures (Regulation 2016/1052/EU)). **B.5.18**

To meet these requirements, the issuer must have mechanisms in place that allow him to fulfil this reporting obligation (Article 2(2) Commission Delegated Regulation for Buy-back Programmes and Stabilisation Measures (Regulation 2016/1052/EU)). **B.5.19**

The reporting requirement of Article 5(1)(b) must be fulfilled no later than by the end of the seventh daily market session following the date of execution of such transactions (Article 2(3) Commission Delegated Regulation for Buy-back Programmes and Stabilisation Measures (Regulation 2016/1052/EU)). **B.5.20**

Compliance with adequate limits (Article 5(1)(c))

In addition, the issuer must comply with adequate limits with regard to price and volume. These limits are set out in Article 3(2) and (3) of the Commission Delegated Regulation for Buy-back Programmes and Stabilisation Measures (Regulation 2016/1052/EU)). **B.5.21**

---

20 See n 5 for the background to the safe harbour.

21 See n 24.

22 See n 26.

B.5.22 The price limit is governed by Article 3(2) of the Commission Delegated Regulation for Buy-back Programmes and Stabilisation Measures (Regulation 2016/1052/EU)), according to which the issuer cannot purchase shares at a price higher than the higher of the price of the last independent trade and the highest current independent purchase bid on the trading venue where the purchase is carried out, including when the shares are traded on different trading venues. By requiring that the purchase price cannot exceed the price of the last independent trade and the highest current independent purchase bid, the influence of the buy-back-programme on the price of the shares is thereby limited.

B.5.23 In addition, on any trading day the issuer is not permitted to purchase more than 25 per cent of the average daily volume of the shares on the trading venue on which the purchase is carried out (Article 3(3) Commission Delegated Regulation for Buy-back Programmes and Stabilisation Measures (Regulation 2016/1052/EU)). For the calculation of the average daily volume, see Article 3(3)(2) of the Commission Delegated Regulation for Buy-back Programmes and Stabilisation Measures (Regulation 2016/1052/EU) for the calculation of the average daily volume.

Compliance with the objectives referred to in Article 5(2) (Article 5(1)(d))

B.5.24 Furthermore, the buy-back-programme must be carried out in accordance with the objectives referred to in Article (5)(2)[23] and the conditions set out by the Commission Delegated Regulation for Buy-back Programmes and Stabilisation Measures (Regulation 2016/1052/EU). These conditions are that the shares shall be purchased by the issuer on a trading venue where the shares are admitted to trading or traded (Article (3)(1)(a) Commission Delegated Regulation for Buy-back Programmes and Stabilisation Measures (Regulation 2016/1052/EU)). Also, for shares traded continuously on a trading venue, the orders shall not be placed during an auction phase and orders placed before the start of the auction phase shall not be modified during that phase (Article (3)(1)(a) Commission Delegated Regulation for Buy-back Programmes and Stabilisation Measures (Regulation 2016/1052/EU)). Finally, for shares traded solely on a trading venue through auctions, orders shall be placed and modified by the issuer during the auction, provided that other market participants have sufficient time to react to them (Article (3)(1)(a) Commission Delegated Regulation for Buy-back Programmes and Stabilisation Measures (Regulation 2016/1052/EU)).

[23] See n 25.

Purpose of the buy-back programme (Article 5(2))

In addition, the safe harbour applies only if the buy-back-programme includes one of the purposes set out in Article 5(2). These purposes are to reduce the capital of an issuer (Article 5(2)(a)), to meet obligations arising from debt financial instruments that are exchangeable into equity instruments (Article 5(2)(b)) or to meet obligations arising from share option programmes, or other allocations of shares, to employees or to members of the administrative, management, or supervisory bodies of the issuer or of an associate company (Article 5(2)(c)). These purposes are the same as in the (former) Buy-back Programmes and Stabilisation Regulation (2273/2003/EC). **B.5.25**

Reporting requirements for buy-back programmes (Article 5(3))

Finally, the issuer must report each transaction relating to the buy-back-programme to the competent authority of the trading venue. With this additional reporting requirement, the competent authorities of the Member States should be granted powers to supervise whether the conditions of the safe harbour are met. The issuer must include in the report given to the competent authority the information specified in Article 25(1) and (2) and 26(1) to (3) of the MiFIR (Regulation 600/2014/EU). **B.5.26**

Additional requirements set by corporate law

The safe harbour for buy-back programmes of Article 5(1) to (3) does not require that the requirements for a buy-back of own shares of the applicable national corporate law must be met. The same applies for the requirement set out in Articles 21 to 27 of the Capital Maintenance Directive (2012/30/EU), since they are not directly applicable. However, the definition in Article 3(17)[24] relates explicitly to Articles 21 to 27 of the Capital Maintenance Directive (2012/30/EU) and states that the buy-back programme must be executed in accordance with Articles 21 to 27 of the Capital Maintenance Directive (2012/30/EU). Therefore, a buy-back programme is not automatically exempt from the prohibitions of Articles 14 and 15 if the requirements set out in Article 5(1) to (3) but not those under European corporate law are met. Requirements set by national corporate law exceeding those of Articles 21 to 27 of the Capital Maintenance Directive (2012/30/EU) are—for the purpose of the safe harbour of Article 5(1) to (3)—of no relevance since the definition of a buy-back programme in Article 3(17)[25] refers explicitly to the Capital Maintenance Directive (2012/30/EU) and **B.5.27**

---

24 See art 3 n 22.

25 See art 3 n 22.

not to the national law of the Member States implementing it. These principles also apply to non-European issuers outside the scope of the Capital Maintenance Directive.

B.5.28 Moreover, the safe harbour for buy-back programmes of Article 5(1) to (3) applies only to the prohibition set by Articles 14 and 15 and therefore does not restrict any sanctions set by national law for the violation of the provisions on the acquisition of own shares by a stock corporation.

Other capital market regulations

B.5.29 The execution of a buy-back programme usually also affects other aspects of capital markets law. This is especially the case with regard to the prohibition of insider trading (Article 8), which is explicitly exempt since Article 5 refers not only to the prohibition of market manipulation (Article 15) but also to the prohibition of insider dealing and of unlawful disclosure of inside information (Article 14).

B.5.30 However, the safe harbour for buy-back programmes of Article 5(1) to (3) does not apply to the public disclosure of inside information as required by Article 17. Consequently, the execution of a buy-back programmes in violation of the requirements of Article 17 can be sanctioned by the competent authorities. The disclosure system set out in Article 17 applies even though Article 5(1)(a)[26] and Article 5(1)(b)[27] establish their own set of rules for the disclosure of the buy-back programme. However, these rules cannot be seen as *lex specialis* to the rules of Article 17.

B.5.31 Moreover, the safe harbour for buy-back programmes of Article 5(1) to (3) does not apply to the requirements set out in national law on the notification of the acquisition or disposal of major holdings, as provided by the Transparency Directive (2013/50/EU). Therefore, the execution of a buy-back programme must comply with these requirements, which usually means that the issuer must publish the information that it reached, exceeded, or fell below the thresholds pursuant to Article 9 of the Transparency Directive (2013/50/EU).

B.5.32 Finally, the requirements set down by national takeover law as an implementation of the Takeover Directive (2004/25/EC) must be respected. This is especially the case for the mandatory bid pursuant to Article 5 of the Takeover Directive (2004/25/EC), if a person or persons acting in concert with that person gains control of the issuer owing to the execution of the buy-back-programme. This could be the case where, pursuant to Article 24(1)(a) of the Capital Maintenance Directive (2012/30/EU), the right to vote is suspended when the issuer acquires his own shares.

[26] See n 16 ff.
[27] See n 18 ff.

III. Stabilization (Article 5(4) and (5))

Definition

Stabilization is defined in Article 3(2)(d)[28] as a purchase or offer to purchase securities, or a transaction in associated instruments equivalent thereto, which is undertaken by a credit institution or an investment firm in the context of a significant distribution of such securities, exclusively for supporting the market price of those securities for a predetermined period of time, owing to selling pressure in such securities. Although several other forms of stabilization exist, the safe harbour for stabilization is limited to the measures mentioned in Article 3(2)(d). All other stabilization measures (note 7 ff) that are not covered by this definition do not provide a safe harbour and can constitute a violation of the prohibitions in Articles 14 and 15. **B.5.33**

Scope of application

In contrast to buy-back-programmes (note 10 ff) the scope of application for the safe harbour for stabilization measures is broader, since Article 5(4) and (5) apply to all securities (Article 3(2)(a)[29]) and associated instruments (Article 3(2)(b)[30]), and not only to shares. Although Article 5(4) refers to securities and associated instruments, the safe harbour applies only to the stabilization of securities. Associated instruments are only covered by Article 5(4), since trading in these types of financial instruments can be used as a stabilization measure for (other) securities. **B.5.34**

Exemption for stabilization measures (Article 5(4))

Article 5(4) sets out the general requirements necessary for stabilization measures not to violate the prohibitions in Articles 14 and 15. Also in this regard, the general characteristics are to establish broad and complete transparency of the stabilization measures to the market[31] and to limit their impact on the market price of the financial instruments in question.[32] These conditions are very similar to those of the (former) Buy-back Programmes and Stabilisation Regulation (Regulation 2273/2003/EC). **B.5.35**

Limitation of the programme (Article 5(4)(a))

The safe harbour of Article 5 requires that the stabilization is carried out for a limited period (Article 5(4)(a)). This so-called stabilization period is set out in **B.5.36**

[28] See art 3 n 52 ff.
[29] See art 3 n 49.
[30] See art 3 n 50.
[31] See n 37 ff.
[32] See n 40.

Article 5 of the Commission Delegated Regulation for Buy-back Programmes and Stabilisation Measures (Regulation 2016/1052/EU) and is limited to thirty days for initial or secondary offerings of shares and up to sixty days for bonds and other forms of securitized debt.

Disclosure of the programme (Article 5(4)(b))

B.5.37 The stabilization measures must be fully disclosed to the market. Pursuant to Article 5(4)(b), all details of the programme must be disclosed prior to the start of trading. If this requirement is complied with, other market participants will have been informed about it and can anticipate that a certain amount of the trading volume in the market will be attributable to the stabilization measures and not to an increasing demand by other market participants.[33] In contrast to buy-back-programmes, the issuer must disclose the information not only before the initial or secondary offering of the securities[34] but also after the execution of the transactions.[35] The details for the disclosure are set out in Article 6(1) of the Commission Delegated Regulation for Buy-back-Programmes and Stabilisation Measures (Regulation 2016/1052/EU).

B.5.38 Before the start of the initial or secondary offering of the securities, the person acting as the central point must, pursuant to Article 6(1) of the Commission Delegated Regulation for Buy-back Programmes and Stabilisation Measures (Regulation 2016/1052/EU), ensure adequate disclosure of:

- the fact that stabilization may not necessarily occur and that it may cease at any time;
- the fact that stabilization transactions aim at supporting the market price of the securities during the stabilization period;
- the beginning and the end of the stabilization period, during which stabilization may be carried out;
- the identity of the entity undertaking the stabilization, unless unknown at the time of disclosure, in which case it shall be subject to adequate public disclosure before the stabilization begins;
- the existence of any overallotment facility or Greenshoe option and the maximum number of securities covered by that facility or option, the period during which the Greenshoe option may be exercised and any conditions for the use of the overallotment facility or exercise of the Greenshoe option; and
- the place where the stabilization may be undertaken including, where relevant, the name of the trading venue(s).

---

33 See n 7 ff for the background of the safe harbour.

34 See n 36.

35 See n 36.

During the stabilization period the person acting as central point shall pursuant to Article 6(2) and (3) of the Commission Delegated Regulation for Buy-back Programmes and Stabilisation Measures (Regulation 2016/1052/EU) within one week of the end of the stabilization period ensure adequate disclosure of: **B.5.39**

- whether or not the stabilization was undertaken;
- the date on which stabilization started;
- the date on which stabilization last occurred;
- the price range within which stabilization was carried out, for each of the dates during which stabilization transactions were carried out; and
- the trading venue(s) on which the stabilization transactions were carried out, where applicable.

See Article 5(5) for further details.

Compliance with adequate limits (Article 5(4)(c))

Stabilization measures must comply with adequate price limits. These price limits are set out in Article 7 of the Commission Delegated Regulation for Buy-back Programmes and Stabilisation Measures (Regulation 2016/1052/EU), which states that the stabilization shall not be carried out above the offering price. In the case of bonds and other forms of securitized debt, the stabilization shall not be carried out above the market price of those instruments at the time of the public disclosure of the final terms of the new offer. **B.5.40**

Compliance with the regulatory technical standards (Article 5(4)(d))

Also, the stabilization measures must, pursuant to Article 5(4)(d), comply with the conditions set out by Article 8 of the Commission Delegated Regulation for Buy-back Programmes and Stabilisation Measures (Regulation 2016/1052/EU). These conditions are that: **B.5.41**

- securities shall be overallotted only during the subscription period and at the offer price;
- a position resulting from the exercise of an overallotment facility by an investment firm or credit institution which is not covered by the Greenshoe option shall not exceed 5 per cent of the original offer;
- the Greenshoe option shall be exercised by the beneficiaries of such an option only where the securities have been overallotted;
- the Greenshoe option shall not amount to more than 15 per cent of the original offer;
- the period during which the Greenshoe option may be exercised shall be the same as the stabilization period pursuant to Article 5;
- the exercise of the Greenshoe option shall be disclosed to the public promptly, together with all appropriate details, including in particular the date of exercise of the option and the number and nature of securities involved.

Reporting requirements for stabilization (Article 5(5))

B.5.42 The reporting requirements set out by Article 5(4)(b) must be fulfilled by the issuer, the offeror, or entities undertaking the stabilization no later than the end of the seventh daily market session following the date of execution of such transactions (Article 5(5)).

Other capital market regulations

B.5.43 The safe harbour for stabilization measures of Article 5(4) does not apply to the public disclosure of inside information, as required by Article 17. Consequently, the execution of stabilization measures in violation of the requirements of Article 17 can be sanctioned by the competent authorities. The disclosure system set out in Article 17 applies even though Article 5(4)(b)[36] and Article 5(1)(b)[37] also establish their own set of rules for the disclosure of the stabilization measures. However, these rules do not affect the requirement of public disclosure of insider information pursuant to Article 17.

B.5.44 Moreover, the safe harbour for stabilization measures of Article 5(4) does not apply to the requirements set out in national law on notification of the acquisition or disposal of major holdings, as provided by the Transparency Directive (2013/50/EU). Therefore, the execution of stabilization measures must comply with these requirements, which usually means that the issuer must publish the information that it reached, exceeded, or fell below the thresholds pursuant to Article 9 of the Transparency Directive (2013/50/EU).

IV. Competence to Develop Regulatory Technical Standards (Article 5(6))

B.5.45 ESMA has, pursuant to Article 5(6), the competence to develop regulatory technical standards to specify the conditions that buy-back programmes and stabilization measures referred to in Article 5(1) and (4) must meet, including conditions for trading, restrictions regarding time and volume, disclosure and reporting obligations, and price conditions. The power to adopt the regulatory technical standard is delegated to the Commission (Article 5(6)(3)). This technical standard (Commission Delegated Regulation (EU) No 2016/1052) was adopted by the Commission on 8 March 2016.

---

[36] See n 37 ff.
[37] See n 18 ff.

Article 6: Exemption for monetary and public debt management activities and climate policy activities

1. This Regulation does not apply to transactions, orders or behaviour, in pursuit of monetary, exchange rate or public debt management policy by:
   (a) a Member State;
   (b) the members of the ESCB;
   (c) a ministry, agency or special purpose vehicle of one or several Member States, or by a person acting on its behalf;
   (d) in the case of a Member State that is a federal state, a member making up the federation.
2. This Regulation does not apply to transactions, orders or behaviour carried out by the Commission or any other officially designated body or by any person acting on its behalf, in pursuit of public debt management policy. This Regulation does not apply to such transactions, orders or behaviour carried out by:
   (a) the Union;
   (b) a special purpose vehicle of one or several Member States;
   (c) the European Investment Bank;
   (d) the European Financial Stability Facility;
   (e) the European Stability Mechanism;
   (f) an international financial institution established by two or more Member States which has the purpose to mobilise funding and provide financial assistance to the benefit of its members that are experiencing or threatened by severe financing problems.
3. This Regulation does not apply to the activity of a Member State, the Commission or any other officially designated body, or of any person acting on their behalf, which concerns emission allowances and which is undertaken in pursuit of the Union's climate policy in accordance with Directive 2003/87/EC.
4. This Regulation does not apply to the activities of a Member State, the Commission or any other officially designated body, or of any person acting on their behalf, that are undertaken in pursuit of the Union's Common Agricultural Policy or of the Union's Common Fisheries Policy in accordance with acts adopted or with international agreements concluded under the TFEU.
5. The Commission shall be empowered to adopt delegated acts in accordance with Article 35 to extend the exemption referred to in paragraph 1 to certain public bodies and central banks of third countries.

To that end, the Commission shall, by 3 January 2016, prepare and present to the European Parliament and to the Council a report assessing the international treatment of public bodies charged with, or intervening in, public debt management and of central banks in third countries.

The report shall include a comparative analysis of the treatment of those bodies and central banks within the legal framework of third countries, and the risk management standards applicable to the transactions entered into by those bodies and central banks in those jurisdictions. If the report concludes, in particular in regard to the comparative analysis, that the exemption of the monetary responsibilities of those third-country central banks from the obligations and prohibitions of this Regulation is necessary the Commission shall extend the exemption referred to in paragraph 1 also to the central banks of those third countries.

6. **The Commission shall also be empowered to adopt delegated acts in accordance with Article 35 to extend the exemption set out in paragraph 3 to certain designated public bodies of third countries that have entered into an agreement with the Union pursuant to Article 25 of Directive 2003/87/EC.**
7. **This Article shall not apply to persons working under a contract of employment or otherwise for the entities referred to in this Article where those persons carry out transactions or orders, or engage in behaviour, directly or indirectly, on their own account.**

Relevant Technical Standards:
Commission Delegated Regulation (EU) 2016/522 of 17 December 2015 supplementing Regulation (EU) No 596/2014 of the European Parliament and of the Council as regards an exemption for certain third countries public bodies and central banks, the indicators of market manipulation, the disclosure thresholds, the competent authority for notifications of delays, the permission for trading during closed periods and types of notifiable managers' transactions (OJ L 88 (5 April 2016) 1).

I. General Principles

Overview

Since Article 2 states that the Market Abuse Regulation applies to all financial instruments admitted to certain markets,[1] it also covers financial instruments being issued by public entities. While there is a need for a prohibition of insider dealing and market manipulation regarding financial instruments being issued by public entities, unlimited application of the Market Abuse Regulation also creates a significant risk for public entities and their representatives to violate these prohibitions. Therefore, Article 6 provides a broad exemption for certain public entities. This value of this privilege is, however, debatable, since it creates a significant risk for market abuse in the markets for these financial instruments and therefore a higher risk of market failure. **B.6.01**

Historical development

The (former) Market Abuse Directive (2003/6/EC) had previously provided in its Article 7 an exemption for transactions carried out in pursuit of monetary, exchange-rate, or public debt-management policy by a Member State, by the European System of Central Banks, by a national central bank, or by any other officially designated body, or indeed by any person acting on their behalf. Moreover, Member States were free to extend this exemption to their federated states or similar local authorities in respect of the management of their public debt. **B.6.02**

II. Exemption of Monetary, Exchange Rate, or Public Debt Management (Article 6(1))

Article 6(1) exempts all transactions, orders, or behaviour, in pursuit of monetary, exchange rate, or public debt management policy by the Member States, the member of European Central Bank (ECB), a ministry, agency, or special purpose vehicle of one or several Member States, or by a person acting on its behalf and in the case of a Member State that is a federal state, a member making up the federation from the application of the Market Abuse Regulation. **B.6.03**

III. Exemption for Transactions, Orders, or Behaviour Carried Out by the Commission (Article 6(2))

Moreover, Article 6(2) exempts all transactions, orders, or behaviour carried out by the Commission or any other officially designated body or by any person **B.6.04**

[1] See art 2 n 3 ff.

acting on its behalf, in pursuit of public debt management policy from the application of the Market Abuse Regulation. Also, all transactions, orders, or behaviour carried out by the Union, a special purpose vehicle of one or several Member States, the European Investment Bank, the European Financial Stability Facility, and the European Stability Mechanism are exempt. Finally, transactions, orders, or behaviour carried out by an international financial institution established by two or more Member States, which is intended to mobilize funding and provide financial assistance for the benefit of its members that are experiencing or threatened by severe financing problems, is also exempt.

IV. Exemption for Climate Policy (Article 6(3))

B.6.05 Activities of Member States, the Commission, or any other officially designated body, or of any person acting on their behalf, which concerns emission allowances and which is undertaken in pursuit of the Union's climate policy in accordance with the Greenhouse Gas Emission Allowances Directive (2003/87/EC) are exempt (Article 6(3)).

V. Exemption for Agricultural and Fisheries Policy (Article 6(4))

B.6.06 Finally, Article 6(4) exempts activities of Member States, the Commission, or any other officially designated body, or of any person acting on their behalf, that are undertaken in pursuit of the Union's Common Agricultural Policy or of the Union's Common Fisheries Policy, in accordance with acts adopted or with international agreements concluded under the Treaty on the Functioning of the European Union (TFEU) from the application of the Market Abuse Regulation.

VI. Adoption of Delegated Acts to Certain Public Bodies and Central Banks of Third Countries (Article 6(5))

B.6.07 Pursuant to Article 6(5)(1), the Commission is empowered to adopt delegated acts to extend the exemption referred to in Article 6(1) to certain bodies and central banks of third countries. Such a delegated act (Commission Delegated Regulation (EU) No 2016/522) was adopted by the Commission on 1 March 2016, extending the exemption to all public bodies and central banks of third countries set out in Annex I of the Commission Delegated Regulation (EU) No 2016/522.

B.6.08 Also, the Commission is obliged—pursuant to Article 6(5)(2)—to prepare and present to the European Parliament and to the Council a report assessing the international treatment of public bodies charged with, or intervening in, public debt management and of central banks in third countries. This report was published on 16 December 2015 (COM(2015) 647 final[2]).

VII. Adoption of Delegated Acts to Public Bodies of Third Countries (Article 6(6))

The Commission is also empowered by Article 6(6) to adopt delegated acts to extend the exemption set out in Article 6(3) to certain designated public bodies of third countries that have entered into an agreement with the Union pursuant to Article 25 of the Greenhouse Gas Emission Allowances Directive (2003/87/EC). To date, the Commission has not adopted such a delegated act. **B.6.09**

VIII. No Application to Persons Working for the Entities (Article 6(7))

Finally, Article 6(7) makes it clear that the exemption of Article 6(1)–(6) does not apply to persons working under a contract of employment or otherwise for the entities referred to in Article 6 where those persons carry out transactions or orders, or engage in behaviour, directly or indirectly, on their own account. Therefore, the Market Abuse Regulation applies within its scope set out in Article 2 to all transactions, orders, or behaviour carried out by these persons on their own account. **B.6.10**

[2] European Commission, Report from the Commission to the European Parliament and the Council 'The international treatment of public bodies charged with, or intervening in, public debt management and of central banks in third countries under Regulation (EU) No 596/2014 on Market Abuse' COM(2015) 647 final.

2

INSIDE INFORMATION, INSIDER DEALING, UNLAWFUL DISCLOSURE OF INSIDE INFORMATION, AND MARKET MANIPULATION

Article 7: Inside information

1. For the purposes of this Regulation, inside information shall comprise the following types of information:
   (a) information of a precise nature, which has not been made public, relating, directly or indirectly, to one or more issuers or to one or more financial instruments, and which, if it were made public, would be likely to have a significant effect on the prices of those financial instruments or on the price of related derivative financial instruments;
   (b) in relation to commodity derivatives, information of a precise nature, which has not been made public, relating, directly or indirectly to one or more such derivatives or relating directly to the related spot commodity contract, and which, if it were made public, would be likely to have a significant effect on the prices of such derivatives or related spot commodity contracts, and where this is information which is reasonably expected to be disclosed or is required to be disclosed in accordance with legal or regulatory provisions at the Union or national level, market rules, contract, practice or custom, on the relevant commodity derivatives markets or spot markets;
   (c) in relation to emission allowances or auctioned products based thereon, information of a precise nature, which has not been made public, relating, directly or indirectly, to one or more such instruments, and which, if it were made public, would be likely to have a significant effect on the prices of such instruments or on the prices of related derivative financial instruments;

(d) for persons charged with the execution of orders concerning financial instruments, it also means information conveyed by a client and relating to the client's pending orders in financial instruments, which is of a precise nature, relating, directly or indirectly, to one or more issuers or to one or more financial instruments, and which, if it were made public, would be likely to have a significant effect on the prices of those financial instruments, the price of related spot commodity contracts, or on the price of related derivative financial instruments.

2. For the purposes of paragraph 1, information shall be deemed to be of a precise nature if it indicates a set of circumstances which exists or which may reasonably be expected to come into existence, or an event which has occurred or which may reasonably be expected to occur, where it is specific enough to enable a conclusion to be drawn as to the possible effect of that set of circumstances or event on the prices of the financial instruments or the related derivative financial instrument, the related spot commodity contracts, or the auctioned products based on the emission allowances. In this respect in the case of a protracted process that is intended to bring about, or that results in, particular circumstances or a particular event, those future circumstances or that future event, and also the intermediate steps of that process which are connected with bringing about or resulting in those future circumstances or that future event, may be deemed to be precise information.
3. An intermediate step in a protracted process shall be deemed to be inside information if, by itself, it satisfies the criteria of inside information as referred to in this article.
4. For the purposes of paragraph 1, information which, if it were made public, would be likely to have a significant effect on the prices of financial instruments, derivative financial instruments, related spot commodity contracts, or auctioned products based on emission allowances shall mean information a reasonable investor would be likely to use as part of the basis of his or her investment decisions.

   In the case of participants in the emission allowance market with aggregate emissions or rated thermal input at or below the threshold set in accordance with the second subparagraph of Article 17(2), information about their physical operations shall be deemed not to have a significant effect on the price of emission allowances, of auctioned products based thereon, or of derivative financial instruments.
5. ESMA shall issue guidelines to establish a non-exhaustive indicative list of information which is reasonably expected or is required to be disclosed in accordance with legal or regulatory provisions in Union or national law, market rules, contract, practice or custom, on the relevant commodity derivatives markets or spot markets as referred to in point (b) of paragraph 1. ESMA shall duly take into account specificities of those markets.

I. General Remarks

Overview of Article 7 *

For the purposes of the Market Abuse Regulation, inside information is defined as information of a precise nature concerning directly or indirectly one or more issuers or one or more financial instruments, which has not been made public yet and which, if it were made public, would be likely to have a significant effect on the price of the financial instruments it refers to or on that of the related derivative securities. **B.7.01**

* Although this comment is the result of the discussion among the authors, paragraphs B.7.08–B.7.24 (Historical development), paragraphs B.7.31–B.7.48 (Information of a precise nature) and paragraphs B.7.75–B.7.82 (Concluding Remarks) shall be attributed to Chiara Picciau, whilst paragraphs B.7.01 (Overview of Article 7), B.7.02–B.7.07 (Structure of Article 7), B.7.25–B.7.30 (Introduction), and B.7.49–B.7.74 (Non-public information; Price-sensitive information) shall be attributed to Marco Ventoruzzo.

Structure of Article 7

The four constitutive elements

B.7.02 Taking over the wording of former Article 1(1) Market Abuse Implementation Directive (2003/124/EC),[1] Article 7(2) further specifies that information may be deemed to be of a precise nature when it indicates a set of circumstances which exists or may reasonably be expected to come into existence or an event which has already occurred or which may reasonably be expected to occur in the future. As in the past, the information must also be specific enough as to enable a conclusion on its possible effect on the prices of the financial instruments concerned. In addition, however, it is now expressly provided that in case of protracted processes, such as a merger, intermediate steps may be deemed to have a precise nature themselves and that, if all other requirements are met, they can also be considered inside information.

B.7.03 Article 7(4) also clarifies that in order to evaluate whether the information is likely to have a significant effect on prices, the interpreter shall consider whether a reasonable investor would be likely to take the information into consideration when making an investment decision.

B.7.04 The price sensitivity is indeed the fourth element of the definition, which in sum basically requires the information (i) to be precise; (ii) to be non-public; (iii) to concern directly or indirectly one or more issuers, financial instruments, or related financial products; and, as anticipated, (iv) to be likely to have a significant price effect on the instruments, meaning that a reasonable investor would likely take the information into account in her investment decisions.

Information on commodity derivatives and emission allowances

B.7.05 The definition also covers information on commodity derivatives and emission allowances or auctioned products based on emission allowances.

[1] Reference is to the different 'levels' of the Lamfalussy procedure adopted within the EU law-making process in compliance with the *Final Report of the Committee of Wise Men on the Regulation of European Securities Markets* (Brussels, 15 February 2001). On the evolution of the market abuse regime and on the adoption of the Lamfalussy model see Jesper Lau Hansen, 'Say When: When Must an Issuer Disclose Inside Information?' Nordic & European Company Law Working Paper No 16-03 (19 September 2016), 5 https://papers.ssrn.com/sol3/papers.cfm?abstract_id=2795993 (last accessed 12 November 2016); Niamh Moloney, *EU Securities and Financial Markets Regulation* (3rd edn, OUP 2014) 706–12; Carmine Di Noia and Matteo Gargantini, 'Issuers at Midstream: Disclosure of Multistage Events in the Current and in the Proposed EU Market Abuse Regime' (2012) 9 European Company and Financial Law Review 484, 487–9; Mathias M Siems and Matthijs Nelemans, 'The Reform of the EU Market Abuse Law: Revolution or Evolution?' (2012) 19 Maastricht Journal of European and Comparative Law 195, 196; Mathias M Siems, 'The EU Market Abuse Directive: A Case-based Analysis' (2008) 2 Law and Financial Markets Review 39; Panagiotis K Staikouras, 'Four Years of MADness? The New Market Abuse Prohibition Revisited: Integrated Implementation Through the Lens of a Critical, Comparative Analysis' (2008) 19 European Business Law Review 775, 776.

For commodity derivatives, Article 7(1)(b) specifies that the information must be of such type and nature that it is reasonably expected to be disclosed, or required to be disclosed, according to binding legal or regulatory provisions established either at the Union or at the national level, or in any case according to other relevant rules, which, for instance, could be found in market practices, customs, or contractual undertakings. The additional element is, therefore, that the information must concern data, facts, events, or circumstances that market participants may reasonably expect to receive or to be made aware of, either because of market practices and customs or by virtue of binding provisions. Article 7 maintains the reference to accepted market practices that, under the previous regime, had originated some criticism, given the uncertainty as to under which circumstances market participants would reasonably expect to receive the information.[2] However, Article 7(5) allows for Level 3 guidance on the subject and recently, in order to dispel these doubts, ESMA published a non-exhaustive list of information that market operators can reasonably expect to obtain or which is required to be disclosed in accordance with legal or regulatory provisions or with market rules, practices or customs.[3] Essentially the list includes both information that (also indirectly) relates to commodity derivative contracts, including, for example, stock levels of commodities in warehouses or changes in the underlying commodity specifications, and information that (only directly) relates to spot commodity contracts, such as communications on production levels issued by conferences of oil producing countries. **B.7.06**

The inclusion of emission allowances and related auctioned products has, instead, been introduced by the Market Abuse Regulation, provided that under the MiFID II these products of the spot segment of the carbon market are, in fact, expressly classified as financial instruments.[4] In this regard, the Market Abuse Regulation merely restates the general definition. **B.7.07**

Historical development

The twofold notion of inside information

The notion of inside information, broken down in its four components, is obviously a central element of the Market Abuse Regulation.[5] Within the new legislative **B.7.08**

---

[2] See Niamh Moloney, *EC Securities Regulation* (2nd edn, OUP 2008) 960–1.

[3] See the 'Final Report. Guidelines on MAR – Information relating to commodity derivatives markets or related spot markets for the purpose of the definition of inside information on commodity derivatives' ESMA/2016/1412 (30 September 2016), which contains the results of the public consultation on the subject and the related final guidelines.

[4] Annex I, Section C, No 11, Markets in Financial Instruments Directive II (2014/65/EU). In this regard see also Stefano Lombardo, 'L'informazione privilegiata' (2016) Le Società 147, 151, and the Consultation Paper on 'ESMA's guidelines on information expected or required to be disclosed on commodity derivatives markets or related spot markets under MAR', 30 March 2016, ESMA/2016/444, at 13.

[5] See Moloney, *EU Securities* (n 1) 717, observing that the definition of inside information is 'at the heart' of the insider dealing prohibition; and Christian Kersting, 'Insider Dealing and Ad

framework on market abuses, other Market Abuse Regulation provisions rely on this definition. It constitutes the basis for both the issuer's disclosure obligations and the insider dealing prohibition and now it is also used to regulate the unlawful disclosure of inside information pursuant to Article 10. In addition, the definition of inside information is employed by the Market Abuse Directive on Criminal Sanctions (2014/57/EU), which introduced a harmonized European framework for criminal offences committed using inside information or consisting in prohibited market manipulation conducts.[6]

B.7.09 According to some commentators, under the Market Abuse Implementation Directive (2003/124/EC), disclosure obligations arose only after the set of circumstances or the event the information referred to came into existence, while the insider dealing prohibition covered also information concerning future circumstances and events, regardless of whether they would actually happen at a later time.[7]

B.7.10 At the European level, this interpretation was justified on the basis of the text of Article 2(2) Market Abuse Implementation Directive (2003/124/EC), according to which issuers could be deemed to have complied with their disclosure obligations under the (former) Market Abuse Directive (2003/6/EC)[8] 'where, upon the coming into existence of a set of circumstances or the occurrence of an event, albeit not yet formalised, the issuers have promptly informed the public thereof'.

B.7.11 Correspondingly, some Member States including the UK, Italy, Spain, Sweden, and Finland adopted a twofold definition of inside information; one applicable to disclosure obligations, and one to the insider dealing prohibition.[9] To offer an

Hoc Disclosure Requirements in the New EU Market Abuse Regulation' (2014) 33 Banking & Financial Services Policy Report 15, 16, according to whom 'the notion of inside information continues to be a key issue under the draft MAR'.

[6] See art 2(4) Market Abuse Directive on Criminal Sanctions (2014/57/EU). On the criminal offences under the new market abuse framework see Francesco Mucciarelli, '*L'insider trading* nella rinnovata disciplina UE sugli abusi di mercato' (2016) Le Società 193. Recently, for further discussion on the limits in the harmonization of the national criminal provisions on insider dealing with regard to the right of defence and the presumption of innocence see Jochem Reichert, 'Die Kausalität von Insiderinformationen—Entwicklungsstufen eines „europäischen" Tatbestandsmerkmals: Von der Insiderrichtlinie (1989) zur Marktmissbrauchsverordnung (2014)' in Cordula Stumpf, Friedemann Kainer, and Christian Baldus (eds), *Privatrecht, Wirtschaftsrecht, Verfassungsrecht. Festschrift für Müller-Graff* (Nomos 2015) especially at 325–7.

[7] In this sense see Filippo Annunziata, 'Riflessi organizzativi della rinnovata disciplina in materia di *market abuse*' (2016) Le Società 169, 175; Jesper Lau Hansen and David Moalem, 'The MAD Disclosure Regime and the Twofold Notion of Inside Information: The Available Solution' (2009) 4 Capital Markets Law Journal 323, 329.

[8] See art 6(1) (former) Market Abuse Directive (2003/6/EC).

[9] See Hansen, 'Say When' (n 1) 7–8; Kersting, 'Insider Dealing' (n 5) 15; Hartmut Krause and Michael Brellochs, 'Insider Trading and the Disclosure of Inside Information after *Geltl v Daimler*—A Comparative Analysis of the ECJ Decision in the *Geltl v Daimler* Case with a View to the Future European Market Abuse Regulation' (2013) 8 Capital Markets Law Journal 283, 296–7; Di Noia and Gargantini, 'Issuers at Midstream' (n 1) 510–14; Hansen and Moalem, 'The MAD Disclosure Regime' (n 7) 329.

example, under Italian law, Article 181 of the Consolidated Law on Finance[10] adopted a single concept of inside information, theoretically triggering both the insider dealing prohibition, and the issuer's disclosure obligations. However, the Italian supervisory authority, Consob, in its implementing rules and interpretative releases expressly endorsed a two-step definition, according to which, for disclosure obligations, the notion of inside information had to be construed narrowly. More specifically, Article 66, para 1, of Consob Regulation No 11971 of 14 May 1999, as subsequently amended, mirrored the text of Article 2(2) Market Abuse Implementation Directive (2003/124/EC) by expressly providing that the issuer complied with the continuous disclosure obligations when, upon the coming into existence of a set of circumstances or the occurrence of an event, the issuer had promptly informed the public.[11] In addition, in its interpretative documents Consob clarified that only information on circumstances and events that reached a high degree of certainty met this threshold, even though full formalization was not strictly necessary.[12] In Spain the distinction was instead set forth at the statutory level. Articles 81 and 82 of Law No 24/1998 distinguished the concept of '*información privilegiada*' for the ban on insider dealing, and of '*información relevante*' as the subject of the issuer's disclosure obligations. The difference was that the latter was limited to information on events and circumstances that reached a significant level of advancement and development.[13]

The Market Abuse Regulation, however, does not allow a similar conclusion; nor does it contain a provision similar to Article 2(2) Market Abuse Implementation Directive (2003/124/EC). The ambiguity appears therefore to be resolved.[14]

[10] The so-called '*Testo Unico della Finanza*': Italian legislative decree of 24 February 1998, No 58, as subsequently amended.

[11] For the sake of completeness, notice that on 24 October 2016 Consob opened a public consultation on proposed amendments and modifications to its implementing rules in order to comply with the new market abuse framework established by the Market Abuse Regulation: Consob, 'Proposta di modifica dei regolamenti di attuazione del decreto legislativo 24 febbraio 1998, n. 58, concernenti la disciplina degli emittenti e dei mercati, nonché del regolamento in materia di operazioni con parti correlate, per l'attuazione del Regolamento (UE) n. 596/2014 in materia di abusi di mercato' http://www.consob.it/documents/46180/46181/cons_MAR_20161024.pdf/2abb0fd4-00bc-4090-aa19-d7d2e9f11c5c (last accessed 18 November 2016). In this context, Consob proposed to repeal almost the entire text of art 66 of Regulation No 11971 of 14 May 1999, as subsequently amended, including the provision mentioned in the text.

[12] Consob, Communication No DME/6027054 of 28 March 2006, para 5.

[13] Cf art 6, para 1, Royal Decree No 1333, of 11 November 2005, implementing Law No 24/1998, according to which: 'La comunicación a la CNMV deberá hacerse tan pronto como sea conocido el hecho o en cuanto se haya adoptado la decisión o firmado el acuerdo o contrato con terceros de que se trate, sin perjuicio de que, en estos últimos casos, pueda efectuarse con anterioridad si el emisor estima que ello no lesiona sus legítimos intereses o en cumplimiento de lo previsto en el artículo 83 bis 1.f.) de la Ley 24/1988, de 28 de julio'. In this regard see also Di Noia and Gargantini, 'Issuers at Midstream' (n 1) 510, especially at fn 84.

[14] At first the Commission planned to maintain such a twofold structure for the definition of inside information. As a matter of fact, in recital (14) of the Draft Market Abuse Regulation, 2011/0295 (COD), of 20 October 2011, the Commission observed that inside information can be abused before issuers are under the obligation to disclose it, because contractual terms and conditions or the state of negotiations can be relevant for investment choices also if they do not

The main consequence will probably be, at least in some Member States, an anticipation of the moment when an issuer is required to disclose information and, eventually, a broader use of the option to delay the public disclosure according to Article 17(4).

History and evolution of the definition of inside information

B.7.12 Notwithstanding this and other important innovations that we will discuss below, the new definition of inside information is largely shaped on the previous definitions set forth by the Insider Dealing Directive (1989/592/EEC) and by the (former) Market Abuse Directive (2003/6/EC), as complemented by the Market Abuse Implementation Directive (2003/124/EC).

B.7.13 The Insider Trading Directive (1989/592/EEC) of 1989 referred to precise, non-public, price-sensitive information concerning issuers of transferrable securities or transferrable securities. The relevant securities were expressly listed in the directive and consisted essentially in shares, bonds, and debentures, contracts or rights to subscribe, acquire, or dispose of, shares and debt securities, as well as future contracts, options, financial futures, and index contracts that had been admitted to trading on a regulated market.[15]

B.7.14 With minor amendments, the same definition was adopted by the (former) Market Abuse Directive (2003/6/EC). This piece of legislation still required inside information to be precise, non-public, and price sensitive. The reference to transferrable securities was, however, replaced with the broader notion of 'financial instruments', which included all instruments admitted to trading on a regulated market or for which a request of admission to trading on a regulated market had been presented.[16]

B.7.15 The precision and the price sensitivity requirements were further specified through Level 2 implementing measures introducing for the first time the concept of 'reasonable expectation' for information on future events and the 'reasonable investor' criterion as a tool to establish the likelihood of a 'price effect'. Interestingly enough, the price effect was, in fact, linked to the alleged relevance

meet the precision requirement. Accordingly, the definition of inside information should have been widened only for the purposes of the insider dealing prohibition. On this initial proposal see Siems and Nelemans, 'The Reform of the EU Market Abuse Law' (n 1) 201. For further discussion see also Kersting, 'Insider Dealing' (n 5) 17, and, more recently, Hansen, 'Say When' (n 1) 19–27.

[15] In this regard see Paul L Davies, 'The European Community's Directive on Insider Dealing: From Company Law to Securities Markets Regulation?' (1991) 11 Oxford Journal of Legal Studies 92, 101–3; Klaus J Hopt, 'The European Insider Dealing Directive' (1990) 27 Common Market Law Review 51, especially at 57–61; David Moalem and Jesper Lau Hansen, 'Insider Dealing and Parity of Information—Is *Georgakis* Still Valid?' (2008) 19 European Business Law Review 949, 950–1.

[16] See art 1(1) (former) Market Abuse Directive (2003/6/EC). The complete list of financial instruments comprised in the scope of the (former) Market Abuse Directive (2003/6/EC) was provided by art 1(3). It also included, for instance, units in collective undertakings, money-market instruments, and several types of derivatives, such as derivatives on commodities.

of the information for the investment decisions of a reasonable investor.[17] However, no clarification on the notion of 'reasonable investor' was provided. What is nonetheless noticeable is that since the first discipline on insider dealing, inside information has always been defined as precise, not public, and likely to have a significant effect on market prices. These elements have, in fact, now been transposed into the text of Article 7, which extends the scope of the definition to securities traded on multilateral trading facilities (MTFs) and other organized trading facilities (the so-called OTFs) or for which a request for admission on MTFs has been made,[18] in order to include new types of trading venues.[19]

The impact of the ECJ case law on the definition of inside information

The main textual innovation of the definition, however, concerns the explicit reference to the relevance of intermediate steps in a protracted process, which appears to be a codification of the ECJ decision in *Geltl v Daimler*.[20] The issue of the case was the application of the definition of inside information to the determination of Mr Jürgen Schrempp to resign early from the chairmanship of the management board of Daimler AG.[21] More precisely, the ECJ addressed whether in case of a protracted process, such as a director's voluntary termination from office, 'not only may the future circumstance or event be regarded as precise information ... but also the intermediate steps of that process which already exist or have already occurred and which are connected with bringing about the future circumstance or event'.[22] The affirmative response of the Court has now been transposed into Article 7(2). **B.7.16**

---

[17] See art 1 Market Abuse Implementation Directive (2003/124/EC).

[18] See art 2(1)(b) and (c). On the need to extend the scope of application of the Market Abuse Regulation to MTFs and OTFs as a means to enhance investor protection cf also recital (8).

[19] Cf Siems and Nelemans, 'The Reform of the EU Market Abuse Law' (n 1) 204.

[20] Case C-19/11 *Markus Geltl v Daimler AG* [2012] ECLI:EU:C:2012:397. For a description of the facts of the case and a comment on the decision see Hansen, 'Say When' (n 1) 10–13; Krause and Brellochs, 'Insider Trading and the Disclosure of Inside Information' (n 9); Alexander Hellgardt, 'The Notion of Inside Information in the Market Abuse Directive: *Geltl*' (2013) 50 Common Market Law Review 861.

[21] The facts of the case are well known: following a general meeting of Daimler AG held on 6 April 2005, Mr Schrempp started thinking about resigning from the office of chairman and director of the management board of the company before the expiry of his mandate in 2008. At first, he shared thoughts only with his wife. Then, on 17 May 2005 he talked to the chairman of the supervisory board about his intentions and in the months of June and July 2005 other members of the supervisory board were made aware of Mr Schrempp's plan to resign. Accordingly, on 10 July 2005 Daimler AG started working on a press release to inform the company's employees about Mr Schrempp's intendment and three days later the meetings of the presidential committee of the supervisory board and of the supervisory board itself were formally convened (even though no information on Mr Schrempp's resignation was given on their agenda). Mr Schrempp finally resigned as director of Daimler AG and was substituted by a decision of the supervisory board on 28 July 2005. Public notice of his resignation was given only at this point.

[22] See *Markus Geltl v Daimler AG* (n 20) para 27. In order to justify this interpretation, the ECJ referred to the previous wording of the (former) Market Abuse Directive (2003/6/EC), to the examples of inside information provided by art 3(1) Market Abuse Implementation Directive (2003/124/EC), which already included intermediate steps in protracted processes, and to the general regulatory aim of the market abuse discipline (see paras 31–40 of the decision).

B.7.17 Indeed, over the years, the ECJ examined on several occasions the outer boundaries of the notion of inside information, clarifying, for example, when an insider commits an infringement of the insider dealing prohibition by trading in possession of inside information, as in *Spector Photo Group NV v CBFA*,[23] or when a non-public piece of information may be deemed to be of a precise nature, as in *Lafonta v Autorité des marchés financiers*.[24] We will come back in due course to these landmark decisions; for now we simply want to underline that they continue to be relevant in the interpretation of Article 7, because even if rendered before the enactment of the currently applicable body of law, they refer to provisions and concepts that have not been substantively altered by the new rules.

The application of pre-existing Level 3 guidance under the Market Abuse Regulation

B.7.18 By the same token, prior Level 3 guidelines will continue to provide useful guidance in shaping the notion of inside information. Reference is to be made, for instance, to the advice reports issued under the (former) Market Abuse Directive (2003/6/EC) by the Committee of European Securities Regulators (CESR), now substituted by ESMA, on the Commission's prospective Level 2 implementing measures; and to all published Level 3 guidance and information documents for issuers and market operators which dealt with the interpretative issues arisen in connection with the (former) Market Abuse Directive (2003/6/EC).[25]

---

[23] Case C-45/08 *Spector Photo Group NV v CBFA* [2009] ECLI:EU:C:2009:806. On this ECJ decision see also Justice Mary Arden, 'Spector Photo Group and Its Wider Implications', Keynote Address at the UCL Laws Conference on Corporate Finance Law: UK and EU Perspectives (28 April 2010) (2010) 7 European Company and Financial Law Review 342; Jesper Lau Hansen, 'Insider Dealing Defined: The EU Court's Decision in *Spector Photo Group*' (2010) 7 European Company Law 98. For a critical opinion towards the ECJ's decision see, recently, Reichert, 'Die Kausalität von Insiderinformationen' (n 6) 323–5.

[24] Case C-628/13 *Lafonta v Autorité des marchés financiers* [2015] ECLI:EU:C:2015:162. For more detail on the facts of the case and a comment see Lars Klöhn, 'Inside Information without an Incentive to Trade? What's at Stake in "*Lafonta v AMF*"' (2015) 10 Capital Markets Law Journal 162; Toni Atrigna, 'Il carattere preciso dell'informazione privilegiata secondo la Corte di Giustizia UE: osservazioni alla sentenza 11 marzo 2015, Seconda Sezione, nella causa C-628/13' (2015) Banca borsa titoli di credito 656.

[25] In the current regulatory framework, Level 1 measures of the European law-maker may be supplemented by Level 2 rules, adopted by the European Commission if so authorized by Level 1 legislation, and ESMA, in turn, may advise the Commission with respect to the preparation of Level 2 measures. The legal basis for this rulemaking procedure is set forth by arts 289–291 of the Treaty on the Functioning of the European Union. Note, in particular, that, according to arts 10–15 of ESMA's founding Regulation (Regulation (EU) No 1095/2010), ESMA may draft delegated or implementing technical standards that are then submitted to the Commission for endorsement. In addition, further guidance, instructions and recommendations can be issued at Level 3 by ESMA (and previously CESR). These Level 3 measures foster convergence on the part of national supervisory authorities and provide useful indications to all market participants. They are essentially non-binding guidelines and advice. However, art 16(3) of Regulation (EU) No 1095/2010 provides that '[t]he competent authorities and financial market participants shall make every effort to comply with those guidelines and recommendations'. For further discussion see Marloes van Rijsbergen, 'On the Enforceability of EU Agencies' Soft Law at the National Level: The Case of the European Securities and Markets Authority' (2014) 10 Utrecht

One of the most important interpretative releases is the 'Second set of CESR Guidance on the Operation of the Market Abuse Directive' of 2007,[26] which laid down the different criteria that identify the concept of inside information. **B.7.19**

In addition, after ESMA took over from CESR, further guidance and implementation measures have been adopted.[27] An example regarding directly the notion of inside information is given by the mentioned guidelines on information concerning commodity derivative markets or related spot markets that were first published on 30 September 2016. **B.7.20**

Preliminary conclusions

As discussed, the Market Abuse Regulation has not significantly changed the definition of inside information. The wording of Article 7 essentially corresponds to the pre-existing versions of Article 1 (former) Market Abuse Directive (2003/6/EC) and Article 1 Market Abuse Implementation Directive (2003/124/EC); the only significant addition being the explicit reference to information on intermediate steps of a protracted process. However, this addition is consistent with, or rather derived from, the ECJ's interpretation of the 'precision' requirement in *Geltl v Daimler*, as well as with earlier CESR guidance on the same issue.[28] Even under the previous market abuse regime each intermediate step of a multi-staged event could in fact, along with its outcome, be deemed sufficiently precise and therefore be subject to disclosure obligations or trade bans. **B.7.21**

Accordingly, the new notion of inside information can be considered the result of an evolutionary process, stemming from judicial interpretation and market authorities' practical instructions. However, it might be also argued that the Market Abuse Regulation missed the opportunity to address some open issues on the constitutive elements of the definition, such as the extent to which the direction and magnitude of the price effect need to be ascertainable in advance, or who is the proverbial 'reasonable investor'. **B.7.22**

On a different note, the provision of a uniform definition directly applicable in all Member States could grant a higher degree of consistency in enforcement within the European Union. The introduction at the national level of a twofold definition of inside information, distinguishing disclosure obligations and prohibitions to trade, seems to be no longer permitted. The greater harmonization is consistent **B.7.23**

Law Review 116. More generally see Edoardo Chiti, 'European Agencies' Rulemaking: Powers, Procedures and Assessment' (2013) 19 European Law Journal 93.

[26] CESR/06-562b (July 2007).

[27] See eg the Market Abuse Regulation Guidelines on 'Persons receiving market soundings' (ESMA/2016/1477, 20 October 2016) and on the 'Delay in the disclosure of inside information' (ESMA/2016/1478, 20 October 2016).

[28] CESR, 'Level 3 second set of CESR guidance and information on the common operation of the Directive to the market' CESR/06-562b (July 2007) para 1.6.

with the choice of a regulation, instead of a directive.[29] More generally, this regulatory approach epitomizes the goal of promoting convergence through directly applicable provisions and of reducing the flexibility granted to Member States in adopting implementing measures.[30]

B.7.24 Needless to say, divergent national interpretations of the now uniform definition of inside information are, however, still possible and indeed probable, considering also the different levels of development of European capital markets and that, while some key concepts remain undefined, the Market Abuse Regulation will be enforced by the competent national authorities and by the courts of each Member State.[31]

II. Constitutive Elements of the (Reformed) Definition of Inside Information

Introduction

The definition in context: the rationale for market abuse rules and the interpretation of Article 7

B.7.25 The definition of inside information is essential to determine the scope of market abuse and, especially, the extension of the insider dealing prohibition and of the disclosure obligations. In the prospective of future reforms one could, in fact, always question whether a broad or a narrow notion of inside information is preferable.[32]

---

[29] Annunziata, 'Riflessi organizzativi' (n 7) 169; Lombardo, 'L'informazione privilegiata' (n 4) 147–8. Observing that the same regulatory aim could have been pursued by transforming all 'Level 2' measures into regulations, in order to ensure greater stability to the regulatory framework see Di Noia and Gargantini, 'Issuers at Midstream' (n 1) 490.

[30] See on this subject Paul L Davies and Sarah Worthington, *Gower's Principles of Modern Company Law* (10th edn, Sweet & Maxwell 2016) para 30-30, arguing that the main innovation of the Market Abuse Regulation may be represented by the choice to remove the need for domestic transposition, which brings about major changes in the structure, but not in the substance, of domestic laws on market abuses. In general, for an analysis of the level of harmonization in EU capital markets regulation, also with an eye to the previous market abuse regime cf Carsten Gerner-Beuerle, 'United in Diversity: Maximum versus Minimum Harmonization in EU Securities Regulation' (2012) 7 Capital Markets Law Journal 317, 327–33.

[31] Siems and Nelemans, 'The Reform of the EU Market Abuse Law' (n 1) 197; Krause and Brellochs, 'Insider Trading and the Disclosure of Inside Information' (n 9) 299.

[32] For instance, if a new regulatory intervention aimed at strongly reducing insiders' opportunities to trade on inside information, the adoption of a broad definition would probably be preferable, because this would avoid 'type II errors', meaning the risk of not detecting the prohibited abusive trading conduct. Instead, from the perspective of the enforcement of disclosure obligations, it would make sense to narrowly construct the elements of the definition in order to avoid that the disclosure of irrelevant, still inaccurate, or underdeveloped information caused noise on the market. Clearly, these observations could also eventually justify a proposal to adopt, at the legislative level, a twofold notion of inside information, on the assumption that it would be desirable (or more effective) to distinguish when the insider dealing ban applies from the moment in which the issuer's disclosure obligations arise.

However, from a purely interpretative standpoint what matters is that market abuse rules and prohibitions, albeit having their own specific grounds, serve the same general purpose.[33]

Market abuse rules have been traditionally justified with the need to ensure the integrity of the financial markets and the public confidence in their proper functioning.[34] Indeed, the ban on insider dealing has often been explained with the principle of equal access,[35] meaning that in order to enhance market confidence investors must be put on a level playing field; and the same rationale lies behind other market abuse prohibitions and, especially, behind the continuous disclosure obligations. It is true that disclosure obligations help preventing insider dealing in the sense that once information is communicated to the public it ceases to be 'monopolistic'.[36] However, they mainly pursue the broader objective of ensuring market integrity and transparency, by giving investors access to information that is material for investment choices. The law-maker considers, in fact, market transparency essential for economic growth and job creating,[37] since it functions as a general 'prerequisite' for confidence on the part of market actors and companies' shareholders.[38] **B.7.26**

Hence, also in the field of market abuse, the European financial regulation and supervision grew at many different interconnected levels that shifted from the simple control and prevention of isolated phenomena to a more comprehensive discipline of the financial sector which aims at ensuring market integrity and public confidence in the financial markets.[39] From a systematic standpoint, **B.7.27**

---

33 See Hansen, 'Say When' (n 1) 4–5.

34 For instance, recital (7) clearly specifies that insider dealing, unlawful disclosure of inside information and market manipulation prevent 'full and proper market transparency, which is a prerequisite for trading for all economic actors in integrated financial markets'. On the subject, also *Spector Photo Group NV v CBFA* (n 23) paras 37 and 47; *Markus Geltl v Daimler AG* (n 20) para 33. On the contrary see Hellgardt, 'The Notion of Inside Information' (n 20) 861–2, who claims that the decision of the ECJ in *Geltl v Daimler* 'clearly endorsed the goal of preventing insider dealing as the leading principle of all insider law' (at 867–8).

35 *Spector Photo Group NV v CBFA* (n 23) paras 47–9; *Markus Geltl v Daimler AG* (n 20) para 33; Case C-384/02 *Grøngaard and Bang* [2005] ECLI:EU:C:2005:708 paras 22–4. Note that within the framework of the Insider Trading Directive (1989/592/EEC) of 1989 the ECJ essentially held that the infringement of the insider dealing prohibition could be avoided by disclosing the inside information to the other trading party: Case C-391/04 *Ipourgos Ikonomikon v Georgakis* [2007] ECLI:EU:C:2007:272. In the legal doctrine see, for instance, Moalem and Hansen, 'Insider Dealing and Parity of Information' (n 15) especially at 956 and 965; Lars Klöhn, 'The European Insider Trading Regulation after *Spector Photo Group*' (2010) 7 European Company and Financial Law Review 347, 354; Marco Ventoruzzo, 'Comparing Insider Trading in the United States and in the European Union: History and Recent Developments' (2014) 11 European Company and Financial Law Review 554, 574–9.

36 See Hansen, 'Say When' (n 1) 5. See also Davies and Worthington, *Gower's Principles* (n 30) paras 26–5, who argue that the continuous disclosure obligation is also a 'way of depriving the information of its "inside" character' and therefore of preventing insider dealing behaviours.

37 See recitals (1), (2), and (7).

38 See recital (58).

39 Market abuse prohibitions (and especially the ban on insider dealing) in European law have developed from the concept of fiduciary duties to a broader market-based approach, aimed at

therefore, the definition of inside information should be interpreted according to these general policy objectives.

A testing ground: the definition applied to the 'insider of himself'

B.7.28 The wider rationale for market abuse rules is also shown by the case in which the insider is the direct source of the information and thus acts as an 'insider of himself'. Basically, this occurs when the person dealing with the inside information is the one that created it or is the very subject of the information, either because the information is the result of his or her own research or because it concerns directly his or her own decisions, plans, intentions, or personal situation. To some extent, *Geltl v Daimler* provides an example, as Mr Schrempp was an insider of himself with regard to his decision, later qualified as inside information, to early resign from the appointment as chairman and director of the management board of Daimler AG. More generally, however, the problem is well illustrated by personal determinations or conditions upon which the insider acts on the market, as will be if the chief executive officer of a listed company sold her shares knowing that she will soon have to resign due to personal reasons. Assuming that the decision to sell the shares was driven by the fact that the insider expected the market to react negatively to her resignation, the insider dealing prohibition would most likely apply because the insider was able to exploit an 'unfair' advantage over other market participants.[40] One could also argue that this would

correcting information asymmetries with regulation. In this regard see Moloney, *EU Securities* (n 1) 700–3; Moalem and Hansen, 'Insider Dealing and Parity of Information' (n 15) 959–61. In the UK, the shift towards the market-based approach has become quite noticeable after the enactment of the Insider Trading Directive (1989/592/EEC). See eg Davies, 'The European Community's Directive' (n 15) 103, who observed that one of the main effects of the Directive was that of putting an emphasis on the protection of the integrity of the financial markets, rather than on the safeguard of the interests of companies, which had been predominant in the early discussion on the subject, at least in the UK. Originally, in fact, the purpose of insider dealing laws in the UK was generally found in the regulation of certain corporate relationships, mainly of fiduciary character, rather than in the regulation of market exchanges, irrespective of the existence of any fiduciary duty towards the issuer. These doubts have been definitively dispelled when the (former) Market Abuse Directive (2003/6/EC) repealed the Insider Trading Directive (1989/592/EEC). The (former) Market Abuse Directive (2003/6/EC) was, in fact, part of a broader project carried out through the EU Financial Services Action Plan (FSAP) of 1999. The aim of the FSAP was to foster the creation of a single market, through the enactment of several interconnected measures. Part of the plan, was, for instance, a more comprehensive regulation on market abuses, prospectuses, transparency, settlement of securities, accounting techniques, corporate insolvency and so on. For a comparative analysis on the evolution of the insider dealing prohibition in the US, the UK, Australia, and Singapore see Alexander F Loke, 'From the Fiduciary Theory to Information Abuse: The Changing Fabric of Insider Trading Law in the UK, Australia and Singapore' (2006) 54 American Journal of Comparative Law 123.

[40] In the opposite sense seems Mucciarelli, '*L'insider trading*' (n 6) 199, who claims that according to art 7 the information must come from 'outside' the insider. Cf on this subject, under the previous regulatory framework, Antonio Morello, 'L'insider che crea ed utilizza l'informazione privilegiata: uso o abuso' (2013) Rivista di diritto bancario http://www.dirittobancario.it/sites/default/files/allegati/morello_a._linsider_che_crea_ed_utilizza_linformazione_privilegiata_uso_o_abuso_2013.pdf (last accessed 19 November 2016).

probably be excessively penalizing for the insider, given that she would be prevented not only to act, for instance, on the basis of corporate operations and issuer-specific facts that she knows because of her relation with the issuer, but also, for instance, on the basis of personal knowledge or conditions that she created or that she even has no control of. However, market transparency could still be hindered if any insider could act on private information on personal situations or decisions that potentially affect the price of the issuer's financial instruments. Indeed, if 'personal' information has the distinctive features of inside information it would be difficult to argue that it should not be included in the scope of the insider dealing prohibition or that it should not be publicly disclosed. Again, in this specific regard *Geltl v Daimler* provides an interesting example.

Market transparency considerations support, however, a somewhat different conclusion for a particular type of information that is the result of personal enquiries. Certain research activities and estimates, in fact, do not fall within the definition of inside information when they are based on publicly available data.[41] By according a more favourable treatment to valuable research and estimates conducted elaborating public data, the law-maker implies that parity of information must be ensured rather upstream and that because they are based on publicly available information these activities do not hinder market transparency. **B.7.29**

Nevertheless, the relevant assessment shall be conducted on a case-by-case basis.[42] The vanishing boundary between inside information on issuers and financial instruments under Article 7, on the one hand, and other personal or private information that, albeit indirectly referring to one of the two, does not qualify as inside information, on the other hand, requires a highly factual analysis in compliance with the four criteria that will now be examined in detail. **B.7.30**

Information of a precise nature

Subject and general understanding of the precision requirement

The justification for requiring a minimum degree of accuracy of information is rooted in the same theoretical foundations that sustain the law as a whole. **B.7.31**

[41] See recital (28). However, in certain cases, even research activities and estimates based on public data could be deemed to be inside information. The recital specifies in this regard that: 'where the publication or distribution of information is routinely expected by the market and where such publication or distribution contributes to the price-formation process of financial instruments, or the information provides views from a recognised market commentator or institution which may inform the prices of related financial instruments, the information may constitute inside information'. Accordingly, the Italian Supreme Cassation Court qualified as inside information a text message concerning the upcoming publication and the results of a study conducted by a qualified expert on a specific financial instrument, which was deemed to likely affect the investment choices of market operators: Corte di Cassazione (2 September 2016) No 17511.

[42] See recital (28).

Imagine, for example, that at a certain point in time the chief executive officer of a listed manufacturing company starts considering the available prospects for entering a new market or launching a new product, but no study or research on the possible different strategies and/or outcomes has yet been undertaken. Arguably, at least until a few projects have been selected or the feasibility of each strategy has been tested, no reasonable investor would trade on such dubious information, nor any insider would be able to exploit a real informative advantage. Market transparency and parity between trading parties are hence not at stake when information falls short of detail. Accordingly, precision narrows down the spectrum of market-relevant information.

B.7.32 Pursuant to Article 7(2) information is precise 'if it indicates a set of circumstances which exists or which may reasonably be expected to come into existence, or an event which has occurred or which may reasonably be expected to occur, where it is specific enough to enable a conclusion to be drawn as to the possible effect of that set of circumstances or event on the prices of the financial instruments or the related derivative financial instruments'.

B.7.33 The first, indeed obvious, observation is that for information to be precise, it must concern either a specific event or a *set* of (factual) circumstances: a single circumstance is not enough.[43] As a matter of fact, even though they are often used as synonyms in the everyday spoken language, from a linguistic perspective there is a difference between events and circumstances. Events are usually combinations of elements, actions, facts or situations that may or may not be affected by one or more circumstances. In fact, while circumstances are basic conditions for something to happen, events are the happening itself. Also intuitively, one could assume that a single event conveys generally more information than isolated circumstances, which acquire significance only when combined with other factors. This is because events usually involve a more complex happening, such as the general meeting of a listed bank in which shareholders are called to decide whether to raise the issuer's share capital, while circumstances generally indicate facts or conditions that are relevant for an event to happen or an action to be taken, as would be the introduction of stricter capital requirements for credit institutions, which, read in conjunction with the bank's most recent financial statements and with its medium-long term strategic plan, may indicate that the bank's shareholders' meeting will soon have to approve a capital increase.

B.7.34 Distinguishing between the two is hence important especially for information that develops in the context of protracted processes. Events allow an easier assessment on the precision of their informative content because they typically occur

[43] Peer Schaumburg-Müller, 'Disclosure of Price-sensitive Information: What Effect Do "Intermediate Steps" Have on the Statutory Disclosure Date?' (2013) 10 European Company Law 7, 9; Di Noia and Gargantini, 'Issuers at Midstream' (n 1) 495.

at the end of the process or at the end of one of its segments. Conversely, when it comes to elementary circumstances it is essential to weigh each one of them up in order to determine at which point in time a '*set*' becomes 'complete' or 'indicative'. That equals asking which new circumstance has a relevant marginal effect on the precision of the overall available data. For obvious reasons there are, however, no strict criteria to follow also in this respect.[44]

Future circumstances and events and the 'reasonable expectation test'

Another implied distinction in the text of Article 7(2) is that between past and future circumstances or events. **B.7.35**

Determining whether an event has already occurred or a set of circumstances has come to existence requires a retrospective analysis, as 'historical' facts are suitable to objective proof and documentation.[45] As a consequence, rumours and speculations do not matter for past situations or happenings.[46] **B.7.36**

On the other hand, a certain degree of conjecture is necessary in order to determine whether a future event or set of circumstances may reasonably be expected to occur. Unanimously, such an assessment, which has sometimes been referred to as 'the reasonable expectation test',[47] must be conducted from an *ex ante* perspective.[48] Establishing if a piece of information had to be considered precise at time X using knowledge that was acquired only at time X+1 would, in fact, undermine the achievement of the European law-maker's regulatory objectives since it would probably give relevance also to sets of insignificant or unpredictable factors whose occurrence acquired meaning only *ex post*. In other words, the risk would be to apply the insider dealing prohibition to cases in which there was no actual possibility for the insider to obtain an unfair advantage over uninformed trading parties or to flood the market with useless information that was not indicative of any future development yet. **B.7.37**

[44] Precision must, in fact, be assessed depending on the specific context of each case: CESR, 'Level 3 second set of CESR guidance and information on the common operation of the Directive to the market' CESR/06-562b (July 2007) para 1.5.

[45] In this regard see Klöhn, 'Inside Information' (n 24) 167, observing that historical information can be qualified as inside information irrespective of 'whether the planned operation is reasonably expected to be successful'.

[46] In this respect see CESR, 'Level 3 second set of CESR guidance and information on the common operation of the Directive to the market', CESR/06-562b (July 2007) para 1.5, clarifying that 'in determining whether a set of circumstances exists or an event has occurred, a key issue is whether there is firm and objective evidence for this as opposed to rumours and speculations'. Cf also Klöhn, 'Inside Information' (n 24) 167; Staikouras, 'Four Years of MADness?' (n 1) 780.

[47] Di Noia and Gargantini, 'Issuers at Midstream' (n 1) 492.

[48] Klöhn, 'Inside Information' (n 24) 165. For further discussion see Di Noia and Gargantini, 'Issuers at Midstream' (n 1) 497, claiming that 'the prognostic evaluation should be made on a rational basis, in light of all the information that could be available' at that moment.

B.7.38 For similar reasons, under 'the reasonable expectation test' the general consensus is also that a mere possibility of future events happening is not enough. The event must be more likely to happen than not, which requires a positive probability (of at least 50 per cent + 1) that the event will occur or that the action will be taken,[49] even though this does not mean that the information must be complete or fully developed. It could even concern alternative events with a similar outcome or a single transaction or operation that could be structured in two different ways,[50] as long as it is likely that one of the two alternatives will actually take place. The test is therefore highly factual and requires evaluating whether there is a realistic chance that the expected outcome occurs. This marks an important difference with the US approach applied also in insider dealing cases. As we will see shortly, in the United States the probability of the event happening must, in fact, be balanced with the magnitude of its anticipated consequences,[51] so that even possible (but not probable) events or circumstances could be deemed relevant if their expected outcome is of significant magnitude.

The direction of the price effect

B.7.39 Provided that the reasonable expectation test is satisfied, for information to be considered sufficiently precise it shall also be specific enough to enable a conclusion on the possible effect of the event or of the set of circumstances on the price of the financial instruments. The main issue is therefore whether the direction or the type of price effect should be predictable in advance as well.

B.7.40 On a preliminary note, it must be borne in mind that price 'effect' does not necessarily mean price 'movement'. For instance, information that confirms market expectations has arguably an effect on prices without causing any significant price movement or a change in the way prices are already moving (eg a steady growth

[49] Among many, Krause and Brellochs, 'Insider Trading and the Disclosure of Inside Information' (n 9) 288–9; Di Noia and Gargantini, 'Issuers at Midstream' (n 1) 495–6. For a different opinion cf Hellgardt, 'The Notion of Inside Information' (n 20) 872–3, who argues that the expression 'realistic prospect' used by the ECJ in *Geltl v Daimler* to interpret the reasonable expectation test does not require an evaluation in terms of probability, but rather demands to assess whether, on the basis of the existing factors, one can realistically expect that the future event or set of circumstances which the information refers to will actually occur. After all, what the ECJ presumably meant is only that a high degree of probability or a probability close to certainty is not necessary. It is indeed true that when the set of possible outcomes is unknown the use of statistical probabilities in the strict sense is inapt to describe the necessary evaluation on the likelihood of an outcome to occur: Hansen, 'Say When' (n 1) 18–19. However, one could still employ a broader concept of probability to indicate the likelihood of an outcome, as opposed to a mere possibility, assessed on the basis of past experiences and of the circumstances of the particular case.

[50] Staikouras, 'Four Years of MADness?' (n 1) 780.

[51] Reference is to the 'probability–magnitude test' under US law, according to which in order to determine the materiality of a statement or of a piece of information one would have to balance the probability that the event will occur with its expected magnitude: see *SEC v Texas Gulf Sulphur Co*, 401 F2d 833, 849 (2d Cir, 1968); *Basic v Levinson*, 485 US 224, 238 (1988), recently confirmed in *Halliburton Co v Erica P John Fund, Inc*, 134 S Ct 2398 (2014).

or decline).[52] It is true, however, that inside information is such usually because it contrasts market expectations, thereby causing price movement, but the distinction helps clarify that the relevant aspect is essentially whether the information potentially sets the price at a level (significantly) different from that which would have prevailed on the market if the information was not disclosed or otherwise publicly available and, consequently, if this effect should be identifiable in advance.

CESR's original proposal to the Commission regarding the enactment of Level 2 implementing measures made explicit reference to the need to anticipate the 'direction' of the price effect.[53] However, the Market Abuse Implementation Directive (2003/124/EC) adopted a different solution taking into consideration the results of a public consultation on the subject, as well as CESR's final advice.[54] Arguably, the law-maker's intent was to require only that the holder of the information could anticipate any price effect, irrespective of whether reasonable predictions on its trajectory were possible or not,[55] especially for cases in which contrasting forecasts could still be made. Accordingly, in *Lafonta v Autorité des marchés financiers* the ECJ argued that a piece of information may be considered sufficiently precise even if it is not clear in which direction the price is likely to move, as long as the holder of the information can reasonably anticipate that there will be a change in price.[56] Such a conclusion, however, is not clearly inferable from the definition of inside information and, from another perspective, needs to be further specified by reading it in conjunction with the mentioned explicit regulatory objectives of the European law-maker and to a certain extent with the case law of the ECJ itself. **B.7.41**

In this respect, the wording of Article 7 now mirrors that of Article 1(1) Market Abuse Implementation Directive (2003/124/EC). However, this does not necessarily imply that the precision requirement must at all times be considered satisfied even when there are no plausible indicators of the type of expected price effect in the **B.7.42**

[52] For a similar observation in the context of the materiality requirement see Hansen, 'Say When' (n 1) 16–17.

[53] Consultation Paper on 'CESR's Advice on Level 2 Implementing Measures for the Proposed Market Abuse Directive' CESR/02-089d (July 2002) paras 32–3.

[54] CESR's Advice on Level 2 Implementing Measures for the Proposed Market Abuse Directive, CESR/02-089d (December 2002) paras 19–20.

[55] *Lafonta v Autorité des marchés financiers* (n 24) para 37.

[56] According to the ECJ, this conclusion could be inferred from the wording of art 1(1) Market Abuse Implementation Directive (2003/124/EC): cf *Lafonta v Autorité des marchés financiers* (n 24) paras 31–2. The more compelling argument in this regard seems, however, to rest on the observation that for complex transactions or operations it might be very hard to predict how the stock prices will move in the particular case: cf Klöhn, 'Inside Information' (n 24) 164–5; Di Noia and Gargantini, 'Issuers at Midstream' (n 1) 500. However, this observation is generally made on an *ex post* basis, by looking at the diverging price movements caused by similar transactions. Nevertheless, as will be explained below, the fact that after the information is made public the price of the financial instruments did not move at all or did not move in the anticipated direction does not undermine the proposed interpretation, since the relevant assessment must in any case be conducted from an *ex ante* perspective.

particular case. Article 7 could also suggest the exact opposite, since it refers to the possible 'effect' and not to the possible 'effects' of the information on market prices.[57]

B.7.43 In addition, if the purpose of the market abuse discipline is 'to protect the integrity of the EU financial markets and to enhance investor confidence in those markets'[58] it becomes clear that the ECJ's conclusion needs some fine-tuning. As the ECJ itself previously recognized, if the insider cannot predict which effect the information will have on prices when it is made public there is no unfair advantage to exploit to the detriment of uninformed trading parties.[59] The distinguishing feature here is the possibility to exploit an informative advantage. Generally, this happens when the information is precise enough to enable its holder to anticipate the direction of the price movement or in any case the specific price effect, so that the investment decision can be taken without, or at a very low, risk compared to other market participants.[60] However, it could also occur when the information suggests greater or lower price volatility—which, by definition, would not make it possible to anticipate the direction of the price effect—as this information could be used, for example, to trade in derivatives to either hedge or speculate with an advantage over uninformed trading parties. Similarly, market transparency would probably be better served if the issuer was mandated to disclose only information that could recognizably be used in an investment decision because, for instance, a reasonable investor would know if she would be better off buying, selling, or even holding onto the securities in the specific case. Disclosure obligations lower the cost to search for new information and make independent analyses of publicly available data more attractive if they convey knowledge that is somehow relevant for the correct pricing of financial instruments, and this requires drawing a conclusion on the course of the price effect to be at least possible.[61]

---

[57] Precisely in this sense, Klöhn, 'Inside Information' (n 24) 170.

[58] As the ECJ explicitly does: see *Lafonta v Autorité des marchés financiers* (n 24) paras 21 and 33.

[59] See recital (23). See also *Spector Photo Group NV v CBFA* (n 23) para 52, whereby the Court argued that 'inside information grants the insider in possession of such information an advantage in relation to all the other actors on the market who are unaware of it' because 'it enables the insider . . . to expect to derive an economic advantage from it without exposing himself to the same risks as the other investors on the market'. Accordingly the 'essential characteristic of insider dealing . . . consists in an unfair advantage being obtained from information to the detriment of third parties who are unaware of it and, consequently, the undermining of the integrity of financial markets and investor confidence'.

[60] Cf CESR's Advice on Level 2 Implementing Measures for the Proposed Market Abuse Directive, CESR/02-089d (December 2002) para 20.

[61] For further discussion see Klöhn, 'Inside Information' (n 24) 171–5, who also warns against the danger of employing an excessively wide concept of inside information, as this would probably bury investors with a large amount of irrelevant information and, in the end, reduce informational efficiency within the European financial markets; Atrigna, 'Il carattere preciso' (n 24) 661. See also *FCA v Hannam* [2014] UKUT 0233 (TCC) para 121, in which the Upper Tribunal interpreted the expression 'possible effect' as to require the information to indicate the direction of the price movement; and *Massey v FSA* [2011] UKUT 49 (TCC) para 39.

In other words, inside information qualifies as such only if it gives the holder of the information an incentive to trade.[62]

Precision applied to intermediate steps in a protracted process

According to Article 7(2), also intermediate steps in a protracted process, which are connected with bringing about future circumstances or resulting in future events, may be deemed to be precise information.[63] This occurs if they make the final event not simply possible but also probable[64] and, of course, if they enable a conclusion to be drawn as to their possible price effect. On paper, then, if intermediate steps are sufficiently precise and also show the three other common features of inside information, they may constitute inside information per se.[65] In practice, when this happens is far less clear. **B.7.44**

Applying these rules to corporate information raises a first contradiction. The probability of bringing about a future event or set of circumstances usually increases after 'formal' decisions have been taken by corporate bodies or corporate functions, but the whole point of attaching significance to preparatory stages and preliminary phases is precisely to broaden the formalistic approach. Typical examples of relevant intermediate stages are, in fact, a promising state of the negotiations regarding a merger or the reaching of a quasi-final, but not binding yet, agreement on the conditions under which certain financial instruments will be marketed.[66] **B.7.45**

Aside from this, the most problematic issue seemingly concerns potential or future intermediate steps because they may require assessing the probability of a probability.[67] Transitional stages that are likely to result in future events or circumstances are, in fact, relevant also if they have not yet occurred, as long as the holder of the information can anticipate their happening,[68] so that in addition to the probability of the future final event one would have to factor in the probability of the intermediate stage, adding further speculation to the reasonable expectation test. For example, in a company's acquisition, the holder of the information would have to evaluate whether an intermediate step, such as the decision to acquire a 5 per cent share in a competing company, of a protracted process eventually ending up in the purchase of a controlling share in that same company, can reasonably be **B.7.46**

62 Klöhn, 'Inside Information' (n 24) 180.

63 As anticipated, this addition to the wording of the definition of inside information is consistent with CESR's Level 3 Guidance of 2007 and with the decision of the ECJ in *Markus Geltl v Daimler AG* (n 20).

64 See para B.7.16 above and the ECJ decision in *Markus Geltl v Daimler AG* (n 20) paras 46–9. On this topic, also Krause and Brellochs, 'Insider Trading and the Disclosure of Inside Information' (n 9) 287–8.

65 As expressly stated by art 7(3).

66 See recital (17).

67 Di Noia and Gargantini, 'Issuers at Midstream' (n 1) 498.

68 Cf *Markus Geltl v Daimler AG* (n 20) para 38.

expected to come into existence, before considering whether it is likely that the future final event (ie the acquisition of control) will actually take place.

B.7.47 The practical consequence is that determining which piece of information is precise (and thus relevant for the purposes of the definition) is not really possible in purely abstract terms.

B.7.48 In our example, would the inside information arise as soon as an executive director confronts the board with the future prospect of buying a share in a competing company, or would that happen only after negotiations have started or even later? In other words, at which stage of the preparatory work or of the negotiations is the precision requirement met? Evidently, all the more for multi-staged processes the necessary assessment must be conducted on a case-by-case basis, and this casts some serious doubt on the definition's capacity to dispel ambiguities. The adoption of a flexible approach that, following the United States model, balances the uncertainty of the information with its expected price effect could probably provide some guidance. However, as we will explain in short, this model does not seem fully compatible with the definition of inside information provided by Article 7 (see para B.7.71 below).

Non-public information

The non-public character of inside information

B.7.49 The second element of the definition of inside information is its non-public character. However, also under the current market abuse regime it is not entirely clear when the information loses its non-public nature and thus stops qualifying as inside information. In particular, questions arise as to what type of disclosure makes a piece of information 'public', provided that the dissemination can also occur because of the incorrect or unlawful disclosure by the issuer or through third parties. The de facto dissemination of precise price-sensitive information covers, in fact, a wide range of hypotheses, spanning from market rumours to the breach of confidentiality obligations by professionals who have worked for the issuer.

B.7.50 The question has important practical implications since it concerns the possibility to trade on the issuer's securities, and might determine whether a certain conduct is lawful or not.

B.7.51 Under the previous market abuse regime, the European law-maker adopted a flexible approach. Even a de facto dissemination of the information was sufficient for the information to lose its non-public character for the purposes of the insider dealing prohibition.[69] However, publication in the issuer's website and

[69] In the 'Level 3 second set of CESR guidance and information on the common operation of the Directive to the market', CESR/06-562b (July 2007) para 1.9, CESR observed that 'for the purposes of determining whether a transaction was made using inside information, it should be

compliance with the disclosure rules established by the competent supervisory authorities were mandated in order to fulfil the disclosure obligations.[70]

Even now, an explicit provision regulates the 'moment' in which the information becomes 'public' with respect to the fulfilment of the issuer's disclosure obligations. Under Article 17(1) 'the issuer shall ensure that the inside information is made public in a manner which enables fast access and complete, correct and timely assessment of the information by the public and, where applicable, in the officially appointed mechanism referred to in Article 21 of Directive 2004/109/EC of the European Parliament and the Council'. Consistency with other provisions of the Market Abuse Regulation could thus suggest that the public or non-public character of the information should be assessed as a general rule according to strictly objective criteria, and possibly with respect to the disclosure mechanisms set forth by the Transparency Directive (Directive 2004/109/EC as amended by Directive 2013/50/EU). There is, however, a difference between simply requiring that the information *be given* to the public and actually requiring that the information *be* public.[71] **B.7.52**

The relevance of the de facto dissemination of inside information

Provided that the rationale of market abuse rules is to create a level playing field for investment decisions, it follows that the non-public character of the information should substantially depend on its actual availability to the investing public. But which investors should be made aware of the information and which communication means would be appropriate for the purpose? **B.7.53**

In practice, when investors in a certain market have a wide and easy access to the information through common means of disclosure (eg through press releases, large spreading newspapers, the internet, etc) this problem loses much of its relevance. In fact, when the information is capable of reaching a wide audience it is far more likely that even those who did not have a first-hand knowledge of the information trade on an equal footing, because in a fairly efficient market the price of the financial instruments should have already incorporated the information. This certainly constitutes a simplification of pricing mechanisms, as there will always be a period of time, even if (very) limited, during which the information is still in the process of being incorporated in market prices and **B.7.54**

noted that information can be publicly available even if it was not disclosed by the issuer' in the prescribed manner and that this applies when 'the information became public through an incorrect disclosure by the issuer or through a third party'. In this regard cf, also for references and for a comparative analysis on national provisions under the previous market abuse regime, Staikouras, 'Four Years of MADness?' (n 1) 781–5. In the Italian case law, for a recent decision which, however, applied the previous market abuse rules: Corte di Cassazione (20 January 2010) No 8588.

[70] See especially art 6(1), (7), and (10) (former) Market Abuse Directive (2003/6/EC). In this respect see also Staikouras, 'Four Years of MADness?' (n 1) 781.

[71] Hopt, 'The European Insider Dealing Directive' (n 15) 58.

insiders still have an advantage over uninformed trading parties. However, from a market transparency perspective, if the market *has* corrected the price and thus if the price already reflects the information, even absent 'formal' disclosure, the information should be considered public, irrespective of how it was disseminated.[72]

B.7.55 It follows that since the extent and speed at which market prices reflect new information are positively correlated with the degree of dissemination of the information, when the information is disclosed to a smaller number of selected recipients one would have to consider where the information has been published, whether other sources have contributed to spread it further and, most importantly, which audience will probably acquire knowledge of the information.[73] The public or non-public character of the information must in fact be assessed having regard to the potential recipients of the information and of the dissemination channels used in each case. Imagine, for instance, that information regarding an innovative pharmaceutical try-out conducted by a German issuer listed in the French stock exchange is published only in a Swiss medical journal printed in a limited number of copies and available only in Switzerland and in certain regions of Germany. It could be argued that the information has not lost its non-public character yet, as market operators are unlikely to acquire knowledge of the information. Conversely, selective disclosure to a high number of institutional investors or influential market participants through specialized journals or databases could be sufficient to affect trading prices,[74] even though it is intended only for a sophisticated audience. In such a case, it would be probably reasonable to assume that also unsophisticated uninformed investors would benefit from the information simply because those who make the market price know it.

Information on issuers or financial instruments

The subject of inside information

B.7.56 Article 7(1) specifies that the definition covers information concerning directly or indirectly one or more issuers or one or more financial instruments, including commodity derivatives,[75] emission allowances, and auctioned products based on emission allowances. As a consequence, inside information is generally intended as any information that somehow relates to the market position of the issuer,[76] either by referring to corporate events and operations or to sector-specific circumstances.

[72] In this regard see Klöhn, 'The European Insider Trading Regulation' (n 35) 364.

[73] Similarly, Staikouras, 'Four Years of MADness?' (n 1) 783–4.

[74] In the same sense Moloney, *EU Securities* (n 1) 721. For further discussion and a clarifying example see Siems, 'The EU Market Abuse Directive' (n 1) 41.

[75] With the exception of information on spot commodity contracts, which is relevant only if there is a direct connection between the information and the spot commodity contract.

[76] CESR's Advice on Level 2 Implementing Measures for the Proposed Market Abuse Directive, CESR/02-089d (December 2002) para 31.

As in the previous regulatory regime, however, only information that shows a *direct* connection to one or more issuers or to one or more financial instruments is subject to the disclosure requirements set forth by Article 17, while *indirect* correlations also contribute to shape the insider dealing prohibition. **B.7.57**

Corporate information v market information

The commonly accepted distinction between corporate information and market information helps clarify the difference.[77] Although this may on occasion constitute an oversimplification,[78] information indirectly relating to one or more issuers or financial instruments could be classified as market information, as opposed to corporate information that generally shows a direct connection. As a matter of fact, while the latter includes data and knowledge of issuer-specific facts, such as corporate decisions taken by the issuer's board of directors or by the general meeting, the issuer's on-going negotiations with third parties or the prospective changes in control; the former generally depicts market-wide data potentially affecting several issuers and financial institutions, such as regulatory or taxation information or data otherwise produced by third parties, including credit ratings, market indexes, decisions of market authorities, investment analysts' reports, and other similar material. Indeed, CESR's 2007 Level 3 Guidance also found examples of information indirectly referring to issuers in central bank decisions on interest rates, data, and statistics published by institutions, credit merit reports, and government decisions, which are all common illustrations of market information. **B.7.58**

Most of the time market information, while showing an indirect connection to the issuer or to one or more financial instruments, is immediately available to the public and thus does not qualify, under the second criterion provided by Article 7, as inside information. Especially information provided by public authorities is often communicated to the media and given broad visibility, usually right after the information becomes 'complete' (*rectius*, precise). Accordingly, as all elements of the definition must be read in conjunction with one another, information only indirectly referring to issuers or financial instruments is in practice confined to **B.7.59**

---

[77] In the same sense see Di Noia and Gargantini, 'Issuers at Midstream' (n 1) 493, according to whom information directly concerning the issuer can be qualified as corporate information, as opposed to information indirectly referring to the issuer, which would fall under the category of market information; Staikouras, 'Four Years of MADness?' (n 1) 78; Guido A Ferrarini, 'The European Market Abuse Directive' (2004) 41 Common Market Law Review 711, 720. A similar distinction in US insider trading law is that between 'inside information', coming from internal corporate sources, and 'market information', originating from sources other than the issuer: Stephen M Bainbridge, 'An overview of US Insider Trading Law: Lessons for the EU?' (2004) University of California, Los Angeles School of Law. Law & Economics Research Paper Series No 05-5, 6 https://papers.ssrn.com/sol3/papers.cfm?abstract_id=654703 (last accessed 12 November 2016).

[78] For example, solicited issuer ratings (ie credit ratings that evaluate the overall creditworthiness of an issuer), which have been communicated only to the issuer, possibly because the internal 'appeal process' is still pending, do not squarely fall into the category of 'corporate information' although they could be regarded as relating directly to the issuer.

data, events, and circumstances that are not specific to the issuer, only for the period of time that they actually remain confidential, which often restricts the range of potentially relevant information.

Price-sensitive information

The concepts of price sensitivity and materiality

B.7.60 The fourth element of the definition of inside information is the price sensitivity. Article 7, in fact, requires the information to be likely to have, if it were made public, a significant effect on the price of the financial instruments it refers to.

B.7.61 In the United States this requirement is explained by employing the concept of 'materiality', which indicates that the information must be 'material' or otherwise 'a significant component' of an investment decision. This generally includes not any information that might be considered important for investment choices, but specifically only information that is likely to be taken into consideration by a reasonable investor,[79] because it alters the total knowledge available at that moment. Although it employs a different expression, the Market Abuse Regulation intends the price sensitivity requirement in a similar sense. In fact, pursuant to Article 7(4) a piece of information is price sensitive if a reasonable investor would be likely to use it as part of his or her investment decisions.

B.7.62 The underlying assumption is that publicly available information that reasonable investors would use to take investment decisions is usually reflected on market prices; therefore, if the information is such that a reasonable investor would trade on it or otherwise take it into consideration, one could posit its price effect.

B.7.63 A (first) possible hidden paradox is, however, that, at least in theory, some information might arguably have a significant effect on prices even if a reasonable investor would not be likely to use it. Imagine for example that there is irrational speculation

[79] The extent of the materiality requirement has been largely shaped by the 'might-or-would-debate', which has developed over a large variety of securities regulation topics since disclosure obligations under US law do not rest on a single provision, but rather can be found in several regulatory sources which all make reference to the element of 'materiality'. Originally, the US Supreme Court regarded as material any information that 'might have been considered important by a reasonable shareholder': *Mills v Electric Auto-lite Co*, 396 US 375, 384 (1970). Accordingly, under this broad interpretation, even information that had little or no relevance for investment decisions could have been considered material. Later on, however, the Supreme Court construed the materiality requirement in a narrower sense, by specifying that the distinctive element was whether there was a substantial likelihood that the information would have been viewed as relevant for the decision: *TSC Industries, Inc v Northway, Inc*, 426 US 438, 449 (1976). While these cases all dealt with the concept of materiality within the meaning of Rule 14a-9 on the disclosure duties in proxy solicitation procedures, the most recent 'would-test' was also adopted by the Supreme Court in the interpretation of Rule 10b-5, which has traditionally constituted the basis for the insider dealing prohibition in the United States. See in this regard the landmark decision in *Basic v Levinson* (n 51) 231–2; recently confirmed in *Halliburton Co v Erica P John Fund, Inc* (n 51). On this subject also for references see Klöhn, 'Inside Information' (n 24) 168–9; Hansen, 'Say When' (n 1) 16.

on the markets and therefore that speculators are going to overreact to news that should not rationally be considered relevant, eg a reduction of sales of 0.5 per cent in a year. The concern is that, provided that the presence of irrational speculation, or irrational exuberance, or irrational pessimism on the markets is a known fact, one could argue that when the law says 'reasonable' investor, it also includes investors anticipating and reacting to 'unreasonable' behaviours by other market participants. In fact, one could assume that a reasonable investor, thanks to this knowledge, would also become sensitive to how unreasonable investors react to information and thus also unreasonable investors would become relevant for the purposes of the definition. This, however, should not be the case because otherwise, in a way, the reference to the 'reasonable investor' would be useless or provide very little guidance. The point might appear highly theoretic, but it is in fact relevant. For instance, irrational or herding behaviours might constitute an easy defence for insiders who failed to comply with market abuse prohibitions by claiming that, because the market reacted to news that should not have been considered important, there was no inside information in the particular case. More generally, there would be a great deal of difference if defendants could argue that the 'market' reacted or might have reacted to the information, but only due to irrational (ie 'unreasonable') forces, and that a 'reasonable' investor would not have attached any importance to the information. The text of the Regulation seems, then, to evoke the approach of a reasonable investor, so to speak, 'stand-alone', looking at the fundamentals of the issuer rather than at potential irrational market reactions.

Conversely, it is also a known fact that markets may not show sufficient informational efficiency at all times and that therefore it is possible that publicly available information is not immediately and effectively reflected in the market price. Even so, the use of this and other conceptual simplifications appears necessary to provide a model of conduct, as any other standard could show to a certain extent some inconsistencies with market reality. Irrational market reactions, herding phenomena among market players, or structural or contingent market inefficiencies should thus not be taken into account in establishing the relevant benchmark. The key issue is rather which information may be theoretically relevant for stand-alone 'reasonable' investment decisions.[80] **B.7.64**

The 'reasonable investor' criterion

Relevant information for 'reasonable' investment decisions must somehow substantially change the total mix of publicly available information[81] and—at least **B.7.65**

[80] In this regard see Krause and Brellochs, 'Insider Trading and the Disclosure of Inside Information' (n 9) 291–3, who address the different national interpretations of the 'reasonable investor test' under the previous market abuse regime in Germany, the UK, the Netherlands, France, and Italy.

[81] Cf recital (1) Market Abuse Implementation Directive (2003/124/EC) and Klöhn, 'Inside Information' (n 24) 165. In this regard see also recitals (14) and (15), which clarify that whether

indirectly—concern the positive or negative returns that an investor might obtain from purchasing or selling the securities, since according to the teachings of corporate finance the present value (and thus the price) of any certain financial instrument is discounted from the future value of the expected returns of the investment.

B.7.66 This, however, does not clarify what kind of investor the price sensitivity requirement refers to. Some question, for instance, whether the reasonable investor should be of a particular gender,[82] a professional investor, or any investor, including unsophisticated or retail investors. Empirical and behavioural studies show, in fact, that there is a great deal of difference between a retail investor, a fund manager, a hedge fund, and a high-frequency trader or even between men and women, who are generally less risk prone and aggressive than men when it comes to investment decisions (it might sound as a stereotype, but it appears confirmed empirically).[83]

B.7.67 The one thing that is certain is that reference to the 'reasonable' investor presumably indicates an investor who thinks and behaves in a rational way[84] and who is able to distinguish information that might affect the economic returns of the investment from information that does not have such an outcome. Adding this to the fact that professional (institutional) investors usually make the market price,[85] the relevant model seems to be that of the 'reasonable professional investor'.[86]

B.7.68 The definition, however, does not allow any significant distinction among reasonable professional investors. The reality is certainly more complex than the definition, as different qualified investors show different skills, expertise, and strategies and could react to the same piece of information in different manners. For instance, the definition does not consider—and to some extent maybe it should not—that in today's world a significant percentage of trades is done with high-frequency techniques, employing algorithms that are capable of reacting

information is likely to be taken into account by a reasonable investor in her investment decisions should be assessed looking at all *ex ante* available information, and especially at 'the anticipated impact of the information in light of the totality of the related issuer's activity, the reliability of the source of information and any other market variables likely to affect the financial instruments, the related spot commodity contracts, or the auctioned products based on the emission allowances in the given circumstances'. For the same reason *ex post* information can only be used to check whether the assumption that the information was price sensitive was correct.

[82] Joan MacLeod Heminway, 'Female Investors and Securities Fraud: Is the Reasonable Investor a Woman?' (2009) 15 William & Mary Journal of Women and the Law 291.

[83] ibid 312–9; A Can Inci, M P Narayanan, and H Nejat Seyhun, 'Gender Differences in Executives' Access to Information' (2015) 3 https://papers.ssrn.com/sol3/papers.cfm?abstract_id=2847906 (last accessed 13 November 2016).

[84] CESR's Advice on Level 2 Implementing Measures for the Proposed Market Abuse Directive, CESR/02-089d (December 2002) para 27 (especially at fn 1).

[85] See extensively Ronald J Gilson and Reinier H Kraakman, 'The Mechanisms of Market Efficiency' (1984) 70 Virginia Law Review 549, 569–72.

[86] Cf Stefan J Padfield, 'Who Should Do the Math? Materiality Issues in Disclosures that Require Investors to Calculate the Bottom Line' (2007) 34 Pepperdine Law Review 927, 939–40.

to new information in milliseconds.[87] Does this mean that since most trades are governed by complex automated software one would also have to include, in defining what a reasonable investor is, the software engineer writing the algorithms? Probably such a conclusion would be far-fetched and, in the absence of explicit textual indications, somehow arbitrary. Accordingly, the 'reasonable investor' probably constitutes a necessary simplification of the far more complex reality of market trading practices.

Precision and price sensitivity as overlapping components of the definition of inside information

On a final note, it is important to point out that precision and price sensitivity seem to overlap.[88] As mentioned above, information can be considered 'precise' if it enables a conclusion to be drawn on its possible price effect, while it is material only if it is actually likely to have a significant effect on market prices. **B.7.69**

The distinction is clearly subtle, since both elements of the definition require an *ex ante* assessment of the potential impact of the information on market prices, which entails to some extent a probabilistic evaluation. However, with respect to precision, such probabilistic estimate is irrelevant for historical facts and concerns the occurrence of a future event or the coming to existence of a future set of circumstances that might in turn have an impact on prices. Instead, with regard to the price sensitivity requirement, the relevant assessment is, as explained earlier, whether the expected price effect is probable or not. **B.7.70**

Under Article 7, precision and price sensitivity are thus two distinct, albeit overlapping, criteria. For information to be qualified as inside information it has to be *both* precise in its content and relevant for investment choices. As a consequence, unlike in the United States,[89] the already mentioned 'probability–magnitude approach', according to which even not perfectly defined events or sets of circumstances could be relevant if the probability of their occurrence was high enough (and vice versa), does not apply to the definition of inside information.[90] **B.7.71**

---

[87] Consob, 'Il *trading* ad alta frequenza. Caratteristiche, effetti, questioni di *policy*' (December 2012) Quaderno No 5. See also, among many, Charles R Korsmo, 'High-Frequency Trading. A Regulatory Strategy' (2014) 48 University of Richmond Law Review 523; Matt Prewitt, 'High-Frequency Trading: Should Regulators Do More?' (2012) 19 Michigan Telecommunications and Technology Law Review 131; Peter Gomber and others, 'High-frequency Trading' (2011) https://papers.ssrn.com/sol3/papers.cfm?abstract_id=1858626 (last accessed 19 November 2016).

[88] In the same sense see Klöhn, 'Inside Information' (n 24) 166; Staikouras, 'Four Years of MADness?' (n 1) 787.

[89] *SEC v Texas Gulf Sulphur* (n 51) 849; *Basic v Levinson* (n 51) 238; recently confirmed in *Halliburton Co v Erica P John Fund, Inc* (n 51). See also para B.7.38.

[90] Specifically on this point see *Markus Geltl v Daimler AG* (n 20) paras 50–5. See also Krause and Brellochs, 'Insider Trading and the Disclosure of Inside Information' (n 9) 290. For further discussion see Di Noia and Gargantini, 'Issuers at Midstream' (n 1) 496, and Hansen, 'Say When' (n 1) 13 and 18, who argues that in excluding the probability–magnitude approach the ECJ only referred to the precision requirement and not to the meaning of 'significant effect' on prices.

B.7.72 Magnitude is, however, not completely disregarded by the European law-maker since Article 7 requires the likelihood of a *significant* effect on market prices. Small or otherwise negligible price effects therefore do not count. However, drawing a clear line between minimal and significant price effects may be possible, once again, only on a case-by-case basis.[91]

The price sensitivity of intermediate steps in a protracted process

B.7.73 The difference between precision and price sensitivity must be borne in mind also in the assessment of the intermediate steps in a protracted process.

B.7.74 In *Geltl v Daimler* the ECJ only addressed whether intermediate phases of a multi-staged process could qualify as precise information.[92] However, as now clarified by Article 7(3), 'an intermediate step in a protracted process shall be deemed to be inside information if, by itself, it satisfies the criteria of inside information', which include also the price sensitivity element. In order to qualify as inside information, intermediate stages must thus also be likely to have, if made public, a significant effect on the price of the financial instruments. It might seem obvious, but the emphasis here is on the separate assessment of whether the transitional stages alone are likely to be material for investment choices.

III. Concluding Remarks

B.7.75 The most significant addition introduced by the Market Abuse Regulation to the definition of inside information is the explicit reference to the fact that intermediate stages in a protracted process may qualify as inside information. What is interesting to notice, however, is not the mere textual change, but that, as already observed, paragraphs 2 and 3 of Article 7 are essentially a codification of the ECJ ruling in *Geltl v Daimler* (and of previous Level 3 guidance). Indeed, this sheds some light on the dynamics between policy-makers and the judiciary at the European level and on the prominent role of the ECJ in the European legal order.[93]

[91] See *Spector Photo Group NV v CBFA* (n 23) paras 66–9, in which the ECJ was asked also to define the threshold above which the influence on prices may be regarded as significant. The ECJ held that 'the capacity to have a significant effect on prices must be assessed, a priori, in the light of the content of the information at issue and the context in which it occurs. It is thus not necessary ... to examine whether its disclosure actually had a significant effect on the price of the financial instruments to which it relates'. No fixed or even indicative threshold thus appeared appropriate. Cf also CESR, 'Level 3 second set of CESR guidance and information on the common operation of the Directive to the market', CESR/06-562b (July 2007) paras 1.13–1.14.

[92] Krause and Brellochs, 'Insider Trading and the Disclosure of Inside Information' (n 9) 286.

[93] On this subject see eg Karen J Alter and Sophie Meunier-Aitsahalia, 'Judicial Politics in the European Community. European Integration and the Pathbreaking *Cassis de Dijon* Decision' (1994) 26 Comparative Political Studies 535.

Despite these few additional clarifications on the treatment of multi-staged processes, however, the main innovation of the Market Abuse Regulation in respect to the notion of inside information may very well be that it does not provide any longer a clear regulatory basis for the adoption at the State level of a twofold concept of inside information, establishing two different trigger points for the insider dealing prohibition and the issuer's continuous disclosure obligations. Accordingly, this will probably lead, at least in some cases, to anticipate the moment in time in which the issuer's disclosure obligations arise. In reality, however, the Market Abuse Regulation does not even explicitly reject this dual approach and consequently the different stages of evolution of the European financial markets and/or the foreseeable practical demands for increased certainty coming from the issuers could push the national supervisory authorities and the national courts to preserve, at least to some extent, the status quo. After all, Article 17(1) simply requires the issuer to disclose inside information 'as soon as possible', implicitly admitting that immediate disclosure might not be feasible. In addition, aside from the fact that even recognizing the existence of a piece of inside information within the issuer may take some time, failure to establish when information becomes precise or price sensitive may alternatively lead issuers to anticipate the disclosure when the information is still inaccurate or underdeveloped or to a broader use of the option to delay disclosure pursuant to Article 17(4), creating an uncertainty in this matter that national authorities may try to solve. **B.7.76**

As for the definition's shortcomings, the Market Abuse Regulation fails to explicitly address other pressing issues that were debated under the (former) Market Abuse Directive (2003/6/EC). The definition, for instance, does not strike an actual and unique balance between the issuer's interest in confidentiality and the market's interest in the flow of material information, which is essentially left to the rules on delayed disclosure.[94] In addition, ambiguities remain especially regarding when the inside information can be considered fully formed and, therefore, when the ban on insider dealing and the disclosure obligations apply. In particular, precision and price sensitivity are still not easily identifiable in advance. **B.7.77**

In this respect, the analysis clearly shows that a case-by-case approach is essential in determining whether a specific piece of information qualifies as inside information. Even though there are certain facts, events, and data that are generally deemed to fall easily within the definition, such as, for instance, profit **B.7.78**

[94] In this regard, cf Hansen and Moalem, 'The MAD Disclosure Regime' (n 7) 328. Interestingly, Davies and Worthington, *Gower's Principles* (n 30) para 26–6, observe that under the Market Abuse Regulation 'investors' interests appear to receive more weight than issuers' concerns'.

warnings, credit ratings, or changes in control,[95] also typical examples of inside information need to be examined having regard to the factual circumstances of the specific case, provided that a non-public piece of information might constitute inside information only if it is sufficiently precise and material.[96] In the event, for example, of information concerning the risk of an unfavourable court ruling for the issuer, the holder of the information would have to consider, among others things, the state of the proceeding and the likelihood of reaching a transaction, the probability and magnitude of each possible compensation scenario in respect of the issuer's liquidity and assets, the existence of funds to cover the risk, the potential negative repercussions for the issuer's image, and the like.

B.7.79 Apart from an inherent level of vagueness, the definition also conceals a few hidden theoretical issues, the main being a disengagement of the assumptions it employs from market reality. The reasonable investor criterion in itself rests on the underlying assumption that in efficient markets publicly available information that reasonable investors would use to take investment decisions is usually reflected in market prices. However, this interpretation does not always come to terms with the fact that inefficient markets exist (with the consequence that not all relevant information is always timely incorporated in market prices), and that when irrational speculation drives the market some information might arguably have a significant effect on prices even if a reasonable investor would not be likely to use it.

B.7.80 The problem loses, however, much of its relevance considering that the definition of inside information provides only an abstract model to determine from an *ex ante* perspective if a piece of non-public information is relevant for investment choices and should thus be disclosed to the public and/or be subject to stricter regulation on who should be able to trade with it and when. Accordingly, it does not really matter whether the price was not actually affected when the information was disclosed, nor is it important that the definition refers to a model—that of the 'reasonable' investor—which does not always exist in reality. The definition identifies who should be protected when trading on the market, ie the reasonable investor, not who actually trades in it.

B.7.81 In any case, the model must be read in compliance with the theoretical underpinnings of the market abuse discipline. Consequently, as the main goal of market abuse rules is that of ensuring market transparency and establishing a level

[95] In its 'Level 3 second set of CESR guidance and information on the common operation of the Directive to the market', CESR/06-562b (July 2007) paras 1.15 and 1.16, CESR even listed, on a purely non-exhaustive and indicative basis, examples of inside information. Other valuable examples on the application of the market abuse rules under the (former) Market Abuse Directive (2003/6/EC) are provided by Siems, 'The EU Market Abuse Directive' (n 1).

[96] CESR, 'Level 3 second set of CESR guidance and information on the common operation of the Directive to the market', CESR/06-562b (July 2007) para 1.15.

playing field for 'reasonable' investors, a strict interpretation of the four requirements listed above is crucial.[97] Inside information can thus only be a piece of information that would allow an insider to actually benefit from it to the detriment of uninformed third parties and that, if made public, would actually help rational investment choices.

Finally, from a corporate law perspective an open question concerns the consciousness of the existence of inside information within the issuer. Especially for protracted processes, the necessary degree of awareness of the competent corporate bodies on the existence of such information is still debatable. Deciding whether information qualifies as inside information is undoubtedly a managerial call. However, since formal decisions by corporate bodies and especially by the board of directors are normally not required for information to be precise, as the new rules on preparatory stages now seem to imply, the question of who is responsible for determining whether inside information exists becomes even more pressing. To put it otherwise, in the case of *Geltl v Daimler*, when could the issuer reasonably expect that Mr Schrempp would have resigned and which corporate body or function was competent to detect the existence of an inside information? Should the board of directors always be invested with such an assessment or, as it appears, the necessary appraisal must be conducted at an earlier stage?[98] A possible solution would be to consider which corporate structures usually deal with that specific piece of information and who would be responsible at the management level for that matter. Accordingly, the issuer would have to establish effective procedures for ensuring that each function timely reports to the operating management and that the information is correctly and promptly handled within the issuer as soon as those responsible for the information are made aware of its existence.[99] It is doubtful, in fact, that the management could in any way decline such responsibility. **B.7.82**

[97] A similar proposal for interpretation is upheld by Krause and Brellochs, 'Insider Trading and the Disclosure of Inside Information' (n 9) 294, whereby they observe that: '[a]s long as the insider prohibitions and the obligation to disclose inside information are triggered simultaneously once "inside information" exists . . ., it is essential that the early stages of protracted decision-making processes do not automatically constitute inside information just because the protracted process is designed to be completed by a future event which is highly significant for the issuer'.

[98] The same issues could arise with regard to who has the power and responsibility within the issuer to decide to delay the disclosure of inside information according to art 17(4) and to the timing of the decision. On this subject cf also Krause and Brellochs, 'Insider Trading and the Disclosure of Inside Information' (n 9) 295; Di Noia and Gargantini, 'Issuers at Midstream' (n 1) 494.

[99] On the importance of establishing organizational schemes, structures and procedures in order to comply with the new regulatory framework on market abuses see Annunziata, 'Riflessi organizzativi' (n 7), especially at 170 and 172.

Article 8: Insider dealing

1. For the purposes of this Regulation, insider dealing arises where a person possesses inside information and uses that information by acquiring or disposing of, for its own account or for the account of a third party, directly or indirectly, financial instruments to which that information relates. The use of inside information by cancelling or amending an order concerning a financial instrument to which the information relates where the order was placed before the person concerned possessed the inside information, shall also be considered to be insider dealing. In relation to auctions of emission allowances or other auctioned products based thereon that are held pursuant to Regulation (EU) No 1031/2010, the use of inside information shall also comprise submitting, modifying or withdrawing a bid by a person for its own account or for the account of a third party.
2. For the purposes of this Regulation, recommending that another person engage in insider dealing, or inducing another person to engage in insider dealing, arises where the person possesses inside information and:
   (a) recommends, on the basis of that information, that another person acquire or dispose of financial instruments to which that information relates, or induces that person to make such an acquisition or disposal, or
   (b) recommends, on the basis of that information, that another person cancel or amend an order concerning a financial instrument to which that information relates, or induces that person to make such a cancellation or amendment.
3. The use of the recommendations or inducements referred to in paragraph 2 amounts to insider dealing within the meaning of this Article where the person using the recommendation or inducement knows or ought to know that it is based upon inside information.
4. This Article applies to any person who possesses inside information as a result of:
   (a) being a member of the administrative, management or supervisory bodies of the issuer or emission allowance market participant;
   (b) having a holding in the capital of the issuer or emission allowance market participant;
   (c) having access to the information through the exercise of an employment, profession or duties; or
   (d) being involved in criminal activities.

This Article also applies to any person who possesses inside information under circumstances other than those referred to in the first subparagraph where that person knows or ought to know that it is inside information.

5. Where the person is a legal person, this Article shall also apply, in accordance with national law, to the natural persons who participate in the decision to carry out the acquisition, disposal, cancellation or amendment of an order for the account of the legal person concerned.

I. General Remarks

Overview of Article 8

Article 8 and the other relevant articles in the Market Abuse Regulation

Article 8 describes what constitutes insider dealing; however, to understand the provision fully it is necessary to understand both its internal structure and its position in the Market Abuse Regulation, since Article 8 is supplemented by other provisions in the Market Abuse Regulation that have a direct bearing on the understanding of what constitutes insider dealing. **B.8.01**

Most importantly, Article 8 concerns the abuse of 'inside information', which is defined in the preceding Article 7. The definition of inside information is crucial to the application of the insider dealing ban, because it strikes the necessary balance between information that legitimately can, respectively cannot, be used when forming an investment decision. The latter kind of information, that is deemed to be inside information, is not only *material* enough to be of interest to a market participant when pricing the security that the information concerns, but it is also *monopolistic*, that is, unavailable to other market participants and thus outside the competition for information that is one of the main functions of the securities markets. It is the abuse of such material monopolistic information **B.8.02** that hurts not only the counterparty to the specific transaction, but also carries negative consequences of a more general societal nature as the unrestrained possibility of such abuse damages the faith in the fair competition for information that market participants expect, notably that all market participants engage in the competition for information on an equal footing. A loss of this confidence may cause them to abandon the market which in turn will lead to suboptimal resource allocation.

B.8.03 Article 8 concerns a particular 'use' of inside information that amounts to abuse. To help fill out this particular and crucial concept of use, several of the recitals in the preamble of the Market Abuse Regulation offer useful examples, notably recital (23). As always when construing legal instruments of EU law, the recitals in the preamble are intended as guidance to the interpretation of the articles and while the recitals are not cited directly as the legal basis themselves, since only the articles can serve that function, the recitals may be cited in connection with the article they concern.

B.8.04 The reach of Article 8 is limited by other provisions of the Market Abuse Regulation. Article 9 describes what constitutes legitimate behaviour and consequently the full scope of the offence of insider dealing is only clear if both Articles are taken into consideration.

B.8.05 Article 5 continues the safe harbour that was offered by Buy-Back Programmes and Stabilisation Regulation (2273/2003/EC) under the (former) Market Abuse Directive (2003/6/EC) in respect of buy-back programmes and stabilization and is now repealed. Another limitation is made by Article 6 to ensure that public bodies may execute political decisions and strategies without being caught by the concept of insider dealing in Article 8, or for that matter the concept of market manipulation as laid out in Article 12.

B.8.06 The scope of Article 8 is not universal. Article 8 only concerns certain securities traded on certain markets, cf Article 2. These securities and markets are defined in Article 3 and, although these provisions display a more technical and objective character, they are of course important to the correct application of Article 8. It should be noted that the offence of insider dealing, that is, taking advantage of material monopolistic information in a transaction to the detriment of the counterparty, is often illegal in national law albeit under other names, such as deceit or fraud, which may make such behaviour illegal under private or criminal law, even when the Market Abuse Regulation does not apply.

B.8.07 Closely related to Article 8 is Article 10 that under certain conditions prohibits selective disclosure of inside information, which in the Market Abuse Regulation is labelled *unlawful disclosure*. It effectively serves as a preventive auxiliary measure to the prohibition on insider dealing in Article 8 by limiting the dissemination of inside information and thereby limiting the risk that such information is abused by insider dealing. Inside information is typically important information and for that reason it is often necessary to disclose it to other parties. Consequently, Article 10 offers an exemption whereby selective disclosure is lawful when done 'in the normal exercise of an employment, a profession or duties'. In its decision of 22 November 2005 in *Grøngaard and Bang*,[1] the Court of Justice of the EU[2] explored the scope of the ban on unlawful disclosure as it was drafted in Article 3(a) Insider Dealing Directive (1989/592/EEC) taking into consideration its exemption, which in this respect was drafted in the same way as Article 10 is drafted today. Although the CJEU emphasized that exemptions should generally be narrowly construed, it also accepted when construing the exemption that one would have to take into account the relevant provisions of national law.[3] In the case at hand, which concerned selective disclosure made by an employee director of a Danish listed issuer, who had been appointed subject to the Danish law on co-determination, to the head of the trade union outside the board that represented a majority of the employees of the company, the legality would depend on how the Danish corporate governance system defined the duties of directors. As it happens, Danish law allows for considerable interaction between major shareholders and management, known and encouraged as 'active ownership',[4] and equally applies to employee appointed directors who usually represent major trade unions with whom they are known to share important information confidentially. Consequently, in the Danish criminal case the two defendants, the director, and the recipient of the disclosure, were eventually acquitted by the Danish Supreme Court, because the selective disclosure of inside information was deemed to be within the scope of duty of the director in question.[5]

Although the case was decided in respect of Article 3(a) of the Insider Dealing Directive (1989/592/EEC), the continuation of the prohibition in first Article 3(a) (former) Market Abuse Directive (2003/6/EC) and then in Article 10 with almost identical wording suggests that it is still valid case law. Also, recital (19) emphasizes that communication between shareholders and management is not necessarily caught by the ban in Article 10. The recital is limited to 'discussions of a general nature', which reflects that the corporate governance systems of the EU Member States are different and that not all jurisdictions may allow the kind of communication that was legal according to Danish law. To understand the **B.8.08**

---

[1] Case C-384/02 *Criminal proceedings against Knud Grøngaard and Allan Bang* [2005] ECR I-9939.

[2] The Court has been operating under different names according to the different treaties, but its present name will be used here throughout.

[3] *Grøngaard and Bang* (n 1) para 40.

[4] On the nature of the almost identical corporate governance systems of the Nordic countries see Per Lekvall (ed), *The Nordic Corporate Governance Model* (SNS Förlag 2014) http://papers.ssrn.com/sol3/papers.cfm?abstract_id=2534331 (last accessed 1 October 2016).

[5] The case is reported in Danish in the legal periodical *Ugeskrift for Retsvæsen* 2009.2142.

scope of Article 10 on unlawful disclosure fully, it may thus be necessary to take national law into consideration. Furthermore, Article 10 is limited by Article 11 on market soundings, which permits selective disclosure when part of a market-sounding exercise.

B.8.09 Finally, Article 8 is supplement by Article 14, which serves to declare that conduct covered by Article 8 is prohibited. Article 14 also prohibits attempts to engage in insider dealing.

Level 2 instruments

B.8.10 The legislative level 1 text of the Market Abuse Regulation is supplemented by several level 2 instruments according to Articles 290 and 291 of the Treaty on the Functioning of the EU (hereafter TFEU) that must be taken into consideration when construing its provisions. However, no level 2 text applies in respect of Article 8.

B.8.11 Furthermore, the European Securities and Markets Authority (hereafter ESMA) may issue guidance and recommendations according to Article 16 of the ESMA Regulation. So far no guidance in respect of Article 8 has been issued.

B.8.12 ESMA also issues a communication called Questions and Answers (Q&A), which is an instrument that purports to answer questions about the application of EU law. This instrument is not regulated by the ESMA Regulation (1095/2010) and is consequently non-binding, but it is very useful as a flexible tool to convey the dominant opinion of ESMA and of the national competent authorities (hereafter NCAs) that constitute the Board of Supervisors, which is the decision-making body of ESMA that adopts the Q&A. At present, the Q&A on the Market Abuse Regulation dated 30 May 2017 only addresses one small aspect of the application of Article 8 directly.

The structure of Article 8

B.8.13 Article 8 itself is composed of several sections. Article 8(1) is the primary provision as it lays out what behaviour constitutes insider dealing. It concerns securities transactions whereby a person who is in possession of inside information (hereafter the insider) abuses the inside information. Behaviour caught by Article 8(1) is prohibited, according to Article 14(a).

B.8.14 Although the title of Article 8 is simply 'insider dealing', the Article comprises in Article 8(2) a behaviour that is subject to a separate prohibition in Article 14(b). This behaviour concerns recommending or inducing another person to engage in insider dealing, where 'engage' is a reference to the behaviour described in Article 8(1). This kind of recommendation or inducement is sometimes referred to as tipping and the person so encouraged is known as a tippee. As Article 14 makes a distinction between insider dealing according to Article 8(1) and the behaviour mentioned in Article 8(2), the latter behaviour will here be termed 'tipping' as a separate offence.

Article 8(3) concerns the actions of the tippee that received recommendations or inducements according to Article 8(2). Article 8(3) declares that if the tippee so engage, it will constitute insider dealing in the sense of Article 8(1) by the tippee. **B.8.15**

Article 8(4) makes in its first subsection a distinction between persons engaging in insider dealing based on their access to the inside information, which is supplemented by a second subsection that covers all other persons who have come into possession of the inside information in other ways. As will be explored in V below, the distinction made within Article 8(4) between the two groups of insiders probably reflects the origin of the insider dealing ban in US law, where a distinction was drawn at an early point in the development of the ban between *primary insiders* and *secondary insiders*, which distinction later found its way into the law of some EU Member States, although its continued relevance in EU law is questionable. **B.8.16**

Finally, Article 8(5) concerns the liability of legal persons and the natural persons employed by them. As a legal person is a figment of our legal imagination, it is obvious that only natural persons can act on their behalf and consequently only natural persons can commit insider dealing. Article 8(5) addresses the problem of when to ascribe the liability of natural persons to a legal person, but appears at first look to have turned the question on its head as it presupposes the liability of the legal person and seeks to expand that liability to the natural persons where they have engaged in the behaviour that constitutes insider dealing. **B.8.17**

Historical development

The origin of insider dealing

Markets flourish in most countries of the world and generally serve to enhance the economic wellbeing of societies, because they enable voluntary transactions. When people voluntarily enter into a transaction, it is usually because the transaction makes them better off, known in economic theory as Pareto efficiency. In this way, markets ensure an efficient allocation of resources to the mutual benefit of all parties. **B.8.18**

However, sometimes a transaction does not make both parties better off. In some cases a transaction can serve as a zero-sum game, where the advantage of one party to the transaction is matched by a loss to the other. Whether in these cases to prevent one person from obtaining an unfair advantage from the transaction at the detriment of the counterparty is an old problem within the regulation of markets, irrespectively of the goods or services traded on the market. On the one hand, it is normally considered fair that the better businessperson is rewarded by his or her superior talents or efforts even where it implies a loss to others, on the other, in some cases it is nevertheless considered unfair. These cases mostly concern instances where the two parties to the transaction are not **B.8.19** considered to be on an equal footing. That competition may produce a winner and a loser is acceptable only if the competition is seen as fair and conducted on a level playing ground. Often in business transactions, unfair outcomes involve transactions where the relevant information about the goods or services is only available to one party but not to the other, known as an information asymmetry. In the regulation of product markets, such as the law on the sale of goods, a distinction between lawful and unlawful transactions is made by emphasising the information available to the parties, and similar outcomes are known from the area of contract law.

B.8.20 For example in the case of a sale of goods that suffers from a condition that the buyer finds unfortunate, the buyer cannot later state a claim on this condition if it was available and recognizable for the buyer at the time when he or she entered into the transaction, which is known as the principle of buyer beware (*caveat emptor*). On the other hand, a claim can be made by the buyer if the condition was a hidden defect known only to the seller. This distinction is well known in the various areas of law concerning the regulation of markets and, although the distinction remains the same, the actual application of it may vary depending on the market in question.

B.8.21 In the securities markets, similar rules have developed in securities regulation independently of other areas of market law and are grouped together under the not entirely apt title of *insider dealing*.[6] Again, the distinction made between lawful and unlawful transactions appears to be much the same across jurisdictions such as the United States, Europe, and Australia, but national law may offer variations. As was the case in the example just offered, emphasis is placed on the information available to the parties. If information is *material*, that is, of importance to the pricing of the securities, and *monopolistic*, that is, only available to one party of the transaction, then the informed party is not allowed to abuse this informational advantage. The information just described is in securities regulation called *inside information* and is defined in Article 7.[7]

The US origin of insider dealing

B.8.22 The ban on insider dealing in securities regulation appears to have originated in US federal law. The substantial federal regulation of securities trading that was brought about by the New Deal legislation of the 1933 Securities Act and the 1934 Securities Exchange Act (the latter hereafter 1934 SEA) was made on the backdrop of the Great Depression that had been triggered by the Stock Market

[6] Although the terms 'insider', 'inside information', and 'insider dealing' all refer to company insiders and are used in most jurisdictions, the actual application of the terms in modern regulation does not rely on the persons or the information actually being 'inside' the issuer of the securities, as will be made clear in this chapter on art 8.

[7] See art 7 n 25 ff.

Crash of 1929. From the hearings in Congress that accompanied the legislation, it was clear that among the malpractices identified some cases appeared to imply the abuse of confidential price-sensitive information that was usually only available to company insiders. However, the disclosure regime at the time was not such that it was seen as unfair in itself to take advantage of an informational advantage; information was not generally distributed among market participants and, consequently, it was not deemed unfair as such to take advantage of information irrespectively of its uneven distribution in the market. This opinion was widely shared not just in the United States, and when the ban on insider dealing was later introduced in Europe, it was by some market practitioners derided as 'the crime of being somebody in the market', that is, a penalization of being important enough to get access to material non-public information. This perception changed, although slowly, as the law on securities trading began to make disclosure and distribution of price-sensitive information more widespread and frequent, which eventually made the use of non-public material information appear unfair.

In the 1934 SEA there was no outright ban on insider dealing, but it is apparent that Section 16(b), known as *the short-swing profit rule*, was intended to prevent 'the unfair use of information', that is: insider dealing, by requiring company insiders to account for profits made by first buying and then selling, or vice versa, securities of their company within a short period of time. This 'short-swing' would often be made to exploit material non-public information in the insider's possession and by obliging the insider to hand over any profits made to the company, a disincentive to insider dealing was created. **B.8.23**

In the 1960s, the Securities and Exchange Commission (SEC) tried to expand Section 16(b) 1934 SEA to cover other persons than company insiders, but was rebuffed by the US Supreme Court in the *Lehman* case.[8] As an alternative route, the SEC used Rule 10b-5 promulgated under the anti-fraud provision of Section 10(b) 1934 SEA two decades before to address the use of inside information in transactions carried out on the secondary market. This was successful in the 1961 administrative decision of *Cady, Roberts & Co*,[9] and would eventually develop through case law into a ban on insider dealing. **B.8.24**

The development in European law

The view present in Section 16(b) 1934 SEA focused on company insiders, that is, primary insiders, and the same view is evident in the 1966 Report by the Segré Group on the development of a European capital market as it primarily addressed information possessed by management, that is, company insiders, although it also mentioned considerations of competition and the need to ensure investors **B.8.25**

[8] US Supreme Court, *Blau v Lehman*, 368 US 403 (1962), decided 22 January 1962.

[9] *Cady, Roberts & Co*, 40 SEC (1961).

were placed on an equal footing.[10] About this time, France introduced rules in 1967–68 that were clearly inspired by the US Rule 16(b) 1934 SEA, and their company law nature ensured that they found their way into the 1970 proposal for an SE Regulation,[11] although they were later deleted before the Regulation was adopted. Sweden and Finland would also introduce similar provisions into national law.

B.8.26 This approach of seeing insider dealing as closely connected to company law and fiduciary duties of primary insiders appears to have changed when a task force was established by the Commission's Directorate General XV, which covered Economic and Financial Affairs. It produced a Working Paper on insider dealing in 1976 that emphasized competition more than the company law aspect of directors' loyalty.[12] The Commission first opted not to pursue with a directive, but instead issued the 1977 Recommendation on a European Code of Conduct for securities trading,[13] which as a recommendation was not binding but only advised the Member States of the regulation in national law that the Commission deemed necessary or prudent in this area. The Recommendation addressed insider dealing by persons who had come into possession of non-public price-sensitive information by way of their profession or their duties and unlawful disclosure by the same persons in point 9 of the Supplementary Principles.

The Market Abuse Regulation and its predecessors

B.8.27 When in 1987, the Commission adopted its Insider Dealing Directive Proposal, it noted that by this time four of the then Member States of the EEC had rules on insider dealing: Denmark, France, and the United Kingdom had provisions in criminal law, while Germany had introduced a voluntary regime. Three other Member States, Belgium, Ireland, and the Netherlands, were in the process of legislating. Other Member States had no regulation at all, which probably explains the cautious approach in what became the 1989 Insider Dealing Directive (1989/592/EEC). The Insider Dealing Directive (1989/592/EEC) was a minimum harmonization directive with the express permission in Article 6 of the Insider Dealing Directive (1989/592/EEC) for Member States to implement stricter provisions. The Insider Dealing Directive (1989/592/EEC) provided harmonization of insider dealing and certain auxiliary provisions deemed related to the offence of insider dealing, but it did not include market manipulation.

[10] Commission, Working Document by C Segré, The development of a European capital market. Report of a Group of Experts appointed by the EEC Commission, Brussels (November 1966) 249.

[11] Commission, Proposal for a Regulation Embodying a Statute for the European Company COM(70) 600, OJ C 124 (10 October 1970); see art 82(5) of the Proposal.

[12] Commission Working Paper No 1, Coordination of the Rules and Regulations Governing Insider Trading, XV/206/76-E.

[13] Commission Recommendation of 25 July 1977 concerning a European Code of Conduct relating to Transactions in Transferable Securities, Brussels (77/534).

The euro was envisaged as the new EU wide currency in the 1992 Maastricht Treaty and in anticipation of its effects the Commission was tasked with presenting its policy for integrating the financial markets of the Member States. The Commission's 1999 Financial Services Action Plan (hereafter FSAP) presented an ambitious programme of legislative initiatives, among them a proposal for a directive on market manipulation to supplement the existing Insider Dealing Directive (1989/592/EEC).[14] The Forum of European Securities Commissions (FESCO), which was an organization of national competent authorities put together to enhance cooperation on their supervision of national financial markets in anticipation of the introduction of the euro, supported the initiative, but also recommended that the initiative should imitate the recent reform in the United Kingdom that had led to the Financial Services and Markets Act 2000, which presented a combined regulation of 'market abuse' in section 118, which covered insider dealing, market manipulation, and unlawful disclosure.[15] **B.8.28**

This idea was followed by the Commission and in 2001, it presented its proposal[16] for what would in 2003 become the (former) Market Abuse Directive (2003/6/EC). In (former) Market Abuse Directive (2003/6/EC), the insider dealing ban and the auxiliary provisions were expanded and further supplemented by a ban on market manipulation in Article 5 (former) Market Abuse Directive (2003/6/EC) and an obligation on issuers to disclose inside information to the market in Article 6 of the (former) Market Abuse Directive (2003/6/EC); the latter had in fact been suggested in the Commission's Insider Dealing Directive Proposal but had not been adopted.[17] **B.8.29**

The ambitious legislative programme presented in the FSAP necessitated a new approach to legislation and the Commission established the Lamfalussy Group, which in its 2001 Report[18] presented a new approach based on four different levels of action, notably the increased use of delegation by way of the comitology procedure whereby legal instruments adopted by the Council and, increasingly since the 1992 Maastricht Treaty, also the European Parliament would be implemented by legal texts adopted by the Commission on level 2. To assist the Commission in this new procedure, FESCO was changed into the Committee of **B.8.30**

---

[14] Commission, Financial Services: Implementing the Framework for Financial Markets: Action Plan, Brussels (11 May 1999) 6.

[15] FESCO, 'Market Abuse: FESCO's Response to the Call for Views From the Securities Regulators Under the EU's Action Plan for Financial Services' Paris, Fesco/00-0961 (29 June 2000).

[16] Commission, Proposal for a Directive of the European Parliament and of the Council on insider dealing and market manipulation (market abuse) COM(2001) 281, Brussels (30 May 2001).

[17] Art 7 Insider Dealing Directive Proposal.

[18] Final Report of the Committee of Wise Men on the Regulation of European Securities Markets, Brussels (15 February 2001).

European Securities Regulators (CESR) by a decision of the Commission.[19] The (former) Market Abuse Directive (2003/6/EC) became the first directive to be adopted following the new Lamfalussy procedure and was supplemented by three directives and a regulation on level 2.[20]

B.8.31 Following the Financial Crisis of 2008–2009, much of the regulation of the financial markets, including its overall structure, was changed. In 2011, the Commission presented its Market Abuse Regulation Proposal for what would become the 2014 Market Abuse Regulation. Many provisions of the (former) Market Abuse Directive (2003/6/EC) were restated in the Market Abuse Regulation, including some but not all of the provisions that were previously found in the level 2 instruments, which would be repealed alongside (former) Market Abuse Directive (2003/6/EC) itself when the Market Abuse Regulation entered into force.

B.8.32 What was known as the Lamfalussy procedure had at that time been codified by the Lisbon Treaty and now forms part of the ordinary legislative procedure, where level 1 instruments according to Article 289 TFEU may delegate regulatory or implementing powers to the Commission according to Articles 290–291 TFEU respectively. Consequently, the level 1 instrument the Market Abuse Regulation is supplement by a large number of level 2 instruments issued by the Commission and these level 2 instruments take the form of directly applicable regulations as is the level 1 instrument itself. The Market Abuse Regulation is supplemented by the Market Abuse Directive on Criminal Sanctions (2014/57/EU), which aims to harmonize the criminal sanctions applied by the Member States to combat market abuse such as insider dealing.

II. Section 1: Behaviour that Constitutes Insider Dealing

Two elements: possession and use

B.8.33 Article 8(1) defines the form of market abuse known as insider dealing and states that insider dealing arises 'where a person possesses inside information and uses that information' to engage in certain transactions, the nature of which are explored in para B.8.52 ff below.

B.8.34 Consequently, the insider dealing ban is divided into two separate elements: the possession of inside information and the use of inside information. The first element of 'possession' will be explored next and then the requirement of 'use'.

[19] Commission Decision (2001/527) of 6 June 2001 establishing the Committee of European Securities Regulators, OJ L 191/43 (13 July 2001).

[20] Commission Directives 2003/124, 2003/125, and 2004/72, and Commission Regulation 2273/2003.

It is, of course, extremely important to make clear what constitutes the kind of behaviour that amounts to abuse in the sense of Article 8(1), which is prohibited by Article 14(a) and usually subject to criminal sanctions. It is important not only to appreciate the proper application of the ban in Article 8(1) itself, but also because Article 9 relies on this understanding to distinguish behaviour that may be equally detrimental to the functioning of the securities markets from the behaviour that should be deemed lawful. Article 9 thus provides several examples of behaviour that is deemed legitimate, but according to Article 9(6) the NCA may still consider the behaviour an infringement of Article 14 if there was an 'illegitimate reason'. This concept can only be understood if it is clear what exactly is the concept of abuse applied in Article 8(1), since that is what distinguishes the legitimate behaviour from the illegitimate. **B.8.35**

The behaviour that qualifies as insider dealing according to Article 8(1) is prohibited by Article 14(a), which also includes any attempt to commit insider dealing.[21] **B.8.36**

Possession of inside information—a monopolistic position

In this part, the first element of insider dealing, to possess inside information, is explored. While possession of inside information obviously entails a mental component, that is, when can a person be said to possess a certain piece of information in the sense of being aware of or to understand the information, this subjective requirement is analysed in Section VII below and what is explored here is the more objective character of the possession requirement. **B.8.37**

When deciding the *Grøngaard and Bang* case,[22] that concerned selective disclosure, the CJEU recognized that the ban on unlawful disclosure in Article 3(a) Insider Dealing Directive (1989/592/EEC) served as a preventive measure to the insider dealing ban in Article 2 Insider Dealing Directive (1989/592/EEC) and consequently focused on how to understand the ban on insider dealing. Applying its usual teleological style of interpretation, the CJEU noted that according to recitals (2)–(5) Insider Dealing Directive (1989/592/EEC) the purpose of the ban on insider dealing was to 'ensure the proper functioning of the secondary market in transferable securities and to protect investors' confidence, which depends, in particular, on their being placed on an equal footing and protected against the improper use of inside information'.[23] As the case concerned the separate offence of unlawful disclosure that is now dealt with in Article 10, it is not of further relevance here, except that its emphasis of equal position was later quoted in another case which more directly concerned the ban on insider dealing as it was drafted under the Insider Dealing Directive (1989/592/EEC). **B.8.38**

---

21 See art 14 Section III.

22 *Grøngaard and Bang* (n 1).

23 *Grøngaard and Bang* (n 1) para 33.

B.8.39 That was the *Georgakis* case, which was decided by the CJEU on 10 May 2007 and concerned the ban on insider dealing in Article 2 Insider Dealing Directive (1989/592/EEC).[24] *Georgakis* concerned an instance of market manipulation in the Greek securities markets, whereby a circle of wealthy individuals conspired to buy and sell to each other certain securities in companies where they were substantial investors at prices above what they would fetch in the market, also known as *painting the tape*, to support the price of the securities and prevent them from falling. However, the defendant had been charged with insider dealing and appealed on the grounds that this was an erroneous application of the ban on insider dealing as laid down by Article 2 Insider Dealing Directive (1989/592/EEC). The CJEU was consequently asked by the referring national court whether the actions amounted to insider dealing, that is, if the actions corresponded to the relevant wording of Article 2 of the Insider Dealing Directive (1989/592/EEC) of 'taking advantage of [the inside information] with full knowledge of the facts'.[25]

B.8.40 The decision of the CJEU in *Georgakis* can be divided into three steps. First, the CJEU rejected that the defendants had acted on inside information when they relied on the advice provided by their financial advisors to begin the concerted effort to keep up the price by trading within their circle.[26] Secondly, the CJEU acknowledged that the decision made by the defendants to act in this way to keep up the price could constitute inside information in the sense of Article 1(1) Insider Dealing Directive (1989/592/EEC).[27] Third, the CJEU concluded that the defendants did not 'take advantage' of the inside information.[28]

B.8.41 It is this third part of the CJEU's reasoning that is relevant to the issue examined here. In examining the meaning of 'taking advantage' in Article 2 Insider Dealing Directive (1989/592/EEC), the CJEU restated its prior observation in *Grøngaard and Bang*[29] that recitals (2)–(5) Insider Dealing Directive (1989/592/EEC) state as the purpose of the Directive 'to ensure the proper functioning of the secondary market in transferable securities and to protect investors' confidence, which depends, in particular, on their being placed on an equal footing and protected against the improper use of inside information'.[30] Based on this, the CJEU concluded: 'Consequently, the purpose of the prohibition laid down by Article 2 of Directive 89/592 is to ensure equality between the contracting parties in stock-market transactions by preventing one of them who possesses inside

---

[24] Case C-391/04 *Ipourgos Ikonomikon, Proistamenos DOI Amfissas v Charilaos Georgakis* [2007] ECR I-3741 (*Georgakis*).

[25] The wording was considered to have a bearing on the subjective condition (*mens rea*) of the prohibition, which is not relevant here. See further on the subjective condition Section VII.

[26] *Georgakis* (n 24) paras 30–31.

[27] ibid para 33.

[28] ibid para 35.

[29] *Grøngaard and Bang* (n 1).

[30] *Georgakis* (n 24) para 37.

information and who is, therefore, in an advantageous position vis-à-vis the other investors, from profiting from that information, to the detriment of the other party who is unaware of it.'[31]

B.8.42 Thus, in *Georgakis* the CJEU defined the essence of insider dealing as that of being in an advantageous position by possessing information that is not available to the counterparty of the relevant transaction, that is, the parties are not on an equal footing. In other words, the person possessing the inside information, that is the insider, is in an advantageous position because he or she possesses information that is monopolistic.[32]

B.8.43 This understanding of the ban corresponded to the original intent behind the Insider Dealing Directive (1989/592/EEC) as laid out by the Commission in its proposal for the Insider Dealing Directive (1989/592/EEC).[33] Here, the Commission states that the Insider Dealing Directive (1989/592/EEC) should ensure equality of opportunity for all investors.[34] Equality of opportunity is what is colloquially referred to as a level playing field, or, as it was put in recital (5) of the Insider Dealing Directive Proposal, that investors are placed on an equal footing.

B.8.44 It is important to note that equality of opportunity does not presume full equality among the parties of a transaction, that is, a parity of information. If information is legally available to market participants, the market participants enjoy equality of opportunity and it is irrelevant whether the two parties to a particular transaction have in fact made themselves acquainted with the information as they enter into the transaction. Equality of opportunity is thus a term that emphasizes the competition for information in the securities markets: if information is legally available and thus subject to open competition, it may legally be exploited by a market participant even if that participant's counterparty has failed to learn of the information. This understanding influences the definition of inside information and as the subsequent new legislation has not challenged this view but has restated the importance of having all investors on an equal footing, cf today recital (24), it still applies to Article 7 on the definition of inside information.

B.8.45 In the case at hand, the CJEU observed that trading was only done among the informed circle and consequently they had all been on an equal footing and unable to take advantage of the inside information that was shared among them.[35] Thus, the CJEU concluded that no insider dealing had taken place.

[31] ibid para 38.

[32] As is apparent from the cited para 38 from *Georgakis* (n 24) the CJEU also defined the other element of 'use', or as it was then phrased 'taking advantage', which is explored further below.

[33] Insider Dealing Directive Proposal, COM(87) 111.

[34] ibid 2.

[35] *Georgakis* (n 24) para 39.

B.8.46 In passing the CJEU also mentioned that the inside information 'ceases to be inside information for them' because the inside information was known by them, that is, there was a parity of information among the participants in the circle.[36] What is of importance here is not that the information ceased to be inside information, but that it ceased to be inside information *among the parties*. This implies that outside the circle of informed traders, the information would retain its character of inside information. Probably, the CJEU intended to express that if one of the parties to the informed circle had engaged in trading with an uninformed third person outside the circle, it could have constituted insider dealing, if the inside information, that is, the knowledge of the ploy to keep prices up, had been taken advantage of. In that case, the inside information would not have 'ceased' to be inside information; it only ceased to be in the context of the informed circle that shared the inside information.

B.8.47 In this way, *Georgakis* suggests that the essence of inside information is its monopolistic character in the way that it constitutes an informational advantage that can be abused to the detriment of uninformed parties. Where there is no monopoly, because there is a parity of information among two or more parties, there is no advantage in the form of an informational asymmetry inter partes, and the inside information ceases to qualify as inside information among the informed parties, while it may retain its character as inside information vis-à-vis uninformed parties. The observation that a parity of information cannot give way to insider dealing is, by the way, comparable to the position known in US federal securities regulation, where it is expressed as *disclose or abstain*. Disclosure of the inside information, where this is permissible and practically feasible, will create a parity of information with the insider that makes it impossible for the insider to take advantage of the inside information.

B.8.48 The observation of the CJEU in *Georgakis* may further suggest that the qualification of inside information depends on the specific transaction, so that a piece of information may constitute inside information in respect of one transaction but not in respect of another, depending on the distribution of information among the parties engaged in these transactions.

B.8.49 In the Market Abuse Regulation, inside information is defined in Article 7, and readers are referred to the commentary of that article. Here, suffice it to point out that *Georgakis* settled that, according to the Insider Dealing Directive (1989/592/EEC), possession concerned information that was monopolistic to the insider in the sense that it was not available to the other party of the relevant transaction. This reasoning was based on recitals (2)–(5) Insider Dealing Directive (1989/592/EEC). However, recital (5) on 'equal footing' was not replicated in the (former) Market Abuse Directive (2003/6/EC). This omission did not influence the

[36] ibid.

outcome in the later decision of 23 December 2009 in case C-45/08 *Spector Photo Group NV*,[37] which concerned insider dealing according to Article 2 (former) Market Abuse Directive (2003/6/EC), and in its decision the CJEU quoted by analogy *Grøngaard and Bang* in its finding that the purpose of the ban on insider dealing was to ensure that parties to a securities transaction are placed on an equal footing.[38]

In the Market Abuse Regulation, the reference to 'equal footing' has been reinstated in recital (24) in what is clearly a reference to the decision in *Spector* and consequently it appears to be valid law that the requirement to possess inside information in Article 8(1) concerns the situation where the insider possesses information that is monopolistic in respect of the other party or parties to the relevant transaction. Or to use the phrase from *Georgakis*, where the insider is in an advantageous position vis-à-vis the other investors. **B.8.50**

Equally, we can assume as was the case in *Georgakis*, that where there is a parity of information among the parties of the relevant transaction, no insider dealing can take place among them. **B.8.51**

Using the inside information—detrimental action

It is clear from the way the ban on insider dealing has been worded through time from the Insider Dealing Directive (1989/592/EEC) over (former) Market Abuse Directive (2003/6/EC) to the Market Abuse Regulation, that it consists of two elements: to possess inside information and to abuse the inside information. **B.8.52**

In *Georgakis*, the CJEU concluded that the essence of insider dealing as defined in Article 2 Insider Dealing Directive (1989/592/EEC) was to be in an advantageous position by possessing monopolistic (inside) information *and* profiting from that information to the detriment of the other uninformed party. Both elements had to be fulfilled and consequently trading while in possession of inside information was not enough to constitute abuse; the transaction would also have to inflict a detriment to the other party, which constituted the 'taking advantage' of the inside information required in Article 2 Insider Dealing Directive (1989/592/EEC). **B.8.53**

That taking advantage of the inside information means to profit to the detriment of the uninformed party to the transaction also reflects the position taken originally by the Commission in the Insider Dealing Directive Proposal, where the Commission remarked that insider dealing is defined by making 'gains at the expense of other investors'.[39] **B.8.54**

---

[37] Case C-45/08 *Spector Photo Group NV v CBFA* [2009] ECR I-12073.
[38] ibid para 47.
[39] Insider Dealing Directive Proposal COM(87) 111, 2.

B.8.55 However, when the Commission in 2001 brought forward its (former) Market Abuse Directive (2003/6/EC) Proposal to replace the Insider Dealing Directive (1989/592/EEC),[40] the wording of the ban on insider dealing in Article 2(1) was changed from 'taking advantage of [the inside information] with full knowledge of the facts' as it had been in Article 2 Insider Dealing Directive (1989/592/EEC). In the (former) Market Abuse Directive (2003/6/EC) Proposal, Article 2(1) deleted 'with full knowledge of the facts' but maintained the words 'taking advantage of', and in the final version of Article 2(1) (former) Market Abuse Directive (2003/6/EC) that was further changed to 'using'. The change was made because some Member States had construed the previous wording as mandating a high degree of the subjective condition (*mens rea*).[41]

B.8.56 This raised the question whether the change from 'taking advantage', which in *Georgakis* had been construed as acting to the detriment of the other party of the relevant transaction, to 'use' meant that the condition of a detrimental effect was no longer required under the (former) Market Abuse Directive (2003/6/EC).

B.8.57 The Commission did not appear to have contemplated a change, since in its original (former) Market Abuse Directive (2003/6/EC) Proposal it stated that the content of the old Insider Dealing Directive (1989/592/EEC) was continued except for this change,[42] and described insiders as using inside information 'to their own advantage',[43] which suggest a detrimental disadvantage to others affected by the transaction. That no material change was in fact contemplated in the (former) Market Abuse Directive (2003/6/EC) compared to the old Insider Dealing Directive (1989/592/EEC) and that a condition of detriment to the uninformed parties was still part of the insider dealing offence was made clear in the decision by the CJEU of 23 December 2009 in the *Spector* case.[44]

B.8.58 *Spector* concerned a Belgian company that engaged in a buy-back scheme while the management of the company was in possession of positive inside information.[45] Among the questions before the national court was how to construe the concept of 'use' and in its referral to the CJEU, the national court asked among other things whether the mere fact that a person is in possession of inside information when trading constitutes such use as covered by Article 2 (former) Market Abuse Directive (2003/6/EC).

---

[40] Commission, Proposal for a Regulation of the European Parliament and of the Council on insider dealing and market manipulation (market abuse) COM(2011) 651 final.

[41] See Section VII on the subjective condition.

[42] Commission, Proposal for a Regulation of the European Parliament and of the Council on insider dealing and market manipulation (market abuse) COM(2011) 651 final, 7.

[43] ibid 2.

[44] *Spector* (n 37).

[45] Positive inside information is information that indicates an increase in the price of the security, while negative inside information would indicate a price decrease.

The CJEU began its reasoning by addressing the question of the subjective condition, which it saw as the reason the wording had been changed in Article 2 (former) Market Abuse Directive (2003/6/EC) compared to that of Article 2 Insider Dealing Directive (1989/592/EEC) into a more objective wording. This line of argument will be explored in Section VII below on the subjective condition. The CJEU then addressed the question of how to construe the concept of 'use'. **B.8.59**

It is clear that the CJEU was concerned that the new objective wording of the prohibition should not lead to an excessive application. The CJEU cites approvingly the interventions of the governments of Italy and the United Kingdom in this respect,[46] and expressly notes the importance of not extending the scope of the prohibition beyond what is appropriate and necessary and to ensure that the use of inside information is 'actually unfair' in order for it to be unlawful.[47] **B.8.60**

To understand what kind of use is unfair, that is, abusive in the sense of Article 2 (former) Market Abuse Directive (2003/6/EC), the CJEU begins by observing that not every instance of trading while in possession of inside information is unlawful,[48] and that it is necessary to distinguish between use of inside information that is unlawful and that which is not.[49] In other words, not every instance where inside information is in possession at the time of the trade or even where the inside information has been used is necessarily unlawful. **B.8.61**

Applying its teleological style of interpretation, the CJEU highlights the purpose of the prohibition and makes a reference by analogy to its prior decision in *Georgakis*: 'Thus, the purpose of the prohibition laid down by Article 2(1) of Directive 2003/6 is to ensure equality between the contracting parties in stock-market transactions by preventing one of them who possesses inside information and who is, therefore, in an advantageous position vis-à-vis other investors, from profiting from that information, to the detriment of those who are unaware of it . . .'[50] **B.8.62**

Based on this purpose, the CJEU concludes: 'The essential characteristic of insider dealing thus consists in an unfair advantage being obtained from information to the detriment of third parties who are unaware of it and, consequently, the undermining of the integrity of financial markets and investor confidence.'[51] **B.8.63**

The fact that the CJEU cited its older case law under Insider Dealing Directive (1989/592/EEC) in *Spector* suggests that the CJEU saw the ban on insider dealing **B.8.64**

46 *Spector* (n 37) para 46.
47 ibid para 55.
48 ibid para 45.
49 ibid para 46.
50 ibid para 48.
51 ibid para 52.

as essentially unchanged by the subsequent adoption of (former) Market Abuse Directive (2003/6/EC).[52]

B.8.65 Considering that Article 8(1) uses effectively the same wording as Article 2(1) (former) Market Abuse Directive (2003/6/EC), it is likely that the CJEU would find that the insider dealing ban is essentially the same in the Market Abuse Regulation. This is supported by the fact that guidance to what is meant by the phrasing in Article 8(1) about 'using' inside information is provided by recital (23), which begins:

> The essential characteristic of insider dealing consists in an unfair advantage being obtained from inside information to the detriment of third parties who are unaware of such information and, consequently, the undermining of the integrity of financial markets and investor confidence. Consequently, the prohibition against insider dealing should apply where a person who is in possession of inside information takes unfair advantage of the benefit gained from that information by entering into market transactions in accordance with that information ...

B.8.66 The wording of recital (23) is clearly taken from the CJEU's decision in *Spector* and it was inserted very early in the legislative procedure by the EU legislators, apparently to make a direct reference to *Spector* as a guide to understand the concept of illegal use applied in Article 8(1).[53] Consequently, *Spector* must be considered valid case law in respect of the Market Abuse Regulation.

B.8.67 To understand fully the ban on insider dealing in Article 8, it is important to note the important role played by the concept of inside information. In *Spector*, the CJEU noted that there is a close link between the prohibition on insider dealing and the concept of inside information.[54] This is because the essence of insider dealing is to abuse an informational advantage and that advantage is defined by the concept of inside information. When Article 8(1) states two conditions for insider dealing, possession of inside information and use of that inside information, the first condition of possession is effectively filled out by Article 7 on the definition of inside information. What remains in Article 8(1) is to determine when a person 'possesses' inside information and when the insider is 'using' that inside information. Thus, in order to construe the concept of *inside information* in Article 7 correctly, it is necessary to conform to the overall purpose of the prohibition on insider dealing of which the concept of inside information forms an integral part.[55]

[52] ibid, where the CJEU states that the relevant recitals of the Market Abuse Regulation on insider dealing were 'following the example of Directive 89/592', that is the Insider Dealing Directive (1989/592/EEC), cf para 47 of *Spector* (n 37), and reference is made to its case law under Insider Dealing Directive (1989/592/EEC) 'by analogy'; see inter alia paras 47–8, which refers to *Grøngaard and Bang* (n 1) and *Georgakis* (n 24), respectively.

[53] Recital (23) was inserted as recital (16b) in the first Presidential Compromise of 2 May 2012, Interinstitutional file 2011/0295(COD) No 9435/12.

[54] *Spector* (n 37) para 50.

[55] See art 7 n 25 ff.

Lawful or unlawful use

As explored above, the ban on insider dealing in Article 8(1) consist of two elements: possession of monopolistic (inside) information and the abuse of such information to the detriment of other parties. This is, by the way, a familiar characteristic from a related field of law concerning markets, that of competition law, where possession of a dominant position is not in itself unlawful, only the abuse of a dominant position is. **B.8.68**

Both elements have to be fulfilled and consequently trading while in possession of inside information is not enough to constitute abuse; the transaction must also inflict a detriment to the other party and this detrimental action is what is meant by 'use' in Article 8(1). **B.8.69**

As already established in *Georgakis*,[56] the possession of inside information is not enough to establish insider dealing, it is only the starting point. The inside information constitutes the informational advantage enjoyed by the insider, or in the parlance of competition law: the dominant position enjoyed by the insider by his or her possession of monopolistic information. Only if the insider engages in a transaction, which is detrimental to other parties, has the insider taken unfair advantage and thus committed insider dealing. Using inside information in the sense applied in Article 8(1) is to engage in a transaction, whereby the other party is put at a disadvantage. The need to distinguish between lawful and unlawful use of inside information pointed out by the CJEU in *Spector*, and which is also of relevance to Article 9(6), thus concerns whether the transaction was detrimental to other parties.[57] **B.8.70**

Both the CJEU in *Spector* and recital (23) speak of 'obtaining an unfair advantage' to the detriment of third parties. This raises the question of whether it is a necessary requirement to establish that an advantage was obtained. Considering how the CJEU in its case law has focused on the need to protect investors, it is likely that the emphasis is on the detriment to third parties affected by the insider's transaction and not on any advantage enjoyed by the insider. Often, what constitutes a detriment to third parties will accrue as an advantage of the insider who exploits his or her informational advantage or persons favoured by the insider. It is probably not necessary to establish that the insider or others obtained an advantage from the relevant transaction that exactly corresponds to the detriment of the third parties caused by the transaction. The indispensable requirement in Article 8(1) appears to be that it can be established that a detriment was caused to third parties and the causal requirement that this detriment was caused by the insider's possession of inside information. In one case, however, the offence of insider dealing has been expanded in a rather curious way in the **B.8.71**

[56] *Georgakis* (n 24).

[57] See paras B.8.52–B.8.54 above.

Market Abuse Regulation, whereby the emphasis appears to be on the advantage enjoyed by the insider of his or her possession of inside information even where no detriment is present.[58]

B.8.72 It is probably not necessary either that the detriment is inflicted on the party directly participating in the transaction. Indeed, the CJEU in *Spector* speaks of 'third parties' and not only of contractual counterparties. Where, for example, management agrees with a major shareholder to issue shares directed at that shareholder at the market price, although both the management and the shareholder know due to their possession of positive inside information that this price will go up when the market learns of the information, there would not be any insider dealing in the relationship between the insider and the management or, by extension, the company that they represent, because there is a parity of information among them, but the transaction is likely nevertheless to be detrimental to the other shareholders of the company and may, for that reason, constitute insider dealing committed by the insider and the members of management.[59]

B.8.73 That insider dealing requires a detriment to one or more parties is common sense. If a person is in possession of inside information that the price of his shares is about to go up by next week, but he sells today at the current lower market price, that person was obviously in possession of inside information when he engaged in the transaction, but nobody was hurt by the transaction and so it cannot constitute inside dealing, because it cannot negatively affect investor confidence in the integrity of the market. In other words, this behaviour does not harm investor confidence which it is the purpose of the Market Abuse Regulation to protect and for that reason it should not be made unlawful by an expansive reading of Article 8(1).

B.8.74 Equally, it should be obvious that nor is investor confidence disturbed by a transaction that is not detrimental, even though the inside information was in fact used. This point was made by the CJEU in *Spector* when it emphasized that not all use of inside information is necessarily unlawful.[60] In that case, the CJEU offered an example on how inside information may be used without causing any harm and for that reason such use should be considered lawful. Observing that the preamble of the (former) Market Abuse Directive (2003/6/EC) provided several examples where there is no 'use' in the unlawful sense applied in Article 2 (former) Market Abuse Directive (2003/6/EC),[61] the CJEU mentioned recital (29) (former) Market Abuse Directive (2003/6/EC) which stated that the use of inside information in the context of a public take-over bid or a merger proposal 'should

[58] See n 84 ff on cancellations and amendments of orders.

[59] That the members of management may also be liable for breaking their duty of loyalty is another matter.

[60] See paras B.8.61–B.8.63 above.

[61] *Spector* (n 37) para 56.

not in itself be deemed to constitute insider dealing'.[62] On that background, the CJEU concluded: The operation whereby an undertaking, after obtaining inside information concerning a specific company, subsequently launches a public take-over bid for the capital of that company at a rate higher than the market rate cannot, in principle, be regarded as prohibited insider dealing since it does not infringe the interests protected by that directive.[63]

What the CJEU here confirms is the practice whereby the bidder will often perform a due diligence of the target company and may easily obtain inside information in the process. The bidder may be contractually prohibited from disclosing information provided by the target company and the target company itself may be allowed not to disclose the inside information.[64] Nonetheless, as long as the bidder takes into account any inside information in its possession when calibrating its bid to ensure that the offer price reasonably reflects all information in the bidder's possession, the bidder does not seek to take unfair advantage of the inside information and the bid will be lawful, even though the inside information was in fact used to establish the offer price. **B.8.75**

This has been a long standing practice in the market for takeovers and mergers and there are different ways to justify what is obviously a reasonable result. Some would argue that the inside information ceases to be inside information when the offer is made, because if the offer takes the inside information into account, the inside information cannot any longer affect the pricing of the target company's shares, which is a necessary characteristic of inside information.[65] Others may argue that if the offer takes into account the inside information, that is, the inside information is reasonably priced in, then there is no detriment to the target company's shareholders and consequently the bidder has not taken unfair advantage of the inside information and no insider dealing has been committed. The latter explanation would appear to be the closest to the ruling in *Spector* and enjoys the analytical benefit that the inside information retains its qualification as inside information which makes it subject to the insider dealing ban if somebody else than the bidder were to use and abuse it. **B.8.76**

It is important to note that the CJEU uses this example to highlight the general requirement that unlawful use of inside information must 'infringe the interests protected by [MAD]' and so this principle applies also outside the context of takeovers and mergers. If a person is in possession of inside information for some **B.8.77**

[62] ibid para 59.

[63] ibid.

[64] The disclosure of certain inside information can be delayed according to art 17.

[65] It is doubtful, however, whether it is a requirement that the information can change the market price when disclosed in order to qualify as inside information according to art 7. It would appear to suffice if the information would take part of the basis of a reasonable investor's investment decision, cf art 7(4), irrespectively of whether the information would be likely to result in a price change. See art 7 n 5 ff for further details.

reason or other, that person is not prevented from trading with an uninformed party. The insider is only prevented from taking unfair advantage of the inside information and if the insider ensures that the transaction is conducted at a price that reasonably reflects the inside information in such a way that the transaction is not detrimental to the other party for that reason, no insider dealing has been committed. Such instances where one party may be in possession of inside information but not at liberty or able to disclose it to one or more uninformed counter parties are probably more widespread than generally perceived. They may frequently occur where professionals engage with consumers, or even in transactions among professionals, and consequently it is useful to remember that such instances do not amount to insider dealing where no unfair advantage is taken to the detriment of the uninformed parties.

B.8.78 The realization that inside information may be more widespread in the market than was understood when the previous directives were drafted is probably also behind the inclusion in the Market Abuse Regulation of Article 11 on market sounding, which enables market professionals to selectively disclose inside information under certain conditions to the parties that may contemplate entering into a transaction with them. That Article 11 marks a narrow and very detailed exemption to the ban on unlawful disclosure is testament to the fact that often such disclosure according to Article 11 is not possible and then it is useful to remember that possession of inside information and trading while in possession of inside information is not unlawful in itself; only when the inside information is used to the detriment of others does it amount to insider dealing.

The relevant transactions

Acquisitions or disposals

B.8.79 According to Article 8(1), insider dealing arises when inside information is used by the insider in certain transactions (hereafter relevant transactions) defined in this way: '... acquiring or disposing of, for its own account or for the account of a third party, directly or indirectly, financial instruments to which that information relates'.

B.8.80 It is clear that the EU legislator was anxious to make the scope of relevant transactions as wide as possible. Not only are the relevant transactions determined by the very open concepts of 'acquiring or disposing', they also include transactions that directly or indirectly result in acquisition or disposal.

B.8.81 Considering the teleological style of interpretation of the CJEU which emphasizes the purpose of the prohibition in Article 8(1), it is helpful to remember that the essence of insider dealing is defined as obtaining an unfair advantage to the detriment of third parties, cf also recital (23).[66] Consequently, any transaction

[66] See para B.8.52 ff.

that may produce a detriment to third parties is likely to be covered by the scope of relevant transactions in Article 8(1). As mentioned in para B.8.52 ff above, emphasis appears to be on the protection of investors and consequently it is less important whether an advantage can be shown to be obtained by the insider as long as it is clear that a detriment was suffered by a third party due to the transaction. This is further emphasized by the fact that the advantage does not have to be obtained by the insider him- or herself, it may accrue to a third party, which is signified by the notion of acting 'for the account of a third party' in Article 8(1). To act for the account of a third party probably just means to act in the interest or to the benefit of that third party and probably does not require any formal arrangement such as an agreement or authorization to act.

Acquisition would include not just buying securities on organized trading venues or over-the-counter, but also signing up for securities upon emission as well as buying securities by open public offers. Acquisition by use of derivatives (futures, options, warrants, etc) or by way of a merger must also be covered. Considering the purpose of the ban, which is to avoid investor detriment, it is probably not relevant whether the transaction conveys specified benefits in the form of economic benefits, ownership rights, or other benefits to the insider or a third party, if it is capable of causing harm to some identified parties. The word 'detriment' in recital (23) is most likely an economic concept, so transactions that only cause emotional harm or discomfort or which may cause public outrage are probably not covered by Article 8(1), unless they are accompanied by a pecuniary loss of some kind. The purpose of the Market Abuse Regulation is to protect the integrity of securities markets as economic transactions mechanisms of great societal importance, not to pamper the moral sentiments of the public. **B.8.82**

Disposing of the relevant financial instruments is naturally also covered by Article 8(1) and must be construed in the same wide sense as acquisition again relying upon whether the transaction caused harm to identifiable third parties. Since detriment as used in recital (23) is most likely an economic concept, the concept of disposing would probably cover all transactions whereby the insider disposes of a financial instrument in consideration of an economic benefit. **B.8.83**

Gifts are made without consideration, and disposing of a financial instrument by making a gift is probably not covered by Article 8(1) if no consideration is offered even if the insider is in possession of inside information when making the gift. If the inside information is negative,[67] the recipient of the gift may become disappointed when the price of the financial instrument falls, but as the recipient offered no consideration this disappointment probably does not amount to a detriment in the sense of recital (23). If, on the other hand, the inside information is positive, the recipient of the gift will enjoy an increase in the value of the gift **B.8.84**

[67] On the concept of positive or negative inside information; see n 45.

when the inside information becomes publicly known and has obviously not been harmed, and consequently there is no insider dealing. However, if the insider in this case has acquired the financial instrument from a third party, this may in itself constitute insider dealing by the insider even though the financial instrument is no longer owned by the insider once the gift is made and the benefit falls on the recipient, but the insider's subsequent presentation of the financial instrument as a gift does not in itself constitute another instance of insider dealing and consequently cannot affect the recipient of the gift. On the other hand, if the insider has acquired the financial instrument from an uninformed third party in order to pass on the instrument to the recipient as a gift, this may constitute acquisition for the account of a third party and in that case the recipient may be liable of insider dealing if he or she knew that the acquisition by the insider constituted insider dealing.

Cancellations and amending orders

B.8.85 The second sentence of Article 8(1) expands the concept of unlawful use of inside information to the act of *cancelling or amending an order* concerning a financial instrument, where the order was placed before the insider possessed the inside information.

B.8.86 This is an expansion in the Market Abuse Regulation of the concept of 'use' that has otherwise remained unchanged since the Insider Dealing Directive (1989/592/EEC) because it applies to circumstances where there is yet no transaction but only an order and consequently there is no detriment to other parties that may harm public confidence in markets, which is otherwise singled out by the CJEU as the *raison d'être* of the prohibition.[68]

B.8.87 Before exploring this expansion of the scope of the prohibition further, it should be noted that the expansion only concerns the *active* use of the inside information where inside information has subsequently come into the possession of the person who placed the order. Where the person remains passive after coming into possession of the inside information, the transaction that will result if a third party accepts the order will be legal. This is evident from recital (25), which states that: 'Orders placed before a person possesses inside information should not be deemed to be insider dealing. However, where a person comes into possession of inside information, there should be a presumption that any subsequent change relating that information to orders placed before possession of such information, including the cancellation or amendment of an order, or an attempt to cancel or amend an order, constitutes insider dealing. That presumption could, however, be rebutted if the person establishes that he or she did not use the inside information when carrying out the transaction.'

[68] See para B.8.52 ff.

The recital makes it clear that only a 'subsequent change ... to orders placed' is covered by the expansion of the prohibition. Thus, once an order has been placed, it will be legal to leave the order even after coming into possession of inside information that would have made it illegal to place the order had the inside information been in possession at that time. **B.8.88**

This understanding is further supported by the catalogue of 'legitimate behaviour' in Article 9(3)(a), which covers transactions carried out in the discharge of an obligation that has become due in good faith and not to circumvent the prohibition against insider dealing and: '(a) that obligation results from an order placed or an agreement concluded before the person concerned possessed inside information; ...'. **B.8.89**

Here, it is a requirement that the order was placed without possession of inside information and the subsequent possession of inside information is then deemed irrelevant. Article 9(3)(a) only concerns transactions that are made in the 'discharge of an obligation that has become due', which may be construed as covering only transactions that obliges the insider to trade, for example a futures contract. Recital (25) is not limited in the same way but would apply to all orders and thus the support offered by Article 9(3)(a) is less manifest but does support the view that it may be legal for the insider to enter into a transaction in possession of inside information, if that information has only arisen after the order was placed that led to the transaction. This is probably a principle that applies more generally.[69] **B.8.90**

It could be argued that the insider should cancel his or her order upon coming into possession of the inside information. This would effectively amount to an obligation to cancel orders upon coming into possession of inside information and the justification would be to protect the third parties who may otherwise risk accepting an order, which is now in the light of the new inside information unknown to them detrimental to their interests. **B.8.91**

However, there is no support for this view in recital (25) and the absence of any indication of such an obligation to cancel leads to the conclusion that the contention must be rejected. On the contrary, there is positive affirmation in Member States' jurisdictions that passivity after placing an order is legitimate as suggested by the first sentence of recital (25) regardless of the arrival of inside information.[70] This is normally founded on principles of criminal law whereby the subjective condition (*mens rea*) of a person should be judged at the time when that person **B.8.92**

[69] See in this respect art 9 Section IV.

[70] Under the former Market Abuse Directive (2003/6/EC) regime, it was established in a public Green Paper (betænkning 1521/2010, 91) as Danish law in accordance with the CJEU's decision in *Spector* that orders placed before coming into inside information could legally be left for acceptance. A similar view is expressed in the Swedish government's bill (proposition 2016/17:22, 275) in respect of the Market Abuse Regulation.

performs the last action depending on him or her to bring about a certain outcome. Information received after this point is irrelevant and so if a person places an order at a regulated market to bring about a transaction, the subjective condition should be evaluated at the time the order was placed. According to this reasoning, it would require a special basis in law to infer on the person a duty to safeguard the interests of others, for example by cancelling orders given, and no such basis is visible in the Market Abuse Regulation.

B.8.93 In this context, it should be remembered, as emphasized by the CJEU in *Spector*, that it is not in itself illegal to possess inside information at the time of entering into a transaction, as long as the insider has not sought to 'take advantage' of it, which suggests an action on behalf of the insider to actively obtain the advantage. Also, the acceptance that an insider may accidentally enjoy an advantage that he or she could not foresee at the time the order was placed is not likely to damage public confidence in securities markets.

B.8.94 Finally, a separate justification for this result may also be based on the way securities markets operate. A regulated market is an exchange for 'anonymous transactions', where communication among the parties is limited to the issuance of orders that convey only the most essential information of price and volume. Contrary to face-to-face transactions (off-exchange), where both parties may expect the other party to provide all relevant information up and until the transaction is concluded, on-exchange transactions are based on order execution that does not allow for such communication. To introduce an obligation on market participants to cancel orders once placed, must require a firm basis in law that is absent in the Market Abuse Regulation. This latter argument points to the fact that recital (25) only applies to 'orders', which in the absence of a definition in Article 3 must mean orders placed on a trading venue covered by the Market Abuse Regulation. The principle may not be applicable in off-exchange transactions, where the parties may expect to receive all relevant information up and until the conclusion of the transaction.

B.8.95 When examining the expansion of the scope of the prohibition in Article 8(1) by the second sentence, it should be noted that it applies to amendments and cancellations of orders, but effectively it only represents an expansion in respect of the latter.

B.8.96 Where the insider amends an order placed before the insider came into possession of the inside information in order to take advantage of new inside information that has subsequently come into his or her possession, this would clearly constitute 'use' in the sense of recital (23). In this respect, the new second sentence in Article 8(1) is unnecessary and does not expand the scope of the prohibition.

B.8.97 However, the second sentence also comprises the act of 'cancellation' of an order that was placed before the inside information came into possession and in this respect it does mark an expansion of the prohibition, because without this text such a cancellation would be regarded as lawful, which indeed was the case under the (former) Market Abuse Directive (2003/6/EC). To cancel an order does not affect any third party and, consequently, cannot lead to the detriment that may harm public confidence. But the inclusion of the second sentence of Article 8(1) has expanded the scope of the prohibition to such cancellations of preplaced orders.

Apparently, the EU legislator has found that the active use of inside information, that is, the cancellation of a preplaced order, to provide an advantage to the insider should be illegal on par with insider dealing in general irrespectively of the fact that no harm to others was caused by the action. It is a bit like outlawing swearing, even when one is alone and nobody can hear it. Thus, whereas detriment to third parties is generally required in order for the use of inside information to be illegal, in this particular case it suffices that the use of the inside information provides an advantage to the insider. **B.8.98**

The use of inside information must, however, provide an advantage to the insider. Although this is not mentioned directly in the second sentence of Article 8(1), it must be assumed in line with the general outlay of the prohibition as demonstrated in the *Spector* decision. Consequently, if the insider cancels a buy order, because he or she comes into possession of negative inside information indicating a later fall in the price of the security, this will constitute insider dealing. If, on the other hand, the insider's decision to cancel the order is not done to take advantage of the new inside information, the cancellation would be legal. This may be the case, where the person subsequently to the placing of the order receives inside information that would only provide an advantage if the order was indeed executed as originally placed. This is equivalent to the situation where the insider trades 'against' his or her inside information, which is of course legal.[71] **B.8.99**

That an insider may wish to annul an order to avoid taking advantage of inside information that has subsequently come into his or her possession is not as unlikely as some may think. For example, a situation may occur where a major shareholder has placed an order to buy shares in his company and subsequently learns of positive inside information suggesting a price increase. Although the insider is entitled to leave the order as it is, the insider may still want to avoid being seen as taking advantage of the inside information that has now come into his possession, which may cause a public outrage irrespectively of its formal legality, and may for that reason want to change the order. Consequently, as no unfair advantage is obtained by the cancellation of the order, it cannot constitute insider dealing according to Article 8(1). This view is supported by the Q&A issued by **B.8.100**

[71] See para B.8.73.

ESMA and dated 30 May 2017. Q4.1 asks whether a 'blanket cancellation of orders policy', whereby all orders are cancelled if inside information is obtained, is legal. ESMA answers that it has to been determined on a case-by-case basis, whether such cancellations are lawful. The reasoning behind this statement must be that the cancellation will be lawful, where the new inside information is advantageous to the firm making the order, because the cancellation will then hurt nobody but the firm itself. Contrary, it would be illegal to cancel an order, if the new inside information indicated that the order would now be unfavourable and the cancellation would thus constitute an advantage obtained by use of the inside information. ESMA's position appears correct as the law stands, but it does raise the question of the wisdom in expanding the ban on insider dealing in this way to cover cancellations, where nobody gets hurt. Such a policy of generally cancelling all orders when new inside information arises is a simple way to ensure that no orders are affected whereby third parties may get hurt, and since it is applied generally, advantages and disadvantages from cancellations should even themselves out, but the policy is not possible to apply because the EU-legislators want to make sure that even in this case no one can benefit from inside information.

Relevant financial instruments

B.8.101 The financial instruments that are covered by Article 8(1) are defined by Article 3(1)(1) if they are subject to trading, or admission for trading has been sought, on a trading venue, cf Article 2(1)(a)–(c). The trading venues are regulated markets, multilateral trading facilities (MTF) and organized trading facilities (OTF).

B.8.102 Financial instruments also cover instruments, which depend or have an effect on the price or value of financial instruments traded on these venues, cf Article 2(1)(d), which are often referred to as derivatives. The provision especially mentions credit default swaps (CDS) and contracts for difference (CFD) as examples.

Emission allowances

B.8.103 The third sentence of Article 8(1) concerns emission allowances that are subject to the auctioning system set up by the Greenhouse Gas Emission Allowances Regulation. The term 'emission allowances' is defined in Article 3(1)(19) by reference to the definition in point (11) of Section C of Annex I to Directive 2014/65.

B.8.104 It follows from the last subsection of Article 2(1), that the Market Abuse Regulation also applies to behaviour or transactions, including bids, relating to the auctioning on an auction platform authorized as a regulated market of emission allowances or other auctioned products based thereon, including when auctioned products are not financial instruments, pursuant to Greenhouse Gas Emission Allowances Regulation and that all requirements and prohibitions referring to orders to trade shall apply to such bids. The text in Article 8(1) is supplemented by recital (54), but it provides no further guidance to the use of the provision.

The purpose of the third sentence of Article 8(1) is to apply the concept of 'use' from the first sentence, where it is used in the context of traditional financial instruments such as equity or debt, to the special regime applicable to emission allowances. It does so by equalling use with 'submitting, modifying or withdrawing a bid by a person for its own account or for the account of a third party'. As was the case with the second sentence of Article 8(1),[72] it is likely that the concept of use must be construed as it is in recital (23) and in the case law of the CJEU that is still valid law in this area, which means that the use must at least constitute taking advantage of the inside information. Submitting, modifying, or withdrawing a bid in order not to take advantage of the inside information cannot be seen as a use of the inside information and is lawful. **B.8.105**

III. Section 2: Tipping

Article 8(2) concerns the act of recommending or inducing another person to engage in insider dealing, which must be seen as a reference to the activities covered by Article 8(1). In US parlance, the act of recommending someone to engage in insider dealing is called tipping and the recipient is known as a tippee. Tipping may involve disclosure of inside information to the tippee, which is a separate offence according to Article 10. Here, the term 'tipping' is used for the behaviour covered by Article 8(2). **B.8.106**

Although the act of recommending or inducing in this way does not in itself amount to insider dealing, unless the tippee subsequently acts to take advantage of the tip, the activity of tipping is treated similarly to insider dealing in Article 14(b), which declares the activity of tipping unlawful. **B.8.107**

Article 8(2) on tipping must be distinguished from Article 10 on unlawful disclosure. Both can be seen as preventive measures that serve to prevent insider dealing and both are deemed unlawful by Article 14(b) and Article 14(c), respectively. Nevertheless, their different basis in the Market Abuse Regulation requires a distinction and although both are unlawful, it is probably justified to regard tipping as a more serious breach of the law compared to unlawful disclosure, because the risk of insider dealing taking place is greater in the former instance than in the latter. Unlawful disclosure increases the risk of insider dealing taking place, but tipping actively encourages the tippee to engage in insider dealing, making that outcome more likely. The more serious character of tipping probably also explains why tipping is placed in Article 8(2) next to Article 8(1) that concerns insider dealing, whereas unlawful disclosure is provided with its own provision in Article 10. **B.8.108**

---

[72] See para B.8.52 ff.

B.8.109 Tipping has not yet been tried before the CJEU, nor is there any guidance to be found in the preamble of the Market Abuse Regulation. Both Article 8(2) and Article 10 would appear to include a communication from the insider to another person. In the case of tipping, the insider recommends or induces the tippee to engage in insider dealing, which may include disclosing the inside information, but not necessarily as it may suffice if the insider makes it clear to the tippee that the transaction would be beneficial without disclosing the actual content of the inside information. In the case of unlawful disclosure, there is no such recommendation or inducement, since the unlawful disclosure may be made for other reasons. As with tipping, it is probably not a requirement that the insider discloses the full content of the inside information in order to commit an act of unlawful disclosure. It probably suffices if the insider discloses enough information to enable the other person to engage in insider dealing based on the disclosed information. The distinctive feature of tipping appears to be the purpose of the insider's communication: to make the tippee engage in insider dealing.

B.8.110 Consequently, Article 8(2) should be applied where the insider recommends or induces another person to engage in insider dealing, irrespectively of whether any inside information is disclosed in the process.

B.8.111 Article 8(2) is divided into two subsections (a) and (b), which concern acts to acquire or dispose of financial instruments, or acts to cancel or amend a preplaced order, respectively. The understanding of acquisition and disposal is explored in para B.8.79 ff above and the understanding of cancellations or amendments in para B.8.85 ff above to which reference is made.

B.8.112 Subsections (a) and (b) were probably motivated by the inclusion in the Market Abuse Regulation of the second sentence in Article 8(1), which expands the notion of use to cover the act of cancellation and amendment. This subdivision is unfortunate, because it appears that the subsections both concern 'financial instruments', whereas in Article 8(1), the first two sentences concern such financial instruments but are then supplemented by a third sentence concerning emission allowances.[73] This raises the question of whether emission allowances are also covered by Article 8(2) on tipping even though the provision only mentions financial instruments.

B.8.113 It is likely that this is the case. Article 8(2) on tipping refers to the conduct of engaging in insider dealing, which is clearly a reference to the activities described in Article 8(1). While it is true that Article 8(1) itself makes a distinction between financial instruments and emission allowances, this distinction is mainly to make clear that what constitutes use in respect of traditional financial instruments may take certain different forms in respect of emission allowances. Combined, it is

[73] See para B.8.103 ff on emission allowances.

reasonable to see all of Article 8(1) as concerning insider dealing thus covering both markets for traditional financial instruments and emission allowances, and consequently the reference in Article 8(2) to behaviour that amounts to engaging in insider dealing must cover insider dealing in respect of emission allowances as well. Consequently, tipping in respect of such emission allowances must be included in Article 8(2) despite the omission to mention these instruments directly in subsections (a) and (b).

IV. Section 3: Tippee Liability

Whereas Article 8(2) concerned recommending or inducing somebody to engage in insider dealing, known as tipping, Article 8(3) concerns the liability of the tippee if the recommendation or inducement is acted upon. **B.8.114**

Article 8(3) declares that to use a recommendation or an inducement amounts to insider dealing, which is a reference to the offence defined in Article 8(1) and made unlawful by Article 14(a). **B.8.115**

The concept of use is not defined in Article 8(3), but since the provision makes a reference to the concept of insider dealing in Article 8(1), it must be construed as indicated by recital (23).[74] Consequently, the tippee must take advantage of the recommendation or inducement to obtain an unfair advantage to the detriment of third parties. In so doing, the tippee has committed insider dealing according to Article 8(1). It must further be assumed that if the tippee uses the recommendation or inducement to cancel or amend a preplaced order, that would also amount to insider dealing. **B.8.116**

As explored when construing Article 8(2), the recommendations or the inducements are not necessarily accompanied by a disclosure of the facts that constitute inside information, and the tippee may be ignorant of why he is encouraged to trade by the insider. Article 8(3) only requires that the tippee knows or ought to know that the recommendations or inducements are based on inside information. This is a special subjective condition applicable only to tippees that supplements the subjective conditions that generally applies to the offence of insider dealing and is discussed in greater detail in Section VII below. It could be said that it replaces the condition that an insider must understand that the information in his or her possession qualifies as inside information according to Article 7. **B.8.117**

It follows from Article 8(4)(2) that the recipient of an unlawful disclosure according to Article 10 would commit insider dealing according to Article 8(1) if he or she took unfair advantage of the inside information unlawfully disclosed to the detriment of third parties. The same outcome is provided by Article 8(3) **B.8.118**

[74] See para B.8.52 ff on use.

on tippee liability. Consequently, irrespectively of how a person comes into possession of inside information, either by tipping according to Article 8(2) or by unlawful disclosure according to Article 10, if that person uses the communicated information to obtain an unfair advantage to the detriment of third parties, that person has engaged in insider dealing according to Article 8(1), which is prohibited by Article 14(a).

B.8.119 Tipping is prohibited by Article 14(b). That provision does not include attempt, and consequently the act of tipping must have been concluded to be punishable, unless national law has extended the scope of Article 14(b).[75]

V. Section 4: Primary and Secondary Insiders

B.8.120 Article 8(4) singles out in subsections (a)–(d) certain persons based on their access to the inside information that is in their possession and declares that these insiders are covered by Article 8. In the second subsection of Article 8(4), it is then noted that so are all other persons who possess inside information under other circumstances than those mentioned in subsections (a)–(d). Traditionally, the first group of persons are known as *primary insiders* and the second groups as *secondary insiders*.

B.8.121 Considering that both primary and secondary insiders are covered by Article 8 and that the essential condition for applying Article 8 is not Article 8(4) but whether a person is in possession of inside information as defined by Article 7, it begs the question what motivates the division in Article 8(4) and what function it serves.[76]

B.8.122 The division probably originates from US federal securities regulation, which inspired the first European Member States that sought to prohibit insider dealing.[77] In US law, the insider dealing ban was developed from Rule 10b-5 derived from Section 10b 1934 SEA, which is an anti-fraud measure. As such, the ban was developed in case law from notions of the duty of loyalty owed by company insiders, which would later name the offence of 'insider dealing', and it was only gradually expanded to encompass persons who were not company insiders. In *Chiarella*, the US Supreme Court thus established an understanding of insider dealing based on fraud, which presupposed an existing duty of loyalty

---

[75] See art 14 Section II.

[76] While it is argued here that the distinction between primary and secondary insiders is practically moot, except perhaps for a presumption that primary insiders know better when information qualifies as inside information, it is argued by S Gilotta, 'The Regulation of Outsider Trading in EU and the US' (2016) 13 ECFR 631, that this outcome in EU law is unfortunate compared to US law because the latter allows trading by 'outsiders', ie primary insiders, that is efficient.

[77] See para B.8.22 ff on the US origin of the ban on insider dealing.

that limited the offence to company insiders or others who were subject to such a duty of loyalty.[78] Later, in *Dirks*, the US Supreme Court recognized that also others than company insiders could commit insider dealing, but only if they had been tipped by an insider, who by tipping had breached his or her duty of loyalty, and only if the tippee knew or should have known of the breach.[79]

When the Commission presented its Insider Dealing Directive Proposal in 1987, four years after *Dirks*, insider dealing was only regulated in some Member States and of these some had been inspired by the US approach to distinguish between primary insiders and secondary insiders (tippees). However, in its proposal the Commission made it clear that it favoured a broader approach effectively covering both categories of insiders.[80] In the adopted version of Insider Dealing Directive (1989/592/EEC), primary insiders were mentioned in Article 2(1) Insider Dealing Directive (1989/592/EEC) as part of the ban on insider dealing. In Article 4 Insider Dealing Directive (1989/592/EEC), the ban on insider dealing in Article 2 Insider Dealing Directive (1989/592/EEC) was expanded to 'any person other than those', that is, secondary insiders. The ban on unlawful disclosure and on recommending (tipping) in Article 3 Insider Dealing Directive (1989/592/EEC) applied to the primary insiders in Article 2 of the Insider Dealing Directive (1989/592/EEC), but not to secondary insiders. This probably reflected that many Member States were at that time yet unfamiliar with insider dealing and favoured a narrow application that covered only trading and not tipping, and in Article 6 Insider Dealing Directive (1989/592/EEC) those Member States that favoured a broader application as originally proposed by the Commission were allowed to expand the ban on tipping in Article 3 of the Insider Dealing Directive (1989/592/EEC) to the secondary insiders mentioned in Article 4 Insider Dealing Directive (1989/592/EEC). **B.8.123**

Article 4 Insider Dealing Directive (1989/592/EEC), which expanded the ban on insider dealing in Article 2 Insider Dealing Directive (1989/592/EEC) to secondary insiders, used similar wording to define the possession of inside information ('with full knowledge of the facts possesses inside information') but furthermore required that 'the direct or indirect source of which could not be other than a person referred to in Article 2', that is, a primary insider. This reflected the position in US law according to which the secondary insider knew or should have known that the inside information derived from a breach of loyalty by the primary insider. This was deemed necessary in US law to maintain the requirement of a fraud based offence, where the fraud depended on the violation of the primary insider's duties, but it was not strictly necessary in the context of Insider Dealing Directive **B.8.124**

[78] US Supreme Court, *Chiarella v United States*, 445 US 222 (1980), No 78-1202, decided 18 March 1980.
[79] US Supreme Court, *Dirks v SEC*, 463 US 646 (1983). No 82-276, decided 1 July 1983.
[80] Insider Dealing Directive Proposal COM(87) 111, 4.

(1989/592/EEC), where the central requirement was to possess inside information and to understand that the information qualified as inside information, and where it was consequently irrelevant from whom the inside information was derived.

B.8.125 When the (former) Market Abuse Directive (2003/6/EC) was adopted, both primary and secondary insiders were subjected to the same prohibitions as originally intended by the Commission in its Insider Dealing Directive Proposal. This was achieved by expanding Article 4 (former) Market Abuse Directive (2003/6/EC) on secondary insiders to include both the insider dealing ban in Article 2 (former) Market Abuse Directive (2003/6/EC) and the ban on tipping in Article 3, which already applied to primary insiders. As mentioned in respect of 'possession' in Article 8(1),[81] the Commission changed the wording of the ban on insider dealing in Article 2(1) (former) Market Abuse Directive (2003/6/EC) compared to the old ban in Article 2(1) Insider Dealing Directive (1989/592/EEC) by removing the condition 'with full knowledge of the facts'. It is interesting in the present context that the Commission justified the change by stating in its proposal: '... the expression "with full knowledge of the facts" applied in the Insider Dealing Directive to the primary insiders is suppressed in Article 2 of the present Directive, as by nature these insiders may have access to inside information on a daily basis and are aware of the confidential nature of the information that they receive;'[82]

B.8.126 Apparently the Commission wanted to lower the subjective condition in respect of primary insiders. In respect of secondary insiders, no change was made in this respect, and in Article 4 of the (former) Market Abuse Directive (2003/6/EC) it was still required that he or she 'with full knowledge of the facts possesses inside information', which in the adopted version became 'who possesses inside information while that person knows, or ought to have known, that it is inside information'. This corresponds to the present Article 8(4), second subsection, which reads 'where the [secondary insider] knows or ought to know that it is inside information'.

B.8.127 Since the prohibitions in Article 8 apply equally to both primary and secondary insiders, the purpose of making a distinction between the two groups of insiders in Article 8(4) must be to make a distinction in the subjective condition applying to the two groups. Primary insiders are supposed to be 'aware' of the special character of inside information due to their privileged access to it, whereas secondary insiders, who have no such direct access, are only subject to the prohibitions in Article 8 if it is proven that they knew or ought to have known that the information in their possession was in fact inside information as defined by Article 7. This subjective condition will be explored in Section VII below.

B.8.128 The categories of primary insiders in Article 8(4) covers in subsection (a) persons who are members of the administrative, management, or supervisory bodies of

---

[81] See para B.8.37 above.

[82] Commission, Proposal for a Regulation of the European Parliament and of the Council on insider dealing and market manipulation (market abuse) COM(2011) 651 final, 8.

either the issuer or the emission allowance market participant, that is, they are directors or executives of these enterprises. The reference to the issuer or emission allowance market participant must be to the enterprise that has issued the securities or emission allowances to which the inside information relates. Subsection (b) concerns shareholders and other owners who have a holding in these issuers or emission allowance market participants. Subsection (c) concerns persons whose access to the inside information was through their employment, profession, or duties, where duties considering in respect of employment and profession must involve a contractual relationship.

The presumed awareness of primary insiders stems from 'the nature' of their specified relationship and their understanding of the information that this relationship may produce. Consequently, it is likely that for primary insiders according to subsections (a)–(c) the inside information must have been accessed as part of the specified relationship and not coincidently. For example, a lawyer visiting an issuer will be a primary insider if he is instructed with inside information by the issuer, whereas it is not necessarily the case if he accidently happens to overhear some information while visiting the issuer. **B.8.129**

The (former) Market Abuse Directive (2003/6/EC) was negotiated in the aftermath of the terrorist atrocities perpetrated in the US on 9/11 2001. At that time, it was debated whether the terrorists had taken advantage of their knowledge of the terrorist acts by going short in airline securities. Consequently, in recital (14) (former) Market Abuse Directive (2003/6/EC) reference was made to terrorism and in Article 2(1)(d) (former) Market Abuse Directive (2003/6/EC) criminal acts were mentioned as a source of inside information. This is maintained in Article 8(4)(d) and to qualify as a primary insider, the criminal must have access to the inside information as a part of or as a result of his criminal activities. **B.8.130**

As already mentioned, the qualification as a primary insider has an effect on the subjective condition as the primary insiders are supposed to be 'aware' that the information in their possession qualify as inside information according to Article 7. Even if a person is not qualified as a primary insider, for example because the inside information was not accessed directly through the specified relationship, the person may still be qualified as a secondary insider if he or she knew or ought to have known that the information was inside information. This is dealt with in Section VII below on the subjective condition. **B.8.131**

VI. Section 5: Legal Persons as Insiders

Article 8(5) states that where insider dealing is made by a legal person, the natural persons who participated in the decision to carry out the relevant transaction are also covered by Article 8. The purpose of the provision seems to be to ensure that **B.8.132** not only the legal person but also the natural persons participating in the decision shall be liable as well.

B.8.133 Article 8(5) appears to be a simple restatement of a principle that was also included in Article 2(2) (former) Market Abuse Directive (2003/6/EC) and Article 2(2) Insider Dealing Directive (1989/592/EEC), but its repositioning in Article 8(5) may be problematic. The relevant transactions mentioned in Article 8(5) are the transactions mentioned in Article 8(1), but do not appear to cover recommendation or inducement as mentioned in Article 8(2) on tipping. It could be argued that when Article 8(5) states that 'this Article shall also apply', it is a reference also to these activities because they too are part of Article 8; however, Article 8(5) is very specific in detailing the behaviour that may make the natural persons liable. A literal reading of Article 8(5) would thus lead to the conclusion that natural persons cannot be held liable for participating in decisions whereby the legal person recommends or induces according to Article 8(2). A very strict reading would even question whether the legal person itself can be liable, when Article 8(5) only concerns the transactions mentioned in Article 8(1). This, however, is obviously too strict an understanding, as Article 8(5) only concerns the liability of natural persons who participate in the decision-making of a legal person and does not address the question of the liability of the legal person itself, and since 'person' used in Articles 8(1), 8(2), and 8(3) must encompass legal persons it is reasonable to understand that the legal person itself may be liable according to these provisions directly, even if the natural persons participating in the decision are not liable.

B.8.134 Since Article 8(5) cannot be taken to mean that the legal person itself is not liable according to Article 8(2), it is likely, although subject to uncertainty, that Article 8(5) is merely expressing a general principle that natural persons should be held liable where they participate in decisions on the account of a legal person, whereby the legal person violates Article 8, and that Article 8(5) can be used by analogy where the legal person has violated Article 8(2). The uncertainty arises from the fact that Article 8(2) on tipping is deemed a criminal offence by Article 3(1) Market Abuse Directive on Criminal Sanctions (2014/57/EU), which may make the CJEU apply a narrow interpretation of Article 8(5) in regard of the natural persons who participated in the decision.

B.8.135 To the extent that Article 8(5) can be relied upon, the provision makes a reference to national law to determine when natural persons have participated in the decision. This must be understood as a reference to national law on corporate governance, company law, and similar disciplines that determine which natural persons have the power to make decisions on behalf of the legal person.

B.8.136 It is a separate question when a legal person can be deemed to have violated the prohibitions of Article 8 by the actions carried out by natural persons acting on its behalf. This is determined by national law, not by the Market Abuse Regulation itself, and national law is to some extent harmonized by the Market

Abuse Directive on Criminal Sanctions (2014/57/EU), although it does not apply to some Member States due to reservations made by these Member States. Nonetheless, many Member States will apply it and consequently it can be expected that national law will conform to the standards set out in Article 8 Market Abuse Directive on Criminal Sanctions (2014/57/EU) on the liability of legal persons, which reads:

> 1. Member States shall take the necessary measures to ensure that legal persons can be held liable for offences referred to in Articles 3 to 6 committed for their benefit by any person, acting either individually or as part of an organ of the legal person, and having a leading position within the legal person based on:
>   (a) a power of representation of the legal person;
>   (b) an authority to take decisions on behalf of the legal person; or
>   (c) an authority to exercise control within the legal person.
> 2. Member States shall also take the necessary measures to ensure that legal persons can be held liable where the lack of supervision or control, by a person referred to in paragraph 1, has made possible the commission of an offence referred to in Articles 3 to 6 for the benefit of the legal person by a person under its authority.
> 3. Liability of legal persons under paragraphs 1 and 2 shall not exclude criminal proceedings against natural persons who are involved as perpetrators, inciters or accessories in the offences referred to in Articles 3 to 6.[83]

Some further assistance to the proper construing of the liability of legal persons for violating Article 8 is provided by Article 9(1) on legitimate behaviour. This provision is dealt with in more detail in the commentary to Article 9, but it should be noted here that it provides two situations where the legal person is not liable. **B.8.137**

First, according to Article 9(a), if the legal person has established, implemented, and maintained adequate and effective internal arrangements and procedures known as information barriers, or in older parlance Chinese Walls, that effectively ensures that the persons making a decision to engage in transactions mentioned in Article 8(1) or having an influence on that decision, were not in possession of inside information. This instance appears to address the question of whether a legal person is deemed to be 'in possession' of inside information simply because a person working for the legal person is in such possession irrespectively of whether that person had any influence on the decision to trade. It should be noted that this question is less important than it might have been previously, because the CJEU has established in *Spector* that possession is not enough to commit insider dealing and that the inside information must be taken unfairly advantage of to **B.8.138**

[83] The offences listed in arts 3–6 Market Abuse Directive on Criminal Sanctions (2014/57/EU) are insider dealing and tipping; unlawful disclosure; and market manipulation. These offences are mentioned in the Market Abuse Directive on Criminal Sanctions (2014/57/EU), but must be applied according to the Market Abuse Regulation, which as a regulation has direct effect in the national law of the Member States.

the detriment of third parties, which hardly can be done if the decision-makers are not themselves in possession of the inside information. However, Article 9(1) may be of relevance where it is not clear whether persons with inside information have been close to the decision-making process, for example, where employees working in one department have inside information and are located in the same building as the employees in another department, who make the decision. If the employees are kept apart by effective procedures, the legal person can prove that it has not engaged in insider dealing despite the presence of inside information among its work force.

B.8.139 Secondly, according to Article 9(b), if the legal person is in possession of inside information because one or more of the natural persons working for the legal person are in such possession, the legal person has not engaged in insider dealing, where it has not encouraged, recommended, induced, or otherwise influenced the natural person, who made the decision to trade. Subsection (b) is less clear than subsection (a) above, but probably concerns the incentives offered by the legal person to the natural persons making decisions on its behalf and can be seen basically as an application of the instances covered by subsection (a), that is, the legal person should not in any way encourage or permit conduct whereby inside information in the possession of some of its employees is transmitted directly or indirectly to those who make trading decisions. Indirect transmission can take place, where the employee making the decision is not informed of the inside information as such, but it is made sufficiently clear that a certain decision would be welcomed. In this way, the relationship between subsections (a) and (b) resembles the relationship between Articles 8(1) and 8(3), where the former concerns decisions made by persons who possess inside information and the latter concerns decisions made by persons who know or ought to know that their decisions are based on inside information.

VII. Section 6: The Subjective Condition—*Mens Rea*

The applicable standard

B.8.140 The two offences mentioned in Article 8, that of insider dealing and tipping, both presuppose the possession of inside information in combination with a special action, either to engage in insider dealing according to Article 8(1) or to engage in tipping according to Article 8(2). The subjective condition (*mens rea*) must be established in respect of each element, which is examined in turn below.

B.8.141 It should be remembered that insider dealing and tipping are normally criminal offences under national law, which indeed the Market Abuse Directive on Criminal Sanctions (2014/57/EU) tries to harmonize for the Member States that apply it, cf Article 3 Market Abuse Directive on Criminal Sanctions (2014/57/EU).

Consequently, it is likely that the CJEU will require clear proof of the subjective condition in all national criminal cases, cf Article 48(1) of the Charter of Fundamental Rights of the EU (hereafter the European Charter), whereas the absence of a subjective condition may be acceptable if only subject to administrative sanctions.

The subjective condition concerns the question of when a certain action can be attributed to the person who carried out the action. Traditionally, the standards applied in most jurisdictions would involve different degrees of attribution and furthermore they would usually apply differently depending on whether the assessment was done in respect of claims in tort or in criminal cases. These standards have not been harmonized in the EU and national law will determine the standards applied by national courts. This poses a challenge as to how to describe these elements in a way that is understandable in all Member State jurisdictions. In respect of the Market Abuse Regulation, however, some general guidance is possible. **B.8.142**

The standard applied consistently in the Market Abuse Regulation is *to know or ought to know.*[84] The knowledge in question must be of the particular action that is prohibited, for examples, in respect of insider dealing, the standard would apply to the possession of inside information and to engage in insider dealing. In each respect, it must be determined whether the persons knew or ought to have known that they were in possession of inside information and whether they knew or ought to have known that their actions constituted a use of the inside information according to Article 8(1). **B.8.143**

The standard of knowing or ought to have known covers two very different standards of mental attribution. The standard of knowing of a certain fact or circumstance requires proof that the fact or circumstance was understood by the person, whereas ought to have known is a lower standard, where it is sufficient to prove that the person had opportunity to know it and can be applied even if it remains uncertain whether the person actually knew of it. Where the former standard is strictly subjective and depends on an assessment of the individual person's mental condition, the latter standard is more objective and circumstantial and may rely on what other people would have inferred under similar circumstances. This is also pointed out in recital (26), which makes a reference to 'what a normal and reasonable person knows or should have known in the circumstances'. **B.8.144**

It could be argued that when the Market Abuse Regulation applies both standards, effectively it endorses the standard of ought to have known, because this standard requires a less onerous burden of proof and will be sufficient to determine violations of the Market Abuse Regulation. However, by stating both standards the Market Abuse Regulation allows national courts to apply the standards of subjective attribution that are customary to their jurisdiction, which typically entails a **B.8.145**

[84] Cf recitals (26) and (54); arts 8(3) and 8(4) on insider dealing; art 10(2) on unlawful disclosure; and art 12(1)(c)–(d) on market manipulation.

stricter sanction for the higher standard of knowing than for the lesser standard of ought to have known. The limit of discretion for the national courts is that on the one hand, the lesser standard of ought to have known must be sufficient to find the defendant guilty of violating an offence in the Market Abuse Regulation and it is not possible to require the higher standard of having known of the violation, while on the other hand it is not possible to attribute the violation unless at least the perpetrator ought to have known that he or she violated the Market Abuse Regulation.

Possession of inside information

B.8.146 The subjective condition required to establish that a person is in possession of inside information must be divided into two separate questions: when does a person 'possess' inside information (*actus reus*) and when does that person possess 'inside information' (*mens rea*).

B.8.147 To possess information, inside or otherwise, must mean to know the information, that is, the information must be located in the brain of that person. The state of neuroscience is such that it is not yet possible to verify this condition objectively and as defendants tend to deny inconvenient facts, the knowledge of a person must be established by circumstantial evidence. In respect of possession, it is probably not necessary that the person has the information at his or her command. It is sufficient if it is established that the information was known by that person at the relevant time.[85] A claim that the information had been forgotten by the time of the transaction or tip may be relevant for the subjective condition pertaining to this action, but should not be relevant in respect of the question of possession.

B.8.148 Normally in the Market Abuse Regulation, the subjective standard for attributing a violation is to have known or ought to have known of the facts or circumstances that constitute the violation. However, in this instance Articles 8(1) and 8(2) are clear in demanding that the person *possesses* the inside information. Consequently, the inside information must have become known to the person. It is not enough that the person ought to have known of it, for example, if a director was supposed to read a brief containing the inside information but did in fact not, then the director was not in possession of the information despite the fact that he ought to have been.

B.8.149 The observation made by the Commission in the (former) Market Abuse Directive (2003/6/EC) Proposal that by the nature of their privileged access primary insiders 'are aware' of the confidential nature of the information they receive,[86]

[85] The burden of proof will be on the prosecutor.

[86] Commission, Proposal for a Regulation of the European Parliament and of the Council on insider dealing and market manipulation (market abuse) COM(2011) 651 final, 8.

which lies behind the wording of the insider dealing ban as it was in Article 2(1) of the (former) Market Abuse Directive (2003/6/EC) and as it is now in Article 8(1), cannot change this. The inside information must be known and the offence cannot include cases where the person only ought to have known of it. This is not to deny that in certain cases the fact that a person ought to have known of certain facts may be taken as evidence that he or she did in fact know of it. For example, if a brief containing inside information was sent to a director who was supposed to read it on the night before a board meeting and the director later claims not to have read it although he ought to have read it, a court of law may find under the circumstances that he probably did read it.

The Commission's observation about primary insiders being 'aware' of the nature of the information they receive is on the other hand relevant in respect of the other question, that of when a person possesses 'inside information'. The person must understand that the information in his or her possession qualifies as inside information according to Article 7. Here, it will suffice to prove that the person ought to have understood that the information in possession qualified as inside information. **B.8.150**

It is in this respect that the Commission's observation becomes relevant. In respect of information that the primary insider is accustomed to receive and handle, which is information that he or she receives in the specified relationships mentioned in Article 8(4)(a)–(d), it is reasonable to suppose that the primary insider is capable of correctly assessing its character as inside information. Considering the position of the CJEU in respect of the subjective condition necessary in respect of the actual act of insider dealing or tipping, as laid out in *Spector* and explored in para B.8.152 below, it is probably not possible to conclude that a primary insider is always aware when information in his or her possession qualifies as inside information. It is more likely that the special relationship enjoyed by the primary insider creates a rebuttable presumption that he or she knew or ought to have known that it could be qualified as inside information. **B.8.151**

Engaging in insider dealing or tipping

A presumption of use

The act of insider dealing means to use inside information in one's possession in a certain way. Recital (23) describes it as obtaining an unfair advantage from the inside information to the detriment of third parties who are unaware of such information. This particular use of the inside information must be attributable to the insider and in its decision in *Spector*, the CJEU not only laid out what constituted such use, as is now restated in recital (23), but also made clear what the applicable subjective condition was. **B.8.152**

B.8.153 In *Spector*,[87] the question was to which extent the change from the wording applied in Article 2(1) of the Insider Dealing Directive (1989/592/EEC) to that applied in Article 2(1) of the (former) Market Abuse Directive (2003/6/EC), notably changing 'taking advantage with full knowledge of the facts' to simply 'using the inside information', signified a change from the understanding of the offence of inside dealing displayed by the CJEU in *Georgakis*.[88] The CJEU made it clear in *Spector* that while the change of 'taking advantage' to 'using' did not change the essential meaning of engaging in insider dealing, the deletion of 'with full knowledge of the facts' did affect the subjective condition. The former observation has already been explored in para B.8.59 ff above to which reference is made, and in the following this change of the subjective condition is examined in greater detail.

B.8.154 In this respect, the CJEU begins its analysis by observing that the phrase 'with full knowledge of the facts' had been construed by some Member States as requiring a certain mental element and that the EU legislator in the (former) Market Abuse Directive (2003/6/EC) strived to remove any element of purpose and intent.[89] Then, the CJEU observed that Article 2(1) of the (former) Market Abuse Directive (2003/6/EC) defined insider dealing without explicitly referring to the intent behind such action,[90] that is, the EU legislator had removed the intentional element that had caused some Member States to apply a too narrow understanding of Article 2(1) of the Insider Dealing Directive (1989/592/EEC). However, this development was not seen by the CJEU as completely removing the need for a subjective condition. On the contrary, the CJEU continues its analysis by pointing out that due to the specific nature of insider dealing, a *presumption* of the mental element arises once the constituent elements referred to in the legislative text of the (former) Market Abuse Directive (2003/6/EC) are present.[91]

B.8.155 In its explanation of how this presumption arises,[92] the CJEU points to the relationship of confidence that normally exists for primary insiders, which implies a special responsibility. The CJEU is not specific here, but it is probably arguing that due to the special relationship, primary insiders must be presumed to know when information in their position is inside information and to know that they should not use this information for their own advantage. Furthermore, the CJEU mentions that trading involves a series of decisions, which makes it unlikely that the insider could have acted without being aware of his or her actions. Finally, and this is probably the more important observation, the CJEU concludes that

87 *Spector* (n 37).
88 *Georgakis* (n 24).
89 *Spector* (n 37) para 34.
90 ibid para 35.
91 ibid para 36.
92 ibid.

when an insider enters into a transaction while in possession of inside information, that information 'must, in principle, be deemed to have played a role' in the insider's decision-making.

To comprehend this part of the analysis fully, reference should be made to what was then Article 1(2) of the Commission Directive 2003/124, which was a level 2 instrument issued according to the (former) Market Abuse Directive (2003/6/EC).[93] This Article implements point 1 of Article 1 of the (former) Market Abuse Directive (2003/6/EC) on the definition of inside information that the inside information must be 'information which, if it were made public, would be likely to have a significant effect on the prices of financial instruments or related derivative financial instruments', which is then in the level 2 instrument deemed to mean information which 'a reasonable investor would be likely to use as part of the basis of his investment decisions'. In other words, since inside information is by definition information that a reasonable investor would be likely to use as part of the basis for an investment decision, the possession of inside information, so defined, must create a presumption that the inside information was used in this way. **B.8.156**

Since Article 1(2) of the Commission Directive 2003/124 has now been restated as Article 7(4), the analysis of the CJEU on a presumption of use when acting in possession of inside information is still valid law. Furthermore, since this presumption is prompted by the very definition of inside information, which is common to both primary and secondary insiders, the presumption in respect of use will arise in cases involving either of the two groups.[94] Finally, it should be observed that the CJEU's establishment of a presumption of the subjective condition must imply that such a subjective condition is necessary and cannot be dispensed with. Although the EU legislator strived to make the offence of insider dealing as objective as possible, it still requires a subjective condition, which is hardly surprising considering its nature as a criminal offence. **B.8.157**

A rebuttable presumption

Although the CJEU concludes that it is possible to 'assume an intention',[95] this is probably not to say that it has to be proven that the insider 'knew' and that his or her action was carried out solely with a given purpose. This would go against the EU legislators' express desire to avoid a too narrow application of the ban on insider dealing, which the CJEU had just commented on. **B.8.158**

93 Commission Directive 2003/124/EC of 22 December 2003 implementing Directive 2003/6/EC of the European Parliament and of the Council as regards the definition and public disclosure of inside information and the definition of market manipulation, OJ L 339/70, 24 December 2003.

94 However, the presumption that the insider knew or ought to have known that information in his or her possession qualified as inside information according to art 7 only applies to primary insiders, see para B.8.150 ff, which is also a rebuttable presumption.

95 *Spector* (n 37) para 38.

B.8.159 It is more likely that what the CJEU concludes is that the constitutive element of inside information is defined in such a way as to enable a presumption that the inside information was used. It should be noted that a presumption is something different from the standard used to determine the subjective condition of the insider. That standard is more likely the 'knew or ought to have known' standard, which is applicable in determining whether the insider's transaction constituted an unfair advantage to the detriment of third parties, for example by assessing whether the insider knew or ought to have known that the transaction would be detrimental to third parties. Presumptions like the one established by the CJEU in *Spector* concern another matter, that of proof.

B.8.160 In criminal law, a presumption of innocence prevails, which in European law is codified in Article 48(1) of the European Charter. What the CJEU pointed out in *Spector* was that the constituent element of inside information has been defined to create a presumption of use, which still holds true, cf Article 7(4). In other words, where the insider has entered into a relevant transaction or tipped a third party while in possession of inside information, there is a presumption that that activity was carried out while using the inside information, because inside information is defined as information that is normally used by a reasonable investor.

B.8.161 This effectively shifts the burden of proof once the possession of inside information has been proven, and the CJEU spends the remainder of its analysis in this area to explain that such a reversal is permissible both according to the 1950 European Convention for the Protection of Human Rights and Fundamental Freedoms and its own case law on fundamental rights.[96] In passing, the CJEU correctly observes that market abuse, including insider dealing and tipping, must be subjected to a convention autonomous interpretation of the 1950 European Convention, that is, the notion of a criminal offence in that Convention must be construed autonomously according to the Convention itself and independently of how the notion is defined in national law. In other words, it is irrelevant that an offence is not deemed to be subject to criminal proceedings in national law if in the understanding of the 1950 European Convention it is.[97] Most likely, all cases of market abuse are likely to be deemed criminal under the 1950 European Convention and thus that Convention and its safeguards must be taken into due consideration.[98] The CJEU concludes that it is permissible to apply a presumption of use, where that presumption is open to rebuttal and the right of defence is guaranteed.[99]

[96] ibid paras 39–43.

[97] ibid para 42 with references to case law by the European Court of Human Rights under the 1950 European Convention.

[98] See on the need to avoid double jeopardy where an offence is subject to criminal and administrative sanctions, which is contrary to art 6 of the 1950 European Convention and now also art 50 of the European Charter art 14 para B.14.7.

[99] *Spector* (n 37) para 44.

Consequently, where the insider either enters into a relevant transaction according to Article 8(1) or is tipping another person according to Article 8(2) while in possession of inside information, a presumption arises that this activity was done by using the inside information in order to take advantage of it to the detriment of third parties. However, the insider must be allowed to defend him- or herself, which defence can take many forms. For example, the insider may argue that he was not in possession of inside information; that he did not understand that the information qualified as inside information; that the transaction was motivated by other information than the inside information; or that the transaction did not constitute an unfair advantage to the detriment of third parties. In assessing this defence, the national court will apply the double standard of 'knew or ought to have known' as adopted in national law to ascertain whether the defence should be successful or rejected. **B.8.162**

Article 9: Legitimate behaviour

1. For the purposes of Articles 8 and 14, it shall not be deemed from the mere fact that a legal person is or has been in possession of inside information that that person has used that information and has thus engaged in insider dealing on the basis of an acquisition or disposal, where that legal person:
   (a) has established, implemented and maintained adequate and effective internal arrangements and procedures that effectively ensure that neither the natural person who made the decision on its behalf to acquire or dispose of financial instruments to which the information relates, nor another natural person who may have had an influence on that decision, was in possession of the inside information; and
   (b) has not encouraged, made a recommendation to, induced or otherwise influenced the natural person who, on behalf of the legal person, acquired or disposed of financial instruments to which the information relates.
2. For the purposes of Articles 8 and 14, it shall not be deemed from the mere fact that a person is in possession of inside information that that person has used that information and has thus engaged in insider dealing on the basis of an acquisition or disposal where that person:
   (a) for the financial instrument to which that information relates, is a market maker or a person authorised to act as a counterparty, and the acquisition or disposal of financial instruments to which that information relates is made legitimately in the normal course of the exercise of its function as a market maker or as a counterparty for that financial instrument; or
   (b) is authorised to execute orders on behalf of third parties, and the acquisition or disposal of financial instruments to which the order relates, is made to carry out such an order legitimately in the normal course of the exercise of that person's employment, profession or duties.
3. For the purposes of Articles 8 and 14, it shall not be deemed from the mere fact that a person is in possession of inside information that that person has used that information and has thus engaged in insider dealing on the basis of an acquisition or disposal where that person conducts a transaction to acquire or dispose of financial instruments and that transaction is carried out in the discharge of an obligation that has become due in good faith and not to circumvent the prohibition against insider dealing and:
   (a) that obligation results from an order placed or an agreement concluded before the person concerned possessed inside information; or
   (b) that transaction is carried out to satisfy a legal or regulatory obligation that arose, before the person concerned possessed inside information.

4. For the purposes of Article 8 and 14, it shall not be deemed from the mere fact that a person is in possession of inside information that that person has used that information and has thus engaged in insider dealing, where such person has obtained that inside information in the conduct of a public takeover or merger with a company and uses that inside information solely for the purpose of proceeding with that merger or public takeover, provided that at the point of approval of the merger or acceptance of the offer by the shareholders of that company, any inside information has been made public or has otherwise ceased to constitute inside information.

This paragraph shall not apply to stake-building.

5. For the purposes of Articles 8 and 14, the mere fact that a person uses its own knowledge that it has decided to acquire or dispose of financial instruments in the acquisition or disposal of those financial instruments shall not of itself constitute use of inside information.

6. Notwithstanding paragraphs 1 to 5 of this Article, an infringement of the prohibition of insider dealing set out in Article 14 may still be deemed to have occurred if the competent authority establishes that there was an illegitimate reason for the orders to trade, transactions or behaviours concerned.

I. General Remarks

Overview of Article 9

Article 9 follows Article 8 that defines insider dealing, which is prohibited by way of Article 14. Article 9 is closely related to these provisions and must be read in conjunction with them. **B.9.01**

According to its own title, Article 9 describes legitimate behaviour. As such, it appears to serve as a delimitation of the activities that are covered by Article 8 and prohibited by Article 14. However, upon closer inspection Article 9 does not conclusively determine behaviour as legitimate, but should be understood as a supplement rather than an exemption to Article 8. This is explored in para B.9.06 below. **B.9.02**

B.9.03 Article 9 covers different situations, which appear to have as their common denominator the fact that persons are acting when directly or indirectly in possession of inside information. Article 9(1) concerns the liability of a legal person in respect of natural persons that are in its service, when one or more of these persons are in possession of inside information. Article 9(2) concerns the liability of market makers and persons authorized to execute orders on behalf of third parties, when the market maker or the trader are in possession of inside information. Article 9(3) concerns trading in discharge of an obligation assumed before coming into possession of inside information. Article 9(4) concerns takeover bids and mergers conducted after coming into possession of inside information. Article 9(5) concerns the situation where a person's decision to engage in a transaction in itself constitutes inside information. Finally, Article 9(6) allows a national competent authority (hereafter NCA) to disregard Article 9(1)–(5) if it establishes that there were, after all, illegitimate reasons at play.

B.9.04 Article 9 is related to Article 5, which also limits the reach of Article 8 by providing an exemption for buy-back programmes and stabilization. However, their natures appear to be different, since Article 5 makes its exemption in regard of Article 14, which is the provision that prohibits activities covered by Article 8. Consequently, if behaviour is covered by Article 5 it is legitimate, which is not quite the effect of Article 9. Article 9 is also related to Article 6, which makes an exemption for monetary and public debt management activities and climate policy activities. Again, there is a visible difference between Articles 9 and 6, because the latter exempts these activities entirely from the scope of the Market Abuse Regulation and not only from Article 14.

B.9.05 Guidance for construing Article 9 is provided by recitals (30)–(31).

The nature and function of Article 9

B.9.06 The nature of Article 9 is important to grasp in order to determine its relationship with Article 8. If Article 9 is understood as an exemption, then it should be construed narrowly. This is a general principle when construing legal provisions and in the *Grøngaard and Bang* case,[1] the Court of Justice of the EU (CJEU)[2] expressed this principle in respect of the exemption to Article 3 Insider Dealing Directive (1989/592/EEC) on unlawful disclosure. It is likely that the same principle would be applied by the CJEU by analogy to exemptions found in the Market Abuse Regulation.

B.9.07 If, on the other hand, Article 9 is not seen as an exemption but as a delineation of behaviour that is legitimate, then it assumes the character of a supplement to

[1] Case C-384/02 *Criminal proceedings against Knud Grøngaard and Allan Bang* [2005] ECR I-9939 para 27.

[2] The Court has been operating under different names according to the different treaties, but its present name will be used here throughout.

the description of insider dealing in Article 8, in which case there is no need to construe it differently than Article 8 itself.

The difference between the two ways of construing Article 9 is that an exemption restricts the scope of the main rule, here the offence of insider dealing, and consequently the exemption must be construed narrowly in order not to eliminate the main rule entirely. It must be assumed that the legislator wanted the main rule observed, and so any exemption should be construed narrowly. Even in criminal law, which is traditionally subject to a narrow application due to the legality principle (*lex certa*), the exemption to a criminal offence would normally be construed stricter than the main rule prohibiting the behaviour. But if Article 9 is not an exemption but forms a supplement to Article 8, then it ranks *pari passu* with that Article, and should not be subject to a narrow application, as both provisions are necessary to understand the full scope of the offence of insider dealing, which is prohibited by Article 14. **B.9.08**

Lacking clear indication from the EU legislator of the purpose that Article 9 should serve and as long as the CJEU has not had the opportunity to construe it, any interpretation remains subject to some uncertainty. However, it is likely that Article 9 should be seen as a supplement to Article 8, which is supported by the following observations. **B.9.09**

First, it is not likely that Article 9 is an exemption, when in fact it is provided with its own exemption by way of Article 9(6), whereby a NCA may declare the behaviour illegitimate regardless of the circumstances stated in the Article. **B.9.10**

Secondly, some of the elements of Article 9 were part of the Article that defined insider dealing in the Commission's original Market Abuse Regulation Proposal,[3] which suggests that they were seen as ranking *pari passu* with the other provisions of the said Article. **B.9.11**

Thirdly, the various situations covered by Article 9 appear to be designed to counter the presumption established by the CJEU in *Spector*,[4] that acting when in possession, directly or indirectly, of inside information constitutes insider dealing.[5] Where such possession occurs, Article 9 sets out certain conditions that make it likely that the activity did not amount to insider dealing despite the possession of inside information. It is clear from the inclusion of Article 9(6) that this may not fully rebut the presumption of use and make the behaviour legitimate, since the NCA may find it illegal, but it does appear to cancel the presumption of use. **B.9.12**

[3] See proposal (n 1), Article 6(7) on the liability of legal persons and national persons employed by them, and Article 6(8) on discharging obligations entered into before coming into possession of inside information.

[4] Case C-45/08 *Spector Photo Group NV v CBFA*, ECR I-12073.

[5] See on this presumption art 8 para B.8.152 ff.

B.9.13 Fourthly, it is likely that the provisions that now make up Article 9 were grouped together in a separate Article to collect the various provisions that had been scattered about in the (former) Market Abuse Directive (2003/6/EC) and its level 2 instruments in order to increase their visibility and ensure that the ban on insider dealing, which was now directly applicable in national law by way of a regulation, would not become too far reaching. This view is supported by the reference to 'defence' in the title of Article 9, when it was first introduced in the Presidency Compromise[6] during the negotiations. It is also supported by the fact that the CJEU in *Spector* emphasized the need to avoid an overly expansive use of the insider dealing ban.[7] Finally, the proposition is supported by the wording used in the various sections of Article 9 where the insider's possession of inside information is regarded as a 'mere fact', which appears to counsel against drawing too wide conclusions of use in the described circumstances.

B.9.14 This would suggest that Article 9 actually serves as a supplement to Article 8 and should not be subject to a narrow interpretation.

B.9.15 The function of Article 9 is to describe certain particular situations where possession of inside information does not, after all, produce a presumption that the inside information had been taken advantage of to the detriment of third parties. See also recitals (23)–(24). If Article 9(1)–(5) is applicable, there is no presumption of use; however, the NCA may still find the behaviour illegitimate by way of Article 9(6), which means that the behaviour would be prohibited by Article 14.

B.9.16 The assessment that the NCA must make is to apply Article 8 and its description of what constitutes insider dealing, but now without the aid of the presumption on use established in *Spector*. If the NCA can prove that despite the conditions described in Article 9(1)–(5) the insider did in fact take unfair advantage of the inside information to the detriment of third parties, which constitutes the essence of insider dealing as remarked by recital (23), then Article 9 can be disregarded and the behaviour falls within the scope of Article 8(1) after all and as such is prohibited by Article 14(a).

B.9.17 By this understanding, it becomes clear how Article 9 differs from Articles 5 and 6, although they too in a way serve to limit the scope of Article 8. Article 5 on buy-back programmes and stabilization makes an exemption not to Article 8 but to Article 14, which means that the behaviour described in Article 5 may well fall within Article 8, but the behaviour would not be prohibited by Article 14. Whereas Article 6 on monetary and public debt management activities and climate policy activities makes an exemption from the Market Abuse Regulation as such, which means that the behaviour should not be qualified at all as insider

---

6 See on the historical development of art 9 para B.9.19.

7 *Spector* (n 4) para 55.

dealing according to Article 8 or market manipulation according to Article 12, because these provisions are inapplicable.

There is some similarity between Articles 5, 6, and 9 as well. None of them can be seen as exemptions in the way that they must be construed narrowly or strictly. They limit the scope of what is deemed illegal in the Market Abuse Regulation not in such a way that a narrow understanding is necessary to respect and maintain the main rule of prohibiting certain behaviour intended by the EU legislator, but because the EU legislator found that behaviour of this kind should not be illegal as such. Another similarity is that although the behaviour has to be covered by the particular description of each Article in order to be considered legitimate, it is not possible to make conclusions *au contraire*. Even if behaviour is not covered by Articles 5, 6, and 9, it does not follow that the behaviour is illegitimate per se and the NCA would in each case have to establish a case to convict by using the relevant provisions of the Market Abuse Regulation. **B.9.18**

Historical development

Article 9 is a new provision compared to the (former) Market Abuse Directive (2003/6/EC). However, some of its elements are restatements of text that was either found in the preamble of the (former) Market Abuse Directive (2003/6/EC) or in the level 2 instruments issued according to the (former) Market Abuse Directive (2003/6/EC) and some can be traced back to the Insider Dealing Directive (1989/592/EEC). Article 9 was not part of the Commission's Market Abuse Regulation Proposal[8] and was inserted under the title 'Defences to insider dealing' at the beginning of the legislative negotiations,[9] which was later changed into the present title of 'legitimate behaviour'. The title is not entirely apt, since behaviour is not necessarily legitimate just because it complies with the Article, as a NCA may find that the behaviour was illegitimate.[10] **B.9.19**

II. Section 1: Liability of Legal Persons

Article 9(1) concerns the liability of legal persons that engage in acquisitions and disposals of securities that would be covered by Article 8(1) and concerns the situation where one or more natural persons who serve the legal person are in possession of inside information. **B.9.20**

The provision begins by observing that the legal person is or has been in possession of inside information and then proceeds to state that this 'mere fact' should **B.9.21**

[8] Commission, Proposal for a Regulation of the European Parliament and of the Council on insider dealing and market manipulation (market abuse) COM(2011) 651, Brussels (20 October 2011).

[9] Presidency compromise, 9435/12, Brussels (2 May 2012).

[10] See on the function of art 9 para B.9.06 ff.

not be deemed to imply that the legal person has used the inside information and engaged in insider dealing if the conditions described in subsection (a) and subsection (b) are fulfilled.

B.9.22 First of all, this raises the question of when a legal person, which after all is a mere figment of our legal imagination without any flesh or mental capacity of its own, can be in possession of inside information.

B.9.23 National law on how to attribute subjective conditions to legal persons may differ among Member States and depend on what is being assessed. If the question is whether the legal person is in possession of a particular piece of information where a natural person in its service has in fact possession of the information, many jurisdictions would take an affirmative view. But if the question was whether the information could be attributed to the legal person in respect of a certain decision, many jurisdictions would only affirm this if the information was possessed by the natural persons who took part in the decision on behalf of the legal person.

B.9.24 Article 9(1) attempts to accommodate both views, but favours the latter. It appears to consider the legal person in possession of inside information simply because a natural person in its service possesses it, but then in subsections (a)–(b) establishes conditions where the possession of inside information among natural persons of the company is irrelevant if they are not making the decision to acquire or dispose of the securities or have been influenced to make it. Taken together, the end result is that a legal person is only liable for violating the ban on insider dealing in Article 8, if the decision to enter into a relevant transaction was made by natural persons in possession of inside information, whereas it is irrelevant if the information was only in the possession of other natural persons employed by the company.

B.9.25 Before examining these conditions further it should thus be observed that Article 9(1) as well as Article 8(5) appear to rest upon an understanding that legal persons will only violate the ban on insider dealing according to Article 8(1), if their decision to enter into a relevant transaction is made by natural persons who are either in possession of inside information or influenced by it. Consequently, even if Article 9(1)(a)–(b) is not complied with, a legal person may rebut the presumption of use that arises where it has been proven that inside information was in the possession of natural persons working for the legal person if the legal person can prove that the natural persons in charge of the decision were in fact not themselves in possession of the inside information, nor influenced by it.

B.9.26 The reasoning behind subsections (a)–(b) is based on this understanding as they establish certain conditions that minimizes the risk that the natural persons participating in the decision on behalf of the legal person are themselves in possession of inside information or are influenced by somebody within the legal person who is. Considering how frequently inside information may be in possession of natural persons employed by legal persons, especially financial institutions, and how many natural persons may possess different kinds of inside information at any one time, this understanding is simply necessary to allow such institutions to operate.

Subsection (a) concerns the situation where the legal person has 'established, implemented and maintained internal arrangements and procedures' known as information barriers, or in older parlance Chinese walls, that effectively ensure that inside information does not come into the possession of the natural persons who participate in the decision on behalf of the legal person. It is clear that the procedures must be maintained and remain efficient in order to cancel the presumption in Article 8(1) that inside information available to other natural persons serving the legal person has been made available to the decision-makers or influenced them. **B.9.27**

Subsection (b) concerns encouragement, recommendations, and inducements to take advantage of the inside information and in this way Article 9(1)(b) is similar to Article 8(2) on tipping, especially in the sense that the natural persons participating in the decision on behalf of the legal person does not have to know or understand the actual content of the inside information as long as they do understand that it would be advantageous for the legal person to trade in a certain way. **B.9.28**

Subsections (a)–(b) are combined conditions, that is, they both must be satisfied in order for the legal person to escape the presumption that inside information in its possession was abused. **B.9.29**

As observed, the failure to comply with Article 9 does not in itself warrant that the behaviour falls within Article 8(1). If the arrangements and procedures are not deemed effective, perhaps due to irregularities, the legal person has not for that reason alone engaged in insider dealing according to Article 8(1). Whether the situation amounts to insider dealing probably depends on the proximity between the natural persons in possession of inside information and the natural persons who participated in the decision on behalf of the legal person. If a decision is demonstrably taken by natural persons without inside information, because the natural persons with inside information were in another building or another country without any access among them, the presumption of use may not arise. But if there is a proximity, whereby inside information could have been transmitted to the decision-makers, it is very likely that a presumption of use will arise. It may still be possible for the legal person to escape liability despite its insufficient safeguards and even if Article 9(1) is not applicable, if it is possible to rebut the presumption of use, for example, or if it can prove that the transaction was not in fact made to take unfair advantage of the inside information to the detriment of third parties. **B.9.30**

Consequently, where Article 9(1) has been observed by the legal person, the outcome is simply to remove a presumption of use, even if it is established that **B.9.31** natural persons serving the legal person were in possession of inside information. This is not necessarily the end of the matter, as the NCA may still investigate whether the natural persons who participated in the decision had or were influenced by inside information.

III. Section 2: Market Makers and Execution of Orders

B.9.32 Article 9(2) concerns certain market professionals that may be in possession of inside information when they engage in the acquisition of disposal of a security according to Article 8(1), but should not necessarily for that reason be deemed to have engaged in insider dealing. The two groups of professionals are market makers in Article 9(2)(a), and persons authorized to execute order in Article 9(2)(b).

B.9.33 An almost similar text to Article 9(2) was found in recital (18) of the (former) Market Abuse Directive (2003/6/EC) and before that in recital (12) of the Insider Dealing Directive (1989/592/EEC), that were used to construe the meaning of the ban on insider dealing in the two directives, which supports the understanding advanced in para B.9.06 ff above, that Article 9 serves to supplement the understanding of Article 8 and is not as such an exemption to that Article.

Market makers

B.9.34 Article 9(2)(a) concerns market makers, that is, persons who continuously display buy and sell orders in a given security, whereby they provide liquidity (make the market). This function can be performed by a person simply trading on his or her own behalf to profit from the transactions if the spread between buy and sell orders so allow, but mostly market making is a service provided by financial institutions for a consideration and at the request of the issuer to ensure liquidity in its securities.

B.9.35 The problem is that market makers may come into possession of inside information about one or more of the securities that they trade, especially if the function is carried out by a financial institution with many employees. The inside information could be information about market conditions and although some of this information may be legal to use according to Article 9(5), where it is derived by the market maker's own deliberations, most inside information of this kind will not be legal to trade on. Since the market maker may be contractually obliged to continue trading and is generally serving the liquidity of the market, the EU legislator has since the 1989 Insider Dealing Directive (1989/592/EEC) provided that mere possession of inside information does not amount to insider dealing and consequently the market makers may continue their activities despite their possession of inside information as long as they do not abuse their advantage.

The purpose of subsection (a) is to describe when the market maker acts in a way that should be considered legitimate. This is described as when the market maker acquires or disposes of securities to which the inside information relates and does it 'in the normal course' of the exercise of the function as a market maker. **B.9.36**

Before exploring this condition further, it should be noted that where the market maker is organized as a legal person, the principles derived from Article 9(1) should be applied to ascertain whether the natural person actually making the acquisition or disposal on behalf of the market maker was in possession of inside information. It may be that the inside information is in the possession of a natural person employed by the market maker, but demonstrably not in the possession of the natural person acting on behalf of the market maker, in which case Article 9(2)(a) becomes moot. If, on the other hand, it is not possible to exclude that the natural person acting is in possession of inside information or influenced by it, then Article 9(2)(a) becomes relevant. **B.9.37**

The previous wording in the Insider Dealing Directive (1989/592/EEC) and the (former) Market Abuse Directive (2003/6/EC) used the phrase that market makers had 'to confine themselves' to their legitimate business. The phrase has not been restated in Article 9(2)(a), but is still employed in recital (30). It may have been intended as a strict requirement, but more likely it simply means that the market maker should perform the activity of making a market without taking account of the inside information. **B.9.38**

To ascertain whether a market maker is acting in the 'normal course' of his or her business it is probably necessary to examine both the trading pattern of the market maker and that of other market makers trading in the same or very similar securities at the same time. The offence of insider dealing according to Article 8(1) is to use the inside information to obtain an unfair advantage to the detriment of third parties. Only if the examination of the market maker's trading pattern discloses that it has offered prices that deviate from its normal trading pattern in such a way as to take advantage of the inside information, would the market maker have engaged in insider dealing. **B.9.39**

This assessment is basically the same assessment that must be made according to Article 8(1) and it is thus not obvious whether Article 9(2)(a) serves any independent purpose. To the extent that it does, it is probably because it draws attention to the fact that market makers are obliged to trade and cannot cease simply because they come into possession of inside information and for that reason consideration should be paid to the trading pattern of what can be seen as 'normal' market making of the security at that particular time in order to determine whether the market maker actually took advantage of the inside information by displaying orders that did not conform to this pattern. **B.9.40**

Persons authorized to execute orders

B.9.41 Article 9(2)(b) concerns persons authorized to execute orders on behalf of third parties as part of that person's employment, profession, or duties, where such persons acquire or dispose of securities according to Article 8(1) while in possession of inside information.

B.9.42 The problem here is related to that examined in subsection (a) above that the person is contractually obliged to trade and should be allowed to perform the execution if it does not entail the use of the inside information. Subsection (b) employs the same phrase, that it is legitimate behaviour where it is done 'in the normal course' of that person's duties. Much of what was stated in respect of subsection (a) in para B.9.34 ff above can be used here as well, notably to determine whether a legal person authorized to execute orders on behalf of others does in fact possess inside information.

B.9.43 However, contrary to the problem of market makers examined in subsection (a), the persons covered by subsection (b) do not themselves set the price at which acquisition or disposal is made. This, in a way, makes the issue easier to handle. If the person simply executes an order issued by a third party and on that party's account without having any influence on the order, then it is irrelevant that the person was in possession of inside information. This result would follow directly from Article 8(1), because the presumption of use applicable in that Article would be rebutted by the fact that the order was made entirely by somebody else and only executed by the person in question. Again, and even more so than in subsection (a), it is questionable whether subsection (b) has any independent relevance outside Article 8(1). To the extent that it does, it serves to point out that the mere execution of an order does not amount to insider dealing even if the person handling its execution happens to be in possession of inside information, if that information does not affect the order in any way.

B.9.44 Finally, it should be observed in respect of Article 9(2)(b) that it does not change this outcome if the third party that issued the order was in fact in possession of inside information and made the order to take unfair advantage of it to the detriment of others. That would constitute insider dealing according to Article 8(1) on behalf of that party, but it would not amount to insider dealing for the person who simply executed the order. This scenario raises a further question of whether the person executing the order could be held liable for assisting the insider in committing insider dealing. This possible liability for a party that knowingly assists in an offence is not directly covered by Article 9(2)(b) and must be determined by national law. If the dealer does not simply execute a given order but actively encourages a third party to trade in a way that takes advantage of inside information in the dealer's possession, it would constitute tipping, according to Article 8(2) as prohibited by Article 14(b).

IV. Section 3: Subsequent Possession of Inside Information

Article 9(3) concerns acquisitions and disposals of a security by a person in possession of inside information (the insider) according to Article 8(1), when the relevant transaction is derived from arrangements that existed before the insider came into possession of the inside information. A similar text was found in Article 2(3) of the (former) Market Abuse Directive (2003/6/EC). **B.9.45**

The problem at issue concerns a question of great practical importance, which is situations where a person is obliged to enter into a securities transaction due to some pre-existing arrangement, but subsequently comes into possession of inside information before he or she can enter into the transaction. The purpose of Article 9(3) is to enable the person to perform this transaction if the inside information is not used. **B.9.46**

The first condition is that the transaction is carried out in the discharge of an obligation that has become due. In Article 9(3) it is furthermore required that it has become due 'in good faith and not to circumvent' the prohibition against insider dealing, which goes further than the original wording of Article 2(3) of the (former) Market Abuse Directive (2003/6/EC). **B.9.47**

The next condition that must be fulfilled as well follows from subsection (a) which states that the obligation results from an order placed or an agreement concluded before the insider came into possession of inside information. **B.9.48**

In combination it is clear that Article 9(3)(a) would apply, for example, to the performance of a futures contract, where the insider has entered into the contract to buy or sell a security at a specified time in the future and subsequently comes into possession of inside information before that date. In this case, the insider may legitimately acquire or dispose of the security according to the contractual obligation regardless of the inside information in his or her possession, because the insider is effectively only performing an obligation that was entered into without possession of inside information and consequently there has been no abuse of the inside information when the contract was formed. In other words, the performance that was conditioned on the pre-existing arrangement does not in itself entail a use of the inside information, because the conditions of the transaction were all determined before the inside information came into possession, that is, the performance was done in good faith and not to circumvent the prohibition against insider dealing. **B.9.49**

The same reasoning must also apply to other pre-existing arrangements, where the obligation to trade at a later time is assumed without the benefit of inside information, which only arises later. As such, Article 9(3)(a) would also cover the situation where a seller of an option comes into possession of inside information after the option was sold but before the option's strike date. If the buyer of the **B.9.50** option wants to exercise the option, the seller is entitled to perform the option regardless of any inside information that may have come into his or her possession after the conclusion of the option. It cannot be assumed that the insider as the seller of the option is required to warn the buyer of the option that exercising the option would be contrary to his own interest. There is no basis to assume such an obligation to protect the interest of the other party and obliging the insider to make such a warning may disclose the inside information, which would increase the risk of insider dealing and go against the purpose of the ban in Article 10 on unlawful disclosure.

B.9.51 Article 9(3)(a) only applies to situations where the transaction is made in the discharge of a pre-existing *obligation*. Consequently, the buyer of the option could not apply this provision directly, since the buyer only has a right to exercise the option but no obligation to do so. However, if the buyer can prove that he or she bought the option without possession of inside information, which only arose subsequently, the buyer would not have engaged in insider dealing according to Article 8(1), because the presumption of use of the inside information in that Article would have been rebutted by the fact that there was no inside information at the time when the option contract was entered into by the parties. This reasoning would be the same, irrespective of whether the option was European, that is, with a set strike date, or American, that is, exercisable at a time chosen by the buyer of the option. Again, there is no basis to assume that the buyer of the option must refrain from exercising the option to protect the interest of the option seller, because the option was entered into without possession of inside information.

B.9.52 Consequently, even in pre-existing arrangements that do not involve a legal obligation to transact at a later point and which may for that reason fall outside the strict wording of Article 9(3)(a), would it be legitimate to enter into such a pre-planned transaction in possession of inside information if all relevant circumstances of the transaction, notably that of price, had been established by the pre-existing arrangement. In these cases, there is no use of the inside information, and the fact that one party subsequently happens to come into possession of inside information after the conclusion of the arrangement does not prevent that person from entering into the pre-planned transaction.

B.9.53 Furthermore, in all these cases of pre-existing arrangements, where a party is contractually entitled subsequently to enter into the pre-planned transaction on its pre-existing conditions, that person's entitlement is not affected by the fact that the inside information now in that person's possession is favourable to him or her. Thus, the seller of an option who is obliged to enter into the pre-planned transaction if the buyer of the option decides to exercise the option, will be covered by Article 9(3)(a) even if the new inside information that is now in his or her possession makes the transaction favourable. Equally in respect of the buyer of the option, although here the result is reached by using either Article 8(1) directly or an analogy of Article 9(3)(a). For example, the seller of a put-option is entitled to buy the security at the pre-arranged strike price if the buyer wants to exercise the put-option even though the seller may have come into possession of positive inside information indicating an imminent price increase. The outcome would be the same, if it is the buyer of the put-option who has come into possession of negative inside information indicating a fall in prices. The fact that the buyer's motivation to exercise the put-option was in fact the negative inside information that later came into his possession does not constitute use in the sense of Article 8(1) because it cannot have affected the conditions of the trade and is therefore irrelevant. What matters is whether the inside information was used to settle the conditions of the transaction, notably the price, which it cannot have been, because at that point it was not in his or her possession.

If the exercise of options was not possible due to the subsequent possession of inside information it would seriously impair the functioning of securities markets, which it is the express purpose of the Market Abuse Regulation to protect.[11] Options are often sold as a kind of insurance, or in the parlance of the financial markets: hedging. For example, a party who owns a certain share may fear that its price may fall and for that reason invests in a put-option giving him the right to sell the share at a predetermined time and price. If later his fears are justified and the price does drop, he should be able to exercise the option that he has paid for. It is irrelevant that he is not under any obligation to sell the share; it is a right that he has acquired in good faith and for which he has paid good money. Whether the entitled person after entering into the option in good faith subsequently happens to come into possession of inside information is irrelevant as long as the inside information was not taken advantage of in the first place. **B.9.54**

The same applies for the seller of the option. This is normally a professional financial institution and like an insurance company it will calculate the risk of the options that it sells and the premium that it has to collect to set-off this risk. It makes no sense to deny it a favourable deal, simply because it happens to have come into possession of inside information that makes the exercise of the option more financially rewarding that originally planned, nor is it sensible or even feasible to require it to disclose its inside information to the buyer of the option in order to prevent the exercise of the option as this could entail unlawful disclosure contrary to Article 10. **B.9.55**

In all these instances, there is simply not the abuse of inside information that may damage the functioning of the securities markets or harm its integrity. Abuse only arises when inside information is taken advantage of to the detriment of third parties and in order to take advantage of the inside information **B.9.56**

[11] Cf recitals (1)–(2).

it has to be in a party's possession when that party negotiates the conditions of the relevant transaction. After that point, inside information becomes irrelevant among the parties, just as it was irrelevant in the *Georgakis* case that the parties shared the same inside information, when they traded with each other.[12] As stated in the *Spector* case, not all trading done while in possession of inside information amounts to insider dealing.[13]

B.9.57 It is different, of course, if the option was entered into while in possession of inside information. Although the option would then determine the date and price it could be exercised, the conditions of the pre-planned transaction would not come due in good faith and would consequently constitute insider dealing according to Article 8(1). The same would apply where important conditions of the transaction were not settled and thus subject to be determined when the transaction takes place. In that case, possession of inside information that has come into possession before the transaction is finally settled will produce a presumption that it has been used in determining these conditions to obtain an unfair advantage.

B.9.58 The principle that actions only amount to insider dealing if the inside information is actively taken advantage of to the detriment of third parties also lies behind the acceptance that an order placed without inside information does not have to be cancelled or amended if inside information subsequently comes into possession of the person who placed the order.[14]

B.9.59 By subsection (b) the same result is extended to situations where it is not a pre-existing arrangement to enter into a securities transaction, but a pre-existing legal or regulatory obligation. The term legal obligation is vague, because strictly speaking the obligations covered by subsection (a) are also 'legal', but it probably refers to contractual arrangements made outside the securities markets for other purposes than securities trading, for example, according to company law. As such it may cover incentive programmes of the issuer, which may necessitate that the issuer acquires its own shares in the market at a given point in time even though the issuer is in possession of positive inside information about itself that it is not obliged to disclose according to Article 17. Regulatory obligations may cover transactions mandated by law or by a NCA. The reasoning behind Article 9(3)(b) is naturally the same in all respects, so what is important is that the insider cannot use his or her inside information to affect the conditions of the transaction involving the acquisition or disposal of securities according to Article 8(1) if the insider is to fulfil the legal or regulatory obligation. If there is any possibility to use the inside information, Article 9(3)(b) is not applicable, but the transaction only constitutes insider dealing if the conditions in Article 8(1) are fulfilled.

---

[12] Case C-391/04 *Ipourgos Ikonomikon, Proistamenos DOI Amfissas v Charilaos Georgakis* [2007] ECR I-3741 (*Georgakis*). See on this case art 8 n 37 ff.

[13] *Spector* (n 4) para 45.

[14] See on this art 8 para B.8.85 ff.

Subsection (b) is probably less frequent in practice than the situations covered by subsection (a) and since the pre-existing legal or regulatory obligation normally would not determine the conditions of the subsequent securities transaction as they would in situations covered by subsection (a), there may be greater scope for the insider to use the inside information and thus less scope to apply subsection (b). Nonetheless, it is important to remind of the CJEU's dictum that not all trading done in possession of inside information constitutes insider dealing and subsection (b) serves an important purpose where the insider is obliged to act in good faith despite the possession of inside information. **B.9.60**

V. Section 4: Takeovers and Mergers

Inside information obtained in the conduct of a bid or merger

Article 9(4) concerns the conduct of a takeover bid or a merger, when the bidder or one of the merging companies is in possession of inside information. A similar text was found in recital (29) of the (former) Market Abuse Directive (2003/6/EC) and formed part of the argumentation of the CJEU in the *Spector* case.[15] As that decision has clearly inspired recital (23), the decision must be considered valid law under the Market Abuse Regulation as well. **B.9.61**

The problem arises from the fact that takeovers and mergers are usually conducted after a fact-finding mission (due diligence), which may uncover inside information that is in the possession of the target company. Taking into account the broad interpretation used by the CJEU on the definition of inside information according to Article 7, which appears to include basically all non-public information that may affect the pricing of a security, it is very likely that a due diligence will uncover information that qualifies as inside information. For the initial analysis, it is irrelevant whether the target company should have disclosed this inside information or was allowed to delay disclosure according to Article 17. The problem concerns whether the bidder can continue the takeover or merger when in possession of inside information. **B.9.62**

Article 9(4) is limited to situations, where the inside information is obtained in 'the conduct' of the takeover or merger, that is, by way of due diligence or similar information retrieving exercise involving the target company. It would not cover inside information obtained in other ways, for example, from third parties. However, if the management of the target company provides the inside information to the bidder or the merging company hoping that its possession of inside information may now frustrate the bid, this should not succeed, as the information provided must be handled in the same way as any inside information **B.9.63**

[15] *Spector* (n 4) para 59.

uncovered by the bidder or the merging company itself while examining the target company and thus be seen as obtained in 'the conduct' of the takeover or merger.

B.9.64 Furthermore, the inside information must be obtained legally in the conduct of the takeover or merger, and it is thus not enough that the information was provided by somebody engaged in the transaction, for example by an indiscretion from financial intermediaries involved in the transaction. It should be remembered that cases which fall outside the scope of Article 9 do not necessarily constitute insider dealing according to Article 8(1); this is only the case if Article 8(1) is satisfied on its own conditions. Consequently, the following analysis may also apply to situations where the inside information was not obtained in the conduct of the takeover or merger and thus fall outside the scope of Article 9(4).

B.9.65 In its decision in the *Spector* case, the CJEU elaborated on what it meant when it said that not all trading done while in possession of inside information is necessarily insider dealing. Reference is here made to the commentary of Article 8, see para B.8.68 ff, where this is analysed in greater detail. Suffice to say here that, as long as the bidder or the merging company takes into account any inside information in its possession when calibrating its bid to ensure that the offer price reasonably reflects all information in its possession, the bidder or the merging company does not seek to take unfair advantage of the inside information and the bid will be lawful, even though the inside information was in fact used to establish the offer price. This view is also reflected in recital (30), which appears to restate recital (29) of the (former) Market Abuse Directive (2003/6/EC) in this respect.

Inside information after the bid or merger

B.9.66 Article 9(4) deviates from recital (29) of the (former) Market Abuse Directive (2003/6/EC), and thereby from the present recital (30), in requiring as a further condition that 'at the point of approval of the merger or acceptance of the offer by the shareholders of that company, any inside information has been made public or has otherwise ceased to constitute inside information'.

B.9.67 This condition is probably the reason why stake-building, that is, the gradual acquisition of shares in the target company, is excluded from Article 9(4) by its 2nd subsection, because in a stake-building there is no public presentation of the bid or merger plan to the shareholders of the target company, where such disclosure could take place.

B.9.68 This further condition is not necessary according to the understanding applied by the CJEU in *Spector*, which has shaped the understanding of the insider dealing ban in Article 8(1), see also recital (23) on the essence of insider dealing. The essence of insider dealing is to use the inside information to obtain an unfair advantage to the detriment of third parties. If no such unfair advantage is sought, because the bidder or the merging company calibrates its bid to reasonably reflect the inside information and thereby no third parties are harmed, then it is irrelevant in relation to Article 8 whether the inside information was eventually made public or not. Consequently, the purpose of this provision is more likely to serve as a disclosure obligation and not as a condition the violation of which may be qualified as insider dealing.

The purpose of Article 9(4) as a disclosure obligation is probably to ensure that no abuse of the inside information took place. This is done by providing that if the inside information was disclosed at the point in time specified, then the bidder or the merging company will not be subject to the presumption of use that would otherwise arise according to Article 8(1) due to its possession of inside information. The reasoning appears to be that if the inside information is disclosed, it will be possible to determine whether the takeover bid or merger takes account of the inside information and so the act of disclosure serves to prove the good intent of the bidder or the merging company. **B.9.69**

However, if the bidder or merging company does not disclose the inside information, it cannot be concluded by this fact alone that the company has engaged in insider dealing according to Article 8(1) simply because of its failure to comply with Article 9(4). The failure to disclose inside information may give rise to the presumption inherent in Article 8(1) that the inside information was taken advantage of unfairly. But if the bidder or the merging company can prove that the offer or merger price reasonably reflected the inside information in their possession, they will have rebutted the presumption of use and the behaviour is legitimate, regardless of whether Article 9(4) has been complied with. **B.9.70**

It should be noted in this connection, that the bidder or merging company may be prevented from disclosing the inside information, for example where it has signed a confidentiality agreement with the target company. Equally, where the target company is allowed to delay disclosure of a particular inside information according to Article 17(4), for example to protect intellectual property rights such as patents, then Article 9(4) cannot be seen as an obligation to disclose it anyway and thereby harm the legitimate interest of the target company. Article 17(4) on delay of disclosure must be the applicable provision (*lex specialis*) in regard of disclosure that overrules the disclosure obligation following from Article 9(4). **B.9.71**

It is also possible, but not clear, that Article 9(4) does not actually warrant disclosure of any inside information at all. This is because the provision calls for the disclosure of inside information unless it has 'otherwise ceased to constitute inside information'. Some may argue that where the bidder or merging company calibrate its offer to reflect the inside information that has come into its possession in order to protect the interests of the target company's shareholders, then the publication of the bid will make the inside information cease to be inside information in the relationship between the bidder or the merging company and **B.9.72** the shareholders of the target company. The argument is that if the bid reflects the inside information, then the inside information will no longer be able to affect the pricing of the shares, which is part of its definition according to Article 7. Some support may be taken from *Georgakis*, which stated that inside information may 'cease' to be inside information among certain parties due to the circumstances.[16]

B.9.73 This understanding is, however, not very likely. For one thing, it would imply that the bidder or merging company could choose whether to reflect the inside information in its possession or just disclose the inside information. If inside information in the possession of the bidder or the merging company is not reflected in the bid, it will constitute insider dealing according to Article 8(1), regardless of any subsequent disclosure made. Furthermore, it would deprive the provision of any independent meaning next to Article 8(1), which already requires a calibration of the bid to reflect the inside information. It is more likely that this part of the provision simply refers to inside information that by its own nature ceases to be inside information before the takeover or the merger is concluded, for example, the target company's confidential negotiations about a major contract that are abandoned before any contract is made.

B.9.74 Consequently, if a bidder or a merging company comes into possession of inside information about the target company, for example by way of a due diligence, it must take care to reasonably calibrate its offer to reflect the inside information so as not to harm the shareholders of the target company. This follows directly from Article 8(1) as supported by the CJEU's decision in *Spector*. Furthermore, if the bidder or the merging company disclose all inside information in its possession by the time the takeover or the merger is concluded, there will not be any presumption that it took unfair advantage of the inside information disclosed. If it fails to make such disclosure, it may still be able to rebut the presumption of use if it can demonstrate that the offer was calibrated to reasonably reflect the inside information. If it has actively tried to hide inside information, this may be detrimental to the assessment, whereas if the failure to disclose is justified by the fact that it were not at liberty to disclose or the inside information was legitimately delayed according to Article 17(4), no such detrimental effect should arise. Finally, this assessment is probably not a question of all or nothing. The suspicion that inside information was used to the detriment of the shareholders of the target company will only arise in respect of inside information that was not disclosed, so even where disclosure is made only of some inside information but not all, Article 9(4) may still serve its purpose.

VI. Section 5: Own Knowledge

B.9.75 Article 9(5) concerns instances where the decision by a person to engage in acquisitions or disposals of securities according to Article 8(1) constitutes inside

[16] *Georgakis* (n 12) para 39.

information in itself, which may be the case if the transaction is substantial enough to affect the pricing of the security. The typical example is a takeover bid, but other transactions can qualify as well. The text is similar to recital (30) of the (former) Market Abuse Directive (2003/6/EC) and recital (11) of the Insider Dealing Directive (1989/592/EEC), which are now restated in recital (31).

The problem is whether the person engages in insider dealing according to Article 8(1) when using his or her 'own knowledge'. The answer is unsurprisingly no, but this is not to suggest that the problem is irrelevant. Naturally, it is not reasonable to outlaw securities transactions carried out in possession of inside information, when that information only concerns one's own decision to trade. But it is nevertheless important to safeguard the interests of the other market participants in cases that involve information of major importance. This is achieved by obliging disclosure by the insider in some instances of major importance, for example, to disclose that a takeover bid has been decided.[17] Equally, the disclosure of major stakes are mandated to ensure that the market is kept informed of any stake-building that may take place, although the disclosure in these cases only concerns the holdings and does not include the strategic intent behind such transactions.[18] **B.9.76**

Since Article 7 on the definition of inside information and Article 8 on insider dealing do not distinguish among inside information that is own knowledge and other forms, Article 9(5) serves the practical purpose of ensuring that the presumption of use in Article 8(1) does not apply to inside information that is own knowledge. However, the same view that was expressed in the recitals of the previous directives is restated in recital (31) and so, even without Article 9(5), it would be possible to construe Article 8(1) in such a way as to include these instances simply by relying on recital (31). **B.9.77**

It is important to note that Article 9(5) only concerns 'own' knowledge of a decision to engage in a transaction, as does recital (31). This means that it becomes relevant to determine who the information belongs to. If the knowledge is attributed to a legal person, Article 9(5) and recital (31) will only apply to that legal person and to that transaction. If another person, be that other persons than the legal person or a natural person working for the legal person, uses the information to their own unfair advantage and to the detriment of third parties, they will have engaged in insider dealing according to Article 8(1) in the form known as front-running, which is mentioned in recital (30) as unlawful behaviour. **B.9.78**

On the other hand, it is legal to suggest an action, for example a takeover, to another person which would then amount to inside information if that other party accepts the proposition and acts upon it. To make such a proposition is not illegal, because at the time the proposition is made, the proposition is not in **B.9.79**

[17] Article 6(1) Takeover Directive (2004/25/EC).
[18] Transparency Directive (2013/50/EU).

itself inside information. It does, however, become inside information, once the proposition is accepted and from that moment, the proposition now qualifies as inside information belonging to the party that will act on it and that party will be allowed to act on it according to Article 9(5), for example making a takeover bid, although originally the proposition to make such a bid was suggested by somebody else.

VII. Section 6: Illegitimate Reasons

B.9.80 Article 9(6) enables an NCA to set aside the provisions in Article 9(1)–(5) if it establishes that there were illegitimate reasons for the securities transaction in question. As already observed, behaviour does not amount to insider dealing according to Article 8(1) just because it does not fall within the conditions outlined in Article 9(1)–(5); it further requires that the conditions in Article 8(1) are fulfilled. Consequently, the purpose of Article 9(6) appears to be the wish by the EU legislator to avoid a perception of Article 9(1)–(5) as exemptions or safe harbours whereby a behaviour that apparently fulfils the conditions must be deemed lawful as this may enable a formalism that would facilitate circumvention of the prohibition against insider dealing. That this is not the purpose of these provisions is also visible from the fact that they are all worded in the same way to emphasize that in the instances described the 'mere fact' that inside information is in possession at the time of the securities transaction does not trigger the presumption of use inherent in Article 8(1).

B.9.81 It is likely that Article 9(6) will not be of any greater importance in itself compared to Article 8(1). If a case arises, where a person has engaged in a securities transaction according to Article 8(1) while in possession of inside information this may trigger a presumption of use and in that case the insider may claim that the presumption is unjustified because the instance is covered by Article 9(1)–(5). If, on closer inspection, the NCA establishes that the inside information was in fact used to obtain an unfair advantage to the detriment of third parties and in this way constituted insider dealing, this conclusion will be reached by use of Article 8(1) directly in which case it becomes less important for the NCA to justify its result by use of Article 9(6).

Article 10: Unlawful disclosure of inside information

1. For the purposes of this Regulation, unlawful disclosure of inside information arises where a person possesses inside information and discloses that information to any other person, except where the disclosure is made in the normal exercise of an employment, a profession or duties.

This paragraph applies to any natural or legal person in the situations or circumstances referred to in Article 8(4).

2. For the purposes of this Regulation the onward disclosure of recommendations or inducements referred to in Article 8(2) amounts to unlawful disclosure of inside information under this Article where the person disclosing the recommendation or inducement knows or ought to know that it was based on inside information.

I. General Remarks

The improper use of inside information consists of three types of conduct: two of them, known as 'insider dealing' (or insider trading), are described under Article **B.10.01**

8(1)(2), while the third concerns the 'unlawful disclosure of inside information', according to Article 10. As a whole they pursue the main objective of the Market Abuse Regulation, which is the protection of 'inside information' as defined in Article 7.

B.10.02 Following a short introduction on unlawful behaviours connected to the improper uses of inside information (Section I), the present comment addresses the main issues raised by Article 10. Both insider trading and the unlawful disclosure of inside information are prohibited by Article 14, even if the discipline of the two types of misconduct unveils significant differences.

B.10.03 While the prohibition of insider trading is absolute, the transmission to third parties of inside information is sometimes necessary and, thus, legitimate without impairing the effectiveness of the equal access of information principle (Section II). In order to understand Article 10, cases of legitimate and illegitimate transmission of inside information from primary or secondary insiders must be carefully distinguished (Section III). Within the overall picture of a strongly market-oriented discipline, unlawful disclosure of inside information not only reduces insider trading opportunities, but aims to impose a duty of confidentiality for all persons possessing inside information (Section IV).

Historical developments

B.10.04 Article 10 came into force on 3 July 2016.[1] It reproduces the approach taken by Article 3 of the (former) Market Abuse Directive (2003/6/EC) in prohibiting the unlawful disclosure of inside information. Its origin can be traced back to Article 3 of Council Directive 89/592/EEC of 13 November 1989, coordinating regulations on insider trading.

Overview on the improper uses of inside information in the Market Abuse Regulation

Acquiring or disposing of financial instruments

B.10.05 The actions that fall under 'insider trading' are related to transactions of financial instruments listed on a regulated market or traded in other venues[2] (multilateral or organized trading facilities) among counterparties who have a dissimilar amount of information concerning the financial instruments involved. However, it can also concern a transaction carried out privately.

B.10.06 The banning of insider trading is based on the presumption that legal or natural persons possessing 'inside information' can exploit such an informational

[1] Article 39(2).
[2] Article 2(1) and (3).

advantage by acquiring or disposing of the related financial instruments.[3] From an individual transaction perspective, this prohibition prevents all unfair trading activities arising from the asymmetrical distribution of inside information. Overall, insider trading regulation introduces an element of integrity of financial transactions, setting out fair rules for all market operators.[4]

Tuyautage

The second profile of insider trading, described in Article 8(2), is commonly known as 'tuyautage'. It concerns the conduct of a person who, without performing any trading operation, recommends a transaction to another person (or induces others to trade) where the recommendation (or inducement) is based on inside information. Even though such information is not disclosed, it may lead to (unfair) trading activity. **B.10.07**

Prohibition of this behaviour is strict. The mere transmission of the recommendation to another person, regardless of the use the recipient may make of it, is considered insider trading. In this respect, any form of advice or inducement capable of influencing the decision process, if considered the principal motivator of the investment decision, should be considered a recommendation.[5] **B.10.08**

Insider trading also occurs if a person who receives a recommendation acquires or disposes of the financial instruments related to it. However, punishment requires awareness that the recommendation is based on inside information, even if its precise content remains unknown.[6] **B.10.09**

Omission to trade

A completely new element in the catalogue of insider trading is the case of omission to trade by a person in possession of inside information. Not all hypothetical **B.10.10**

[3] Emilios Avgouleas, 'A Critical Evaluation of the New EC Financial-Market Regulation: Peaks, Troughs, and the Road Ahead' (2005) 18 Transnational Lawyer 179, 202; cf recital (24); on the rebuttable presumption that trading while in possession of inside information normally constitutes *use* of inside information, see Lars Klöhn, 'The European Insider Trading Regulation after *Spector Photo Group*' (2010) 2 European Company and Financial Law Review 347, 350–3; Jesper Lau Hansen, 'Insider Dealing Defined: The EU Court's Decision in *Spector Photo Group*' (2010) 7 European Company Law 98, 101–3; Martin Böse, 'Case C-45/08, *Spector Photo Group NV v CBFA*, Judgment of the European Court of Justice (Third Chamber) of 23 December 2009' (2011) 48 Common Market Law Review 190, 191–4.

[4] Niamh Moloney, *EU Securities and Financial Markets Regulation* (3rd edn, Oxford University Press 2014) 700–2, 705. Cf recital (2).

[5] Francesco Mucciarelli, 'Articolo 184' in Marco Fratini and Giorgio Gasparri (eds), *Il Testo Unico della Finanza* (Utet 2012) 2367; Luigi Foffani, 'Articolo 184' in Francesco Vella (ed), *Commentario T.U.F.* (Giappichelli 2012) 1779.

[6] Article 8(3) and art 3(7) of the Market Abuse Directive on Criminal Sanctions (2014/57/EU) require a different degree of awareness by the person that trades on the basis of the recommendation. In order to impose an administrative sanction, it is enough that this person 'knows or ought to know that it is based upon inside information'; however, the criminal sanction requires that this person 'knows' (definitively) that the recommendation is based on the inside information.

omissions of this kind are significant, and enforcement would be otherwise impossible,[7] but in one identified situation, the direct link between the omission and the inside information is quite clear. Such cases may happen where an order is placed *before* the person possessed inside information, and, subsequently, in light of the inside knowledge, the order is cancelled or amended. Similarly, recommending or inducing another person, based on inside information, to cancel or modify a previously submitted order falls under this definition of insider trading.[8]

B.10.11 As a general rule, orders entered into the system can still be modified or cancelled. The risk of committing insider trading occurs only when the decision not to complete the transaction derives from knowledge of inside information obtained after the order was placed but before its execution. However, the risk of market manipulation should be at least mentioned when, by virtue of the significance (in quantitative or economic terms) of the order cancelled, the market was affected by this conduct.[9]

Structure of Article 10

B.10.12 Within the framework of the Market Abuse Regulation, unlawful disclosure may be classified, together with insider trading and recommending to engage or inducing in insider trading, among the improper uses of inside information. According to Article 10, disclosure of inside information is always unlawful—except for the cases discussed in Section III—even if the recipient neither uses the information for any act of disposal of related financial instruments nor intends to induce others to do so. Moreover, this conduct does not require the exploitation of inside information since, even in the absence of any personal profit or benefit, the disclosing person has nevertheless committed unlawful disclosure.

B.10.13 In order to be charged with unlawful disclosure of inside information, the disclosing person should (or ought to) be aware of the specific nature of the information involved. This requirement, which implies personal capacity to discern the inside information, is presumed for primary insiders, while it will need to be proven when disclosure is made by secondary insiders.[10]

---

[7] In general, omissions (which do not coincide with the cancellation of orders previously placed on trading platforms) are not considered acts of insider trading, even though the choice of investment (not to sell or not to buy) may directly follow knowledge of inside information; this topic is poorly explored in the literature, but see Barbara J Watson, 'Prohibiting Insider Trading: Is It All Worth It?' (1995) European Journal of Crime, Criminal Law and Criminal Justice 122, 144.

[8] Article 8(1) and (2). The underlying rationale of these provisions is to avoid people receiving information and systematically inserting orders with different execution dates so that, once aware of the inside information, they might decide whether to allow the order to be executed or, alternatively, to delete it; see Paolo Cioppa, 'Unexpected Insider Trading Abuses and the Need for Revision of Rule 10b5-1(c)' (2009) 9 Global Jurist 1, 8; André Betzer and others, 'Stealth Trading and Trade Reporting by Corporate Insiders' (2014) 19 Review of Finance 865, 870.

[9] Article 12(2) and Annex 1.

[10] Articles 10 and 8(4); art 3(3) and (4) Market Abuse Directive on Criminal Sanctions (2014/57/EU).

Meaning of disclosure

The person who possesses inside information should not disclose it to others. Disclosure implies the communication of inside information to one or more parties, either verbally or through a written message, physically or technologically delivered. Unlawful disclosure also includes the conduct of sharing access codes or passwords that make inside information available to others. **B.10.14**

Conversely, forgetting documents containing inside information or being overheard in a price-sensitive conversation does not appear to be proper *disclosure* to third parties. The same can be said when documents or technical devices are stolen and inside information is seized by others. **B.10.15**

However, a subtle distinction can be made here. Intentionality, as a requirement of unlawful transmission of inside information under Article 4 of the Market Abuse Directive on Criminal Sanctions (2014/57/EU), is clearly lacking in these situations, thus excluding the risk of incurring criminal penalties.[11] **B.10.16**

Instead, from the Market Abuse Regulation's perspective, the significance of these cases requires more attention. In principle, theft of inside information does not technically correspond to a form of disclosure or to a behaviour directly (even not intentionally) causing the transmission of information. The same conclusion of irrelevance might be reached with respect to an overheard conversation, since the disclosing party may not be aware that a third party is listening. But such a conclusion might differ in strong cases of negligence where, even without intentionality, the disclosing person does not pay sufficient attention to avoid undue disclosure (as may happen, for example, in a crowded elevator, where the inside information is gathered by third parties from a cell phone call). **B.10.17**

An issue arises in case of transmission to larger groups of people, as it may happen during a meeting with financial analysts or during a professional conference, where, inadvertently, a person possessing inside information, as the issuer's chief executive officer, discloses such information. According to the opinion[12] that this information is not public unless it was disseminated 'to the investing public in general' and not only 'to a limited segment of market participants only—for example, a group of market professionals (such as analysts)', this conduct might be qualified as unlawful disclosure of inside information, since it leads to the asymmetrical distribution of information.[13] **B.10.18**

---

[11] Article 4(1) Market Abuse Directive on Criminal Sanctions (2014/57/EU) providing that unlawful disclosure 'constitutes a criminal offence at least in serious cases and when committed intentionally'.

[12] Panagiotis K Staikouras, 'Four Years of MADness? The New Market Abuse Prohibition Revisited: Integrated Implementation Through the Lens of a Critical, Comparative Analysis' (2008) 19 European Business Law Review 775, 782.

[13] Article 17(7) and (8) provides remedies to restore parity of information to the market. The issuer shall disclose to the public the (delayed) inside information 'as soon as possible' if

Exemption and safeguards

B.10.19 Any disclosure of inside information is unlawful, unless it 'is made in the normal exercise of an employment, a profession or duties'. This is the only exception, provided by Article 10(1), legitimating specific cases of transmission. This may happen, for instance, when an executive officer provides the issuing company's advisers with necessary sensitive information in order to implement a specific deal.

B.10.20 Disclosure made within the framework of the exemption in Article 10(1) requires specific safeguards, intended to preserve the confidentiality of inside information and to facilitate the article's enforcement by competent national authorities. In this respect, insider lists are particularly important. Persons who receive inside information from an issuer (or on its behalf) are traced in lists related to such information, and the issuer ensures that each insider 'acknowledges in writing the legal and regulatory duties entailed' with specific reference to the sanctions applicable to insider dealing and unlawful disclosure.[14]

B.10.21 Insider lists only include persons who have access to inside information (for example, directors) or who legitimately receive it due to their working activity

confidentiality 'is no longer ensured'. Moreover, if the issuer or a person acting on its behalf unintentionally 'discloses any inside information to any third party in the normal course of the exercise of an employment, a profession or duties' to a person that does not owe a duty of confidentiality (as may be the case during a meeting with financial analysts), 'effective and public disclosure' should be made promptly.

[14] According to art 18(1), issuers shall 'draw up a list of all persons who have access to inside information and who are working for them under a contract of employment, or otherwise performing tasks through which they have access to inside information, such as advisers, accountants or credit rating agencies'. An issue arises regarding the obligation to register the counterparty of a deal carried out with the issuer if, during the negotiation, inside information is transmitted. Registration is in line with the view that insider lists are tools to trace all inside information communicated under the control of the issuer, even if the issuer cannot be responsible for the onward transmission of the information made by the counterparty to its advisers or other third parties. However, this requires a wide interpretation of art 18(1)(a) that only includes in the list persons who 'are working ... under a contract of employment, or ... performing tasks ... such as advisers, accountants or credit rating agencies'. In this respect, under the (former) Market Abuse Directive (2003/6/EC), the Italian Supervisory Authority, which excluded that counterparties of a deal should be registered on an insider list, still retains the power to require from the issuer all relevant information about such counterparties (Consob: see Comunicazione no DEM/6027054, 28 March 2006 www.Consob.it (last accessed 7 November 2016)). In light of past experience, and also considering the very limited amendments to insider list regulation in the transition from the (former) Market Abuse Directive (2003/6/EC) to the Market Abuse Regulation, as well as the wording of art 18, the narrow interpretation deserves to be supported. As a matter of fact, the exclusion of counterparties from the issuer insider list does not correspond to a decrease in inside information protection, since confidentiality is granted by the contractual non-disclosure agreement (the so-called 'NDA'), which must be signed between the issuer and the receiving party according to art 17(8). In this respect, the inclusion of counterparties on the insider list may only be considered a cautionary measure—one that by no means may extend issuer liability beyond the transmission of inside information made to the counterparty's advisers. This interpretation also supports the view that the main objective of the insider lists is to provide an organizational tool that the issuer shall put in place to comply, within its internal structure, with the duties of confidentiality and the protection of inside information.

(advisers).[15] However, unlawful disclosure of inside information under Article 10 also extends to those persons who possess inside information for any reason, even if not recorded on the appropriate insider list. In fact, although the issuer is responsible for the drawing and updating of insider lists, transmission of inside information can reach persons who are not reported inside them, outside of the issuer's control.

Onward disclosure of recommendations

The prohibition of recommending or inducing another person to engage in insider trading, stated in Article 8(2), is reflected in Article 10(2), which aims to prevent the subsequent transmission of a recommendation based on inside information. **B.10.22**

Like the chain communication of inside information, the transmission of recommendations falls under the conduct described in Article 10, even if it occurs after a series of steps. This provision is applicable to any person who receives a recommendation and passes it onward, if this person knows (or ought to know) that such guidance was based on inside information. Proving this knowledge may be difficult when the disclosure takes place far from the source of the inside information and when transmission is second-hand or even further, but it is still possible that the receiving person is able, in light of other available clues, to trace back its origins to the possessor of the inside information or to derive that the recommendation was formulated on the basis of such information. **B.10.23**

Prohibition and sanctions

Protection of inside information strictly relies on the effectiveness of the regulation on insider trading and unlawful disclosure. Article 14 encompasses all possible misconduct concerning inside information and prohibits insider trading, the 'attempt to engage in insider trading', unlawful disclosure of inside information, and recommendations, and their transmission. **B.10.24**

Along this line, Article 30 confers on Member States the power to issue administrative sanctions applicable to all prohibited behaviours under Article 14.[16] As a result of this mandate, administrative pecuniary sanctions may diverge at the national legislative level, within the maximum thresholds set differently for natural or legal persons by Article 30(2)(i)–(j). **B.10.25**

The amount of administrative sanction may be influenced by the provision of Article 30(1), which allows Member States 'not to lay down rules for administrative **B.10.26**

[15] Article 8(1)(a), and see recital (56); Carmine Di Noia, Mateja Milič, and Paola Spatola, 'Issuers Obligations under the New Market Abuse Regulation and the Proposed ESMA Guideline Regime: A Brief Overview' (2014) Zf Bankrecht & Bankwirtschaft 96, 104.

[16] Unlike the provisions mentioned in the Market Abuse Regulation, which are all directly applicable to Member States as of 3 July 2016, art 30 requires them to intervene on the sanctions within each national legal system.

sanctions ... where the infringements ... are already subject to criminal sanctions in their national law'.[17] The overlapping of administrative and criminal sanctions also concerns the misconduct of unlawful disclosure of inside information, which may be subject to the latter 'at least in serious cases and when committed intentionally', and when the disclosure does not qualify 'as a market sounding'.[18]

II. Equal Access of Information and Unlawful Disclosure of Inside Information

B.10.27 The making of any disclosure of inside information unlawful, and providing harsh sanctions, functions to prevent insider trading and increase the reliability of financial markets. It boosts confidentiality, renders violations less frequent, and enforcement more plausible. The assumption is that in a legal system containing such promise, the propensity to invest in financial instruments is stronger.[19]

Asymmetric distribution of (general) information

B.10.28 Symmetry of information available to investors is, in its broadest sense, a utopia. Corporate insiders always have a broader knowledge of the issuer because of their privileged business position. However, when in possession of *inside* information, they must comply with the no-trading rule. Based on their qualified knowledge, when it does not involve inside information, they can otherwise freely trade,[20] but past a certain threshold, these transactions are subject to a specific notification process.[21] Knowledge of certain corporate insiders, especially of those who discharge managerial responsibilities, is always deeper than outsiders' knowledge

[17] Article 30(1) and (2) clearly aims to avoid double jeopardy by coordinating criminal and administrative sanctions (see Matteo Gargantini, 'Public Enforcement of Market Abuse Bans: The ECtHR *Grande Stevens* Decision' (2015) 1 Journal of Financial Regulation 149, 157). The application of the *ne bis in idem* principle broke down in the 2014 decision of the European Court of Human Rights in the case *Grande Stevens and Others v Italy* (see Marco Ventoruzzo, 'Do Market Abuse Rules Violate Human Rights? The Grande Stevens v Italy Case' (2014) ECGI Law Working Paper No 269/2014 and Bocconi Legal Studies Research Paper No 2517760 https://ssrn.com/abstract=2517760 (last accessed 7 November 2016)), according to which sanctions aimed at punishing the same single offence have been considered criminal in nature by the Court, in spite of their formal labelling as administrative sanctions.

[18] Article 4(1) and (2) Market Abuse Directive on Criminal Sanctions (2014/57/EU) also deals with criminal sanctions applicable in cases of onward recommendation, requiring that the persons transmitting 'know it was based on inside information', while for administrative sanction, it suffices that this person 'ought to know' the nature of the information involved (art 8(3)).

[19] Luca Enriques and Sergio Gilotta, 'Disclosure and Financial Market Regulation' in Niamh Moloney, Eilís Ferran, and Jennifer Payne (eds), *The Oxford Handbook of Financial Regulation* (Oxford University Press 2015) 514; Marco Ventoruzzo, 'Insider Trading' in Marco Ventoruzzo and others (eds), *Comparative Corporate Law* (West Academic Publishing 2015) 580.

[20] The prohibition for persons discharging managerial responsibility to conduct any transactions (the no-trading rule) is also applicable in the closed period, which lasts for 30 days before an annual or interim report which the issuer is obliged to make public; see art 19(11) and recital (61).

[21] Article 19.

and transactions executed in this light represent powerful signals for the market.[22] Intuitively, a buying trend on the issuer's shares is an indicator that the company's managers trust the company strategy and feel positively about its results; the opposite can be deduced in cases of massive selling.

Equal access to (inside) information

European regulation is clearly inspired by the 'parity-of-information' theory that focuses on the dissemination (or strict confidentiality) of those specific pieces of information that are qualified as inside information and are particularly important because of their impact on market prices. A proper symmetrical distribution does not involve all knowledge and information regarding issuers, which would not be a plausible goal, but it can be achieved with regards to specific information identified by the issuer, according to an internal process, as inside (price-sensitive) information. **B.10.29**

Two instruments have been traditionally used in Europe in order to ensure full compliance with the principle of equal access to (inside) information. **B.10.30**

The first one is the obligation for the issuer to disclose all (corporate) inside information as soon as possible,[23] as a measure to shorten the time frame during which insider trading and information leaks may take place.[24] Thus, the market is provided with all inside information under the issuer's control, which is relevant for the pricing of its financial instruments.[25] **B.10.31**

The second tool aimed at fostering 'equal access of information' derives from Article 10, and consists of protecting the confidentiality of both corporate and market information (direct and indirect information),[26] until it is publicly available. **B.10.32**

---

22 See recital (58); Mårten Knuts, 'The Optimal Scope of Disclosure by Association Regime Under MAR' (2016) 24 European Company and Financial Law Review 495, 500 ff; Guido Ferrarini, 'La nuova disciplina europea dell'abuso di mercato' (2004) Rivista delle società 43, 68; Chiara Mosca, 'Internal Dealing e Corporate Governance' in *Amministrazione e controllo nel diritto delle società* (Giappichelli 2010) 669 ff.

23 See recital (49); Jesper Lau Hansen, 'Say When: When Must an Issuer Disclose Inside Information?' (2016) 16 Nordic & European Company Law Working Paper No 16-03 https://papers.ssrn.com/sol3/papers.cfm?abstract_id=2795993 (last accessed 7 November 2016) 3–4 and 16.

24 Takis Tridimas, 'Insider Trading: European Harmonisation and National Law Reform' (1991) 40 International and Comparative Law Quarterly 919, 923; Carmine Di Noia and Matteo Gargantini, 'The Market Abuse Directive Disclosure Regime in Practice: Some Margins for Future Actions' (2009) Rivista delle società 782, 792 and 795; Mathias Siems, Matthijs Nelemans, 'The Reform of the EU Market Abuse Law: Revolution or Evolution?' (2012) 19 Maastricht Journal of European and Comparative Law 195, 201 https://papers.ssrn.com/sol3/papers.cfm?abstract_id=2037727 (last accessed 7 November 2016).

25 Watson, 'Prohibiting Insider Trading' (n 7) 127 and 144.

26 Market information concerns the issuer indirectly; for a non-exhaustive list of direct and indirect inside information, see *CESR's Advice on Level 2 Implementing Measures for the proposed Market Abuse Directive* (December 2002) 12; Guido Ferrarini, 'The European Market Abuse Directive' (2004) 41 Common Market Law Review 711, 720.

B.10.33 Inside (corporate) information, the disclosure of which may be delayed by issuers,[27] requires special attention and appropriate organizational measures in order to be kept confidential.

B.10.34 In addition, the confidentiality regime extends to inside market information—that is, to information that is not available (or immediately available) to the issuer but which, in compliance with the parity-of-information theory, must be similarly protected. For instance, this consideration applies to inside information like the imminent enactment of laws that could favour or penalize a specific company, a change in interest rates, or assessment notices or sanctions under preparation by tax agencies or supervisory authorities for which the issuer has not yet been notified. Any disclosure to a third party made by a person who possesses this kind of (indirect or market) inside information is considered to be unlawful.

Investors' protection

B.10.35 Processes of public disclosure aim to ensure that identical information is made available to all investors. However, less experienced investors (retail clients) may lack the necessary skills and competences to use all the available information,[28] and they may turn to financial intermediaries for support in their investment decisions.

B.10.36 This side of the investors' protection regime owes much to the MiFID[29] principles that, together with the Market Abuse Regulation, represent the backbone of the entire European regulation of financial markets. While the aim of the Market Abuse Regulation is to make relevant information publicly available, the MiFID reinforces the protection granted to vulnerable investors by imposing on intermediaries the duty to work in the best interest of their clients (investors) while rendering financial services.[30]

Comparative remarks

B.10.37 Article 10 expresses the commitment of European legislators to the effective transposition of the parity-of-information theory, sketching a distance from the US approach.

B.10.38 In the 1960s, North American courts theorized the equal-access-of-information principle; however, the following decisions reduced its original scope.[31] In a

[27] Article 17(4) and (5).

[28] See Klöhn, 'European Insider Trading' (n 3) 359; Enriques and Gilotta, 'Disclosure' (n 19) 528.

[29] Directive 2004/39/EC of the European Parliament and of the Council of 21 April 2004 on markets in financial instruments (MiFID I); reference is also made to Directive 2014/64/EU of the European Parliament and of the Council of 15 May 2014 (MiFID II, applicable by Member States from 3 January 2018).

[30] Niamh Moloney, 'Regulating the Retail Markets' in Niamh Moloney, Eilís Ferran, and Jennifer Payne (eds), *The Oxford Handbook of Financial Regulation* (Oxford University Press 2015) 754 ff; Hansen, 'Say When' (n 23) 25.

[31] Marco Ventoruzzo, 'Comparing Insider Trading in the United States and in the European Union: History and Recent Developments' (2014) 11 European Company and Financial Law

nutshell, the American system sanctions trading when carried out on the basis of price-sensitive information, should it be proven that the possession of such information derived from a breach of a fiduciary duty or a misappropriation of the information itself.[32] Consequently, in the US, tippers and tippees are not automatically subject to the same prohibitions as they would be in Europe,[33] and tippees might be immune from the risk of insider trading if unaware of the violation of fiduciary duties referring to the tipper.[34] In Europe, irrespective of the reason of possession, the sheer availability of the inside information establishes the strict protection regime that punishes both dealing and transmission.

III. Possession of Inside Information and Disclosure to Third Parties

Primary and secondary insiders

Prohibiting the unlawful disclosure of inside information 'applies to any natural or legal person in the situation(s) or circumstance(s) referred to in Article 8(4)'. Such a heterogeneous group can be internally divided into primary insiders and secondary insiders, based on their proximity to the source of inside information, which for primary insiders is normally much closer.[35] **B.10.39**

Review 555, 556 and Ventoruzzo, 'Insider Trading' (n 19) 138; Watson, 'Prohibiting Insider Trading' (n 7) 133 ff; Tridimas, 'Insider Trading' (n 24) 920; Klöhn, 'European Insider Trading' (n 3) 358.

[32] Saikrishna Prakash, 'Our Dysfunctional Insider Trading Regime' (1999) 99 Columbia Law Review 1491, 1500 ff.

[33] Alexander F Loke, 'From the Fiduciary Theory to Information Abuse: The Changing Fabric of Insider Trading Law in the UK, Australia and Singapore' (2006) 54 American Journal of Comparative Law 123, 134.

[34] Steven R Salbu, 'A Critical Analysis of Misappropriation Theory in Insider Trading Cases' (1992) 2 Business Ethics Quarterly 465, 466; Cioppa, 'Unexpected Insider Trading Abuses' (n 8) 5; Ventoruzzo, 'Comparing Insider Trading' (n 31), 564. The leading case on tipper and tippee liability is *Dirks v SEC*, 463 US 646 (1983); *Dirks v SEC*, 103 S Ct 3255 (1983) (also mentioned by Ventoruzzo 'Insider Trading' (n 19) 589). However, the strict conditions required to sanction tippers for breaches of the insider trading prohibition have been somehow relaxed in the case *United States v Newman* 773 F 3d 438 (2d Cir, 2014), whose decision was subsequently reversed by the Court of Appeal (see Jon Eisenberg, 'How *United States v Newman* Changes The Law' (2015) https://corpgov.law.harvard.edu and Stephen Bainbridge, 'US v Newman: A Big Win for Coherence and Fairness in Insider Trading Law' (2014) http://www.professorbainbridge.com/professorbainbridgecom/2014/12/us-v-newman-a-big-win-for-coherence-and-fairness-in-insider-trading-law.html (last accessed 7 November 2016)). For recent expansion of doctrinal constraints on imposing insider trading liability on tippees see John C Coffee Jr, 'Mapping the Future of Insider Trading Law: Of Boundaries, Gaps, and Strategies' (2013) ECGI Law Working Paper No 204 http://ssrn.com/abstract_id=2221475 (last accessed 7 November 2016) and for judicial recent developments on the personal benefit requirement met by the insider tipper see the Supreme Court's unanimous decision in *United States v Salman* 792 F 3d 1087 (9th Cir, 2015).

[35] For the distinction between primary and secondary insiders, see Klaus J Hopt, 'The European Insider Dealing Directive' (1990) 27 Common Market Law Review 51, 62; Caspar Rose, 'Impact of

B.10.40 Primary insiders represent a qualified group of individuals, listed on the basis of certain distinctive characteristics in Article 8(4)(a)–(c). Due to their proximity to the source of the inside information or due to the activities they perform, knowledge of the sensitive nature of inside information is generally presumed for primary insiders.

B.10.41 Primary insiders should be further divided into corporate insiders, who fulfil a function within the issuer (such as a company's directors), or temporary insiders, who occasionally possess inside information transmitted to them 'through the exercise of an employment, a profession or duties' (such as attorneys, bankers, or advisers). By reason of other types of employment (for instance, in governmental agencies, central banks, or supervisory authorities), inside information may also be available to other (non-corporate) primary insiders.[36]

B.10.42 Persons involved in criminal activities are also considered primary insiders. The criminal episode itself might adversely affect financial markets (as has happened in past years, in the aftermath of terrorist attacks) and informed persons may exploit their knowledge by taking a short position on financial instruments or index betting on the market reaction.

B.10.43 The category of secondary insiders is less defined: they are provided, for whatever reason, with inside information[37] and they know (or ought to know) that it is sensitive information. A secondary insider might receive the information from a primary insider who unlawfully transmits it directly or after a long series of steps. However, after several transmissions, distinguishing true inside information from unverified rumours might be a strenuous task for the receiving person, especially if the source of the information is unknown.

B.10.44 Any individual who possesses inside information, even incidentally, could be considered a 'secondary insider'. It may be a case of a person unexpectedly finding some relevant documents forgotten by someone else, or of documents accidentally sent to the wrong recipients (which is not unlikely to happen in sending emails). Moreover, inside information might be incidentally heard from a conversation or inferred from the overall context during interpersonal communications.[38]

Investor Meetings/Presentations on Share Prices, Insider Trading and Securities Regulation' (2003) 23 International Review of Law and Economics 227, 229; Tridimas, 'Insider Trading' (n 24) 924.

[36] See Moloney, '*EU Securities*' (n 4) 724.

[37] Article 8(4), last paragraph; cf with regard to criminal sanctions, art 3(3), last paragraph of Market Abuse Directive on Criminal Sanctions (2014/57/EU) requires that insiders should 'know' that the information is considered inside, thus strengthening the awareness test on the nature of secondary insiders' possession of inside information.

[38] The examples of documents left in a taxi and found by a taxi driver, or a conversation overheard during the ride (thus causing the taxi driver to become an insider) have been debated since the initial introduction of insider dealing discipline. As a matter of fact, in this example drivers have access to inside information simply through the exercise of the profession, and in theory they could be included in the category of primary insiders (when they have inside information). The

Secondary insiders may also be close-knit family members of a primary insider (for example, the spouse of a director), to whom the inside information is unlawfully transmitted.[39] **B.10.45**

In conclusion, the duty of confidentiality arising from Article 10 applies to all secondary insiders who ought to know that they possess inside information, irrespective of how they obtained it. It does not particularly matter whether it was communicated by a primary insider,[40] found in a completely incidental way, or even reconstructed from different sources. Therefore, secondary insiders include tippees but do not end with them. In this respect, the scope of the 'secondary insiders' category in European legislation is evidently wider in comparison to the narrower interpretation traced in US courts' decisions.[41] **B.10.46**

Disclosure of inside information among corporate governance members

Boards of directors

Normally, the 'members of the administrative, management or supervisory bodies of the issuer or emission allowance market participant' are in possession of inside information and, hence, are considered as 'primary insiders'. **B.10.47**

Focusing on corporate governance members, the transmission of inside information during or in preparation of meetings of boards of directors or supervisory bodies is legitimate, to the extent that sharing inside information is necessary for the decision-making and evaluative functions that these bodies must perform. **B.10.48**

Within the board, the chief executive's position differs from that of other directors, since not all of the non-executives may receive inside information at the same time. According to Article 17(4) and (5), all members must dispose of inside information if a delay in disclosure has been decided by the entire board. However, if only the chief executive officer has made a decision, non-executive directors might be unaware of this specific inside information.[42] In other words, **B.10.49**

literature is split into two positions: some scholars consider this view correct (Watson, 'Prohibiting Insider Trading' (n 7) 140), while others affirm that to qualify as a primary insider, the person's professional commitment mentioned under art 8(4)(c) should be more closely connected with the issuer or with financial instruments (Tridimas, 'Insider Trading' (n 24) 926–8); see Moloney, '*EU Securities*' (n 4) 724.

[39] Hopt, 'The European Insider Dealing Directive' (n 35) 65.

[40] Katja Langenbucher, 'Insider trading in European law' in Stephen Bainbridge (ed), *Research Handbook on Insider Trading* (Edward Elgar Publishing 2013) 429, 432.

[41] Donald C Langevoort, 'What Were They Thinking? Insider Trading and the Scienter Requirement' in Stephen Bainbridge (ed), *Research Handbook on Insider Trading* (Edward Elgar Publishing 2013) 52, 56; Eric Engle, 'Global Norm Convergence: Capital Markets in US and EU Law' (2010) 21 European Business Law Review 465, 486.

[42] Hartmut Krause and Michael Brellochs, 'Insider Trading and the Disclosure of Inside Information after *Geltl v Daimler*—A Comparative Analysis of the ECJ Decision in the *Geltl v*

directors may not all receive inside information simultaneously; some of them will obtain the information at a later time.

B.10.50 Communication hierarchies among board members are reflected in the structure of insider lists. Directors are normally considered permanent insiders and they are entered into the pertinent section of the list.[43] However, this choice also depends on the policy pursued by the company. When access to inside information is restricted to the executive directors and a few managers who possess information by reason of their activity, the list of permanent insiders does not include all board members.

B.10.51 It may also happen that a member of the management or supervisory board occasionally gathers inside information from outside of the company. A classic example is the member who, during a social event, receives information on takeover plans regarding the issuer and, consequently, should avoid any unlawful communication of this information.[44] However, the decision to share it confidentially with the other members of the issuer's board may fall within the exemption of Article 10(1), at least where such disclosure responds to the director's duty to act in the best interest of the issuer.

Supervisory boards

B.10.52 For members of supervisory boards, the availability of inside information depends to some extent on the corporate governance rules applicable in each context and results from the powers and duties of their office. Legitimate possession of inside information may be a consequence of their duty to attend board meetings, since they will receive the same documents sent to directors. Powers of investigation and inspection, when granted to members of supervisory bodies and even when carried out individually, may be the source of possession of inside information. In addition, the power to make inquiries to board members about company affairs, including the directors of the corporations within the same group of companies, represents another source of inside information.

Duty of loyalty and duty of confidentiality

B.10.53 Members of administrative, management, or supervisory bodies must keep all inside information concerning the issuer confidential, even in the absence of a specific company's interest in the information (as, for example, for the results

---

Daimler Case with a View to the Future European Market Abuse Regulation' (2013) 8 Capital Markets Law Journal 283, 295.

[43] ESMA, 'Final Report: Draft technical standards on the Market Abuse Regulation' No 1455, (28 September 2015) 61.

[44] Klaus J Hopt, 'Conflict of Interest, Secrecy and Insider Information of Directors—A Comparative Analysis' (2013) 2 European Company and Financial Law Review 167, 184.

of important research, or for a technological innovation, the exploitation of which requires the issuer to have exclusive knowledge, and many efforts are generally deployed to keep it secret).[45] From the perspective of the Market Abuse Regulation, the general duty of confidentiality imposed on corporate governance members until public disclosure does not necessarily realize an interest of the issuer, but it derives from the general goal of financial markets' integrity. It may be argued that, while the duty of secrecy is a tangible expression of the duty of loyalty to corporate bodies, Article 10 introduces a more general duty towards investors.[46]

Disclosure of inside information to shareholders

Having a holding in the capital of the issuer

The Market Abuse Regulation's inclusion of any person 'having a holding in the capital of the issuer' in the list of those who are normally considered primary insiders remains ambiguous.[47] **B.10.54**

Article 8(4)(b) does not specify the extent of participation that gives a shareholder an insider position. A closer proximity to directors, from which a privileged knowledge of inside information descends, can plausibly distinguish the position of the controlling shareholder. More generally, a similar conclusion can be reached with respect to those shareholders with a significant holding in the company, or to the participants of a shareholders' agreement, because of their influence over the company, by virtue of their contribution in selecting and appointing directors.[48] **B.10.55**

Institutional investors, in their monitoring of the investee company, may be willing to establish a dialogue with the board of directors and, in turn, the board may fulfil requests to comply with best practices in corporate governance and with stewardship codes. The possibility that this dialogue may involve the transmission of inside information is undeniable, thus rendering the institutional investor a primary insider subject to the no-trading rule.[49] **B.10.56**

---

[45] Sergio Gilotta, 'Disclosure in Securities Markets and the Firm's Need for Confidentiality: Theoretical Framework and Regulatory Analysis' (2012) 13 European Business Organization Law Review 45, 53–4.

[46] Hopt, 'Conflict of Interest' (n 44) 186.

[47] Article 8(4)(b).

[48] See Moloney, '*EU Securities*' (n 4) 723; Hopt, 'The European Insider Dealing Directive' (n 35) 63.

[49] See Financial Reporting Council, 'The UK Stewardship Code' (September 2012), Principle 3, page 7. It is worth noting that this principle suggests that an institutional investor 'should indicate in its stewardship statement its willingness [to become an insider], and the mechanism by which this could be done'. An issue arises as to whether the market sounding of article 11 (see para B.10.60) represents the only possible mechanism that may allow a flow of information from the issuer to investors, as suggested by recital (32).

Reasons to disclose

B.10.57 In any case, the legitimacy of a flow of information from a board to its shareholders (or to some qualified shareholders) should not be taken for granted. This dialogue is not always allowed. Indeed, as a general rule, directors must avoid any asymmetric distribution of information and treat investors according to the principle of equal treatment.

B.10.58 Engaging in a privileged dialogue, conducted by the initiative of the board in which inside information is shared with shareholders (or some of them), may be legitimate only if it satisfies a specific interest of the company. A typical company's interest is identified when, during a particular transaction or operation, the board needs to get the opinion of the shareholders, as it may arise, for example, during the process that leads to a share capital increase, when major shareholders are consulted in advance with regard to their intention to underwrite. A flow of inside information may also be involved in the setup of accelerated book-building transactions, when the issuer enters into a close and privileged dialogue with some of its investors, usually but not necessarily through an intermediary.[50]

B.10.59 More generally, including persons 'having a holding in the capital of the issuer' in the list of primary insiders displays legislative attention to corporate governance practices. It is recognized that a dialogue involving both directors and shareholders is a phenomenon that may occur in the world of listed companies, whose legitimacy depends on the board's assessment on the need for selective disclosure in order to satisfy a company's interests. In any case, such dialogue must always take place within specific safeguards to preserve confidentiality.

Market sounding

B.10.60 Market sounding, a novelty of the Market Abuse Regulation, allows an issuer or a secondary offeror 'prior to the announcement of a transaction, to gauge the interest of potential investors' using a procedure that carefully protects the confidentiality of the information transmitted, requiring overwhelming attention when inside information is involved.[51]

B.10.61 Even if not strictly necessary, an intermediary (disclosing market participant) may be appointed to oversee the procedure and manage the flow of information from the issuer or secondary offeror (beneficiary market participants) to the interviewed investors (receiving market participants). Most important among safeguards to preserve confidentiality is *wall crossing*—namely, a query about the investor's consent to receive inside information.[52] The consent obtained should

[50] See Stefano Lombardo, 'I sondaggi di mercato: prime riflessioni' (2016) Società 159, 160, who suggests the application of market sounding to accelerate book-building.

[51] Article 11, and see ESMA, 'Final Report' (n 43) 21(64) and 23(74).

[52] Although market sounding is a new normative tool, it has long been a common practice in the industry. In particular, wall crossing was the procedure applied for asking another person to

be recorded digitally or in writing and the transmitted content should be clearly identified.

One may suppose that the complexity of market sounding is justified by the risk raised by the transmission of inside information. However, this procedure should apply irrespective of the evaluation made by market participants regarding the involvement of inside information. The extended use of market sounding in dialogues with investors can be understood by observing the evolution in the nature of the information as a result of the sounding. In fact, non-inside information—lacking the requirement of precision of Article 7—may nevertheless become inside information depending on the positive reactions of investors to the sounding, implying a high probability of completing a significant transaction.[53] **B.10.62**

In this light, market sounding offers reasonable, but not absolute, protection against sanctions for potential violations of Article 10.[54] From the perspective of the Market Abuse Directive on Criminal Sanctions (2014/57/EU), market sounding operates as a safe harbour that hampers the imposition of criminal sanctions, while, with respect to administrative sanctions, 'disclosure of inside information made in the course of a market sounding shall be deemed to be made in the normal exercise of a person's employment, a profession or duties'.[55] The strength of this presumption depends on consistency between the issuer's motivation leading to the market sounding and the communication of inside information. Thus, the issuer's board of directors still must weigh carefully the decision to implement market sounding and to identify a precise interest of the issuer that needs to be satisfied through this channel. **B.10.63**

Groups of companies

According to Article 8(4)(b), a parent company is classified as a primary insider, by virtue of its 'holding in the capital of the issuer' with respect to the inside information of the controlled company. Broadly speaking, disclosure of inside information that flows from the controlled company may be considered legitimate when it satisfies the need of the holding to carry out a precise business **B.10.64**

---

agree to the terms of a non-disclosure agreement, where acceptance may imply the transmission of inside information. In this respect, the case reported in the Financial Conduct Authority's decision of 12 January 2012 https://www.fca.org.uk in the section 'Publications/Final notices' (last accessed 7 November 2016) is of particular interest. It concerns a sanction for insider trading to a president and owner of a US investment management firm who refused to be wall crossed but nevertheless derived inside information from various conversations, and who did not abstain from trading.

[53] Lombardo, 'I sondaggi' (n 50) 163; Di Noia, Milič, and Spatola, 'Issuers Obligations' (n 15) 102.

[54] See recital (35). Jake Green and Emily Torrens, 'The European Market Abuse Regulation: MAR Ado about Everything' (2016) 17 Journal of Investments Compliance 1, 6.

[55] See art 11(4) Market Abuse Regulation and art 4 Market Abuse Directive on Criminal Sanctions (2014/57/EU).

strategy at a group level or to comply with the law. Typical cases of the upward transmission of inside information include the preparation of consolidated financial statements, or compliance with the disclosure obligations of the controlling company, which may require detailed information from the controlled entity.[56]

B.10.65 Instead, confidentiality should be kept towards all other companies within the group. The transmission of inside information along various lines may be carried out only as strictly necessary to manage the company. Even in this case, any communication of information must be justifiable through the exemption under Article 10(1), in the light of the reality of the group.[57]

Disclosure of inside information in the exercise of an employment, a profession, or duties

The exemption and its strict interpretation

B.10.66 Primary insiders, who own the inside information 'through the exercise of an employment, a profession or duties',[58] received this particular knowledge in accordance with Article 10(1), which provides an exemption to unlawful disclosure when the transmission of the inside information 'is made in the normal exercise of an employment, a profession or duties'.

B.10.67 This provision allows the normal flow of information in the context of business and professional transactions, towards persons or entities like attorneys, bankers, advisers, intermediaries, suppliers of goods and services, or unions. All persons receiving the inside information are subject to a duty of confidentiality, whose source is the Market Abuse Regulation, often reproduced in articles of association, or in contracts.[59]

B.10.68 It is easy to understand why, in order to follow the principle of equal access of information, the prohibition of disclosure is extremely rigorous while, at the same time, it cannot be absolute.

B.10.69 Sometimes the disclosure of information, including inside information, is necessary. This occurs, for instance, when the issuers' board of directors transmits inside information to the issuer's advisers entrusted with the analysis and implementation of a corporate transaction, as well as when it is communicated within the corporate structure, to executives, employees, or agents in charge of an operation or deal not yet disclosed to the public.

---

[56] Hopt, 'Conflict of Interest' (n 44) 184; Mucciarelli, 'Articolo 184' (n 5) 2362.
[57] Hopt, 'The European Insider Dealing Directive' (n 35) 65.
[58] Article 8(4).
[59] Article 17(8).

The requirement of normality should be reasonably understood through the specific filter offered by the Market Abuse Regulation's commitment to shield confidentiality. 'Normality' might hardly be inferred in a theoretical standard communication that may occur in the exercise of a profession or employment. Likewise, normality may not be seen as a simple coincidence between the moment of the disclosure and the exercise of the employment, profession, or duties. **B.10.70**

As a general criterion, the exemption should be applied narrowly, as 'a close link between that disclosure and the exercise of that employment, that profession or those duties in order to justify such disclosure'.[60] In this light, the only consistent reading claims a careful, case-by-case evaluation of the overriding need to effectively establish the transmission of inside information. **B.10.71**

Cases of unlawful and legitimate disclosure

The following hypothetical situations can help to clarify the use of the exemption allowed by Article 10. **B.10.72**

Faced with a tricky question posed by a journalist or an analyst, the issuer's chief executive officer or its investor realtor manager may carelessly reveal, in whole or in part, inside information. Being unnecessary, this disclosure is not covered by the exemption under Article 10(1), even if it occurs during the exercise of the manager's employment. Prompt public disclosure of the inside information, which is the remedy for similar cases provide by Article 17(8), may actually restore informational parity, and it might also justify a soft applicability of the sanctions imposed for this breach of confidentiality. **B.10.73**

The transmission of inside information that may take place within the structure of the issuer (for example among the employees) should not always be considered under the scope of the exemption of Article 10(1). The CEO, if in possession of confidential documents (for example, the timetable of an imminent takeover or the conditions of a public offer that has not yet been announced), should take reasonable care to keep this documentation inaccessible to the issuer's staff unless strictly necessary. In this respect, issuers' internal organizational procedures are of overwhelming importance in avoiding the uncontrolled and damaging spread of inside information, as well as fostering an environment of confidentiality within the company's structure and its employees. **B.10.74**

Sometimes a second-hand transfer of inside information may still fall under the exemption of Article 10(1). This situation typically arises when a professional (banker, attorney, or other adviser) lawfully receives inside information from **B.10.75**

60 See Case C-384/02 *Criminal proceedings against Knud Grøngaard and Allan Bang* (2005) ECR I-9939; see Mathias M Siems, 'The EU Market Abuse Directive: A Case-based Analysis' (2008) 2 Law of Financial Markets Review 39, 41; Engle, 'Global Norm' (n 41) 487; Staikouras, 'Four Years of MADness?' (n 12) 790–1.

corporate insiders for performing an activity that will be carried out with other professionals (such as when a law firm is entrusted by the issuer). The chain of transmission implies disclosure made in the exercise of a profession, and it requires the inclusion of all participants of the professional team on the insiders' list. It is worth noting that the issuer's responsibility to draw and update the insider list may be assumed by 'another person on behalf or on the account of the issuer'; such a provision allows the issuer to delegate the task to maintain the list of all professionals who should receive inside information.[61]

B.10.76 A final situation concerns those shareholders listed among primary insiders under Article 8(4) because of their 'holding in the capital of the issuer'. As mentioned, the directors of an issuer can deem it appropriate to speak to certain shareholders, by virtue of their significant holding, in order to get their opinion on a planned operation or transaction. In turn, these shareholders may receive advice from their personal consultants, as long as this disclosure is in the exercise of a duty and under a stringent confidentiality agreement.

Financial analysts

B.10.77 It is questionable whether financial analysts can be considered primary insiders or not. Although they make use of public information in performing their duties,[62] the content of an investment recommendation may itself be price-sensitive information that, once public, moves supply and demand of financial instruments and thus influences market prices. The issue arises in connection to the actual dissemination of this investment recommendation to a large public. Indeed, selective disclosure before such dissemination obviously resembles the unlawful disclosure of inside information under Article 10, especially when it may lead to movements in market prices of related financial instruments.[63]

Legal persons

B.10.78 The provision that unlawful disclosure of Article 10(1) also applies to legal persons has some implications in the organization of issuers and other players receiving

---

[61] Article 18(2)(2).

[62] See recital (28).

[63] The final notice enacted by the (UK) Financial Conduct Authority on 20 March 2007 https://www.fca.org.uk in the section 'Publications/Final notices' (last accessed 7 November 2016) reports an interesting case of the selective disclosure of a research report made before the date planned for its dissemination. The FCA sanctioned the behaviour of the financial analyst as a breach of the proper standard of market conduct. Interestingly, Italian courts also decided upon the same episode because the information under discussion was related to a financial instrument listed in the Italian regulated market and a fund manager traded on the basis of it. Among other considerations, the most noteworthy for the present analysis is that the court qualified as 'inside information' the event of the dissemination of a financial report prepared by an analyst rated as a top one, especially because of the movements in market prices caused by the investment recommendation (see Corte di Appello di Milano 1220, 14 December 2010; Corte di Cassazione 1782, 10 November 2014).

inside information.[64] Issuers must protect the confidentiality of this information through a procedure aimed at avoiding widespread and uncontrolled disclosure,[65] both inside and outside of its structure. With regard to the receiving entity, a clear example of such organizational measures is set in the ESMA Guidelines addressed to persons receiving market soundings, where the designation of the physical person or a 'contact point' in charge of receiving market soundings is crucial. Furthermore, it should be ensured that internally this information is shared only through predetermined reporting channels and on a need-to-know basis; likewise, the persons dealing with the inside information must be properly trained. The Guidelines point out that each flow of information among the staff of the receiving entity should be in compliance with Articles 8 and 10.[66]

IV. Conclusion

It has been stated that the improper transmission of inside information may find fertile ground in environments that are barely conscious of confidentiality obligations and where the scarce attention to this duty is not necessarily driven by greed or by personal expectations of rapid enrichment.[67] In this light, the prohibition of unlawful disclosure of inside information as set forth in Articles 10 and 14 strongly contributes to a culture of confidentiality. **B.10.79**

The legislation on the unlawful disclosure of inside information, as applicable to all legal or natural persons in possession of inside information (primary or secondary insiders, even when 'remote insiders' receive information through a long chain of transmission),[68] shows the firm belief of European legislators that 'not only must the market be fair, it must be seen to be fair and no one should be seen to be at a disadvantage'.[69] The result is a highly market-oriented discipline,[70] where the prohibition of insider trading and unlawful disclosure is crucial in ensuring the public interest.[71] **B.10.80**

64 Filippo Annunziata, 'Riflessi organizzativi della rinnovata disciplina in materia di market abuse' (2016) Società 169, 173; cf n 14.

65 Cf art 8 Market Abuse Directive on Criminal Sanctions (2014/57/EU) and art 9 on the emergence of internal organizational devices to escape punishment for insider trading and unlawful disclosure.

66 ESMA, 'MAR Guidelines. Persons Receiving Market Soundings' No 1477 (10 November 2016).

67 Nancy Reichman, 'Breaking Confidences: Organizational Influences on Insider Trading' (1989) 30 Sociological Quarterly 185, 193.

68 Paul Barnes, 'Insider Dealing and Market Abuse: The UK's Record on Enforcement' (2011) 39 International Journal of Law, Crime and Justice 174, 178.

69 ibid 175.

70 Moloney, '*EU Securities*' (n 4) 724; Paul Davies, 'The European Community's Directive on Insider Dealing: From Company Law to Securities Markets Regulation?' (1991) 11 Oxford Journal of Legal Studies 92, 103.

71 Salbu, 'A Critical Analysis' (n 34) 469.

B.10.81 'Disclose or abstain',[72] as the evocative synthesis of the entire insider trading doctrine, should be declined in light of the priorities of the Regulation on market abuses, which is deeply compelled to strengthen an environment of equal access to information. The general rule is to *abstain* from trading when in possession of inside information, while *disclosure* should always be addressed to the public and aim to an equal footing to all investors. Under the Market Abuse Regulation, disclosure can never be used in a private transaction in a way that supersedes the no-trading rule. Sharing inside information with less-informed parties before trading, as an illusory solution that seeks to restore parity of information, is still in violation of Article 10 ([73]). In other words, lawfulness of selective disclosure never depends on the fairness of a single transaction, and the permitted exemptions to unlawful disclosure are limited.

B.10.82 Confidentiality is also closely related to corporate governance issues. Neither the dialogues between board members, nor those between directors and shareholders, are immune from this discipline, and their legitimacy should be assessed through the lens offered by the exception under Article 10 (and, if necessary, in compliance with Article 11).

[72] Prakash, 'Our Dysfunctional Insider Trading Regime' (n 32) 1508–510.

[73] One important exception is provided, however, by art 9(4), entitled 'legitimate behaviour', which is applicable to the private transactions of the holders of a controlling interest that lead to the obligation to announce a takeover bid. This Article introduces an exception to insider trading sanctions when the inside information is communicated 'for the purpose of proceeding' with a 'public takeover' provided that the information will be made public 'at the point of … acceptance of the offer by the shareholders'. A rational interpretation of art 9(4) is that the insider trading prohibition cannot hinder private transactions involving a change of corporate control when investors' protection is granted by the takeover regulation. Accordingly, private acquisitions are deemed legitimate, even if they imply the selective disclosure of inside information from the vending controlling shareholder to the buyer, as long as the symmetrical distribution of information to the public follows shortly afterwards. It is understood that the inside information should not be transmitted or used for different purposes, such as to increase the holding through market acquisitions (cf art 9(4)(2)).

Article 11: Market soundings

1. A market sounding comprises the communication of information, prior to the announcement of a transaction, in order to gauge the interest of potential investors in a possible transaction and the conditions relating to it such as its potential size or pricing, to one or more potential investors by:
   (a) an issuer;
   (b) a secondary offeror of a financial instrument, in such quantity or value that the transaction is distinct from ordinary trading and involves a selling method based on the prior assessment of potential interest from potential investors;
   (c) an emission allowance market participant; or
   (d) a third party acting on behalf or on the account of a person referred to in point (a), (b) or (c).
2. Without prejudice to Article 23(3), disclosure of inside information by a person intending to make a takeover bid for the securities of a company or a merger with a company to parties entitled to the securities, shall also constitute a market sounding, provided that:
   (a) the information is necessary to enable the parties entitled to the securities to form an opinion on their willingness to offer their securities: and
   (b) the willingness of parties entitled to the securities to offer their securities is reasonably required for the decision to make the takeover bid or merger.
3. A disclosing market participant shall, prior to conducting a market sounding, specifically consider whether the market sounding will involve the disclosure of inside information. The disclosing market participant shall make a written record of its conclusion and the reasons therefor. It shall provide such written records to the competent authority upon request. This obligation shall apply to each disclosure of information throughout the course of the market sounding. The disclosing market participant shall update the written records referred to in this paragraph accordingly.
4. For the purposes of Article 10(1), disclosure of inside information made in the course of a market sounding shall be deemed to be made in the normal exercise of a person's employment, profession or duties where the disclosing market participant complies with paragraphs 3 and 5 of this Article.
5. For the purposes of paragraph 4, the disclosing market participant shall, before making the disclosure:
   (a) obtain the consent of the person receiving the market sounding to receive inside information;
   (b) inform the person receiving the market sounding that he is prohibited from using that information, or attempting to use that information, by

acquiring or disposing of, for his own account or for the account of a third party, directly or indirectly, financial instruments relating to that information;

(c) inform the person receiving the market sounding that he is prohibited from using that information, or attempting to use that information, by cancelling or amending an order which has already been placed concerning a financial instrument to which the information relates; and

(d) inform the person receiving the market sounding that by agreeing to receive the information he is obliged to keep the information confidential.

The disclosing market participant shall make and maintain a record of all information given to the person receiving the market sounding, including the information given in accordance with points (a) to (d) of the first subparagraph, and the identity of the potential investors to whom the information has been disclosed, including but not limited to the legal and natural persons acting on behalf of the potential investor, and the date and time of each disclosure. The disclosing market participant shall provide that record to the competent authority upon request.

6. Where information that has been disclosed in the course of a market sounding ceases to be inside information according to the assessment of the disclosing market participant, the disclosing market participant shall inform the recipient accordingly, as soon as possible.

The disclosing market participant shall maintain a record of the information given in accordance with this paragraph and shall provide it to the competent authority upon request.

7. Notwithstanding the provisions of this Article, the person receiving the market sounding shall assess for itself whether it is in possession of inside information or when it ceases to be in possession of inside information.
8. The disclosing market participant shall keep the records referred to in this Article for a period of at least five years.
9. In order to ensure consistent harmonisation of this Article, ESMA shall develop draft regulatory technical standards to determine appropriate arrangements, procedures and record keeping requirements for persons to comply with the requirements laid down in paragraphs 4, 5, 6 and 8.

ESMA shall submit those draft regulatory technical standards to the Commission by 3 July 2015.

Power is delegated to the Commission to adopt the regulatory technical standards referred to in the first subparagraph in accordance with Articles 10 to 14 of Regulation (EU) No 1095/2010.

10. In order to ensure uniform conditions of application of this Article, ESMA shall develop draft implementing technical standards to specify the systems and notification templates to be used by persons to comply with the requirements established by paragraphs 4, 5, 6 and 8 of this Article, particularly the precise format of the records referred to in paragraphs 4 to 8 and the technical means for appropriate communication of the information referred to in paragraph 6 to the person receiving the market sounding.

ESMA shall submit those draft implementing technical standards to the Commission by 3 July 2015.

Power is conferred on the Commission to adopt the implementing technical standards referred to in the first subparagraph in accordance with Article 15 of Regulation (EU) No 1095/2010.

11. ESMA shall issue guidelines in accordance with Article 16 of Regulation (EU) No 1095/2010, addressed to persons receiving market soundings, regarding:

(a) the factors that such persons are to take into account when information is disclosed to them as part of a market sounding in order for them to assess whether the information amounts to inside information;
(b) the steps that such persons are to take if inside information has been disclosed to them in order to comply with Articles 8 and 10 of this Regulation; and
(c) the records that such persons are to maintain in order to demonstrate that they have complied with Articles 8 and 10 of this Regulation.

I. General Remarks

Overview

As contained in Article 11(1): 'a market sounding comprises the communication of information prior to the announcement of a transaction, in order to gauge the interest of potential investors in a possible transaction and the conditions relating **B.11.01** to it such as its potential size or pricing, to one or more potential investors'.[1] The regime captures communications of information, prior to the announcement of a transaction to either one or more potential investors by an issuer, a secondary offeror of financial instruments, an emissions allowances market participant, or a third-party acting on behalf of these person, in order to gauge the interest of potential investors in a possible transaction and the related conditions.[2]

B.11.02 Owing to a joint initiative by France and the UK, the Market Abuse Regulation includes a new article on market sounding.[3] The Market Abuse Regulation in its stringent nature, establishes a specific new provision for market sounding. The strict nature of the unlawful discloser obligation has, to a great extent, been mitigated by the Market Abuse Regulation's novel introduction of the market sounding regime which is designed to protect communications by firms and other actors of certain information pertaining to inside information and to support fund-raising (Article 11): where a disclosure of inside information is 'made in the course of a market sounding', and as long as the relevant conditions are complied with, the disclosure is deemed to have been made in the expected course of the exercise of a person's employment, profession, or duty.[4]

The nature of market sounding

B.11.03 Market soundings are useful protection where there is compliance with all the requirements in the Market Abuse Regulation, the Regulatory Technical Standards and guidelines. However, unless disclosure is made in accordance with the requirements for market soundings, Article 17(8) specifies that where an issuer or a person acting on their behalf discloses any inside information to a third party in the normal course of their employment, profession, or duties, then unless the recipient owes a duty of confidentiality, the information must be treated in the normal way for disclosures of inside information. So, the issuer must disclose the information to the market. This must be done simultaneously with any intentional disclosure or as soon as possible where inside information was inadvertently disclosed.

B.11.04 Recitals (32) and (33) provide an extensive description of market sounding. While the new regime is not dissimilar to market practices under (former) Market Abuse Directive (2003/6/EC) in respect of soundings, in certain respects such as disclosure requirements,[5] it lays out a more prescriptive procedural approach and strict regime, particularly with record keeping requirements. As a result, market

---

1 Article 11(1).
2 Article 11(1).
3 http://www.amf-france.org/en_US/Reglementation/Dossiers-thematiques/Marches/Abus-de-marche/l-europe-renforce-son-dispositif-anti-abus-de-marche.html#title_paragraph_2.
4 Article 11(4).
5 Article 14(c).

soundings procedures need to be updated to reflect the Market Abuse Regulation and the relevant Regulatory Technical Standards and Implementing Technical Standards (ie EU Regulations 2016/960 and 2016/959), and banks are already considering which common communications will or will not be caught.[6] The Market Abuse Regulation sets out detailed duties that, mainly, a disclosing market participants[7] ought to be in compliance. To this extent, the starting point for legal interpretation needs to be the ascertainment of what constitutes 'inside information' and to a large extent, 'insider dealing'.

For the purposes of the Market Abuse Regulation, Article 7[8] is important in that, its provisions describe what constitutes inside information. It stipulates that inside information shall comprise information that is; **B.11.05**

a) of a precise nature, which has not been made public, relating, directly or indirectly;
b) in relation to commodity derivatives, information of a precise nature, which has not been made public, relating, directly or indirectly to one or more such derivatives or relating directly to the related spot commodity[9] contract, and which were it made public would be likely to have a significant effect on the prices such as derivatives or related spot commodity contracts where this information is reasonably expected to be disclosed or is required to be disclosed;
c) in relation to emissions or auctioned products based on information which is of a precise nature, which has not been made public, relating, directly or indirectly, to one or more such instruments, and if it were made public, it is likely to have a significant effect on the prices of such instruments or on the prices of related derivative financial instruments; the price of related spot commodity contracts, or on the price of related derivative financial instruments, and;
d) persons charged with the execution of orders concerning financial instruments, it also means information conveyed by a client and relating to the client's pending orders in financial, which is of a precise nature, which has not been made public, relating, directly or indirectly, to one or more such instruments, and if it were made public, it is likely to have a significant effect on the prices of such instruments or on the prices of related derivative financial instruments, the price of related spot commodity contracts, or on the price of related derivative financial instruments.[10]

[6] http://www.allenovery.com/publications/en-gb/Pages/Romanian-Legal-Update-A-new-Market-Abuse-Regime.aspx.

[7] 'Disclosing market participant' means a person who falls into any of the categories set out in points (a) to (d) of art 11(1) or of art 11(2), and discloses information in the course of a market sounding.

[8] Article 7.

[9] Article 3(1)(14) Commodity means a commodity as defined in point (1) of art 2 of Commission Regulation (EC) No 1287/2006.

[10] Article 7(1)(a), (b), (c), and (d).

II. Contours of Market Sounding

B.11.06 Perhaps, conceptually, Article 7, Article 8(2)(a), (b), Article, 8(4), and Article 10 (unlawful disclosure of inside information) could indeed, be interpreted as the guiding principles that shape the contours of Article 11 on market sounding. Article 7 rather interestingly provides a definition of inside information that moves us closer to recent UK and EU case law, that is, 'information that would be likely to have a significant effect on the prices of those financial instruments or the price of related derivative financial instruments'. Ultimately, information is likely to have a 'significant effect' on price if it is information that a reasonable investor would be likely to use as the basis of his or her investment decision.[11] Notably, this definition is directly in line with the *Ian v Hannam v FCA*[12] and as a result of the *Daimler v Commission of the European Communities*[13] case on the ECJ level. The Market Abuse Regulation provides that an intermediate step in a protracted process shall be deemed to be inside information if by itself it qualifies as inside information.

B.11.07 In relation to takeovers, disclosure of inside information by a person intending to make a takeover bid or merger to parties entitled to the securities will also be a market sounding if: (a) the information is necessary to enable the parties entitled to the securities to form an opinion on their willingness to offer the securities; and (b) their willingness to offer their securities is reasonably required in order to decide whether to make the takeover bid or merger.[14]

B.11.08 Although it is presumed that there is a general understanding of market sounding or wall-crossing, the Market Abuse Regulation outlines specific procedures and time recording requirement including the following:

i) The requirement to assess in advance whether the market sounding in relation to presale/transaction discussions with potential will involve the disclosure of inside information.
ii) Keeping written recordings of the issuer's conclusion and reasons.
iii) Obtain the consent of the recipient of the market sounding to receive inside information and identify the information that happens to be inside information.
iv) Inform the recipient of the restrictions on the inside information for: acquiring or disposing of, for the recipient's own account or for the account of a

---

[11] Slaughter and May, 'The New EU Market Abuse Regulation: An overview for UK issuers' (January 2016) https://www.slaughterandmay.com/media/2535170/the-new-eu-market-abuse-regulation-an-overview-for-uk-issuers.pdf.

[12] *Ian Charles Hannam v FCA* [2014] UKUT 0233 (TCC).

[13] Case T-325/01 *Daimler v Commission of the European Communities* [2005] ECR II-3319.

[14] Article 11(2).

third party, directly or indirectly, the securities relating to that information; or, cancelling or amending an order which has already been placed concerning securities to which the information concerns.

v) If the market sounding is conducted by phone, recorded lines should be used where possible. The issuer is required to makes a clear statement that the conversation is being recorded and obtain consent to record the conversation.

vi) Verify that the individual is the person authorised by the recipient institution to receive the market sounding and also, inform the recipient of its obligation to keep the information confidential.[15]

III. Nature and Functionality

Notwithstanding that the focus of these new requirements is on the disclosing market participant, Article 11(7) also provides that market sounding recipients ought to determine for themselves whether they are in possession or cease to possess inside information, even in the view that they have been told by disclosing market participants that the information is, in their view, no longer inside information. **B.11.09**

In the ESMA's draft guidelines, there is a proposal that market sounding recipients cannot limit assessment simply to information they received from the disclosing market participants, but instead they should also consider any other related information they might be in possession of at the point and after, as the combination may result in inside information.[16] The guidelines apply to all market sounding recipients regardless of whether they are regulated or non-regulated entity, no matter their jurisdiction. For instance, a UK investment manager receiving a market sounding from a UK broker concerning the London Stock Exchange-listed issuer whose securities happen to be admitted to trading on a US multilateral trading facility (MTF) would be subject to ESMA guidelines. Notwithstanding that ESMA guidelines are not enforceable, compliance with these guidelines would help market sounding recipients in demonstrating compliance with the Market Abuse Regulation. To this extent, market participants, regardless of the regulatory status and location, will thus need to consider putting in place internal mechanisms to address the points raised by the ESMA Guidelines. **B.11.10**

Unlike its predecessor, the Market Abuse Directive, the Market Abuse Regulation applies to companies with securities traded on multilateral traded facilities, such **B.11.11**

[15] Shearman & Sterling, 'EU Market Abuse Regulation: Implications for Non-EU Issuers with Securities Traded on an EU Market' (23 June 2016) http://www.shearman.com/~/media/Files/NewsInsights/Publications/2016/06/EU-Market-Abuse-Regulation-Implications-for-Non-EU-Issuers-with-Securities-Traded-on-an-EU-Market-CM-06232016.pdf.

[16] ESMA, 'Final Report: Guidelines on the MAR: Market Soundings and Delay of Disclosure of Inside Information (ESMA/2016/1130)' (13 July 2016) www.esma.org.

as alternative investment market entities to encourage market integrity and across-the-board best practices. In the event that Markets in Financial Instruments Directive II (2014/65/EU) officially comes into force, alternative investment market entities will be able to apply for recognition as a 'Small Growth Market', in which case alternative investment market entities companies would be exempt from drawing up an insider list provided certain conditions are satisfied. Notably, without prejudice to Article 23(3), the provisions on market soundings create a defence to unlawful disclosure of inside information whereby a party intending to make a takeover bid for the securities of a company or a merger with a company to parties entitled to the securities, may effectively carry out a market sounding without infringing the rules on unlawful disclosure, provided that:

(a) the information is necessary to enable the parties entitled to the securities to form an opinion on their willingness to offer their securities; and
(b) the willingness of parties entitled to the securities to offer their securities is reasonably required for the decision to make the takeover bid or merger.

IV. Sections 1, 2, and 3: What Constitutes a Market Sounding

B.11.12 Before the coming into force of the Market Abuse Regulation, the City of London Law Society (CLLS) Company Law Committees' joint working parties on market abuse, share plans and takeovers code prepared a question and answer session to address the more technical elements of the Market Abuse Regulation.[17] Chiefly at discussion was Article 11 on market sounding. The committee rationalised Article 11(2) to be interpreted as the negotiations of the terms of the irrevocable undertaking involving communications between the bidder and target (represented by its directors) and not communications with a 'person entitled to securities' of the target.[18] In this respect, a bidder seeking recommendation from a target board will approach the target board and put forward an indicative offer that is subject to a number of conditions. These will include a requirement that those directors who hold shares will give irrevocable undertakings to accept the offer/vote in favour of the scheme as applicable. If a recommendation is forthcoming, the directors will agree to provide such undertakings.

[17] City of London Law Society and Law Society Company Law Committees' Joint Working Parties on Market Abuse, 'Market Abuse Regulation (EU the Market Abuse Regulation) Q&A Prepared by the City of London Law Society and Law Society Company Law Committees' Joint Working Parties on Market Abuse: Share Plans and Takeovers Code' (5 July 2016) http://www.citysolicitors.org.uk/attachments/category/114/the Market Abuse Regulation%20Takeover%20QA%20Final%20538882375_4.pdf.
[18] CLLS, 'Q&A' (n 17) Q1, A1.

The fact that a decision to recommend is likely to lead to an expectation that the directors will enter into irrevocable undertakings is a consequence and not an objective of the approach, which is not, therefore, a market sounding. The same goes for where the terms of an irrevocable undertaking to accept the offer/vote in favour of the scheme as applicable intended to be given by directors have been agreed between the bidder and target, the provision of the agreed form irrevocable to the target directors does not fall within the market abuse regime. This was construed by the CLLS as a mere ancillary process relating to communications that have already taken place with the target directors (in their capacity as such) in connection with the proposed offer, including the negotiation of a form of irrevocable undertaking as between the bidder and target.[19] In this context, the process (whether conducted directly by the bidder or by the target company) of providing the final form of irrevocable undertaking to the target directors and gathering executed copies of the same does not involve the communication of inside information necessary to enable the target directors to form an opinion on their willingness to offer their securities as referred to in Article 11(2). **B.11.13**

Communication within the market sounding under Article 11(2) is not restricted to only if the bidder makes it even though Article 11(1)(d) does not provide an equivalent. The CLLS analyses this provision to arrive at the conclusion that references to the bidder in Article 12 should be read as including reference to persons clearly acting as the bidder's agent/on its behalf eg its financial adviser or broker.[20] To read the provision of Article 11(2) more restrictively is to produce an anomalous result. The Committee also in their technical interpretation of market sounding affirmed in that market sounding can be conducted other than in the strict compliance with Article 11 and the Implementation Technical Standard.[21] Non-compliance with market sounding requirements (when a communication is within Article 11(1) or (2) and insider information is disclosed) does not automatically mean that the communication is unlawful or that the person making the communication is subject to sanctions simply on the basis of non-compliance. This is subject to complying with Article 11(3), that is, the requirement for the disclosing market participant must consider in advance whether the market sounding will involve disclosure of inside information and make a written record of its conclusion and reasons therefore. The rationale behind this is that, Recital 35[22] provides that 'there should be a presumption that market participants who do not comply with this Regulation when conducting a **B.11.14**

[19] CLLS, 'Q&A' (n 17) Q2, A2.

[20] CLLS, 'Q&A' (n 17) Q4, A4, rationale: 'to read the provisions of Article 11(2) more restrictively would produce an anomalous result'.

[21] CLLS, 'Q&A' (n 17) Q5, A5.

[22] Recital (35).

market sounding have unlawfully disclosed inside information but they should not be able to take advantage of the exemption given to those who have complied with such provisions. The question of whether they have infringed a prohibition against the unlawful disclosure of inside information should be analysed in light of all the relevant provisions of the regulation'.[23]

V. Sections 4 and 5: Unlawful Disclosures

B.11.15 In essence, Article 11(4) provides for the purposes of unlawful disclosure, that is addressed in Article 10(1), disclosure of insider information made during the course of a market sounding, shall be treated as information that is exchanged within normal exercise of the disclosing market participant's employment, profession, or duties where the disclosing market participant is compliant to Article 11(3) and (5)[24]—that is, compliance with the provisions of Article 11 is mandatory to fall within the safe harbour, but non-compliance does not automatically mean a breach for Article 10. Much weight is drawn from Article 30—administrative sanctions, to enhance this analysis. Article 11(3) imposes a stand-alone obligation that is *not* specifically limited to the safe harbour set out in Article 11(4). For the purposes of Article 11(4) which set out the need to establish a more uniform and stronger framework in order to preserve market integrity to avoid potential regulatory arbitrage, to ensure accountability in the event of a market manipulation and to provide legal certainty, Article 11(5) states that the disclosing market participant shall, prior to making the disclosure ensure the following:

(a) Obtain the consent of the person receiving the market sounding to receive the inside information.
(b) Inform the market sounding recipient the he/she is prohibited from using that information, attempting to use that information by acquiring or disposing of, for his own account or for the third party, directly or indirectly, financial instruments relating to that information.
(c) Inform the market sounding recipient that they are prohibited from using the information, attempting to use that information, by cancelling or amending an order which has already been placed concerning a financial sounding to which the information relates.
(d) Inform the receiving party that by agreeing to receive the information they are obliged to keep the information confidential.

[23] Recital (35).
[24] Article 11(4).

VI. Section 7: Market Sounding Recipient to Determine whether They Have Inside Information

Although there is a clear focus of these new requirements on the disclosing market participant, Article 11(7) shifts the attention from market sounding recipients to almost equal measure as that placed on the disclosing participant. Article 11(7) provides that, there is an obligation for a market sounding recipient to determine for themselves whether they have or cease to have inside information, even where they have been told by the disclosing market participants that the information is, in their estimation, no longer inside information. To this extent, ESMA issued guidelines[25] to propose that the market sounding recipients cannot limit this assessment to the information they received from the disclosing market participants on the pretext that it is in their view, no longer insider information. Market sounding recipients should also consider any other related information they might be in possession of at the time and after, as the combination may result in inside information. This may otherwise seem to be a grey area that could lead market sounding recipients to be susceptible to infringing of market sounding provision given the likelihood that most recipients of market sounding are less sophisticated participants. **B.11.16**

VII. Section 11: Receiving Information: Factors to Consider

Perhaps it is appropriate that Article 11(11) provides that ESMA shall issue guidelines in accordance with Article 16 ESMA Regulation (1095/2010/EU), addressed to persons receiving market sounding, regarding; factors the person receiving should take into account when information is disclosed to them as part of the market sounding in order for them to assess whether the information revealed to them amounts to inside information. They should also take into consideration the steps that such persons take if inside information has been disclosed to them in order to comply with Article 8 and Article 10, and; ultimately, the records that such persons are to maintain in order to demonstrate that they have complied with Articles 8 and 10. **B.11.17**

Furthermore, where an issuer or a person acting on their behalf discloses any inside information to a third party in the normal course of their employment, profession, or duties, Article 17(8) specifies that, unless the recipient owes a duty **B.11.18**

[25] ESMA, 'Q&A on the Market Abuse Regulation (ESMA/2016/1129)' (13 July 2016) 9 www.esma.org.

of confidentiality, the information must be treated in the normal way for disclosures of inside information. It follows that the issuer must, therefore, disclose the information to the market. This must be done simultaneously with any intentional disclosure or as soon as possible where inside information was inadvertently disclosed.

Article 12: Market manipulation

1. For the purposes of this Regulation, market manipulation shall comprise the following activities:
   (a) entering into a transaction, placing an order to trade or any other behaviour which:
      (i) gives, or is likely to give, false or misleading signals as to the supply of, demand for, or price of, a financial instrument, a related spot commodity contract or an auctioned product based on emission allowances; or
      (ii) secures, or is likely to secure, the price of one or several financial instruments, a related spot commodity contract or an auctioned product based on emission allowances at an abnormal or artificial level;
      unless the person entering into a transaction, placing an order to trade or engaging in any other behaviour establishes that such transaction, order or behaviour have been carried out for legitimate reasons, and conform with an accepted market practice as established in accordance with Article 13;
   (b) entering into a transaction, placing an order to trade or any other activity or behaviour which affects or is likely to affect the price of one or several financial instruments, a related spot commodity contract or an auctioned product based on emission allowances, which employs a fictitious device or any other form of deception or contrivance;
   (c) disseminating information through the media, including the internet, or by any other means, which gives, or is likely to give, false or misleading signals as to the supply of, demand for, or price of, a financial instrument, a related spot commodity contract or an auctioned product based on emission allowances or secures, or is likely to secure, the price of one or several financial instruments, a related spot commodity contract or an auctioned product based on emission allowances at an abnormal or artificial level, including the dissemination of rumours, where the person who made the dissemination knew, or ought to have known, that the information was false or misleading;
   (d) transmitting false or misleading information or providing false or misleading inputs in relation to a benchmark where the person who made the transmission or provided the input knew or ought to have known that it was false or misleading, or any other behaviour which manipulates the calculation of a benchmark.

2. The following behaviour shall, inter alia, be considered as market manipulation:
   (a) the conduct by a person, or persons acting in collaboration, to secure a dominant position over the supply of or demand for a financial instrument, related spot commodity contracts or auctioned products based on emission allowances which has, or is likely to have, the effect of fixing, directly or indirectly, purchase or sale prices or creates, or is likely to create, other unfair trading conditions;
   (b) the buying or selling of financial instruments, at the opening or closing of the market, which has or is likely to have the effect of misleading investors acting on the basis of the prices displayed, including the opening or closing prices;
   (c) the placing of orders to a trading venue, including any cancellation or modification thereof, by any available means of trading, including by electronic means, such as algorithmic and high-frequency trading strategies, and which has one of the effects referred to in paragraph 1(a) or (b), by:
      (i) disrupting or delaying the functioning of the trading system of the trading venue or being likely to do so;
      (ii) making it more difficult for other persons to identify genuine orders on the trading system of the trading venue or being likely to do so, including by entering orders which result in the overloading or destabilisation of the order book; or
      (iii) creating or being likely to create a false or misleading signal about the supply of, or demand for, or price of, a financial instrument, in particular by entering orders to initiate or exacerbate a trend;
   (d) the taking advantage of occasional or regular access to the traditional or electronic media by voicing an opinion about a financial instrument, related spot commodity contract or an auctioned product based on emission allowances (or indirectly about its issuer) while having previously taken positions on that financial instrument, a related spot commodity contract or an auctioned product based on emission allowances and profiting subsequently from the impact of the opinions voiced on the price of that instrument, related spot commodity contract or an auctioned product based on emission allowances, without having simultaneously disclosed that conflict of interest to the public in a proper and effective way;
   (e) the buying or selling on the secondary market of emission allowances or related derivatives prior to the auction held pursuant to Regulation (EU) No 1031/2010 with the effect of fixing the auction clearing price for the auctioned products at an abnormal or artificial level or misleading bidders bidding in the auctions.

3. For the purposes of applying paragraph 1(a) and (b), and without prejudice to the forms of behaviour set out in paragraph 2, Annex I defines non-exhaustive indicators relating to the employment of a fictitious device or any other form of deception or contrivance, and non-exhaustive indicators related to false or misleading signals and to price securing.

4. Where the person referred to in this Article is a legal person, this Article shall also apply, in accordance with national law, to the natural persons who participate in the decision to carry out activities for the account of the legal person concerned.

5. The Commission shall be empowered to adopt delegated acts in accordance with Article 35 specifying the indicators laid down in Annex I, in order to clarify their elements and to take into account technical developments on financial markets.

Relevant Technical Standards:

Commission Delegated Regulation (EU) 2016/522 of 17 December 2015 supplementing Regulation (EU) No 596/2014 of the European Parliament and of the Council as regards an exemption for certain third countries public bodies and central banks, the indicators of market manipulation, the disclosure thresholds, the competent authority for notifications of delays, the permission for trading during closed periods and types of notifiable managers' transactions (OJ L 88 (5 April 2016) 1).

I. General Remarks

Overview

The Market Abuse Regulation introduces a new regime for market abuse in the form of market manipulation and insider dealing, alongside new rules on disclosure of inside information,[1] insider lists,[2] and restrictions on dealings by persons discharging managerial responsibilities and their associated persons. The new **B.12.01**

[1] Article 7.

[2] In art 18, broadly, the requirements to maintain an insider list remain the same as they were before; however, the format and content of insider lists will change and will be prescribed by technical standards. In particular, more extensive data will need to be recorded for each individual added to an insider list. There will also be a new requirement for the company to send a written note to any person who is added to an insider list.

rules will apply to listed companies and also to companies quoted on AIM, meaning that AIM companies' obligations will be closer to those of companies listed on the Main Market and will be overseen by the Financial Conduct Authority who are charged with enforcing the rules in the UK.

B.12.02 At the heart of the provisions set out in Article 12, market manipulation practice is an inherent pursuit to tackle the misuse of material information; the dissemination of false or misleading information, and behaviour, which distorts the trading price or the trading volume of securities. That being noted, the evolving nature of the marketplace, which sees new products constantly developed, makes it difficult effectively to detect trading avenues designed artificially to increase or decrease a security's trading volumes, to distort its price or interfere with market forces.[3] In the advent of the 2008 financial crisis and the recognition that we live in an intrinsically interconnected world, the possibilities and forms of which market integrity can be undermined are multiple;[4] thus, the Market Abuse Regulation's effort to introduce Article 12 to, at best get rid of, and at worst minimize events of market manipulation.

Comparative remarks

B.12.03 In some EU Member States such as France, an infringement of stock market regulations can lead to prosecution and sanctions. The coexistence of regulatory and criminal sanctions deriving from the same set of facts has increasingly been the subject of challenges from defendants on grounds that it contravenes the double jeopardy rule that is stipulated in Article 50 of the European Charter of Human Rights. Such a dual-trial system has been held to be compliant with France's law provided the penalties awarded do not exceed the maximum threshold that can be incurred under criminal or AMF regulation,[5] and Protocol No 7 to the European Convention on Human Rights (Article 4). As far as French law is concerned on this issue, there is a caveat that states: 'only those offences that which under French law fall within the jurisdiction of French criminal Courts shall be regarded as offences within the scope of Article 2 to 4 of this protocol'.

---

[3] IOSCO, 'Investigating and Prosecuting Market Manipulation, Report of the Technical Committee of IOSCO' (May 2000) 13 http://www.iosco.org/library/pubdocs/pdf/IOSCOPD103.pdf. IOSCO has suggested that: 'The key question is whether there appears to be any logical trading pattern to the security's price and volume, or whether it seems erratic. If erratic, the question is whether pattern coincides with the activities of the promoter, broker, or other participant in the potential manipulation'.

[4] FSA, 'Hedge Funds: A Discussion of Risks and Regulatory Engagement: Discussion Paper 05/4' (2005) 53–4. UK Financial Services Authority (FSA) now the Financial Conduct Authority (FCA), issued a report on hedge fund activities citing that 'managers might be testing limits of acceptable practice in relation to market manipulation', and might be tempted to use their positions to start rumours to move the market deliberately and committed to close surveillance and tough enforcement where necessary.

[5] CC Decision No 89-260 DC (28 July 1989) (Fr), Cass Crim (22 January 2014) *Bull* No 22 (Fr).

In the advent of the Market Abuse Regulation, particularly, the introduction of the Market Abuse Directive on Criminal Sanctions (2014/57/EU) and the feature of being directly applicable to all Member States ensures regulatory uniformity. **B.12.04**

Conceptually, the introduction of Market Abuse Directive on Criminal Sanctions (2014/57/EU) would offer some reprieve to what seems like a legal conundrum in certain countries and here is why: in a recent market abuse decision by the European Court of Human Rights (ECtHR), *Grande Stevens and Others v Italy*,[6] the controversy surrounding dual-trial was intensified and its outcome is likely to have far reaching implications. In this case, the Court contended that the Italian dual-trial system for market abuses, which is identical to the one in France, constituted a breach of Article 4. Essentially, when Italy ratified the Protocol, it made reservations to the effect that Articles 2 to 4 apply only to offences, procedures, and decisions that qualify as criminal offences under Italian law. Notwithstanding this precedent, the Court in *Grande Stevens* handed down a decision to declare the reservation invalid. Following from this decision, it would appear the *Grande* decision has spurred defendants with similar insider trading-related proceeding to file motion of priority ruling; an outcome that would create the kind of legal uncertainty that can only be resolved by the coming into force of Market Abuse Directive on Criminal Sanctions (2014/57/EU) to ensure a consistent legal framework across the board. **B.12.05**

II. Definition of Market Manipulation (Article 12(1))

Market manipulation is committed if a person carries out any of the specified activities or behaviours outlined in Article 12. The list of examples that shall comprise market manipulation under the Market Abuse Regulation is non-exhaustive. Article 12(1) states that market manipulation shall comprise entering into a transaction, placing an order to trade, or any other behaviour which: **B.12.06**

(i) gives or is likely to give, false or misleading signals as to the supply of, or price of, a financial instrument, a related spot commodity contract, or an auctioned product based on emission allowances; or
(ii) secure, or is likely to secure, the price of one or several financial instruments, a related spot commodity contract, or an auctioned product based on emission allowances at an abnormal or artificial level.

In this regard, the Market Abuse Regulation extends its reach beyond the (former) Market Abuse Directive (2003/6/EC) regime by addressing the lack of oversight and visibility of the underlying commodity contracts to which the value of **B.12.07**

[6] *Grande Stevens and Others v Italy* (Application nos 18640/10, 18647/10, and 18698/10).

certain derivative financial instruments is referenced. Generally, market manipulation is prohibited under the Market Abuse Regulation regime, which provides a comprehensive list of behaviours that may amount to a manipulation offence. For instance, market manipulation is defined under Article 12(1a) as any activity of entering into a transaction; placing an order to trade in a way that gives, or is likely to false, misleading signal as to the supply of, demand for, price of, a financial instrument, a related spot commodity shall amount to the offence of market manipulation. It is only for this type of market manipulation that an exemption may be applied, according to which behaviour will not amount to market manipulation if the person acting establishes that their actions conformed with an 'accepted market practice' as determined by a relevant competent authority.

B.12.08 In assessing whether certain behaviour constitutes accepted market practice, the Market Abuse Regulation sets out a list of criteria, such as whether the market practice provides for a substantial level of transparency, whether it ensures a high degree of safeguards to the operation of market forces and the proper interplay of supply and demand, and whether it has a positive impact on market liquidity and efficiency. The Market Abuse Regulation does not permit competent authorities to adopt as accepted market practice certain behaviour, if they are entering in a transaction, placing an order to trade, or any other behaviour that is not legitimate, and does not qualify for accepted market practice in accordance with Article 13. These behaviours include, but are not limited to:

i. the use of a fictitious device or any other form of deception;
ii. the dissemination of information through media or the internet that may lead to false or misleading signals as to the supply of, demand for, or price of, a financial instrument;
iii. false or misleading information in relation to a benchmark—this was already a criminal offence in the UK;
iv. any conduct to secure a dominant position over the supply of or demand for a financial instrument with the effect of fixing prices or creating unfair trading conditions such as the use of highly sophisticated algorithmic trading strategies which disrupt or give an unfair advantage, eg high-frequency trading (HFT)[7] and;
v. the buying or selling of financial instruments at the opening or closing of the market, which is likely to have a misleading effect on investors.

B.12.09 Furthermore, under Article 12(1)(b), market manipulation shall comprise entering into a transaction, placing an order to trade, or any other activity or behaviour which affects or is likely to affect the price of one or several financial instruments, a related spot commodity contract, or an auctioned product based on emission

[7] 'High-frequency trading' means high-frequency algorithmic trading technique as defined in point (40) of art 4(1) of Directive 2014/65/EU.

allowances, which employs a fictitious device or any other form of deception or contrivance; disseminating information through the media, including the internet, or by any other means, which gives, or is likely to give false or misleading signals as to the supply of, demand for, or price of a financial instrument, related to a spot commodity contract, or auctioned contract product based on emissions allowances or secures, or is likely to secure, the price of one or several financial instruments, a related spot commodity contract, or an auctioned product based on emission allowances at an abnormal or artificial level, including the dissemination of rumours, where the person who made the dissemination knew, or ought to have known, that the information was misleading or false;[8] Article 12(1)(d) expands its scope to also capture transmitting false or misleading information or providing false or misleading inputs in relation to a benchmark where the person who made the transmission or provided the input knew or ought to have known that it was false or misleading, or any other behaviour which manipulates the calculation of a benchmark.

III. Additional Actions and Behaviours as Market Manipulation (Article 12(2))

To reflect upon the previous (former) Market Abuse Directive (2003/6/EC) regime, the Market Abuse Regulation specifies certain examples such as strategies using algorithmic trading and high-frequency trading that will fall within the prohibition against market manipulation in Article 12(2). These include engaging in the disruption or delay of the trading system of the trading avenue or being likely to do so; making it more difficult for others to identify genuine orders on the trading system or being likely to do so, including by entering orders which result in the overloading or destabilizing the order books; or creating or being likely to create a false or misleading signal about the supply of, or demand for or price of, a financial instrument, in particular by entering orders to initiate or exacerbate a trend. **B.12.10**

Key to this part is that, regulators have identified certain automated strategies that, if carried out, are manipulative and likely to constitute market abuse. These strategies include: quote stuffing, which is the placing and withdrawing of large orders quickly to flood the market with quotes to be processed. They also cite and take into account the concept of layering, which is the submission of multiple orders, typically on a single stock, to create an exaggerated impression it is highly liquid, and finally, regulators identified spoofing, that is, when a trader with direct market access places an order for a large number of shares then **B.12.11**

[8] Article 12(1)(c).

immediately cancels it, creating the impression the shares are highly liquid and allowing the trader to sell at a higher price.

IV. Article 12: Wider Purview

B.12.12 Although not clearly defined, under Article 15, the Market Abuse Regulation captures the attempt to engage in insider dealing and market manipulation as well as the actual involvement in prohibited conduct. That is, in the event that a transaction is intended for abusive purposes but it is unsuccessfully executed, for example due to a failure in technology or refusal to act on an instruction to trade. Although detecting market abuse practice may prove to be quite complex for firms,[9] the risk that is addressed in Article 2(3) that market manipulation can be achieved more remotely is likely to demand that firms implement high standards in their respect practices. Article 2 appears to give the market abuse regime an almost unlimited geographical reach. The regime will cover behaviour both within and outside the EU in relation to instruments admitted to trading on an EU trading venue. Thus, the extraterritorial effect vested in Article 2(4) could be a welcome deterrent to engaging in market manipulation. Therefore, it is advisable for market participants to interpret Article 12—market manipulation, together with, especially, Articles 15 and 16, both of which set out clear guidelines of prohibited conduct and requirements for market operators and investment firms that operate on a trading venue to establish and maintain effective arrangements, systems, and procedures aimed at preventing and detecting insider dealing, market manipulation, and attempted insider dealing and, also, market manipulation in accordance with Articles 31 and 54 of Directive 2014/65EC.[10]

B.12.13 The prohibitions in Article 12 ought to be read in conjunction with Articles 14 and 15, which for foresight of conduct that is not specifically covered in the Market Abuse Regulation, are drafted widely to capture unforeseen manipulative behaviour. They prohibit engaging in or attempting to engage in insider dealing and market manipulation. The insider dealing prohibition also prohibits persons possessing inside information (insiders) from recommending or inducing another to engage in dealings based on the inside information. If an insider does so, the person acting on the basis of their recommendation or inducement is insider dealing—if they knew or ought to have known the recommendation or inducement is based on inside information.[11] There are exemptions from the market abuse prohibitions from share buy-backs and stabilization. Where persons trade in their own shares in buy-back programmes and stabilization programmes,

---

[9] Recital (46) states that attempted manipulation includes placing orders, which may not be executed.

[10] Articles 31 and 54 Markets in Financial Instruments Directive II (2014/65/EU).

[11] Article 14.

these transactions shall not be caught by the prohibition provided they comply with Article 5.

In addition to the activities mentioned above, certain behaviours also constitute market manipulation. They include collaborating to secure a dominant position over the supply of demand for a financial instrument or creating other unfair trading conditions. Further guidance on forms of activities, and without prejudice to the forms of behaviour set out in Article 12(1)(2) Annex 1 a list of non-exhaustive indicators, which shall not necessarily be deemed, in themselves, to constitute market manipulation, shall be taken into account when transactions or orders to trade are examined by market participants and competent authorities. The extensive scope of this provision will undoubtedly have far-reaching implications for market participants located outside the European Union. For example, transactions by US participants in the commodities market are caught within the remit of the Market Abuse Regulation's regime, where such transactions are likely to have an impact on the price or value of a financial instrument traded on a relevant EU venue—even if the instrument is predominantly traded on a US platform. **B.12.14**

Article 13: Accepted market practices

1. A competent authority may establish an accepted market practice, taking into account the following criteria:
   (a) whether the market practice provides for a substantial level of transparency to the market;
   (b) whether the market practice ensures a high degree of safeguards to the operation of market forces and the proper interplay of the forces of supply and demand;
   (c) whether the market practice has a positive impact on market liquidity and efficiency;
   (d) whether the market practice takes into account the trading mechanism of the relevant market and enables market participants to react properly and in a timely manner to the new market situation created by that practice;
   (e) whether the market practice does not create risks for the integrity of, directly or indirectly, related markets, whether regulated or not, in the relevant financial instrument within the Union;
   (f) the outcome of any investigation of the relevant market practice by any competent authority or by another authority, in particular whether the relevant market practice infringed rules or regulations designed to prevent market abuse, or codes of conduct, irrespective of whether it concerns the relevant market or directly or indirectly related markets within the Union; and
   (g) the structural characteristics of the relevant market, inter alia, whether it is regulated or not, the types of financial instruments traded and the type of market participants, including the extent of retail-investor participation in the relevant market.
2. A market practice that has been established by a competent authority as an accepted market practice in a particular market shall not be considered to be applicable to other markets unless the competent authorities of those other markets have accepted that practice pursuant to this Article.
3. Before establishing an accepted market practice in accordance with paragraph 2, the competent authority shall notify ESMA and the other competent authorities of its intention to establish an accepted market practice and shall provide the details of that assessment made in accordance with the criteria laid down in paragraph 2. Such a notification shall be made at least three months before the accepted market practice is intended to take effect.
4. Within two months following receipt of the notification, ESMA shall issue an opinion to the notifying competent authority assessing the compatibility of the accepted market practice with paragraph 2 and with the regulatory

technical standards adopted pursuant to paragraph 7. ESMA shall also assess whether the establishment of the accepted market practice would not threaten the market confidence in the Union's financial market. The opinion shall be published on ESMA's website.

5. Where a competent authority establishes an accepted market practice contrary to the opinion of ESMA issued in accordance with paragraph 4, it shall publish on its website within 24 hours of establishing the accepted market practice a notice setting out in full its reasons for doing so, including why the accepted market practice does not threaten market confidence.
6. Where a competent authority considers that another competent authority has established an accepted market practice that does not meet the criteria set out in paragraph 2, ESMA shall assist the authorities concerned in reaching an agreement in accordance with its powers under Article 19 of Regulation (EU) No 1095/2010. If the competent authorities concerned fail to reach an agreement, ESMA may take a decision in accordance with Article 19(3) of Regulation (EU) No 1095/2010.
7. In order to ensure consistent harmonisation of this Article, ESMA shall develop draft regulatory technical standards specifying the criteria, the procedure and the requirements for establishing an accepted market practice under paragraphs 2, 3 and 4, and the requirements for maintaining it, terminating it, or modifying the conditions for its acceptance.

ESMA shall submit those draft regulatory technical standards to the Commission by 3 July 2015.

Power is delegated to the Commission to adopt the regulatory technical standards referred to in the first subparagraph in accordance with Articles 10 to 14 of Regulation (EU) No 1095/2010.

8. Competent authorities shall review regularly, and at least every two years, the accepted market practices that they have established, in particular by taking into account significant changes to the relevant market environment, such as changes to trading rules or to market infrastructures, with a view to deciding whether to maintain it, to terminate it, or to modify the conditions for its acceptance.
9. ESMA shall publish on its website a list of accepted market practices and in which Member States they are applicable.
10. ESMA shall monitor the application of accepted market practices and shall submit an annual report to the Commission on how they are applied in the markets concerned.
11. Competent authorities shall notify accepted market practices that they have established before 2 July 2014 to ESMA within three months of the entry into force of the regulatory technical standards referred to in paragraph 7.

The accepted market practices referred to in the first subparagraph of this paragraph shall continue to apply in the Member State concerned until the competent authority has made a decision regarding the continuation of that practice following ESMA's opinion under paragraph 4.

Relevant Technical Standards:
Commission Delegated Regulation (EU) 2016/908 of 26 February 2016 supplementing Regulation (EU) No 596/2014 of the European Parliament and of the Council laying down regulatory technical standards on the criteria, the procedure and the requirements for establishing an accepted market practice and the requirements for maintaining it, terminating it or modifying the conditions for its acceptance (OJ L 153, 10.6.2016, p. 3).

I. General Remarks

B.13.01 The market abuse regulation builds upon the structures of the (former) Market Abuse Directive (2003/6/EC) to ensure it guarantees the integrity of financial markets, transparency, and increases the level of investor confidence with a non-exhaustive list of accepted market practices outlined in Article 13. In accordance with Article 3(1)(9), accepted market practice[1] is described as a specific market practice that is accepted by a 'competent authority'[2] of a given member state in concert with provisions set out in Article 13. It is noteworthy that the prohibition in Article 15, that is, 'a person shall not engage in or attempt to engage in market manipulation', shall not apply to the activities referred to in Article 12(1)(a), provided that the person entering into a transaction, placing an order to trade,

[1] Article 3(1)(9) 'accepted market practice' means specific market practice that is accepted by a competent authority in accordance with Article 13.

[2] Article 22. Inter alia: '[t]he competent authority shall ensure that the provisions of this regulation are applied on its territory, regarding all actions carried out on its territory, and actions carried out abroad relating to instruments admitted to trading on a regulated market, for which a request for admission to trading on such market has been made, auctioned on an auction platform or which are traded on an MFT or on an OTF or for which a request for admission to trading has been made on an MFT operating within its territory'.

or engaging in any other behaviour establishes that such transaction, order, or behaviour have been carried out for legitimate reasons, and conform with an accepted market practice as established in accordance with this Article.

II. Section 2: The Concept of Accepted Market Practice

Article 13(2) concerns the concept of accepted market practice, particularly the criteria that a competent authority must take into account and the process it must follow in order to establish an accepted market practice. At the centre of what a competent authority is expected to take into account to establish accepted market practice is: whether the market practice provides a substantial level of transparency to markets (Article 13(2)(a)); ensuring a high degree of safeguards and the proper interplay of the forces of supply demand (Article 13(2)(b)); whether the market practice has a positive impact on market liquidity and efficiency (Article 13(2)(c)); whether the trading mechanism of the relevant market is taken into account and enables market participant to react properly and in a timely manner to the new market situation and created by that practice (Article 13(2)(d)); avoiding risk for the integrity of, directly or indirectly, related markets, whether regulated or not, in the relevant financial industry within the Union (Article 13(2)(e)); whether the outcome of any investigation of the relevant market practice by any competent authority or by the another authority, in particular, whether the relevant market practice, directly or indirectly infringed rules or regulations designed to prevent market abuse or codes of conduct within the Union (Article 13(2)(f)); and whether regulated or not, the types of financial instruments traded and the type of market participants, including the extent of retail investor participation in the relevant market (Article 13(2)(g)). **B.13.02**

III. Establishing an Accepted Market Practice

Accepted market practices are practices that could be potentially manipulative but that are accepted and authorized to pursue a benefit they bring to market structure, operation, or robustness.[3] A key requirement prior to establishing a market practice as an accepted market practice is for competent authorities to do the following: **B.13.03**

a. Evaluate the market practice against each of the criteria set out in Article 13(2) and specified further in Article 3 Regulation 2016/908/EU.

[3] ESMA, 'Opinion on Intended Accepted Market Practice on Liquidity Contracts Notified by the Comisión Nacional del Mercado de Valore (ESMA/2016/1663)' (16 December 2016), available at www.esma.org.

b. Consult as appropriate with relevant bodies including, at a minimum, representatives of the issuers, investments firms, credit institutions, investors, emission allowance market participants, market operators operating a multilateral trading facility or an organized trading facilities and operators of regulated markets and other authorities on the appropriateness of establishing a market practice as an accepted market practice.[4]

B.13.04 Emphasis is made for where a competent authority establishes and accepts an accepted market practice in a particular market, it shall not be considered to be applicable to other markets unless the competent market authorities of those other markets have indeed accepted that practice pursuant to this Article.

IV. Section 3: Ensuring Functioning Markets and Public Confidence

B.13.05 Before establishing an accepted market practice in accordance with Article 13(2), Article 13(3) provides that the competent authority shall notify ESMA and other competent authorities of its intention to establish an accepted market practice and shall provide the details of that assessment made in accordance with the criteria laid down in Article 13(2). Such a notification shall be made at least three months before that accepted market practice is intended to take effect. It follows from this that, within two months upon receipt of the notification, ESMA shall issue an opinion to the notifying competent authority assessing the compatibility of the accepted market practice and with the regulatory technical standards adopted pursuant to Article 13(7). The assessment will also take into account whether the establishment of the accepted market practice does not threaten the market confidence and the opinion shall be published on ESMA's website.

V. Section 5: Publication of a Notice

B.13.06 Under Article 13(5), a competent authority that establishes an accepted market practice contrary to the opinion of ESMA issued in accordance with Article 13(4), shall publish on its website within twenty-four hours of establishing the accepted market practice a notice setting out in full its reasons for doing so, including why the accepted market practice does not threaten market confidence. A key theme for the Market Abuse Regulation is to ensure a uniform legal framework

[4] Article 2(1) Regulation 2016/908/EU.

establishing more uniform regulation, which more clearly defines rules applicable to all Union Member States (Article 13(5)).

VI. Section 7: Technical Standards

Perhaps the need to ensure consistent harmonization is more evident in Article 13(7), which sets out that ESMA shall develop draft regulatory technical standards specifying the criteria, the procedure, and the requirements for establishing an accepted market practice under Article 13(2) to (4), and the requirements for maintaining it, or modifying the conditions for its acceptance. This empowerment contributes to the development of uniform criteria, procedure, and requirement for accepted market practices, improves the clarity of the legal regime that governs the accepted market practices and promotes their performance by the market participants, thus, it also reinforces the orderly functioning of the market and market integrity. What is deemed as accepted market practice will be subject to regular review by the competent authorities, at least every two years taking into account significant changes to the relevant market environment, such as changes to trading rules or to market infrastructures, with a view to deciding whether to maintain it, to terminate it, or to modify the conditions for its acceptance (Article 13(8)). **B.13.07**

VII. Section 9: Accepted Market Practice

In the spirit of ensuring transparency and good corporate practice, Article 13(9) on accepted market practice, provides that ESMA shall publish on its website a list of accepted market practices and in which Member States they are applicable. It flows from this that ESMA shall submit an annual report to the Commission on how they are applied in the market concerned (Article 13(10)). **B.13.08**

VIII. Section 11: Notification of Accepted Market Practice

Article 13(11) provides the requirement for the competent authorities to notify accepted market practices that they have established before 2 July 2014 to ESMA within three months of the entry into force of the regulatory technical standards referred to in Article 13(7). The accepted market practices referred to in the first sub-paragraph shall continue to apply in the Member States concerned until the competent authority has made a decision regarding the continuation of that practice following ESMA's opinion under Article 13(4). **B.13.09**

B.13.10 To ensure that accepted market practices do not undermine innovation and the continued dynamic development of financial markets, new or emerging market trends that could result in novel market practices should not automatically be assumed to be unacceptable by competent authorities. Rather, those competent authorities should assess whether practices comply with the criteria set out in the Market Abuse Regulation. The Market Abuse Regulation substantially strengthens the transparency requirements that must be followed with respect to the public and competent authorities before, during, and upon completion of implementing an accepted market practice.[5] In line with a 'grandfather clause' for current practice in France, the Market Abuse Regulation requires them to be re-examined by competent authorities in the light of a set of criteria and according to a procedure detailed in the draft RTS, with the results reported to ESMA by the national competent authority.[6]

IX. Legal Protection

B.13.11 The safeguards foreseen in the Market Abuse Regulation by regulators with respect to activities falling within an accepted market practice were anticipated precisely because those activities, for example, placing orders or conducting transactions could, in themselves, constitute market manipulation. The mechanisms for doing so could be either by affecting the price-formation process by giving false or misleading signals as to the supply of, demand for, or price of the financial instrument or by securing the price at an abnormal or artificial level.[7] The accepted market practice grants a specific legal protection to those persons performing it, provided they fulfil two conditions, namely; that they do so in conformity with the conditions of the accepted market practice and that they engage in those activities for legitimate reasons.

B.13.12 The Market Abuse Regulation provides a defence if a transaction is legitimately executed, and in compliance with market practices accepted by the competent authority, that is, accepted market practices. As seen above, Article 13 sets out a list of factors that a competent authority must take into account before deciding whether or not to accept a market practice. The competent authority must in particular consult as appropriate relevant bodies such as representatives of issuers, financial services providers, consumers, other authorities, market operators, and ESMA, before officially accepting an accepted market practice. It follows from this that upon establishing an accepted market practice; the regulation provides a defence for transactions that are carried out in the legitimate course of action.

[5] Article 2 Regulation 2016/908/EU.

[6] http://www.amf-france.org/en_US/Reglementation/Dossiers-thematiques/Marches/Abus-de-marche/l-europe-renforce-son-dispositif-anti-abus-de-marche.html#title_paragraph_4.

[7] ESMA, 'Liquidity Contracts' (n 3).

To this point, the prohibition in Article 15, that is, 'a person shall not engage in or attempt to engage in market manipulation', shall not apply to the activities referred to in Article 12(1)(a), provided that the person entering into a transaction, placing an order to trade, or engaging in any other behaviour establishes that such transaction, order, or behaviour have been carried out for legitimate reasons, and conform with an accepted market practice as established in accordance with this Article.

Article 14: Prohibition of insider dealing and of unlawful disclosure of inside information

A person shall not:

(a) engage or attempt to engage in insider dealing;
(b) recommend that another person engage in insider dealing or induce another person to engage in insider dealing; or
(c) unlawfully disclose inside information.

I. General Remarks

Overview of Article 14

B.14.01 Article 14 is supplemented by Article 15, which serves to prohibit market manipulation according to Article 12. Article 14 is further supplemented by Article 30 on administrative sanctions and administrative measures.

The structure of Article 14

B.14.02 Article 14(a)–(c) prohibits three forms of behaviour: insider dealing according to Article 8(1); tipping according to Article 8(2); and unlawful disclosure according to Article 10, respectively. Each of these provisions defines the specific behaviour and the effect of Article 14 is to make such behaviour illegal. Each of these provisions is matched in the Market Abuse Directive on Criminal Sanctions (2014/57/EU) in order to harmonize the criminal law regime of the Member States to which the Directive applies.

Historical development

B.14.03 Article 14 is a new provision compared to the (former) Market Abuse Directive (2003/6/EC). Although the (former) Market Abuse Directive (2003/6/EC) also contained prohibitions, these were placed directly in the provisions describing the prohibited behaviour and were directed at the Member States due to the legal instrument's nature of a directive and required subsequent implementation in national legislation. As the Market Abuse Regulation is a directly applicable regulation, it was apparently found necessary to supply it with a provision that explicitly announces that these offences are prohibited.

II. Sanctions Provided by Article 14

If behaviour is deemed to fall within one of the three categories mentioned in Article 14(a)–(c), the behaviour is illegal and must be sanctioned by national law. The Market Abuse Directive on Criminal Sanctions (2014/57/EU) tries to harmonize this regime of national criminal law in the Member States where the Directive applies and even where the Directive is not applicable due to the reservations made by some Member States, these Member States are according to the case law of the Court of Justice of the EU (CJEU) obliged to ensure that infringements of EU law are penalized under conditions, both procedural and substantive, which are analogous to those applicable to infringements of national law of a similar nature and importance. Penalties must be effective, dissuasive, and proportionate to the infringement and, furthermore, the national authorities must proceed with respect to infringements of EU law with the same diligence as that which they bring to bear in respect of similar national laws.[1] **B.14.04**

Where the CJEU originally accepted that Member States alone should decide whether sanctions in national law should be of a criminal law nature, more recent case law of the CJEU has accepted that this choice can be made by the EU legislator directly.[2] In regard of market abuse, the Market Abuse Directive on Criminal Sanctions (2014/57/EU) constitutes an attempt to harmonize criminal sanctions, but it is likely that criminal sanctions must be available even in Member States that do not apply the Directive, since a failure to provide for a criminal regime would not provide the 'effective, dissuasive and proportionate' penalties that Member States are obliged to ensure according to the older and more uncontroversial case law of the CJEU. **B.14.05**

Article 30(1) calls on Member States to establish administrative sanctions and measures in respect of infringements of Article 14, that is, Member States are required to operate two parallel regimes, one criminal and one administrative, to sanction market abuse. However, according to the second subsection of Article 30(1), Member States are not obliged to have an administrative regime if they operate a regime of criminal sanctions for these infringements, but they must inform the European Commission and the European Securities and Markets Authority (ESMA) of the applicable criminal regime. **B.14.06**

---

[1] Case C-68/88 *Commission v Greece* [1989] ECR I-2965 paras 24–25.

[2] Case C-176/03 *Commission v Council of the EU* [2005] ECR I-7879. The case concerned environmental law and has since been followed by directives, beginning with Directive 2008/99, OJ L 328/28, 6.12.2008, restating the need for criminal penalties.

B.14.07 If a Member State operates both an administrative regime and a criminal regime, the Member State must ensure that they both observe the principles of fair trial as established in the 1950 European Convention for the Protection of Human Rights and Fundamental Freedoms (hereafter 1950 European Convention). As pointed out by the CJEU in its decision of 23 December 2009 in Case C-45/08 *Spector Photo Group NV*,[3] the 1950 European Convention applies a convention autonomous style of interpretation, that is, the concepts used in the 1950 European Convention should be construed according to the Convention irrespectively of their meaning in the national law of Contracting States. Consequently, even though a sanction is deemed to be administrative in national law, it may qualify as a criminal measure according to the 1950 European Convention in which case a Contracting State must observe the requirements applicable to criminal cases, including the right to a fair trial in Article 6 of the 1950 European Convention, which also includes a ban on self-incrimination developed in the case law of the European Court of Human Rights, and the right not to be subject to sanctions more than once for the same offence in Article 4 of Protocol 7 to the 1950 European Convention, known as the principle of *ne bis in idem* or double jeopardy.

B.14.08 Consequently, even though a sanction is deemed to be administrative in national law, it may qualify as a criminal measure according to the 1950 European Convention and the application of both administrative and criminal sanctions may thus violate the principle as laid out in Article 4 of Protocol 7 to the 1950 European Convention. So far, the European Court of Human Rights in its decision of 4 March 2014 has found the parallel application of both an administrative regime and a criminal regime in the Italian case, *Grande Stevens*, contrary to both Article 6 of the 1950 European Convention on fair trial and to Article 4 of Protocol 7 on double jeopardy.[4] In respect of the latter Article, it was observed that since the two sanctions concerned the same conduct, by the same persons, and on the same date, Article 4 had been violated.

III. Attempt to Engage in Insider Dealing

Attempt or final violation

B.14.09 When behaviour is prohibited, it raises the question of whether an attempt to engage in such behaviour should also be prohibited. An attempt is characterized

---

[3] Case C-45/08 *Spector Photo Group NV v CBFA* [2009] ECR I-12073 para 42, citing the case law of the Court of Human Rights in this area.

[4] European Court of Human Rights, *Grande Stevens et al v Italy*, Application nos 18640/10, 18647/10, 18663/10, 18668/10, and 18698/10. The Court noted, inter alia, that a reservation made by Italy in respect of Article 4 of Protocol 7, which would have upheld the Italian parallel

by behaviour that may bring about the prohibited behaviour but has not realized the crucial endpoint that justifies the prohibition. Once the behaviour has brought about the outcome that the prohibition intends to prevent, the violation is final and actions taken cannot be qualified as attempt. National criminal law of Member States will have their own provisions on what qualifies as attempt, when attempt is punishable, and which subjective conditions are required, and these elements of national law are not harmonized by the Market Abuse Regulation or the Market Abuse Directive on Criminal Sanctions (2014/57/EU) except for stating when attempt must be punishable.

In Article 14, attempt is included in the description of insider dealing according to Article 8(1), but not in respect of tipping according to Article 8(2), or unlawful disclosure according to Article 10. Attempt is not mentioned in Article 30 on administrative sanctions and measures. **B.14.10**

Since sanctions for these three offences are subject to national law, either harmonized by Market Abuse Directive on Criminal Sanctions (2014/57/EU) or independently determined, it is probably within each Member State's discretion to decide whether to also prohibit attempt in respect of tipping and unlawful disclosure. Article 14 does not appear to prohibit such extension of the scope of its prohibitions. **B.14.11**

What constitutes attempt depends on the prohibited behaviour and it is likely that the assessment will be influenced by the legal traditions of the courts in the Member States that have not been harmonized as they form constituent parts of criminal law and criminal procedure. It is possible that a preliminary ruling may eventually be issued by the CJEU according to Article 267 of the Treaty on the Functioning of the EU, which may bring about a common understanding. Until then, traditions of national law will probably be influential in this area. **B.14.12**

Insider dealing

Logically, attempt is no longer relevant when the offence has been committed. In respect of insider dealing according to Article 8(1), and taking into account the guidance offered by Recital (23), which is based on the CJEU's decision in *Spector*,[5] it is likely that the offence of insider dealing has been committed when the use of the inside information has caused a detriment to one or more third parties. It is the detriment to third parties that serves to separate lawful use of inside **B.14.13**

regime, had not been made with the necessary detail and could consequently not prevent the application of the Article. On the decision in respect of the sanctioning of market abuse see M Ventoruzzo, 'When Market Abuse Rules Violate Human Rights: Grande Stevens v Italy and the Different Approaches to Double Jeopardy in Europe and the US' (2014) 11 European Business Organization Law Review 297.

[5] *Spector Photo Group NV v CBFA* (n 3). The case is discussed in the commentary to art 8 para B.8.58 ff.

information from unlawful. Detriment would arise, where a securities transaction has been concluded that would hurt the interests of an uninformed third party, usually because the third party would not have accepted the conditions of the transaction had he or she known of the inside information. Until the transaction is concluded, action to bring such a transaction to its conclusion would constitute an attempt to engage in insider dealing. Typical instances would include forwarding an offer or an acceptance of an offer in order to conclude a securities transaction, but it probably also includes earlier actions by the insider if these actions can be seen as preparing a transaction that would constitute insider dealing, for example instructions to brokers to place an order. If, for some reason, the offer or the acceptance did not lead to a transaction, they could still be viewed as an attempt to conclude the transaction, in which case Article 14 would be violated. It will probably be required that the insider's actions indicate a clear determination to act upon the inside information in such a way as to obtain an advantage to the detriment of the third parties afflicted by the contemplated transaction.

B.14.14 In respect of cancelling or amending preplaced orders according to the second sentence of Article 8(1), the wording in recital (23) that unfair advantage may include 'attempting to cancel or amend' an order means that actions by the insider to cancel or amend the order equally amounts to punishable attempt, for example, providing a securities trader with instructions to cancel or amend the order.

Tipping and unlawful disclosure

B.14.15 In respect of tipping, the offence would appear to have been committed once the tippee comes into possession of the information that constitutes the tip, that is, the recommendation or inducement. To have the inside information in possession must entail to know of the facts that qualifies the information as inside information according to Article 7; it is not enough that the inside information has reached the tippee, but has not yet become known to him or her. From this point, the insider no longer has any control of how the tippee may use the inside information and actions to recommend or induce the tippee will cease to be characterized as attempt, because the offence has been committed.

B.14.16 Where no expansion has been made in national law to cover attempt, the behaviour by the insider is only prohibited by Article 14(b), where this final point has been reached, since behaviour leading up to the point constitutes attempt, which is not punishable according to Article 14(b).

B.14.17 Whether the tippee actually engages in insider dealing as a consequence of the recommendation or inducement is irrelevant in respect of the illegality of the act of tipping, as it concerns the separate offence of insider dealing by the tippee according to Article 8(1) by way of Article 8(3).

Since unlawful disclosure also concerns the passing on of information, here inside information, to another person, the same would apply in respect of Article 10. Again, behaviour would only qualify as unlawful disclosure according to Article 10, where the information has come into possession of one or more recipients, that is, to their knowledge. It is not enough that the inside information has reached them, if it in fact has not yet become known to them. Behaviour leading up to this result is only attempt and as such not punishable according to Article 14(c), unless attempt has been criminalized in the national law of the Member State. **B.14.18**

It is probably irrelevant whether the unlawful disclosure made the inside information known to the specific recipient that the insider intended by his or her disclosure, as long as the insider knew or ought to have known that the disclosure would make the inside information known to one or more recipients. As with tipping, it is also irrelevant whether the recipient of the inside information actually takes advantage of the disclosed inside information to commit insider dealing. The prohibited behaviour is to disclose the inside information to others in such a way that it is no longer within the control of the insider to prevent the abuse of the information by trading or by subsequent passing on to others. Whether the disclosed information is in fact so abused, is irrelevant. **B.14.19**

Article 15: Prohibition of market manipulation

A person shall not engage in or attempt to engage in market manipulation.

I. General Principles

Overview

B.15.01 Article 15 prohibits the engagement or any attempt to engage in market manipulation. It does so without specifying the kind of behaviour that might constitute market manipulation. That is defined in Article 12.

Historical background

B.15.02 The prohibition of market manipulation was already included in the (former) Market Abuse Directive (2003/6/EC), which stated in its Article 5 that Member States should prohibit any person from engaging in market manipulation. Therefore, in contrast to Article 15, the (former) Market Abuse Directive (2003/6/EC) did not cover attempts to engage in market manipulation.

II. Prohibition of Market Manipulation

Engaging in market manipulation

B.15.03 As stated above, pursuant to Article 15, a person shall not engage in market manipulation. The actual behaviour covered by this prohibition is defined in Article 12. See Article 12 for further details.

Attempting to engage in market manipulation

B.15.04 In addition, attempts to engage in market manipulation is forbidden. Recital (41) provides a rather unclear definition of when a person only attempts but does not finally engage in market manipulation. Pursuant to recital (41), such an attempt would include any behaviour where the activity is started but not completed. As an example, recital (41) states that failed technology or an instruction to trade which is not acted upon. However, it remains unclear what the start of any activity (to engage in market manipulation) requires. Also, it remains unclear whether the definition in recital (41) is also binding on national criminal laws imposing criminal sanctions for any attempt to commit market manipulation (Article 6(2) Market Abuse Directive on Criminal Sanctions (2014/57/EU)). Since Article 5 of the Market Abuse Directive on Criminal Sanctions (2014/57/EU) provides a specific definition for market manipulation as the basis for criminal sanctions and since Article 6(2) of the Market Abuse Directive on Criminal Sanctions (2014/57/EU) does not explicitly refer to the definition in recital (41) of the Market Abuse Regulation, the definition of any attempt to engage in market manipulation must be determined by national criminal law.

Inciting, aiding, and abetting

Although not being explicitly mentioned in Article 15, inciting, aiding, and abetting of market manipulation is forbidden under the regime of the Market Abuse Regulation. This prohibition is set out indirectly by Article 6(1) of the Market Abuse Directive on Criminal Sanctions (2014/57/EU), which requires Member States to take the necessary steps to ensure that such behaviour is punishable as a criminal offence. Although limited to criminal sanctions, Article 6(1) of the Market Abuse Directive on Criminal Sanctions (2014/57/EU) makes it clear that inciting, aiding, and abetting of market manipulation is not excluded from the market abuse regime of the Market Abuse Regulation. This is especially relevant for civil liability for a violation of the prohibition of market manipulation.[1] **B.15.05**

III. No Requirement of a Specific Intent

Article 15 states that a person shall not engage in or attempt to engage in market manipulation, although it does not state whether engagement in market manipulation requires a specific intent. Although this requirement is of general importance and has already been described as an unresolved issue under the regime of the (former) Market Abuse Directive (2003/6/EU),[2] its practical impact is marginal. This is particularly the case with regard to criminal sanctions under Article 5(1) of the Market Abuse Directive on Criminal Sanctions (2014/57/EU), which explicitly requires that the market manipulation charged was committed **B.15.06**

[1] See Part A—Private Enforcement of the Market Abuse Regulation in European Law for further details.

[2] See Part A—The Concept of Market Manipulation for further details.

intentionally.[3] As for the civil liability for committing market manipulation, national (civil) law applies, which then can also determine whether specific intent is necessary or not.[4]

IV. Violation of the Prohibition

Administrative sanctions

B.15.07 Violation of the prohibition against market manipulation under Article 15 can be addressed by administrative sanctions, as set out by Articles 30 ff.[5]

Criminal sanctions

B.15.08 Pursuant to Article 5 of the Market Abuse Directive on Criminal Sanctions (2014/57/EU), the Member States must take all necessary steps to ensure that market manipulation constitutes a criminal offence. Although market manipulation is generally defined in Article 12 of the Market Abuse Regulation and forbidden under Article 15 of the Market Abuse Regulation, Article 5(2) of the Market Abuse Directive on Criminal Sanctions (2014/57/EU) provides a separate definition for market manipulation as a basis for the criminal offence referred to in Article 5(1) of the Market Abuse Directive on Criminal Sanctions (2014/57/EU). The differences between the definition of market manipulation in Article 12 of the Market Abuse Regulation and Article 5(2) of the Market Abuse Directive on Criminal Sanctions (2014/57/EU) is because, for criminal law purposes, a narrower approach is necessary in order to meet the requirements of the general criminal law principle of *nulla poena sine lege certa*. However, Article 5 only requires Member States to establish such a criminal offence in a serious case of market manipulation and provided that the market manipulation is committed intentionally. The seriousness of a market manipulation is defined in recital (11) of the Market Abuse Directive on Criminal Sanctions (2014/57/EU), where the impact on the integrity of the market, the actual or potential profit derived or loss avoided, the level of damage caused to the market, the level of alteration in the value of the financial instrument or spot commodity contract, or the amount of funds originally used is high. Moreover, the fact that the person committing the market manipulation is employed or working in the financial sector or in a supervisory or regulatory authority must also be taken into consideration.[6] Also,

---

[3] See note 8 ff.

[4] See Part A—Private Enforcement of the Market Abuse Regulation in European Law for further details.

[5] See Part A—Public Enforcement of the Market Abuse Regulation in European Law for further details.

[6] Recital (12) Market Abuse Directive on Criminal Sanctions (2014/57/EU).

recital (7) of the Market Abuse Directive on Criminal Sanctions (2014/57/EU) cites the LIBOR scandal as an example of a serious case of benchmark market manipulation.

The inciting, aiding, and abetting of engaging in market manipulation must be punishable as a criminal offence under national law (Article 6(1) Market Abuse Directive on Criminal Sanctions (2014/57/EU)). The same applies to attempts to commit market manipulation (Article 6(2) Market Abuse Directive on Criminal Sanctions (2014/57/EU)). Owing to the general reference in Article 6(1) and (2) of the Market Abuse Directive on Criminal Sanctions (2014/57/EU) to Article 5 of the Market Abuse Directive on Criminal Sanctions (2014/57/EU), only serious cases and market manipulations committed intentionally are covered by Article 6 of the Market Abuse Directive on Criminal Sanctions (2014/57/EU). **B.15.09**

The criminal penalties for committing market manipulation must be effective, proportionate, and dissuasive (Article 7 Market Abuse Directive on Criminal Sanctions (2014/57/EU)). Pursuant to Article 7(2) of the Market Abuse Directive on Criminal Sanctions (2014/57/EU), this means that the criminal offence of committing market manipulation must be punishable by a maximum term of imprisonment of at least four years. However, this limitation does not apply to inciting, aiding, and abetting, or attempts to commit market manipulation. **B.15.10**

Member States must also take the measures necessary to ensure that legal as well as natural persons can be held liable for offences committed for their benefit by any person, acting either individually or as part of an organ of the legal person (Article 8(1) Market Abuse Directive on Criminal Sanctions (2014/57/EU)). However, this requires that such a person is in a leading position within the legal entity, as defined by Article 8(1)(a) to (c) of the Market Abuse Directive on Criminal Sanctions (2014/57/EU). Also, the lack of supervision or control must constitute a criminal offence, where such omission made the commission of market manipulation possible (Article 8(2) Market Abuse Directive on Criminal Sanctions (2014/57/EU)). Finally, in these cases a legal person must be subject to effective, proportionate, and dissuasive sanctions, which shall include criminal or non-criminal fines and may include other sanctions, as defined in Article 9 of the Market Abuse Directive on Criminal Sanctions (2014/57/EU). **B.15.11**

The jurisdiction over these offences is governed by Article 10 of the Market Abuse Directive on Criminal Sanctions (2014/57/EU), according to which a Member State shall have jurisdiction over an offence when this offence has been committed in whole or in part within its territory or by one of its nationals, at least in cases where the act is an offence in the place where it was committed. **B.15.12**

Civil liability

B.15.13 Civil liability for the violation of the prohibition of market manipulation is addressed in the Market Abuse Regulation or any of its accompanying directives or regulations. Therefore, in general, the national laws of the Member States apply.[7]

[7] See Part A—Private Enforcement of the Market Abuse Regulation in European Law for further details.

Article 16: Prevention and detection of market abuse

1. Market operators and investment firms that operate a trading venue shall establish and maintain effective arrangements, systems and procedures aimed at preventing and detecting insider dealing, market manipulation and attempted insider dealing and market manipulation, in accordance with Articles 31 and 54 of Directive 2014/65/EU.

A person referred to in the first subparagraph shall report orders and transactions, including any cancellation or modification thereof, that could constitute insider dealing, market manipulation or attempted insider dealing or market manipulation to the competent authority of the trading venue without delay.

2. Any person professionally arranging or executing transactions shall establish and maintain effective arrangements, systems and procedures to detect and report suspicious orders and transactions. Where such a person has a reasonable suspicion that an order or transaction in any financial instrument, whether placed or executed on or outside a trading venue, could constitute insider dealing, market manipulation or attempted insider dealing or market manipulation, the person shall notify the competent authority as referred to in paragraph 3 without delay.
3. Without prejudice to Article 22, persons professionally arranging or executing transactions shall be subject to the rules of notification of the Member State in which they are registered or have their head office, or, in the case of a branch, the Member State where the branch is situated. The notification shall be addressed to the competent authority of that Member State.
4. The competent authorities as referred to in paragraph 3 receiving the notification of suspicious orders and transactions shall transmit such information immediately to the competent authorities of the trading venues concerned.
5. In order to ensure consistent harmonisation of this Article, ESMA shall develop draft regulatory technical standards to determine:
   (a) appropriate arrangements, systems and procedures for persons to comply with the requirements established in paragraphs 1 and 2; and
   (b) the notification templates to be used by persons to comply with the requirements established in paragraphs 1 and 2.

ESMA shall submit those draft regulatory technical standards to the Commission by 3 July 2016.

Power is delegated to the Commission to adopt the regulatory technical standards referred to in the first subparagraph in accordance with Articles 10 to 14 of Regulation (EU) No 1095/2010.

Relevant Technical Standards:
Commission Delegated Regulation (EU) 2016/957 of 9 March 2016 supplementing Regulation (EU) No 596/2014 of the European Parliament and of the Council with regard to regulatory technical standards for the appropriate arrangements, systems and procedures as well as notification templates to be used for preventing, detecting and reporting abusive practices or suspicious orders or transactions (OJ L 160 (17 June 2016) 1).

I. General Principles

Overview

B.16.01 The (public) enforcement of the Market Abuse Regulation is based on a cooperation between ESMA and the supervisory authorities of the Member States. However, since market abuse occurs at trading venues under the supervision of market operators and investments firms, Article 16(1) obliges them to maintain an effective system to prevent and detect insider dealing and market manipulation. Article 16(2) also establishes a reporting requirement for persons professionally arranging or executing transactions concerning suspicious orders or transactions in the Member State in which they are registered (Article 16(3)). The competent authorities then have to transmit such information to the competent authorities of the trading venues concerned (Article 16(4)). Finally, ESMA is empowered to develop regulatory technical standards (Article 16(5)).

Historical background

B.16.02 The (former) Market Abuse Directive (2003/6/EC) already contained an obligation for Member States to ensure that market operators should adopt structural provisions aimed at preventing and detecting market manipulation practices (Article 6(6) Market Abuse Directive (2003/6/EC)). Also, Member States were required to ensure that any person professionally arranging transactions in financial instruments who reasonably suspects that a transaction might constitute insider dealing or market manipulation should notify the competent authority without delay (Article 6(9) Market Abuse Directive (2003/6/EC)). Finally,

Article 6(10) 7th indent of the Market Abuse Directive (2003/6/EC) empowered the Commission to implement technical arrangements, a provision that was used by the Commission to enact the Commission Directive 2004/72/EC.[1] In contrast to this regime established by the (former) Market Abuse Directive (2003/6/EC), Article 16 is more precise in addressing market operators and investment firms operating a trading venue directly and setting out rules to determine the applicable notification rules.

II. Arrangements, Systems, and Procedures to Prevent Market Abuse (Article 16(1))

Pursuant to Article 16(1), market operators (Article 3(1)(5)[2]) and investment firms (Article 3(1)(2)[3]) operating a trading venue (Article 3(1)(10)[4]) must establish and maintain effective arrangements, systems, and procedures aimed at preventing and detecting insider dealing, market manipulation, and attempted insider dealing and market manipulation, in accordance with Articles 31 and 54 of the Markets in Financial Instruments Directive II (2014/65/EU). This means in particular that they must report orders and transactions, including any cancellation or modification thereof, that could constitute insider dealing, market manipulation, or attempted insider dealing or market manipulation to the competent authority of the trading venue without delay (Article 16(1)(2)). In this regard, a reasonable suspicion that an order or transaction constitutes a market abuse is sufficient. Since Article 16(1)(2) establishes only a reporting requirement the standard for this reasonable suspicion is low. In the case of a violation of the obligations under Article 16(1), the competent authorities of the Member States must undertake appropriate administrative sanctions (Article 30(1)[5]). **B.16.03**

III. Detection and Reporting of Suspicious Orders and Transactions (Article 16(2))

Pursuant to Article 16(2), any person professionally arranging or executing transactions (Article 3(1)(28)[6]) must establish and maintain effective arrangements, **B.16.04**

[1] Commission Directive 2004/72/EC of 29 April 2004 implementing Directive 2003/6/EC of the European Parliament and of the Council as regards accepted market practices, the definition of inside information in relation to derivatives on commodities, the drawing up of lists of insiders, the notification of managers' transactions and the notification of suspicious transactions (OJ L 162 (30 April 2004) 70).

[2] See art 3 n 9.

[3] See art 3 n 6.

[4] See art 3 n 14.

[5] See art 30 n 10 ff.

[6] See art 3 n 39.

systems, and procedures to detect and report suspicious orders and transactions. If such a person has a reasonable suspicion that an order or transaction in any financial instrument, whether placed or executed on or outside a trading venue, could constitute insider dealing, market manipulation, or attempted insider dealing or market manipulation, the person must notify the competent authority as set out in Article 16(3) without delay.

IV. Notification System (Article 16(3))

B.16.05 Article 16(3) governs which notification rules are applicable for the persons professionally arranging or executing transactions (Article 3(1)(28)[7]). Pursuant to Article 16(3), persons professionally arranging or executing transactions must comply with the notification rules of the Member State in which they are registered or have their head office. In the case of a branch, the notification rules of the Member States apply where the branch is situated. The persons professionally arranging or executing transactions must address the notification to the competent authority of that Member State. If the persons professionally arranging or executing transactions apply the notification rules of another Member State, they violate their obligations under Article 16(2) and can be subject to sanctions imposed by the competent authority of the Member State in which the notification rules are applicable.

V. Transmission of Notifications (Article 16(4))

B.16.06 Pursuant to Article 16(4), the competent authority as referred to in Article 16(3) must transmit the information immediately to the trading venues concerned.

VI. Development of Technical Regulatory Standards (Article 16(5))

B.16.07 ESMA has, pursuant to Article 16(5), the competence to develop regulatory technical standards to determine appropriate arrangements, systems, and procedures for persons to comply with the requirements established in Article 16(1) and (2) and the notification templates to be used by persons to comply with the requirements established in Article 16(1) and (2). The power to adopt the regulatory technical standard is delegated to the Commission (Article 16(5)(3)). This

[7] See art 3 n 39.

technical standard (Commission Delegated Regulation (EU) No 2016/957) was adopted by the Commission on 9 March 2016.

VII. Prevention and Detection of Market Abuse and Compliance

Article 16 addresses only the reporting obligations of market operators, investment firms, persons professionally arranging or executing transactions, and the competent authorities. However, similar reporting obligations do also exist for officers and directors of listed corporations, although these reporting requirements are not based on the Market Abuse Regulation but on the applicable corporate law of the Member States. Therefore, the obligations and requirements set out in Article 16 have no influence on these corporate duties. **B.16.08**

3

DISCLOSURE REQUIREMENTS

Article 17: Public disclosure of inside information

1. An issuer shall inform the public as soon as possible of inside information which directly concerns that issuer.

   The issuer shall ensure that the inside information is made public in a manner which enables fast access and complete, correct and timely assessment of the information by the public and, where applicable, in the officially appointed mechanism referred to in Article 21 of Directive 2004/109/EC of the European Parliament and the Council. The issuer shall not combine the disclosure of inside information to the public with the marketing of its activities. The issuer shall post and maintain on its website for a period of at least five years, all inside information it is required to disclose publicly.

   This Article shall apply to issuers who have requested or approved admission of their financial instruments to trading on a regulated market in a Member State or, in the case of instruments only traded on an MTF or on an OTF, issuers who have approved trading of their financial instruments on an MTF or an OTF or have requested admission to trading of their financial instruments on an MTF in a Member State.

2. An emission allowance market participant shall publicly, effectively and in a timely manner disclose inside information concerning emission allowances which it holds in respect of its business, including aviation activities as specified in Annex I to Directive 2003/87/EC or installations within the meaning of Article 3(e) of that Directive which the participant concerned, or its parent undertaking or related undertaking, owns or controls or for the operational matters of which the participant, or its parent undertaking or related undertaking, is responsible, in whole or in part. With regard to installations, such disclosure shall include information relevant to the capacity and utilisation of installations, including planned or unplanned unavailability of such installations.

The first subparagraph shall not apply to a participant in the emission allowance market where the installations or aviation activities that it owns, controls or is responsible for, in the preceding year have had emissions not exceeding a minimum threshold of carbon dioxide equivalent and, where they carry out combustion activities, have had a rated thermal input not exceeding a minimum threshold.

The Commission shall be empowered to adopt delegated acts in accordance with Article 35 establishing a minimum threshold of carbon dioxide equivalent and a minimum threshold of rated thermal input for the purposes of the application of the exemption provided for in the second subparagraph of this paragraph.

3. The Commission shall be empowered to adopt delegated acts in accordance with Article 35 specifying the competent authority for the notifications of paragraphs 4 and 5 of this Article.
4. An issuer or an emission allowance market participant, may, on its own responsibility, delay disclosure to the public of inside information provided that all of the following conditions are met:
   (a) immediate disclosure is likely to prejudice the legitimate interests of the issuer or emission allowance market participant;
   (b) delay of disclosure is not likely to mislead the public;
   (c) the issuer or emission allowance market participant is able to ensure the confidentiality of that information.

In the case of a protracted process that occurs in stages and that is intended to bring about, or that results in, a particular circumstance or a particular event, an issuer or an emission allowance market participant may on its own responsibility delay the public disclosure of inside information relating to this process, subject to points (a), (b) and (c) of the first subparagraph.

Where an issuer or emission allowance market participant has delayed the disclosure of inside information under this paragraph, it shall inform the competent authority specified under paragraph 3 that disclosure of the information was delayed and shall provide a written explanation of how the conditions set out in this paragraph were met, immediately after the information is disclosed to the public. Alternatively, Member States may provide that a record of such an explanation is to be provided only upon the request of the competent authority specified under paragraph 3.

5. In order to preserve the stability of the financial system, an issuer that is a credit institution or a financial institution, may, on its own responsibility, delay the public disclosure of inside information, including information which is related to a temporary liquidity problem and, in particular, the need to receive temporary liquidity assistance from a central bank or lender of last resort, provided that all of the following conditions are met:

(a) the disclosure of the inside information entails a risk of undermining the financial stability of the issuer and of the financial system;
(b) it is in the public interest to delay the disclosure;
(c) the confidentiality of that information can be ensured; and
(d) the competent authority specified under paragraph 3 has consented to the delay on the basis that the conditions in points (a), (b) and (c) are met.

6. For the purposes of points (a) to (d) of paragraph 5, an issuer shall notify the competent authority specified under paragraph 3 of its intention to delay the disclosure of the inside information and provide evidence that the conditions set out in points (a), (b) and (c) of paragraph 5 are met. The competent authority specified under paragraph 3 shall consult, as appropriate, the national central bank or the macro-prudential authority, where instituted, or, alternatively, the following authorities:
   (a) where the issuer is a credit institution or an investment firm the authority designated in accordance with Article 133(1) of Directive 2013/36/EU of the European Parliament and of the Council;
   (b) in cases other than those referred to in point (a), any other national authority responsible for the supervision of the issuer.

The competent authority specified under paragraph 3 shall ensure that disclosure of the inside information is delayed only for a period as is necessary in the public interest. The competent authority specified under paragraph 3 shall evaluate at least on a weekly basis whether the conditions set out in points (a), (b) and (c) of paragraph 5 are still met.

If the competent authority specified under paragraph 3 does not consent to the delay of disclosure of the inside information, the issuer shall disclose the inside information immediately.

This paragraph shall apply to cases where the issuer does not decide to delay the disclosure of inside information in accordance with paragraph 4.

Reference in this paragraph to the competent authority specified under paragraph 3 is without prejudice to the ability of the competent authority to exercise its functions in any of the ways referred to in Article 23(1).

7. Where disclosure of inside information has been delayed in accordance with paragraph 4 or 5 and the confidentiality of that inside information is no longer ensured, the issuer or the emission allowance market participant shall disclose that inside information to the public as soon as possible.

This paragraph includes situations where a rumour explicitly relates to inside information the disclosure of which has been delayed in accordance with paragraph 4 or 5, where that rumour is sufficiently accurate to indicate that the confidentiality of that information is no longer ensured.

8. Where an issuer or an emission allowance market participant, or a person acting on their behalf or for their account, discloses any inside information to any third party in the normal course of the exercise of an employment, profession or duties as referred to in Article 10(1), they must make complete and effective public disclosure of that information, simultaneously in the case of an intentional disclosure, and promptly in the case of a non-intentional disclosure. This paragraph shall not apply if the person receiving the information owes a duty of confidentiality, regardless of whether such duty is based on a law, on regulations, on articles of association, or on a contract.
9. Inside information relating to issuers whose financial instruments are admitted to trading on an SME growth market, may be posted on the trading venue's website instead of on the website of the issuer where the trading venue chooses to provide this facility for issuers on that market.
10. In order to ensure uniform conditions of application of this Article, ESMA shall develop draft implementing technical standards to determine:
    (a) the technical means for appropriate public disclosure of inside information as referred to in paragraphs 1, 2, 8 and 9; and
    (b) the technical means for delaying the public disclosure of inside information as referred to in paragraphs 4 and 5.

ESMA shall submit those draft implementing technical standards to the Commission by 3 July 2016.

Power is conferred on the Commission to adopt the implementing technical standards referred to in the first subparagraph in accordance with Article 15 of Regulation (EU) No 1095/2010.

11. ESMA shall issue guidelines to establish a non-exhaustive indicative list of the legitimate interests of issuers, as referred to in point (a) of paragraph 4, and of situations in which delay of disclosure of inside information is likely to mislead the public as referred to in point (b) of paragraph 4.

I. General Remarks

Overview and structure of Article 17

Successor of Article 6 of the (former) Market Abuse Directive (2003/6/EC), Article 17 lays down the general legal regime of the so-called 'ad hoc', 'continuous' or 'ongoing' public disclosure of inside information, aimed at avoiding insider dealing and ensuring that investors are not misled.[1] **B.17.01**

Article 17(1) states that issuers should inform the public as soon as possible of all inside information which directly concerns them. This disclosure should be made in an appropriate way, enabling the information to be accessed quickly for complete, correct, and timely assessment by the public. Kept distinct from the issuer's marketing of its activities, such information must be posted and maintained on a website for a period of at least five years. **B.17.02**

Article 17(2) contains an equivalent provision with reference to emission allowance market participants, required to disclose inside information concerning emission allowances which they hold in respect of their businesses publicly, effectively, and in a timely manner. **B.17.03**

Taking into account conflicting confidentiality imperatives, Article 17(4) and (5) authorizes issuers and emission allowance market participants, under their own responsibility, to delay disclosure to the public of inside information in two types of situations. **B.17.04**

The first situation concerns all issuers and emission allowance market participants, authorized by Article 17(4) to delay disclosure of the inside information when immediate publication is likely to prejudice their legitimate interests, provided that the delay is not likely to mislead the public and that the issuer or emission allowance market participant is able to ensure the confidentiality of that information. The process is subject to an *ex post* reporting to the national competent authority, which must be informed that disclosure was delayed and provided with a written explanation of how the aforementioned conditions were met, unless national law only requires such an explanation upon request of the competent authority. **B.17.05**

Designed to preserve the stability of the financial system, the second situation concerns specifically credit or financial institutions, authorized by Article 17(5) to delay the public disclosure of inside information, notably related to the need to receive temporary liquidity assistance from a central bank, provided that: the disclosure of the inside information entails a risk of undermining the financial stability of the issuer and of the financial system; the delay is in the public interest; the confidentiality of that information can be ensured; and the national competent authority has consented to the delay. **B.17.06**

---

[1] Recital (49).

B.17.07 In both types of situations, where disclosure of inside information has been delayed and the confidentiality of that inside information is no longer ensured, the issuer or the emission allowance market participant shall publicly disclose the said information as soon as possible (Article 17(7)).

B.17.08 Article 17(8) sets the anti-selective disclosure rule, forbidding a lawful passing of inside information to a third party without simultaneously or promptly making a complete and effective public disclosure of that information, unless the third party is bound by a duty of confidentiality.

B.17.09 These level 1 provisions are supplemented by:

- a Regulation 2016/522/EU as regards the disclosure thresholds and the competent authority for notifications of delays;
- a Commission implementing regulation 2016/1055 of 29 June 2016 laying down technical standards with regard to the technical means for appropriate public disclosure of inside information and for delaying the public disclosure of inside information;
- ESMA Guidelines dated of 20 October 2016 on delay in the disclosure of inside information, establishing an indicative list of the legitimate interests of issuers and of situations in which delay of disclosure of inside information is likely to mislead the public.[2]

Although the substance of the provisions remains, the new regime brings in a number of noteworthy changes. Some of the changes are highly visible eg:

- the transfer in Article 17 of provisions previously included in a level 2 directive regarding the technical means of publicly disclosing inside information;[3]
- the possibility for issuers whose financial instruments are admitted to trading on an SME growth market to post their inside information on the trading venue's website instead of on their own website where the trading venue chooses to provide this facility for issuers (Article 17(9));
- the special provision covering the delay of disclosure in a protracted process, as a result of the amendment to the definition of inside information;
- the specification that immediate disclosure is mandated when the confidentiality condition for delaying disclosure is no longer fulfilled, including in the case of rumours (Article 17(7));
- in case of delay, the requirement to inform the national competent authority immediately after the information is disclosed to the public and to provide, if the Member State has elected this option, a written explanation of how the conditions for the delay were met;

[2] ESMA, 'MAR Guidelines: Delay in the disclosure of inside information (ESMA/2016/1478)' (20 October 2016) www.esma.org.

[3] See Market Abuse Implementation Directive (2003/124/EC).

- the introduction of an additional possibility for credit or financial institutions to delay disclosure of inside information in order to preserve the stability of the financial system.

Other changes, at least as important, are less easily apparent to the readers of Article 17. **B.17.10**

Some changes are only indirect as side-effects of amendments in the definitions or in the scope of the Market Abuse Regulation. Regarding the notion of inside information, the codification of the ECJ *Markus Geltl v Daimler AG*[4] ruling necessarily impacts on the perimeter of the disclosure requirement. As for the subjective scope of Article 17, new actors are now included due to the extension of the Market Abuse Regulation to issuers that consented to the trading of their financial instruments on MTFs or OTFs and to emission allowance market participants. **B.17.11**

Other changes result from the new distribution of European provisions between the different levels of regulation, where some ex-level 2 provisions have been transferred to level 1 (means of public disclosure) and to level 3 (legitimate interests for delay), or have simply disappeared (time limit for public disclosure). **B.17.12**

Finally, one should also take into account certain legislative non-changes, which may enlighten the interpretation of Article 17 in the sense that they are eloquently indicative of the legislator's intentions to maintain the legal regime put in place in the (former) Market Abuse Directive (2003/6/EC) despite the criticism. In particular, the rejection of the heavily supported proposal to distinguish the 'inside information' that triggers the prohibition of insider dealing and the 'relevant information' that triggers the public disclosure requirement shows a profound attachment at the European level to the so called 'one-step model', where the same notion of inside information serves both purposes. The tension on this unified system serving two functions that are partially distinct only increases with the expansion of the definition of inside information and the disappearance of the comfort brought to issuers by previous level 2 provisions authorising them to wait to promptly inform the public until the coming into existence of an event. **B.17.13**

Undisputedly, Article 17 is one of the cornerstone provisions of EU securities regulation. Its reach goes far beyond the mere preventative function of insider dealing induced by its inclusion in the Market Abuse Regulation as it forms the European legal general basis for ad hoc disclosure, one of the three pillars of listed issuers' transparency, beside periodic and occasional disclosure.[5] **B.17.14**

---

[4] Case C-19/11 *Markus Geltl v Daimler AG* ECLI:EU:C:2012:397.

[5] See n 3.

Historical development

B.17.15 The history of the issuer ad hoc disclosure regime is as old as the EU securities regulation itself. Its genesis goes back to the very origins and its consecration occurred long before the prohibition of insider dealing.

B.17.16 The importance of such a requirement for the development of a European securities market was underlined by the 1966 Segré Report, where the CEE-Commission insisted on the necessity of ensuring, in addition to the annual publication of accounts, 'a continuous flow of information for shareholders and the public at large, providing accurate facts and figures on company operations', 'a steady flow of intelligence to shareholders and the public ... indispensable if investors and their advisers are to be enabled to take fully informed investment decisions'.[6] The Commission doubted that this objective could be reached without compulsory intervention, as the French example confirmed,[7] and, taking into account the problems that such a legal requirement raises for listed companies in relation to their shareholders, employees, competitors and the tax authorities, considered essential to place European firms on an equal footing through harmonization. A harmonized principle was therefore suggested according to which 'Any new factor which might have a major bearing on the firm's situation or profit expectations (for instance investment programmes, important agreements of contracts) should be brought to the public's notice almost at once'.[8]

B.17.17 Putting this doctrine in action, the Commission formulated in its recommendation to the Member States of 25 July 1977 concerning a European code of conduct relating to transactions in transferable securities, the two following supplementary principles:

> 12. Every company whose securities are dealt in on the market should publish periodically, and at least every six months, information which is clear, precise, complete and up-to-date concerning its business operations, results, and financial position. Any fact or important decision capable of having an appreciable effect on the price of securities should also be made public without delay.
> 13. When a fact or important decision, referred to in the preceding provision, cannot be made public without delay, for example because certain formalities have not yet been completed or because the company would be seriously prejudiced as a result, but the company nevertheless considers that there is a risk of leaks, the company should inform the competent authorities of the position. The latter should take the necessary steps to safeguard the market's proper operation until the relevant fact or decision can be made public. In particular they may, if this step appears unavoidable, suspend transactions for the necessary period.

---

[6] European Commission, 'The development of a European capital market—Report of a Group of Experts appointed by the EEC Commission' (1966) 228.

[7] On the development on the ad hoc disclosure requirement in France see A Pietrancosta, 'Le droit des sociétés sous l'effet des impératifs financiers et boursiers, thèse Paris 1' (1999, edn Transactive 2000 (CD-ROM)) and Lulu.com (paper) n° 1116 ff.

[8] ibid 229.

Taken a step further, the continuous disclosure requirement of price-sensitive information found its first legal consecration in the Stock Exchange Listing Directive (79/279/EEC) coordinating the conditions for the admission of securities to an official stock exchange listing. In a paragraph 5 entitled 'Additional information', Schedule C of the directive dedicated to the 'obligations of companies whose shares are admitted to official listing on a stock exchange' stated the following: **B.17.18**

> The company must inform the public as soon as possible of any major new developments in its sphere of activity which are not public knowledge and which may, by virtue of their effect on its assets and liabilities or financial position or on the general course of its business, lead to substantial movements in the prices of its shares.
>
> The competent authorities may, however, exempt the company from this requirement, if the disclosure of particular information is such as to prejudice the legitimate interests of the company.

For issuers whose debt securities are admitted to official listing on a stock exchange, the Schedule D para 4 of the directive contained an analogous but not identical requirement: **B.17.19**

> The undertaking must inform the public as soon as possible of any major new developments in its sphere of activity which are not public knowledge and which may significantly affect its ability to meet its commitments.
>
> The competent authorities may, however, exempt the undertaking from this obligation at its request if the disclosure of particular information would be such as to prejudice the legitimate interests of the undertaking.

Article 17 of the directive defined the process through which the required disclosure had to be made available to the public. **B.17.20**

Interestingly, the Insider Dealing Directive (1989/592/EEC) was exclusively devoted to the prohibition and made no reference to—much less integrated—the positive prescription of issuer ongoing disclosure. Further evidence of this absence of coordination could be found in the different notions of information triggering the new-born prohibition and the ten-year-old positive requirement. **B.17.21**

The Stock Exchange Listing Directive (79/279/EEC) was later on replaced by Stock Exchange Listing Directive (2001/34/EC) with two articles (Article 68 for shares and Article 81 for debt securities) reproducing literally the 1979 Schedules C and D provisions. Details relating to the means of publication were consolidated in Articles 102 ff and 69/82 for equivalence of information. **B.17.22**

Soon after the adoption of the Stock Exchange Listing Directive (2001/34/EC), the DG Internal Market suggested aligning the definition of price-sensitive information to be published on an ad hoc basis with the definition of material information to be included in the listing particulars or prospectuses required **B.17.23** respectively by Directive 80/390 of 17 March 1980 on admission to listing and Directive 89/298 of 17 April 1989 on public offerings of securities.[9]

B.17.24 This option was finally abandoned and replaced by a totally different option, enshrined in the (former) Market Abuse Directive (2003/6/EC). Departing from the path initiated and followed from the outset, it was decided to put an end to the two-step model: the issuer ad hoc disclosure regime was consequently transferred to the new market abuse directive[10] and based on the same notion of inside information, which became the single triggering event for all the duties set out in the (former) Market Abuse Directive (2003/6/EC) ie the prohibition to enter into transactions, the confidentiality duty and the disclosure duty placed upon the issuers.

B.17.25 Thus, Article 6(1) of the (former) Market Abuse Directive (2003/6/EC) mandated Member States to 'ensure that issuers of financial instruments inform the public as soon as possible of inside information which directly concerns the said issuers' and 'that issuers, for an appropriate period, post on their Internet sites all inside information that they are required to disclose publicly'. However, according to Article 6(2), an issuer 'may under his own responsibility delay the public disclosure of inside information, as referred to in paragraph 1, such as not to prejudice his legitimate interests provided that such omission would not be likely to mislead the public and provided that the issuer is able to ensure the confidentiality of that information. Member States may require that an issuer shall without delay inform the competent authority of the decision to delay the public disclosure of inside information'. For its part, Article 6(3) introduced an anti-selective disclosure rule, forbidding an issuer to lawfully pass inside information to a third party without simultaneously or promptly making a complete and effective public disclosure of that information, unless the third party is bound by a duty of confidentiality.

B.17.26 Article 6 was supplemented by the Market Abuse Implementation Directive (2003/124/EC), whose Article 2 defined the means of public disclosure of inside information, by reference to Article 102(1) and Article 103 Stock Exchange Listing Directive (2001/34/EC) and the time-limit of the disclosure, providing issuers with a deferred mechanism until the occurrence of the relevant event; and whose Article 3 contained a non-exhaustive list of legitimate interests justifying the delay of public disclosure and set the conditions for ensuring the confidentiality of inside information. In July 2007, the CESR issued a set of guidance dealing

[9] European Commission, 'Towards an EU Regime on Transparency Obligations of Issuers whose Securities are Admitted to Trading on a Regulated Market: Consultation Document of the Services of the Internal Market Directorate General' (11 July 2001).

[10] See art 20 of the (former) Market Abuse Directive (2003/6/EC), repealing art 68(1) and 81(1) Stock Exchange Listing Directive (2001/34/EC).

with situations in which there are legitimate interests for an issuer to delay the publication of inside information.[11]

With the adoption of the Transparency Directive (2013/50/EU), inside information disclosed under Article 6 of the (former) Market Abuse Directive (2003/6/EC) by issuers whose securities are traded on a regulated market fell into the category of 'regulated information'[12] and became subject to the legal consequences attached in terms of home Member State control, languages, public access and equivalence, instead of the prescriptions provided in the Stock Exchange Listing Directive (2001/34/EC).[13] **B.17.27**

II. The Requirement to Disclose Inside Information Publicly

The general requirement of continuous disclosure

The concerned issuers

Article 17(1)(3) specifies the subjective scope of the public disclosure requirement laid down in the first subparagraph, which covers: **B.17.28**

> issuers who have requested or approved admission of their financial instruments to trading on a regulated market in a Member State;

or, in the case of instruments exclusively traded on an MTF or on an OTF:

> issuers who have approved trading of their financial instruments on an MTF or an OTF or have requested admission to trading of their financial instruments on an MTF in a Member State.

This coverage is more extensive than in the (former) Market Abuse Directive (2003/6/EC), owing to the inclusion of issuers whose financial instruments are traded on MTFs and OTFs, but more restrictive than the Market Abuse Regulation's general scope in the sense that it is limited to financial instruments admitted to trading with the issuer's consent and leaves out unlisted financial derivatives.[14] **B.17.29**

For issuers whose financial instruments are traded on MTFs, this inclusion entails major consequences from an organizational viewpoint.[15] Since on MTFs **B.17.30**

---

[11] 'Second set of CESR guidance on the MAD, CESR/06-562 b' (July 2007).

[12] Article 2(1)(k) of the Transparency Directive (2013/50/EU).

[13] See art 32 of the Transparency Directive (2013/50/EU), deleting arts 68, 69, 102, and 103 Stock Exchange Listing Directive (2001/34/EC).

[14] Article 2.

[15] For a critical view on such extension, C di Noia, 'Pending Issues in the Review of the European Market Abuse Rules' ECMI Policy Brief No (19 February 2012).

financial instruments may more easily be admitted and traded without the issuer's consent, it was nonetheless considered inappropriate to burden these issuers and their managers with additional publication obligations.

B.17.31 Recital (55) recognizes that the requirement to disclose inside information can be burdensome for SMEs whose financial instruments are admitted to trading on SME growth markets, 'given the costs of monitoring information in their possession and seeking legal advice about whether and when information needs to be disclosed. Nevertheless, prompt disclosure of inside information is essential to ensure investor confidence in those issuers. Therefore, ESMA should be able to issue guidelines which assist issuers to comply with the obligation to disclose inside information without compromising investor protection'.

B.17.32 No further distinction is made among issuers, which are all covered by the disclosure requirement regardless of their nationality,[16] their size, the types of markets their instruments are listed on, the types of instruments that they chose to list, their corporate form or their ownership structure. Since the Market Abuse Regulation defines an issuer as a legal entity, governed by either private or public law,[17] the disclosure requirement should in principle be analysed individually in a group context.[18]

The concerned information: reference to the notion of 'inside information', indicative of a one-step model

B.17.33 As evidenced in the historical development,[19] the decision was taken with the (former) Market Abuse Directive (2003/6/EC) to abandon the previous two-step model legislative framework, where the definition of information used for the ad hoc disclosure requirement differs from the one triggering the market abuse prohibitions, and to replace it with a one-step model, where the notion of inside information is a common constituent element from which derive all the duties set out in the Directive.

B.17.34 As a matter of principle, the Market Abuse Regulation walks in the footsteps of the (former) Market Abuse Directive (2003/6/EC) and continues to make the notion of inside information the cornerstone of its negative and positive requirements. The meaning of the 'inside information' whose disclosure is made compulsory by Article 17(1) should therefore be looked for in the general definition of the notion, set in Article 7, basically referring to private, precise and price-sensitive information.[20]

[16] As a result of the Market Abuse Regulation expansion to MTFs, many more non-EU issuers have become subject to its requirements: see Gibson Dunn, 'New European Market Abuse Regime: What Do non-EU Incorporated Issuers Need to Know?' (21 June 2016); Shearman & Sterling, 'EU Market Abuse Regulation: Implications for Non-EU Issuers with Securities Traded on an EU Market' (23 June 2016).

[17] According to art 3(1)(21) '"issuer" means a legal entity governed by private or public law, which issues or proposes to issue financial instruments, the issuer being, in case of depository receipts representing financial instruments, the issuer of the financial instrument represented'.

[18] See Philipp Koch, 'Disclosure of Inside Information' in Rüdiger Veil (ed), *European Capital Markets Law* (1st edn, Hart Publishing 2012) para 19 n 30 and 49 ff.

[19] See n 8.

[20] See the chapter on inside information.

In fact, the one-step model initiated in 2003 comes out strengthened through the Market Abuse Regulation, for two main reasons. **B.17.35**

First, the dual function of inside information is maintained in spite of the extension of the said notion, now including intermediate steps in a protracted process.[21] A priori, this inclusion obeys a logic of transparency since it consolidates the interpretation of the ECJ in *Markus Geltl v Daimler AG*, which was not an insider dealing case, but a disclosure case.[22] Indeed, the ECJ based its literal and teleological interpretation on the fact that several situations eligible for a delay in disclosure, specified by the Market Abuse Implementation Directive (2003/124/EC), were 'typical examples of intermediate steps in processes',[23] with the risk that the exclusion of intermediate steps in a protracted process would undermine the transparency objective of the (former) Market Abuse Directive (2003/6/EC),[24] this risk being all the greater given 'that it would be possible, in certain circumstances, to regard the outcome of a specific process as an intermediate step in another, larger process'.[25] However, the *Geltl* preliminary ruling amply evidences the weight of insider dealing considerations in the reasoning of the ECJ, particularly the importance for the integrity of capital markets that investors be 'placed on an equal footing and protected against the improper use of insider information',[26] and therefore the interpretation bias and the contamination effect embedded in a one-step model. **B.17.36**

Secondly, and more importantly, the Market Abuse Regulation strongly reaffirms the change of path brought in 2003 despite widespread criticism.[27] Considered to be a lesser burden for its users, the one-step model was clearly reaffirmed. Legally, this reaffirmation is all the stronger that the replacement of the (former) Market Abuse Directive (2003/6/EC) by a European regulation will leave less room for manoeuvre in two-step-model countries. **B.17.37**

However, in addition to the aforementioned limit in the subjective scope of the disclosure requirement,[28] the reference to the general definition of inside information should be made under an important restriction: Article 17(1) only mandates **B.17.38**

---

[21] Article 7(2) and (3), recitals (16) and (17). Interestingly, the specific provisions inserted in the context of the *Geltl* case to differ disclosure when the inside information relates to a process that occurs in stages were removed, as well as the ones relaxing the conditions to delay such disclosure, see Jesper Lau Hansen, 'Say When: When Must an Issuer Disclose Inside Information?' Nordic & European Company Law Working Paper No 16-03 (19 September 2016) 19–27 https://papers.ssrn.com/sol3/papers.cfm?abstract_ id=2795993.

[22] See n 4; already, in the Second set of CESR guidance (n 11) 1.6.

[23] Case C-19/11 *Markus Geltl v Daimler AG* (n 4) para 32.

[24] ibid para 35.

[25] ibid para 37.

[26] ibid para 33; see also paras 34 and 36.

[27] See n 7.

[28] See n 10.

an issuer to publish inside information 'which directly concerns that issuer', when Article 7(1)(a) encompasses information 'relating, directly or indirectly, to one or more issuers'.

B.17.39 Unfortunately, this legal restriction leads to a distinction that is not easy to undertake in all certainty. As a first approximation, one could think of drawing the line between 'corporate information' and 'market information'. Inspired by the interpretation of the famous US SEC Rule 10b-5, corporate information 'typically comes from internal corporate sources and involves events or developments affecting the issuer's assets or earnings', whereas market information 'typically originates from sources other than the issuer and involves events or circumstances concerning or affecting the price or market for the issuer's securities and does not concern the issuer's assets or earning power'.[29] Although useful in most cases, the source-of-information criterion may not always be reliable since an 'outside' but private information, emanating from an external source, may also directly concern an issuer[30] and consequently be taken into account, under the implicit condition that the issuer holds it. A more objective delimitation, drawn from the first provision included in the Stock Exchange Listing Directive (79/279/EEC),[31] would include all information related to developments in the issuer's 'sphere of activity', which does not necessarily correspond with its sphere of influence, provided of course that the issuer has knowledge of the information.[32] However, a level of specificity regarding the impact of such developments on a particular issuer should be required in order to avoid excessive and redundant disclosure.[33] Thus, a combination of the two criteria could be advisable, resulting in the exclusion of any inside information that neither originates from within the issuer nor specifically affects it.[34]

B.17.40 This conclusion seems to reflect the opinion CESR expressed in its 2007 second set of guidance on the (former) Market Abuse Directive (2003/6/EC).[35] In this

---

[29] See S M Bainbridge, 'The Law and Economics of Insider Trading: A Comprehensive Primer' (2001) Working Paper University of California, Los Angeles. http://papers.ssrn.com/sol3/papers.cfm?abstract_id=261277. See also C di Noia and M Gargantini, 'Issuers at Midstream: Disclosure of Multistage Events in the Current and in the Proposed EU Market Abuse Regime' (2012) European Company and Financial Law Review 484.

[30] See Koch, 'Disclosure of Inside Information' (n 18) para 19 at 37 ff; for credit institutions see the results of the Supervisory Review and Evaluation Process (SREP) to be conducted in accordance with art 97 of Directive 2013/36/EU (CRD IV), 'Q&A, ESMA70-145-11' (6 July 2017) 10.

[31] See n 8.

[32] See for the UK, B McDonnell, 'Inside Information: A Guide to the Disclosure Rules' Compliance Officer Bulletin (2013) 108 (Aug) 1–42 at para 3.3.3.

[33] See P Staikouras, 'The Conundrum of the Market Abuse Directive Preventative Measures for EU Financial Services' Integration: In Search of Equilibrium between Market Integrity Enhancement and Undue Regulatory Encumbrance' (2008) 35 Legal Issues of Economic Integration 351, 356.

[34] See di Noia and Gargantini, 'Issuers at Midstream' (n 29); Staikouras, 'The Conundrum of the Market Abuse Directive Preventative Measures for EU Financial Services' Integration' (n 33) 356.

[35] CESR/06-562b (July 2007).

non-binding document, CESR presented two non-exhaustive lists of events that might constitute 'information which directly concerns the issuer' or 'information which indirectly concerns the issuer'.

The former consisted mostly but not exclusively in information stemming from the issuer: **B.17.41**

> Operating business performance; Changes in control and control agreements; Changes in management and supervisory boards; Changes in auditors or any other information related to the auditors' activity; Operations involving the capital or the issue of debt securities or warrants to buy or subscribe securities; Decisions to increase or decrease the share capital; Mergers, splits and spin-offs; Purchase or disposal of equity interests or other major assets or branches of corporate activity; Restructurings or reorganizations that have an effect on the issuer's assets and liabilities, financial position or profits and losses; Decisions concerning buy-back programmes or transactions in other listed financial instruments; Changes in the class rights of the issuer's own listed shares; Filing of petitions in bankruptcy or the issuing of orders for bankruptcy proceedings; Legal disputes; Revocation or cancellation of credit lines by one or more banks; Dissolution or verification of a cause of dissolution; Changes in the assets' value; Insolvency of relevant debtors; Reduction of real properties' values; Physical destruction of uninsured goods; New licences, patents, registered trade marks; Decrease or increase in value of financial instruments in portfolio; Decrease in value of patents or rights or intangible assets due to market innovation; Receiving acquisition bids for relevant assets; Innovative products or processes; Product liability or environmental damages cases; Changes in expected earnings or losses; Orders received from customers, their cancellation or important changes; Withdrawal from or entry into new core business areas; Changes in the investment policy of the issuer; Ex-dividend date, changes in dividend payment date and amount of the dividend; changes in dividend policy.[36] The breadth of this list seems to contradict the view that issuers are only expected to inform of matters that will be made public at a certain time, either because the event to which the information is pertaining will become publicly known, or, more importantly, because the facts will appear in the public accounts published annually, semi-annually or quarterly.[37]

The information which 'indirectly' concerns the issuer consisted mostly but not exclusively in information stemming from outside the issuer: **B.17.42**

> Data and statistics published by public institutions disseminating statistics; The coming publication of rating agencies' reports; The coming publication of research, recommendations or suggestions concerning the value of listed financial instruments; Central bank decisions concerning interest rates; Government's decisions concerning taxation, industry regulation, debt management, etc.; Decisions concerning changes in the governance rules of market indices, and especially as regards their composition; Regulated and unregulated markets' decisions concerning rules governing the markets; Competition and market authorities' decisions

[36] On dividends see 'Q&A, ESMA/2012/9' (9 January 2012).

[37] J L Hansen, 'The New Proposal for a European Union Directive on Market Abuse' (2002) 23(2) University of Pennsylvania Journal of International Economic Law 241. For France see the AMF, 'Guide to permanent information and management of inside information (DOC-2016-08)' (2016) 6 www.amf.fr.

concerning listed companies; Relevant orders by government bodies, regional or local authorities or other public organizations; A change in trading mode (e.g., information relating to knowledge that an issuer's financial instruments will be traded in another market segment: e.g. change from continuous trading to auction trading); a change of market maker or dealing conditions.

CESR noted that there is no legal basis to require prompt disclosure of such events because 'the issuer would usually either not be aware of the information before it was publicly announced, or, if they were aware, would be precluded from making any disclosure themselves until the other agency had made its announcement', adding, nevertheless, that 'if such events when they become public knowledge would have consequences directly affecting the issuer which would meet the tests for inside information, the disclosure requirement in Article 6 of MAD would apply at the relevant point'.

B.17.43 By contrast, CESR stated that 'in general, other than in exceptional circumstances or unless requested to comment by the competent regulator ... issuers are under no obligation to respond to speculation or market rumours which are without substance', explicitly distinguished from leaks,[38] which call for issuer action.[39] This distinction would apply to 'publications, eg articles published in the press or internet postings, which are not resulting from the issuer's initiative in relation to its disclosure obligations and that the issuer is aware of or ought reasonably to be aware of'.[40] ESMA follows the same path when it restricts the impossibility for an issuer to delay disclosure of inside information regarding the likelihood that the issuer will not meet its financial objectives to situations where such financial objectives were previously publicly announced, or when it rejects the delay of disclosure of inside information that is inconsistent with the market's expectations, if such expectations are based on the issuer's signals.[41] As explained in legal literature, true rumours are in general used by insiders to maximize their trading gains, while false rumours may be spread by opportunistic traders, thus potentially constituting different market abuses.[42] Besides the existence of grey areas between both categories, the treatment of rumours, in particular regarding issuers' reactions, significantly diverges among Member States,[43] as a reflection of

[38] See n 20.

[39] 'Third set of CESR guidance on the MAD, CESR/09-219' (15 May 2009) paras 64 ff. For a critical comment see di Noia and Gargantini, 'Issuers at Midstream' (n 29); di Noia, 'Pending Issues in the Review of the European Market Abuse Rules' (n 15); see for the UK: DTR 2.7; McDonnell, 'Inside information' (n 32) para 3.10.

[40] 'Third set of CESR guidance on the MAD, CESR/09-219' (15 May 2009) para 66.

[41] See n 19. On the requirement for issuers to publish profit warnings see for France, the AMF 'Guide to permanent information' (n 37) § 1.4.2.

[42] C di Noia and M Gargantini, 'The Market Abuse Directive Disclosure Regime in Practice' (2009) Rivista delle Società 24 (di Noia and Gargantini, 'Disclosure Regime in Practice').

[43] ibid; see also Koch, 'Disclosure of Inside Information' (n 18) para 19 at 93 ff; L Legein, *Le nouveau règlement Abus de Marché et ses conséquences pour les sociétés cotées belges* (TRV-RPS 2016) p. 479 spec no 46.

different national corporate and financial cultures, which could call for further European guidance.[44]

Absent a substantial definition, the condition that the information should directly concern the issuer was interpreted and implemented differently under the (former) Market Abuse Directive (2003/6/EC). Additional lists of events were sometimes drawn at national level, notably through competent authorities' guidelines, as in Germany.[45] Stock exchange rulebooks could also contain indications about the kinds of information that could qualify as inside information and that should consequently be disclosed publicly.[46] The replacement of a directive by a regulation, in reducing the room for national manoeuvre, somewhat undermines the value of these specifications. **B.17.44**

Except for the direct connection with the issuer, Article 17(1) does not contain any other limitation as to the type of inside information that must be disclosed. For instance, the existence of other disclosure rules, whether periodic or related to a specific transaction, should not exempt an issuer from complying with the obligation to make inside information public.[47] Conversely, the Market Abuse Regulation remains silent on a potentially sensitive issue, namely the articulation of its general inside information disclosure requirement with specific legal confidentiality requirements that may apply to issuers. Difficulties may arise when such situations cannot be dealt with through a delay in disclosure as they are, for example, in certain pre-insolvency proceedings.[48] Comparatively, an issuer could not escape publication owing to a mere confidentiality agreement.[49] **B.17.45**

The determination of the other legal elements conditioning the existence of inside information may also be a source of uncertainty, absent any binding secondary provisions. Without even mentioning the difficulty of assessing the price-sensitiveness of information based on the likely behaviour of a reasonable investor,[50] especially in volatile markets, issuers have to consider many kinds of circumstances or events, all together or separately, that exist or that may reasonably be expected to come into existence. As most circumstances and events **B.17.46**

---

[44] See di Noia and Gargantini, 'Disclosure Regime in Practice' (n 42).

[45] See Koch, 'Disclosure of Inside Information' (n 18) para 19 at 37.

[46] See eg NASDAQ First North Nordic: Rulebook 1 January 2016, citing: orders or investment decisions; co-operation agreements or other agreements of major importance; price or exchange rate changes; credit or customer losses; new joint ventures; research results; commencement or settlement of, or decisions rendered in, legal disputes; financial difficulties; decisions taken by authorities; shareholder agreements known to the company which pertain to the use of voting rights or transferability of the shares; market rumours; market making agreements; information regarding subsidiaries and affiliated companies; and significant deviation in financial result or financial position.

[47] See Koch, 'Disclosure of Inside Information' (n 18) para 19 at 52 ff.

[48] See for France, the AMF 'Guide to permanent information' (n 37) 21 ff.

[49] For France see AMF, Sanctions committee (1 October 2009) SAN-2009-30.

[50] See the chapter on inside information.

develop over time, the assessment of the point in time when they amount to inside information can be a delicate exercise and lead to several publications for the same event. By itself, disclosure of an anticipated negative outcome may also weaken an issuer's position, as it is the case when involved in ongoing legal proceedings.[51] Even spot operations/decisions may require some forms of internal or external approval, monitoring or checking. If the solution, previously based on level 2 provisions, requiring disclosure of an event not yet formalized[52] is likely to survive, the extent to which substance should supersede form is problematic because of the potential disruption effect of premature disclosure notably on corporate and governance decision-making processes.[53]

B.17.47 From a legal certainty viewpoint, the European Union approach, based on a principle-based disclosure requirement, contrasts with the event-specific approach favoured in the US, where there exists a number of particular events that issuers should report under the 1934 Securities and Exchange Act, through a Form 8-K.[54] Even if the number of the reportable events increased significantly in 2004,[55] after the passing of the Sarbanes-Oxley Act, somewhat reducing the gap between the two systems, these events remain specifically defined and detailed at length. Under the famous Rule 10b-5, prohibiting any act or omission resulting in fraud or deceit in connection with the purchase or sale of securities, and incidentally the primary instrument for regulating insider trading, the US Supreme Court decided in 2011 that companies are not subject to 'an affirmative duty to disclose any and all material information', disclosure being only required 'when necessary 'to make … statements made, in the light of the circumstances under which they were made, not misleading'.[56] The reluctance to create such a general duty precisely lies in the uncertainty as to when information becomes material and must be disclosed, and the risks of judicial second-guessing and of excessive liability imposed on listed companies owing to an effective private litigation system.[57]

---

[51] See Europeanissuers, 'Response to the European commission's call for evidence on the review of the MAD' (April 2009) Position 15 June 2009.

[52] Article 2(2) Market Abuse Implementation Directive (2003/124/EC).

[53] See K Langenbucher, 'Insider Trading: An Exercise in (Economic and Legal) Transplants' RTDF 2013/2014, 35.

[54] See T L Hazen, *The Law of Securities Regulation* (7th edn West Academic Publishing 2017) 330 ff.

[55] See SEC, 'Additional Form 8-K Disclosure Requirements and Acceleration of Filing Date' (25 March 2004).

[56] *Matrixx Initiatives, Inc. v Siracusano*, 131 S Ct 1309 (2011). See ESMA, reminding 'that when there is a change in a published inside information, and the change itself constitutes a new inside information, this new information is covered by the inside information's provisions within the Market Abuse Regulation, and the full process of public disclosure would have to take place (again)'. ESMA, 'Draft technical standards on the Market Abuse Regulation (ESMA/2015/1455)' para 223 (28 September 2015) www.esma.org.

[57] E Greene and O Schmid, 'Duty-Free Insider Trading?' (2013) Columbia Business Law Review 369.

In the EU, this uncertainty could be usefully reduced using level 2 measures or ESMA guidance in order to specify for instance the elements that make the most significant business operations precise enough to trigger the public disclosure requirement, based on the US Form 8-K or the UK Disclosure and Transparency Rules ('DTRs')[58] models. The replacement of the (former) Market Abuse Directive (2003/6/EC) with a Regulation even casts doubt on the compatibility of national detailed implementing prescriptions bringing some relief to issuers. In the meantime, since the responsibility lies on their shoulders, issuers would be well advised to implement appropriate internal procedures for assessing whether the information they hold is privileged or not, in order to determine whether and when such information should be published.[59] **B.17.48**

The timing of the disclosure

When inside information comes into existence, the concerned issuer is required to disclose it '*as soon as possible*'. The timing of the process is obviously one of the 'essential' conditions to ensure market integrity (recital (49)) but also market efficiency, since timely dissemination of information allows for accurate and quick valuation of securities. Against this background, one could be surprised by the lack of precision regarding the time-limit of the publication, knowing that the notion of 'possibility' can be interpreted more or less stringently, depending on the degree of relativity owing to factors internal or external from the issuer's viewpoint. This uncertainty of the *dies ad quem* adds to the aforementioned uncertainty of the *dies a quo*. The situation contrasts with the US, where a Form 8-K has to be filed, for most items, within four business days after the occurrence of an event triggering the disclosure requirement. **B.17.49**

Although the expression 'as soon as possible' has been in place since the Stock Exchange Listing Directive (79/279/EEC), little European guidance has been provided on the matter. In its 2007 report, the ESME group confirmed, unsurprisingly, the disharmony of national situations in Europe and sometimes the lack of enforcement of this legal requirement: 'The speed with which facts are considered as relevant and any necessary announcement is made varies from jurisdiction to jurisdiction; information is not always disclosed as soon as possible … Nowadays, in some jurisdictions acceptable delays are measured in hours; in others, days. Many regulators are not, in practice, applying the test as **B.17.50**

[58] See DTR 2 on 'Disclosure and control of inside information by issuers' (December 2016); McDonnell, 'Inside Information' (n 32).

[59] For France see the AMF 'Guide to permanent information' (n 37) 6. Note that recital (11) of the recent directive 2016/943 of 8 June 2016 on the protection of undisclosed know-how and business information (trade secrets) against their unlawful acquisition, use and disclosure (OJEU L 157/1, 15 June 2016) provides that the directive 'should not affect the application of Union or national rules that require the disclosure of information, including trade secrets, to the public or to public authorities'. For the UK see DTR 2.2.7.

written: they are not requiring disclosure as soon as possible'.[60] Divergent behaviours were particularly noticed relating to the publication of inside information arising within or without non-business hours or days, during or outside trading hours or days. Contrasting with the UK position,[61] in countries like France or Belgium, the NCA has traditionally favoured issuer disclosure outside trading hours, save exceptional circumstances,[62] although in France, this recommendation has not been reproduced in the 2016 AMF Guide to permanent disclosure, with the view to being fully compliant with the Market Abuse Regulation.

B.17.51 With regard to events that have not yet occurred, Article 2(2) of the Market Abuse Implementation Directive (2003/124/EC) provided issuers with some legal comfort, ordering Member States to 'ensure that issuers are deemed to have complied with [the disclosure requirement of inside information] where, upon the coming into existence of a set of circumstances or the occurrence of an event, albeit not yet formalized, the issuers have promptly informed the public thereof'. Following what has been called in some countries a 'principle of reality',[63] issuers were accordingly allowed to postpone disclosure until the triggering event came into existence, provided that they disclosed 'promptly' once this level of certainty is reached. Unlike the ordinary delay in disclosure, this deferred disclosure mechanism did not require any reporting to the authorities or proof of a legitimate interest.

B.17.52 This informal delay no longer exists, reinforcing the logic of a one-step model. Consequently, disclosure is required as soon as possible even for relatively uncertain events, unless formal delay can be used under public supervision. For some commentators, the call for disclosure 'as soon as possible' is not a call 'for immediate or prompt disclosure, but allows the issuer some latitude to analyse the development and in timing its disclosure and the content hereof'.[64] It indicates 'some tolerance for the fact that the disclosure could take some time to prepare'.[65] The requirement should indeed be understood as mandating that disclosure not be deferred unnecessarily[66] and the temptation be resisted to interpret a contrario

[60] AMF, 'Guide to permanent information' (n 37) 7.

[61] See McDonnell, 'Inside Information' (n 32) para 3.9.

[62] See for France, COB, 'Vade-mecum à l'attention des dirigeants des sociétés cotées sur la diffusion de l'information' Bull no 272 (September 1993); and for Belgium, FSMA, 'Obligations incombant aux émetteurs cotés sur un marché réglementé (Circulaire Émetteurs)' (30 June 2016); Legein, *Le nouveau règlement* (n 43) n 40.

[63] L Hellstén, 'Disclosure and delayed disclosure of inside information in the light of the EU Market Abuse Regulation' (University of Helsinki Faculty of Law, Master's thesis, February 2015).

[64] J L Hansen and D Moalem, 'The MAD Disclosure Regime and the Two-Fold Notion of Inside Information: The Available Solution' (2009) 4 Capital Markets Law Journal 323; Hansen, 'Say When' (n 21).

[65] NASDAQ, 'The Market Abuse Regulation and the Duty to Disclose Inside Information, Q&A on the Application of the MAR' (2016) para 2.8 www.nasdaq.com.

[66] On the questionability of the practice, previously accepted in some jurisdictions, offering issuers the possibility to postpone the disclosure of inside information until the next trading day if the markets have closed at the time of the event see NASDAQ (n 65) para 2.9.

the condition laid down in Article 17(4) that a delay in disclosure is only possible when 'immediate' disclosure is likely to prejudice the legitimate interests of the issuer.[67] As a result, the acceptability of the timing should depend on a case-by-case assessment of the appropriateness of the issuer's internal procedures for managing and publishing inside information[68] and of their application to a particular occurrence, with account taken of the issuer's anticipations regarding the likelihood of an event[69] or of the information's nature and significance for the issuer and investors.[70] There is a case for bringing at the EU level such precisions on the timely moment to disclose inside information, in order to avoid a costly disharmony that represents an obstacle to the creation of a single financial market.

The means for appropriate disclosure

On this matter, three main requirements emerge from Article 17(1)(2). The issuer shall (i) 'ensure that the inside information is made public in a manner which enables fast access and complete, correct and timely assessment of the information by the public'; (ii) 'not combine the disclosure of inside information to the public with the marketing of its activities'; and (iii) 'post and maintain on its website for a period of at least five years, all inside information it is required to disclose publicly'. **B.17.53**

The first requirement is directly inspired by Article 2(1) of the Market Abuse Implementation Directive (2003/124/EC) and by Article 12 of Directive 2007/14 implementing the 2004 Transparency Directive. Its content is specified by implementing Regulation 2016/1055 of 29 June 2016. Thus, Article 2 of this regulation mandates the use of technical means ensuring that inside information (a) be disseminated to as wide a public as possible on a non-discriminatory basis; free of charge; simultaneously throughout the Union and (b) be communicated electronically, reliably, and explicitly to the media which are reasonably relied upon by the public to ensure its effective dissemination. Consequently, a disclosure made directly by the issuer only via other ways of publication (eg issuer's website, mobile, or web-based social media such as blogs, social network sites), or only through a subscription system would not meet Market Abuse Regulation **B.17.54**

[67] See ESMA referring to an 'immediate disclosure requirement': ESMA, 'Technical Standard' (n 56) para 172. See also the use of the expression 'immediate disclosure' in art 17(6) regarding the delaying possibility reserved to financial institutions.

[68] On the consideration that disclosure decisions are normally part of the day-to-day administration of the issuer rather than a matter for the board, which could justify postponing disclosure see NASDAQ (n 65) para 2.10.

[69] See the UK DTR 2.2.9, whose enforcement has demonstrated that: 'subject to extraordinary circumstances, the FCA has a delay of minutes and hours in mind, rather than days'; McDonnell, 'Inside information' (n 32) para 3.5; the rule ends with an invitation to issuers that are in any doubt as to the timing of announcements required under the Market Abuse Regulation to consult the FCA at the earliest opportunity.

[70] NASDAQ (n 65) para 2.8; see the UK DTR 2.

requirements.[71] The communication clearly states: '(i) that the information communicated is inside information'; '(ii) the identity of the issuer'; '(iii) the identity of the person making the notification'; '(iv) the subject matter of the inside information'; '(v) the date and time of the communication to the media'. Even if, contrasting once again with the US Form 8-K model, no further guidance is given concerning the content of the communication, issuers are expected, according to the general goal of Article 17, to allow complete and correct assessment of the information in order to enable reasonable investors to make enlightened investment decisions.[72]

B.17.55 Since the Transparency Directive (2013/50/EU) requirements regarding 'regulated information', which includes disclosure made under Article 17,[73] do not apply outside the realm of regulated markets, the rapprochement of disclosure requirements realized by the Market Abuse Regulation has the advantage of 'capitalising on existing and reliable channels, already known by the market' and of levelling the playing field among European trading venues.[74] However, Article 17(1) introduces an explicit distinction between trading venues as prescribing that inside information also be made available in the 'officially appointed mechanism' (OAM) referred to in Article 21 Transparency Directive (2013/50/EU). Since the Transparency Directive (2013/50/EU) only applies to issuers that have requested or approved admission of their financial instruments to trading on a regulated market, this requirement does not reach issuers of financial instruments only traded on MTFs or OTFs, which may use the OAM solely on a voluntary basis or as the result of a national prescription.[75]

B.17.56 The second requirement, namely the prohibition of combining the disclosure of inside information to the public with the marketing of its activities, is also inspired by Article 2(1) of the Market Abuse Implementation Directive (2003/124/EC). Its wording appears even stronger since the latter only forbad such combination when made 'in a manner likely to be misleading'.

B.17.57 The third requirement, imposing that an issuer posts and maintains on its website, for a period of at least five years, all inside information to be disclosed publicly, did not exist in the (former) Market Abuse Directive (2003/6/EC) framework. As the first requirement, it is also specified by Regulation 2016/1055 of 29 June

[71] ESMA, 'Technical Standard' (n 56) paras 188 and 189.

[72] See NASDAQ (n 65) § 2.11: 'In conjunction with a deal or transaction, it is generally required that issuers disclose both the identity of the counterparty and the total value of the transaction or deal. However, in some cases it may be possible to omit those details while still enabling the public to comprehend the economic implications the event will have on the issuer's business and financial position'.

[73] With the attached consequences, laid down in art 19 ff of the Transparency Directive, in terms of home Member State control, languages, European electronic access point, and international equivalence.

[74] ESMA, 'Technical Standard' (n 56) para 186.

[75] ibid para 179.

2016, whose Article 3 mandates that the said website (a) allow users to access the inside information posted in a non-discriminatory basis and free of charge; (b) allow users to locate the inside information in an easily identifiable section; (c) ensure that the disclosed inside information clearly indicates date and time of disclosure and that the information is organized in chronological order. In order to stick with the standard practice of an 'investor relations' section on the website, including all regulatory announcements, ESMA modified its draft in such a way that 'there is no requirement for the section of the website, to include "only" inside information, although this has to be clearly and easily identifiable'.[76]

An issuer whose financial instruments are admitted to trading on an SME growth market may, however, under Article 17(9), only post its inside information on the trading venue's website, provided this venue chooses to provide such facility. In such a case, the aforementioned technical requirements laid down in Regulation 2016/1055 apply to the trading venue's website. Only Article 17(9) does not explicitly extend the five-year maintenance obligation in this particular situation. **B.17.58**

The anti-selective disclosure rule

Whereas any person other than an issuer may unconditionally disclose inside information privately as long as the disclosure is made in the normal exercise of his or her employment, profession, or duties (Article 10(1)), issuers are bound by a specific public disclosure obligation when they do. Indeed, Article 17(8) requires that in such cases an issuer, or a person acting on its behalf or for its account, 'make complete and effective public disclosure of that information, simultaneously in the case of an intentional disclosure, and promptly in the case of a non-intentional disclosure'. Such obligation is only waived where 'the person receiving the information owes a duty of confidentiality, regardless of whether such duty is based on a law, on regulations, on articles of association, or on a contract'. This logically amounts to the creation of an autonomous triggering event for mandatory public disclosure, leading issuers to disclose inside information publicly, even when the concerned information could have remained momentarily private in ordinary circumstances.[77] **B.17.59**

Article 17(8) is the exact reproduction of Article 6(3) of the (former) Market Abuse Directive (2003/6/EC), which introduced this anti-selective disclosure provision. The 2003 European legislator took direct inspiration from the SEC Regulation FD (Fair Disclosure), adopted in 2000, that requires listed companies disclosing material non-public information to enumerated outside professionals (brokers or dealers, investment advisers, investment companies) or holders of the issuer's securities, 'under circumstances in which it is reasonably foreseeable that the person will purchase or sell the issuer's securities on the basis of the information', **B.17.60**

---

[76] ibid paras 220 ff.

[77] See Hansen and Moalem, 'The MAD Disclosure Regime' (n 64).

to make public disclosure of that information 'simultaneously, in the case of an intentional disclosure' and 'promptly, in the case of a non-intentional disclosure', unless the information is passed to a person 'who owes a duty of trust or confidence to the issuer (such as an attorney, investment banker, or accountant)' or 'expressly agrees to maintain the disclosed information in confidence', or to 'an entity whose primary business is the issuance of credit ratings, provided the information is disclosed solely for the purpose of developing a credit rating and the entity's ratings are publicly available', or unless the communication is made in connection with most registered securities offerings.[78]

B.17.61 The adoption of these anti-selective disclosure rules is clearly motivated by the desire to level the playing field between retail investors and market professionals. The objective is to forbid the practice whereby issuers disclose important non-public information, such as advance warnings of earnings results, to securities analysts or selected institutional investors, before making full disclosure of the same information to the general public, as the creation of such unequal access to the source of corporate information leads to a loss of confidence in the integrity and fairness of capital markets.[79] Incidentally, the prohibition helps address perverse behaviours either from issuers, who could be tempted to use inside information as a commodity in order to gain or maintain favour with particular analysts or investors, or from analysts, who may feel pressured to report favourably about a company in order to keep access to selectively disclosed information.[80]

B.17.62 However, the ban on selective disclosure does not come without costs. From a capital markets' viewpoint, it is accused of 'chilling' corporate disclosures to market professionals, especially analysts, whose role is crucial for efficient price formation.[81] From an issuer's viewpoint, it is a source of internal organizational costs, relating to the procedures and controls put in place in order to avoid any breaches, as well as external business costs, incurred by a more systematic use of confidential agreements, at the risk of losing market professionals unwilling or unable to agree to such restrictions, and the disclosure costs themselves. The consideration of these adverse effects has led the US SEC to introduce several safeguards, limiting the scope of Regulation FD to communications with an exhaustive group of persons, protecting communications made in connection with securities offerings and excluding private rights of action.

B.17.63 The Market Abuse Regulation does not—and as far as private litigation is involved, could not—contain any of these limitations and simply sets out a

---

[78] SEC, 'Selective Disclosure' 17 CFR Part 243; Hazen, *Securities* (n 54) 530 ff.

[79] SEC, 'Selective Disclosure' 17 CFR Part 243.

[80] ibid.

[81] See S Choi, 'Selective Disclosure in the Public Capital Markets' (2002) 35 University of California (Davis) Law Review 533; See Niamh Moloney, *EU Securities and Financial Markets Regulation* (3rd edn, OUP 2014) 735.

general, and on several points elusive, ban on selective disclosure, which can be a source of concerns and practical difficulties for issuers. It may lead to additional risks and precautions surrounding, notably, the practice of selective disclosure in the context of corporate acquisitions or takeover bids involving data rooms and due diligence.[82] The notion of 'intentional disclosure' may also result in divergent interpretations[83], as well as the requirement to disclose the inside information 'promptly' and not 'as soon as possible'. As for the means of publication, Article 17(8) remains curiously silent. According to ESMA, 'the way and manner in which the inside information transmitted to a third party should be made public, should not be different from any other disclosure of inside information pursuant to Article 17(1)'.[84]

The emission allowance market participants' tailor-made regime

The expansion of the Market Abuse Regulation's objective scope to emission allowances (EA), logically following their legal reclassification as financial instruments under MiFID II[85] and practically intended to address a range of fraudulent practices in EA spot secondary markets,[86] results in an expansion of the Market Abuse Regulation's subjective scope of its disclosure requirements to emission allowance market participants (EAMPs), as defined in Article 3(20) of the Market Abuse Regulation.[87] This expansion does not, however, translate into a mere extension of issuers' disclosure requirements to EAMPs. To a large extent, a tailor-made regime is designed in order to accommodate the specificities of EAMPs, EAs, and the related markets. Consideration had to be devoted to the fact that the duty to disclose lies not on an issuer but on a market participant; that inside information related to EAs is, at least partly, defined in different terms;[88] that such information normally concerns the EAMP's physical activity; or that **B.17.64**

[82] Regarding takeover bids, the protection for bidders resulting from the exclusion that communication of inside information from a potential target could be deemed to constitute insider dealing has been reinstituted in the Market Abuse Regulation recital (30), after its elimination in the 2011 draft Regulation see I Molinari, 'Grande assalto alla diligence' *Economy* (1 August 2007); di Noia, 'Pending Issues in the Review of the European Market Abuse Rules' (n 15); di Noia and Gargantini, 'Disclosure Regime in Practice' (n 42); Legein, *Le nouveau règlement* (n 43) n 60 ff; See AMF, 'Guide to permanent information' (n 37) para 3.2.

[83] According to Regulation FD, 'A selective disclosure of material nonpublic information is "intentional" when the person making the disclosure either knows, or is reckless in not knowing, that the information he or she is communicating is both material and nonpublic'.

[84] ESMA, 'Technical Standard' (n 56) para 182.

[85] See Annex I, Section C, point (11).

[86] See EC, 'Review of the Markets in Financial Instruments Directive (MiFID) and Proposals for a Regulation on Market Abuse and for a Directive on Criminal Sanctions for Market Abuse: FAQ on Emission Allowances' Memo/11/719, Brussels (20 October 2011).

[87] '"[e]mission allowance market participant" means any person who enters into transactions, including the placing of orders to trade, in emission allowances, auctioned products based thereon, or derivatives thereof and who does not benefit from an exemption pursuant to the second subparagraph of Article 17(2).'

[88] Article 7(1)(c).

some EAMPs may already be subject to special disclosure requirements of inside information, which is the case for electricity and gas market participants covered by the Wholesale Energy Market Integrity and Transparency Regulation (2011/1227/EU). Additionally, policy and cost-efficiency reasons, especially the desire 'to avoid exposing the market to reporting that is not useful', justified the reservation of the disclosure requirement to only those EAMPs 'which, by virtue of their size and activity, can reasonably be expected to be able to have a significant effect on the price of emission allowances'.[89]

B.17.65 Thus, according to Article 17(2)(1): 'An emission allowance market participant shall publicly, effectively and in a timely manner disclose inside information concerning emission allowances which it holds in respect of its business', including aviation activities as specified in Annex I Greenhouse Gas Emission Allowances Directive (2003/87/EC) or installations within the meaning of Article 3(e) Greenhouse Gas Emission Allowances Directive (2003/87/EC). With regard to these installations, disclosure must include 'information relevant to the capacity and utilisation of installations, including planned or unplanned unavailability of such installations'. Following the example of recital (12) of the Wholesale Energy Market Integrity and Transparency Regulation (2011/1227/EU), recital (51) of the Market Abuse Regulation adds that the information to be disclosed 'should concern the physical operations of the disclosing party and not own plans or strategies for trading emission allowances, auctioned products based thereon, or derivative financial instruments relating thereto'. The precision that the EAMP should itself hold the information is all the more important in that the inside information also relates to activities and installations that the participant owns, controls, or is responsible for indirectly, through 'its parent undertaking or related undertaking', or 'in part'.[90] The content of the Market Abuse Regulation disclosure requirement is obviously and deliberately inspired from the requirement set out in Article 4(1) of the Wholesale Energy Market Integrity and Transparency Regulation (2011/1227/EU).[91] Notwithstanding, for EAMPs covered by the Wholesale Energy Market Integrity and Transparency Regulation (2011/1227/EU), the respective scope of the Market Abuse Regulation and the Wholesale Energy Market Integrity and Transparency Regulation (2011/1227/EU) disclosure requirements do not coincide exactly given the existence of certain differences in their respective definitions of inside information.[92]

---

[89] Recital (51).

[90] See the condition of knowledge under the Wholesale Energy Market Integrity and Transparency Regulation (2011/1227/EU); P Mäntysaari, *The Law of Corporate Finance: General Principles and EU Law* (Springer 2010) 275.

[91] See also ACER, *Guidance on the Application of REMIT* (4th edn, 17 June 2016); Mäntysaari, *Corporate Finance* (n 90) 275.

[92] See ESMA, 'Technical Standard' (n 56) para 197 ff.

However, Article 17(2)(2) provides for an exemption where the installations or aviation activities that a participant in the emission allowance market 'owns, controls or is responsible for, in the preceding year have had emissions not exceeding a minimum threshold of carbon dioxide equivalent and, where they carry out combustion activities, have had a rated thermal input not exceeding a minimum threshold'. Article 5 Regulation 2016/522/EU sets the minimum threshold of carbon dioxide (CO2) equivalent to 6 million tonnes a year and the minimum threshold of rated thermal input at 2,430 MW, specifying that they both 'apply at group level and relate to all business, including aviation activities or installations, which the participant in the emission allowance market concerned, or its parent undertaking or related undertaking owns or controls or for the operational matters of which the participant concerned, or its parent undertaking or related undertaking is responsible, in whole or in part'. Below these materiality thresholds, such a participant falls out of the EAMP definition[93] and therefore escapes the disclosure requirement pursuant to Article 17(2), unless of course it is an issuer of financial instruments subject to Article 17(1).[94] These thresholds allow for the exemption of a large majority of emitters but still capture the majority of emissions.[95] The exemption also affects market abuse prohibitions since the information about the participant's physical operations no longer qualifies as inside information.[96] **B.17.66**

Finally, with regard to the EAMPs' publication itself, the Market Abuse Regulation aims at promoting equivalence and preventing redundancy.[97] On the one hand, some equivalence is ensured between issuers and EAMPs as both categories have to use the same technical means for public disclosure of inside information under Article 2 of Regulation 2016/1055. It remains that the Market Abuse Regulation does not mandate that inside information relating only to an emission allowance product be posted on a website and made available in the officially appointed mechanism. On the other hand, in order to avoid 'the duplication of mandatory disclosures with substantially the same content',[98] Article 2 of Regulation 2016/1055 authorizes EAMPs required to disclose inside information in accordance with Article 4 of the Wholesale Energy Market Integrity and Transparency Regulation (2011/1227/EU)[99] to use the same technical means **B.17.67**

---

[93] Article 3(20).

[94] EMSA, 'Draft technical advice on possible delegated acts concerning the Market Abuse Regulation, Consultation Paper (ESMA/2014/808)' (11 July 2014) www.esma.org, para 34; ESMA, 'ESMA's technical advice on possible delegated acts concerning the Market Abuse Regulation (ESMA/2015/224)' (3 February 2015) para 42 www.esma.org.

[95] '70 companies would be captured by the threshold (approximately 56% being energy producers and the rest other industrial emitters) accounting for 70% of the total verified emissions, and 857 companies would be exempted;' Consultation paper para 46.

[96] Article 7(4).

[97] See ESMA, 'Technical Standard' (n 56) para 194 ff.

[98] Recital (51).

[99] Supplemented by art 10 of Regulation 1348/2014 of 17 December 2014 on data reporting OJEU (18 December 2014) L 363/121.

for the disclosure of inside information under Article 17(2), 'provided the inside information required to be disclosed has substantially the same content and the technical means used for the disclosure ensure that the inside information is communicated to the relevant media'. However, ESMA publicly criticized the Commission for relaxing its draft technical standard provisions designed to ensure the active dissemination of inside information and the marking of that information as inside information under Market Abuse Regulation, and for simply considering that the Wholesale Energy Market Integrity and Transparency Regulation (2011/1227/EU) website-based disclosure regime meets Market Abuse Regulation requirements.[100]

The limited right to delay disclosure

The necessary limits to ad hoc disclosure and the legislative tipping point

B.17.68 From the outset, before insider dealing law even emerged, the European compromise between the investors' need for permanent transparency and the issuers' need for temporary secrecy[101] took the form of the possibility for issuers to delay public disclosure where such disclosure would jeopardize their legitimate interests, under the supervision of their national competent authorities (NCAs).[102] Only the definition of such legitimate interests and the role devoted to NCAs changed over time. The Commission recommendation of 25 July 1977 referred to 'a fact or important decision' that 'cannot be made public without delay, for example because certain formalities have not yet been completed or because the company would be seriously prejudiced as a result', alluded to 'a risk of leaks', and insisted on the information of the NCAs, encouraged to 'take the necessary steps to safeguard the market's proper operation until the relevant fact or decision can be made public'. The Directive of 5 March 1979, in a more concise but interventionist way, conditioned the exemption upon prior approval of the NCA where 'the disclosure of particular information is such as to prejudice the legitimate interests of the company'. Article 6(2) of the (former) Market Abuse Directive (2003/6/EC), implicitly recognizing that temporary privacy may at times legitimately prevail over the risk of insider dealing, gave this exemption its modern structure, providing that issuer 'may under his own responsibility delay the public disclosure of inside information, as referred to in paragraph 1, such as not to prejudice his legitimate interests provided that such omission would not be likely to mislead the public and provided that the issuer is able to ensure the confidentiality of that information', and merely offered to Member States

[100] See Opinion—Draft Implementing Technical Standards on the technical means for appropriate public disclosure of inside information and for delaying the public disclosure of inside information (17 June 2016) ESMA/2016/982.

[101] See n 9.

[102] See n 7.

the option to 'require that an issuer shall without delay inform the competent authority of the decision to delay the public disclosure of inside information'.

Despite the calls to relax the pre-requisites to delay disclosure,[103] Article 17 largely maintains the previous legislative framework, only changing the distribution of competences between level 2 and level 3 authorities, explicitly underlining its exceptionality,[104] setting forth a rule on rumours as well as on protracted processes, mandating the *ex post* information of NCAs and introducing a specific case of delay based on financially systemic reasons. **B.17.69**

As the vast majority of the rules composing the delaying regime apply both to issuers and EAMPs,[105] the presentation will follow another line of distinction, separating the common rules for delaying from the additional possibilities designed to preserve the stability of the financial system. **B.17.70**

General regime

Conditions for delaying: Overview Article 17(4) reinstates the three substantial and cumulative conditions set out in Article 6(2) of the (former) Market Abuse Directive (2003/6/EC) for delaying public disclosure of inside information, only changing their formal presentation as they are now placed on equal footing: **B.17.71**

> An issuer or an emission allowance market participant, may, on its own responsibility, delay disclosure to the public of inside information provided that all of the following conditions are met:
> (a) immediate disclosure is likely to prejudice the legitimate interests of the issuer or emission allowance market participant;
> (b) delay of disclosure is not likely to mislead the public;
> (c) the issuer or emission allowance market participant is able to ensure the confidentiality of that information.

Taking into account the corresponding amendment of the definition of inside information, Article 17(4)(2) logically extends the right to delay to cover the situations where inside information relates to a protracted process. Understandably, delay is of paramount importance where inside information is only an intermediate step of multi-stage process.[106] **B.17.72**

Following Article 6(2) of the (former) Market Abuse Directive (2003/6/EC), Article 17(4) makes it explicit that the decision to delay is taken by the issuer at **B.17.73**

---

103 See ESME, 'Report EC Call for evidence: Review of the MAD' (2007) 8 and 10 www.ec.europa.eu.

104 See recital (49) referring to 'special circumstances'.

105 Therefore, the word issuer will be used in this context to cover both categories, unless stated otherwise.

106 For a commentator, the insertion in art 17(4) of a subparagraph specifically providing for a delaying possibility in case of protracted processes 'should be construed as extending the access to delay in the special circumstance of a protracted process that occurs in stages' as it 'is reasonable to construe this wide access taking into account the special circumstances of such a process', Hansen, 'Say When' (n 21).

its own risk. In the Market Abuse Regulation framework, the idea to leave the whole responsibility for the decision to issuers is reinforced by the mandatory postponing of NCA notification, and therefore possible intervention, until the delayed information is publicly disclosed.

B.17.74 However, the detailed information expected to be recorded by the issuer about the delay practically compels issuers to resort to highly formal decision-making and monitoring processes.[107] Indeed, Article 4 of implementing Regulation 2016/1055 of 29 June 2016 requires that, for the purpose of delaying the public disclosure of inside information, issuers use 'technical means that ensure the accessibility, readability, and maintenance in a durable medium' of information including: the dates and times when the inside information first existed and the decision to delay was made; the identity of the persons within the issuer responsible for making the decision to delay disclosure and ensuring the ongoing monitoring of the conditions for the delay; and evidence of the fulfilment of the legal conditions for delaying. As further specified by ESMA, '[t]here should be person(s) appointed within the issuer responsible for taking such decision. This person(s) should be clearly identified within the issuer and should have the necessary decision-making power (eg a managing board member or a senior executive director), considering the major importance of the decision ... In addition, before taking a decision allowing the delay of publication of inside information, this person(s) should conduct an assessment on whether the three conditions set forth in Article 17(4) for delaying are fulfilled'.[108] Issuers should also ensure that the legal conditions for the delay are fulfilled throughout the period of delay.[109] This legal change is likely to affect significantly the day-to-day life of listed issuers and increase accordingly their regulatory burden, especially for SME issuers.

B.17.75 **Existence of legitimate interests** Since its introduction in 2003, the notion of 'legitimate interests' has not been substantially defined. In its advice to the Commission, CESR explained that: 'a definition would have to be extremely accurate, in order not to widen the scope of this article' and that '[r]eality will probably be more creative than CESR can foresee and new cases will appear that will be on "the wrong side" of the definition'. Therefore, advocating flexibility, CESR suggested to go forward through 'examples of situations that might justify delaying disclosure'.[110]

---

107 On the previous discussion in Germany about the necessity for the issuer to make a conscious decision delaying disclosure see Koch, 'Disclosure of Inside Information' (n 18) para 19 n 99 ff.

108 See ESMA, 'Technical Standard' (n 56) para 239.

109 ibid para 242.

110 CESR's Advice on Level 2 Implementing Measures for the proposed Market Abuse Directive, CESR/02-089d (December 2002) paras 68 and 69.

Following CESR's advice, the Commission adopted the Market Abuse Implementation Directive (2003/124/EC) whose Article 3(1) laid down an indicative list of legitimate interests referring to: **B.17.76**

(a) negotiations in course, or related elements, where the outcome or normal pattern of those negotiations would be likely to be affected by public disclosure. In particular, in the event that the financial viability of the issuer is in grave and imminent danger, although not within the scope of the applicable insolvency law, public disclosure of information may be delayed for a limited period where such a public disclosure would seriously jeopardise the interest of existing and potential shareholders by undermining the conclusion of specific negotiations designed to ensure the long-term financial recovery of the issuer;
(b) decisions taken or contracts made by the management body of an issuer which need the approval of another body of the issuer in order to become effective, where the organisation of such an issuer requires the separation between these bodies, provided that a public disclosure of the information before such approval together with the simultaneous announcement that this approval is still pending would jeopardise the correct assessment of the information by the public.

From the indicative nature of the list, two opposite consequences were drawn: the situations described did not automatically qualify for a delay in disclosure, as further examination could reveal that the legal conditions for delaying were not met in a particular instance; conversely, the list being non-exhaustive, issuers could resort to delaying disclosure in other types of circumstances. Later on, in its second set of guidelines on the (former) Market Abuse Directive (2003/6/EC), CESR provided 'illustrative examples' of the two types of circumstances mentioned in Article 3(1), while reaffirming the view that 'the right to delay the disclosure of inside information is a derogation from the general rule rather than the norm'.[111] **B.17.77**

The Market Abuse Regulation builds on the (former) Market Abuse Directive (2003/6/EC) acquis, while changing its legal structure. Its recital (50) reproduces Article 3(1) of the Market Abuse Implementation Directive (2003/124/EC) word for word. Thus by-passing the need for a level 2 directive, Article 17(11) empowers ESMA to issue guidelines in order to 'establish a non-exhaustive indicative list of the legitimate interests of issuers'.[112] ESMA published the expected list in its Guidelines dated of 20 October 2016 and effective from 20 December 2016.[113] Indicating typical cases where immediate disclosure of the inside information is likely to prejudice the issuers' legitimate interests, the list compiles the situations previously enshrined in Article 3(1) of the Market Abuse Implementation **B.17.78**

[111] 'Second set of CESR guidance on the MAD, CESR/06-562 b' (July 2007) para 2.1 ff.
[112] Note that EAMPs are not mentioned in art 17(11).
[113] See ESMA, 'MAR Guidelines: Delay in the disclosure of inside information (ESMA/2016/1478)' (n 2).

Directive (2003/124/EC) and CESR guidelines, with some formal rearrangement and some non-insignificant updating in substance. The following circumstances are enumerated:

a. the issuer is conducting negotiations, where the outcome of such negotiations would likely be jeopardised by immediate public disclosure. Examples of such negotiations may be those related to mergers, acquisitions, splits and spin-offs, purchases or disposals of major assets or branches of corporate activity, restructurings and reorganisations.
b. the financial viability of the issuer is in grave and imminent danger, although not within the scope of the applicable insolvency law, and immediate public disclosure of the inside information would seriously prejudice the interests of existing and potential shareholders by jeopardising the conclusion of the negotiations designed to ensure the financial recovery of the issuer;
c. the inside information relates to decisions taken or contracts entered into by the management body of an issuer which need, pursuant to national law or the issuer's bylaws, the approval of another body of the issuer, other than the shareholders' general assembly, in order to become effective, provided that:
    i. immediate public disclosure of that information before such a definitive decision would jeopardise the correct assessment of the information by the public; and
    ii. the issuer arranged for the definitive decision to be taken as soon as possible.
d. the issuer has developed a product or an invention and the immediate public disclosure of that information is likely to jeopardise the intellectual property rights of the issuer;
e. the issuer is planning to buy or sell a major holding in another entity and the disclosure of such an information would likely jeopardise the implementation of such plan;
f. a transaction previously announced is subject to a public authority's approval, and such approval is conditional upon additional requirements, where the immediate disclosure of those requirements will likely affect the ability for the issuer to meet them and therefore prevent the final success of the deal or transaction.

B.17.79 The preparatory work to these Guidelines[114] provides interesting information about the changes ESMA decided to make. For instance, further to the feedback received during the consultation process, ESMA decided in the first listed type of situations, relating to negotiations, to provide some specific examples (mergers, acquisitions, splits and spin-offs etc). In the second type of situations, concerning the viability of the issuer, ESMA chose not to refer, unlike recital (50), to the 'long-term' financial recovery of the issuer, as the 'successful conclusion of negotiations aimed at ensuring the "short term" financial

[114] See ESMA, 'Consultation Paper: Draft guidelines on the MAR (ESMA/2016/162)' (28 January 2016) www.esma.org; ESMA, 'Final Report: Guidelines on the MAR: market soundings and delay of disclosure of inside information (ESMA/2016/1130)' (13 July 2016) www.esma.org.

recovery of the issuer could constitute a legitimate interest to delay disclosure of inside information'.[115] In the third type of situations, mainly related to two-tiered board structures, ESMA accepted to delete two additional conditions, criticized for being too restrictive, namely the requirements: that 'an announcement explaining that such approval is still pending would jeopardise the freedom of decision of the other body'; and that 'the decision of the body responsible for such approval is not expected to be in line with the decision of the management body, as for instance it would be where such body is the expression of the same shareholders represented in the management body or in cases where such body has consistently approved the management body's decisions on similar issues'.[116]

At least as importantly, the preparatory work enlightens the interpretation about the changes ESMA refused to make. For example, ESMA refused to consider that, in the case of a CEO's resignation, the disclosure of the information could be legitimately delayed until the appointment of a successor; or that a delay could be needed in order for a parent company to check the accounting information received by the subsidiaries; and refrained from including a wide statement saying that some time may be needed for an issuer to clarify the situation in case of an unexpected and significant event. Against the opinion of its stakeholder group pointing out that 'the right to delay should not be interpreted narrowly' and that 'an issuer should be allowed to keep the information secret if disclosure of the information may be detrimental to him', ESMA reaffirmed that 'the possibility to delay the disclosure of inside information as per Article 17(4) represents the exception to the general rule of disclosure to be made as soon as possible according to Article 17(1), and therefore should be narrowly interpreted'.[117] ESMA concluded that if the list is indicative, '[i]t should be for the issuers to explain that they are in a case where their legitimate interests are likely to be prejudiced by immediate disclosure of inside information, and that each situation, including those listed in the draft Guidelines, should be assessed on a case by case basis'.[118] **B.17.80**

The stated aim of the ESMA Guidelines, specified in their cost-benefit analysis, is to provide clarity and enhance legal certainty by defining a list of legitimate interests of issuers for delaying public disclosure of inside information.[119] The Guidelines should 'assist the issuers in conducting their assessment as to whether they meet the conditions to delay inside information according to MAR' and therefore 'contribute to reduce the number of controversial cases of delay'.[120] **B.17.81**

115 ESMA, 'Final Report' (n 114) para 58.
116 ibid para 64; see the opinion of the SMSG at para 30 ff.
117 ESMA, 'Final Report' (n 114) para 52.
118 ibid para 53.
119 ibid para 53.
120 ibid 24.

To be sure, the higher compelling nature of ESMA Guidelines, compared to CESR's, could help ensure common, uniform and consistent application of the Market Abuse Regulation provisions by NCAs and financial market participants as they are supposed to 'make every effort to comply with guidelines and recommendations'. The result will however depend on the extent to which NCAs intend to comply with the guidelines, only bound to report to ESMA on a comply-or-explain basis, and follow the rather limitative interpretation of ESMA, which seems arguable in light of the extensive notion of inside information subject to disclosure and the explicit provision in Article 17(4)(2) related to delay in protracted processes.[121] Furthermore, besides the fact that these Guidelines may be differently considered in private litigation before national courts, important weaknesses remain within the new framework that create obstacles on the road to uniformity and certainty. The great divergence existing among Member States, notably on the notion of corporate interest, which should logically command a company to delay disclosure, on its possible extension to group or third-party interest in certain circumstances, on the respect for usual practices in certain economic sectors,[122] on the distinction between legitimate and illegitimate interests beyond the mere exclusion of cases where the issuer would selfishly aim at exploiting the ignorance of the public of price-sensitive information, on the usefulness of a dogmatic definition of a legitimate interest based on the comparison between the issuer's private interest in delaying disclosure and the capital markets' public interest in disclosure,[123] or on the possibility for an NCA to second-guess the decision of a company's representatives to delay disclosure, will likely continue and reflect national legal traditions and corporate cultures either favouring disclosure or issuers' interests.[124]

B.17.82 **Absence of public misleading** Delaying disclosure is only permissible, under Article 17(4)(b), where it 'is not likely to mislead the public'. Already present in Article 6(2) of the (former) Market Abuse Directive (2003/6/EC), although formulated in the conditional tense, this second requirement seems prima facie to defy logic. Since inside information is characterized by the fact that it is likely to be used by a reasonable investor, delaying its disclosure could by definition be regarded as misleading.[125] Also, during the (former) Market Abuse Directive (2003/6/EC) review process, it was suggested to either delete this circular condition altogether or, at least, introduce additional specifications, which could underline for example that a delay is likely to mislead the public 'only when the relevant information could run counter to a market consensus, ie only when the

[121] See Legein, *Le nouveau règlement* (n 42).

[122] See Europeanissuers, 'Response to the European commission's call for evidence on the review of the MAD' (n 51).

[123] See for Germany, Koch, 'Disclosure of Inside Information' (n 18) para 19 n 75.

[124] ibid para 19 n 73 ff.

[125] See di Noia and Gargantini, 'Issuers at Midstream' (n 29) 506.

investment community clearly shows (through market prices, analysts coverage or others) expectations that are contradicted by the information directly regarding the issuer'.[126]

The Market Abuse Regulation takes this second option and empowers ESMA, in Article 17(11), to issue guidelines in order to bring the necessary precisions, through the establishment of 'a non-exhaustive indicative list of ... situations in which a delay of disclosure of inside information is likely to mislead the public'. ESMA published the expected list in the abovementioned Guidelines dated of 20 October 2016 and effective from 20 December 2016.[127] The said situations 'include at least' the three following circumstances: **B.17.83**

a. the inside information whose disclosure the issuer intends to delay is materially different from the previous public announcement of the issuer on the matter to which the inside information refers to;
b. the inside information whose disclosure the issuer intends to delay regards the fact that the issuer's financial objectives are not likely to be met, where such objectives were previously publicly announced;
c. the inside information whose disclosure the issuer intends to delay is in contrast with the market's expectations, where such expectations are based on signals that the issuer has previously sent to the market, such as interviews, roadshows or any other type of communication organized by the issuer or with its approval.

The three illustrative situations are based on a common articulation of the same two restrictions: the delay in the disclosure of inside information is considered misleading only where the concerned information differs from market expectations and only where such expectations are based on the concerned issuer's previous communication. In so restricting the perimeter of the listed exclusions, and discharging issuers from reacting to external rumours,[128] ESMA took account of the need to provide more clarity and certainty to issuers, an imperative stressed by the respondents to ESMA's public consultation.[129] The references to the vague and undefined terms or notions 'materially different', 'financial objectives', 'market expectations', or the invitation for issuers 'to take into account the market sentiment, for instance considering the consensus among financial analysts',[130] may somewhat undermine the fulfilment of this objective. Finally, ESMA decided not to include in the list situations where issuers disclose public information that is inconsistent with the information **B.17.84**

[126] See CESR, 'Second set of guidance on the MAD, CESR/06-562 b' (July 2007) para 2.12; ESME Report (n 103) 8; Commission, 'Staff Working Paper: Impact Assessment' SEC(2011) 12717 final 178.

[127] See ESMA, 'MAR Guidelines: Delay in the disclosure of inside information (ESMA/2016/1478)' (n 2).

[128] See n 10.

[129] See ESMA, 'Final Report' (n 114) para 82 ff.

[130] ibid para 84.

under delay, on the basis that 'such situation is already covered by the prohibition of market manipulation'.[131]

B.17.85 **Preservation of confidentiality** Delaying the disclosure of inside information is conditioned upon the ability of the concerned issuer to 'ensure the confidentiality of that information' (Article 17(4)(c)). If confidentiality can no longer be ensured, including the situation where rumours are sufficiently accurate to indicate that a leak has occurred, the issuer must publicly disclose the inside information as soon as possible (Article 17(7)).[132] This third condition for delay is perfectly in line with the objective of preventing market abuse practices.[133] Its practical satisfaction requires the setting-up of appropriate internal procedures and arrangements enabling issuers to ensure confidentiality, to control access to the inside information throughout the delay period and, if need be, the prompt publication of the information.[134] In the (former) Market Abuse Directive (2003/6/EC) framework, specific requirements related to such precautionary measures were set out in Article 3(2) of the Market Abuse Implementation Directive (2003/124/EC), which referred to 'effective arrangements to deny access to such information to persons other than those who require it for the exercise of their functions within the issuer'; 'necessary measures to ensure that any person with access to such information acknowledges the legal and regulatory duties entailed and is aware of the sanctions attaching to the misuse or improper circulation of such information'; and 'measures which allow immediate public disclosure in case the issuer was not able to ensure the confidentiality of the relevant inside information'.[135] Under the Market Abuse Regulation, these requirements are only laid down indirectly, through the items that an issuer must record when delaying disclosure of inside information.[136] Article 4(1)(c) of implementing Regulation 2016/1055 of 29 June 2016 requires that these items contain 'evidence of the initial fulfilment of the conditions referred to in Article 17(4) of Regulation (EU) No 596/2014, and of any change of this fulfilment during the delay period, including: (i) the information barriers which have been put in place internally and with regard to third parties to prevent access to inside information by persons other than those who require it for the normal exercise of their employment, profession or duties within the issuer or emission allowance market participant; (ii) the

[131] ibid para 86.

[132] 'In such circumstances, which should be the exception rather than the rule and should be examined by the issuer on a case-by-case basis, a policy of staying silent or of "no comment" by the issuer would not be acceptable.' See ESMA 'Q&A, ESMA70-145-11' (6 July 2017) 11.

[133] See ESME Report (n 103) 8.

[134] 'The issuer's reaction or response should be made publicly available in the same conditions and using the same mechanisms as those used for the communication of inside information, so that an ad hoc announcement has to be published without undue delay.' See ESMA 'Q&A, ESMA70-145-11' (n 132) 11.

[135] See CESR, Second set of guidance on the MAD, CESR/06-562 b (July 2007) para 2.11; ESME Report (n 103) 8.

[136] See n 17.

arrangements put in place to disclose the relevant inside information as soon as possible where the confidentiality is no longer ensured'.[137] However, according to ESMA, Article 17(7) does not specify that the leak necessarily has to originate from the 'sphere of the issuer' in order to trigger the duty to disclose. Such an additional condition would lead to a potentially time-consuming investigation, unduly delaying the disclosure of the inside information.[138]

i) Consequences of delaying: ex post *notification of the NCA* As long as its conditions are fulfilled, delaying disclosure of inside information may continue.[139] It may, however, lose its purpose when the inside information ceases to exist before it becomes disclosable, which may be the case of a contemplated event that does not ultimately materialize. Conversely, should the information become disclosable and effectively disclosed, the Market Abuse Regulation requires that the issuer notify the relevant NCA. More precisely, as mandated by Article 17(4) last subparagraph, the issuer 'shall inform the competent authority . . . that disclosure of the information was delayed and shall provide a written explanation of how the conditions set out in this paragraph were met, immediately after the information is disclosed to the public. Alternatively, Member States may provide that a record of such an explanation is to be provided only upon the request of the competent authority'. **B.17.86**

This *ex post* notification represents a significant change in NCAs' involvement in the delaying process. Indeed, Article 6(2) of the (former) Market Abuse Directive (2003/6/EC) provided that 'Member States may require that an issuer shall without delay inform the competent authority of the decision to delay the public disclosure of inside information'. Not only was it merely a national option for Member States to require that the issuer inform the relevant NCA but, in the event this option was exercised, the information had to be sent *ex ante*, since the issuer was bound to inform the NCA of the 'decision to delay the public disclosure' 'without delay'. **B.17.87**

The (former) Market Abuse Directive (2003/6/EC) provision turned out to be a source of great divergence among Member States, as sixteen of them used the option to require such notification, while eleven did not.[140] Furthermore, this divergence seems here to stay as most Member States declared no intention to amend their legislation on this particular point.[141] However, the (former) **B.17.88**

[137] See ESMA, 'Technical Standard' (n 56) para 242 ff; see also the legal requirements relating to insider lists.

[138] ibid.

[139] See Koch, 'Disclosure of Inside Information' (n 18) 290; Hellstén, 'Disclosure and delayed disclosure of inside information in the light of the EU Market Abuse Regulation' (n 63) 41.

[140] See 'Review Panel Report Options and Discretions 2009, CESR/09-1120' (29 March 2010) no 25 ff.

[141] ibid.

Market Abuse Directive (2003/6/EC) review process showed wide support among respondents for a mandatory *ex post* notification system included in the Commission proposal, on the grounds that it set the right balance between the responsibility for assessing whether a delay in disclosure is justified, which should entirely remain with the issuer,[142] and the possibility for the regulator 'to further verify where appropriate whether the conditions for delay were indeed met and to sanction the issuer in the event that this was not the case',[143] the only perceived disadvantage being 'that investors' economic interests could be harmed by a delay to disclosure which was not justified, and there would be no means for them to obtain redress other than through legal action against the issuer'.[144]

B.17.89 The case for a compulsory and uniform *ex post* notification being made, the implementation of the new mechanism led to the adoption of two level 2 regulations designed to address two separate issues: the determination of the NCA to notify and the technical means for notifying it.

B.17.90 First, Article 17(3) empowers the Commission to adopt a delegated act specifying 'the national competent authority' for the notification of Article 17(4). This allocation of national powers exercise was made rather difficult for a series of reasons. Indeed, account had to be taken of: the expansion of the Market Abuse Regulation scope to issuers of financial instruments traded only on a MTF or an OTF, when these issuers have requested admission to trading on a MTF or have approved trading on a MTF or an OTF, as well as to EAMPs; the requirement enshrined in Article 17(3) that the notification is provided to only one NCA, where application of the general definition of competent authorities included in Article 22 could lead to the designation of several NCAs for a single issuer; the inadequacy of the criteria used in other financial directives or regulations; and finally, the necessity to 'ensure that in all instances the single competent authority receiving the notification is the one with the most interests in market supervision and to avoid in all cases the exercise of discretion by the issuer'.[145]

B.17.91 The final result, set out in Article 6 of Regulation 2016/522/EU, could only but reflect the complexity of the premises. Schematically, it designates the NCA of the Member State where the issuer is registered:(i) when this issuer has its equity securities admitted or traded with its consent in its home Member States;[146] (ii) if it does not have equity securities admitted or traded with its consent on any Member States' trading venue, when the issuer has other financial instruments admitted to trading or traded with its consent on a trading venue in its home

[142] See n 17.
[143] Commission, 'Impact Assessment' (n 126) 179.
[144] ibid.
[145] See ESMA, 'Delegated Acts' (n 94) para 62 ff.
[146] ibid para 74: 'By equity securities, ESMA means the class of transferable securities referred to in MiFID II (Article 4(44)(a))'.

Member State. In all other cases, including for third-country issuers, the NCA is that of the Member State where: (i) the issuer has equity securities admitted to trading or traded with its consent on a trading venue for the first time; or (ii) it has any other financial instruments admitted to trading or traded with its consent on a trading venue for the first time. In case of a simultaneous first trading in several Member States, the designated NCA is the one of the trading venue that is 'the most relevant market in terms of liquidity, as determined in the Commission Delegated Regulation to be adopted under Article 26(9)(b)' of MiFIR.[147] For their part, EAMPs are bound to notify the delay in disclosing inside information to the NCA of the Member State where the EAMP is registered.[148]

Secondly, Article 17(10)(b) empowers the Commission to adopt implementing technical standards, drafted by ESMA, in order to uniformly determine the technical means and content of the notifications provided to the NCA. This determination is made by Regulation 2016/1055 of 29 June 2016, whose Article 4(2) requires that issuers inform the NCA of a delay in the disclosure of inside information, 'by means of a written notification', 'using electronic means' of communication accepted by the NCA, including a number of items related to the identity of the issuer, of the person making the notification and of all persons responsible for the decision to delay the public disclosure of inside information; the identification of the concerned inside information; and the date and time of the public disclosure of the inside information and of the decision to delay the disclosure of inside information (Article 4(3)). According to ESMA, the notification of delay to the NCA 'should take place immediately after the delayed inside information has been publicly disclosed'.[149] **B.17.92**

In Member States using the option, offered in Article 17(4), to require issuers to provide a written explanation of how the conditions for delaying were met only upon the NCA request, as it is the case in France,[150] this written explanation, if not provided simultaneously with the notification of delay, should also include the abovementioned elements of information (Article 4(4)). **B.17.93**

Special regime designed to preserve the stability of the financial system

Absent any distinction among firms in Article 17(4), the 'general' delay described above is open to credit or financial institutions. However, drawing lessons from the financial crisis and the difficulties experienced by systemic financial firms, **B.17.94**

[147] Article 26(9) Markets in Financial Instruments Implementation Regulation (1287/2006/EC) empowers ESMA to develop draft RTS to specify the criteria for defining a relevant market in accordance with 26(1); on 28 September 2015, ESMA transmitted to the Commission the draft RTS 22, whose art 16 sets the rules for the determination the most relevant market in terms of liquidity, based on the highest turnover for the previous calendar year.

[148] See ESMA, 'Delegated Acts' (n 94) para 80 ff.

[149] ESMA, 'Technical Standard' (n 56) para 225.

[150] AMF General Regulation, art 223-2, modified by the Arrêté of 14 September 2016.

the European institutions decided to introduce in the Market Abuse Regulation an additional possibility to withhold inside information, which only credit or financial institutions may use in a situation where the stability of the financial system is at risk. As summarized in recital (52), '[i]n order to protect the public interest, to preserve the stability of the financial system and, for example, to avoid liquidity crises in financial institutions from turning into solvency crises owing to a sudden withdrawal of funds, it may be appropriate to allow, in exceptional circumstances, the delay of the disclosure of inside information for credit institutions or financial institutions ... This delay should be conditional upon the issuer obtaining the consent of the relevant competent authority and it being clear that the wider public and economic interest in delaying disclosure outweighs the interest of the market in receiving the information which is subject to delay'.

B.17.95 For some, the introduction of these specific provisions in the Market Abuse Regulation was only a matter of clarification, as the ordinary delaying mechanism seemed per se able to handle the types of situations considered.[151] In reality, judging by its many distinct characteristics, the reform creates a regime in its own right, offering an additional option[152] enshrined in Article 17(5) and (6).

B.17.96 First, as indicated, this regime has a limited subjective scope, since it is reserved to issuers that are 'credit institutions' and 'financial institutions', although the Market Abuse Regulation refrains from defining these expressions. If Article 17(6) mentions the entities covered by Directive 2013/36 of 26 June 2013 on access to the activity of credit institutions and the prudential supervision of credit institutions and investment firms, it makes it clear that there can be other types of eligible firms.

B.17.97 Secondly, the triggering reason for delaying disclosure is not based on considerations exclusively or even mainly related to the issuer itself. This ultimum remedium aims to 'preserve the stability of the financial system' as a whole (Article 17(5)).

B.17.98 Thirdly, the conditions and procedure for delaying reflect the fact that the interest at stake prevails over potentially colliding interests and that this prevailing interest is intrinsically public.

B.17.99 Article 17(5)(a) conditions the use of the special delay upon some evidence that: 'the disclosure of the inside information entails a risk of undermining the financial stability of the issuer and of the financial system'. Recital (52) underlines

[151] For the view that the ordinary rules on delaying disclosure were sufficient to deal with the cases cited by the Commission, especially the one concerning La Société Générale see AMF, 'Réponse à la consultation de la Commission européenne sur la révision de la directive abus de marché' (15 June 2009).

[152] As provided by art 17(6)(4), this regime applies 'to cases where the issuer does not decide to delay the disclosure of inside information in accordance with paragraph 4'.

its availability only in 'exceptional circumstances', mentioning 'temporary liquidity problems' encountered by financial institutions 'where they need to receive central banking lending including emergency liquidity assistance from a central bank where disclosure of the information would have a systemic impact'. The decisive factor lies therefore in the objective systemic risk arising from the financial institution's difficulty and not exclusively in the subjective systemic status of the institution itself.[153]

Article 17(5)(c) requires that the systemically important inside information whose public disclosure is delayed remain confidential. Contrasting with Article 17(4)(c), applicable to the 'general' delay, the condition is expressed here in the form of an objective possibility, and not a subjective obligation for the issuer, to ensure such confidentiality, a difference that can be explained by the particularism of the concerned inside information and the procedure to be followed accordingly. However, the ongoing confidentiality of the information is preserved through application of Article 17(7), requiring the issuer to disclose it publicly as soon as possible when its confidentiality is no longer ensured.[154] **B.17.100**

By way of derogation, because the delay in the disclosure must be dictated by the 'public interest' (Article 17(5)(b)), the absence of misleading the public is not listed among the conditions for delaying disclosure. Furthermore, an *ex ante* approval of the NCA is required. In such exceptional circumstances, financial stability supersedes investor protection and issuers' privacy. As provided by Article 17(5)(d), the NCA specified under Article 17(3)[155] must consent to the delay on the basis that the abovementioned conditions are met. Accordingly, Article 17(6) requires that the financial institution notify the NCA[156] 'of its intention to delay the disclosure of the inside information and provide evidence that the conditions set out in points (a), (b) and (c) of paragraph 5 are met'. The NCA shall then consult as deemed appropriate 'the national central bank or the macro-prudential authority, where instituted, or, alternatively, the following authorities: (a) where the issuer is a credit institution or an investment firm the authority designated in accordance with Article 133 of Directive 2013/36/EU of the European Parliament and of the Council; (b) in cases other than those referred to in point (a), any other national authority responsible for the supervision of the issuer'. Since the information is not yet disclosed, the notification must ensure, according to Article 5 of implementing Regulation 2016/1055 of 29 June 2016, along with its completeness and integrity, the 'confidentiality of the information, through a dedicated contact point within, or designated by, the competent authority'. The NCA must **B.17.101**

[153] The 2011 proposal (art 12(5)) referred to the systemic importance of the inside information.
[154] See n 20.
[155] See n 21.
[156] The reference in art 17(6) to the NCA specified under art 17(3) is without prejudice to the ability of the competent authority to exercise its functions in any of the ways referred to in art 23.

communicate to the issuer its decision whether to consent under the same conditions.[157] When consenting to the delay, the NCA has to ensure that 'disclosure of the inside information is delayed only for a period as is necessary in the public interest' and evaluate at least on a weekly basis whether the conditions set out in points (a), (b), and (c) of Article 17(5) are still met. In case the NCA refuses to consent to the delay of disclosure, the issuer must disclose the inside information 'immediately'.

III. Sanctions

B.17.102 Breaches of disclosure and other requirements set out in Article 17 give rise to the general administrative measures and sanctions defined in Article 30 ff. They do not per se expose their authors to the criminal sanctions provided for in the Market Abuse Directive on Criminal Sanctions (2014/57/EU), which would only be applicable where the infringement comprises all the constituent elements of one of its criminal offences *ie* insider dealing, unlawful disclosure of inside information and market manipulation, notably in the form of a dissemination of false information, including failure properly to disclose inside information to the public.[158] Civil liability rules lie beyond the realm of the Market Abuse Regulation, despite the major role they can play in this area.[159] It should also be kept in mind that, when it enters into force, the MiFID II will mandate NCAs to require that the suspension or removal from trading of a financial instrument that no longer complies with the rules of a trading venue (regulated market, MTF, or OTF), be extended to the other trading venues (regulated markets, MTFs, OTFs, and systematic internalizers) falling under their jurisdiction and trading the same financial instrument or derivatives, 'where the suspension or removal is due to suspected market abuse, a take-over bid or the non-disclosure of inside information about the issuer or financial instrument infringing Articles 7 and 17 of Regulation (EU) No 596/2014 except where such suspension or removal could cause significant damage to the investors' interests or the orderly functioning of the market' (MiFID II Articles 32 and 52).

[157] According to ESMA, these written requirements do not preclude oral discussions between the issuer and the competent authority, ESMA, 'Technical Standard' (n 56) para 255.

[158] See ESMA 'Q&A, ESMA70-145-11' (n 132) 10.

[159] See on the variety of national experience, Koch, 'Disclosure of Inside Information' (n 18) para 19 n 105 ff; see also, for France, A Pietrancosta, 'Délits boursiers: la réparation du préjudice subi par l'investisseur' RTDF 2007 no 3 p 21; N Spitz, *La réparation des préjudices boursiers* (Banque 2010).

Article 18: Insider lists

1. Issuers or any person acting on their behalf or on their account, shall:
   (a) draw up a list of all persons who have access to inside information and who are working for them under a contract of employment, or otherwise performing tasks through which they have access to inside information, such as advisers, accountants or credit rating agencies (insider list);
   (b) promptly update the insider list in accordance with paragraph 4; and
   (c) provide the insider list to the competent authority as soon as possible upon its request.
2. Issuers or any person acting on their behalf or on their account, shall take all reasonable steps to ensure that any person on the insider list acknowledges in writing the legal and regulatory duties entailed and is aware of the sanctions applicable to insider dealing and unlawful disclosure of inside information.
   Where another person acting on behalf or on the account of the issuer assumes the task of drawing up and updating the insider list, the issuer remains fully responsible for complying with this Article. The issuer shall always retain a right of access to the insider list.
3. The insider list shall include at least:
   (a) the identity of any person having access to inside information;
   (b) the reason for including that person in the insider list;
   (c) the date and time at which that person obtained access to inside information; and
   (d) the date on which the insider list was drawn up.
4. Issuers or any person acting on their behalf or on their account shall update the insider list promptly, including the date of the update, in the following circumstances:
   (a) where there is a change in the reason for including a person already on the insider list;
   (b) where there is a new person who has access to inside information and needs, therefore, to be added to the insider list; and
   (c) where a person ceases to have access to inside information.

Each update shall specify the date and time when the change triggering the update occurred.

5. Issuers or any person acting on their behalf or on their account shall retain the insider list for a period of at least five years after it is drawn up or updated.

6. Issuers whose financial instruments are admitted to trading on an SME growth market shall be exempt from drawing up an insider list, provided that the following conditions are met:

(a) the issuer takes all reasonable steps to ensure that any person with access to inside information acknowledges the legal and regulatory duties entailed and is aware of the sanctions applicable to insider dealing and unlawful disclosure of inside information; and

(b) the issuer is able to provide the competent authority, upon request, with an insider list.

7. This Article shall apply to issuers who have requested or approved admission of their financial instruments to trading on a regulated market in a Member State or, in the case of an instrument only traded on an MTF or an OTF, have approved trading of their financial instruments on an MTF or an OTF or have requested admission to trading of their financial instruments on an MTF in a Member State.

8. Paragraphs 1 to 5 of this Article shall also apply to:

(a) emission allowance market participants in relation to inside information concerning emission allowances that arises in relation to the physical operations of that emission allowance market participant;

(b) any auction platform, auctioneer and auction monitor in relation to auctions of emission allowances or other auctioned products based thereon that are held pursuant to Regulation (EU) No 1031/2010.

9. In order to ensure uniform conditions of application of this Article, ESMA shall develop draft implementing technical standards to determine the precise format of insider lists and the format for updating insider lists referred to in this Article.

ESMA shall submit those draft implementing technical standards to the Commission by 3 July 2016.

Power is conferred on the Commission to adopt the implementing technical standards referred to in the first subparagraph in accordance with Article 15 of Regulation (EU) No 1095/2010.

I. General Remarks

Overview of Article 18

Insider lists are a prophylactic measure that have the specific purpose to enforce the ban on insider dealing.[1] While the register of insiders' transactions[2] is a public list that comprises persons 'discharging managerial responsibilities' for purposes connected to disclosure and insider dealing, insider lists are not public but should be available for authorities investigating possible violations more specifically connected to (and possibly preventing) insider dealing.[3] **B.18.01**

Insider lists, introduced with the (former) Market Abuse Directive (2003/6/EC), are beneficial for both the competent authorities, to investigate on potential market abuses effectively,[4] in the view of protecting the market integrity (for example they are helpful when assessing 'the opportunity of opening an investigation should be opened vs. used when a formal investigation has already been opened'),[5] and issuers, 'to control the flow of inside information and thereby help manage their confidentiality duties'.[6] Article 18 requires issuers as well as any person acting on their behalf to create and update insider lists. Such lists shall comply with specific requirements, including a format and a template, that respond to the need of full harmonization at European level. **B.18.02**

Structure of Article 18

Article 18(1)[7] requires issuers, as well as any person acting on their behalf, to create and update insider lists. The new provisions apply to issuers 'who have requested or approved admission of their financial instruments to trading on a regulated market in a Member State' or, in the case of instruments exclusively traded on an MTF or on an OTF, 'issuers who have approved trading of their financial instruments on an MTF or an OTF or have requested admission to trading of their financial instruments on an MTF in a Member State' (Article 18(7)). Such **B.18.03**

---

[1] Jesper Lau Hansen, 'MAD in a Hurry: The Swift and Promising Adoption of the EU Market Abuse Directive' (2004) 15 European Business Law Review 183.

[2] ibid: 'The publication of insiders' transactions was proposed by the Council in its common position (Common position (EC) no 50/2002, (2002/C 228 E/03) but for reasons of privacy it was suggested that the publication of the transactions could be done on an aggregated basis, thereby in effect granting anonymity to the insiders. An anonymous disclosure obligation is close to being an oxymoron, and the concept was overturned by the 2nd reading of the Parliament insisting that the publication must be done at least on an individual basis (Ref 13427/02)'.

[3] ibid.

[4] Recital (56).

[5] ESMA, 'Final Report: Guidelines on the MAR: market soundings and delay of disclosure of inside information (ESMA/2016/1130)' (13 July 2016) 58 www.esma.org.

[6] Recital (57). See also ESMA, 'Final Report' (n 5) 58.

[7] Note that under the 2011 Proposal for a Market Abuse Regulation, the actual art 18 was art 13.

lists should encompass a broad range of actors, not only 'all persons who have access to inside information and who are working for them under a contract of employment', but also those 'performing tasks through which they have access to inside information, such as advisers, accountants or credit rating agencies'. Article 18(8) extends this obligation to emission allowance market participants (EAMPs) and to any auction platform, auctioneer, and auction monitor. Article 18(2) further specifies that issuers or any person acting on their behalf or on their account, shall take all reasonable steps to ensure the written acknowledgement by any person on the insider list of the legal and regulatory duties entailed and the awareness of the sanctions applicable to insider dealing and unlawful disclosure of inside information. The issuer remains fully responsible for the compliance of insider lists, even where another person acting on behalf or on the account of the issuer assumes the task of drawing up and updating the insider list.

B.18.04 Article 18(3) provides a set of information that insider lists shall necessarily contain: data on the identity of the insider as well as the reasons for including such persons in the insider lists and any factual circumstances on the effective access by the insider on the inside information. This information has been further detailed by ESMA, in carrying out its mandate to develop implementing technical standards, as provided by Article 18(9).

B.18.05 Article 18(4) sets forth the duty for issuers or any person acting on their behalf or on their account to update the insider list promptly, including the date of the update, when specific circumstances occur, in particular where a change occurs in the reason for including a person that is already on the insider list, as well as where a new person has access to inside information or ceases to have access to inside information.

B.18.06 Article 18(6) introduces a lighter regime,[8] both on the content of the list and means of transmission, for issuers whose financial instruments are admitted to trading on an SME growth market.[9] If specific conditions[10] are met, such issuers

[8] The decision to provide a lighter regime has been revised: 'The initial approach proposed in the CP was to require SME issuers to provide upon request a similar insider list, in terms of content, to the one used by non-SME issuers, as the risks of non-compliance with the provisions of Market Abuse Regulation by SME issuers are the same (if not higher) than for non-SME issuers. Similarly, the formats proposed to use for transmitting the insider list to the competent authority were the same (electronic and machine readable form using secure electronic means)'. ESMA, 'Draft Technical Standards on the Market Abuse Regulation' (28 September 2015) ESMA/2015/1455.

[9] In accordance with art 3(1)(11) in conjunction with art 4(1)(12) of MiFID II a 'SME growth market' means a MTF that is registered as an SME growth market in accordance with art 33 of MiFID II. One of the conditions of art 33 of MiFID II is that at least 50% of the issuers whose financial instruments are admitted to trading on the MTF are SMEs at the time when the MTF is registered as an SME growth market. Furthermore, art 4(1)(13) of MiFID II states that (for the purposes of that Directive) SMEs means companies that had an average market capitalization of less than €200,000,000 on the basis of end-year quotes for the previous three calendar years.

[10] The Proposal for a Market Abuse Regulation did not require any specific conditions for exempting SME growth market issuers.

shall be exempt from drawing up an insider list. An SME issuer is exempted if it takes all reasonable steps to ensure that any person with access to inside information acknowledges the legal and regulatory duties entailed and is aware of the sanctions applicable to insider dealing and unlawful disclosure of inside information, and it is able to provide the competent authority with an insider list, if it requests that. The insider list shall be drawn up, complying with the template elaborated by ESMA, adopting 'a format that ensures that the completeness, integrity and confidentiality of the information are maintained during the transmission'.[11]

The structure of Article 18 substantially incorporates the provisions of Article 6(3)(3) (former) Market Abuse Directive (2003/6/EC) and Article 5 of the level 2 Directive 2004/72. **B.18.07**

Historical background

Insider lists have been introduced with the (former) Market Abuse Directive (2003/6/EC). Article 6(3), which required the drawing up of such lists by issuers or persons acting on their behalf or for their account. Article 5 of Directive 2004/72 of 29 April 2004 establishes a set of items that an insider list should contain. **B.18.08**

Article 6 of the Proposal for a (former) Market Abuse Directive required issuers and entities acting on their behalf to prepare and update a list of insiders. **B.18.09**

The final version of Article 6 of the (former) Market Abuse Directive (2003/6/EC) adopted a wording closer to the one replicated for Market Abuse Regulation: 'Member States shall require that issuers, or persons acting on their behalf or for their account, draw up a list of those persons working for them, under a contract of employment or otherwise, who have access to inside information. Issuers and persons acting on their behalf or for their account shall regularly update this list and transmit it to the competent authority whenever the latter requests it'. **B.18.10**

Article 5 of Directive 2004/72 required lists to provide information on the identity of the insiders, the reasons why such persons were part of the list as well as the date at which the list of insiders was created and the reasons to update such lists. It also required to promptly update insider lists in the same cases. Insiders had to acknowledge the legal and regulatory duties entailed and be aware of the sanctions attaching to the misuse or improper circulation of such information. Article 5 did not specify the form of such acknowledgement, which was not the case with Article 18. **B.18.11**

[11] Commission Implementing Regulation (EU) 2016/347 of 10 March 2016 laying down implementing technical standards with regard to the precise format of insider lists and for updating insider lists in accordance with art 4.

B.18.12 The view adopted by the European institutions with regard to insider lists has been towards a higher degree of prescription with new information required: name, professional and personal telephone numbers, date of birth and national identification number were not provided by the (former) Market Abuse Directive (2003/6/EC) and the implementing directives.

B.18.13 Given the divergence of national implementation of the (former) Market Abuse Directive (2003/6/EC), CESR emphasized the difficulties encountered by issuers whose financial instruments were admitted to trading on regulated markets in different European jurisdictions. Such issuers had 'to comply with the requirement to draw up and maintain insider list in accordance with the various legal frameworks applicable in the concerned jurisdictions'.[12] CESR clearly stated that the potential overlapping of requirement should be preferred to loopholes, but that at the same time 'such overlapping could prove "burdensome" for issuers'.[13] In such a situation, CESR recommended that 'for an issuer subject to the jurisdiction of more than one EU or EEA Member State with respect to insider list requirements, it is recommended that the relevant competent authorities recognize insider lists prepared by an issuer that has its registered office in another EU or EEA Member State, according to this Member State's requirements'.[14] However, this non-binding recommendation[15] did not challenge the fact that an issuer had an obligation 'in each of the relevant jurisdictions to establish an insider list and the right for the competent authority from any of these jurisdictions to request such list'.[16]

B.18.14 ESME, in its evaluation report on the (former) Market Abuse Directive (2003/6/EC), cast doubts on the effectiveness of insider lists and expressed a rather critical view. First, it noted that, while insider lists have served to identify those in possession of confidential information, under the (former) Market Abuse Directive (2003/6/EC), 'the purpose of the lists has become more confused, while it is questionable if a list can provide guidance as to whether a particular person has in fact received particular information. Lists seldom appear to provide valuable information about the "true" insider traders'.[17] The ESME report distinguished between two situations: a deal-specific case and a general course of business

[12] CESR, 'Market Abuse Directive Level 3: Second set of CESR guidance and information on the common operation of the Directive to the market' (November 2006) 14.

[13] ibid.

[14] ibid.

[15] See L Enriques and M Gatti, 'Is There a Uniform EU Securities Law after the Financial Services Action Plan?' (2008–2009) 14 Stanford Journal of Law, Business and Finance 43, who emphasize that the non-binding nature of level 3 recommendations may have weaken the effectiveness of CESR's guidance.

[16] ibid. CESR also clarified that: 'with respect to the persons acting on behalf of for the account of the issuer, regardless of their nationality or their location or place of incorporation, the rules to follow have to be the rules of the jurisdiction applicable to the issuer'.

[17] ESME Report, 'Market abuse EU legal framework and its implementation by Member States: a first evaluation' (6 July 2007).

situation. In the former, it emphasized that, in principle, 'if the list is being maintained by an issuer then, logically those on the list should be those who possess information in the brief window between the information rising to the level of inside information and its disclosure to the market under the requirement to do so as soon as possible'.[18] Instead, in practice, 'people are added to the list because they possess confidential information and are part of a "deal team"',[19] and therefore the duties contained in the (former) Market Abuse Directive (2003/6/EC) do not have an impact on the market practice and do not provide any additional information that could be valuable for the purposes of the regulators.[20] For those placed on lists because of their occasional access to inside information, the ESME report underlined that the long lists of names, 'do not provide real guidance as to whether a particular person has in fact received particular information'.[21] It also highlighted specific issues related to maintaining one central insider list, with regard to the identification of inside information, the extent to which those employees who have 'occasional' access to inside information were to be placed on the list, as well as 'the way the obligation to keep insiders list has been devised by the relevant directives'.[22]

CESR maintained its position on the relevance of insider lists, 'expected to have raised the importance that companies put on the careful handling of inside information and helped issuers to monitor the flow of inside information and hence to comply with their duties of secrecy'.[23] It also remarked on the quality of information received so far through insider lists, owing to the requirements of completeness and preciseness of the insider list,[24] as well as their relevance for competent authorities in the context of a market abuse enquiry or investigation, where they are used as a 'first glance tool', 'without prejudice for the authority to require additional information from the issuer, as it is usually done, when a case is investigated'.[25] **B.18.15**

CESR also pointed out the risks associated with a large number of people, within an organization, having access to inside information and therefore placed on lists: in the view of CESR, issuers should 'make every effort to keep inside information known to as small a group of people as possible'.[26] It also reminded that 'to be included by a company on its insiders list, the concept of having access to inside information means that the person concerned must have access **B.18.16**

[18] ibid.
[19] ibid.
[20] ibid.
[21] ibid.
[22] ibid.
[23] CESR, 'Market Abuse Directive Level 3: Third set of CESR guidance and information on the common operation of the Directive to the market' (15 May 2009).
[24] ibid.
[25] ibid.
[26] ibid.

to information as a result of his activities or duties within the issuer or persons acting on their behalf, as opposed to obtaining access by other means, such as by accident, of which the issuer is not aware'.[27]

B.18.17 In 2011, the European Commission considered that there was a case for harmonizing insider lists at the European level:[28] 'This option would entail prescribing conclusively the precise data an insider list has to contain in relation to each individual included on the insider list, rather than prescribing only minimum requirements'. In the view of the European Commission, this would be beneficial in terms of lowering administrative burdens, in particular for issuers operating in multiple jurisdictions, while enhancing legal certainty for all issuers and contributing to a further integration and level playing field across the European markets as a whole, without diminishing the investor protection.[29] The European Commission also noted that a disadvantage of harmonization would be the reduction of regulators' discretion with regard to the data fields to be included in insider lists, owing to their experience with their current requirements.

B.18.18 The decision to harmonize insider lists has characterized the further steps that drove the approval of the Market Abuse Regulation as well as its implementing acts. The regulatory strategy was based on the assumption that a homogenous structure for insider lists across the EU would be consistent with the replacement of the directive by a regulation, while achieving considerable cost savings for issuers across Europe.[30]

II. Insider Lists: Information and Template

Introduction

B.18.19 Pursuant to Article 18(3), the list shall contain at least the following elements: the identity of any person having access to inside information; the reason for including that person in the insider list; the date and time at which that person obtained access to inside information; and the date on which the insider list was drawn up.[31]

B.18.20 As Recital (57) emphasized, 'national differences in regard to data to be included in those lists impose unnecessary administrative burdens on issuers. Data fields required for insider lists should therefore be uniform in order to reduce those costs'. Consistently with this, the Market Abuse Regulation now provides more stringent requirements in relation to the minimum elements that a list shall

[27] ibid.
[28] See Commission staff working paper impact assessment.
[29] ibid.
[30] ESMA, 'Final Report' (n 5).
[31] Article 18(3) Market Abuse Regulation.

contain: the identity of any person having access to inside information, the reason for including such persons in the list, as well as more precise information not only on the date but also on the time at which that person obtained and ceased to have access to inside information, the date on which the insider list was drawn up and updated.[32] In addition, ESMA was mandated to 'develop draft implementing technical standards to determine the precise format of insider lists and the format for updating insider lists, with the purpose to ensure uniform conditions of application' of Article 18.[33] ESMA consulted stakeholders by way of a Discussion Paper[34] followed by a Consultation Paper.[35] The Commission Implementing Regulation (level 2) was adopted on 10 March 2016.[36]

The information to be provided in the insider lists

The template proposed by ESMA in the course of the consultation raised concerns at different levels: data protection and privacy, administrative burden, and ability of competent authorities to investigate effectively.[37] **B.18.21**

In terms of data protection and privacy, a large number of respondents highlighted the personal invasiveness for the employees in relation to the information to be included in the insider lists, as well as the possibility of data theft if such personal information is visible on an insider list, and the risks for firms of non-compliance with regulations on data protection and privacy.[38] Concerns were connected to the difficulty to 'maintain a high level of information for all insiders on an on-going basis'.[39] **B.18.22**

With regard to the identity of the insiders, ESMA proposed to include a high number of items,[40] raising concerns among respondents to the public consultation. The reactions to the consultations drove ESMA to shorten the amount of information to be inserted within the list, acknowledging the concerns from both the perspectives of data protection and administrative burden, without reducing their effectiveness as a useful tool when detecting and investigating market abuse practices. The definitive list of items to be provided includes: a. Name: First **B.18.23**

---

32 ibid art 18(3) and (4).

33 ibid art 18(9).

34 ESMA, 'Discussion Paper: ESMA's policy orientations on possible implementing measures under the Market Abuse Regulation' (14 November 2013).

35 Consultation Paper on ESMA's draft technical advice on possible delegated acts concerning the Market Abuse Regulation (ESMA/2014/809) (15 July 2014).

36 Commission Implementing Regulation (EU) 2016/347 of 10 March 2016 laying down implementing technical standards with regard to the precise format of insider lists and for updating insider lists in accordance with the Article 2(1).

37 ESMA, 'Final Report' (n 5) 58.

38 ibid.

39 ibid.

40 ESMA, 'ESMA's policy orientations on possible implementing measures under the Market Abuse Regulation, Discussion Paper (ESMA/2013/1649)' (14 November 2013).

name, surname, birth surname (if different from surname); b. Company name and address; c. Work direct line and work mobile telephone numbers; d. Function and reason for being insider; e. Date and time at which the person obtained inside information; f. Date and time at which the person ceased to have access to inside information; g. Date of birth; 'National Identification Number' (where applicable in the concerned Member State); h. Personal home and personal mobile telephone numbers; i. Personal full address: street name; street number; city; post/zip code; country.

B.18.24 Pursuant to the Market Abuse Regulation, the name of the insider is 'a compulsory first step to ascertain his identity'.[41] Other Level 1 pieces of information are the function and the reason for being an insider, crucial to understand the capacity of the insider when accessing the inside information and to define his role in the context of the deal, as well as the date of obtained and ceased access to inside information, to identify the exact timeframe during which the inside information was available and accessible to the insider.[42] The date of birth, the national identification number and the personal address are further information valuable to identify an individual.[43] Both the personal and professional telephone numbers serve to access communications traffic data.[44] Owing to the 'inferential nature of market abuse cases', traffic data is extremely important to understand the 'connections between people and patterns of behaviour demonstrated by the interplay of contacts and actions following those contacts'.[45]

B.18.25 The company name and address have a function in identifying a person and further understanding his role in the deal, while the precise location of the insider may be helpful for competent authorities to understand his branch or office.[46]

The structure of insider lists

B.18.26 The approach followed by the European regulators has consisted in requiring from an issuer, an EAMP and an auction entity 'to draw up the insider list in the form of Deal-specific/Event based sections, while allowing them to decide to also draw up, in addition, a separate and complementary section that will include only the permanent insiders'.[47]

---

[41] ESMA, 'Final Report' (n 5) 58.
[42] ibid 60.
[43] ibid 59.
[44] ibid.
[45] ibid 59. ESMA further explains that: 'Where these records show telephone numbers for regulated firms, some competent authorities may also be able to access the content of the calls. Where content of calls is available, considering that persons on an insider list in Market Abuse Regulation are subject to a reverse burden of proof, this information could be very useful for their elimination from an investigation or indeed for their defence if necessary'.
[46] ibid 60.
[47] ibid 62.

Consistently with this approach, the Implementing regulation of 10 March 2016 requires that insider list shall be 'divided into separate sections relating to different inside information', further specifying that 'new sections shall be added to the insider list upon the identification of new inside information',[48] accordingly with the definition of Article 7. Each section of the insider list shall only include details of individuals having access to the inside information relevant to that section.[49] Such deal-specific/event-based sections are referred to a particular piece of inside information for occasional insiders, with the inclusion of all the insiders in respect to that specific information: as ESMA clarified, 'the event referred to is the coming into existence of inside information which may or may not correspond to a temporal or contractual event'.[50] These sections typically include employees of the issuers who have access to an inside information, given their specific functions relating to a specific transaction.[51] With regard to the staff of advisers to issuers, substantially in line with the (former) Market Abuse Directive (2003/6/EC), it shall be included in the insider lists only if it performs tasks through which it has access to inside information on the issuer and it is acting on behalf of or for the account of the issuer.[52] Insider lists shall include the deal teams and client-facing staff, if they have access to inside information, as well as senior management receiving management information or sitting on review committees even if not directly involved in the transactions, and secretarial staff and other support staff when they have access to inside information.[53] Analysts as well as financial journalists are not a priori subject to inclusion in insider lists, since in principle issuers' information is not available to them: only in the case of a potential access to the issuers' inside information, should they be included in the issuers' list of insiders.[54] **B.18.27**

In addition, the Implementing Regulation of 10 March 2016 maintains the practice of issuers, providing the possibility of a supplementary section of the insider list for individuals who have access at all times to all inside information ('permanent insiders').[55] The permanent insiders section shall encompass individuals considered insiders in respect of all types of inside information, given **B.18.28**

---

48 Commission Implementing Regulation art 2(1).

49 ibid.

50 ESMA, 'Final Report' (n 5) 61.

51 See eg AMF, 'Établissement des listes d'initiés par les émetteurs d'instruments financiers (Position n 2006–11)' (2006) www.amf.fr.

52 City of London Law Society and Law Society Company Law Committees' Joint Working Parties on Market Abuse, Share Plans and Takeovers Code, Market Abuse Regulation (EU MAR) Q&A (6 July) 18 http://www.lawsociety.org.uk/news/Stories/law-society-and-city-of-london-law-society-query-fca-on-market-abuse-regulation/.

53 ibid. With regard to the secretarial staff, the document specifies that individuals who have access to IT systems but whose duties do not require them to access inside information do not need to be included unless they have actually accessed it.

54 See AMF, 'Position n 2006–11' (n 51) 2.

55 ibid para 2.

the nature of their function or position within the organization.[56] Typically, individuals included in this list are: members of the board of directors, CEOs, relevant persons discharging management responsibility, related staff members (such as secretaries and personal assistants), internal auditors, people having access to databases on budgetary control or balance sheet analyses, and people who work in units that have regular access to inside information (such as IT people).[57]

B.18.29 As CESR explained, the regular and occasional access to inside information is a matter of fact, that triggers the obligation to include a person in an insiders' list and this access to inside information 'means that the person concerned must have access to information as a result of his activities or duties within the issuer or persons acting on their behalf, as opposed to obtaining access by other means, such as by accident, of which the issuer is not aware'.[58]

Potential vs effective insiders

B.18.30 Both Article 18(1) and the Implementing Regulation may cast doubts (as the (former) Market Abuse Directive (2003/6/EC) did) on the persons to be included in the insider list, if such list shall include those who can have access to inside information (potential insiders) or those who effectively have access to inside information (effective insiders).[59] The goal of the rule to provide a support to regulators in the context of potential insider transactions, coupled with the utilization of the term 'insider' to refer all the persons included in the lists, and the information to be provided (in particular date and time of the effective access to the inside information) suggest that only the effective insiders and not the potential ones shall be included in the list.[60]

The definition of permanent insiders

B.18.31 The definition of 'permanent insiders' may raise concerns. Pursuant to the Implementing Regulation, 'permanent insiders' are persons who have access at all times to all inside information,[61] given the nature of their function or position within the organization. Given the restrictive notion of permanent insiders, there are doubts about the categories of persons to include. The formulation of

[56] ESMA, 'Final Report' (n 5) 61. ESMA clarifies that permanent insiders do not need to be included in each and every deal-specific/event-based section.

[57] CESR, 'Third set' (n 23) para 15.

[58] ibid para 11. In this context, CESR recommended that: 'the emphasis should be on the access (regular/occasional) of persons to inside information rather than on the existence, in some jurisdictions, of a distinction between regular and occasional insiders'.

[59] L Legein, 'Le nouveau règlement Abus de Marché et ses conséquences pour les sociétés cotées belges' (TRV–RPS 2016) 502, spec n° 46.

[60] ibid.

[61] Commission Implementing Regulation art 2(2).

this rule leaves open the possibility for an excessively restrictive interpretation, only including persons who, given their role, have access to all inside information and could access the information before it became inside information, ie through inter alia the issuer's executive directors, chairman, general manager, and its staff.[62] On the other hand, the reduction of the insider lists' length may be conducive to enhanced effectiveness of this tool.

The format of insider lists

The format of insider lists is electronic and the Implementing Regulation of 10 March 2016 now provides a template to be followed.[63] The electronic format shall respect three parameters: (i) the confidentiality of the information included by ensuring that access to the insider list is restricted to clearly identified persons from within the issuer, emission allowance market participant, auction platform, auctioneer, and auction monitor, or any person acting on their behalf or on their account that needs that access, owing to the nature of their function or position; (ii) the accuracy of the information contained in the insider list; (iii) the access to and the retrieval of previous versions of the insider list.[64] The insider list shall be submitted using the electronic means[65] specified by the competent authorities, as specified on their website.[66] Those electronic means shall ensure that completeness, integrity, and confidentiality of the information are maintained during the transmission.[67] **B.18.32**

The interpretation of Article 18(2)(2): the full responsibility of the issuers

Article 18(2)(2) provides that where 'another person acting on behalf or on the account of the issuer assumes the task of drawing up and updating the insider list', the issuer remains fully responsible for complying with this Article. The issuer shall always retain a right of access to the insider list. A critical issue has been identified with regard to this provision, which may be interpreted in two different ways. According to a restrictive view, it should only apply to persons who draw up and update the list on behalf of the issuer, as in the case of a company **B.18.33**

62 See Assonime, 'La disciplina sugli abusi di mercato: problemi e incertezze nell'applicazione per le società italiane e alcune ipotesi interpretative' (19 October 2016) 11 www.assonime.it.

63 Commission Implementing Regulation art 2(3) para 3. As provided by art 1, '"electronic means" are means of electronic equipment for the processing (including digital compression), storage and transmission of data, employing wires, radio, optical technologies, or any other electromagnetic means'.

64 ibid art 2(4) para 4.

65 ibid. As provided by art 1: '"electronic means" are means of electronic equipment for the processing (including digital compression), storage and transmission of data, employing wires, radio, optical technologies, or any other electromagnetic means'.

66 ibid art 2(5) para 5.

67 ibid.

within the same group. In a broader interpretation, this provision shall also apply to third-parties such as consultants or intermediaries acting in deals on behalf of the issuer and therefore having access to the issuer's inside information.[68] Under the (former) Market Abuse Directive (2003/6/EC), third-parties acting on behalf of the issuer could draw up their own lists, to register those persons who within their structure had access to issuer's inside information and were fully responsible for the creation and maintenance of such lists. The issuer had a duty to provide in its own list the name of the consultant that drew up the list, as was the case in France,[69] Italy,[70] and Germany.[71] As no intention was expressed to depart radically from the previous framework,[72] it would be reasonable to consider that Article 18(2) only applies to those persons who draw up and update the list on behalf of the issuer.

The impact of the new regulation on permanent insider lists

B.18.34 Issuers have systematically included a large number of individuals in the list of permanent insiders. The Market Abuse Regulation has strengthened the importance of lists to be implemented in connection with new events for each inside information. This approach may potentially have an impact on issuers' practices, making an effective update of the insiders' list more complicated.

B.18.35 To avoid burdensome and inefficient processes, a potential solution would consist in structuring the list of permanent insiders with specific subsections that would correspond to specific recurrent inside information, on the basis of the model of the periodic information. This would make it easier to include in each subsection those permanent insiders who always have access to that specific inside information.[73]

B.18.36 To be compliant with the Market Abuse Regulation, issuers will have to review and update their process for creating and maintaining insider lists. A major issue relates to the availability of the information required and the difficulties connected to the potential consents or approval to be obtained from individuals

---

[68] Assonime, 'La disciplina sugli abusi di mercato' (n 62) 11.

[69] See AMF, 'Position n 2006-11' (n 51) 2.

[70] See Consob, Comunicazione no 6027054, 'Informazione al pubblico su eventi e circostanze rilevanti e adempimenti per la prevenzione degli abusi di mercato: Raccomandazioni e chiarimenti' (28 March 2006) para 103.

[71] See Bafin, 'Issuer Guidelines' (2009) para VII.2.2.

[72] ESMA, 'Consultation Paper: Draft technical standards on the Market Abuse Regulation (ESMA/2014/809)' (15 July 2014) para 303, which only stated that: 'in case of a third party acting on behalf or on the account of the issuer, the EAMP or the auction entity (third party), issuers also could consider whether to provide to the CA: a. a single consolidated insider list, fully and solely maintained by the issuer, the EAMP or the auction entity; or b. separate insider lists (ie the insider list of the issuer, the EAMP or the auction entity itself and the insider list(s) of the third party(ies))'; see www.esma.org.

[73] ibid 12.

not to infringe any national data protection or privacy requirements,[74] starting from 'permanent' insiders as well as any other individuals 'to be listed in connection to any existing transactions which are unlikely to announce prior to Market Abuse Regulation coming into effect'.[75] From a more general perspective, it will be important to implement a full integration of 'the process for gathering the necessary information in respect of other relevant individuals into the company's existing systems and procedures and how the information gathered will be stored and updated'.[76]

III. Sanctions

See comment on Article 17. **B.18.37**

[74] Norton Rose Fulbright, The Market Abuse Regulation: Key considerations for UK listed issuers, February 2016 http://www.nortonrosefulbright.com/knowledge/publications/136820/the-market-abuse-regulation-key-considerations-for-uk-listed-issuers#section5.
[75] ibid.
[76] ibid.

Article 19: Managers' transactions

1. Persons discharging managerial responsibilities, as well as persons closely associated with them, shall notify the issuer or the emission allowance market participant and the competent authority referred to in the second subparagraph of paragraph 2:
   (a) in respect of issuers, of every transaction conducted on their own account relating to the shares or debt instruments of that issuer or to derivatives or other financial instruments linked thereto;
   (b) in respect of emission allowance market participants, of every transaction conducted on their own account relating to emission allowances, to auction products based thereon or to derivatives relating thereto.

Such notifications shall be made promptly and no later than three business days after the date of the transaction.

The first subparagraph applies once the total amount of transactions has reached the threshold set out in paragraph 8 or 9, as applicable, within a calendar year.

1a. The notification obligation referred to in paragraph 1 shall not apply to transactions in financial instruments linked to shares or to debt instruments of the issuer referred to in that paragraph where at the time of the transaction any of the following conditions is met:
   (a) the financial instrument is a unit or share in a collective investment undertaking in which the exposure to the issuer's shares or debt instruments does not exceed 20 per cent of the assets held by the collective investment undertaking;
   (b) the financial instrument provides exposure to a portfolio of assets in which the exposure to the issuer's shares or debt instruments does not exceed 20 per cent of the portfolio's assets;
   (c) the financial instrument is a unit or share in a collective investment undertaking or provides exposure to a portfolio of assets and the person discharging managerial responsibilities or person closely associated with such a person does not know, and could not know, the investment composition or exposure of such collective investment undertaking or portfolio of assets in relation to the issuer's shares or debt instruments, and furthermore there is no reason for that person to believe that the issuer's shares or debt instruments exceed the thresholds in point (a) or (b).

If information regarding the investment composition of the collective investment undertaking or exposure to the portfolio of assets is available, then the person discharging managerial responsibility or person closely associated with such a person shall make all reasonable efforts to avail themselves of that information.

2. For the purposes of paragraph 1, and without prejudice to the right of Member States to provide for notification obligations other than those referred to in this Article, all transactions conducted on the own account of the persons referred to in paragraph 1, shall be notified by those persons to the competent authorities.

The rules applicable to notifications, with which persons referred to in paragraph 1 must comply, shall be those of the Member State where the issuer or emission allowance market participant is registered. Notifications shall be made within three working days of the transaction date to the competent authority of that Member State. Where the issuer is not registered in a Member State, the notification shall be made to the competent authority of the home Member State in accordance with point (i) of Article 2(1) of Directive 2004/109/EC or, in the absence thereof, to the competent authority of the trading venue.

3. The issuer or emission allowance market participant shall ensure that the information, that is notified in accordance with paragraph 1 is made public promptly and no later than three business days after the transaction in a manner which enables fast access to this information on a non-discriminatory basis in accordance with the implementing technical standards referred to in point (a) of Article 17(10).

The issuer or emission allowance market participant shall use such media as may reasonably be relied upon for the effective dissemination of information to the public throughout the Union, and, where applicable, it shall use the officially appointed mechanism referred to in Article 21 of Directive 2004/109/EC.

Alternatively, national law may provide that a competent authority may itself make public the information.

4. This Article shall apply to issuers who:
   (a) have requested or approved admission of their financial instruments to trading on a regulated market; or
   (b) in the case of an instrument only traded on an MTF or an OTF, have approved trading of their financial instruments on an MTF or an OTF or have requested admission to trading of their financial instruments on an MTF.
5. Issuers and emission allowance market participants shall notify the person discharging managerial responsibilities of their obligations under this Article in writing. Issuers and emission allowance market participants shall draw up a list of all persons discharging managerial responsibilities and persons closely associated with them.

Persons discharging managerial responsibilities shall notify the persons closely associated with them of their obligations under this Article in writing and shall keep a copy of this notification.

6. A notification of transactions referred to in paragraph 1 shall contain the following information:
   (a) the name of the person;

(b) the reason for notification;
(c) the name of the relevant issuer or emission allowance market participant;
(d) a description and the identifier of the financial instrument;
(e) the nature of the transaction(s) (e.g. acquisition or disposal), indicating whether it is linked to the exercise of share option programmes or to the specific examples set out in paragraph 7;
(f) the date and place of the transaction(s); and
(g) the price and volume of the transaction(s). In the case of a pledge whose terms provide for its value to change, this should be disclosed together with its value at the date of the pledge.

7. For the purposes of paragraph 1, transactions that must be notified shall also include:
   (a) the pledging or lending of financial instruments by or on behalf of a person discharging managerial responsibilities or a person closely associated with such a person, as referred to in paragraph 1;
   (b) transactions undertaken by persons professionally arranging or executing transactions or by another person on behalf of a person discharging managerial responsibilities or a person closely associated with such a person, as referred to in paragraph 1, including where discretion is exercised;
   (c) transactions made under a life insurance policy, defined in accordance with Directive 2009/138/EC of the European Parliament and of the Council, where:
      (i) the policyholder is a person discharging managerial responsibilities or a person closely associated with such a person, as referred to in paragraph 1,
      (ii) the investment risk is borne by the policyholder, and
      (iii) the policyholder has the power or discretion to make investment decisions regarding specific instruments in that life insurance policy or to execute transactions regarding specific instruments for that life insurance policy.

For the purposes of point (a), a pledge, or a similar security interest, of financial instruments in connection with the depositing of the financial instruments in a custody account does not need to be notified, unless and until such time that such pledge or other security interest is designated to secure a specific credit facility.

For the purposes of point (b), transactions executed in shares or debt instruments of an issuer or derivatives or other financial instruments linked thereto by managers of a collective investment undertaking in which the person discharging managerial responsibilities or a person closely associated with them has invested do not need to be notified where the manager of the collective investment undertaking operates with full discretion, which excludes the manager receiving any instructions or suggestions on portfolio composition directly or indirectly from investors in that collective investment undertaking.

Insofar as a policyholder of an insurance contract is required to notify transactions according to this paragraph, an obligation to notify is not incumbent on the insurance company.

8. Paragraph 1 shall apply to any subsequent transaction once a total amount of EUR 5 000 has been reached within a calendar year. The threshold of EUR 5 000 shall be calculated by adding without netting all transactions referred to in paragraph 1.
9. A competent authority may decide to increase the threshold set out in paragraph 8 to EUR 20 000 and shall inform ESMA of its decision and the justification for its decision, with specific reference to market conditions, to adopt the higher threshold prior to its application. ESMA shall publish on its website the list of thresholds that apply in accordance with this Article and the justifications provided by competent authorities for such thresholds.
10. This Article shall also apply to transactions by persons discharging managerial responsibilities within any auction platform, auctioneer and auction monitor involved in the auctions held under Regulation (EU) No 1031/2010 and to persons closely associated with such persons in so far as their transactions involve emission allowances, derivatives thereof or auctioned products based thereon. Those persons shall notify their transactions to the auction platforms, auctioneers and auction monitor, as applicable, and to the competent authority where the auction platform, auctioneer or auction monitor, as applicable, is registered. The information that is so notified shall be made public by the auction platforms, auctioneers, auction monitor or competent authority in accordance with paragraph 3.
11. Without prejudice to Articles 14 and 15, a person discharging managerial responsibilities within an issuer shall not conduct any transactions on its own account or for the account of a third party, directly or indirectly, relating to the shares or debt instruments of the issuer or to derivatives or other financial instruments linked to them during a closed period of 30 calendar days before the announcement of an interim financial report or a year-end report which the issuer is obliged to make public according to:
    (a) the rules of the trading venue where the issuer's shares are admitted to trading; or
    (b) national law.
12. Without prejudice to Articles 14 and 15, an issuer may allow a person discharging managerial responsibilities within it to trade on its own account or for the account of a third party during a closed period as referred to in paragraph 11 either:
    (a) on a case-by-case basis due to the existence of exceptional circumstances, such as severe financial difficulty, which require the immediate sale of shares; or
    (b) due to the characteristics of the trading involved for transactions made under, or related to, an employee share or saving scheme, qualification

or entitlement of shares, or transactions where the beneficial interest in the relevant security does not change.

13. The Commission shall be empowered to adopt delegated acts in accordance with Article 35 specifying the circumstances under which trading during a closed period may be permitted by the issuer, as referred to in paragraph 12, including the circumstances that would be considered as exceptional and the types of transaction that would justify the permission for trading.

14. The Commission shall be empowered to adopt delegated acts in accordance with Article 35, specifying types of transactions that would trigger the requirement referred to in paragraph 1.

15. In order to ensure uniform application of paragraph 1, ESMA shall develop draft implementing technical standards concerning the format and template in which the information referred to in paragraph 1 is to be notified and made public.

ESMA shall submit those draft implementing technical standards to the Commission by 3 July 2015.

Power is conferred on the Commission to adopt the implementing technical standards referred to in the first subparagraph in accordance with Article 15 of Regulation (EU) No 1095/2010.

Relevant Technical Standards:

Commission Delegated Regulation (EU) 2016/522 of 17 December 2015 supplementing Regulation (EU) No 596/2014 of the European Parliament and of the Council as regards an exemption for certain third countries public bodies and central banks, the indicators of market manipulation, the disclosure thresholds, the competent authority for notifications of delays, the permission for trading during closed periods and types of notifiable managers' transactions (OJ L 88, 5.4.2016, p. 1)

Commission Delegated Regulation (EU) 2016/523 of 10 March 2016 laying down implementing technical standards with regard to the format and template for notification and public disclosure of managers' transactions in accordance with Regulation (EU) No 596/2014 of the European Parliament and of the Council (OJ L 88 (5 April 2016) 19)

I. General Remarks

Overview of Article 19

Article 19 provides for the public disclosure of certain transactions entered into by persons discharging managerial responsibilities within an issuer or closely associated persons with them. It requires that persons discharging managerial responsibilities within an issuer and closely associated persons notify the issuer and the national competent authority of every transaction conducted on their own account relating to the shares or debt instruments of that issuer. In addition, the issuer itself is responsible for ensuring that the information is made public, unless national law provides that the national competent authority makes public the information. **B.19.01**

The main purpose of this disclosure obligation consists in the improvement of the transparency of financial markets.[1] More specifically, it is a preventive measure against market abuse, particularly insider dealing. The public disclosure of such transactions also contributes to the information available to investors and to the effectiveness of the competent authorities' supervision.[2] **B.19.02**

Structure of Article 19

Article 19(1) provides for persons discharging managerial responsibilities within an issuer and closely associated persons a duty to notify the issuer or the emission allowance market participant and the national competent authority. In respect of issuers, they shall notify every transaction conducted on their own account relating to the shares or debt instruments of that issuer or to derivatives or other financial instruments linked thereto. In respect of emission allowance market participants, the notification refers to every transaction conducted on their own account relating to emission allowances, to auction products based thereon, or to derivatives relating thereto. The regulation requires a prompt disclosure, in any case no later than three business days after the date of the transaction. **B.19.03**

Article 19(7) refers to specific transactions subject to notification. It sets a non-exhaustive list including: the pledging or lending of financial instruments by or on behalf of a person discharging managerial responsibilities within an issuer or a closely associated person; transactions undertaken by persons professionally arranging or executing transactions or by another person on behalf of a person discharging managerial responsibilities within an issuer or a closely associated person, as referred to in Article 19(1), including where discretion is exercised; transactions made under a life insurance policy under specific circumstances. **B.19.04**

---

[1] ESMA, 'ESMA's technical advice on possible delegated acts concerning the Market Abuse Regulation (ESMA/2015/224)' (3 February 2015) para 42 www.esma.org.

[2] ibid Annex II, Opinion of the Securities and Markets Stakeholder Group (Extracts) 72.

B.19.05 Article 19(10) enlarges the scope of this provision, including transactions by persons discharging managerial responsibilities within an issuer within any auction platform, auctioneer and auction monitor involved in the auctions held under Regulation (EU) No 1031/2010 and to closely associated persons in so far as their transactions involve emission allowances, derivatives thereof or auctioned products based thereon. Even in these circumstances, and at the same conditions, those persons have a duty of disclosure of their transactions to the auction platforms, auctioneers and auction monitor, as applicable, and to the competent authority where the auction platform, auctioneer or auction monitor, as applicable, is registered.

B.19.06 Moreover, the Commission shall be empowered to adopt delegated acts, specifying types of transactions that would trigger the requirement referred to in Article 19(1).

B.19.07 Such notification requirement is anchored to a *de minimis* threshold, provided by the Market Abuse Regulation: below this threshold, calculated taking into account a calendar year, no disclosure is required. Pursuant to Article 19(8), the disclosure obligation applies to any subsequent transaction once a total amount of €5,000 has been reached within a calendar year, calculated by adding without netting the referred transactions. A national competent authority may increase the threshold to €20,000 and, in such a case, has a duty to inform ESMA of its decision and of the justification for it, providing specific reasons connected to market conditions.

B.19.08 All referred transactions shall be notified to the issuers or the emission allowance market participants and to the national competent authorities (Article 19(1)). The rules applicable to notifications shall be those of the Member State where the issuer or the emission allowance market participant is registered. Notifications shall be made within three working days of the transaction.

B.19.09 Issuers or emission allowance market participants are under the obligation to ensure that the notified information is made public promptly, and in any case no later than three business days after the transaction, in a manner that enables fast access to the disclosed information on a non-discriminatory basis, consistently with the implementing technical standards (Article 19(3)). The dissemination of information shall be effective, otherwise, national law may provide that the national competent authority may itself make public the information.

B.19.10 Article 19(4) defines the perimeter of the entities subject to this provision, ie issuers who have requested or approved admission of their financial instruments to trading on a regulated market or, in the case of an instrument only traded on an MTF or an OTF, have approved trading of their financial instruments on an MTF or an OTF or have requested admission to trading of their financial instruments on an MTF.

B.19.11 In application of Article 19(5), issuers and emission allowance market participants shall notify the persons discharging managerial responsibilities within an issuer of their obligations in writing. In the same way, persons discharging managerial responsibilities within an issuer shall notify the persons closely associated with them of their disclosure obligations in writing and shall keep a copy of this notification. In addition, issuers and emission allowance market participants are required to draw up a list of all persons discharging managerial responsibilities within an issuer and closely associated persons.

Article 19(6) relates to the content of the notification. The required elements refer to the identity of the person and the issuer, as well as information connected to the transaction, including the financial instrument involved, the nature, the date, the place of the transaction, its price and volume. **B.19.12**

Pursuant to Article 19(11) a person discharging managerial responsibilities within an issuer (but not a closely associated person) within an issuer is prohibited from concluding any transactions on its own account or for the account of a third party, directly or indirectly, relating to the shares or debt instruments of the issuer or to derivatives or other financial instruments linked to them during a closed period of 30 calendar days before the announcement of an interim financial report or a year-end report which the issuer is obliged to make public according to: the rules of the trading venue where the issuer's shares are admitted to trading; or national law. **B.19.13**

However, the Market Abuse Regulation provides for specific exemptions: an issuer may decide to allow a person discharging managerial responsibilities within an issuer to trade on its own account or for the account of a third party during a closed period as referred to in § 11 either: on a case-by-case basis due to the existence of exceptional circumstances; or due to the characteristics of the trading involved for transactions made under, or related to, an employee share or saving scheme, qualification or entitlement of shares, or transactions where the beneficial interest in the relevant security does not change. **B.19.14**

In addition, the Commission is empowered to adopt delegated acts specifying the circumstances under which trading during a closed period may be permitted by the issuer, including the circumstances that would be considered as exceptional and the types of transaction that would justify the permission for trading. **B.19.15**

Historical background

The notification of managers' transactions has been provided by the (former) Market Abuse Directive (2003/6/EC), on the assumption that it would increase transparency. While the Proposal for the (former) Market Abuse Directive (2003/6/EC) did not include such a specific requirement, the final version of the (former) Market Abuse Directive (2003/6/EC), taking into account the US experience,[3] adopted a different approach, emphasizing that 'greater transparency of transactions conducted by persons discharging managerial responsibilities within issuers and, where **B.19.16**

[3] See Niamh Moloney, *EU Securities and Financial Markets Regulation* (3rd edn, OUP 2014) para VIII.7.3.

applicable, persons closely associated with them, constitutes a preventive measure against market abuse. The publication of those transactions on at least an individual basis can also be a highly valuable source of information to investors',[4] while the Implementing Directive of 29 April 2004 emphasized its importance as 'an additional means for competent authorities to supervise markets'.[5] Pursuant to Article 6(4) (former) Market Abuse Directive (2003/6/EC), persons discharging managerial responsibilities within an issuer and, where applicable, closely associated persons, had a duty to, at least, notify to national competent authorities the existence of transactions conducted on their own account relating to shares of the said issuer, or to derivatives or other financial instruments linked to them.[6] In addition it was required that Member States 'ensure that public access to information concerning such transactions, on at least an individual basis, is readily available as soon as possible'.[7]

B.19.17 The Commission Directive 2004/72/EC required persons discharging managerial responsibilities within an issuer and closely associated persons to notify the national competent authorities of all transactions related to shares admitted to trading on a regulated market, or to derivatives or other financial instruments linked to them, conducted on their own account.[8] The notification had to be made within five working days of the transaction date.[9] It was also provided a threshold, equal to €5,000, below which Member States could have decided not to require any notification or delaying the terms of such notification until 31 January of the following year.[10] The total amount of transactions had to be calculated 'by summing up the transactions conducted on the own account of persons discharging managerial responsibilities within an issuer with the transactions conducted on the own account of closely associated persons'.[11]

II. Critical Remarks

Persons discharging managerial responsibilities within an issuer and closely associated persons

B.19.18 Article 19 provides for a transparency regime for persons discharging managerial responsibilities within an issuer dealing on their own account with stocks and

[4] Recital (26) (former) Market Abuse Directive (2003/6/EC).
[5] Commission Directive 2004/72/EC of 29 April 2004 implementing the MAD as regards accepted market practices, the definition of inside information in relation to derivatives on commodities, the drawing up of lists of insiders, the notification of managers' transactions and the notification of suspicious transactions.
[6] Article 6(4) (former) Market Abuse Directive (2003/6/EC).
[7] ibid.
[8] Article 6(1) Commission Directive (2004/72/EC).
[9] ibid.
[10] ibid art 6(2).
[11] ibid art 6(1).

extends such duties to closely associated persons. These transactions are considered informative for price formation, while at the same time vulnerable to insider-dealing risk.[12]

A person discharging managerial responsibilities within an issuer is 'a person within an issuer, an emission allowance market participant or another entity referred to in Article 19(10), who is either: a member of the administrative, management or supervisory body of that entity; or a senior executive who is not a member of the administrative, management or supervisory body of that entity, who has regular access to inside information relating directly or indirectly to that entity and power to take managerial decisions affecting the future developments and business prospects of that entity'.[13] **B.19.19**

Persons discharging managerial responsibilities within an issuer are typically corporate managers that do not act in isolation of their social context: natural and legal outside persons connected to persons discharging managerial responsibilities within an issuer can be influenced by the company's managers and may also share with them aligned economic interests.[14] This is the reason why securities law and disclosure regulation provide 'a functional disclosure regime on managers' transactions, one that curbs the possible circumvention by the prime target of the disclosure regime, i.e., the inside manager. To that end, the personal scope of the disclosure obligation is generally extended from the manager to certain "persons closely associated" with such manager'.[15] **B.19.20**

A closely associated person is: '(a) a spouse or a partner [...], (b) a dependent child [...], (c) a relative who has the same household for at least one year on the date of the transaction concerned, (d) a legal person, trust or partnership, the managerial responsibilities of which are discharged by a person discharging managerial responsibilities within an issuer or by a person referred to in point (a), (b) or (c), which is directly or indirectly controlled by such a person, which is set up for the benefit of such a person, or the economic interests of which are substantially equivalent to those of such a person'.[16] **B.19.21**

---

[12] See Moloney, *EU Securities and Financial Markets Regulation* (n 3) para VIII.7.3.

[13] Article 3(1)(25). According to Article 3(1)(26)(d), a closely associated person is, inter alia, 'a legal person, trust or partnership, the managerial responsibilities of which are discharged' by a person discharging managerial responsibilities (PDMR). As ESMA has specified in the 'Q&A on the Market Abuse Regulation (ESMA/2016/1644)' (6 July 2017), www.esma.org, 'the reference to "the managerial responsibilities of which are discharged", contained in Article 3(1)(26)(d) of MAR shall not be read in the same way as the definition of "persons discharging managerial responsibilities" (PDMR) within an issuer contained in Article 3(1)(25) of MAR: in this case the reference to "the managerial responsibilities of which are discharged" should be read to cover those cases where a PDMR within an issuer (or a closely associated natural person) takes part in or influences the decisions of another legal person, trust or partnership to carry out transactions in financial instruments of the issuer'.

[14] M Knuts, 'The Optimal Scope of Disclosure by Association Regime under MAR' (2016) European Company and Financial Law Review 496.

[15] ibid.

[16] Article 3(1)(26).

B.19.22 The question behind the association issue has been correctly synthetized by these words: 'how far into the ambit of outside legal persons the disclosure obligation, the core purpose of which is to increase transparency on inside managers' transactions, may be extended, without causing inefficiencies in the information economics of managerial disclosures and without imposing an overly inclusive disclosure regime which would restrict the integrity of outside actors in a financial markets context'.[17]

Transparency

B.19.23 Recital 58 underlines the relationship between transparency and prevention of market abuse, in particular insider dealing, in the context of transactions conducted by persons discharging managerial responsibilities within an issuer and closely associated persons: the publication of these transactions is beneficial for both the investors, since it is a highly valuable source of information, and the confidence of market actors, in particular the one of the company's shareholders.[18] In addition, the notification of transactions by persons discharging managerial responsibilities within an issuer and closely associated persons is a valuable tool for competent authorities to supervise markets.[19] The rationale for the disclosure measures has been confirmed by a vast literature of empirical studies on capital markets in Europe.[20]

The type of transactions

B.19.24 Article 19(1) refers to transactions related to a broad range of instruments (shares or debt instruments of an issuer, derivatives or other financial instruments linked to them). Doing so, the regulation makes the venue or place where the transaction has been concluded irrelevant for the purposes of reporting it. Therefore, any transaction irrespective of where it was conducted shall be notified to issuers and national competent authorities.[21]

B.19.25 Given the reference to 'every transaction', ESMA took the view that the notification should apply to all transactions, ie any acquisition, disposal, subscription or exchange of financial instrument of an issuer or related financial instruments, without taking into account either the size or the significance relative to the market of the given instrument.[22] According to ESMA, the terms 'acquisition' and

[17] Knuts, 'Optimal Scope' (n 14) 498. The author suggests a model for correctly interpreting the scope of the association regime. According to this model, 'the level of disclosure should be increased only until the marginal costs of disclosure (i.e. of producing and assessing disclosures) exceed its marginal benefits (i.e. the signal value of disclosure to outside investors)', with the further possibility to operationalize this approach adopting a sufficiency test, whose purpose consists in preventing 'a over-inclusive application of the regime which risks increasing disclosure costs disproportionately, while simultaneously inflating the signal value of disclosure'.

[18] See recital (58).

[19] See recital (59).

[20] ESMA, 'Delegated Acts' (n 1) Annex II, para 50.

[21] ibid para 94.

[22] ibid para 95.

'disposal' shall be interpreted in a broad manner, encompassing a wide range of transactions, even those where the role played by the person discharging managerial responsibilities within an issuer/closely associated person was passive, and therefore not decisive for the conclusion of the transaction, for example in connections to gifts, inheritances and donations received by a person discharging managerial responsibilities within an issuer/closely associated person.[23]

Compared to the (former) Market Abuse Directive (2003/6/EC), the Market Abuse Regulation has significantly expanded the scope of the disclosure requirement with respect to two key points. It has enlarged the spectrum of the instruments covered, encompassing financial instruments admitted to trading, or for which a request has been made to trade on a RM and MTF, as well as those exchanged on an OTF or OTC,[24] with the limitation that 'the notification and disclosure requirements of persons discharging managerial responsibilities within an issuer/closely associated persons' transactions will only apply to those issuers that have requested or approved admission to trading of their financial instruments on one of the venues'.[25] Moreover, the provision explicitly mentions both shares and debt instruments of the said issuer, as well as derivatives or other financial instruments linked to them, and emission allowances, related auction products or related derivatives.[26] **B.19.26**

Article 56(1)(a) of the Benchmark Regulation[27] amended Article 19(1), providing for specific exceptions to be included in the following new paragraph 1a of Article 19: **B.19.27**

> 1a. The notification obligation ... shall not apply to transactions in financial instruments linked to shares or to debt instruments of the issuer ... where at the time of the transaction any of the following conditions is met:
> (a) the financial instrument is a unit or share in a collective investment undertaking in which the exposure to the issuer's shares or debt instruments does not exceed 20 % of the assets held by the collective investment undertaking;
> (b) the financial instrument provides exposure to a portfolio of assets in which the exposure to the issuer's shares or debt instruments does not exceed 20 % of the portfolio's assets;
> (c) the financial instrument is a unit or share in a collective investment undertaking or provides exposure to a portfolio of assets and the person discharging managerial responsibilities or person closely associated with such a person does not know, and could not know, the investment composition or exposure of such collective investment undertaking or portfolio of assets

[23] ibid.
[24] ibid para 93.
[25] ibid.
[26] ibid.
[27] Regulation (EU) 2016/1011 of 8 June 2016 on indices used as benchmarks in financial instruments and financial contracts or to measure the performance of investment funds and amending Directives 2008/48/EC and 2014/17/EU and Regulation (EU) No 596/2014.

in relation to the issuer's shares or debt instruments, and furthermore there is no reason for that person to believe that the issuer's shares or debt instruments exceed the thresholds in point (a) or (b).

B.19.28 Article 19(7) specifies the transactions to be notified. It sets out a non-exhaustive list of transactions that includes the pledging or lending of financial instruments. The reason for including this type of transaction depends on the fact that 'the pledging of shares can result in a material and potentially destabilising impact on the company in the event of a sudden, unforeseen disposal. Without disclosure, the market would not know that there was the increased possibility of, for example, a significant future change in share ownership, an increase in the supply of shares to the marketplace or a loss of voting rights in that company. For that reason, notification under this Regulation is required where the pledge of the securities is made as part of a wider transaction in which the manager pledges the securities as collateral to gain credit from a third party'.[28] However, Article 19(7)(2) provides an exemption from the notification for 'a pledge, or a similar security interest, of financial instruments in connection with the depositing of the financial instruments in a custody account [...], unless and until such time that such pledge or other security interest is designated to secure a specific credit facility'.[29]

B.19.29 The list also includes 'transactions undertaken by persons professionally arranging or executing transactions or by another person on behalf of a person discharging managerial responsibilities or a person closely associated with such a person, as referred to in paragraph 1, including where discretion is exercised' and transactions made under a life insurance policy, under specific conditions: the policyholder must be a person discharging managerial responsibilities within an issuer or a closely associated person; he must bear the investment risk; and has the power to make investment decisions in connection to specific instruments in that life insurance policy or execute transactions regarding specific instruments for that life insurance policy at his discretion.[30]

B.19.30 With regard to this list, ESMA considered that 'the scope of the transactions to be covered under the empowerment of Article 14(6)[31] is broad and should not be limited to only the three types of transactions explicitly listed in Article 14(2). Therefore, although these three types of transactions referred to in Article 14(2) will need to be considered individually, ESMA considers it useful to begin by establishing some basic characteristics of any transaction, which must be present in order for the transaction to require reporting. Besides, ESMA understands that transactions referred to in Article 14(2)(b) include transactions executed for the account of the persons discharging managerial responsibilities within an

[28] Recital (58).
[29] Article 19(7)(1).
[30] Article 19(7).
[31] Under the Proposal the actual art 19 was art 14.

issuer within the framework of a fully discretionary asset management contract (meaning that there is no instruction whatsoever from the person discharging managerial responsibilities within an issuer) as regards the investment policy of the contract'.[32] For this reason, it favoured a more extensive list, including examples of transactions triggering notification and publication requirements.[33]

Paragraph 1, let. (b) refers to 'transactions undertaken by persons professionally arranging or executing transactions or by another person on behalf of a person discharging managerial responsibilities or a person closely associated with such a person, as referred to in paragraph 1, including where discretion is exercised'. The Benchmark Regulation at Article 19(1)(b) provided a new subparagraph for this paragraph, specifying that 'For the purposes of point (b), transactions executed in shares or debt instruments of an issuer or derivatives or other financial instruments linked thereto by managers of a collective investment undertaking in which the person discharging managerial responsibilities or a person closely associated with them has invested do not need to be notified where the manager of the collective investment undertaking operates with full discretion, which excludes the manager receiving any instructions or suggestions on portfolio composition directly or indirectly from investors in that collective investment undertaking'. **B.19.31**

The Regulation 2016/522/EU provides a wider list of heterogeneous transactions, including: **B.19.32**

a) Purchases and sales, including short sales, of shares or debt instruments of the concerned issuer or of related derivatives or other financial instruments linked to them, or of emission allowances or related auction products or derivatives.
b) The acceptance and the exercise of a stock-option in case of stock options granted to managers and employees as part of their remuneration package.

---

32 ESMA, 'Discussion Paper: ESMA's policy orientations on possible implementing measures under the Market Abuse Regulation (ESMA/2013/1649)' (14 November 2013) paras 345, 346, and 347 www.esma.org.

33 ESMA, 'Discussion Paper' (n 32) para 353. ESMA proposed a more extensive list including: 'a. The acceptance and the exercise of a stock-option in case of stock options granted to managers and employees as part of their remuneration package. b. The sale of shares stemming from the exercise of a stock option (even in case of stock options granted to managers and employees as part of their remuneration package). c. Equity swaps. The constitutive elements of equity swaps that have to be notified are: name of person discharging managerial responsibilities within an issuer, description of securities, nature of transaction, value of transaction, date of transaction, share's price, maturity/term of the contract. d. Transactions related to derivatives products settled in cash (such as for instance equity swaps with a cash settlement). e. Acquisition, sale or exercise of rights, put and call options traded on a RM and/or a MTF and/or over the counter. If rights, as well as put and call options, are exercised, the date of the exercise of rights has to be taken into account when considering whether there is a notification requirement. f. The subscription to a capital increase (primary market). g. Conditional trades i.e. trades which occur on the basis of a previous contract that stipulates a condition that is now met or on the basis of a contract which establishes that the trade will occur in the future if a condition is met, by persons discharging managerial responsibilities within an issuer. The conversion of a financial instrument into another financial instrument e.g. exchange of convertible bonds to shares'.

c) The sale of shares stemming from the exercise of a stock option (even in case of stock options granted to managers and employees as part of their remuneration package).
d) Equity swaps. The following features of an equity swap should be included in the notification: description of securities, share's price and maturity/term of the contract.
e) Transactions related to derivatives products settled in cash (such as for instance equity swaps with a cash settlement).
f) Entering into a contract for difference on a financial instrument of the issuer.
g) Acquisition, sale or exercise of rights, put and call options, warrants traded on a regulated market, a multilateral trading facility, an organized trading facility, and/or over the counter. If rights, warrants, and put and call options are exercised, the date of transaction is the date of exercise.
h) The subscription to a capital increase.
i) The subscription of a debt instrument issuance.
j) Transactions on derivatives/financial instruments linked to a debt instrument, including credit default swaps.
k) Conditional trades, ie trades which occur on the basis of a previous contract that stipulates a condition that is now met.
l) The (automatic and not automatic) conversion of a financial instrument into another financial instrument, eg exchange of convertible bonds to shares.
m) Gift and donation made or received as well as inheritance.
n) Transactions executed by a third party under a (fully) discretionary portfolio or asset management mandate.
o) Transactions executed in index-related products, baskets and derivatives based thereto, or in shares/units of investment funds (AIFM and UCITS),[34] provided that they are linked to the issuer's shares or debt instruments.
p) Borrowing of shares or debt instruments of the issuer or other financial instruments linked thereto.

B.19.33 ESMA has specified that shares received by a person discharging managerial responsibilities within an issuer as part of a remuneration package have to be notified pursuant to Article 19(1) and Article 10(2)(i) Regulation 2016/522/EU only upon the occurrence of the conditions and the actual execution of the transaction.[35] This is due to the rationale of Article 19(1), consisting in preventing insider dealing and providing investors with a highly valuable source

[34] In relation to these specific transactions, ESMA noted that: 'In the case of funds where the fund managers do not have full discretion and the clients are able to participate in the investment decisions, the closed period referred to in Article 19(11) applies to the fund itself, as it is possible for a person discharging managerial responsibilities within an issuer to influence the investment decision. So, the fund manager would have to be informed, including where relevant by the person discharging managerial responsibilities within an issuer, of the start of this closed period and of the relative investment restriction. The different approach for this sub-case of funds is a consequence of their different functioning, i.e. of the fact that the person discharging managerial responsibilities within an issuer participates in the investment decisions of the fund, and is reflected also in the section "Types of transactions triggering the duty to notify", where these funds are treated with different requirements'. See ESMA, 'Delegated Acts' (n 1) para 147.

[35] ESMA, 'Q&A on the Market Abuse Regulation (ESMA/2016/1644)' (20 December 2016) 9 www.esma.org.

of information: a notification of entering into a remuneration package contract, according to which a person discharging managerial responsibilities within an issuer is entitled to receive shares only upon the occurrence of certain conditions, is not covered by that rationale.[36]

Format and template

As for insider lists, ESMA developed a harmonized format and template for notification and public disclosure of managers' transactions (Regulation 2016/958/EU). Uniform rules regarding how the information shall be notified and made public through a single template foster efficiency in the process of notification while providing comparable information to the public.[37] Pursuant to recital (2) of Regulation 2016/523/EU, 'the template should contain the information on all the transactions conducted on a particular day by persons discharging managerial responsibilities within an issuer or persons closely associated: in order to provide a comprehensive view to the public, the template should allow for the presentation of the transactions on an individual basis and also in an aggregated form. The aggregated information should indicate the volume of all the transactions of the same nature on the same financial instrument that have been carried out on the same trading day and on the same trading venue, or outside any trading venue, as a single figure representing the arithmetical sum of the volume of each transaction. It should also indicate the corresponding volume-weighted average price. When filling in the template transactions of different nature, such as purchases and sales, should never be aggregated nor should be netted between themselves'.[38] **B.19.34**

With regard to the template, ESMA has changed its approach in the course of time. While the Consultation Paper[39] proposed a single template for notification, with two sections (one containing information on a transaction by transaction basis, for the sole use of the competent authority and the issuer and a second for the use of the persons discharging managerial responsibilities within an issuer and closely associated persons to notify transaction in an aggregated form and then by the issuer to proceed to the public disclosure of the information),[40] the final solution adopted consists in a single template (containing the information referred to in recital 2 of the Commission Implementing Regulation), to be publicly disclosed in its entirety, since the Market Abuse Regulation Level 1 text does not distinguish between information to be provided to national competent authorities and issuers and information to be publicly disclosed:[41] this is confirmed by the wording of Article 19(3) of the **B.19.35**

36 ibid.
37 Recital (1) Regulation 2016/958/EU.
38 ibid recital (2).
39 ESMA, 'Discussion Paper' (n 32).
40 ibid para 312.
41 ibid para 313.

Market Abuse Regulation that does not suggest this differentiation ('the issuer or emission allowance market participant shall ensure that the information that is notified in accordance with Article 19(1) is made public promptly …'), and, on the other hand, by the wording of Article 19(5), stating that '[ESMA] shall develop draft implementing technical standards concerning the format and template in which the information referred to in paragraph 1 is to be notified and made public'.[42]

B.19.36 In relation to the content of the notification, it is important to start from the difference existing between Article 19(6) and Article 18(3). While the latter adopts the wording 'shall include at least', the former does not contain such expression. Therefore, the information included in Article 19(6) already indicates the elements that the notification should contain, and should not be extendable with the provision of further items.[43]

Timing and means of notification

B.19.37 The Market Abuse Regulation has significantly reduced the timing provided for notifications from five working days to three business days after the date of the transaction. The notification must be made via secure electronic means, which ensure that completeness, integrity, and confidentiality of the information are maintained. ESMA clarified that 'the notifications to be received by the competent authorities and the issuers, the emission allowance market participants or the auction entities and to be publicly disclosed should detail every transaction. However, it is not expected that a separate notification is sent for each individual transaction. To limit the burden, a person discharging managerial responsibilities within an issuer or a closely associated person should be able to send a single notification listing and detailing multiple transactions carried out, as long as the three working days deadline foreseen in Article 19(2)(2), is complied with'.[44]

Threshold

B.19.38 An important change introduced with the Market Abuse Regulation is the possibility offered to national competent authorities to increase the threshold. Article 19(9) provides that national competent authorities may decide to increase the €5,000 threshold up to €20,000, and inform ESMA of their decisions and of their justifications, making reference to the specific market conditions.

B.19.39 The European Commission, in the Impact Assessment for the Proposal of the Market Abuse Regulation, noticed that: 'An advantage of raising the threshold

---

42 ibid.
43 ibid para 318.
44 ibid para 310.

would be that relatively small and insignificant deals by managers would not need to be reported anymore which would result in a moderate reduction of administrative burdens for issuers. Harmonising the application of the threshold by making it compulsory all over Europe would evidently reduce the number of notifications for issuers in Member States which currently do not apply the threshold and would, in addition, level the European playing field and increase legal certainty for issuers. A disadvantage would be a moderate reduction in market transparency which would not harm investor protection as even a slightly increased threshold would still serve as a deterrent against engaging in insider trading and investors would still be informed about significant deals conducted by managers'.[45]

With regard to the calculation of the threshold, ESMA has specified that 'the transactions carried out by a person discharging managerial responsibilities within an issuer and by closely associated persons to that person discharging managerial responsibilities within an issuer should not be aggregated ... where the overall transactions singularly carried out by either a person discharging managerial responsibilities within an issuer or any closely associated person to that person discharging managerial responsibilities within an issuer do not reach the threshold, those persons should not notify those transactions even where the threshold is reached aggregating all the transactions carried out by the person discharging managerial responsibilities within an issuer and all the closely associated persons to them. A practical example is a CEO buying €4,000 of equity and her spouse buying another €2,000. In such a case, none of them has reached the €5,000 threshold and thus a notification is not required'.[46] **B.19.40**

In addition, for donations, gifts and inheritance, ESMA has also considered that 'the price to consider is the last published price for the financial instrument concerned in accordance with the post trade transparency requirements under Articles 6, 10, 20, and 21 of the Markets in Financial Instruments Implementation Regulation (1287/2006/EC) on the date of acceptance of the donation, gift or inheritance (i.e. the date of the transaction), or where such price is not available that day, the last published price'.[47] **B.19.41**

Closed period

One of the novelties introduced with the Market Abuse Regulation is the ban for persons discharging managerial responsibilities within an issuer (but not for closely associated persons) to conduct any transactions on their own account or for the account of a third party, directly or indirectly, relating to the shares or debt instruments of the issuer or to derivatives or other financial instruments linked **B.19.42**

[45] Commission, 'Staff Working Paper: Impact Assessment' SEC(2011) 12717 final para 5.7.7.
[46] ESMA, 'Q&A' (n 35) 8.
[47] ibid. ESMA provides further indication for the interim period until the entry into force of Markets in Financial Instruments Implementation Regulation (1287/2006/EC).

to them during a closed period of thirty calendar days before the announcement of an interim financial report or a year-end report which the issuer is obliged to make public.[48]

B.19.43 As ESMA clarified, any interim reports (eg quarterly, half yearly), when required, fall within the scope of this provision.[49] Furthermore, it should be noted that the relevant date for the computation of the closed period is the date of publication of such interim and year-end reports, as required by the rules of the relevant trading venue or by the national law. In cases where an issuer is not required to publish the interim and year-end reports, the closed period provisions would not apply.[50]

B.19.44 As already mentioned, this regime provides for exemptions. An issuer may decide to allow a person discharging managerial responsibilities within an issuer to trade on its own account or for the account of a third party during the closed period on a case-by-case basis, determined by the existence of exceptional circumstances (such as severe financial difficulties) or specific characteristics of the trading involved.[51] The issuer's authorization is given without prejudice to Articles 14 and 15, as the person discharging managerial responsibilities within an issuer could not be exempted by the issuer from complying with the insider dealing and market manipulation prohibitions. In addition, the person discharging managerial responsibilities within an issuer shall be able to demonstrate that the particular transaction cannot be executed at another moment in time other than during the closed period.[52]

B.19.45 In case of exceptional circumstances set out in Article 19(12)(a), a person discharging managerial responsibilities within an issuer shall, prior to any trading during the closed period, provide a reasoned written request to the issuer, in order to obtain its permission to proceed with immediate sale of shares of that issuer during a closed period.[53] In the written request, the person discharging managerial responsibilities within an issuer shall describe the envisaged transaction, explaining why the sale of shares is the only reasonable alternative to obtain the necessary financing.[54] The decision of the issuer is based on a case-by-case assessment and it has the right to permit the immediate sale of shares only when the circumstances for such transactions may be deemed exceptional.[55] This is the case of circumstances that are extremely urgent, unforeseen, and compelling, and they have been caused by external reason and the person discharging managerial responsibilities within an issuer has no control over them.[56] To conduct an

[48] Article 19(11).
[49] ESMA, 'Delegated Acts' (n 1) para 137.
[50] ibid.
[51] See Article 19(12).
[52] Article 7(1)(b) Regulation 2016/522/EU.
[53] ibid art 7(1).
[54] ibid art 8(1).
[55] ibid.
[56] ibid art 8(2).

assessment of the exceptionality of such circumstances, the issuer shall consider whether and the extent to which the person discharging managerial responsibilities within an issuer is facing, at the time he submits its request, a legally enforceable financial commitment or claim, or is in a situation entered into before the beginning of the closed period and requiring the payment of sum to a third party, including tax liability, and cannot reasonably satisfy a financial commitment or claim by means other than immediate sale of shares.[57]

The second exception set out in Article 19(12)(b) refers to the specific characteristics of the trading involved for transactions made under, or related to, an employee share or saving scheme, qualification or entitlement of shares, or transactions where the beneficial interest in the relevant security does not change.[58] Article 9 of the Implementing Regulation contains a non-exhaustive list of such transactions, including the situation where a person discharging managerial responsibilities within an issuer had been: 'awarded or granted financial instruments under an employee scheme, provided that… (i) the employee scheme and its terms have been previously approved by the issuer in accordance with national law and the terms of the employee scheme specify the timing of the award or the grant and the amount of financial instruments awarded or granted, or the basis on which such an amount is calculated and given that no discretion can be exercised, and (ii) the person discharging managerial responsibilities does not have any discretion as to the acceptance of the financial instruments awarded or granted';[59] or 'had been awarded or granted financial instruments under an employee scheme that takes place in the closed period provided that a pre-planned and organised approach is followed regarding the conditions, the periodicity, the time of the award, the group of entitled persons to whom the financial instruments are granted and the amount of financial instruments to be awarded, the award or grant of financial instruments takes place under a defined framework under which any inside information cannot influence the award or grant of financial instruments'.[60] **B.19.46**

It is worth noting that the prohibition under the Market Abuse Regulation does not extend to other periods where the company is in possession of inside information (although dealing by insiders during these periods would of course be restricted by the more general prohibition of insider dealing).[61] **B.19.47**

Concerning the precise moment as from which persons discharging managerial responsibilities within an issuer transactions are banned, ESMA explained that 'the relevant date for the computation of the closed period is the date of publication **B.19.48**

57 ibid art 8(3).
58 Article 19(12)(b).
59 Article 9(a) Regulation 2016/522/EU.
60 ibid art 9(b).
61 Norton Rose Fulbright, 'The Market Abuse Regulation: Key Considerations for UK Listed Issuers' (February 2016) http://www.nortonrosefulbright.com/knowledge/publications/136820/the-market-abuse-regulation-key-considerations-for-uk-listed-issuers#section5.

of such interim and year-end reports, as required by the rules of the relevant trading venue or by the national law. In cases where an issuer is not required to publish the interim and year-end reports, the closed period provisions would not apply'.[62] It also noted that: 'if the "preliminary announcement" of annual report is required either by national or trading venue rules, it would start the closing period. In this context, it should be kept in mind that the issuer has an obligation to disclose inside information as soon as possible, and the prohibition of insider dealing applies with no limitation and irrespective of the closed period'.[63] The Q&A of ESMA clarified that 'the term "announcement" of an interim or a year-end financial report ... is the public statement whereby the issuer announces the information included in an interim or a year-end financial report that the issuer is obliged to make public according to the rules of the trading venue where the issuer's shares are admitted to trading or national law. The date when the "announcement" is made is the end date for the thirty-day closed period. With particular reference to the year-end financial report, the "announcement" is the public statement whereby the issuer announces, in advance to the publication of the final year-end report, the preliminary financial results agreed by the management body of the issuer and that will be included in that report. This can apply only if the disclosed preliminary financial results contain all the key information relating to the financial figures expected to be included in the year-end report'.[64]

B.19.49 However, doubts have emerged with regard to the case of an issuer publishing preliminary information, followed by definitive information, as it is not clear whether the closed period ban should apply twice: thirty days before the publication of the preliminary information and thirty days before the publication of the definitive information, substantially impeding the activity on the issuers' shares for the entire period until the publication of the definitive information by

---

[62] ESMA, 'Delegated Acts' (n 1) para 137.

[63] ibid para 138. ESMA in this way replied to the doubts casted by a group of respondents to the Discussion Paper, who explained the market practice in the UK, where 'issuers publish a preliminary announcement of annual results (containing information prescribed by the FCA's Listing Rules) before publishing the year-end report. In some cases, where the preliminary announcement contains inside information, the issuer is obliged to make the preliminary announcement before the year-end report is published (it may not be possible to publish the year-end report at the same time as it will normally contain significantly more information than the preliminary announcement). Under the UK Model Code, the preliminary announcement triggers the end of the closed period as once the inside information has been published, there is no need to impose a prohibition on dealings. Such a practice is also common to other markets. According to the respondents, an inability to use a preliminary announcement as a trigger for the end of a closed period would mean that the 30-day prohibited period would not properly match the period prior to the release of the results to the market. In relation to this issue, MAR level 1 clearly states that a financial report triggers a close period only when it is required to be publicly disclosed according (i) to the rules of the relevant trading venues, or (ii) to national law. It should be noted that the publication of a preliminary announcement is a practice common in other Member States other than the UK'.

[64] ESMA, 'Q&A' (n 35) 8.

the board of directors.[65] Moreover, another issue may refer to the deadline of the closed period, whether it is the day of the public announcement or the day after.[66]

In addition, the Market Abuse Regulation provides closed periods for persons discharging managerial responsibilities within an issuer for any transactions on their own account or for the account of a third party, directly or indirectly. For clarification purposes, ESMA underlines that transactions in the issuer's related instruments within the assets of a UCITS/AIF are not transactions conducted by the person discharging managerial responsibilities within an issuer but by the fund manager, except where the fund manager does not have full discretion.[67] The Feedback Statement takes the same view. **B.19.50**

Impact of Article 19 on issuers, persons discharging managerial responsibilities within an issuer, and closely associated persons

As for insider lists, the issuers have to review their policies as well as brief their persons discharging managerial responsibilities within an issuer on the new regime, and prepare formal communications to persons discharging managerial responsibilities within an issuer and closely associated persons compliant with the new rules in place.[68] For their part, persons discharging managerial responsibilities within an issuer and closely associated persons have to review their existing investment arrangements carefully.[69] Issuers should also encourage persons discharging managerial responsibilities within an issuer to review their lists of closely associated persons and eventually to amend them with any changes under the Market Abuse Regulation.[70] **B.19.51**

Issuers with equity securities listed and admitted to trading in the EU will need to update their disclosure practices in order to comply with the new (and potentially more onerous) obligation in connection with timing, electronic forms, and submission processes that each national competent authority will require for documenting any reporting of persons discharging managerial responsibilities within an issuer transactions. Issuers only listed on MTF markets in the EU will struggle more in rapidly familiarizing themselves with such new forms.[71] **B.19.52**

III. Sanctions

See comment on Article 17. **B.19.53**

---

65 See Assonime, 'La disciplina sugli abusi di mercato: problemi e incertezze nell'applicazione per le società italiane e alcune ipotesi interpretative' (19 October 2016) 15.

66 ibid.

67 ESMA, 'Delegated Acts' (n 1) paras 146 and 147.

68 Norton Rose Fulbright, 'The Market Abuse Regulation' (n 61).

69 ibid.

70 ibid.

71 Skadden Arps, 'EU Market Abuse Regulation—New Requirements for Issuers of Debt Securities Admitted to Trading in Europe' (21 July 2016) 3 www.skadden.com.

Article 20: Investment recommendations and statistics

1. Persons who produce or disseminate investment recommendations or other information recommending or suggesting an investment strategy shall take reasonable care to ensure that such information is objectively presented, and to disclose their interests or indicate conflicts of interest concerning the financial instruments to which that information relates.
2. Public institutions disseminating statistics or forecasts liable to have a significant effect on financial markets shall disseminate them in an objective and transparent way.
3. In order to ensure consistent harmonisation of this Article, ESMA shall develop draft regulatory technical standards to determine the technical arrangements for the categories of person referred to in paragraph 1, for objective presentation of investment recommendations or other information recommending or suggesting an investment strategy and for disclosure of particular interests or indications of conflicts of interest.

ESMA shall submit those draft regulatory technical standards to the Commission by 3 July 2015.

Power is delegated to the Commission to adopt the regulatory technical standards referred to in the first subparagraph in accordance with Articles 10 to 14 of Regulation (EU) No 1095/2010.

The technical arrangements laid down in the regulatory technical standards referred to in paragraph 3 shall not apply to journalists who are subject to equivalent appropriate regulation in a Member State, including equivalent appropriate self-regulation, provided that such regulation achieves similar effects as those technical arrangements. Member States shall notify the text of that equivalent appropriate regulation to the Commission.

Relevant Technical Standards:
Commission Delegated Regulation (EU) 2016/958 of 9 March 2016 supplementing Regulation (EU) No 596/2014 of the European Parliament and of the Council with regard to regulatory technical standards for the technical arrangements for objective presentation of investment recommendations or other information recommending or suggesting an investment strategy and for disclosure of particular interests or indications of conflicts of interest (OJ L 160 (17 June 2016) 15)

I. General Remarks

Overview of Article 20

Article 20 applies to persons who produce or disseminate investment recommendations or other information recommending or suggesting an investment strategy. For this category of individuals, it provides specific requirements connected to the information provided as well as their own role. **B.20.01**

Structure of Article 20

Article 20(1) provides that persons who produce or disseminate investment recommendations or other information recommending or suggesting an investment strategy shall take care of the objectivity of the information presented. In addition, they have an obligation to disclose their interests or indicate conflicts concerning the financial instruments to which the information produced relates. Public institutions disseminating statistics or forecasts liable to have a significant effect on financial markets shall disseminate them in an objective and transparent way. **B.20.02**

Article 20(2) extends to public institutions disseminating statistics or forecasts with a significant impact on financial markets, the same duty to disseminate such information in an objective and transparent way. **B.20.03**

Article 20(3) requires ESMA to develop draft regulatory technical standards in order to determine the technical arrangements in three areas: the categories of persons who produce or disseminate investment recommendations or other information, the objective presentation of investment recommendations or other information recommending or suggesting an investment strategy, and the disclosure of particular interests or indications of conflicts of interest. **B.20.04**

Journalists do not fall within the scope of the technical arrangements laid down in the regulatory technical standards, if they are subject to appropriate equivalent **B.20.05** regulation in a Member State. Article 20 includes appropriate self-regulation in the notion of appropriate equivalent regulation, under the condition that such regulation achieves similar effects as those technical arrangements.

Historical background

B.20.06 In the context that led to the (former) Market Abuse Directive (2003/6/EC) and its implementing acts, significant emphasis was put on the role of financial analysts. In Europe, where relevant scandals happened (eg Parmalat in Italy and Ehold in the Netherlands) the manipulative tactics of inflating the prices of the 'new economies' stocks, contributing to the subsequent markets' bubble, put in place by investment banks and financial analysts, significantly affected the financial markets.[1]

B.20.07 In the US, the revelations by the New York Attorney General Eliot Spitzer concerning the widespread analyst misconduct[2], as well as the collapse of the technology bubble in the stock market, enhanced a strong debate on the regulation and the role of research analysts.[3] The reforms adopted by the US Congress, the SEC and the self-regulatory organizations required certifications of the content of analyst reports, together with a broad range of disclosure requirements and limitation on the possibility to engage in personal trading for analysts.[4] A new structural reform has consisted in requiring the separation of research from the investment banking activity, with the purpose of enhancing analyst independence and reducing conflicts of interests.[5]

B.20.08 Even IOSCO[6] has focused on research analysts and their conflicts of interests: in this regard, the Technical Committee considered that, in general, the conduct and professionalism of securities analysts is monitored and supervised by their employers, self-regulatory organizations, government regulators or other authorized securities regulatory authorities, and/or professional associations.[7] Given the regulatory activity around the analysts and their research, the IOSCO developed some principles with the purpose to pursue three objectives: 'the identification

[1] See G Ferrarini, 'The European Market Abuse Directive' (2004) 41 Common Market Law Review 711, 713.

[2] Press Release, Office of NY Att'y Gen Eliot Spitzer, 'Merrill Lynch Stock Rating System Found Biased by Undisclosed Conflicts of Interests' (8 April 2002) http://www.oag.state.ny.us/press/2002/apr/aprO8b_02.html.

[3] J Fisch, 'Does Analyst Independence Sell Investors Short?' (2007–2008) 55 UCLA Law Review 39, 53. For an overview of the debate in the US see also O H Dombalagian, 'Investment Recommendations and the Essence of Duty' (2010–2011) 60 American University Law Review 1265. See also J M Salmanowitz, 'Broker Investment Recommendations and the Efficient Capital Market Hypothesis: A Proposed Cautionary Legend' (1976–1977) 29 Stanford Law Review 1077.

[4] See Fisch, 'Does Analyst Independence Sell Investors Short?' (n 3).

[5] ibid.

[6] IOSCO, 'Statement of Principles for Addressing Sell-Side Securities Analyst Conflicts of Interest', September 2003 www.iosco.org.

[7] ibid.

and elimination, avoidance, management or disclosure of conflicts of interest faced by analysts; the integrity of analysts and their research; and the education of investors concerning the actual and potential conflicts of interest analysts face'.[8]

In this context, the (former) Market Abuse Directive (2003/6/EC) and the Investment Recommendations Directive (2003/125/EC) have introduced in Europe a disclosure regime for investment recommendations, research and conflicts of interests of persons disseminating such information. The (former) Market Abuse Directive (2003/6/EC) emphasized the importance to 'choose the most appropriate way to regulate persons producing or disseminating research concerning financial instruments or issuers of financial instruments or persons producing or disseminating other information recommending or suggesting investment strategy', encompassing also the possibilities of self-regulation.[9] The Investment Recommendations Directive (2003/125/EC) emphasized the importance of implementing harmonized standards for a fair, clear and accurate presentation of information and disclosure of interests and conflicts of interest, to be complied with by those persons. From a market integrity perspective, the Commission highlighted the need of 'high standards of fairness, probity and transparency when information recommending or suggesting an investment strategy is presented',[10] and risks connected to 'the own interests or conflicts of interest of persons recommending or suggesting investment strategy may influence the opinion that they express in investment recommendations'.[11] These potential own interests or conflicts of interest could have undermined the objectivity and reliability of the information, and for this reason the Investment Recommendations Directive (2003/125/EC) required 'appropriate disclosure of significant financial interests in any financial instrument which is the subject of the information recommending investment strategies, or of any conflicts of interest or control relationship with respect to the issuer to whom the information relates, directly or indirectly'.[12] **B.20.09**

The Investment Recommendations Directive (2003/125/EC) provided definitions for 'recommendations', 'research or other information recommending or suggesting investment strategy', 'distribution channel'.[13] It specified that 'recommending or suggesting an investment strategy is either done explicitly (such as "buy", "hold" or "sell" recommendations) or implicitly (by reference to a price target or otherwise)',[14] while investment advice, in the form 'a personal recommendation **B.20.10**

[8] ibid.
[9] Recital (22) (former) Market Abuse Directive (2003/6/EC).
[10] Recital (1) Investment Recommendations Directive (2003/125/EC).
[11] ibid recital (7).
[12] ibid recital (7).
[13] ibid art 1.
[14] ibid recital 2.

to a client in respect of one or more transactions relating to financial instruments (in particular informal short-term investment recommendations originating from inside the sales or trading departments of an investment firm or a credit institution expressed to their clients), which are not likely to become publicly available' did not fall within the definition of recommendation.[15] Even the credit rating agencies' opinions on the creditworthiness of a particular issuer or financial instrument as of a given date did not fall within the notion of recommendation within the meaning as given by the Directive.[16]

B.20.11 Under the Investment Recommendations Directive (2003/125/EC), two sets of rules were provided: the first one for the 'production of recommendations', with provisions on fair presentation of recommendations and the disclosure of interests or conflicts of interest (Articles 2–6); the second one for the 'dissemination of recommendations produced by third parties' (Articles 7–9),[17] both including 'general standards' applicable to all so-called 'relevant persons', ie 'a natural or legal person producing or disseminating recommendations in the exercise of his profession or the conduct of his business, and additional obligations for a specific sub-set of persons, namely independent analysts, investment firms, credit institutions, any other person whose main business is to produce recommendations or any natural person working for them, that, directly or indirectly, expresses a particular investment recommendation (financial analysts)'.[18]

II. Critical Remarks

The definitions provided by the Market Abuse Regulation

B.20.12 The Market Abuse Regulation now provides the definitions relevant for Article 19, which used to be included in the Investment Recommendations Directive (2003/125/EC).

B.20.13 The concept of 'information recommending or suggesting an investment strategy' is defined as 'information: (i) produced by an independent analyst, an investment firm, a credit institution, any other person whose main business is to produce investment recommendations or a natural person working for them under a contract of employment or otherwise, which, directly or indirectly, expresses a particular investment proposal in respect of a financial instrument or an issuer; or (ii) produced by persons other than those referred to in point (i), which directly

[15] ibid recital (3).

[16] ibid recital (10).

[17] ESMA, 'Consultation Paper: Draft technical standards on the Market Abuse Regulation (ESMA/2015/809)' (28 September 2015) para 325 www.esma.org.

[18] ibid para 326.

proposes a particular investment decision in respect of a financial instrument'[19] (ie 'qualified persons' and 'non-qualified persons', adopting the qualification provided by ESMA).[20]

Investment recommendations are defined as 'information recommending or suggesting an investment strategy, explicitly or implicitly, concerning one or several financial instruments or the issuers, including any opinion as to the present or future value or price of such instruments, intended for distribution channels or for the public'.[21] In practice, information recommendations include any buy, sell, or relative value recommendation, for any in-scope instrument, regardless of whether any time horizon for the trade is specified and irrespective of whether there is a specific price target.[22] With regard to the definition of investment recommendations, ESMA has clarified that: **B.20.14**

- communications to clients containing purely factual information on one or several financial instrument or issuers would not constitute an investment recommendation under the Market Abuse Regulation, provided that it does not explicitly or implicitly recommend or suggest an investment strategy. In this context, factual information might, among other things, include recent events or news relating to one or several financial instruments or issuers;[23]
- material intended for distribution channels or for the public concerning one or several financial instruments containing statements on the concerned financial instruments (eg 'undervalued', 'fairly valued', or 'overvalued') falls within the definition of 'investment recommendation' under the Market Abuse Regulation: it is considered as information implicitly recommending or suggesting an investment strategy pursuant to Article 3(1)(34), insofar as it contains a valuation statement as to the price of the concerned financial instruments;[24] the same view shall be taken with respect to material containing an estimated value such as a 'quantitative fair value estimate' that is providing a projected price level or 'price target', or any other elements of opinion on the value of the financial instruments.[25]
- communications intended for distribution channels or for the public which only report or refer to previously disseminated investment recommendation and do not include any new elements of opinion or valuation or confirmation of a previous opinion or valuation do not constitute investment recommendations

[19] Article 3(1)(34). The (former) Market Abuse Directive (2003/6/EC) provided the definition of 'research or other information recommending or suggesting an investment strategy'.

[20] ESMA, 'Technical Standard' (n 17) para 328.

[21] ibid.

[22] ICMA, 'Market Abuse Regulation: Investment Recommendations: An ICMA Q&A', 2016 www.icmagroup.org.

[23] ESMA, 'Q&A on the Market Abuse Regulation (ESMA/2016/1644)' (20 December 2016) 12 www.esma.org.

[24] ibid.

[25] ibid.

under the Market Abuse Regulation. If a communication reports or refers to a former investment recommendation but contains either confirmation of the previous opinion or valuation or new elements of opinion or valuation, which may be based on new facts or events concerning the issuer which are considered in the valuation, it will be viewed as a new investment recommendation and all aspects of Commission Delegated Regulation (EU) 2016/958 would need to be considered;[26]

- a communication that does not refer to either a financial instrument or an issuer, should generally not be considered an investment recommendation. However, the producer's assessment as to whether the above communication may be investment recommendation should be conducted on a case-by-case basis;[27]
- where a standardized communication, including oral or electronic communication, is structured and pre-planned for distribution channels and it implicitly or explicitly suggests an investment strategy in relation to a financial instrument or issuer, it should be regarded as 'investment recommendation'.[28]

B.20.15 Article 1 Regulation 2016/958/EU defines an 'expert' as 'a person ... who repeatedly proposes investment decisions in respect of financial instruments and who: (i) presents himself as having financial expertise or experience; or (ii) puts forward his recommendation in such a way that other persons would reasonably believe he has financial expertise or experience'.

B.20.16 With regard to 'qualified persons' (the persons under Article 3(1)(34)(i)), ESMA considered it important to continue to submit them to the rules set out for financial analysts by the Investment Recommendations Directive (2003/125/EC).[29] The category of non-qualified persons under Article 3(1)(34)(ii) represents a wide and diverse group of persons, including both professionals, whose main business is not related to the production of investment recommendations, as well as non-professional persons 'which directly propose a particular investment decision in respect of a financial instrument'.[30]

B.20.17 ESMA also stressed the importance of a 'twofold approach', based on 'a first general set of requirements applying to any person in mentioned in Article 3(1)(34)(i) and

[26] ibid.

[27] ibid.

[28] ibid.

[29] ESMA, 'Technical Standard' (n 17) para 329.

[30] ibid para 330. ESMA underlines that some respondents, in the course of the consultation process, 'highlighted the risk that the full set of requirements envisaged by Implementing Directive 2003/125/EC for "relevant persons" could apply, if transposed in MAR technical standards, to an extremely wide set of circumstances, particularly given the current technological platforms that allow virtually anyone (whether an employee of a regulated firm or not) to disseminate his opinions to a potentially large audience. ESMA is aware of the issue, but does not believe that the spectrum of people mentioned in Article 3(1)(34)(i) and (ii) of MAR can be limited through Level 2 measures to only relevant persons as defined under the current MAD regime'.

(ii); and II. on applying a set of additional requirements to any person mentioned in Article 3(1)(34)(i) and also to those persons mentioned in Article 3(1)(34)(ii) that are considered "experts" '.[31] ESMA clarifies that: 'for this purpose, an "expert" should be considered a person who falls outside Article 3(1)(34)(i) and who repeatedly proposes particular investment decisions in respect of financial instruments and: presents himself as having financial expertise or experience; or puts forward his recommendation in such a way that other persons would reasonably believe he has financial expertise or experience'.[32] The 'twofold approach' is beneficial since, given the extended scope of the Market Abuse Regulation in terms of persons covered by the provisions on investment recommendations, it ensures a proportionate approach, providing more stringent requirements on persons posing higher risks in terms of market integrity and investor protection, de facto implementing a risk-based approach for the enforcement of the rules while avoiding the creation of onerous monitoring obligations in areas of little or low risk.[33]

Under MiFID, two categories of investment research can be identified. A first category is presented as objective or independent, whereas a second one, not meeting the standards of objectivity and independence, is labelled as marketing communication. Recital (28) of the MiFID Implementing Directive 2006/73/EC includes both these categories under the Market Abuse Regulation definition of investment recommendations.[34] **B.20.18**

It was stressed that the wording of Article 20(1) ('persons who produce or disseminate investment recommendations or other information recommending or suggesting an investment strategy shall take reasonable care to ensure that such information is objectively presented') fails to include non-independent research.[35] ESMA has specified that this requirement is not intended to apply only to those recommendations that are held out as being objective or independent.[36] In addition, it has confirmed that a note meeting the Market Abuse Regulation definition of 'investment recommendations' (Article 3(1)(35)) or of 'information recommending or suggesting an investment strategy' (Article 3(1)(34)) would fall within the scope of Article 20(1) and (3), irrespective of the label of that note.[37] **B.20.19**

General standard of objective presentation of investment recommendations

As ESMA explained, 'the general standard of objective presentation of investment recommendations can be based on the current general standard for **B.20.20**

[31] ibid para 331.
[32] ibid.
[33] ibid para 333.
[34] ibid para 335.
[35] ibid para 336.
[36] ibid para 337.
[37] ibid para 338.

fair presentation of recommendations',[38] contained at Article 3 Investment Recommendations Directive (2003/125/EC): 'the general standard of fair presentation of recommendations for all relevant persons includes that: a) facts are clearly distinguished from interpretations, estimates or opinions, b) all sources are reliable or, where there is any doubt as to whether a source is reliable, this is clearly indicated, c) all projections, forecasts and price targets are clearly labelled as such and that the material assumptions made in producing or using them are indicated'.[39] Article 3 of the 2016 Implementing Regulation has maintained this approach providing: '(a) facts are clearly distinguished from interpretations, estimates, opinions and other types of non-factual information; (b) all substantially material sources of information are clearly and prominently indicated; (c) all sources of information are reliable or, where there is any doubt as to whether a source is reliable, this is clearly indicated; (d) all projections, forecasts and price targets are clearly and prominently labelled as such, and the material assumptions made in producing or using them are indicated; (e) the date and time when the production of the recommendation was completed is clearly and prominently indicated'.[40]

Distribution channels

B.20.21 Following Article 1(3) Investment Recommendations Directive (2003/125/EC), Article 3(1)(35) Market Abuse Regulation establishes that investment recommendations falling under the Market Abuse Regulation's scope are those 'intended for distribution channels or for the public'. The definition of 'distribution channels', provided by Article 1(7) Investment Recommendations Directive (2003/125/EC), qualifies those as channels 'through which information is, or is likely to become, publicly available. "Likely to become publicly available information" shall mean information to which a large number of persons have access'.[41] ESMA has taken the view that: 'an investment recommendation is intended for distribution channels or for the public not only when it is intended or expected to be made available to the public in general, but also when it is intended or expected to be distributed to clients or to a specific segment of clients, whatever their number, as a non-personal recommendation, ie without the provision of the investment service of investment advice'.[42] Further, ESMA has considered that: 'a too narrow definition of "investment recommendation intended for distribution channels or

[38] ESMA, 'Discussion Paper: ESMA's policy orientations on possible implementing measures under the Market Abuse Regulation (ESMA/2013/1649)' (14 November 2013) para 394 www.esma.org.

[39] ibid para 395.

[40] Article 3(1) Regulation 2016/958/EU.

[41] ESMA, 'Technical Standard' (n 17) para 339. Examples of 'distribution channels' are, among others, the following: a Regulatory Information System, media specialized in disseminating information (news agency, news provider, a newspaper etc), or the website of the producer.

[42] ibid para 340.

for the public" would entail the risk of leaving some investment recommendations provided to investors unregulated, without investors being in a position to know that the recommendation received is not regulated. In other words, ESMA believes that a "large number of persons" should have access to the recommendation irrespective of the nature of the channels through which the recommendation is distributed'.[43] Finally, with respect to persons who are financial analysts, economists, experienced or professional investors or experts assumed to regularly analyse companies or markets, ESMA emphasized the fact that 'their recommendations are likely to reach a large number of persons even when this information is transmitted through short messages to their followers', with an immediate impact on the market when they are disseminated during trading hours, especially on less liquid financial instruments.[44]

Non-written recommendations

With regard to non-written recommendations, the 2016 Implementing Regulation maintains the same approach as the Investment Recommendations Directive (2003/125/EC). ESMA did not indicate in the RTS the adaptation necessary for non-written recommendations, opting for an approach whereby an assessment is made on a case-by-case basis.[45] Moreover, after considering the possibility to clarify the meaning of non-written recommendations ESMA concluded that the risk of not being complete, thus allowing for circumvention and arbitrage opportunities, should be taken into account. With the intention to enhance more clarity on that definition and harmonize current practices, a first step has consisted in considering that 'non-written recommendations refer to recommendations given according to a wide range of modalities: meetings, road shows, audio/video conference calls, radio, TV or website interviews, or similar ones'.[46] **B.20.22**

However, it is reasonable to assume that non-written recommendations should follow the same rules as set out for written recommendations, albeit with some elements of flexibility, as introduced by Article 6(4): 'Where the disclosure of the information referred to in paragraphs 1 and 2 is disproportionate in relation to the length or form of the recommendation, including in the case of a non-written recommendation that is made using modalities, such as meetings, road shows or audio or video conferences, as well as radio, television or website interviews, the person who produces recommendations shall state in the recommendation where the required information can be directly and easily accessed by the persons receiving the recommendation free of charge'. Similar provisions have been included in Article 3(2) and Article 4.[47] **B.20.23**

[43] ibid para 341.
[44] ibid para 342.
[45] ESMA, 'Technical Standard' (n 17) para 387.
[46] ibid paras 388 and 389.
[47] ibid para 390.

Identity of the producers of recommendations

B.20.24 The 2016 Commission Implementing Regulation has confirmed the requirements provided by the Investment Recommendations Directive (2003/125/EC) for the identity of the producers of recommendations requiring these persons to 'disclose clearly and prominently in all the recommendations they produce their identity and the following information about the identity of any other person(s) responsible for the production of the recommendation: (a) the name and the job title of all the natural persons involved in the production of the recommendation; (b) where a natural or a legal person involved in the production of the recommendation is acting under contract, including a contract of employment, or otherwise for a legal person, the name of such legal person'.[48]

B.20.25 Persons producing recommendations have a duty to present them objectively. For this reason the Commission Implementing Regulation provides that they shall ensure the compliance of their recommendations with specific requirements: 'facts shall be clearly distinguished from any other subjective interpretation, estimate, opinions and other types of non-factual information; all substantially material sources of information are clearly and prominently indicated; all sources of information are reliable or, where there is any doubt as to whether a source is reliable, this is clearly indicated; all projections, forecasts and price targets are clearly and prominently labelled as such, and the material assumptions made in producing or using them are indicated; the date and time when the production of the recommendation was completed is clearly and prominently indicated'.[49]

B.20.26 For the persons referred to Article 3(1)(34)(i) of the Market Abuse Regulation and experts, the Commission Implementing Regulation requires, in addition to the general information, specific information in a clear and prominent manner. Among others, more specific information on the methodology adopted shall be provided. On this specific point, different views have emerged: on the one hand, market actors stressed the need for a more adequate discussion on research methodologies at the regulatory level; they also highlighted the importance in this context of transparency, often insufficient; other market actors have underlined that existing market incentives for financial analysts

[48] Article 2(1). Article 2(2) and (3) Regulation 2016/958/EU also require that: 'Where the person who produces recommendations is an investment firm, a credit institution, or a natural person working for an investment firm or a credit institution under contract of employment or otherwise, that person shall, in addition to the information laid down in paragraph 1, state the identity of the relevant competent authority in the recommendation. Where the person who produces recommendations is not a person referred to in paragraph 2, but is subject to self-regulatory standards or codes of conduct for the production of recommendations, that person shall, in addition to the information laid down in paragraph 1, state a reference to those standards or codes in the recommendation'.

[49] Article 3(1) Regulation 2016/958/EU.

have naturally been brought to more transparency, even in absence of strict regulatory requirements.[50]

Disclosure of interests or of conflicts of interests

In this regard the Commission Implementing Regulation provides a first layer of general obligations applicable to all persons who produce recommendations and a second layer for qualified persons. **B.20.27**

With regard to the general obligations, persons who produce recommendations shall disclose 'all relationships and circumstances that may reasonably be expected to impair the objectivity of the recommendation, including interests or conflicts of interest, on their part or on the part of any natural or legal person working for them under a contract, including a contract of employment, or otherwise, who was involved in producing the recommendation, concerning any financial instrument or the issuer to which the recommendation directly or indirectly relates'.[51] **B.20.28**

The second layer of disclosure for qualified persons includes, inter alia, information on the net long or short position exceeding the threshold of 0.5 % of the total issued share capital of the issuer (included on the initiative of ESMA),[52] with a statement to that effect specifying whether the net position is long or short; or, in case of holdings exceeding 5 % of its total issued share capital are held by the issuer, a statement to that effect.[53] **B.20.29**

Dissemination of information produced by third parties

As the Investment Recommendations Directive (2003/125/EC) did, the 2016 Implementing Regulation provides a section for regulating the dissemination of information produced by third parties. First, Article 8(1) of the Implementing Regulation requires that persons disseminating recommendations produced by a third party should communicate to the persons receiving the recommendations the following information: '(a) their identity, in a clear and prominent manner; (b) all relationships and circumstances that may reasonably be expected to impair the objective presentation of the recommendation, including interests or conflicts of interest concerning any financial instrument or the issuer to which the recommendation, directly or indirectly, relates; (c) the date and time when **B.20.30**

---

[50] ESMA, 'Technical Standard' (n 17) para 360. ESMA emphasized the importance of providing both qualitative and quantitative analysis and, to protect their investments, when producers of recommendations adopt a proprietary model they do not need to disclose the underlying methodology in detail.

[51] Article 5(1) Regulation 2016/958/EU. Article 5(2) and (3) Regulation 2016/958/EU require further information to be disclosed for natural and legal persons.

[52] ESMA, 'Technical Standard' (n 17) para 376.

[53] Article 6 Regulation 2016/958/EU.

the recommendation is first disseminated'.[54] Article 8(2) requires specific information to be provided for investment firms, credit institutions, or a natural or legal person working for an investment firm or a credit institution. Articles 9 and 10 provide additional requirements for arrangements for the dissemination of summaries or the extraction of recommendations and for the dissemination of substantially altered recommendations.

The impact of the Market Abuse Regulation disclosure obligations for investment recommendations

B.20.31 While the (former) Market Abuse Directive (2003/6/EC) disclosure obligation with respect to investment recommendation applied to a standardized equity market 'buy/hold/sell' research template, the Market Abuse Regulation enlarges the scope, encompassing a broader spectrum of less standardized sales recommendations.[55] This different regime will enhance the disclosure obligations for both the investment firms and their investment employees: specifically, they shall record every single investment recommendation at the security and issuer level, and make the last twelve months of this data available whenever making new recommendations.[56] This may be particularly difficult for investment firms that do not systematically record all the investment recommendations. It is likely that there will be consequences at a different level: a reduction in number of investment recommendations provided from investment firms for clients, the adoption of the electronic form instead of vocal communications, relevant investments in information technology, and high level staff training.[57]

III. Sanctions

B.20.32 See comment on Article 17.

[54] ibid art 8.
[55] ICMA, 'Market Abuse Regulation' (n 22).
[56] ibid.
[57] ibid.

Article 21: Disclosure or dissemination of information in the media

For the purposes of Article 10, Article 12(1)(c) and Article 20, where information is disclosed or disseminated and where recommendations are produced or disseminated for the purpose of journalism or other form of expression in the media, such disclosure or dissemination of information shall be assessed taking into account the rules governing the freedom of the press and freedom of expression in other media and the rules or codes governing the journalist profession, unless:

the persons concerned, or persons closely associated with them, derive, directly or indirectly, an advantage or profits from the disclosure or the dissemination of the information in question; or

the disclosure or the dissemination is made with the intention of misleading the market as to the supply of, demand for, or price of financial instruments.

I. General Remarks

Overview of Article 21

Article 21 focuses on the case of disclosure or dissemination of information and recommendation produced or disseminated for the purpose of journalism or any other form of expression in the media, and the application of the rules governing the freedom of the press and freedom of expression in other media, as well as the rules or codes governing the journalist profession. **B.21.01**

Structure of Article 21

Article 21 provides that for the purposes of Article 10 on unlawful disclosure of inside information, Article 12(1)(c) on market manipulation related to the media, Article 20 on investment recommendations and statistics, where information is disclosed or disseminated and where recommendations are produced or disseminated for the purpose of journalism or any other form of expression in the media, such disclosure or dissemination of information shall be assessed taking into account the rules governing the freedom of the press and freedom of expression in other media and the rules or codes governing the journalist profession. **B.21.02**

B.21.03 This assessment on the basis of the rules governing the freedom of the press and the freedom of expression in any other media and the rules or codes governing the journalist profession will be taken into account only if specific conditions do not apply.

B.21.04 A first exclusion refers to the situation of persons concerned, or other persons closely associated with them, deriving, directly or indirectly, an advantage or profits from the disclosure or the dissemination of the information in question. A second exclusion refers to the disclosure or the dissemination made with the intention of misleading the market as to the supply of, demand for, or price of financial instruments.

Historical background

B.21.05 The Proposal for the (former) Market Abuse Directive (2003/6/EC) referred to journalists at Article 5 in these terms: 'Member States may decide to introduce specific provisions to cover persons acting for journalistic purposes in the normal course of the exercise of their profession. By this the Directive separates clearly professional—journalistic—behaviour from personal behaviour for market abuse purposes'.[1]

B.21.06 Under the (former) Market Abuse Directive (2003/6/EC), the content of the current Article 21 was included in the definition of 'market manipulation', laid down in Article 1(2)(c), referring to, inter alia: 'dissemination of information through the media, including the Internet, or by any other means, which gives, or is likely to give, false or misleading signals as to financial instruments, including the dissemination of rumours and false or misleading news, where the person who made the dissemination knew, or ought to have known, that the information was false or misleading. In respect of journalists when they act in their professional capacity such dissemination of information is to be assessed, without prejudice to Article 11, taking into account the rules governing their profession, unless those persons derive, directly or indirectly, an advantage or profits from the dissemination of the information in question'.

B.21.07 The same wording of the (former) Market Abuse Directive (2003/6/EC) was adopted for the Market Abuse Regulation Proposal, whereas Article 21, as it is now, has been introduced only in the final version of the Regulation.

II. Freedom of Press versus Transparency Rules

B.21.08 Article 21 excludes journalists from the scope of the market manipulation regime. This article has a function of safeguard: given the nature of their professional

[1] It also provided a reference with respect to the professional secrecy: 'Only particular professions may be authorised to oppose, partly or completely, professional secrecy to competent authorities, according to national legislation (e.g. lawyers or journalists)'.

activity, journalists could be easily exposed to the accusation of market manipulation, against the principles of freedom governing their profession and the press, when publishing information with a substantial impact on the market of a given financial instrument.[2] Following Article 1(2)(c) of the (former) Market Abuse Directive (2003/6/EC), Article 21 makes an exception for the rules governing journalism as a profession, which have to be taken into account when assessing the journalists' conduct.

This exception is subject to two conditions. First, journalists do not 'derive, directly or indirectly, an advantage or profits from the dissemination of the information in question'. This confirms their economic independence from the topic treated in their information, thus enhancing the objectivity and transparency of the information journalists provide. Second, such activity shall not be put in place with the intention of misleading the market as to the supply of, demand for, or price of financial instruments. **B.21.09**

Article 21 emphasizes the difficulties to identify a 'fair balance between professional rules, often of a self-regulatory nature, and anti-manipulation rules, subject to public enforcement'.[3] While on the one hand, it is crucial to adequately protect the freedom and objectivity of information, it is on the other hand important to establish rules on financial investments by journalists and their conflicts of interest.[4] **B.21.10**

III. Sanctions

See comment on Article 17. **B.21.11**

---

[2] See G Ferrarini, 'The European Market Abuse Directive' (2004) 41 Common Market Law Review 711.

[3] ibid.

[4] ibid.

4

ESMA AND COMPETENT AUTHORITIES

Article 22: Competent authorities

Without prejudice to the competences of the judicial authorities, each Member State shall designate a single administrative competent authority for the purpose of this Regulation. Member States shall inform the Commission, ESMA and the other competent authorities of other Member States accordingly. The competent authority shall ensure that the provisions of this Regulation are applied on its territory, regarding all actions carried out on its territory, and actions carried out abroad relating to instruments admitted to trading on a regulated market, for which a request for admission to trading on such market has been made, auctioned on an auction platform or which are traded on an MTF or an OTF or for which a request for admission to trading has been made on an MTF operating within its territory.

I. General Remarks

Overview of article

Article 22 has two main intentions: on the one hand, it obliges the Member States to designate a single administrative authority responsible for the implementation of the Market Abuse Regulation, and to inform the Commission, the ESMA, and the authorities of the other Member States about this decision. On the other **B.22.01** hand, this provision determinates the jurisdiction of each national administrative authority, especially when it comes to cross-border cases.

Structure of article

B.22.02 Article 22 contains the obligation for each Member State to establish an administrative authority for the purposes of the Market Abuse Regulation. The subsequent Articles (23–29) govern the powers and the duties of these national authorities: Article 23 lays down the powers of the competent authority; Articles 24–26 entail the obligation of those authorities to cooperate with ESMA, other competent authorities of the other Member States (Article 25) and with third-country authorities (Article 26); Article 27 provides for the obligation to maintain the professional secrecy concerning any confidential information a competent authority has received; Articles 28 and 29 regulate the disclosure and protection of personal data.

B.22.03 Unlike other provisions of the Market Abuse Regulation, Article 22 is not directly applicable. The Member States have—as laid down in Article 39(3)—to take the necessary measures to comply with the Market Abuse Regulation.

Historical development and comparative remarks

B.22.04 The regulatory content of Article 22 of the Market Abuse Regulation was previously split into Arts 10 and 11(1) of the (former) Market Abuse Directive (2003/6/EC). Notably, the rules previously laid down in Article 11(1) of the (former) Market Abuse Directive (2003/6/EC) were transferred using almost identical wording. Only the obligation of the Member States to inform the Commission, the ESMA, and the authorities of the other Member States about the designated authority has been newly introduced and was not previously laid down in the (former) Market Abuse Directive (2003/6/EC).

B.22.05 The material scope of application has been remarkably extended in the new Market Abuse Regulation, compared to the (former) Market Abuse Directive (2003/6/EC): It now includes not only actions concerning financial instruments that are admitted to trading on a regulated market but also actions relating to instruments auctioned on an auction platform or instruments that are traded on a MTF or an OTF.

II. Establishment of the Competent Authority

Designation

B.22.06 Each Member State has to designate one single administrative authority entrusted with the power to enforce the Market Abuse Regulation. In light of the Market

Abuse Regulation, the Member States are free to decide what kind of authority will fulfil this function.

However, with regard to the duties and the required supervisory and investigatory powers of this authority, the Member States have to make sure that the designation of one particular authority complies with the national legal framework. **B.22.07**

The designation of one single administrative authority does not undermine the powers of the national judicial authorities: Even after the establishment of an authority in the sense of Article 22, the national judicial authorities retain their competence to impose criminal sanctions if the national law provides for them. Depending on the national law of each Member State, it is possible that two different authorities can punish violations of provisions of the Market Abuse Regulation. **B.22.08**

Information

According to the second sentence of Article 22, each Member State has to inform the Commission, the ESMA, and the competent authorities of the other Member States about the designation of the competent authority. Neither the date for informing the Commission, ESMA, and the other authorities, nor the minimum content of this disclosure, are mentioned in Article 22. **B.22.09**

Nevertheless, the above parties must at least be informed about the fact that a single competent authority within the meaning of Article 22 was established, and the name of this authority. According to the aims of the Market Abuse Regulation, the Member States have to inform the parties mentioned above immediately in order to guarantee a proper cooperation with ESMA and the authorities of the other Member States. **B.22.10**

The competent authorities of the Member States: **B.22.11**

Member State	Competent authority
Austria	Finanzmarktaufsichtsbehörde (FMA)
Belgium	Financial Services and Markets Authority (FSMA)
Bulgaria	Financial Supervision Commission
Croatia	Croatian Financial Services Supervisory Agency (HANFA)
Cyprus	Cyprus Securities and Exchange Commission (CySEC)
Czech Republic	Czech National Bank (CNB)
Denmark	Danish Financial Supervisory Authority
Estonia	Estonian Financial Supervision Authority (EFSA)
Finland	Financial Supervision Authority (FIN-FSA)
France	Autorité des marchés financiers (AMF)
Germany	Bundesanstalt für Finanzdienstleistungsaufsicht (BaFin)

Member State	Competent authority
Greece	Hellenic Capital Market Commission (HCMC)
Hungary	Central Bank of Hungary (MNB)
Ireland	Central Bank of Ireland
Italy	Commissione Nazionale per le Società e la Borsa (CONSOB)
Latvia	Financial and Capital Market Commission (FCMC)
Lithuania	Bank of Lithuania
Luxembourg	Commission de Surveillance du Secteur Financier (CSSF)
Malta	Malta Financial Services Authority (MFSA)
The Netherlands	Autoriteit Financiële Markten (AFM)
Poland	Polish Financial Supervision Authority (PFSA)
Portugal	Portuguese Securities Market Commission (CMVM)
Romania	Financial Supervisory Authority (ASF)
Slovakia	National Bank of Slovakia (NBS)
Slovenia	Securities Market Agency
Spain	Spanish National Securities Market Commission (CNMV)
Sweden	Swedish Financial Supervisory Authority
United Kingdom	Financial Conduct Authority (FCA)

III. Jurisdiction of the Administrative Authority

B.22.12 The third sentence of Article 22 determines the international jurisdiction of the authority in question. Unfortunately, the wording of this provision is not as clear as it should be. Doubtless the national authority within the meaning of Article 22 is responsible for the application of the provisions of the Market Abuse Regulation on its territory. Accordingly, this Member State authority has the power to investigate, supervise, and impose administrative sanctions regarding all actions carried out on its territory irrespective of the location of the market to which the instruments are admitted.

B.22.13 The authority is also responsible for the application of the provisions of the Market Abuse Regulation with respect to actions carried out abroad insofar as they relate to instruments admitted to trading on a regulated market. It is not sufficiently clear whether only actions (carried out abroad) that relate to instruments admitted to trading on a regulated market operating within the Member State's territory fall within the scope of this provision. However, there has to be a clear boundary between the competences of the different national authorities and this can only be achieved by restricting the competence of one authority to actions (carried out abroad) relating to instruments admitted to trading on a regulated market operating within the Member State's territory. Thus, in my view, the competent authority of a Member State is only responsible for the application of the provisions of the Market Abuse Regulation regarding actions carried out abroad relating to instruments admitted to trading on a regulated market of this Member State.[1] It is irrelevant that those instruments have not yet been admitted to trading on a regulated market, when a request for admission to trading on a market of this kind has been made. The authority is also responsible for actions carried out on its territory or abroad insofar as they relate to instruments auctioned on an auction platform within the Member State's territory, as well as for those actions that relate to instruments that are traded on a MTF or an OTF within the Member State's territory. The request for admission to trading is equal to the trading on a MTF or an OTF.

[1] See para 1(2) of the German Wertpapierhandelsgesetz.

Article 23: Powers of competent authorities

1. Competent authorities shall exercise their functions and powers in any of the following ways:
   (a) directly;
   (b) in collaboration with other authorities or with the market undertakings;
   (c) under their responsibility by delegation to such authorities or to market undertakings;
   (d) by application to the competent judicial authorities.
2. In order to fulfil their duties under this Regulation, competent authorities shall have, in accordance with national law, at least the following supervisory and investigatory powers:
   (a) to access any document and data in any form, and to receive or take a copy thereof;
   (b) to require or demand information from any person, including those who are successively involved in the transmission of orders or conduct of the operations concerned, as well as their principals, and if necessary, to summon and question any such person with a view to obtain information;
   (c) in relation to commodity derivatives, to request information from market participants on related spot markets according to standardized formats, obtain reports on transactions, and have direct access to traders' systems;
   (d) to carry out on-site inspections and investigations at sites other than at the private residences of natural persons;
   (e) subject to the second subparagraph, to enter the premises of natural and legal persons in order to seize documents and data in any form where a reasonable suspicion exists that documents or data relating to the subject matter of the inspection or investigation may be relevant to prove a case of insider dealing or market manipulation infringing this Regulation;
   (f) to refer matters for criminal investigation;
   (g) to require existing recordings of telephone conversations, electronic communications or data traffic records held by investment firms, credit institutions or financial institutions;
   (h) to require, insofar as permitted by national law, existing data traffic records held by a telecommunications operator, where there is a reasonable suspicion of an infringement and where such records may be relevant to the investigation of an infringement of point (a) or (b) of Article 14 or Article 15;

(i) to request the freezing or sequestration of assets, or both;
(j) to suspend trading of the financial instrument concerned;
(k) to require the temporary cessation of any practice that the competent authority considers contrary to this Regulation;
(l) to impose a temporary prohibition on the exercise of professional activity; and
(m) to take all necessary measures to ensure that the public is correctly informed, inter alia, by correcting false or misleading disclosed information, including by requiring an issuer or other person who has published or disseminated false or misleading information to publish a corrective statement.

Where in accordance with national law prior authorization to enter premises of natural and legal persons referred to in point (e) of the first subparagraph is needed from the judicial authority of the Member State concerned, the power as referred to in that point shall be used only after having obtained such prior authorization.

3. Member States shall ensure that appropriate measures are in place so that competent authorities have all the supervisory and investigatory powers that are necessary to fulfil their duties.

This Regulation is without prejudice to laws, Regulations and administrative provisions adopted in relation to takeover bids, merger transactions and other transactions affecting the ownership or control of companies regulated by the supervisory authorities appointed by Member States pursuant to Article 4 of Directive 2004/25/EC that impose requirements in addition to the requirements of this Regulation.

4. A person making information available to the competent authority in accordance with this Regulation shall not be considered to be infringing any restriction on disclosure of information imposed by contract or by any legislative, regulatory or administrative provision, and shall not involve the person notifying in liability of any kind related to such notification.

I. General Remarks

Overview of article

B.23.01 One the one hand, Article 23 enumerates the minimum supervisory and investigatory powers that the authority of each Member State must have. It also obliges the Member States to ensure that the authorities concerned have all necessary powers to fulfil their duties. On the other hand, Article 23 determines the way in which the domestic authority shall exercise its functions and powers. Furthermore, Article 23(4) provides that restrictions on disclosure of information imposed by contract or by law shall not apply to a person making this information available to the competent authority.

Historical development and comparative remarks

B.23.02 Comparing Article 12 and 6(7) of the (former) Market Abuse Directive (2003/6/EC) and Article 23 demonstrates that all the provisions of the (former) Market Abuse Directive (2003/6/EC) were transferred into the Market Abuse Regulation, notwithstanding some extensions that had been added to the Market Abuse Regulation. First and foremost, the competent authorities now have the power to enter the premises of natural and legal persons in order to seize documents and data in any form. Nevertheless, there has to be a reasonable suspicion that these documents or data may be relevant to prove an infringement of the Market Abuse Regulation. Furthermore, this provision does not suspend national law requiring a prior authorization by the judicial authority for these actions.

B.23.03 Also, pursuant to Article 23, the administrative authority is now competent to refer matters for criminal investigation and has the power to request information concerning commodity derivatives from the market participants.

B.23.04 Persons may not be held liable for making information available to the competent authority in accordance with the Market Abuse Regulation. This is a significant change, as national legal provisions on professional secrecy remained unaffected by the (former) Market Abuse Directive (2003/6/EC).

Scope of application

B.23.05 Article 23(3) governs the relation between the Market Abuse Regulation and the Takeover Directive (2004/25/EC). According to this provision, the Market Abuse Regulation does not prejudice laws and regulations concerning takeover bids, merger transactions and other transactions affecting the ownership or the control of companies. However, Article 23(3) only refers to the laws and regulations supervised by a national takeover commission and imposing additional requirements. To illustrate, the special duties of disclosure and of notification imposed by the Takeover Directive (2004/25/EC) are left untouched by the Market Abuse Regulation.

II. Guidelines for the Exercise of the Powers

General remarks

Article 23(1) determines the different ways in which the authority shall exercise its functions and powers. This exercise of its competences depends on the specific task and the relevant context. It lies in the discretion of the authority to choose the optimal type of action. However, this decision has to be made in accordance with the national law. **B.23.06**

Direct exercise

According to Article 23(1)(a), the competent author may exercise its functions and powers directly. In other words, the authority takes the necessary measures independently, without the support of other (national or international) judicial or other, non-judicial, authorities. **B.23.07**

If the authority does not exercise its powers and functions directly, it can either collaborate with other authorities or market undertakings, or delegate its functions to other authorities or market undertakings. It can also request the competent judicial authorities to take adequate measures. **B.23.08**

Collaboration

According to Article 23(1)(b) the competent authority may also fulfil its tasks by collaborating with other authorities or market undertakings. In this case, the competent authority fulfils its tasks not fully independently but receives support from other authorities or market undertakings. **B.23.09**

The meaning of the term 'market undertaking' is vague. The German version of Article 23(1)(c) uses the term *Marktteilnehmer*. According to Article 3(1)(5), *Marktteilnehmer* refers to a market operator as defined in Article 4(1)(18) of the Markets in Financial Instruments Directive II (2014/65/EU). However, Article 4(1)(18) of the Markets in Financial Instruments Directive II (2014/65/EU) defines the meaning of the term *Marktbetreiber*, which is not identical to *Marktteilnehmer*. In the English version, Article 23(1)(c) uses the term 'market undertaking'; Article 3(1)(5) defines the meaning of 'market operator' but not the meaning of 'market undertaking'. **B.23.10**

In my view, it is better to read Article 23(1)(c) in the meaning of market operator: as a rule, only a market operator is given sovereign powers and, thus, can support **B.23.11** the competent authority in fulfilling its duties. Hence, the competent authority is allowed to collaborate only with market operators.

Delegation

B.23.12 Instead of collaborating with other authorities, the competent authority may also delegate its tasks to other authorities or market undertakings. Article 23 does not explain the distinction made between delegation and collaboration. Evidently, if the competent authority delegates its tasks, it remains responsible for the exercise of powers and functions of the other authorities or market undertakings. Its competences and responsibilities are not transferred, as the other authorities or market undertakings act on behalf of the competent authority.

B.23.13 Also in the context of Article 23(1)(d), market undertaking has to be understood within the meaning of Article 3(1)(5) of the Markets in Financial Instruments Directive II (2014/65/EU). Hence, the competent authority may only collaborate with market operators.

Application

B.23.14 The competent authority may also fulfil its duties by making applications to the competent judicial authorities. Involving judicial authorities is especially important whenever infringements of the Market Abuse Regulation result in criminal sanctions imposed by judicial authorities. Thus, the competent authority can apply for imposition of criminal sanctions. Depending on the national law of each Member State, applications to the competent judicial authorities may also be necessary for onsite inspections and investigations.

III. Supervisory and Investigatory Powers

B.23.15 Article 23(2) enumerates the minimum supervisory and investigatory powers of a competent authority. Additionally, Article 23(3) obliges the Member States to ensure that the authorities concerned have all required supervisory and investigatory powers. Hence, on the one hand, Article 23(3) emphasizes that Article 23(2) does not contain an exhaustive list of the supervisory and investigatory powers of the authority; moreover, Article 23(2) provides solely for a minimum set of powers of a competent authority. On the other hand, Article 23(3) can be understood as obliging the Member States to ensure that a competent authority receives adequate support from other national authorities.

B.23.16 **General clause:** In addition to the supervisory and investigatory powers listed in Article 23(2), Article 23(3) obliges the Member States to take appropriate measures to ensure that the authorities have all required supervisory and investigatory powers to fulfil their duties. In particular, it can be necessary to guarantee that the competent authority receives support of other national authorities while fulfilling its duties.

For example, it may be appropriate that the police or another security agency assists the competent authority in its investigation. **B.23.17**

Special powers: As a minimum, the competent authorities have to have the following supervisory and investigatory powers: **B.23.18**

- According to Article 23(1)(a), competent authorities have to be granted unrestricted access to any type of documents or data; additionally, they can request copies thereof.
- The second Article 23(1)(b) provides for the competence to require or demand information from any person, and, if necessary, to summon and question any such person.
- With regard to commodity derivatives, Article 23(3)(c) provides that the authority concerned may request information from market participants as well as reports on transaction; it also has direct access to traders' systems. The power to gain direct access to traders' systems in particular gives the competent authority broad investigatory powers.
- Article 23(3)(d) and (e) are closely related: On the one hand, Article 23(4) permits the authority to carry out on-site inspections and investigations without an existing reasonable suspicion. However, these measures may only be carried out at sites other than at the private residences of natural persons. Nevertheless, if there is a reasonable suspicion, authorities do have the competence to enter the premises of natural and legal persons in order to seize documents and data in any form.
- Article 23(2)(g) and (h) provide for the power of competent authorities to require existing recordings of telephone conversations from specific institutions, in addition to requesting existing data traffic records held by a telecommunication operator. Confining the requests solely to the already existing material substantially restricts the scope of these requests.
- Further important powers and competences of the authorities are provided in Article 23(2)(f) and (i) to (l), including the permission to refer matters for criminal investigation, to request the sequestration of assets, or to suspend trading of the financial instrument concerned. On top of this, authorities may also issue provisional orders.
- Finally, authorities are allowed to take all the necessary measures to ensure that the public is adequately informed, eg by correcting disclosed information if it is false or misleading.

IV. 'Whistle-blowing'

B.23.19 Article 23(4) protects 'whistle-blowers'. If a person makes information available to the competent authority according to Article 23(4), this person shall neither be prosecuted nor held liable in any way. A disclosure of information shall not be considered as an infringement of contract, even if this particular agreement prohibits such a disclosure. According to Article 23(4), this privilege applies only to persons supplying the information *in accordance with this Regulation*. This provision evidently refers to Article 32. The latter obliges the Member States as well as their competent authorities to establish effective reporting mechanisms enabling the reporting of actual or potential infringements of the Market Abuse Regulation.

B.23.20 Although Article 23(4) does not mention it explicitly, this provision will mainly apply to the employees of the issuer. If an employee informs the competent authority about an actual or potential infringement of the Market Abuse Regulation, this disclosure shall not be considered as an infringement of the employee's duties. This person can be neither dismissed nor be held liable for any damage caused by the disclosure of information.

B.23.21 Although its wording is relatively broad, Article 23(4) does not affect the professional secrecy rules applicable to attorneys, tax consultants, and others who are bound to professional secrecy by law. If these persons receive information concerning the infringement of the Market Abuse Regulation, they are bound not to disclose it.

Article 24: Cooperation with ESMA

1. The competent authorities shall cooperate with ESMA for the purposes of this Regulation, in accordance with Regulation (EU) No 1095/2010.
2. The competent authorities shall, without delay, provide ESMA with all information necessary to carry out its duties, in accordance with Article 35 of this Regulation (EU) No 1095/2010.
3. In order to ensure uniform conditions of application of this Article, ESMA shall develop draft implementing technical standards to determine the procedures and forms for exchange of information as referred to in paragraph 2.

The ESMA shall submit those draft implementing technical standards to the Commission by 3 July 2016.

Power is conferred on the Commission to adopt the implementing technical standards referred to in the first subparagraph in accordance with Article 15 of this Regulation (EU) No 1095/2010.

I. General Remarks

Overview of article

Article 24(1) obliges the competent authorities of the Member States to cooperate with ESMA. Article 24(2) stipulates that the national competent authorities are to provide ESMA all information necessary to fulfil its duties in accordance with Article 35 ESMA Regulation (1095/2010/EU). Furthermore, this Article seeks to ensure uniform conditions of its application. To this end, ESMA is obliged to develop implementing technical standards and submit those to the Commission. **B.24.01**

The duty of cooperation with EMSA is laid down not only in Article 24. Similarly, Article 25 provides for cooperation between national authorities and the ESMA. **B.24.02**

However, in contrast to Article 24, Article 25 mainly governs the cooperation between the competent authorities of different Member States. Nevertheless, there is some overlapping: Article 25(1) obliges the national authorities (just as the preceding provision) to cooperate with ESMA in accordance with the ESMA Regulation (1095/2010/EU). Article 24 appears to constitute a general provision for the cooperation between the different competent authorities and ESMA, whereas Article 25 governs the methods of cooperation in a more specific way. **B.24.03**

Historical development

B.24.04 Compared to Article 15a (former) Market Abuse Directive (2003/6/EC), Article 24 of this Regulation entails only one significant addition: To ensure effective cooperation with ESMA, the latter is obliged to develop draft implementing technical standards to determine the procedure of information exchange.

II. Cooperation with ESMA

B.24.05 According to Article 24(1), the competent authorities of the Member States are obliged to cooperate with ESMA. As mentioned above, this duty of cooperation is also established in Article 25(1). The cooperation with ESMA has to comply with the ESMA Regulation (1095/2010/EU) and guarantee effective and uniform compliance with the Market Abuse Regulation.

B.24.06 The central element of the cooperation between the competent authorities and ESMA encompasses the duty to provide all relevant information to ESMA in order to enable it to fulfil its duty according to Article 24(2). The latter provision refers to Article 35 ESMA Regulation (1095/2010/EU). Article 35 ESMA Regulation (1095/2010/EU) authorizes ESMA to demand all information necessary to fulfil its duties. For example, ESMA may request information needed for the drafting of recommendations within the meaning of Article 17 ESMA Regulation (1095/2010/EU). ESMA may also inquire about information necessary for establishing the guidelines in line with Article 17 ESMA Regulation (1095/2010/EU).

B.24.07 In essence, ESMA may only demand information that is related to the nature of its respective duties. However, according to Article 35(2) of the ESMA Regulation (1095/2010/EU), ESMA has the competence to request information at recurring intervals without having to rely on a specific incident or case as a basis for its requests.

III. Technical Standards

B.24.08 According to Article 24(3), ESMA shall develop draft implementing technical standards to ensure uniform conditions of the cooperation between ESMA and the different national authorities. The Commission is empowered to adopt these standards.

B.24.09 Although the deadline for the submission of the draft standards ended on 3 July 2016, ESMA has—according to its website[1]—not yet submitted these standards to the Commission.

[1] See https://www.esma.europa.eu/convergence/guidelines-and-technical-standards.

Article 25: Obligation to cooperate

1. Competent authorities shall cooperate with each other and with ESMA where necessary for the purposes of this Regulation, unless one of the exceptions in paragraph 2 applies. Competent authorities shall render assistance to competent authorities of other Member States and ESMA. In particular, they shall exchange information without undue delay and cooperate in investigation, supervision and enforcement activities.

The obligation to cooperate and assist laid down in the first subparagraph shall also apply as regards the Commission in relation to the exchange of information relating to commodities which are agricultural products listed in Annex I to the TFEU.

The competent authorities and ESMA shall cooperate in accordance with Regulation (EU) No 1095/2010, in particular Article 35 thereof.

Where Member States have chosen, in accordance with Article 30(1), second subparagraph, to lay down criminal sanctions for infringements of the provisions of this Regulation referred to in that Article, they shall ensure that appropriate measures are in place so that competent authorities have all the necessary powers to liaise with judicial authorities within their jurisdiction to receive specific information related to criminal investigations or proceedings commenced for possible infringements of this Regulation and provide the same to other competent authorities and ESMA to fulfil their obligation to cooperate with each other and ESMA for the purposes of this Regulation.

2. A competent authority may refuse to act on a request for information or a request to cooperate with an investigation only in the following exceptional circumstances, namely where:
   (a) communication of relevant information could adversely affect the security of the Member State addressed, in particular the fight against terrorism and other serious crimes;
   (b) complying with the request is likely adversely to affect its own investigation, enforcement activities or, where applicable, a criminal investigation;
   (c) judicial proceedings have already been initiated in respect of the same actions and against the same persons before the authorities of the Member State addressed; or
   (d) a final judgment has already been delivered in relation to such persons for the same actions in the Member State addressed.
3. Competent authorities and ESMA shall cooperate with the Agency for the Cooperation of Energy Regulators (ACER), established under Regulation (EC) No 713/2009 of the European Parliament and of the Council (1), and

the national regulatory authorities of the Member States to ensure that a coordinated approach is taken to the enforcement of the relevant rules where transactions, orders to trade or other actions or behaviours relate to one or more financial instruments to which this Regulation applies and also to one or more wholesale energy products to which Article 3, 4 and 5 of Regulation (EU) No 1227/2011 apply. Competent authorities shall consider the specific characteristics of the definitions of Article 2 of Regulation (EU) No 1227/ 2011 and the provisions of Article 3, 4 and 5 of Regulation (EU) No 1227/ 2011 when they apply Articles 7, 8 and 12 of this Regulation to financial instruments related to wholesale energy products.

4. Competent authorities shall, on request, immediately supply any information required for the purpose referred to in paragraph 1.
5. Where a competent authority is convinced that acts contrary to the provisions of this Regulation are being, or have been, carried out on the territory of another Member State or that acts are affecting financial instruments traded on a trading venue situated in another Member State, it shall give notice of that fact in as specific a manner as possible to the competent authority of the other Member State and to ESMA and, in relation to wholesale energy products, to ACER. The competent authorities of the various Member States involved shall consult each other and ESMA and, in relation to wholesale energy products, ACER, on the appropriate action to take and inform each other of significant interim developments. They shall coordinate their action, in order to avoid possible duplication and overlap when applying administrative sanctions and other administrative measures to those cross-border cases in accordance with Articles 30 and 31, and shall assist each other in the enforcement of their decisions.
6. The competent authority of one Member State may request assistance from the competent authority of another Member State with regard to on-site inspections or investigations.

A requesting competent authority may inform ESMA of any request referred to in the first subparagraph. In the case of an investigation or an inspection with cross-border effect, ESMA shall, if requested to do so by one of the competent authorities, coordinate the investigation or inspection.

Where a competent authority receives a request from a competent authority of another Member State to carry out an on-site inspection or an investigation, it may do any of the following:

(a) carry out the on-site inspection or investigation itself;
(b) allow the competent authority which submitted the request to participate in an on-site inspection or investigation;
(c) allow the competent authority which submitted the request to carry out the on-site inspection or investigation itself;

(d) appoint auditors or experts to carry out the on-site inspection or investigation;
(e) share specific tasks related to supervisory activities with the other competent authorities.

Competent authorities may also cooperate with competent authorities of other Member States with respect to facilitating the recovery of pecuniary sanctions.

7. Without prejudice to Article 258 TFEU, a competent authority whose request for information or assistance in accordance with paragraphs 1, 3, 4 and 5 is not acted upon within a reasonable time or whose request for information or assistance is rejected may refer that rejection or absence of action within a reasonable timeframe to ESMA.

In those situations, ESMA may act in accordance with Article 19 of Regulation (EU) No 1095/2010, without prejudice to the possibility of ESMA acting in accordance with Article 17 of Regulation (EU) No 1095/2010.

8. Competent authorities shall cooperate and exchange information with relevant national and third-country regulatory authorities responsible for the related spot markets where they have reasonable grounds to suspect that acts, which constitute insider dealing, unlawful disclosure of information or market manipulation infringing this Regulation, are being, or have been, carried out. Such cooperation shall ensure a consolidated overview of the financial and spot markets, and shall detect and impose sanctions for cross-market and cross-border market abuses.

   In relation to emission allowances, the cooperation and exchange of information provided for under the first subparagraph shall also be ensured with:
   (a) the auction monitor, with regard to auctions of emission allowances or other auctioned products based thereon that are held pursuant to Regulation (EU) No 1031/2010; and
   (b) competent authorities, registry administrators, including the Central Administrator, and other public bodies charged with the supervision of compliance under Directive 2003/87/EC.

ESMA shall perform a facilitation and coordination role in relation to the cooperation and exchange of information between competent authorities and regulatory authorities in other Member States and third countries. Competent authorities shall, where possible, conclude cooperation arrangements with third-country regulatory authorities responsible for the related spot markets in accordance with Article 26.

9. In order to ensure uniform conditions of application of this Article, ESMA shall develop draft implementing technical standards to determine the procedures and forms for exchange of information and assistance as referred to in this Article.

ESMA shall submit those draft implementing technical standards to the Commission by 3 July 2016.

Power is conferred on the Commission to adopt the implementing technical standards referred to in the first subparagraph in accordance with Article 15 of Regulation (EU) No 1095/2010.

I. General Remarks

Overview of article

B.25.01 Article 25(1) obliges the competent authorities to cooperate with the respective authorities of the other Member States as well as with ESMA. Under special circumstances, there is also an obligation to cooperate with the Commission or with the Agency for the Cooperation of Energy Regulators (ACER).

B.25.02 According to Article 25(2), the competent authorities may, under exceptional circumstances, refuse a request to cooperate. Article 25 also regulates the ways in which the different national authorities cooperate with each other or with ESMA, and the consequences of refusing to cooperate. Moreover, Article 25 obliges ESMA to develop draft implementing technical standards in order to ensure uniform conditions of the cooperation.

B.25.03 The duty of cooperation shall make compliance with the rules of the Market Abuse Regulation more efficient, as many infringements of the Market Abuse Regulation will affect more than one Member State.

Historical development and comparative remarks

B.25.04 With regard to the obligation to cooperate, the Market Abuse Regulation introduces numerous changes compared to the (former) Market Abuse Directive (2003/6/EC). Some of them were necessary, since two new EU-wide authorities—ESMA and ACER—have been established in the period between 2011 and 2012. Further, the material scope of application was extended, whereby the Market Abuse Regulation also sanctions actions relating to instruments auctioned on an auction platform or instruments that are traded on an MTF or an OTF.

Article 25(1) stipulates a general obligation of the competent authorities to cooperate with the competent authorities of other Member States as well as with ESMA. Moreover, under the Market Abuse Regulation, Member States which have chosen to lay down criminal sanctions for infringements of the Market Abuse Regulation are to guarantee adequate measures empowering the competent authorities to receive information from judicial authorities on criminal investigations or proceedings relating to these infringements, and to provide the same to other competent authorities and ESMA in order to fulfil their obligation to cooperate. **B.25.05**

As regards the possibility of refusing to act on a request for information, one exemption has been added, namely when complying with a request is likely to affect the authority's own investigation and measures. **B.25.06**

The new Article 25(3) implements the obligation to cooperate with ACER and national regulatory authorities of the Member States. **B.25.07**

When a competent authority receives a request from a competent authority of another Member State, seeking to carry out an on-site inspection or investigation, the requested authority now has additional options. Specifically, it may: **B.25.08**

- allow the other authority to carry out the on-site actions itself
- appoint auditors or experts or
- share specific tasks with the other competent authority.

According to Article 25(8), the competent authorities shall cooperate and exchange information with relevant national and third-country regulatory authorities if they have reasonable grounds to suspect that acts violating the Market Abuse Regulation are being carried out. **B.25.09**

II. Duty of Cooperation with Authorities

Cooperation with competent authorities, ESMA, and Commission

According to Article 25(1), the national authorities are obliged to cooperate. In particular, the competent authorities have to cooperate with each other and—if necessary—with ESMA, thereby rendering assistance to each other and to ESMA. The competent authorities also have to cooperate with, and render assistance to, the Commission for the purpose of exchanging information regarding agricultural products listed in Annex I to the TFEU. **B.25.10**

B.25.11 According to Article 25(3), the competent authorities and ESMA are, further, obliged to cooperate with ACER and, under special circumstances, with the regulatory authorities of the Member States. This special duty of cooperation applies only to transactions, orders to trade or other actions or behaviours that concern one or more financial instruments related to wholesale energy products within the meaning of Articles 3, 4, and 5 of the Wholesale Energy Market Integrity and Transparency Regulation (2011/1227/EU). This special form of cooperation shall ensure coordinated enforcement of the relevant rules enshrined in both Regulations.

B.25.12 In particular, the authorities mentioned above shall cooperate by exchanging information without undue delay during investigation, supervision, and enforcement activities. Hence, the competent authorities are not only obliged to cooperate; they must carry out this duty within a reasonable time. Whether an authority cooperates without undue delay, depends on the concrete circumstances, mainly on the requested assistance.

B.25.13 If a competent authority refuses to cooperate, although the exception within the meaning of Article 25(2) does not apply, this authority can refer this matter to ESMA (Article 25(7)).

B.25.14 If competent authorities cooperate with each other or with ESMA or the Commission, the question of the applicable law arises. Each authority is to fulfil its duties in compliance with the law of its respective Member State.

Exceptions

B.25.15 Article 25(2) enumerates the circumstances under which a competent authority may refuse to cooperate and to disclose information. According to the wording of Article 25(2), the list of exceptions is exhaustive; only under the circumstances enumerated in this provision may a competent authority refuse to cooperate.

B.25.16 A competent authority may refuse to cooperate or disclose information if this disclosure could affect the security of the Member State concerned. In particular, this exception is applicable if the duty of cooperation and disclosure of information is liable to obstruct the fight against terrorism or against other serious crimes.

B.25.17 Furthermore, a competent authority may refuse to cooperate if the compliance with the request of information could affect its own investigation or enforcement activities.

B.25.18 A request to cooperate may also be refused if complying with it would be liable to affect criminal investigations. A refusal to cooperate can be compatible with the provisions of the Market Abuse Regulation if negative effects to investigative or enforcement activities are merely likely to arise; these negative effects do not have to be considered as certain.

Moreover, a competent authority is not obliged to cooperate (within the meaning of Article 25(1)) if judicial proceedings against the person concerned and in respect of the same actions have already been initiated in the Member State of the authority that received a request to cooperate. This exception seeks to ensure compliance with Article 50 of the Charter of Fundamental Rights of the European Union (right not to be tried or punished twice in criminal proceedings for the same criminal offence). **B.25.19**

Moreover, a request may be refused if a final judgment has already been delivered in relation to the person concerned, with regard to the same action. Notably, this exception applies only to final judgments adopted in the Member State of the addressed competent authority. As noted above, this exception is also necessary to ensure compliance with Article 50 of the Charter of Fundamental Rights. **B.25.20**

III. Cooperation with the Judicial Authorities

If a Member State has decided, in accordance with Article 30(1), to prescribe criminal instead of administrative sanctions for infringements of the Market Abuse Regulation, this Member State has to ensure adequate cooperation between the judicial authority within its jurisdiction and the competent authority, as required in Article 25(1)(4). In particular, the Member State must take the necessary measures to grant the competent authority all the powers needed to receive the relevant information related to criminal investigations or proceedings commenced for possible infringements of the Market Abuse Regulation. The Member State also has to guarantee that the information mentioned above is available to competent authorities of other Member States and ESMA if this information is needed to fulfil the obligation to cooperate with other competent authorities or with ESMA. **B.25.21**

IV. Nature of Cooperation

General remarks

There are many methods of cooperation available to different authorities as well as ESMA. These methods include the supply of information on request (Article 25(4)), assistance by the competent authority of another Member State (Article 25(6)), or the notification of possible infringements of this Regulation (Article 25(5)). Although the competent authorities may independently determine the way of cooperating with each other or with ESMA, they have to avoid undue delay, as stipulated under Article 25(1). **B.25.22**

Supply of information (Article 25(4))

B.25.23 Article 25(4) requires the competent authority of a Member State to supply information to the other competent authorities and to ESMA.

B.25.24 At the very least, the competent authorities must comply with a request of the competent authority of another Member State or that of ESMA. Even though the wording of Article 25(4) is rather unclear, the Commission and ACER may also request information (within the meaning of Article 25(4)), in light of the competent authority's duty to cooperate with these authorities. In my view, Article 25 does not impose upon the competent authorities the duty to comply with a request for information from a judicial authority.

B.25.25 The competent authorities only have to disclose information that is required for the purposes referred to in Article 25(1).

Assistance from the competent authority (Article 25(6))

B.25.26 The competent authority of a Member State may request assistance from a competent authority of another Member State regarding investigations or on-site inspections. According to the last sentence of Article 25(6), the competent authority may also request assistance from the competent authorities of other Member States in order to facilitate the enforcement of pecuniary sanctions. The competent authority receiving this request is to act in line with the law of its respective Member State. The decision-making power remains with the competent authority and is not transferred to the authority that received this request.

B.25.27 The competent authority may also inform ESMA about this request. This may be useful insofar as it can prompt the competent authority that received the request to fulfil its duties at the earliest possible opportunity.

B.25.28 If the request of the competent authority concerns investigations or on-site inspections with cross-border effects, the competent authority may also approach ESMA to coordinate those actions. The coordination by ESMA is likely to accelerate the investigations, making the compliance with the Market Abuse Regulation more efficient.

B.25.29 According to Article 25(2)(3), the authority that was approached with a request has a number of options in fulfilling its duty:

- It may carry out the requested on-site inspection or investigation by itself. In this case, the requesting competent authority will not participate in the requested actions.
- It may also allow the requesting competent authority to participate in the requested investigation or on-site inspection. In this case, both competent authorities are involved. The requesting authority investigates according to the

provisions of the laws of its Member State. The decision-making power remains with the requesting competent authority.

- Moreover, it may allow the competent authority from another Member State, which submitted the request, to carry out the requested investigation or on-site inspection independently. In this case, the requesting competent authority acts alone. Also in this case the decision-making power stays with the requesting competent authority acting in accordance with the laws of its respective Member State.
- It may, further, appoint auditors or experts to carry out the investigation or on-site inspections.
- Finally, it is also allowed to share specific supervisory activities with other competent authorities. If a competent authority chooses this option, more than one competent authority will carry out on-site inspections or investigations; the involved competent authorities will act in collaboration.

Notification of infringements

A special method of cooperation is laid down in Article 25(5): If the competent authority of a Member State is convinced of the existence of an infringement of the Market Abuse Regulation concerning another Member State, it should inform the competent authority of the other Member State, ESMA and, with regard to wholesale energy products, the ACER about the proceedings in question. The competent authority shall, in particular, inform the above authorities when actions violating the Market Abuse Regulation are being or have been carried out in the territory of another Member State or if those actions affect financial instruments traded on a trading venue situated in another Member State. **B.25.30**

The involved competent authorities of the Member States shall consult each other and ESMA on the appropriate actions to be taken and assist each other in their decision-making. These authorities shall also inform each other of new developments and coordinate their measures to avoid duplication and overlapping administrative sanctions. **B.25.31**

If the infringements of the Market Abuse Regulation concern a wholesale energy product, the ACER should be informed and consulted as well. **B.25.32**

V. Consequences of Violating the Obligation to Cooperate

Article 25(7) governs the consequences of violating the duty to cooperate. This provision stipulates that a competent authority whose request for information or assistance remained unanswered within a reasonable time or was rejected may appeal to ESMA. **B.25.33**

B.25.34 Article 25(7) explicitly refers only to a request for information or assistance within the meaning of Article 25(1), (3), (4), and (5). However, a request for assistance regarding investigations or on-site inspections (as understood under Article 25(6)) is also covered by Article 25(7).

B.25.35 After receiving information about the rejection or a delay in action, ESMA may settle a disagreement between the competent authorities in cross-border situ ations in line with Article 19 ESMA Regulation (1095/2010/EU). In this case, ESMA has the competence to set a time limit for conciliation between the competent authorities. If the competent authorities fail to reach an agreement within this time limit, ESMA may make a decision requiring these authorities to take specific actions or to refrain from certain actions in order to settle the matter concerned.

B.25.36 Irrespective of Article 19 ESMA Regulation (1095/2010/EU), ESMA may also investigate the alleged breach or non-application of the EU law under Article 17 ESMA Regulation (1095/2010/EU).

B.25.37 After initiating an investigation, ESMA has to address a recommendation to the competent authorities specifying the actions necessary to comply with the EU law. If the competent authority does not comply with the relevant provisions of *acquis communautaire* within one month from the receipt of ESMA's recommendation, the latter may inform the Commission, which may consequently issue a formal opinion.

B.25.38 Article 25(7) does not prejudice Article 258 TFEU, leaving open the option of initiating a Treaty infringement proceeding.

VI. Special Provisions for Spot Markets and Emissions Allowances

B.25.39 Article 25(8) entails special provisions for the cooperation with the national and third-country regulatory authorities responsible for the related spot markets.

B.25.40 With regard to emission allowances, there is also an obligation to cooperate with the auction monitor as well as with the competent authorities, registry administrators (including the Central Administrator) and other public bodies charged with the supervision of compliance under the Greenhouse Gas Emission Allowances Directive (2003/87/EC).

B.25.41 According to Article 25(8)(1), the duty of cooperation and exchange of information arises in the case of a justified suspicion that insider dealing, unlawful disclosure of information, or market manipulation contrary to the Market Abuse Regulation is taking place.

VII. Technical Standards

According to Article 25(9), ESMA shall develop draft implementing technical standards in order to ensure uniform conditions of cooperation between different national authorities and between competent authorities and ESMA. The Commission has the competence to adopt these standards. **B.25.42**

Although the deadline for the submission of the draft of implementing technical standards has ended on 3 July 2016, ESMA has, according to its website,[1] not yet submitted these technical standards to the Commission. **B.25.43**

[1] URL: https://www.esma.europa.eu/convergence/guidelines-and-technical-standards.

Article 26: Cooperation with third countries

1. The competent authorities of Member States shall, where necessary, conclude cooperation arrangements with supervisory authorities of third countries concerning the exchange of information with supervisory authorities in third countries and the enforcement of obligations arising under this Regulation in third countries. Those cooperation arrangements shall ensure at least an efficient exchange of information that allows the competent authorities to carry out their duties under this Regulation.

A competent authority shall inform ESMA and the other competent authorities where it proposes to enter into such an arrangement.

2. ESMA shall, where possible, facilitate and coordinate the development of cooperation arrangements between the competent authorities and the relevant supervisory authorities of third countries.

In order to ensure consistent harmonisation of this Article, ESMA shall develop draft regulatory technical standards containing a template document for cooperation arrangements that are to be used by competent authorities of Member States where possible.

ESMA shall submit those draft regulatory technical standards to the Commission by 3 July 2015.

Power is delegated to the Commission to adopt the regulatory technical standards referred to in the second subparagraph in accordance with Articles 10 to 14 of Regulation (EU) No 1095/2010.

ESMA shall also, where possible, facilitate and coordinate the exchange between competent authorities of information obtained from supervisory authorities of third countries that may be relevant to the taking of measures under Articles 30 and 31.

3. The competent authorities shall conclude cooperation arrangements on exchange of information with the supervisory authorities of third countries only where the information disclosed is subject to guarantees of professional secrecy which are at least equivalent to those set out in Article 27. Such exchange of information must be intended for the performance of the tasks of those competent authorities.

I. General Remarks

Overview of article

While Article 25 governs provisions concerning the cooperation between the competent authorities of the Member States, Article 26 provides for the rules on the cooperation between competent authorities of the Member States and supervisory authorities of third countries. Moreover, Article 29 regulates the transfer of personal data, which can also be part of a cooperation agreement in meaning of this Article. **B.26.01**

According to Article 26(1), cooperation with authorities of third countries has to be based on a special agreement among the competent authority (of one Member State) and the supervisory authority of the third country. ESMA has to be informed about the plans to cooperate, whereby it is obliged to facilitate and coordinate the development of cooperation agreements (Article 26(2)). **B.26.02**

Historical development

Article 26 is completely new. There have not been similar provisions in the (former) Market Abuse Directive (2003/6/EC). **B.26.03**

II. Cooperation Agreements

General remarks

The competent authorities of the Member States can conclude cooperation agreements with the supervisory authorities of third countries if there is a corresponding need for this. **B.26.04**

ESMA is obliged to support the competent authorities concluding such cooperation agreements (Article 26(2)). To this end, ESMA shall develop draft regulatory technical standards for these cooperation agreements.[1] The power to conclude such agreements is not delegated to ESMA, but remains with the Member States and their competent authorities. **B.26.05**

If the competent authority of a Member State proposes the conclusion of a cooperation agreement with a third country, this authority has to inform ESMA and the competent authorities of the other Member States. This pre-information is intended to enable ESMA to fulfil its duties according to Article 26(2), ie the coordination of the development of cooperation agreements. **B.26.06**

[1] See para B.26.13 ff below.

Equivalent guarantees of professional secrecy

B.26.07 According to Article 26(3), cooperation agreements regarding the exchange of information may only be concluded if the information disclosed is subject to guarantees of professional secrecy. If the law of the third country does not provide any guarantees of professional secrecy or only offers guarantees that are not equivalent to those set out in Article 27, cooperation within the meaning of Article 26 may not be arranged.

Content of the agreement

B.26.08 According to Article 26(1), cooperation agreements have to relate to the exchange of information between the supervisory authorities of third countries and the competent authorities of the Member States. These agreements, or arrangements, shall cover, at the minimum, all information needed by the competent authorities to fulfil their duties under the Market Abuse Regulation. Accordingly, these agreements have to include at least the exchange of information about actions infringing the provisions of the Market Abuse Regulation carried out in third countries and relating to instruments admitted to trading on regulated markets of the specific Member State.

B.26.09 The exchange of information must, according to Article 26(3), be intended for the performance of the tasks of the competent authorities. Therefore, the exchange of additional information that is unnecessary to carry out the authority's duties is prohibited. The transfer of personal data is governed by the special provisions laid down in Article 29.

B.26.10 The cooperation agreements shall also deal with the enforcement of obligations of a competent authority arising under Market Abuse Regulation.

III. Duties of ESMA

Facilitation and coordination

B.26.11 According to Article 26(2), ESMA is obliged to facilitate and coordinate the development of cooperation agreements between the competent authorities and supervisory authorities of third countries. To this end, ESMA shall develop draft regulatory technical standards[2].

B.26.12 ESMA shall also coordinate and facilitate the exchange of certain information between the competent authorities of the Member States. This duty only refers to information obtained from supervisory authorities of third countries that might

[2] ibid.

be relevant for imposing sanctions in accordance with Articles 30 and 31. In other words, ESMA only has to coordinate and facilitate the exchange of information that concerns possible infringements of the Market Abuse Regulation, possibly leading to sanctions according to Articles 30 and 31.

Technical standards

According to Article 26(2)(2), ESMA is obliged to develop draft regulatory technical standards for the cooperation of the competent authorities and the supervisory authorities of third countries. **B.26.13**

If possible, these technical standards must contain a template document for a cooperation agreement that should be used by the competent authorities. These standards and in particular the template document shall ensure uniform cooperation agreements between the competent authorities and the supervisory authorities of third countries. The Commission is empowered to adopt these standards according to Articles 10 to 14 ESMA Regulation (1095/2010/EU). **B.26.14**

Although the deadline for the submission of the draft of regulatory technical standards has ended on 3 July 2016, ESMA has—according to its website[3]—not yet submitted those technical standards to the Commission. **B.26.15**

[3] See https://www.esma.europa.eu/convergence/guidelines-and-technical-standards.

Article 27: Professional secrecy

1. Any confidential information received, exchanged or transmitted pursuant to this Regulation shall be subject to the conditions of professional secrecy laid down in paragraphs 2 and 3.
2. All the information exchanged between the competent authorities under this Regulation that concerns business or operational conditions and other economic or personal affairs shall be considered to be confidential and shall be subject to the requirements of professional secrecy, except where the competent authority states at the time of communication that such information may be disclosed or such disclosure is necessary for legal proceedings.
3. The obligation of professional secrecy applies to all persons who work or who have worked for the competent authority or for any authority or market undertaking to whom the competent authority has delegated its powers, including auditors and experts contracted by the competent authority. Information covered by professional secrecy may not be disclosed to any other person or authority except by virtue of provisions laid down by Union or national law.

I. General Remarks

Overview of article

B.27.01 Article 27 governs the question of professional secrecy in relation to confidential information received, exchanged, or transmitted pursuant to the Market Abuse Regulation. Paragraph 2 of Article 27 defines the information that is subject to professional secrecy.

B.27.02 Addressees of the obligation relating to professional secrecy are, according to Article 27(3), all persons who work for the competent authority, any other authority, or a market operator to whom powers of the competent authority have been delegated.

Historical development and comparative remarks

B.27.03 The provisions on professional secrecy were transferred from Article 13 of the (former) Market Abuse Directive (2003/6/EC), inserting them into Article 27(3).

In addition, a definition of confidential information was incorporated into this provision of the Market Abuse Regulation.

However, there are exceptions to the obligation of professional secrecy, namely when the competent authority states at the time of communication that confidential information may be disclosed or such disclosure is necessary for legal proceedings. **B.27.04**

II. Confidential Information

Subject to professional secrecy within the meaning of Article 27 is all the confidential information received, exchanged, or transmitted pursuant to the Market Abuse Regulation. Therefore, information exchanged between the competent authorities of different Member States, between a competent authority and the ESMA or between a competent authority and any other authority is subject to the rules governing professional secrecy insofar as this information is confidential. **B.27.05**

According to Article 27(2), information is deemed confidential within the meaning of this provision if it concerns business or operational conditions and other economic or personal affairs. **B.27.06**

III. Addressees

According to Article 27(3), professional secrecy applies to all persons working for the competent authority. It is also applicable to any other authority to which the competent authority has delegated its powers. Although Article 27(3) appears to refer only to Article 23(1)(c), in my view, professional secrecy is not only applicable in the case of delegation but also in cases of collaboration (Article 23(1)(b)). **B.27.07**

Only when Article 27(3) is understood in a broad sense can the confidentiality of all relevant information be guaranteed. **B.27.08**

Professional secrecy also applies to persons working for a 'market undertaking' to which the competent authority has delegated its powers. As mentioned in the commentary on Article 23, 'market undertaking' has to be understood within the meaning of market operator. **B.27.09**

According to Article 27(3), professional secrecy not only applies to persons who work for a competent authority or for a market operator but also to those who have worked for them in the past.

In addition to current and former employees of the competent authority, any other authority, or a market operator, professional secrecy also bears upon auditors and experts with whom the competent authority has a contractual relationship. **B.27.10**

B.27.11 Although the relevant provision does not mention this explicitly, professional secrecy also applies to the competent authority itself. Accordingly, the latter may not disclosure information that falls within the meaning of Article 27(2).

IV. Ban on Disclosure

B.27.12 In line with Article 27(3), the above persons may not disclose any information covered by professional secrecy to any other person or authority. Disclosure is only allowed if national or EU law provides for it.

B.27.13 To illustrate, disclosure is allowed in accordance with Article 25(5) when competent authorities of different Member States exchange information concerning possible infringements of the Market Abuse Regulation; disclosure is, for example, also allowed in accordance with Article 26(3). Information may also be disclosed if this is necessary for legal proceedings.

B.27.14 Article 27(3) only prohibits the disclosure of information itself. The wording of this provision does not ban the use of confidential information by an employee. Hence, an employee may benefit from the information falling within the meaning of Article 27(1).

B.27.15 However, in my view, the use of this confidential information should be prohibited as well.

Article 28: Data protection

With regard to the processing of personal data within the framework of this Regulation, competent authorities shall carry out their tasks for the purposes of this Regulation in accordance with the national laws, regulations or administrative provisions transposing Directive 95/46/EC. With regard to the processing of personal data by ESMA within the framework of this Regulation, ESMA shall comply with the provisions of Regulation (EC) No 45/2001.

Personal data shall be retained for a maximum period of five years.

I. General Remarks

Overview of article

The exchange of information is part of the cooperation between the competent authorities, between a competent authority and the ESMA, or between a competent authority and authorities of third countries.[1] The exchanged information may contain personal data; therefore, special provisions concerning the processing of this information are required. Articles 28 and 29 contain special rules for the overall processing and especially for the transfer of personal data. **B.28.01**

Article 28 obliges the competent authorities to carry out their duties specified in this Regulation in accordance with the national laws, regulations, and administrative provisions transposing the Data Protection Directive (95/46/EC). The ESMA is further obliged to comply with the ESMA Regulation (1095/2010/EU) when personal data are processed. **B.28.02**

According to the last sentence of Article 28, personal data may not be retained for more than five years. **B.28.03**

Historical development

Article 28 is completely new. There have been no similar provisions in the (former) Market Abuse Directive (2003/6/EC). **B.28.04**

[1] See arts 25 and 26.

II. Personal Data

B.28.05 The Market Abuse Regulation does not define the term 'personal data'. However, Article 28 refers to the Data Protection Directive (95/46/EC), thus, personal data has to be understood within the meaning of Article 2(2) Data Protection Directive (95/46/EC). According to this Article, 'any information relating to an identified or identifiable natural person ('data subject')' constitutes personal data.

B.28.06 An identifiable person is defined as a person 'who can be identified, directly or indirectly, in particular by reference to an identification number or to one or more factors specific to his physical, physiological, mental, economic, cultural or social identity'.[2]

III. Processing of Personal Data

General remarks

B.28.07 Article 28 does not stipulate new rules for the processing of personal data. It obliges the competent authorities of each Member State as well as ESMA to comply with already existing relevant rules concerning the processing of personal data: These authorities have to comply with the national laws, regulations, and administrative provisions transposing the Data Protection Directive (95/46/EC). With regard to ESMA, the provisions of the ESMA Regulation (1095/2010/EU) are also applicable.

Competent authorities

B.28.08 Any exchange or transmission of information containing personal data by the competent authorities has to comply with the national laws, regulations, and administrative provisions transposing the Data Protection Directive (95/46/EC).

B.28.09 Accordingly, each competent authority that is processing personal data in light of its duties arising from the Market Abuse Regulation has to comply with the laws of its respective Member State. If different competent authorities cooperate, each authority has to comply with its own national law. The Data Protection Directive (95/46/EC) aims to harmonize these diverse national provisions. Nevertheless, possible differences between the provisions laid down in diverse domestic laws remain. These discrepancies could lead to conflicts when applying the national provisions to cross-border cases. If the competent authorities do not act in conformity with the national provisions transposing the Data Protection Directive

[2] See also para 4(1) Austrian Data Protection Act of 2000; para 3(1) German Data Protection Act.

(95/46/EC), individuals whose personal data have been processed unlawfully may demand compensation (based on Article 23 of the Data Protection Directive (95/46/EC)).

ESMA

Any exchange or transmission of personal data by ESMA has to adhere to the relevant rules laid down in the Regulation (EC) No 45/2001.[3] This Regulation contains special provisions regarding the processing of personal data by the Community institutions and bodies, such as Article 7 on the transfer of personal data within or between Community institutions and bodies. **B.28.10**

IV. Storage of Personal Data

According to the last sentence of Article 29, personal data shall only be retained for a maximum of five years. This period appears to begin to run after specific personal data has been received and/or recorded. **B.28.11**

[3] Regulation (EC) No 45/2001 of the European Parliament and of the Council of 18 December 2000 on the protection of individuals with regard to the processing of personal data by the Community institutions and bodies and on the free movement of such data (OJ L 8 (12 January 2001) 1).

Article 29: Disclosure of personal data to third countries

1. The competent authority of a Member State may transfer personal data to a third country provided the requirements of Directive 95/46/EC are fulfilled and only on a case-by-case basis. The competent authority shall ensure that the transfer is necessary for the purpose of this Regulation and that the third country does not transfer the data to another third country unless it is given express written authorization and complies with the conditions specified by the competent authority of the Member State.

2. The competent authority of a Member State shall only disclose personal data received from a competent authority of another Member State to a supervisory authority of a third country where the competent authority of the Member State concerned has obtained express agreement from the competent authority which transmitted the data and, where applicable, the data is disclosed solely for the purposes for which that competent authority gave its agreement.

3. Where a cooperation agreement provides for the exchange of personal data, it shall comply with the national laws, regulations or administrative provisions transposing Directive 95/46/EC.

I. General Remarks

Overview of article

B.29.01 Article 29 governs rules concerning the disclosure of personal data to third countries. According to this provision, the transfer of personal data to the supervisory authorities of third countries is not generally forbidden but it must occur on a case-by-case basis. A competent authority may, according to Article 29(1), transfer personal data obtained through its own activities to third countries only if the requirements of the Data Protection Directive (95/46/EC) are fulfilled.

B.29.02 Special requirements are listed in Article 29(2) on the disclosure of personal data received from the competent authorities of another Member State: This provision lays down the circumstances in which a competent authority may disclose personal data received from the competent authority of another Member State.

Article 29(3) stipulates special provisions for cooperation arrangements within the meaning of Article 26; these arrangements also facilitate the exchange of personal data. **B.29.03**

Historical development

Article 29 is completely new. There were no similar provisions in the (former) Market Abuse Directive (2003/6/EC). **B.29.04**

Personal data

In defining the term 'personal data' for the purposes of the Market Abuse Regulation, the remarks on Article 28 may also be considered. **B.29.05**

II. Disclosure to Third Countries

General remarks

In the particular case of an information exchange with the supervisory authorities of third countries, a distinction has to be made between personal data obtained from another competent authority and self-obtained information. This distinction is necessary because Article 29 specifies stricter conditions for the transfer of personal information: In essence, a competent authority of a Member State may transfer personal data to a supervisory authority of a third country based only on a case-by-case decision (Article 29(1)). For the transfer of personal data obtained from the competent authority of another Member State, Article 29(2) stipulates additional requirements. **B.29.06**

Exchange of personal data in general

Article 29(1) is a general provision for the exchange of personal data between a competent authority of a Member State and a supervisory authority of a third country. It lays down the conditions under which a transfer of personal data to third countries is permitted. First of all, the decision has to be made for each case individually. Hence, the competent authority of a Member State may not carry out a general disclosure of personal data. Additionally, the competent authority has to ensure that the authorities of a third country who have received the data do not transfer them to another third country. A transfer to another third country is only permitted if the competent authority of a Member State has given its written authorization for this disclosure and the third country complies with the conditions specified by the competent authority of the Member State concerned. For **B.29.07** example, the competent authority of a Member State may impose the condition that the personal data transferred to the third country may be stored only for a restricted period of time. This provision aims to ensure that only the competent authority retains the power to decide whether personal data are transferred to authorities or not.

B.29.08 Furthermore, a competent authority may only transfer personal data if this disclosure is necessary for the purposes of the Market Abuse Regulation. In other words, the transfer of personal data must be essential for the integrity of the markets within the European Union. It is insufficient to argue that the transfer of personal data would contribute to the strengthening of the integrity of third countries' markets. Moreover, the transfer of personal data to third countries has to comply with the requirements of the Data Protection Directive (95/46/EC), in particular, with Articles 25 and 26 Data Protection Directive (95/46/EC).

Exchange of personal data obtained from another competent authority

B.29.09 If a competent authority has obtained personal data from a competent authority of another Member State, this information may be transferred to supervisory authorities of third countries only in compliance with additional restrictions.

B.29.10 In addition to the requirements mentioned above, the competent authority which transmitted the data must expressly agree to the disclosure of the personal data in question. It may also constrain the purposes for which this information may be disclosed to supervisory authorities of third countries.

B.29.11 Although it is not mentioned explicitly in Article 29(2), a data transfer from a supervisory authority of a third country to a supervisory authority of another third country is, in my view, permitted only if the competent authority which transmitted the data and the competent authority which obtained it have given their written authorization to this transfer of data.

III. Cooperation Agreements

B.29.12 According to Article 29(3), a cooperation agreement (within the meaning of Article 26) may also determine rules for the exchange of personal data. Notably, this part of a cooperation agreement also has to comply with the national laws, regulations, and administrative provisions transposing the Data Protection Directive (95/46/EC).

B.29.13 Although Article 29(3) generally permits cooperation agreements that deal with the transfer of personal data, the decision whether personal data may be transferred to the supervisory authority of a third country has to be made on a case-by-case basis.

5

ADMINISTRATIVE MEASURES AND SANCTIONS

Article 30: Administrative sanctions and other administrative measures

1. Without prejudice to any criminal sanctions and without prejudice to the supervisory powers of competent authorities under Article 23, Member States shall, in accordance with national law, provide for competent authorities to have the power to take appropriate administrative sanctions and other administrative measures in relation to at least the following infringements:
   (a) infringements of Articles 14 and 15, Article 16(1) and (2), Article 17(1), (2), (4) and (5), and (8), Article 18(1) to (6), Article 19(1), (2), (3), (5), (6), (7) and (11) and Article 20(1); and
   (b) failure to cooperate or to comply with an investigation, with an inspection or with a request as referred to in Article 23(2).

Member States may decide not to lay down rules for administrative sanctions as referred to in the first subparagraph where the infringements referred to in point (a) or point (b) of that subparagraph are already subject to criminal sanctions in their national law by 3 July 2016. Where they so decide, Member States shall notify, in detail, to the Commission and to ESMA, the relevant parts of their criminal law.

By 3 July 2016, Member States shall notify, in detail, the rules referred to in the first and second subparagraph to the Commission and to ESMA. They shall notify the Commission and ESMA without delay of any subsequent amendments thereto.

2. Member States shall, in accordance with national law, ensure that competent authorities have the power to impose at least the following administrative sanctions and to take at least the following administrative measures in

the event of the infringements referred to in point (a) of the first subparagraph of paragraph 1:

(a) an order requiring the person responsible for the infringement to cease the conduct and to desist from a repetition of that conduct;
(b) the disgorgement of the profits gained or losses avoided due to the infringement insofar as they can be determined;
(c) a public warning which indicates the person responsible for the infringement and the nature of the infringement;
(d) withdrawal or suspension of the authorisation of an investment firm;
(e) a temporary ban of a person discharging managerial responsibilities within an investment firm or any other natural person, who is held responsible for the infringement, from exercising management functions in investment firms;
(f) in the event of repeated infringements of Article 14 or 15, a permanent ban of any person discharging managerial responsibilities within an investment firm or any other natural person who is held responsible for the infringement, from exercising management functions in investment firms;
(g) a temporary ban of a person discharging managerial responsibilities within an investment firm or another natural person who is held responsible for the infringement, from dealing on own account;
(h) maximum administrative pecuniary sanctions of at least three times the amount of the profits gained or losses avoided because of the infringement, where those can be determined;
(i) in respect of a natural person, maximum administrative pecuniary sanctions of at least:
    (i) for infringements of Articles 14 and 15, EUR 5 000 000 or in the Member States whose currency is not the euro, the corresponding value in the national currency on 2 July 2014;
    (ii) for infringements of Articles 16 and 17, EUR 1 000 000 or in the Member States whose currency is not the euro, the corresponding value in the national currency on 2 July 2014; and
    (iii) for infringements of Articles 18, 19 and 20, EUR 500 000 or in the Member States whose currency is not the euro, the corresponding value in the national currency on 2 July 2014; and
(j) in respect of legal persons, maximum administrative pecuniary sanctions of at least:
    (i) for infringements of Articles 14 and 15, EUR 15 000 000 or 15% of the total annual turnover of the legal person according to the last available accounts approved by the management body, or in the Member States whose currency is not the euro, the corresponding value in the national currency on 2 July 2014;

(ii) for infringements of Articles 16 and 17, EUR 2 500 000 or 2% of its total annual turnover according to the last available accounts approved by the management body, or in the Member States whose currency is not the euro, the corresponding value in the national currency on 2 July 2014; and

(iii) for infringements of Articles 18, 19 and 20, EUR 1 000 000 or in the Member States whose currency is not the euro, the corresponding value in the national currency on 2 July 2014.

References to the competent authority in this paragraph are without prejudice to the ability of the competent authority to exercise its functions in any ways referred to in Article 23(1).

For the purposes of points (j)(i) and (ii) of the first subparagraph, where the legal person is a parent undertaking or a subsidiary undertaking which is required to prepare consolidated financial accounts pursuant to Directive 2013/34/EU, the relevant total annual turnover shall be the total annual turnover or the corresponding type of income in accordance with the relevant accounting directives – Council Directive 86/635/EEC for banks and Council Directive 91/674/EEC for insurance companies – according to the last available consolidated accounts approved by the management body of the ultimate parent undertaking.

3. Member States may provide that competent authorities have powers in addition to those referred to in paragraph 2 and may provide for higher levels of sanctions than those established in that paragraph.

I. General Remarks

Overview of Article 30

While the Market Abuse Regulation, like the (former) Market Abuse Directive (2003/6/EC), leaves enforcement up to national authorities, Article 30 aims at a greater harmonization of the sanctioning regimes. Article 30(1) starts off by repeating the (former) Market Abuse Directive (2003/6/EC) requirement that Member States ensure that competent authorities have the power to take **B.30.01** 'appropriate administrative sanctions and other administrative measures'. It goes on to specify for which infringements of the Market Abuse Regulation such sanctions must be provided, including not only breaches of the main substantive prescriptions of the Market Abuse Regulation but also the failure to cooperate or to comply with an investigation, with an inspection or with a request as referred to in Article 23(2).[1] Non-compliance with information and recording obligations in connection with market soundings, however, does not require a specific sanction, to the extent this non-compliance would not constitute an infringement of Articles 14–15. Where criminal sanctions apply under national law, Member States may refrain from providing for administrative sanctions.

B.30.02 Article 30(2) details the sanctions and measures that must at least be available to the national competent authorities for all breaches referred to above (not including the failure to cooperate or to comply with an investigation). Most striking are the minimum prescriptions for the upper level of administrative pecuniary sanctions, which will lead to profound increases in the potential sanctions in almost all Member States. This development evokes comparisons with the high fines that have been applied for some time in competition law, another area of law of high public interest that is similarly plagued with information asymmetries and difficulties in private enforcement, and that therefore displays a heavy reliance on administrative sanctions.[2] However, as will be shown further,[3] the sanctions for market abuse may even exceed those in the competition law area.

B.30.03 Although being part of a Regulation, the provisions of Article 30 are minimum requirements that must be transposed into national law. This follows from the wording 'at least' in Article 30(2) and from the clarification in Article 30(3) that Member States may provide for additional powers and more severe sanctions than those established in Article 30. Accordingly, Article 30(1) requires Member States to notify the Commission and ESMA of the administrative (or criminal) measures and sanctions available in their national laws.

Historical development

B.30.04 With Article 30, the Market Abuse Regulation introduces a noticeably more prescriptive sanctioning regime than its predecessors. While the Insider Dealing

[1] Theoretically, if the potential sanctions are considered criminal in nature from a human rights perspective, sanctioning non-compliance with requests for information could be considered contrary to the rule against self-incrimination. In practice, the competent authorities have other means available to obtain information, see the chapter on public enforcement. See also, with regard to competition law: Richard Whish and David Bailey, *Competition Law* (8th edn, Oxford University Press 2015) 284–5.

[2] Jörn Axel Kämmerer, 'Bemessung von Geldbußen im Wettbewerbs- und Kapitalmarktrecht: Eine komparative Betrachtung' in *Festschrift für Klaus J. Hopt zum 70. Geburtstag*, vol II (De Gruyter 2010) 2050–1; Philipp Maume, 'Staatliche Rechtsdurchsetzung im deutschen Kapitalmarktrecht: eine kritische Bestandsaufnahme' [2016] ZHR 389.

[3] See para B.30.12.

Directive (1989/592/EEC) merely instructed the Member States to determine penalties that are 'sufficient to promote compliance' with the directive,[4] the (former) Market Abuse Directive (2003/6/EC) went only slightly further, requiring appropriate administrative measures that are 'effective, proportionate and dissuasive', allowing the imposition of criminal sanctions, and specifically requiring sanctions only for failure to cooperate in investigations.[5] In its recitals, the (former) Market Abuse Directive (2003/6/EC) alerted the Member States to the need to ensure some uniformity between Member States with regard to administrative measures and sanctions.[6] However, without more concrete provisions and in the absence of a clarification as to what is meant by administrative measures and administrative sanctions,[7] the directive did little to curb Member States' discretion in this regard. As a result, in 2007, CESR found large disparities between Member States with regard to the range of sanctions available, the size of pecuniary sanctions, and the infringements for which they were applied.[8] That these differences were also noticeable in actual sanctioning practices was later confirmed by ESMA.[9]

In 2009, the de Larosière Group urged the EU to strengthen and harmonize sanctions for all financial crimes generally, but with specific reference to insider trading.[10] It also noted the striking differences between the level of fines that can be levied in the competition arena and those of financial fraud fines.[11] The Commission answered this call with a 2010 communication entitled 'Reinforcing sanctioning regimes in the financial services sector', in which it envisaged promoting convergence and reinforcement of national sanctioning regimes in the financial services sector. In particular, the Commission considered introducing a core set of administrative sanctions, rendering the level of any fines provided for by national law sufficiently high to allow national authorities to impose effective, proportionate, and dissuasive fines, and providing for sanctions for both the individuals responsible for a violation and the financial institution in whose benefit they were acting.[12] **B.30.05**

---

[4] Article 13 Insider Dealing Directive (1989/592/EEC).

[5] Article 14(1) and 14(3) (former) Market Abuse Directive (2003/6/EC).

[6] ibid recital (39).

[7] See Commission, 'Staff Working Paper: Impact Assessment' SEC(2011) 1217 final 122.

[8] CESR, An evaluation of equivalence of supervisory powers in the EU under the Market Abuse Directive and the Prospectus Directive (June 2007) 07-334, 3–4. See also ESME, 'Market abuse EU legal framework and its implementation by Member States: a first evaluation' (6 July 2007) 19 http://ec.europa.eu/finance/securities/docs/esme/mad_070706_en.pdf. See also CESR, 'Report on administrative measures and sanctions as well as criminal sanctions available in Member States under the Market Abuse Directive' (17 October 2007) (CESR/07-693) http://www.esma.europa.eu/sites/default/files/library/2015/11/07_693_u_2_.pdf.

[9] ESMA, 'Report Actual Use of Sanctioning Powers under MAD' (26 April 2012) ESMA/2012/270, 44–55.

[10] High-Level Group on Financial Supervision in the EU, 'Report' (25 February 2009) 23 http://ec.europa.eu/internal_market/finances/docs/de_larosiere_report_en.pdf.

[11] ibid 23.

[12] Communication from the Commission to the European Parliament, the Council, the European Economic and Social Committee and the Committee of the Regions, Reinforcing

B.30.06 The Commission's Market Abuse Regulation proposal of 20 October 2011[13] pursued these objectives with the goals of contributing to deterrence, creating a level playing field, and reducing regulatory arbitrage.[14] It contained the main elements of the final text of Article 30, albeit with some administrative measures still missing (especially disgorgement of profits, and a permanent ban from management functions) and with pecuniary sanctions, that were not as severe as in the final text, although they already represented a significant increase compared with the (former) Market Abuse Directive (2003/6/EC).[15] During the parliamentary debates, disagreement arose among Member States in terms of the appropriate level of the sanctions, which resulted in a solution that still left some flexibility to the Member States,[16] namely minimum prescriptions for maximum sanctions.[17] Nevertheless, the first reading resulted in drastically harsher sanctions than in the original proposal, with penalties to up to ten times the profits gained or losses avoided, unlimited amounts for natural persons, and up to 20 per cent of the annual (consolidated) turnover for legal persons.[18] As a compromise between the Parliament and the Council, administrative sanctions were again lowered and were differentiated depending on the type of infringement; additionally, Member States retained the option of not laying down administrative sanctions where breaches were already subject to criminal sanctions.[19]

Comparative remarks

B.30.07 With its harsher administrative sanctions, the European market abuse regime approaches the US insider trading regime, from which the Commission has explicitly drawn inspiration.[20] This is clear as regards the newly introduced possibility to order penalties up to three times the amount of profits that were realized,

sanctioning regimes in the financial services sector (8 December 2010) COM(2010) 716 final. See also Commission, 'Public Consultation on a Revision of the Market Abuse Directive' (MAD) (25 June 2010) 9–10 http://ec.europa.eu/finance/consultations/2010/mad/docs/consultation_paper_en.pdf.

[13] Proposal for a Regulation on insider dealing and market manipulation (market abuse) 2011/0295 (COD), arts 24–26.

[14] Commission, 'Impact Assessment' (n 7) 51.

[15] Article 26(1)(k)–(m) of the Commission Proposal (n 13) provided for administrative pecuniary sanctions of up to twice the amount of the profits gained or losses avoided because of the breach where those can be determined; and of up to €5,000,000 for natural persons and of up to 10 per cent of the total (if applicable, consolidated) annual turnover for legal persons.

[16] Danish Presidency Progress Report (21 June 2012), 2011/0295 (COD) 4.

[17] See para B.30.10.

[18] Market Abuse Regulation Plenary Committee Report (22 October 2012), A7-0347/2012, 53–7. See Amendment 373, Draft Report Arlene McCarthy, Amendments 332–401 (11 May 2012) 2011/0295(COD) 29 (arguing that twice the profits is not dissuasive enough, given the difficulty in establishing exactly what they are).

[19] Council, 'Validation of the provisional agreement with the European Parliament' (26 June 2013) 2011/0295(COD) http://register.consilium.europa.eu/doc/srv?l=EN&f=ST%2011384%20 2013%20INIT.

[20] See Commission, 'Impact Assessment' (n 7) Annex 9.

or losses that were avoided, through insider trading activities. The American SEC has had the power to obtain such penalties, in addition to disgorgement or any criminal fine, since the Insider Trading Sanctions Act of 1984.[21] Its power to impose other civil penalties is rather limited,[22] with criminal penalties playing a much larger role (up to US$5 million for an individual and US$25 million for a corporate entity).[23] Finally, many of the non-monetary sanctions that the Market Abuse Regulation prescribes, such as cease-and-desist orders, disgorgement and bans from exercising managerial functions, are also available to the SEC.[24]

Economic analysis

The rationale behind the hefty fines in the Market Abuse Regulation is a standard law and economics reasoning: there will be insufficient deterrence when the potential gains from an infringement exceed the expected sanctions. The expected sanction is not simply the sanction that would be imposed in the event the wrongful behaviour is detected and punished; rather, it is lower, as it is multiplied by the probability that the authorities will in fact detect and punish it (which will always be less than one). The sanction therefore needs to be higher than the potential gain from an infringement, in order to offset the possibility of no punishment, and the more so as the probability of detection and punishment decreases.[25] Moreover, increasing the sanctions allows public authorities to save on enforcement efforts (thus lowering the probability of punishment), while avoiding dilution of deterrence.[26] An obvious side-effect of higher sanctions is that the addressees of the new rules will be willing to spend more time and money on compliance and litigation, thus eventually benefiting their lawyers. **B.30.08**

The introduction of new types of non-monetary sanctions also aims to improve deterrence. Having a wide range of sanctions available renders it possible for the authorities to fine-tune their response to individual infringements, thus improving the effectiveness, proportionality, and dissuasiveness of the sanction.[27] Moreover, non-monetary sanctions are recommended when monetary sanctions stop short of **B.30.09**

---

[21] Exchange Act s 21A.

[22] ibid s 21B.

[23] ibid s 32(a). In addition, insider traders may also face other charges, such as aiding and abetting.

[24] Alan R Palmiter, *Securities Regulation* (6th edn, Kluwer 2014) 562–3.

[25] See Communication from the Commission to the European Parliament, the council, the European Economic and Social Committee and the Committee of the Regions, Reinforcing sanctioning regimes in the financial services sector (8 December 2010) COM(2010) 716 final 7; Commission, 'Impact Assessment' (n 7) 123; Steven Shavell, *Foundations of Economic Analysis of Law* (Harvard University Press 2004) 483. See, however, H Neyat Seyhun, 'The Effectiveness of the Insider-Trading Sanctions' (1992) 35 Journal of Law and Economics 149.

[26] Shavell, *Foundations of Economic Analysis of Law* (n 25) 484.

[27] Communication from the Commission to the European Parliament, the Council, the European Economic and Social Committee and the Committee of the Regions, Reinforcing sanctioning regimes in the financial services sector (8 December 2010) COM(2010) 716 final 7.

deterring potential offenders, eg where their personal wealth is less than possible monetary sanctions.[28]

II. Pecuniary Sanctions

B.30.10 The pecuniary sanctions detailed in items (h) through (j) of Article 30(2) are minimum amounts for maximum sanctions under national law. Member States may thus prescribe higher maximum sanctions[29] and also retain complete freedom in setting minimum sanctions. The 2012 ESMA study had actually revealed substantial differences across Member States with regard to minimum sanctions, with several having no minimum at all.[30] The responses to the public consultation generally supported imposing minimum levels as well, but they also pointed to the need for flexibility in determining sanctions,[31] an idea which eventually prevailed.[32] Nevertheless, it is often assumed that the new prescriptions will in practice trigger an increase in the sanctions that are effectively imposed.[33] Such a development has already taken place in the UK[34] and would also fit in with the general trend towards stricter enforcement.[35]

B.30.11 The absence of a definition of administrative sanctions[36] may give rise to practical questions, for instance, whether the term also covers settlements. An affirmative answer seems to follow from the recitals in the Market Abuse Regulation, where it is considered that 'fines significantly lower than the maximum level may be applied to minor infringements or in case of settlement'.[37] Under the national laws of a majority of the Member States where settlement is available to deal with market abuse, however, settlements are not categorized as sanctioning decisions.[38]

B.30.12 Items (i) and (j) of Article 30(2) set out the minimum maximum fines and thereby differentiate between natural persons and legal persons.[39] The former risk having to pay up to €5 million for insider dealing, unlawful disclosure of

[28] See Shavell, *Foundations of Economic Analysis of Law* (n 25) 509–10.
[29] Article 30(3), recital (71) Market Abuse Regulation.
[30] ESMA, 'Actual Use of Sanctioning Powers' (n 9) 11–12 and 179–80.
[31] Commission, 'Impact Assessment' (n 7) 84.
[32] See also Danish Presidency Progress Report (n 16) 4.
[33] Seibt, '20 Thesen zur Binnenverantwortung im Unternehmen im Lichte des reformierten Kapitalmarktsanktionsrechts' [2015] Neue Zeitschrift für Gesellschaftsrecht 1098.
[34] Iain MacNeil, 'Enforcement and Sanctioning' in Niamh Moloney, Eilís Ferran, and Jennifer Payne (eds), *The Oxford Handbook of Financial Regulation* (Oxford University Press 2015) 298.
[35] See the chapter on public enforcement.
[36] See Commission, 'Impact Assessment' (n 7) 122.
[37] Recital (71) Market Abuse Regulation.
[38] ESMA, 'Actual Use of Sanctioning Powers' (n 9) 11.
[39] Even before enactment of the Market Abuse Regulation, in all Member States that provided for administrative sanctions for market abuse, administrative sanctions could be imposed on both natural and legal persons (ESMA, 'Actual Use of Sanctioning Powers' (n 9) 9–10).

inside information or market manipulation; up to €1 million for not complying with the obligations aimed at prevention and detection of market abuse and the rules regarding public disclosure of inside information; and up to €500,000 for breaching obligations concerning insider lists, reporting of managers' transactions or the dissemination of investment recommendations, statistics, and forecasts.[40] Legal entities can face fines that may even jeopardize their continued existence, with the three named categories of infringements carrying fines of, respectively, €15 million or 15 per cent of their total annual turnover, €2.5 million or 2 per cent of their total annual turnover and €1 million. Importantly, but in line with the maximum sanctions provided for in other European financial regulation instruments and in competition law,[41] the turnover is to be calculated on a consolidated basis for parent companies or subsidiaries that are required to prepare consolidated financial accounts. The resulting high maximum fines leave more room to take into consideration the financial strength of the perpetrator, as provided for in Article 32. However, with a maximum fine of 15 per cent of the (consolidated) turnover the Market Abuse Regulation largely exceeds the already severe maximum fines in competition law[42] and other areas of financial regulation,[43] which do not exceed 10 per cent of the group turnover. Not surprisingly, some authors have advanced an interpretation of Article 30(2)(j) that would limit the amounts, namely that, in setting the maximum fines, the national legislator can choose between the fixed amount and the turnover-related amount. In their view, the word 'or' in items (j)(i) and (j)(ii) does not imply that the higher of both is to be prescribed as a maximum fine.[44] Their main argument is that similar sanctioning provisions in the Transparency Directive (2013/50/EU) explicitly specify that the higher of both must be prescribed,[45] whereas the Market Abuse Regulation does not contain such a clarification.[46] However, an argument

[40] Or the corresponding values in the national currency on 2 July 2014.

[41] See the next two footnotes.

[42] Article 23(2) Regulation 1/2003 on the implementation of the rules on competition laid down in Articles 81 and 82 of the Treaty [2003] OJ L1/1.

[43] Article 28b(1)(a) Transparency Directive (2013/50/EU) (maximum 5%); art 67(2)(e) Capital Requirements Directive (CRD IV) (2013/36/EU) (maximum 10%); art 24(2)(e)(i) PRIIPs-Regulation (2014/1286/EU) (maximum 3%); art 99(6)(e) UCITS V (2014/91/EU) (maximum 10%); art 70(6)(f) Markets in Financial Instruments Directive II (2014/65/EU) (maximum 10%); art 22(4)(g) Securities Financing Transaction Regulation (2015/2365/EU) (maximum 10%); art 33(2)(e) Insurance Distribution Directive (2016/97/EU) (maximum 5%); art 38(2)(d) Prospectus Regulation (2017/1129/EU) (maximum 3%); art 18(1) SSM Regulation (1024/2013/EU) (maximum 10%).

[44] Lars Teigelack and Christian Dolff, 'Kapitalmarktrechtliche Sanktionen nach dem Regierungsentwurf eines Ersten Finanzmarktnovellierungsgesetzes—1. FimanoG' [2016] Betriebs-Berater 390; Deutsches Aktieninstitut, 'Finanzmarktnovellierungsgesetz sollte nicht über EU-Recht hinausgehen' (18 November 2015) 14–15 www.dai.de/files/dai_usercontent/dokumente/positionspapiere/2015-11-18%20DAI-Stellungnahme%20FimanoG.pdf.

[45] Article 28b(1)(c) Transparency Directive (2013/50/EU).

[46] Lars Teigelack and Christian Dolff, 'Kapitalmarktrechtichle Sanktionen nach dem Regierungsentwurf eines Ersten Finanzmarktnovellierungsgesetzes—1. FimanoG' [2016] BB 390.

per analogiam would be at least as convincing as their argument *a contrario*. In light of the minimum harmonization envisaged by Article 30, it is in any case clear that Member States are at least allowed to prescribe that the higher of both amounts will be the maximum penalty.[47]

B.30.13 In some cases, the fine may exceed the maximum amounts described above. Indeed, item (h) of Article 30(2) requires 'maximum administrative pecuniary sanctions of at least three times the amount of the profits gained or losses avoided because of the infringement, where those can be determined'. This is a fine, to be distinguished from a pure disgorgement of profits as foreseen by Article 30(2)(b).[48] The words 'at least' in both item (h) and items (i) or (j) respectively indicate that maximum fines can be defined as the higher of the amounts resulting from both applicable items. Again, this sanction is high in comparison to similar sanctions in other areas of financial regulation, which are almost all limited to twice the profits gained or losses avoided.[49]

III. Other Administrative Sanctions and Measures

B.30.14 Under the (former) Market Abuse Directive (2003/6/EC), non-pecuniary sanctions were not frequently imposed,[50] and many competent authorities even lacked important sanctioning powers, such as withdrawal of licenses and disqualification or dismissal of managers.[51] Article 30(2) therefore requires that competent authorities have a range of measures and non-pecuniary sanctions available, in addition to the pecuniary sanctions just described. These include a cease and desist order; the disgorgement of profits gained or losses avoided; a public warning; withdrawal or suspension of the authorization of an investment firm; a temporary or permanent ban from exercising management functions in investment firms; and a temporary ban from dealing on own account. This provision is one

[47] Dörte Poelzig, 'Durchsetzung und Sanktionierung des neuen Marktmissbrauchsrechts' [2016] NZG 498.

[48] See para B.30.16 below.

[49] Capping the fine at two times the amount of the profits: art 28b(1)(c) Transparency Directive; art 67(2)(g) CRD IV; art 24(2)(e) PRIIPs Regulation (2014/1286/EU); art 99(6)(g) UCITS V (2014/91/EU); art 70(6)(h) Markets in Financial Instruments Directive II (2014/65/EU); art 18(1) SSM Regulation (1024/2013/EU); art 33(2)(e) and (f) Insurance Distribution Directive (2016/97/EU); art 38(2)(c) Prospectus Regulation (2017/1129/EU). See however art 22(4)(e) Securities Financing Transaction Regulation (2015/2365/EU) (also capping the fine at three times the amount of the profits).

[50] ESMA, 'Actual Use of Sanctioning Powers' (n 9) 63–4.

[51] Communication from the Commission to the European Parliament, the Council, the European Economic and Social Committee and the Committee of the Regions, Reinforcing sanctioning regimes in the financial services sector (8 December 2010) COM(2010) 716 final 7. See also CESR, 'Report on administrative measures and sanctions as well as criminal sanctions available in Member States under the Market Abuse Directive' (17 October 2007) CESR/07-693 http://www.esma.europa.eu/sites/default/files/library/2015/11/07_693_u_2_.pdf.

of minimum harmonization (as follows from the words 'at least'), and Member States are free to grant additional powers to their competent authorities.[52]

The cease and desist order has become a common sanction in European financial regulation, and can also be found in the Transparency Directive (2013/50/EU), the Capital Requirements Directive (CRD IV) (2013/36/EU), UCITS V (2014/91/EU), the Markets in Financial Instruments Directive II (2014/65/EU), the Securities Financing Transaction Regulation (2015/2365/EU), and the Insurance Distribution Directive (2016/97/EU).[53] The words 'in the event of the infringements [listed above in Article 30]' at the beginning of paragraph 2 indicate that competent authorities do not need to be able to intervene at a time that a person is still about to engage in those infringements, as the American SEC can do.[54] **B.30.15**

In contrast to the other sanctions of Article 30(2), disgorgement is a relatively new sanction in European financial regulation. Article 30(2)(b) does not identify the disgorgement of profits gained or losses avoided as a sanction (like the Market Abuse Regulation does for fines). Disgorgement may indeed also serve another purpose, namely preventing unjust enrichment of the offender in the absence of identifiable victims who could resort to private enforcement.[55] Disgorgement differs from private enforcement, though, in that it is imposed by the competent authority in the public interest and not initiated by the victim on his own behalf and in that the amount to be paid corresponds with the profits made or the losses avoided by the offender rather than with the losses made or profits foregone by the victim.[56] The Market Abuse Regulation does not specify whether disgorgement should be imposed in addition to possible compensation payments to victims following private suits, but it seems to suggest that it does supplement the above described pecuniary sanctions.[57] In any case, disgorgement alone would not be a sufficient sanction. Otherwise, a potential offender would in any event risk no more than the potential gains, while having a chance at remaining undetected or being un- or under-punished (eg because the gain was not assessed accurately) and thus at being able to keep the gains, at least partially.[58] **B.30.16**

---

52 Article 30(3) Market Abuse Regulation.

53 Article 28b(1)(b) Transparency Directive (2013/50/EU); art 67(2)(b) CRD IV; art 99(6)(b) UCITS V (2014/91/EU); art 70(6)(b) Markets in Financial Instruments Directive II (2014/65/EU); art 22(4)(a) Securities Financing Transaction Regulation (2015/2365/EU); art 33(2)(b) Insurance Distribution Directive (2016/97/EU). See also art 38(2)(b) Prospectus Regulation (2017/1129/EU), and art 24(2) (a), (b), and (d) PRIIPs Regulation (2014/1286/EU).

54 Exchange Act s 21C.

55 Vassilios D Tountopoulos, 'Market Abuse and Private Enforcement' (2014) 11 European Company and Financial Law Review 318.

56 ibid 319.

57 In the UK, disgorgement is part of the pecuniary sanction, whereas in other jurisdictions it is a distinct measure. See Lev Bromberg, George Gilligan, and Ian Ramsay, 'The Extent and Intensity of Insider Trading Enforcement: An International Comparison' (2016) Journal of Corporate Law Studies 12.

58 See Shavell, *Foundations of Economic Analysis of Law* (n 25) 477.

B.30.17 The possibility of a public warning (or public statement), as provided for by Article 30(2)(c), has become part of the standard sanctioning package in European financial regulation.[59] It is to be distinguished from the publication of sanctions as provided for by Article 34. The latter is in principle mandatory, whereas a warning is merely an option for the competent authority. As follows from the wording of Article 30(2)(c), a public warning also does not necessarily include mention of the imposed sanction, as it is normally issued at an earlier stage in the enforcement proceedings. This difference in timing provides a compelling argument a fortiori for competent authorities to take into account the grounds for exceptions and mitigation listed in Article 34 when considering issuing a public warning. For further discussion on possible exceptions and grounds for mitigation; the qualification of a publication as a sanction or as a preventive measure; its actual sanctioning effect in terms of reputational damage; and concerns regarding fair trials and data protection, see the commentary to Article 34.

B.30.18 Finally, items (d)–(g) of Article 30(2) list a series of disqualification sanctions. These can serve two purposes. First, they punish the offender by barring him (or it) from exercising his profession or pursuing a source of income and by inflicting reputational damage, which can be particularly severe in financial circles.[60] Secondly, they aim to prevent recidivism. In order to be effective, the law must on the one hand render it impossible for the offender to continue his activities de facto (eg as a paid consultant or employee, or by joining a partnership) without carrying the official title of the job from which he has been disqualified;[61] on the other hand it must not overly restrict the offender's professional possibilities.

IV. Relationship with Criminal Sanctions

Criminal sanctions as an alternative for administrative sanctions

B.30.19 Article 30(1), second subparagraph stipulates that Member States are allowed not to introduce administrative sanctions for the infringements referred to in point (a) or point (b) of that subparagraph if these were already subject to criminal sanctions in their national law by 3 July 2016. This concession was made to accommodate different legal traditions with regard to the division between administrative sanctions and criminal sanctions, which has been a point of

[59] It is also provided for by art 28b(1)(a) Transparency Directive; art 67(2)a CRD IV; art 24(2)(c) PRIIPs Regulation (2014/1286/EU); art 99(6)(a) UCITS V (2014/91/EU); art 70(6)(a) Markets in Financial Instruments Directive II (2014/65/EU); art 33(2)(a) Securities Financing Transaction Regulation (2015/2365/EU); art 33(2)(a) Insurance Distribution Directive (2016/97/EU); art 38(2)(a) Prospectus Regulation (2017/1129/EU).

[60] See commentary to art 34.

[61] Jacob Öberg, 'Is It "Essential" to Imprison Insider Dealers to Enforce Insider Dealing Laws?' (2014) 14 Journal of Corporate Law Studies 133.

discussion during the preparation of the Market Abuse Regulation.[62] Denmark and Sweden, for instance, had a well-functioning system based solely on criminal sanctions.[63] Member States that did not have criminal sanctions in place by 3 July 2016 are, however, precluded from still introducing them *instead of* administrative sanctions.[64] The Market Abuse Regulation thus displays a preference for administrative sanctions over criminal sanctions, even with regard to very harsh punishments (except for the most serious infringements, referred to in the Market Abuse Directive on Criminal Sanctions (2014/57/EU)[65]). In its recitals, the Market Abuse Regulation warns that the choice of criminal instead of administrative sanctions 'should not reduce or otherwise affect the ability of competent authorities to cooperate and access and exchange information in a timely manner with competent authorities in other Member States for the purposes of this Regulation, including after any referral of the relevant infringements to the competent judicial authorities for criminal prosecution'.[66]

The Market Abuse Regulation's preference for administrative sanctions for all but the most serious offences raises the question of the appropriate scope of administrative versus criminal sanctions. Criminal courts are often congested, slower, and less specialized than administrative authorities.[67] For those reasons, criminal proceedings have traditionally been reserved for the most severe breaches of the law. Nevertheless, both in the area of market abuse and in other fields of law, regulators are increasingly opting to also address severe infringements with administrative sanctions.[68] However, administrative sanctions are accompanied by fewer protections for the offender, even if they are subject to Article 6 of the European Convention on Human Rights (ECHR) because of their punitive character.[69] **B.30.20**

Criminal sanctions in addition to administrative sanctions

Article 30(1) begins with the qualification 'without prejudice to any criminal sanctions'. Member states can thus lay down both administrative and criminal sanctions for the same offence, as one of its recitals states, 'if their national law so permits'.[70] For some of the offences for which administrative sanctions are **B.30.21**

[62] Danish Presidency Progress Report (n 16) 4. See also ESMA, 'Actual Use of Sanctioning Powers' (n 9) 9.

[63] ESMA, 'Actual Use of Sanctioning Powers' (n 9) 38.

[64] Regarding additional sanctions see paras B.30.21–B.30.24 below.

[65] See para B.30.21 below.

[66] Recital (72) Market Abuse Regulation. With regard to such cooperation see the chapter on public enforcement.

[67] A G Mein, 'Van licht naar zwaar, de evolutie van de bestuurlijke boete in het financieel toezicht' [2015] Tijdschrift voor Sanctierecht en Onderneming 257–8.

[68] ibid 260.

[69] G A Biezeveld, 'Bestraffend bestuur hoort thuis in het strafrecht' [2015] Tijdschrift voor Toezicht 67.

[70] Recital (72) Market Abuse Regulation.

prescribed, namely 'at least' for those that are serious and committed intentionally, Market Abuse Directive on Criminal Sanctions (2014/57/EU) even obliges Member States to institute criminal sanctions in addition to the administrative sanctions.[71] The words 'at least' confirm that, for less serious or unintentional offences, Member States are free to lay down criminal sanctions in addition to the administrative sanctions mandated by Article 30.

B.30.22 The overlap of administrative and criminal sanctions for the same offences begs the question of how they relate to each other. In its recitals, the Market Abuse Directive on Criminal Sanctions (2014/57/EU) merely alerts Member States that the application of, on the one hand, national law transposing the Market Abuse Directive on Criminal Sanctions (2014/57/EU) and, on the other hand, of administrative sanctions in accordance with the Market Abuse Regulation must not lead to a breach of the principle of *non bis in idem*,[72] ie the right not to be persecuted or sanctioned twice for the same facts. This principle is set out in Article 4 of Protocol 7 to the ECHR, Article 50 of the Charter of Fundamental Rights of the European Union (CFR), and Article 54 of the Convention implementing the Schengen Agreement.[73] Under the Engel criteria of the European Court of Human Rights (ECtHR), which are also applied by the ECJ,[74] and in particular under the criterion of the severity of the actual and potential penalty,[75] the administrative sanctions for market abuse will usually qualify as criminal sanctions in the sense of the ECHR. In the recent *Grande Stevens* case, the ECtHR confirmed this for administrative fines under the old market abuse regime.[76] The Court also reaffirmed its earlier holding[77] that double jeopardy also exists when the violations punished by different rules are described differently, if the facts on which the sanctions are based are substantially the same, as is the case for the violations in the Market Abuse Directive on Criminal Sanctions (2014/57/EU) and the Market Abuse Regulation.[78]

B.30.23 The principle of *non bis in idem* does not enjoin law-makers from specifying both administrative and criminal sanctions for the same behaviour, as long as someone who has been convicted with one type of sanction will not also be prosecuted or sanctioned with the other type of sanction.[79] How this is to be

---

[71] Articles 3–6 Market Abuse Directive on Criminal Sanctions (2014/57/EU).

[72] Recital (23) Market Abuse Directive on Criminal Sanctions (2014/57/EU) (see also recital (27) Market Abuse Directive on Criminal Sanctions (2014/57/EU)).

[73] Convention of 19 June 1990 implementing the Schengen Agreement [2000] OJ L239/19.

[74] *Aklagaren v Akerberg Fransson* [2013] ECLI:EU:C:2013:105 para 35.

[75] ECtHR, *Engel and Others v Netherlands* Application nos 5100/71, 5101/71, 5102/71, 5354/72, and 5370/72 (8 June 1976) paras 82–3.

[76] ECtHR, *Grande Stevens and Others v Italy*, Application nos 18640/10, 18647/10, 18668/10, and 18698/10 (4 March 2014).

[77] ECtHR, *Zolotukhin v Russia* Application no 14939/03 (10 February 2009).

[78] ibid.

[79] Françoise Lefèvre and Anne-Louise Servais, 'La procédure devant la Commission des sanctions de la FSMA: quelques considérations au regard de l'article 6 de la Convention européenne

achieved is a puzzle that both the Market Abuse Regulation and the Market Abuse Directive on Criminal Sanctions (2014/57/EU) leave up to the Member States to solve. The underlying reason for this indecisiveness is that, during the negotiations on the Market Abuse Regulation and the Market Abuse Directive on Criminal Sanctions (2014/57/EU), most Member States were keen on their financial authorities retaining investigatory power for as long as possible, as they are less hindered by restrictions and safeguards for the suspect's rights than judicial prosecuting authorities and are thus able to undertake a more thorough investigation.[80] Article 30(1) opened up a possibility for a solution, stipulating that Member States may decide not to lay down rules for administrative sanctions where the infringements were already subject to criminal sanctions in their national law on 3 July 2016. Member states thus had two years after the entry into force of the Market Abuse Directive on Criminal Sanctions (2014/57/EU) to apply its provisions and to make exceptions in their administrative sanctioning regime for those cases where criminal sanctions applied. In Member States that did not make use of this possibility, criminal and administrative authorities will need to find flexible solutions on a case by case basis, although this solution could be hindered by constitutional obligations regarding criminal prosecution.[81]

An even thornier issue is how to avoid double prosecution by different authorities from different Member States.[82] This problem of coordination is discussed in the chapter on public enforcement. **B.30.24**

des droits de l'Homme' in AEDBF/EVBFR (ed), *Market Abuse/Les abus de marché* (Intersentia 2016) 156. See, however, Marco Ventoruzzo, 'When Market Abuse Rules Violate Human Rights: Grande Stevens v Italy and the Different Approaches to Double Jeopardy in Europe and the US' (2015) 16 European Business Organization Law Review 162.

[80] Robert Kert, 'The Relationship Between Administrative and Criminal Sanctions in the New Market Abuse Provisions' in Francesca Galli and Anne Weyembergh (eds), *Do Labels Still Matter?* (Editions ULB 2014) 105.

[81] Matteo Gargantini, 'Public Enforcement of Market Abuse Bans: The ECtHR *Grande Stevens* Decision' (2015) 1 Journal of Financial Regulation 149, 157.

[82] See especially art 50 CFR; art 54 Convention of 19 June 1990 implementing the Schengen Agreement [2000] OJ L 239/19.

Article 31: Exercise of supervisory powers and imposition of sanctions

1. Member States shall ensure that when determining the type and level of administrative sanctions, competent authorities take into account all relevant circumstances, including, where appropriate:
   (a) the gravity and duration of the infringement;
   (b) the degree of responsibility of the person responsible for the infringement;
   (c) the financial strength of the person responsible for the infringement, as indicated, for example, by the total turnover of a legal person or the annual income of a natural person;
   (d) the importance of the profits gained or losses avoided by the person responsible for the infringement, insofar as they can be determined;
   (e) the level of cooperation of the person responsible for the infringement with the competent authority, without prejudice to the need to ensure disgorgement of profits gained or losses avoided by that person;
   (f) previous infringements by the person responsible for the infringement; and
   (g) measures taken by the person responsible for the infringement to prevent its repetition.

2. In the exercise of their powers to impose administrative sanctions and other administrative measures under Article 30, competent authorities shall cooperate closely to ensure that the exercise of their supervisory and investigative powers, and the administrative sanctions that they impose, and the other administrative measures that they take, are effective and appropriate under this Regulation. They shall coordinate their actions in accordance with Article 25 in order to avoid duplication and overlaps when exercising their supervisory and investigative powers and when imposing administrative sanctions in respect of cross-border cases.

I. General Remarks

Overview of Article 31

B.31.01 The long list of possible sanctions and the high maximum fines of Article 30 would, without further measures, risk increasing legal uncertainty. Article 31(1) therefore introduces a minimum set of criteria that competent authorities should use in choosing the type of sanctions and setting the level of any pecuniary sanctions. These should prompt competent authorities to adapt sanctions to the specific characteristics of the infringement and the offender, so as to maintain not only their deterrent effect, but also their proportionality. Although the list of criteria is part of a regulation, it is not directly applicable, instead needing specification in national law.[1] Together with the absence of minimum requirements for minimum penalties,[2] this is likely to moderate the degree of convergence in the actual sanctions that will result from the Market Abuse Regulation.

Article 31(2) requires the competent authorities of the various Member States to cooperate '[i]n the exercise of their powers to impose administrative sanctions and other administrative measures under Article 30' with regard to supervision, investigation, and sanctioning. Without such cooperation, sanctions could be ineffective or inappropriate, or public resources could be wasted on duplicated or overlapping enforcement efforts. Contrary to Article 31(1), Article 31(2) is formulated so as to have direct applicability. **B.31.02**

Historical developments

In its 2010 Communication on sanctioning regimes in the financial services sector, the Commission observed divergences in most financial sectors as to which factors competent authorities take into account when determining the type and/or the amount of administrative sanctions in specific cases. Using common key criteria would improve the effectiveness, proportionality, and dissuasiveness of the imposed sanctions and would allow competent authorities to adapt their sanctions to the nature and the impact of the violation as well as to the personal conditions of the offenders.[3] Specifically, the Commission suggested that competent authorities should at least consider the following factors: (i) the seriousness of the violation; (ii) the financial benefits for the author of the infringement derived from the violation (if calculable); (iii) the financial strength of the author of the violation; (iv) the cooperative behaviour of the author of the violation; and (v) the duration of the violation.[4] In its response, ESMA proposed adding the criteria of (i) the impact on the market and on consumers; (ii) the loss incurred by those impacted; (iii) the steps taken by the offender to compensate those impacted by the violation; (iv) the degree of culpability; (v) the repetitive nature of the **B.31.03**

[1] See Amendment 383, Draft Report Arlene McCarthy, Amendments 332–401 (11 May 2012) 2011/0295(COD), 34–5.

[2] See commentary to art 30.

[3] Communication from the Commission to the European Parliament, the Council, the European Economic and Social Committee and the Committee of the Regions, Reinforcing sanctioning regimes in the financial services sector (8 December 2010) COM(2010) 716 final 8 and 13.

[4] ibid 13–14.

violation; (vi) the compliance history of the offender if it is a regulated entity; and (vii) the level of responsibility or seniority of an individual.[5]

B.31.04 Along these lines, the Commission's proposal for a market abuse regulation included all but the last factor found in the final text of Article 31(1).[6] Article 31(1) largely corresponds to the template used more generally in European financial law, with many of the criteria also appearing in the Transparency Directive (as amended by directive 2013/50/EU), the Capital Requirements Directive (CRD IV) (2013/36/EU), the PRIIPs Regulation (2014/1286/EU), UCITS V (2014/91/EU), the Markets in Financial Instruments Directive II (2014/65/EU), the Securities Financing Transaction Regulation (2015/2365/EU), the Insurance Distribution Directive (2016/97/EU), and the Prospectus Regulation (2017/1129/EU).[7]

B.31.05 The Commission proposal also contained a provision on the need for competent authorities to cooperate with regard to administrative sanctions and measures,[8] that without major changes was eventually relocated to Article 31(2). The Parliament's suggestion to extend the cooperation duty to criminal authorities[9] was discarded in the final text.[10]

II. Relevant Circumstances

B.31.06 Article 31(1) lists a number of circumstances that competent authorities must take into account when determining the type and level of administrative sanctions. These criteria largely correspond with the common denominator of previously existing law and practice in many Member States,[11] although there was

5 See ESMA, 'Actual Use of Sanctioning Powers under MAD' (26 April 2012) ESMA/2012/270, 55.

6 Article 27 Proposal for a Regulation on insider dealing and market manipulation (market abuse) 2011/0295 (COD).

7 Article 28c(1) Transparency Directive (2013/50/EU); art 70 Capital Requirements Directive (CRD IV) (2013/36/EU); art 25 PRIIPs Regulation (2014/1286/EU); art 99c UCITS V (2014/91/EU); art 72(2) Markets in Financial Instruments Directive II (2014/65/EU); art 23 Securities Financing Transaction Regulation (2015/2365/EU); art 34 Insurance Distribution Directive (2016/97/EU); art 39 Prospectus Regulation (2017/1129/EU).

8 Article 24(2) Commission Proposal (n 6).

9 Article 24(2a) in the Report on the proposal for a regulation of the European Parliament and of the Council on insider dealing and market manipulation (market abuse) (22 October 2012), A7-0347/2012 ('Plenary Committee Report') 54.

10 See also the discarded proposal to include criteria on the basis of which the maximum fines could be exceeded (art 26(2) in Plenary Committee Report (n 9), 57) and to include possible pressure on an employee as a criterion for determining the level of a fine (art 27(1)(ba) in Plenary Committee Report (n 9), 58).

11 ESMA, 'Actual Use of Sanctioning Powers' (n 5) 55–62 and 64–7 (preventing re-offence was used less often as a criterion: 62).

also significant variation in national practices.[12] They also bear great resemblance to the factors that the European Commission uses in setting fines for competition law infringements. There, the Commission is legally obliged to take into account the gravity and duration of the infringement,[13] but on a voluntary basis it also applies many of the other factors listed in Article 31(1). According to the Commission's 2006 guidelines, the basic amount of the fine is calculated as a proportion of the value of the sales of the goods or services to which the infringement relates, depending on the degree of gravity of the infringement, and multiplied by the number of years the infringement went on. The basic amount can then be adjusted upwards or downwards on the basis of aggravating and mitigating circumstances that to a large extent overlap with the remaining criteria of Article 31(1).[14]

The first circumstance that Article 31(1) specifies, is the gravity and duration of the infringement. While the meaning of 'duration' may be clear in the context of market manipulation, it is less so for insider trading. One could argue that it does not apply to the instantaneous act of insider trading, or one could interpret it as referring to insider trading being committed a few times over several days.[15] The latter interpretation may at first sight blur the distinction between this circumstance and the one specified in Article 31(1)(f), namely potential previous infringements by the offender. However, in using the word 'previous', the latter criterion indicates that the authorities should take into account infringements that are not currently being sanctioned, eg infringements that have already been sanctioned earlier or that have expired. **B.31.07**

The second circumstance listed in Article 31(1), namely the degree of responsibility of the responsible person, speaks for itself. A leader of a so-called 'insider dealing ring' will deserve a harsher punishment than someone giving some practical help on the side for the same offence. **B.31.08**

The next relevant factor is 'the financial strength of the person responsible for the infringement, as indicated, for example, by the total turnover of a legal person or the annual income of a natural person' (Article 31(1)(c)). It is a well-known economic tenet that the degree of risk aversion of potential offenders varies according to their wealth. The wealthy are less averse to financial risks and thus tend to be deterred less by a penalty of a given amount than persons with fewer financial means.[16] A small fine may thus be enough to dissuade smaller financial **B.31.09**

[12] Commission, 'Staff Working Paper: Impact Assessment' SEC(2011) 1217 final 124.

[13] Article 23(3) Regulation 1/2003 on the implementation of the rules on competition laid down in arts 81 and 82 of the Treaty [2003] OJ L1/1.

[14] Commission, 'Guidelines on the method of setting fines imposed pursuant to Article 23(2)(a) of Regulation No 1/2003' [2006] OJ C210/2.

[15] See ESMA, 'Actual Use of Sanctioning Powers' (n 5) 57.

[16] Steven Shavell, *Foundations of Economic Analysis of Law* (Harvard University Press 2004) 482.

institutions, while a larger sanction is necessary to have an effect on large financial institutions.[17] Exceptionally, the level of a fine may need to be modified where a high fine would otherwise result in the company becoming economically unviable.[18] Authorities should, however, exercise caution in downwardly adapting a fine in accord with the limited financial means of the offender. Doing so may in some cases reduce the deterrent effect towards such offenders, as they stand to gain more from an infringement than they can possibly lose in the event of detection. In those cases, nonmonetary sanctions are recommended.[19] This is a nice example of how the circumstances listed in Article 31(1) are relevant not only in determining the level of the sanctions, but also in choosing the types of sanctions imposed.

B.31.10 Fourth, competent authorities must take into consideration the importance of the profits made or losses avoided by the offender, to the extent they can be determined (Article 31(1)(d)). Under the (former) Market Abuse Directive (2003/6/EC), not even half of the Member States provided for sanctions corresponding to at least the profits made or losses avoided, which could seriously affect their dissuasive effect.[20] Article 31(1)(d) should be read in conjunction with Article 30(2), items (b) and (h), which provide for disgorgement and for maximum fines of three times profits made or losses avoided. The purposes of Article 30(2)(h) and Article 31(1)(d) is different, however. While the former simply sets out minimum amounts for the maximum pecuniary sanctions laid down in national law, the latter prescribes (or better: mandates Member States to prescribe) criteria to be used by competent authorities in determining the level of pecuniary sanctions within the statutory minima and maxima.

B.31.11 The next criterion, namely the level of cooperation by the offender with the competent authority (Article 31(1)(e)), does not directly aim at deterrence, but is in the first place to be taken into account in order to encourage offenders to cooperate and thus to contribute to the investigation.[21] In exceptional cases, where the offender goes above and beyond mere cooperation and delivers important information and/or evidence, the criterion of cooperation by the offender might serve

[17] Communication from the Commission to the European Parliament, the Council, the European Economic and Social Committee and the Committee of the Regions, Reinforcing sanctioning regimes in the financial services sector (8 December 2010) COM(2010) 716 final 8.

[18] In competition law, the Commission may exceptionally take such a risk into account to reduce the fine. See Richard Whish and David Bailey, *Competition Law* (8th edn, Oxford University Press 2015) 294.

[19] See Shavell, *Foundations of Economic Analysis of Law* (n 16) 509–10.

[20] Communication from the Commission to the European Parliament, the Council, the European Economic and Social Committee and the Committee of the Regions, Reinforcing sanctioning regimes in the financial services sector (8 December 2010) COM(2010) 716 final 8; Commission, 'Impact Assessment' (n 12) 124.

[21] Communication from the Commission to the European Parliament, the Council, the European Economic and Social Committee and the Committee of the Regions, Reinforcing sanctioning regimes in the financial services sector, (8 December 2010) COM(2010) 716 final 8–9.

to allow an informal form of leniency. This would be in line with the finding made elsewhere in this book[22] that Article 32 provision on whistle-blowers may be extended to include leniency programmes. From the words 'without prejudice to the need to ensure disgorgement of profits gained or losses avoided by that person', it appears in any case that the fine itself can be reduced to zero, as long as a separate measure of disgorgement of profits gained or losses avoided is ordered.

The last two circumstances named by Article 31(1) relate to recidivism, with item (f) referring to past infringements and item (g) to the risk of future infringements. With regard to the former, it is not specified if the previous infringement needs to be of the same type as the one currently under scrutiny, as is required for treating a previous infringement as an aggravating factor in competition law.[23] When both were committed intentionally, there is a good argument that even an earlier infringement of another type reveals the same sort of contempt for fair play in financial markets, the difference between market manipulation and insider trading being arguably smaller than the difference between participating in cartel and abusing a dominant position. As in competition law,[24] one can assume that there is no limitation period for previous infringements to be taken into account. Item (g), in turn, focuses on the measures taken by the offender to prevent repetition of the infringement. These measures must be concrete interventions taken after learning of the infringement; the mere continuation of a pre-existing compliance programme is unlikely to suffice. **B.31.12**

Pursuant to Article 31(1), Member States must ensure that competent authorities take into account not only the above described circumstances, but also all other relevant circumstances. The list is therefore not exhaustive. For instance, the authorities should probably acknowledge that the publication of sanctions may for some offenders cause huge reputational damage, whereas for others its effect is limited.[25] **B.31.13**

III. Cooperation between Competent Authorities

In today's globalized financial markets, market abuse is rarely confined to national borders.[26] Crossing the territorial jurisdiction of several competent authorities is often even part of a conscious strategy to disguise market abuse.[27] Article 31(2) addresses the risk that this leads to duplication and overlap in enforcement efforts **B.31.14**

---

22 See commentary to art 32.

23 See Whish and Bailey, *Competition Law* (n 18) 294.

24 ibid.

25 See commentary to art 34.

26 See recital (67) Market Abuse Regulation.

27 Janet Austin, 'Protecting Market Integrity in an Era of Fragmentation and Cross-Border Trading' (2014–2015) 46 Ottawa Law Review 41.

and/or to ineffective or inappropriate administrative sanctions and measures. For on the one hand, competent authorities in different Member States risk simultaneously engaging in the same supervisory, investigatory, or enforcement efforts, while being barred from parallel effective enforcement owing to the principle of *non bis in idem*. On the other hand, a competent authority might impose too low a sanction, thereby similarly barring further proceedings under the rule of *non bis in idem*.[28]

B.31.15 The most effective solution to these problems would consist of a priority rule with regard to which jurisdiction can take the lead in enforcement of market abuse. The Market Abuse Regulation does not go this far, but it attempts to limit the potential damage through enhanced cooperation between national authorities, with a facilitating role for ESMA. Specifically, Article 31(2) requires competent authorities to cooperate with a view to the effectiveness and appropriateness of the administrative sanctions and measures they impose and to avoid duplication and overlaps. To a large extent, this provision is a repetition of Article 25, albeit specifically for administrative sanctions and measures.[29] The latter imposes a more general obligation on competent authorities to cooperate with, and render assistance to, each other and ESMA where necessary for the purpose of the Market Abuse Regulation.[30] In addition, in almost the same wording as Article 31(2), second sentence, Article 25 obliges competent authorities to 'coordinate their action, in order to avoid duplication and overlap when applying administrative sanctions and other administrative measures'.[31] In accordance with the ESMA Regulation, Article 25 also grants ESMA a coordination role in investigations and inspections,[32] as well as broad conciliation and enforcement powers in case of requests for information or assistance.[33]

[28] Michiel Luchtman and John Vervaele, 'Enforcing the Market Abuse Regime: Towards an Integrated Model of Criminal and Administrative Law Enforcement in the European Union?' (2014) 5 New Journal of European Criminal Law 192, 201.

[29] With regard to cooperation with criminal authorities, see the chapter on public enforcement.

[30] Article 25(1) and (2) Market Abuse Regulation.

[31] Article 25(5), last sentence Market Abuse Regulation.

[32] Article 25(6) Market Abuse Regulation.

[33] Article 25(7) Market Abuse Regulation.

Article 32: Reporting of infringements

1. Member States shall ensure that competent authorities establish effective mechanisms to enable reporting of actual or potential infringements of this Regulation to competent authorities.

2. The mechanisms referred to in paragraph 1 shall include at least:

(a) specific procedures for the receipt of reports of infringements and their follow-up, including the establishment of secure communication channels for such reports;

(b) within their employment, appropriate protection for persons working under a contract of employment, who report infringements or are accused of infringements, against retaliation, discrimination or other types of unfair treatment at a minimum; and

(c) protection of personal data both of the person who reports the infringement and the natural person who allegedly committed the infringement, including protection in relation to preserving the confidentiality of their identity, at all stages of the procedure without prejudice to disclosure of information being required by national law in the context of investigations or subsequent judicial proceedings.

3. Member States shall require employers who carry out activities that are regulated by financial services regulation to have in place appropriate internal procedures for their employees to report infringements of this Regulation.

4. Member States may provide for financial incentives to persons who offer relevant information about potential infringements of this Regulation to be granted in accordance with national law where such persons do not have other pre-existing legal or contractual duties to report such information, and provided that the information is new, and that it results in the imposition of an administrative or criminal sanction, or the taking of another administrative measure, for an infringement of this Regulation.

5. The Commission shall adopt implementing acts to specify the procedures referred to in paragraph 1, including the arrangements for reporting and for following-up reports, and measures for the protection of persons working under a contract of employment and measures for the protection of personal data. Those implementing acts shall be adopted in accordance with the examination procedure referred to in Article 36(2).

Relevant Technical Standards:

Commission Implementing Directive (EU) 2015/2392 of 17 December 2015 on Regulation (EU) No 596/2014 of the European Parliament and of the Council as regards reporting to competent authorities of actual or potential infringements of that Regulation (OJ L 332, 18.12.2015, p. 126)

I. General Remarks

Subject matter and principle

B.32.01 To facilitate detection of market abuse, Article 32(1) mandates the establishment of whistle-blower programmes at the competent authorities,[1] which is a novelty in the enforcement toolbox in European capital markets law. For the whistle-blower programmes to work effectively, Article 32(2) stipulates that the receipt and follow-up of whistle-blower reports must follow a specific procedure. For the remaining part, Article 32(2) largely focuses on protection of the whistle-blower (who risks being exposed and maltreated) and, to a lesser extent, of the reported person (who risks being accused unrightfully). In accordance with Article 32(5), the provisions on reporting procedures are amplified by an Implementing Directive (EU/2015/2392).[2] Not only this directive, but also Article 32(1) itself requires national measures of implementation. This deviation from the rule of direct applicability of regulation provisions follows from the wording 'member states shall ensure that competent authorities establish' and is relatively common for procedural measures aimed at securing full enforcement of a regulation.[3]

B.32.02 Particularly innovative is Article 32(4), which allows Member States to go beyond offering protection to whistle-blowers, and to promise financial rewards. On this point, the European legislator has clearly drawn inspiration from the American SEC's whistle-blower bounty programme. Because this would be something of a revolution in most Member States, the provision is optional and thus not directly applicable as regulation provisions normally are.

B.32.03 The above described provisions all deal with whistle-blowing to competent authorities and seem to overlook and possibly even undermine the potential benefits from companies' internal compliance programmes. During the trialogues, a provision was therefore added to the effect that employees of employers who carry

[1] Recital (74) Market Abuse Regulation.

[2] See ESMA, 'Technical advice on possible delegated acts concerning the Market Abuse Regulation' (3 February 2015) ESMA/2015/224 60–7.

[3] See Richard Kral, 'National Normative Implementation of EC Regulations: An Exceptional or Rather Common Matter?' (2008) 33 European Law Review 243 (also discussing the direct and indirect effect of improperly implemented regulations that required national implementation).

out activities that are regulated by financial services regulation should be able to report market abuse through appropriate internal procedures. Article 32(4) does not elaborate on this and does not refer to the procedures and protections of the previous paragraphs, but again[4] requires national implementation measures.

History and trends

Article 32 follows an international trend among regulators to increasingly rely **B.32.04** on whistle-blowers (and, more generally, private market actors)[5] as part of their enforcement programme.[6] Such a development presupposes a cultural shift—one that has taken place earlier in the US than in Europe. The elemental idea of whistle-blowing is embedded in the American practice of plea bargaining.[7] As long ago as in the nineteenth century, American law featured some form of whistle-blower rewards in the context of false claims for payment against the government.[8] In 1988, the SEC was authorized to pay bounties for information on insider trading,[9] but this has not been a success.[10] The Sarbanes-Oxley Act of 2002 introduced protection from retaliation for employees who report potential violations of SEC rules or regulations or securities fraud, but no financial incentives.[11] Since then, whistle-blowers have in the US more and more been considered as courageous citizens acting from a sense of public duty and less as traitors or trouble-makers.[12] In 2010, the provisions of the Dodd-Frank Act[13] that improved whistle-blower protection and provided for powerful monetary incentives did not stir much debate any more.[14] Europe, in contrast, is still

[4] See para B.32.01 above.

[5] See the chapter on public enforcement in this volume.

[6] See Anthony Heyes and Sandeep Kapur, 'An Economic Model of Whistle-Blower Policy' (2009) 25 Journal of Law, Economics and Organization 157–8.

[7] Sarah Wilson, 'The New Market Abuse Regulation and Directive on Criminal Sanctions for Market Abuse: European Capital Markets Law and New Global Trends in Financial Crime Enforcement' (2015) 16 ERA Forum 444.

[8] The False Claims Act of 1863 provided for a type of private enforcement of public rights (so-called *qui tam* procedures) by anyone who has knowledge of fraud on behalf of the government, for which the state would financially reward the claimant. See Tom Faunce, Kim Crow, Tony Nikolic, and Frederick M Morgan Jr, 'Because They Have Evidence: Globalizing Financial Incentives for Corporate Fraud Whistleblowers' in A J Brown, David Lew, Richard Moberly, and Wim Vandekerckhove (eds), *International Handbook on Whistleblowing Research* (Edward Elgar Publishing 2014) 382–5.

[9] Insider Trading and Securities Enforcement Act of 1988.

[10] SEC Office of Inspector General, 'Assessment of the SEC's Bounty Program' (Rep No 474, 26 March 2010) 4–5 www.sec.gov/oig/reportspubs/474.pdf; Justin Blount and Spencer Markel, 'The End of the Internal Compliance World as We Know It, or An Enhancement of the Effectiveness of Securities Law Enforcement? Bounty Hunting under the Dodd-Frank Act's Whistleblower Provision' (2012) 17 Fordham Journal of Corporate Finance Law 1031–2.

[11] Section 806 Sarbanes-Oxley Act of 2002, Pub L 107–204.

[12] Michael Delikat and Renee Phillips, *Corporate Whistleblowing in the Sarbanes-Oxley/Dodd-Frank Era* (2nd edn, PLI 2011, Supp 2015) para 1-1.

[13] Dodd-Frank Wall Street Reform and Consumer Protection Act of 2010, Pub L 111-203.

[14] Dave Ebersole, 'Blowing the Whistle on the Dodd-Frank Whistleblower Provisions' (2011) 6 Ohio State Entrepreneurial Business Law Journal 127.

characterized by a preference for trust and cooperation between employer and employee,[15] which is only slowly giving way to a growing acceptance of whistle-blowing. Another inhibiting factor in Germany and in Eastern Europe is the abhorrence of denouncing fellow citizens that grew in Nazi and Stasi times resp. the imposed communist regime.[16] Still, heavily mediatized whistle-blowing affairs, which exposed scandals in companies such as Enron and WorldCom and in governmental bodies including the NSA and the Luxembourg tax authorities, as well as successful leniency programmes in cartels are influencing the public opinion.[17] The passage of the first comprehensive whistle-blower law in an EU Member State, namely the Public Interest Disclosure Act of 1998 in the UK, has taught that legislation introducing protection for whistle-blowers can in fact ameliorate the public perception of whistle-blowing.[18]

B.32.05 Neither the Insider Dealing Directive (1989/592/EEC) nor the (former) Market Abuse Directive (2003/6/EC) contained any provisions on whistle-blowing. In the EU Member States protection of whistle-blowers either did not exist at all or was confined to horizontal employment laws.[19] Drawing from the American Dodd-Frank Act, the European Commission expressed its interest in exploring the possibility of whistle-blowing and leniency programmes in the financial services sector in 2010[20] and included the first option in its proposal for a Market Abuse Regulation.[21] Although this spawned a debate during the trialogues, the proposed text was largely accepted and complemented with a requirement for employers regulated by financial services regulation to set up internal whistle-blowing procedures. In the same period, other legal instruments in European financial regulation also embraced whistle-blowing, albeit without enabling

[15] Thomas Berndt and Ivo Hoppler, 'Whistleblowing: ein integraler Bestandteil effektiver Corporate Governance' (2005) Betriebs-Berater 2623; Uwe H Schneider and Claudia Nowak, 'Sind die Einrichtung einer Whistleblowing-Stelle und der Schutz des Whistleblowers Teil guter Corporate Compliance?' in G Hoenn and others (eds), *Festschrift für Peter Kreutz zum 70. Geburtstag* (Luchterhand 2010) 855, 863.

[16] Wim Vandekerckhove, Tina Uys, Michael T Rehg, and A J Brown, 'Understandings of Whistleblowing: Dilemmas of Societal Culture' in A J Brown, David Lew, Richard Moberly, and Wim Vandekerckhove (eds), *International Handbook on Whistleblowing Research* (Edward Elgar Publishing 2014) 40–1.

[17] See also Mark Worth, *Legal Protections for Whistleblowers in the EU* (Transparency International 2013) 15–16.

[18] Holger Fleischer and Klaus Ulrich Schmolke, 'Financial Incentives for Whistleblowers in European Capital Markets Law' (2012) 9 European Company Law 255; James Gobert and Maurice Punch, 'Whistleblowers, the Public Interest, and the Public Interest Disclosure Act 1998' (2000) 63 Modern Law Review 54.

[19] Commission, 'Staff Working Paper: Impact Assessment' SEC(2011) 1217 final 120 and 155.

[20] Commission Communication, 'Reinforcing sanctioning regimes in the financial services sector' (8 December 2010) COM(2010) 716 final 15.

[21] Article 29 Proposal for a Regulation on insider dealing and market manipulation (market abuse) 2011/0295 (COD), 'The influence of the Dodd-Frank Act surfaces in Market Abuse Regulation Proposal' 121.

financial rewards.[22] More recently, the Prospectus Regulation follows the Market Abuse Regulation template with regard to whistle-blowing, including financial rewards,[23] which may hint at its gradually becoming a standard tool of public enforcement.

II. External Whistle-blowing Mechanisms

Rationale, criticism, and effectiveness

Market abuse is often extremely difficult, if not impossible, for the government to detect from outside. Besides, its victims are remote (ie they do not have a relationship with the offender) and unaware of the offence. As a consequence, they do not deposit a complaint, which for other violations of law is an important avenue through which the state finds out about them.[24] In contrast, employees and other persons related to the offender may discover the latter's unlawful practice in the course of their ordinary business, without any special effort.[25] By harnessing them to uncover market abuse and lay hands on evidence, by means of whistle-blowing, the European legislator hopes to boost detection rates, and thus also to increase deterrence.[26] **B.32.06**

While whistle-blowing can be very fruitful for supervision authorities, it can be profoundly damaging for the whistle-blower himself. Denouncing an employer, a colleague, or an acquaintance frequently provokes reprisals by the employer (in the form of dismissal, demotion, inconvenient working hours, reduced salary, etc), blacklisting from future employers and social ostracism from colleagues and the larger community. Whistle-blowing also risks entailing prolonged interactions with enforcement authorities as well as immense public attention and criticism.[27] In order to encourage potential whistle-blowers to surmount their understandable **B.32.07**

[22] See art 73 Markets in Financial Instruments Directive II (2014/65/EU); art 1(17) UCITS V (2014/91/EU), inserting art 99d into the UCITS Directive; art 71 Capital Requirements Directive (CRD IV) (2013/36/EU); art 23 SSM Regulation (1024/2013/EU); art 28 PRIIPs-Regulation (2014/1286/EU); art 24 Securities Financing Transaction Regulation (2015/2365/EU); art 35 Insurance Distribution Directive (2016/97/EU).

[23] Article 41 Prospectus Regulation (2017/1129/EU).

[24] Theresa Pfeifle, *Finanzielle Anreize für Whistleblowers im Kapitalmarktrecht* (Nomos 2016) 60.

[25] Alexander Dyck, Adair Morse, and Luigi Zingales, 'Who Blows the Whistle on Corporate Fraud?' (2010) 65 Journal of Finance 2214.

[26] Commission, 'Impact Assessment' (n 19) 49.

[27] Commission, 'Impact Assessment' (n 19) 120, 121; Recital (74); Dyck and others, 'Who Blows the Whistle' (n 25) 2240–5; Yuval Feldman and Orly Lobel, 'The Incentives Matrix: The Comparative Effectiveness of Rewards, Liabilities, Duties, and Protections for Reporting Illegality' (2010) 88 Texas Law Review 1157–8; Joyce Rothschild and Terance D Miethe, 'Whistle-Blower Disclosures and Management Retaliation: The Battle to Control Information about Organization Corruption' (1999) 26 Work and Occupations 107. See, however, Rodney Smith, 'Whistleblowers and Suffering' in A J Brown, David Lew, Richard Moberly, and Wim Vandekerckhove (eds),

reluctance to come forward with allegations, the Market Abuse Regulation attempts to protect them from retaliation and to offer accessible and confidential reporting procedures. Appropriate processes should also avoid that competent authorities fail to adequately examine the information provided by whistle-blowers, as happened in the case of the Ponzi scheme hedge fund run by Bernard Madoff, for which the SEC had received and neglected six substantial complaints.[28]

B.32.08 An objection that is sometimes raised against whistle-blowing and that seems related to the cultural disposition against whistle-blowing (see para B.32.04), is that it could foster a culture of fear and mistrust in enterprises.[29] Provided the law is designed so as to discourage frivolous reporting, this should not be a major concern. Proceedings that involve whistle-blowers would also take longer than other procedures, thus increasing the costs to the state. However, the infringement might otherwise have gone unnoticed, and proceedings with whistle-blowers also lead to significantly higher monetary penalties, thus compensating for the higher procedural costs.[30]

B.32.09 Whistle-blowing is in any case a highly effective enforcement tool, as the associated costs for the government are very limited,[31] while it is a major or even the most important way to detect fraudulent behaviour. Even before the Frank-Dodd act, the SEC's and other external auditors' rate of detection (a mere 4.1 per cent of uncovered fraud schemes) paled in comparison to the growing success of whistle-blowing, which brought to light not less than 54.1 per cent of uncovered fraud schemes in public companies.[32] In its Impact Assessment for the Market Abuse Regulation, the European Commission cited more moderate, but still very convincing figures, according to which whistle-blowing accounted for 25 per cent of the general fraud cases across Europe, the Middle East, and Africa, and for 30 per cent of the market abuse investigations in the UK.[33]

Requirements

B.32.10 The whistle-blower regime of the Market Abuse Regulation is an open one, ie Article 32 does not set out any requirements for obtaining and maintaining the

International Handbook on Whistleblowing Research (Edward Elgar Publishing 2014) 230 (arguing that most whistle-blowers do not suffer).

[28] Commission, 'Impact Assessment' (n 19) 120–1 and 155–6.

[29] Deutsches Aktieninstitut, 'The Review of the EU-Market Abuse Regime at the Start of the Trialogues' (30 January 2013) 14 www.dai.de/files/dai_usercontent/dokumente/positionspapiere/2013-01-30%20DAI-Comment_MAR_at_the_start_of_the%20trialogues_final.pdf; Ebersole, 'Blowing the Whistle' (n 14) 139; Pfeifle, *Finanzielle Anreize* (n 24) 152–3.

[30] Andrew C Call, Gerald S Martin, Nathan Y Scharp, and Jaron H Wilde, 'Whistleblowers and Outcomes of Financial Misrepresentation Enforcement Actions' (1 May 2016) papers.ssrn.com/sol3/papers.cfm?abstract_id=2506418.

[31] Commission, 'Impact Assessment' (n 19) 49.

[32] Report of the Senate Committee on Banking, Housing and Urban Affairs (S. Rep. No 111-176, 30 April 2010) 110.

[33] Commission, 'Impact Assessment' (n 19) 121.

status of a 'reporting person'.[34] Nevertheless, its preamble specifies that that status and the concomitant protection should not be granted to those who knowingly report wrong or misleading information to competent authorities.[35]

Pursuant to Article 32(2)(a), Member States must ensure that competent authorities set out specific procedures for the receipt and follow-up of reports of infringements. The Implementing Directive details that this should include dedicated staff members, record-keeping for every report, and dedicated communication channels, including dedicated electronic and postal addresses, telephone lines and the possibility for informants to have a physical meeting with the dedicated staff members.[36] In order to allow potential whistle-blowers to make informed decisions with regard to reporting, the website of the competent authority must contain easily accessible information regarding the reporting procedures, the applicable confidentiality regime and its exceptions, the possibility to report anonymously, and an explanation that whistle-blowing is not considered a breach of any confidentiality obligation and does not trigger liability of any kind.[37] The latter is important in light of the American experience with employers attempting to contractually impede whistle-blowing.[38] **B.32.11**

Article 32(2)(b) clarifies that the whistle-blowing mechanisms of the competent authorities should include appropriate protection for employees against retaliation. On this point, the Implementing Directive limits itself to calling for effective exchange of information and cooperation between relevant authorities and access to information, advice and assistance, further referring to legal procedures available under national law.[39] **B.32.12**

Article 32(2)(c) requires whistle-blowing mechanisms to protect the personal data of both the whistle-blower and the alleged wrongdoer. Confidentiality must be ensured in the competent authority's communication channels for whistle-blowing, record keeping and transmission of data related to a report of infringement and also the identity of reported persons must be protected.[40] Competent authorities must of course comply with their national data protection law (including provisions transposing Directive 95/46/EC) and with Articles 28 and 29.[41] Nevertheless, competent authorities cannot guarantee absolute confidentiality, as **B.32.13**

---

[34] ESMA, 'Technical advice on possible delegated acts concerning the Market Abuse Regulation' (3 February 2015) ESMA/2015/224, 62.

[35] Recital (1).

[36] Articles 3, 4(2)(a)(2), 6(1), and 7 Implementing Directive (EU/2015/2392).

[37] Articles 4 and 5, recital (4) Implementing Directive (EU/2015/2392).

[38] SEC, 'Annual Report on the Dodd-Frank Whistleblower Program' (2015) 19–20; Richard Moberly, Jordan A Thomas, and Jason Zuckerman, 'De Facto Gag Clauses: The Legality of Employment Agreements that Undermine Dodd-Frank's Whistleblower Provisions' (2014) 30 American Bar Association Journal of Labor and Employment Law 87.

[39] Article 8, recital (6) Implementing Directive (EU/2015/2392).

[40] ibid Articles 4(2)(a)(2), 6, 9, 10(2), and 11.

[41] ESMA, 'Technical advice on possible delegated acts concerning the Market Abuse Regulation' (3 February 2015) ESMA/2015/224, 63.

disclosure might exceptionally be necessary pursuant to Articles 27, 28, and 29, in the context of investigations or judicial proceedings, or to safeguard the right of defence of the reported person.[42] This uncertainty is likely to hold back some potential whistle-blowers or to make them opt for anonymous reporting, which may reduce the efficacy of their reporting as the competent authority can then not make further inquiries with the whistle-blower.

III. Rewards for Whistle-blowers

Rationale, criticism, and effectiveness

B.32.14 Mere legal protection of a whistle-blower is likely to reduce but not exclude the potentially enormous accompanying costs to the whistle-blower (see para B.32.07 above). By promising financial rewards for whistle-blowing, the legislator can attempt to win over an hesitant potential whistle-blower.

B.32.15 More than the establishment of whistle-blowing mechanisms per se (see para B.32.08), premiums for whistle-blowers encountered a lot of criticism.[43] A first objection is that financial incentives threaten to erode intrinsic motivation,[44] which normally plays a significant role in the decision to volunteer information to an external authority.[45] Generally, this risk materializes most in matters that cause only low moral outrage,[46] as may well be the case in the so-called 'victimless' offence of market abuse.[47] A countervailing argument is that low moral motivation in itself (ie without financial incentives) is unlikely to be sufficient to make a potential whistle-blower actually report anyway, given the large personal risks. In any case, it has been shown that a morally driven potential whistle-blower will still report in case of financial rewards, provided they are high enough.[48] A second and related objection is that people may refrain from reporting out of fear that others will think they reported for their own financial gain,[49] a problem that can easily be overcome by renouncing the reward. Thirdly, critics point to the risk that unreliable submissions will be made by persons seeking to strike gold, which would waste government resources on the verification of false submissions.[50] Indeed, the SEC has been plagued by a couple of individuals

[42] Article 5(1) Implementing Directive (EU/2015/2392).

[43] With regard to the claim that whistle-blower rewards undermine internal compliance programmes see paras B.32.22–B.32.23.

[44] Ebersole, 'Blowing the Whistle' (n 14) 130.

[45] Adam Waytz, James Dungan, and Liane Young, 'The Whistleblower's Dilemma and the Fairness–Loyalty Tradeoff' (2012) 49 Journal of Experimental Social Psychology 1027.

[46] Feldman and Lobel, 'The Incentives Matrix' (n 27) 1202.

[47] Fleischer and Schmolke, 'Financial Incentives for Whistleblowers' (n 18) 255.

[48] Feldman and Lobel, 'The Incentives Matrix' (n 27) 1202.

[49] ibid 1200–1.

[50] Ebersole, 'Blowing the Whistle' (n 14) 135. See Commission, 'Impact Assessment' (n 19) 156.

who have been making large numbers of fictitious statements.[51] This risk can be minimized by enabling competent authorities to verify the status or the identity of the whistle-blower,[52] refusing protection for wilful false submissions (see para B.32.10), requiring sworn affidavits,[53] and, in extreme cases, declaring fraudulent reporters ineligible for any reward regarding pending or future claims for whistle-blower rewards.[54]

The empirical evidence indicates that the above concerns are probably overblown. Rewards have been found to improve the willingness to report infringements and not to lead to more frivolous suits.[55] Overall, the Dodd-Frank whistle-blowing programme has also been successful until now.[56] **B.32.16**

Eligibility requirements

According to Article 32(4), Member States may provide for financial incentives to whistle-blowers provided they meet four conditions. First, the information they offer must be 'relevant'. This is rightfully less restrictive than the requirement of 'salient' information in the original Commission Proposal,[57] as it would probably hold back some potential whistle-blowers for whom it is difficult to assess whether the information will be salient.[58] Secondly, the whistle-blower must not have a pre-existing legal or contractual obligation to report. The fulfilment of an obligation should indeed not need a reward. Thirdly, the information of the whistle-blower must be 'new'. This is to be understood as not only not publicly known, but also not known by the competent authority.[59] For the information to be 'new', it is not necessary for the violation to be unknown by the competent authority. It suffices that the information significantly contributes to an ongoing investigation.[60] Non-public information that is deduced from an own examination of publicly available information should also be considered new.[61] The newness requirement encourages potential whistle-blowers to address the competent **B.32.17**

---

[51] SEC, 'Annual Report on the Dodd-Frank Whistleblower Program' (2015) 14.

[52] Commission, 'Impact Assessment' (n 19) 156.

[53] See rule 21F-9(b), 17 CFR § 240.21F-9(b).

[54] As the SEC did in 2015: SEC, Annual report on the Dodd-Frank Whistleblower Program (2015) 14.

[55] Dyck and others, 'Who Blows the Whistle' (n 25) 2246.

[56] Andrew Ceresney, 'The SEC's Whistleblower Program: The Successful Early Years' (14 September 2016) www.sec.gov/news/speech/ceresney-sec-whistleblower-program.html#_ftn27.

[57] Article 29(2) Proposal for a Regulation on insider dealing and market manipulation (market abuse) 2011/0295 (COD).

[58] See SEC, 'Securities Whistleblower Incentives and Protections' 76 Fed Reg 34323–34324.

[59] Pfeifle, *Finanzielle Anreize* (n 24) 164.

[60] Such information amounted to approximately half of the cases in which whistle-blowers received monetary awards under the Dodd-Frank program: SEC, 'Annual Report on the Dodd-Frank Whistleblower Program' (2015) 16.

[61] Under the Dodd-Frank programme, such 'independent analysis' is eligible for a whistle-blower bounty: 15 USC § 78u-6(a)(3); 17 CFR § 240.21F-4(b).

authority as soon as possible, as it may otherwise obtain the information from other sources.[62] Finally, the information made available by the whistle-blower must '[result] in the imposition of an administrative or criminal sanction, or the taking of another administrative measure, for an infringement of [the Market Abuse Regulation]'. Unlike the Dodd-Frank Act (see para B.32.19), the Market Abuse Regulation does not limit whistle-blower premiums to cases that result in monetary sanctions.[63]

B.32.18 Article 32(4) does not exclude whistle-blowers who played a role in the reported market abuse themselves. Member States are therefore free to introduce a leniency programme for market abuse offenders (which is also supported by the wording of Article 31).[64] This could be a particularly helpful (if not the only) way to get hold of so-called 'insider dealing rings', which involve small groups of individuals committing insider trading on a sophisticated and paperless basis.[65] Excluding ring members with remorse gives them an incentive to keep things quiet, as they only stand to lose from reporting. The UK has been a forerunner in this regard, as already in 2009, it authorized the FSA (predecessor of the FCA) to enter into plea-bargaining agreements with, or even grant immunity from prosecution to, offenders who assisted in the investigation or prosecution of others.[66] However, the FSA has not made extensive use of these powers. The SEC has achieved more success with its whistle-blowing programme, in which culpability is not a ground for ineligibility but merely for reduction of the award.[67]

B.32.19 It follows from Article 32(4) that Member States may or may not provide financial incentives to whistle-blowers who meet the four above described conditions, and thus that they can also restrict incentives to a more limited number of cases, by imposing additional conditions.[68] Two possible limitations follow from the legislative history of the Market Abuse Regulation. First, as the preamble to the Market Abuse Regulation denies protection to whistle-blowers who deliberately provided false information or documents to the competent authority (see para B.32.10), they should a fortiori not be entitled to a monetary reward. They are also excluded from rewards in the Dodd-Frank regime.[69] Secondly, in its Impact

---

[62] Fleischer and Schmolke, 'Financial Incentives for Whistleblowers' (n 18) 257.

[63] One could, however, read an implicit assumption in that sense in the Commission's suggestion to 'set a minimum level of monetary sanction for which a whistle blower would receive financial incentives' (Commission, 'Impact Assessment' (n 19) 156).

[64] See commentary to art 31.

[65] Christine Astaniou, Shoshana Wainer, and Nikunj Kiri, 'UK Market Abuse Update: FSA Continues to Demonstrate Resolve to Tackle Market Abuse' (2010) 4 Law and Financial Markets Review 583.

[66] Coroners and Justice Act 2009 s 113 (adding the FSA as a 'specified prosecutor' in section 71(4) of the Serious Organised Crime and Police Act 2005).

[67] 17 CFR § 240-21F-6(b)(1).

[68] ESMA, 'Technical advice on possible delegated acts concerning the Market Abuse Regulation' (3 February 2015) ESMA/2015/224, p 62.

[69] 17 CFR § 240.21F8(c)(7).

Assessment, the Commission also suggested allowing financial incentives only for information that lead to monetary sanctions exceeding a certain amount.[70] Such a floor on the monetary sanction would ensure that competent authorities can focus resources on the important cases, that employees will report internally for smaller matters and that potential whistle-blowers can count on receiving a substantial award that is worth the pain.[71]

Member States could also consider limiting awards to reports that lead to sanctioning of legal entities, because they are likely to be involved in market abuse more systematically and to be imposed larger monetary sanctions and there is a higher risk of retaliation that potential informants must overcome.[72] Some scholars go a step further and make a case for limiting rewards to employees and contract parties of the company, because they are in a position to obtain incriminating information, whereas including others may lead to the development of a market for professional whistle-blowers.[73] While relevant information is often found by employees and contract parties, it may be overly restrictive to exclude other whistle-blowers. In fact, under the American Dodd-Frank whistle-blower programme, a large number of award recipients are investors who have been victims of the fraud, professionals working in a related industry, or people who had a personal relationship with the reported person.[74] Other exclusions that have been advocated relate to the source of information.[75] For instance, competent authorities should not reward obtaining information by means of crime.[76] In the US, the SEC Rules also exclude information from attorney-client privileged communication,[77] but not information learnt in the performance of auditing or compliance tasks.[78] **B.32.20**

Determination of the reward

Whistle-blower premiums are commonly framed as a percentage of the monetary sanction imposed for the reported infringement. The Dodd-Frank whistle-blower programme rewards range from 10 per cent to 30 per cent of the imposed monetary sanctions.[79] This proportionality has the advantage of giving a stronger incentive for large violations and of not causing any costs to the State. At the same time, **B.32.21**

[70] Commission, 'Impact Assessment' (n 19) 156. The American Dodd-Frank Act sets out a minimum sanction of US$1 million (§ 21F(a)(1) SEA).

[71] Commission, 'Impact Assessment' (n 19) 156; Blount and Markel, 'End of Internal Compliance' (n 10) 1055–6.

[72] Pfeifle, *Finanzielle Anreize* (n 24) 159.

[73] Fleischer and Schmolke, 'Financial Incentives for Whistleblowers' (n 18) 257; Ebersole, 'Blowing the Whistle' (n 14) 159.

[74] SEC, Annual report on the Dodd-Frank Whistleblower Program (2015) 16.

[75] Fleischer and Schmolke, 'Financial Incentives for Whistleblowers' (n 18) 257.

[76] Compare 17 CFR para 240.21F-4(b)(4)(iv).

[77] 17 CFR s 240.21F-4(b)(4)(i) and (ii).

[78] 17 CFR s 240.21F-4(b)(4)(iii) and (v).

[79] Section 21F(b)(1) SEA, introduced by s 922 Dodd-Frank Act.

this approach leaves enough flexibility to the authority to take into account the specific circumstances of the case.[80] For instance, the SEC increases the reward where the information provided was particularly significant, the informant has actively assisted throughout the investigation, or the informant has experienced unique hardships as a result of blowing the whistle. The SEC reduces the reward when the whistle-blower has unreasonably delayed his reporting, contributed to the infringement or interfered with internal compliance systems.[81] Limiting the flexibility through minimum and maximum percentages reduces the uncertainty and the minimum percentage ensures that a potential whistle-blower has some assurance that it is worth disclosing the information to the authorities.

IV. External versus Internal Whistle-blowing

Rationale, criticism, and effectiveness

B.32.22 In the debate on whistle-blowing, internal compliance structures are frequently said to deserve preference on the grounds that they would be more effective, less adversarial, and sufficiently protective of the reporting person.[82] Because financial rewards incentivize employees to bypass internal compliance programmes and directly address the competent authorities,[83] some argue that external whistle-blowing should not be encouraged with monetary rewards.[84] Another proposal that is frequently put forward is to require potential whistle-blowers to first utilize the internal reporting mechanisms.[85]

B.32.23 Whistle-blowing to competent authorities can, however, serve as a necessary complement to internal reporting procedures, without making the latter redundant. First, whistle-blowers who are not employed by, or members of, the focal organization, but may have another relationship with it (such as clients, customers, or competitors) do not have the internal channels available.[86] For them,

---

[80] Fleischer and Schmolke, 'Financial Incentives for Whistleblowers' (n 18) 258.

[81] 17 CFR § 240.21F-6.

[82] ESMA, 'Technical advice on possible delegated acts concerning the Market Abuse Regulation' (3 February 2015) ESMA/2015/224, 62.

[83] Commission, 'Impact Assessment' (n 19) 156; Delikat and Phillips, *Corporate Whistleblowing* (n 12) 17–18.

[84] Ebersole, 'Blowing the Whistle' (n 14) 151.

[85] Commission, 'Impact Assessment' (n 19) 156; Consultation paper respondents comments as summarized in ESMA, 'Technical advice on possible delegated acts concerning the Market Abuse Regulation' (3 February 2015) ESMA/2015/224, 62; Ebersole, 'Blowing the Whistle' (n 14) 151; Holger Fleischer, 'Whistleblower Bounties in European Capital Markets Law?' (2012) 9 European Company Law 200.

[86] Marcia P Miceli, Suelette Dreyfus, and Janet P Near, 'Outsider "Whistleblowers": Conceptualizing and Distinguishing "Bell-ringing" Behavior' in A J Brown, David Lew, Richard Moberly, and Wim Vandekerckhove (eds), *International Handbook on Whistleblowing Research* (Edward Elgar Publishing 2014) 79.

competent authorities play a vital role[87], and so may financial rewards. Secondly, even for employees in companies with internal reporting mechanisms, competent authorities are the last resort when an issue was raised internally without success[88] or in case internal compliance programmes are likely to be ineffective.[89] Indeed, it has been shown that internal compliance programmes often do not deter infringements within firms and merely serve a window-dressing function.[90] Enterprises may also fail to communicate important information from internal reporting to public authorities. Especially when employers face a sanction, they have an interest in keeping prohibited conduct quiet.[91] Finally, an employee risks refraining from accessing external reporting when he is obliged to first report internally, due to the increased risk of subsequent reprisals.[92] Possibly this explains the repeated empirical finding that internal reporting works best for infringements by rank-and-file employees and less so for infringements by those higher in the hierarchy, although they are more likely to be involved.[93] In fact, financial fraud by management has been shown to be the least likely to be reported at all, whether internally or externally.[94] Easy access to external reporting, supported by financial rewards, then seems particularly suited for market abuse.

Requirements

Article 32(3) stipulates that Member States shall require employers who carry out activities that are regulated by financial services regulation to have in place appropriate internal whistle-blowing schemes for their employees.[95] The implementation of this obligation implies a processing of data which must comply with the data protection rules of Directive 95/46/EC. In 2006, the Article 29 Working Party issued an opinion containing guidance as to how these rules apply to internal whistle-blowing programmes, drawing particular attention to the need to protect the reported person, who may otherwise risk being victimized before **B.32.24**

[87] Commission, 'Impact Assessment' (n 19) 120 .

[88] ibid.

[89] See Blount and Markel, 'End of Internal Compliance' (n 10) 1056–7.

[90] Kimberly D Krawiec, 'Cosmetic Compliance and the Failure of Negotiated Governance' (2003) 81 Washington University Law Quarterly 487; Blount and Markel, 'End of Internal Compliance' (n 10) 1044–7.

[91] A B Schoonbeek, 'Een klokkenluidersregeling in het financiële toezicht; point of no return!?' (2014) Tijdschrift voor Compliance 313.

[92] ESMA, 'Technical advice on possible delegated acts concerning the Market Abuse Regulation' (3 February 2015) ESMA/2015/224, 62.

[93] Blount and Markel, 'End of Internal Compliance' (n 10) 1053.

[94] ibid.

[95] The Commission Proposal did not yet contain such a provision (Proposal for a Regulation on insider dealing and market manipulation (market abuse) 2011/0295 (COD), art 29), which was proposed in the parliamentary debates (Amendments 332–401 (11 May 2012) on the proposal for a regulation of the European Parliament and of the Council on insider dealing and market manipulation (market abuse) 2011/0295(COD) 40).

the allegations have even been investigated.[96] Notably, identified (rather than anonymous) reports should be promoted; the reported person is to be informed as soon as practicably possible after the data concerning them are recorded, provided this does not jeopardize the investigation; and the reported person must in principle be enabled to check the accuracy of the registered data (without having access to information about the identity of the whistle-blower).

B.32.25 Whereas the Market Abuse Regulation does not clarify the relationship between internal and external reporting, the preamble of the Implementing Directive notes that, where internal reporting procedures exist, whistle-blowers should still be free whether to use them or to directly go to the competent authority with concerns of violations.[97] Member States that wish to grant monetary rewards for external whistle-blowing without undermining internal compliancy systems, may find inspiration in the SEC rules. These do not require reporting internally first, but attempt to incentivize employees to do so when appropriate[98] in the following ways: (i) to avoid a race to the SEC, the date of (prior) internal reporting will be considered as the date of the external report for determining the reward, provided the difference does not exceed 120 days;[99] (ii) if the company passes on internally reported information to the SEC, the reporting employee will be eligible for a reward as the original source of the information, including the information the employer added to the report, thus increasing the award;[100] and (iii) voluntary participation in internal reporting can increase the amount of an award, while interfering with it can decrease the amount of an award.[101]

---

[96] Article 29 Working Party Opinion 1/2006 on the application of EU data protection rules to internal whistle-blowing schemes in the fields of accounting, internal accounting controls, auditing matters, fight against bribery, banking and financial crime, 6–7. See Article 29 Data Protection Working Party, Comments on possible delegated acts relating to MiFID and Market Abuse Regulation implementing measures (7 July 2015) 7 (referring to its 2006 opinion).

[97] Recital (2) Implementing Directive (EU/2015/2392). See also ESMA, 'Technical advice on possible delegated acts concerning the Market Abuse Regulation' (3 February 2015) ESMA/2015/224, 62 (rejecting a requirement to report internally first).

[98] See SEC, Securities Whistleblower Incentives and Protections, 76 Fed Reg 34300–34301.

[99] SEC Rule 21F-4(b)(7), 17 CFR § 240.21F-4(b)(7).

[100] SEC Rule 21F(4)(b)(5) and Rule 21F-4(c)(3), 17 CFR § 240.21F-4(b)(5) and 17 CFR § 240.21F-4(c)(3).

[101] Rule 21F-6, 17 CFR § 240.21F-6.

Article 33: Exchange of information with ESMA

1. Competent authorities shall provide ESMA annually with aggregated information regarding all administrative sanctions and other administrative measures imposed by the competent authority in accordance with Articles 30, 31 and 32. ESMA shall publish that information in an annual report. Competent authorities shall also provide ESMA annually with anonymised and aggregated data regarding all administrative investigations undertaken in accordance with those Articles.

2. Where Member States have, in accordance with the second subparagraph of Article 30(1), laid down criminal sanctions for the infringements referred to in that Article, their competent authorities shall provide ESMA annually with anonymised and aggregated data regarding all criminal investigations undertaken and criminal penalties imposed by the judicial authorities in accordance with Articles 30, 31 and 32. ESMA shall publish data on criminal sanctions imposed in an annual report.

3. Where the competent authority has disclosed administrative or criminal sanctions or other administrative measures to the public, it shall simultaneously notify ESMA thereof.

4. Where a published administrative or criminal sanction or other administrative measure relates to an investment firm authorised in accordance with Directive 2014/65/EU, ESMA shall add a reference to that published sanction or measure in the register of investment firms established under Article 5(3) of that Directive.

5. In order to ensure uniform conditions of application of this Article, ESMA shall develop draft implementing technical standards to determine the procedures and forms for exchange of information as referred to in this Article.

ESMA shall submit those draft implementing technical standards to the Commission by 3 July 2016.

Power is conferred on the Commission to adopt the implementing technical standards referred to in the first subparagraph in accordance with Article 15 of Regulation (EU) No 1095/2010.

Relevant Technical Standards:

Commission Implementing Regulation (EU) 2017/1158 of 29 June 2017 laying down implementing technical standards with regards to the procedures and forms for competent authorities exchanging information with the European Securities Market Authority as referred to in Article 33 of Regulation (EU) No 596/2014 of the European Parliament and of the Council (OJ L 167 (30 June 2017) 22)

I. General Remarks

Subject matter and principle

B.33.01 With a view to increasing transparency and enhancing ESMA's oversight of the national sanctioning practices, Article 33 contains annual and immediate reporting obligations for national competent authorities with regard to sanctions, measures and investigations imposed in accordance with Articles 30 to 32.[1] First, the national competent authorities must annually provide ESMA with aggregated information regarding administrative and (if applicable) criminal investigations, sanctions, penalties, and other measures. With regard to administrative investigations and criminal penalties and investigations Article 33(1) and (2) explicitly state that these data must be anonymized. The aggregation and anonymization of the data clearly differentiates the obligation under Article 33 from the cooperation duty in concrete investigations, as covered by Article 25. ESMA must publish the aggregated data on administrative and criminal sanctions in an annual report, which will first be the case in its annual report for 2017. This publication is not prescribed for investigations.

B.33.02 Secondly, pursuant to Article 33(3) national competent authorities must notify ESMA whenever they publish administrative or criminal sanctions or other administrative measures. Under the amended (former) Market Abuse Directive (2003/6/EC),[2] ESMA included these notifications in its public sanctions register. Where a published administrative or criminal sanction or other administrative measure relates to an investment firm authorized in accordance with the Markets in Financial Instruments Directive II (2014/65/EU), Article 33(4) prescribes that ESMA add a reference to that published sanction or measure in its register of investment firms. This register thus not only informs the market about authorizations and withdrawals; by including sanctions under the Market Abuse Regulation (and the Markets in Financial Instruments Directive II (2014/65/EU)),[3] it also adds to the naming and shaming effects of the publication of those sanctions.[4]

B.33.03 Article 33(5) finally mandates ESMA to draft implementing technical standards (ITS) to determine the procedures and forms for the exchange of information

[1] See recital (78) Market Abuse Regulation.

[2] See para B.33.04 below.

[3] Article 71(6) Markets Financial Instruments Directive II (2014/65/EU).

[4] With regard to legal questions surrounding this form of naming and shaming see the commentary to art 34.

regarding administrative and criminal investigations, sanctions, penalties and other measures. ESMA submitted these for endorsement to the European Commission on 26 July 2016[5], and on 29 June 2017, the Commission adopted these with minor changes in its Implementing Regulation (2017/1158 /EU).[6]

History and trends

The mandatory delivery of information about investigations, sanctions, and measures to a European supervisory authority is of relatively recent origin. It existed neither in the Insider Dealing Directive (1989/592/EEC) nor in the original (former) Market Abuse Directive (2003/6/EC), but was part of the EU's response to the financial crisis of 2007–2008. As part of a complete overhaul of the European System of Financial Supervision in 2010–2011 upon recommendation by the de Larosière Group, ESMA was established with stronger powers than CESR, its predecessor, in order to enhance investor protection, promote orderly markets, and improve financial stability. Among others, ESMA must play a general coordination role, promote a common supervisory culture, and collect information.[7] In that vein, the Omnibus I Directive (2010/78/EU), which made the necessary changes to EU legal acts in the field of operation of ESMA (and the two other new supervisory authorities), inserted the essence of the above described information exchange obligations for national authorities, at least with regard to administrative measures and sanctions, into the (former) Market Abuse Directive (2003/6/EC).[8] The Omnibus I Directive (2010/78/EU) also introduced a single consolidated register of authorized investment firms in the Union, maintained by ESMA, as well as the obligation for ESMA to include in this register a reference to published sanctions with regard to the investment firms.[9] **B.33.04**

[5] ESMA, 'Final Report: Draft Implementing Technical Standards on sanctions and measures under Regulation (EU) No 596/2014 on market abuse' (26 July 2016) ESMA/2016/1171. Because the draft ITS and the obligations contained therein are addressed to national competent authorities and ESMA only, ESMA did not hold open public consultations on them (ibid 9). Cf recital (15) Omnibus I Directive (2010/78/EU) and art 15 ESMA Regulation (1095/2010/EU).

[6] Commission Implementing Regulation (EU) 2017/1158 of 29 June 2017 laying down implementing technical standards with regards to the procedures and forms for competent authorities exchanging information with the European Securities Market Authority as referred to in Article 33 of Regulation (EU) No 596/2014 of the European Parliament and of the Council (OJ L 167 (30 June 2017) 22).

[7] ESMA Regulation (1095/2010/EU).

[8] Article 14(5) Consolidated Market Abuse Directive (2003/6/EC), as introduced by art 3(4) Omnibus I Directive (2010/78/EU) as a result of an amendment to the Commission proposal (Amendments By Parliament (7 July 2010) P7_TA(2010)0269, art 3). For the (less elaborate) amendment originally proposed in the Committee discussions, see Committee on Economic and Monetary Affairs, Amendments – draft report (19 March 2010) 2009/0161(COD), Amendment 385 and Amendment 58 in the Committee on Economic and Monetary Affairs' Report to the Plenary (18 May 2010) A7-0163/2010.

[9] Article 14(5) Consolidated Market Abuse Directive (2003/6/EC); art 5(3) Markets in Financial Instruments Directive II (2014/65/EU), as originally introduced by art 6 Omnibus I Directive (2010/78/EU). See also recital (29) Omnibus I Directive (2010/78/EU).

B.33.05 Upon its establishment, ESMA was also empowered to draft and propose technical standards to the Commission in the areas specifically set out in the relevant legislation.[10] The goal was to supplant national differences in the application of EU legislation with a single rulebook applicable to all financial market participants in the internal market.[11] ESMA has thereby been given an important role in the legislative process (its large powers vis-à-vis the European Commission stirred some debate),[12] and has produced a broad panoply of technical standards in recent years. The Omnibus I Directive (2010/78/EU) identified a first set of areas in which ESMA may develop draft technical standards, among others with regard to market abuse by amending the (former) Market Abuse Directive (2003/6/EC). The power (and obligation) for ESMA to develop technical standards with regard to reporting of sanctions, however, is new since the Market Abuse Regulation.

II. Implementing Technical Standards

B.33.06 The Implementing Regulation stipulates that the competent authorities and ESMA must designate contact points specifically for communications relating to the submission of information under Article 33.[13] If not physical persons, these may be mailboxes or other means that ensure effective reception.[14] The Implementing Regulation also includes in its annexes specific forms that competent authorities must use for reporting the information, so as to enable ESMA to correctly register the data and to include meaningful information in its annual report.[15] These forms are to be completed and submitted electronically. For the immediate reporting of published sanctions and measures, ESMA must provide an information technology system and database.[16]

B.33.07 In their annual submissions, competent authorities must for administrative and criminal sanctions and measures separately, provide ESMA with the number of decided, published and under appeal measures; the number of measures imposed on natural persons and on legal persons; the number of each type of sanctions and of settlements, broken down by the type of infringements. With regard to administrative and criminal investigations, the report must specify for each the total number of cases, the number of opened cases and the number of closed cases, as well as the number of cases that resulted in the initiation of administrative

[10] Article 15 ESMA Regulation (1095/2010/EU).

[11] See recital (22) ESMA Regulation (1095/2010/EU).

[12] See Pierre Schammo, 'The European Securities and Markets Authority: Lifting the Veil on the Allocation of Powers' (2011) 48 Common Market Law Review 1882.

[13] Article 2(1) Implementing Regulation (n 6).

[14] ESMA, Final Report (n 5) 4.

[15] Articles 3 and 4 and recital (3) Implementing Regulation (n 6).

[16] ibid art 4.

enforcement proceedings (including settlement), the number of referrals to criminal authorities, the number of cases that led to other actions (eg prohibitions) and the number of cases that were closed without further action.[17] The numbers should reflect the actual investigatory work carried out by the national authorities in a given year, by including only cases in which the authorities have effectively been active during that year.[18]

[17] ibid Annex I. See also recital (78) Market Abuse Regulation.

[18] Recital (4) Implementing Regulation (n 6).

Article 34: Publication of decisions

1. Subject to the third subparagraph, competent authorities shall publish any decision imposing an administrative sanction or other administrative measure in relation to an infringement of this Regulation on their website immediately after the person subject to that decision has been informed of that decision. Such publication shall include at least information on the type and nature of the infringement and the identity of the person subject to the decision.

The first subparagraph does not apply to decisions imposing measures that are of an investigatory nature.

Where a competent authority considers that the publication of the identity of the legal person subject to the decision, or of the personal data of a natural person, would be disproportionate following a case-by-case assessment conducted on the proportionality of the publication of such data, or where such publication would jeopardise an ongoing investigation or the stability of the financial markets, it shall do any of the following:

(a) defer publication of the decision until the reasons for that deferral cease to exist;
(b) publish the decision on an anonymous basis in accordance with national law where such publication ensures the effective protection of the personal data concerned;
(c) not publish the decision in the event that the competent authority is of the opinion that publication in accordance with point (a) or (b) will be insufficient to ensure:
   (i) that the stability of financial markets is not jeopardised; or
   (ii) the proportionality of the publication of such decisions with regard to measures which are deemed to be of a minor nature.

Where a competent authority takes a decision to publish a decision on an anonymous basis as referred to in point (b) of the third subparagraph, it may postpone the publication of the relevant data for a reasonable period of time where it is foreseeable that the reasons for anonymous publication will cease to exist during that period.

2. Where the decision is subject to an appeal before a national judicial, administrative or other authority, competent authorities shall also publish immediately on their website such information and any subsequent information on the outcome of such an appeal. Moreover, any decision annulling a decision subject to appeal shall also be published.
3. Competent authorities shall ensure that any decision that is published in accordance with this Article shall remain accessible on their website for a

period of at least five years after its publication. Personal data contained in such publications shall be kept on the website of the competent authority for the period which is necessary in accordance with the applicable data protection rules.

I. General Remarks

Subject matter and principle

Mandatory publication of administrative measures

Article 34 in principle requires competent authorities to publish their decisions on administrative sanctions or other administrative measures in relation to an infringement of the Market Abuse Regulation. It prescribes neither publication of decisions imposing measures that are of an investigatory nature, nor publication of criminal sanctions.[1] The minimum content of such publication consists of the type and nature of the infringement, as well as the identity of the person subject to the decision. **B.34.01**

With regard to the form of publication, Article 34 merely states that this publication must be made on the website of the competent authorities. It would be good practice for the competent authorities to publish the decisions on a dedicated section of their website, and to include a translation or summary in a commonly understood language when the original decision is not drafted in such a language. This would be in line with recommendations made by the European Banking Authority in the context of administrative sanctions imposed by national competent authorities under the Capital Requirements Directive (CRD IV) (2013/36/EU).[2] **B.34.02**

The decisions of the competent authority must be published immediately, without awaiting their taking legal effect. Article 34(2) stipulates in that regard that where the decision is subject to an appeal before a national judicial, administrative, or **B.34.03**

[1] In its Report of 26 April 2012 on the Actual Use of Sanctioning Powers under MAD (ESMA/2012/270, 133) ESMA advocated that competent authorities should be permitted to publish investigations.

[2] EBA, 'Report on the publication of administrative penalties on an anonymous basis' EBA/Op/2015/18, 3–4.

other authority, this fact, as well as any subsequent information on the outcome of such an appeal (including an annulment of the original decision) must be published as well. Furthermore, Article 34(3) sets out a minimum period of five years during which the decision must remain accessible on the website of the competent authority.

Exceptions and mitigations

B.34.04 Article 34(1) mitigates the above described obligation where the publication of the identity of the legal person subject to the decision, or of the personal data of a natural person, would be disproportionate in the concrete case, or where such publication would jeopardize an ongoing investigation or the stability of the financial markets. In those cases, the competent authority can defer the publication for as long as the above conditions are fulfilled or anonymize it in accordance with national law. If it is foreseeable that the grounds for an anonymous publication will cease to exist after a certain time, the competent authority may postpone 'the publication of the relevant data'. One could interpret this as a postponement of the identity of the subject of the decision, but, in the same context, the Capital Requirements Directive (CRD IV) (2013/36/EU) more clearly allowed postponement of the entire publication.[3] If postponement and/or anonymization would be insufficient to safeguard the stability of the financial markets or the proportionality of the publication of decisions on measures of a minor nature, the competent authority may decide to abstain from publication altogether.

History and trends

B.34.05 The introduction of mandatory publication of sanctions in the European rules on market abuse fits in the general post-crisis movement in financial regulation towards tougher enforcement (which has also been described in the chapter on public enforcement). The Insider Dealing Directive (1989/592/EEC) did not make any mention of publication of sanctions. At the time, such disclosures were largely confined to other areas of law, such as environmental regulation, or to other jurisdictions, such as the United States.[4] The Financial Services Action Plan measures introduced publication of sanctions in European capital markets law on an optional basis.[5] The (former) Market Abuse Directive (2003/6/EC) required Member States to allow competent authorities to disclose their sanctions and measures to the public if doing so would not seriously jeopardize the financial markets or cause disproportionate damage to the parties involved.[6] Similar

[3] Article 68 Capital Requirement Directive (CRD IV) (2013/36/EU).

[4] See eg Securities Exchange Act s 15(b)(4) (authorizing the SEC to censure brokers and dealers).

[5] Niamh Moloney, *EU Securities and Financial Markets Regulation* (Oxford University Press 2014) 967.

[6] Art 14(4) (former) Market Abuse Directive (2003/6/EC) ('Member States shall provide that the competent authority may disclose to the public every measure or sanction that will be imposed for infringement of the provisions adopted in the implementation of this Directive, unless such

provisions could be found in the Markets in Financial Instruments Directive I (2004/39/EC), the Prospectus Directive, the original Transparency Directive (2004/109/EC), and the UCITS IV Directive.[7] Nonetheless, not all national authorities made much use of this discretionary power.[8]

The financial crisis prompted regulators to toughen the enforcement of financial law. To that end, the European Commission issued a communication in which it expressed its belief that competent authorities should, as a rule, be obliged to publicly disclose their sanctions,[9] an approach that was subsequently endorsed by ESMA in the context of market abuse.[10] The Market Abuse Regulation proposal was the first post-crisis reform with a noticeably stronger and more prescriptive sanctioning regime, including the publication of sanctions.[11] The latter has been a major point of discussion in the trialogues leading up to the Market Abuse Regulation. While in some Member States this measure was highly controversial, others considered it indispensable for information and deterrence purposes.[12] In fact, by 2012, slightly more than half of the Member States already had some form of mandatory publication of sanctions for market abuse.[13] Publication of sanctions has since become a standard requirement in European financial law reforms, appearing in the Transparency Directive (2013/50/EU),[14] the Capital Requirements Directive (CRD IV) (2013/36/EU),[15] the PRIIPs Regulation (2014/ **B.34.06**

disclosure would seriously jeopardise the financial markets or cause disproportionate damage to the parties involved').

[7] Article 51(3) Directive 2004/39/EC on markets in financial instruments amending Council Directives 85/611/EEC and 93/6/EEC and Directive 2000/12/EC of the European Parliament and of the Council and repealing Council Directive 93/22/EEC [2004] OJ L145/1; art 25(2) Directive 2003/71/EC on the prospectus to be published when securities are offered to the public or admitted to trading and amending Directive 2001/34/EC [2003] OJ L345/64; art 28(2) Directive 2004/109/EC on the harmonisation of transparency requirements in relation to information about issuers whose securities are admitted to trading on a regulated market and amending Directive 2001/34/EC [2004] OJ L 390/38; art 99(3) Directive 2009/65/EC on the coordination of laws, regulations and administrative provisions relating to undertakings for collective investment in transferable securities (UCITS) [2009] OJ L 302/32.

[8] See eg for Germany: Rüdiger Veil, 'Sanktionsrisiken für Emittenten und Geschäftsleiter im Kapitalmarktrecht' [2016] ZGR 305, 318.

[9] Commission Communication, 'Reinforcing sanctioning regimes in the financial services sector' (8 December 2010) COM(2010) 716 final 12.

[10] ESMA, Report of 26 April 2012, 'Actual Use of Sanctioning Powers under MAD' ESMA/ 2012/270, 133. Its predecessor, CESR, had already described naming and shaming as an important measure (CESR, An evaluation of equivalence of supervisory powers in the EU under the Market Abuse Directive and the Prospectus Directive, 07-334, June 2007, 9).

[11] Niamh Moloney, *EU Securities and Financial Markets Regulation* (Oxford University Press 2014) 967. The Commission Proposal for a Market Abuse Regulation was relatively concise with regard to publication of sanctions (art 26(3) Proposal for a Regulation on insider dealing and market manipulation (market abuse) 2011/0295 (COD)).

[12] Presidency Progress Report on the Market Abuse Regulation, 2011/0295 (COD) (21 June 2012) 4.

[13] ESMA Report of 26 April 2012, 'Actual Use of Sanctioning Powers under MAD' ESMA/ 2012/270, 134–1.

[14] Article 29 Transparency Directive (2013/50/EU).

[15] Article 68 Capital Requirements Directive (CRD IV) (2013/36/EU).

1286/EU),[16] UCITS V (2014/91/EU),[17] the Markets in Financial Instruments Directive II (2014/65/EU),[18] the Securities Financing Transaction Regulation (2015/2365/EU),[19] the Insurance Distribution Directive (2016/97/EU),[20] and the Prospectus Regulation (2017/1129/EU).[21]

II. Sanction or Preventive Measure

Legal nature

B.34.07 The legal nature of the publication of sanctions can be twofold. In positive terms, the publication of administrative sanctions is a form of disclosure by the competent authority, which makes its enforcement practice more transparent and thus also enhances its own accountability. It also demonstrates to the public that offences are effectively detected and punished and thus contributes to general prevention, to the legitimacy of the supervising authority, and to investor confidence.[22] Finally, the theory of responsive regulation emphasizes the role publication of sanctions plays in constituting consciences and strengthening the community's shared values ('moral education').[23] When the publication of administrative sanctions includes the name of offenders, however, it is typically referred to as 'naming and shaming'. Such a publication may be considered as a sanction rather than as mere disclosure, as the ensuing reputational damage is often more severe than the underlying pecuniary sanction.[24]

B.34.08 The Commission used the term naming and shaming in its impact assessment for the Market Abuse Regulation[25] and explicitly mentioned the effects of naming and shaming in terms of reputational damage and further punishment by the market's avoiding the use of the offender's services in its impact assessment for the Capital Requirements Directive (CRD IV) (2013/36/EU).[26] As part of the

---

16 Article 29 PRIIPs Regulation (2014/1286/EU).

17 Article 1(17) UCITS V (2014/91/EU), inserting art 99b(1) into the UCITS Directive.

18 Article 71 Markets in Financial Instruments Directive II (2014/65/EU).

19 Article 26 Securities Financing Transaction Regulation (2015/2365/EU).

20 Article 32 Insurance Distribution Directive (2016/97/EU).

21 Article 42 Prospectus Regulation (2017/1129/EU).

22 See Judith van Erp, 'Naming and Shaming of Corporate Offenders' in *Encyclopedia of Criminology and Criminal Justice* (Springer 2014) 3210.

23 Ian Ayres and John Braithwaite, *Responsive Regulation: Transcending the Deregulation Debate* (Oxford University Press 1992).

24 See para B.34.11 below.

25 Commission, 'Staff Working Paper: Impact Assessment' SEC(2011) 1217 final 54.

26 Commission staff working paper, impact assessment accompanying the document proposal for a Directive of the European Parliament and the Council on the access to the activity of credit institutions and the prudential supervision of credit institutions and investment firms and amending Directive 2002/87/EC of the European Parliament and of the Council on the supplementary supervision of credit institutions, insurance undertakings and investment firms in a financial conglomerate, SEC(2011) 952 final (20 July 2011) 13.

compromise between radically different Member States' views on naming and shaming,[27] however, the Market Abuse Regulation frames publication of sanctions as an informational rather than a punitive measure.[28] The Market Abuse Regulation justifies the publication obligation in its preamble with reference to its dissuasive effect on the public and heralded it as 'an important tool for competent authorities to inform market participants of what behaviour is considered to be an infringement of this Regulation and to promote good behaviour amongst market participants'.[29] Hence the possibility to anonymize the published decision.[30] Also, in the structure of the Market Abuse Regulation, the publication of sanctions is not included in, or does not immediately follow, the list of possible sanctions and measures. Instead, it is dealt with separately in Article 34, which comes after a provision on the exchange of information, which is in unison with the transparency perspective on publication of sanctions. In the same vein, whether or not a sanction is published is not a factor competent authorities must take into account in setting the type and level of sanctions according to Article 31. Such a possibility would nevertheless come close to the UK regime, where the FCA may decide to limit its sanctions to a statement that a person has committed market abuse.[31]

Irrespective of the formulation of the Market Abuse Regulation, the nominative publication of sanctions for infringements that are not yet known to the public may in practice operate as a sanction. To what extent it does so and whether it constitutes a criminal punishment in the meaning of Article 6 of the European Convention on Human Rights (ECHR), will be discussed in paras B.34.10 et seq and B.34.14 respectively. **B.34.09**

Effectiveness as a sanction

As the Commission noted in its Impact Assessment, naming and shaming is a low-cost measure.[32] Unlike imprisonment, publishing sanctions hardly costs the state anything. This is true even when it operates as a sanction, because it does so indirectly. It is not the state, but the offender's community (its investors and customers, the financial press etc) that carries out the punishment.[33] **B.34.10**

Several empirical studies have revealed that naming and shaming is a highly effective sanction, with reputational penalties causing a loss that amounts to over **B.34.11**

[27] See para B.34.06 above.

[28] Presidency Progress Report on the Market Abuse Regulation, 2011/0295 (COD) (21 June 2012) 4. See also Commission Communication, Reinforcing sanctioning regimes in the financial services sector (8 December 2010) COM(2010) 716 final 7, 12.

[29] Recital (73) Market Abuse Regulation.

[30] See para B.34.04 above.

[31] Barry Rider and others, *Market Abuse and Insider Dealing* (3rd edn, Bloomsbury Publishing 2016) 305–6.

[32] Commission, 'Impact Assessment' (n 25) 170.

[33] David A Skeel, 'Shaming in Corporate Law' (2001) 149 University of Pennsylvania Law Review 1811, 1816.

7.5 or almost nine times the sum of the traditional penalties.[34] For that reason, some authors warn that naming and shaming might work too well as a sanction and result in overdeterrence.[35] Moreover, because the sanction is carried out by the public on a voluntary basis, the degree of punishment is unpredictable and risks getting out of hand.[36]

B.34.12 A large body of empirical studies indicates that the effects of naming and shaming are profoundly different depending on the type of misconduct it aims to curb. The publication of corporate misconduct that inflicts harm upon customers, suppliers and/or investors—so-called related-party (or second party) crimes—triggers a negative stock price reaction that reflects large reputational damage. However, for third-party crimes, where the injured parties do not trade with the firm (eg in the case of breach of environmental regulations), the reputational loss from naming and shaming is negligible.[37] Insider trading will often constitute a third-party crime, since it only affects a few anonymous investors, in which case the publication of sanctions causes little or no harm to the offender.

B.34.13 The above differences were found in studies of infringements by corporate enterprises and do not seem relevant for flesh-and-blood individuals, who have a professional reputation to uphold with a view to their career and personal relationships. A better predictor of the effectiveness of naming and shaming for an individual's misconduct is probably whether the offender is part of a closely-knit community with frequent interaction and shared values.[38] Corporate directors will thus be more likely to suffer reputational damage than someone accidentally overhearing a conversation containing inside information outside the work context. In the case of corporate enterprises, the cohesive community is likely to exist in the form of media coverage and professionals with whom they deal.[39]

---

[34] John Armour, Colin Mayer, and Andrea Polo, 'Regulatory Sanctions and Reputational Damage in Financial Markets' (2016) 22 Journal of Financial and Quantitative Analysis 1385; Jonathan M Karpoff, D Scott Lee, and Gerald S Martin, 'The Cost to Firms of Cooking the Books' (2008) 43 Journal of Financial and Quantitative Analysis 581.

[35] Michal G Faure and Claire Leger, 'The Directive on Criminal Sanctions for Market Abuse: A Move Towards Harmonizing Insider Trading Criminal Law at the EU Level?' (2014–2015) 9 Brooklyn Journal of Corporate, Financial & Commercial Law 387.

[36] Nikolaos A Vervessos, 'Das naming und shaming als Sanktion gegen kapitalmarktrechtliches Fehlverhalten' in Klaus J Hopt and Dimitris Tzouganatos (eds), *Das Europäische Wirtschaftsrecht vor neuen Herausforderungen* (Mohr Siebeck 2014) 168.

[37] Cindy R Alexander, 'On the Nature of the Reputational Penalty for Corporate Crime: Evidence' (1999) 42 Journal of Law and Economics 489; Armour, Mayer, and Polo, 'Regulatory Sanctions and Reputational Damage in Financial Markets' (n 34); Deborah L Murphy, Ronald E Shrieves, and Samuel L Tibbs, 'Understanding the Penalties Associated with Corporate Misconduct: An Empirical Examination of Earnings and Risk' (2009) 44 Journal of Financial and Quantitative Analysis 55. See also Jonathan M Karpoff, John R Lott, and Eric W Wehrly, 'The Reputation Penalties for Environmental Violations: Empirical Evidence' (2005) 48 Journal of Law and Economics 653.

[38] See Skeel, 'Shaming in Corporate Law' (n 33) 1811.

[39] Vervessos, 'Das naming und shaming als Sanktion gegen kapitalmarktrechtliches Fehlverhalten' (n 36) 167.

III. Fair Trial and Data Protection

Presumption of innocence

Unlike the Capital Requirements Directive (CRD IV) (2013/36/EU), the PRIIPs Regulation (2014/1286/EU), UCITS V (2014/91/EU), and the Insurance Distribution Directive,[40] but like the Transparency Directive, the Markets in Financial Instruments Directive II (2014/65/EU), the Securities Financing Transaction Regulation (2015/2365/EU), and the Prospectus Regulation (2017/1129/EU),[41] the Market Abuse Regulation does not limit the publication obligation to decisions 'against which there is no appeal'. Instead, Article 34(2) requires competent authorities to include in the publication a notice that the decision is subject to an appeal and to publish information on the outcome of the appeal.[42] This begs the question of the compatibility of a duty to publish sanctions before they are final with the right to a fair trial and in particular the presumption of innocence with regard to criminal charges, which are enshrined in Articles 47 and 48 of the Charter of Fundamental Rights of the European Union (CFR) and Article 6 of the ECHR.[43] These rights must be observed for administrative penalties for market abuse as well, because under the Engel criteria of the European Court of Human Rights (ECtHR), and in particular the criterion of the severity of the actual and potential penalty,[44] they will normally qualify as criminal sanctions in the meaning of the ECHR.[45] **B.34.14**

In *Janosevic v Sweden*, the ECtHR denied that the presumption of innocence would systematically exclude enforcement measures being taken before a final court decision. Such early enforcement, especially if pursued before any court **B.34.15**

---

[40] Article 68 Capital Requirements Directive (CRD IV) (2013/36/EU); art 29 PRIIPs Regulation (2014/1286/EU); art 99b(1) UCITS V (2014/91/EU); art 32 Insurance Distribution Directive (2016/97/EU).

[41] Article 29 Transparency Directive (2013/50/EU); Markets in Financial Instruments Directive II (2014/65/EU); art 26 Securities Financing Transaction Regulation (2015/2365/EU); art 42 Prospectus Regulation (2017/1129/EU).

[42] A few Member States, such as Italy and Austria, provided for publication of non-definitive sanctions under the (former) Market Abuse Directive (2003/6/EC), and have been criticized for doing so. See Susanne Kalss and Janine Oelkers, 'Öffentliche Bekanntgabe: ein wirksames Aufsichtsinstrument im Kapitalmarktrecht?' (2009) Österreichisches BankArchiv 123.

[43] Pursuant to art 6 TEU, the CFR is legally binding on EU institutions and national governments. Article 52(3) CFR refers to the meaning and scope of the ECHR for rights which correspond to rights guaranteed by the ECHR, such as the presumption of innocence. Recital (77) affirms that the Market Abuse Regulation is to be interpreted and applied in accordance with the rights and principles of the CFR.

[44] ECtHR, *Engel and Others v Netherlands*, Application nos 5100/71, 5101/71, 5102/71, 5354/72, 5370/72 (8 June 1976) paras 82–83.

[45] Recently, the ECtHR did indeed qualify administrative fines for market abuse (under the old regime, but in the range of those mentioned in the Market Abuse Regulation) as criminal sanctions in the sense of the ECHR (ECtHR, *Grande Stevens and Others v Italy*, Application nos 18640/10, 18647/10, 18668/10 and 18698/10, 4 March 2014).

assessment, requires states to strike a fair balance between the various interests at stake.[46] From this perspective, publication of sanctions before the final judgment would be permissible if it passes a proportionality test. In its Impact Assessment for the Market Abuse Regulation, the Commission carried out such a test in general terms and also specifically with regard to minimum rules for administrative measures and sanctions,[47] but it did not do so for the publication of sanctions.[48] Article 34 leaves room for the competent authorities to carry out their own proportionality test. How they should do this, remains debatable. An important factor in the ECtHR's reasoning in *Janosevic v Sweden* was that Swedish law provided for the possibility, in the event of a successful appeal, of reimbursement of the fines paid in enforcement proceedings. The reputational damage engendered by a publication of a sanction, in contrast, is virtually irreversible. Competent authorities should therefore carefully assess in every case if the publication of a non-definitive decision would cause significant harm.

Data protection and privacy

B.34.16 The obligation for competent authorities to publish their decisions also triggers questions from a data protection perspective. The Court of Justice qualified the mandatory publication of administrative decisions including the identity of the persons subject to it as a processing of personal data that are protected by Articles 7 and 8 of the CFR. Derogations are permissible only if and to the extent that they are strictly necessary, which requires a clear goal and a proportionate measure.[49] After the European Data Protection Supervisor had raised concerns both with regard to the purpose of the publication obligation and the assessment of proportionality,[50] the draft Market Abuse Regulation was amended in order to provide for a case-by-case assessment of the proportionality exception.

B.34.17 The European Data Protection Supervisor had also alerted the Commission that the Market Abuse Regulation proposal should safeguard both the right of the person subject to the decision to challenge a decision before a court and the presumption of innocence. It considered that this could be achieved by delaying the publication or by indicating that the decision can still be appealed and that, until the decision becomes final, the subject of the decision must be presumed innocent and publishing a rectification if the decision is annulled by a court.[51] Article

[46] ECtHR, *Janosevic v Sweden*, Application nos 34619/97 (23 July 2002).
[47] Commission, 'Impact Assessment' (n 25) 36, 162–3.
[48] Commission, 'Impact Assessment' (n 25) 169–70.
[49] ECJ, Joined Cases C-92/09 and C-93/09 *Schecke*, paras 56–64.
[50] Opinion of the European Data Protection Supervisor on the Commission proposals for a Regulation of the European Parliament and of the Council on insider dealing and market manipulation, and for a Directive of the European Parliament and of the Council on criminal sanctions for insider dealing and market manipulation [2012] OJ C177/7–8.
[51] ibid C-177/8–9.

34(2) follows the latter option, save for the mention of the presumption of innocence. After the enactment of the Market Abuse Regulation, however, Article 29 of the Data Protection Working Party advised the Commission that, generally, only the publication of sanctions that are definitive because they no longer can be legally appealed passes the proportionality test.[52] This should be another reason for competent authorities to carefully consider, for every single case, the effective impact of a publication of a non-definitive decision (cf para B.34.14).

The European Data Protection Supervisor also voiced concerns about the time period during which the information on administrative sanctions would remain accessible.[53] Article 34(3) partially solves this problem with a reference to applicable data protection rules. However, the Article 29 Data Protection Working Party suggested that the implementing acts include a maximum data retention period and made a case for setting up a monitoring mechanism to guarantee that publications do not remain in place for longer than necessary.[54] **B.34.18**

[52] Article 29 Data Protection Working Party, Comments on possible delegated acts relating to MiFID and Market Abuse Regulation implementing measures (7 July 2015) 6 (this remark was made with regard to the MiFID proposal, which used similar wording to the Commission Proposal (n 11)).

[53] Opinion of the European Data Protection Supervisor on the Commission proposals for a Regulation of the European Parliament and of the Council on insider dealing and market manipulation, and for a Directive of the European Parliament and of the Council on criminal sanctions for insider dealing and market manipulation [2012] OJ C177/9.

[54] Article 29 Data Protection Working Party, Comments on possible delegated acts relating to MiFID and Market Abuse Regulation implementing measures (7 July 2015) 7.

6

DELEGATED ACTS AND IMPLEMENTING ACTS

Article 35: Exercise of the delegation

1. The power to adopt delegated acts is conferred on the Commission subject to the conditions laid down in this Article.
2. The power to adopt delegated acts referred to in Article 6(5) and (6), Article 12(5), the third subparagraph of Article 17(2), Article 17(3), and Article 19(13) and (14) shall be conferred on the Commission for an indeterminate period of time from 2 July 2014.
3. The delegation of power referred to in Article 6(5) and (6), Article 12(5), the third subparagraph of Article 17(2), Article 17(3), Article 19(13) and (14), and Article 38 may be revoked at any time by the European Parliament or by the Council. A decision of revocation shall put an end to the delegation of the power specified in that decision. It shall take effect the day following the publication of the decision in the *Official Journal of the European Union* or at a later date specified therein. It shall not affect the validity of any delegated acts already in force.
4. As soon as it adopts a delegated act, the Commission shall notify it simultaneously to the European Parliament and to the Council.
5. A delegated act adopted pursuant to Article 6(5) or (6), Article 12(5), the third subparagraph of Article 17(2), Article 17(3), Article 19(13) or (14), or Article 38 shall enter into force only if no objection has been expressed either by the European Parliament or the Council within a period of three months of notification of that act to the European Parliament and the Council or, if, before the expiry of that period, the European Parliament and the Council have both informed the Commission that they will not object. That period shall be extended by three months at the initiative of the European Parliament or the Council.

B.35.01 Article 35 sets out the power for the Commission to adopt delegated acts. The power to adopt delegated acts is conferred on the Commission for an indeterminate period of time (Article 35(2)) but may be revoked by the European Parliament or the Council (Article 35(3)). As soon as the Commission adopts a delegated act it shall notify the European Parliament and the Council (Article 35(4)). A delegated act enters into force only if no objection has been expressed by the European Parliament and the Council within a period of three months of notification of that act (Article 35(5)). So far, the Commission has adopted the following regulations:

- Commission Implementing Regulation (EU) 2016/378 of 11 March 2016 laying down implementing technical standards with regard to the timing, format, and template of the submission of notifications to competent authorities according to Regulation (EU) No 596/2014 of the European Parliament and of the Council (OJ L 72 (17 March 2016) 1)[1].
- Commission Delegated Regulation (EU) 2016/522 of 17 December 2015 supplementing Regulation (EU) No 596/2014 of the European Parliament and of the Council as regards an exemption for certain third countries public bodies and central banks, the indicators of market manipulation, the disclosure thresholds, the competent authority for notifications of delays, the permission for trading during closed periods and types of notifiable managers' transactions (OJ L 88 (5 April 2016) 1)[2].
- Commission Implementing Directive (EU) 2015/2392 of 17 December 2015 on Regulation (EU) No 596/2014 of the European Parliament and of the Council as regards reporting to competent authorities of actual or potential infringements of that Regulation (OJ L 332 (18 December 2015) 126).
- Commission Delegated Regulation (EU) 2016/523 of 10 March 2016 laying down implementing technical standards with regard to the format and template for notification and public disclosure of managers' transactions in accordance with Regulation (EU) No 596/2014 of the European Parliament and of the Council (OJ L 88 (5 April 2016) 19).[3]
- Commission Delegated Regulation (EU) 2016/908 of 26 February 2016 supplementing Regulation (EU) No 596/2014 of the European Parliament and of the Council laying down regulatory technical standards on the criteria, the procedure and the requirements for establishing an accepted market practice and the requirements for maintaining it, terminating it or modifying the conditions for its acceptance (OJ L 153 (10 June 2016) 3).[4]

[1] For further details see art 4 n 8 ff.
[2] See art 6 nn 7–8, art 12, art 17, and art 19.
[3] See art 19.
[4] See art 13.

- Commission Delegated Regulation (EU) 2016/909 of 1 March 2016 supplementing Regulation (EU) No 596/2014 of the European Parliament and of the Council with regard to regulatory technical standards for the content of notifications to be submitted to competent authorities and the compilation, publication and maintenance of the list of notifications (OJ L 153 (10 June 2016) 13)[5].
- Commission Delegated Regulation (EU) 2016/957 of 9 March 2016 supplementing Regulation (EU) No 596/2014 of the European Parliament and of the Council with regard to regulatory technical standards for the appropriate arrangements, systems and procedures as well as notification templates to be used for preventing, detecting and reporting abusive practices or suspicious orders or transactions (OJ L 160 (17 June 2016) 1).[6]
- Commission Delegated Regulation (EU) 2016/958 of 9 March 2016 supplementing Regulation (EU) No 596/2014 of the European Parliament and of the Council with regard to regulatory technical standards for the technical arrangements for objective presentation of investment recommendations or other information recommending or suggesting an investment strategy and for disclosure of particular interests or indications of conflicts of interest (OJ L 160 (17 June 2016) 15).[7]
- Commission Delegated Regulation (EU) 2016/959 of 17 May 2016 laying down implementing technical standards for market soundings with regard to the systems and notification templates to be used by disclosing market participants and the format of the records in accordance with Regulation (EU) No 596/2014 of the European Parliament and of the Council (OJ L 160 (17 June 2016) 23)[8].
- Commission Delegated Regulation (EU) No 2016/1052 of 8 March 2016 supplementing Regulation (EU) No 596/2014 of the European Parliament and of the Council with regard to regulatory technical standards for the conditions applicable to buy-back programmes and stabilization measures (OJ L 173 (30 June 2016) 34).[9]
- Commission Delegated Regulation (EU) 2016/1055 of 29 June 2016 laying down implementing technical standards with regard to the technical means for appropriate public disclosure of inside information and for delaying the public disclosure of inside information in accordance with Regulation (EU) No 596/2014 of the European Parliament and of the Council (OJ L 173 (30 June 2016) 47).[10]

---

[5] See art 4 n 8 f.
[6] See art 16.
[7] See art 20.
[8] See art 11.
[9] See art 5 n 45.
[10] See art 17.

Article 36: Committee procedure

1. **The Commission shall be assisted by the European Securities Committee established by Commission Decision 2001/528/EC(1). That committee shall be a committee within the meaning of Regulation (EU) No 182/2011.**
2. **Where reference is made to this paragraph, Article 5 of Regulation (EU) No 182/2011 shall apply.**

B.36.01 Article 36 sets out the framework for the assistance for the Commission by the European Securities Committee[2] being established in 2001.

[1] Commission Decision 2001/528/EC of 6 June 2001 establishing the European Securities Committee (OJ L 191 (13 July 2001) 45).

[2] See http://ec.europa.eu/info/business-economy-euro/banking-and-finance/financial-reforms-and-their-progress/regulatory-process-financial-services/expert-groups-comitology-and-other-committees/european-securities-committee_en for further details.

7

FINAL PROVISIONS

Article 37: Repeal of Directive 2003/6/EC and its implementing measures

Directive 2003/6/EC and Commission Directives 2004/72/EC, 2003/125/EC([1]) and 2003/124/EC([2]) and Commission Regulation (EC) No 2273/2003([3]) shall be repealed with effect from 3 July 2016. References to Directive 2003/6/EC shall be construed as references to this Regulation and shall be read in accordance with the correlation table set out in Annex II to this Regulation.

Article 37(1) repeals the (former) Market Abuse Directive (2003/6/EC) and the three Commission directives for its implementation. Also, the Buy-back Programmes and Stabilisation Regulation 2273/2003/EC is repealed by Article 37(1). In contrast to the (former) Market Abuse Directive (2003/6/EC), the safe harbour for buy-back-programmes and stabilization measures is not governed by a separate regulation but integrated into the Market Abuse Regulation in Article 5 (see Article 5 for further details). Pursuant to Article 37(2), all references to the (former) Market Abuse Directive (2003/6/EC) shall be construed with reference to the Market Abuse Regulation, in accordance with its Annex II. **B.37.01**

[1] Commission Directive 2003/125/EC of 22 December 2003 implementing Directive 2003/6/EC of the European Parliament and of the Council as regards the fair presentation of investment recommendations and the disclosure of conflicts of interest (OJ L 339 (24 December 2003) 73).

[2] Commission Directive 2003/124/EC of 22 December 2003 implementing Directive 2003/6/EC of the European Parliament and of the Council as regards the definition and public disclosure of inside information and the definition of market manipulation (OJ L 339 (24 December 2003) 70).

[3] Commission Regulation (EC) No 2273/2003 of 22 December 2003 implementing Directive 2003/6/EC of the European Parliament and of the Council as regards exemptions for buy-back programmes and stabilisation of financial instruments (OJ L 336 (23 December 2003) 33).

Article 38: Report

By 3 July 2019, the Commission shall submit a report to the European Parliament and to the Council on the application of this Regulation, together with a legislative proposal to amend it if appropriate. That report shall assess, inter alia:

(a) **the appropriateness of introducing common rules on the need for all Member States to provide for administrative sanctions for insider dealing and market manipulation;**
(b) **whether the definition of inside information is sufficient to cover all information relevant for competent authorities to effectively combat market abuse;**
(c) **the appropriateness of the conditions under which the prohibition on trading is mandated in accordance with Article 19(11) with a view to identifying whether there are any further circumstances under which the prohibition should apply;**
(d) **the possibility of establishing a Union framework for cross-market order book surveillance in relation to market abuse, including recommendations for such a framework; and**
(e) **the scope of the application of the benchmark provisions.**

For the purposes of point (a) of the first subparagraph, ESMA shall undertake a mapping exercise of the application of administrative sanctions and, where Member States have decided, pursuant to the second subparagraph of Article 30(1), to lay down criminal sanctions as referred to therein for infringements of this Regulation, of the application of such criminal sanctions within Member States. That exercise shall also include any data made available under Article 33(1) and (2).

By 3 July 2019, the Commission shall, after consulting ESMA, submit a report to the European Parliament and to the Council on the level of the thresholds set out in Article 19(1a)(a) and (b) in relation to managers' transactions where the issuer's shares or debt instruments form part of a collective investment undertaking or provide exposure to a portfolio of assets, with a view to assessing whether that level is appropriate or should be adjusted.

The Commission shall be empowered to adopt delegated acts in accordance with Article 35 adjusting the thresholds in Article 19(1a)(a) and (b), if it determines in that report that those thresholds should be adjusted.

B.38.01 Article 38 establishes the obligation for the Commission to submit a report to the European Parliament and to the Council on the application of the Market Abuse Regulation, which must be fulfilled by 3 July 2019. Article 38(a) to (e) sets out the topics that must be addressed in the report.

Article 39: Entry into force and application

1. This Regulation shall enter into force on the twentieth day following that of its publication in the *Official Journal of the European Union*.
2. It shall apply from 3 July 2016 except for:
(a) Article 4(2) and (3), which shall apply from 3 January 2018; and
(b) Article 4(4) and (5), Article 5(6), Article 6(5) and (6), Article 7(5), Article 11(9), (10), and (11), Article 12(5), Article 13(7) and (11), Article 16(5), the third subparagraph of Article 17(2), Article 17(3), (10), and (11), Article 18(9), Article 19(13), (14), and (15), Article 20(3), Article 24(3), Article 25(9), the second, third, and fourth subparagraphs of Article 26(2), Article 32(5), and Article 33(5), which shall apply from 2 July 2014.
3. Member States shall take the necessary measures to comply with Articles 22, 23 and 30, Article 31(1) and Articles 32 and 34 by 3 July 2016.
4. References in this Regulation to Directive 2014/65/EU and Regulation (EU) No 600/2014 shall, before 3 January 2018, be read as references to Directive 2004/39/EC in accordance with the correlation table set out in Annex IV to Directive 2014/65/EU in so far as that correlation table contains provisions referring to Directive 2004/39/EC.

Where reference in the provisions of this Regulation is made to OTFs, SME growth markets, emission allowances or auctioned products based thereon, those provisions shall not apply to OTFs, SME growth markets, emission allowances or auctioned products based thereon until 3 January 2018.

The concluding Article of the Market Abuse Regulation declares that it is binding by the twentieth day following that of its publication in the Official Journal of the European Union. Since the Market Abuse Regulation was published in the Official Journal of the European Union on 12 June 2014, it entered into force on 2 July 2014. **B.39.01**

Except for the Articles mentioned in Article 39(2), which have to be applied by 2 July 2014, it applies only from 3 July 2016 (Article 39(2)). This means that the Market Abuse Regulation has no retrospective effect. **B.39.02**

However, pursuant to Article 39(3) the Member States shall take the necessary measures to comply with Articles 22, 23, and 30, Article 31(1), and Articles 32 and 34, by 3 July 2016. **B.39.03**

Since the Markets in Financial Instruments Directive II (2014/65/EU) and MiFIR (600/2014/EU) only apply from 3 January 2018, Article 39(4)(1) states **B.39.04** that all references in the Market Abuse Regulation shall be read as references to MiFID I (2004/39/EC), with the correlation table set out in Annex IV of the Markets in Financial Instruments Directive II (2014/65/EU). The provisions of the Market Abuse Regulation for OTFs, SME growth markets, emission allowances, or auctioned products apply only from 3 January 2018 (Article 39(4)(2)).

INDEX